CHARLES II

Charles II

JOHN MILLER

Weidenfeld and Nicolson
London

First published in Great Britain in 1991 by
George Weidenfeld and Nicolson Limited
91 Clapham High Street, London SW4 7TA

British Library Cataloguing-in-Publication Data is
available on request.

ISBN 0 297 81214 9

Printed and bound in Great Britain by
Butler and Tanner Ltd, Frome and London

Contents

For Carol, James and Nik

Illustrations

George Villiers, Second Duke of Buckingham, by Lely (*National Portrait Gallery, London*)

Anthony Ashley Cooper, First Earl of Shaftesbury, after John Greenhill (*National Portrait Gallery, London*)

John Maitland, First Duke of Lauderdale, by Jacob Huysmans (*National Portrait Gallery, London*)

Charles, painted by Godfrey Kneller in 1670 (*Walker Art Gallery, Liverpool*)

Preface

Why yet another biography of Charles II? Nobody would claim that his life, loves and reign are *terra incognita* and many of the major sources have been in print for a long time, even if in some cases – most notably that of Pepys's diary – we have had to wait until recently for a definitive edition. The question might seem even more pertinent for the author of a biography of James II, who might seem to have spent much of Charles's reign as either understudy or 'reversionary interest'. That book, however, focused primarily on James's reign, so I did not use some major sources relating exclusively to Charles's reign: for example the Essex papers. In the fourteen years since I completed my life of James, some new sources have become readily available for the first time, such as the Althorp and Clifford papers and the draft of Burnet's *History*. Others I discovered on a somewhat random progress through county record offices, notably the splendid volume of letters on 'Titus Oates's Plot' at Warwick. History, moreover, is a matter not only of sources but also of interpretation. Charles II was the most slippery of kings, a complex and evasive character. It is quite possible, using the same sources, to interpret his character and motivation in very different ways. Experience has convinced me that historical biographers all too often take a narrow, two-dimensional view of their subjects. Some become frenziedly protective, fending off any criticism, real or imagined, of their chosen person. Others seem to regard inconsistency as a mortal sin and embark on a herculean and procrustean struggle to show that their subject's conduct conformed to a clear and logical pattern. The result might be neat, but artefacts based on neatness, like Le Nôtre's gardens, tend to be somewhat distant from real life, a fact that novelists often seem to understand better than historians. Fielding or Stendhal or Tolstoy or George Eliot understood that people can behave in ways which others regard as illogical for reasons that make sense to them. The heart, whether it be driven by love, fear, hatred, panic, caprice or a fondness for deceit, can rule the head. Weak mortals are also all too often dominated by the stronger personalities around them: reason may indeed point towards a certain line of action, but weakness or sloth may lead them to do the opposite.

From the foregoing, it will be clear that I do not think that Charles II pursued consistent objectives or even that he was normally the dominant figure within his own administration. This was not necessarily surprising. Louis XIV, a much more forceful figure, in many areas chose between options defined by his ministers and even in the area which mattered most to him, foreign policy, could oscillate alarmingly: between 1668 and 1671 he was set on war, but was uncertain whether to make war on the Spanish or the Dutch. Kingship was difficult: one had to choose between unpalatable alternatives, while being subjected to importunities and self-interested advice. To remain in overall control required superhuman concentration and willpower, which most kings did not possess: certainly Charles II did not. To accept this does not make the history of his reign any tidier: it may make it more plausible.

These strictures on historians' simple-mindedness are not intended to apply to Charles's recent biographers. J. R. Jones's *Charles II: Royal Politician* displayed a shrewd understanding of Restoration politics and his comment that no king thought less in the future tense than Charles II sums up his character in a single phrase. By the time Professor Jones's book appeared, I discovered that – to our mutual consternation – Dr Ronald Hutton and I were also both committed to write biographies. We agreed that, to minimize the degree of overlap, he would devote far more attention than I would to the period before 1660 and to Scotland and Ireland, while I would concentrate on the reign and deal at greater length with foreign policy, particularly Anglo-French relations. In that way, we would produce books that could reasonably be called biographies, but would cover rather different ground. I did not read Dr Hutton's book until I had finished my first draft. It seems to me that we agree that Charles pursued no master plan, but that conclusion leaves room for considerable differences of opinion. I think that in general I see Charles as being weaker and more vacillating than Dr Hutton does, but becoming much firmer in his last years. Because Dr Hutton's focus is very different from mine, it would be finicky and unproductive to set out in the notes every point where we differ. Instead, I have tried to let the sources determine both the shape of the book and the interpretation. I have not ignored the existing secondary literature, but have tended to refer to it only on points of detail or in areas where my own expertise is limited: in particular, certain aspects of foreign policy, finance and the navy. I should also like to stress that this is essentially a political biography, which addresses military and administrative issues only tangentially.

In writing a book of this size, one is bound to incur many debts of gratitude. Some relate to access to documents: almost two decades ago, the Arundell family kindly allowed me access to their papers; more recently, the Warden and Fellows of All Souls College allowed me to use some of the manuscripts in their library: my thanks to both. In my travels I have constantly been impressed by the helpfulness and friendliness of librarians and archivists, even in these difficult times. If I can pick out a few, without the selection seeming invidious, I should like to thank the staffs of the British Library Manuscripts Room (with a special word of thanks to Frances Harris), the Public Record Office (Chancery Lane), Duke Humfrey's Library in the Bodleian, Durham University Library and the students' room at the Archives des Affaires Etrangères. I am also very grateful to David Davies for allowing me to cite some of the conclusions of his forthcoming book on the Restoration navy; to Rob Stradling for permission to make extensive use of his unpublished thesis; and to Henry Horwitz for lending me his photocopies of the Finch MSS. Professor Horwitz was one of a delightful and distinguished group of historians with whom I worked at the Center for the History of Freedom at Washington University, St Louis, under the genial direction of James Jones. Not only did my visit to St Louis give me a chance to visit a number of American libraries, but my discussions with my colleagues about the causes, consequences and significance of the Revolution of 1688 did much to broaden my intellectual horizons. Apart from Professors Jones and Horwitz, I should like to express my particular thanks to Kathleen Wilson, Graham Gibbs and Gordon Schochet. My visits to these American libraries and to Paris, not to mention numerous libraries and record offices within England, were made possible by a research grant from the Leverhulme Trust, for which I am extremely grateful. I also owe a deep debt of gratitude to Professor Ken Haley, for reading the greater part of the book in draft: I am especially grateful for his advice on areas where his expertise is much greater than mine, notably foreign policy. Any errors which remain are, of course, my own. The latter stages of printing out were bedevilled by computer problems: heartfelt thanks to Angie Watson, Carol Toms and Kathryn Antwi for helping me to extricate myself from them. Finally, my family has lived with the writing of this book for almost two years and will be glad when it is finished. I am most grateful for their patience and tolerance.

John Miller
London, January 1991

A Note on Spellings and Dates

All spellings have been modernized and all quotations from foreign languages have been translated. Dates in the text are old style, but with the year starting on 1 January. (In the seventeenth century, the English calendar was ten days behind that used on the continent and the year was taken as starting on 25 March.)

A Wandering Prince

One August morning in 1628 George Villiers, Duke of Buckingham, was breakfasting at a tavern in Portsmouth. The room was crowded with army officers; the duke was immersed in preparations for the forthcoming expedition to the French port of La Rochelle. Suddenly a newcomer strode through the throng and stabbed the duke to the heart. He made no attempt to escape. He turned out to be a disgruntled and somewhat deranged officer, by name John Felton, who blamed Buckingham for his failure to achieve promotion. In his pocket was a copy of a remonstrance of the House of Commons, describing the duke as the source of all the ills of the kingdom.

When the news reached London there were bonfires in the streets; citizens drank Felton's health. One person, however, did not join in the rejoicing. King Charles I had long idolized the man who in everything but birth seemed his superior. Where Charles was small and nondescript, Buckingham was dashing and charismatic; where Charles was timid and unimaginative, Buckingham's brain teemed with bold and ambitious schemes. Starting as a page at the court of Charles's father, James I, with (apparently) little more than good looks to commend him, he came in time to show a talent for administration and by the time Charles became king, in 1625, the duke was the effective director of English foreign policy. As one disaster followed another, Buckingham's schemes became bolder and more improbable: a born gambler, he remained confident that if he kept raising the stakes, the big win would eventually come that would make it all worthwhile. Then all the humiliations and broken promises would be forgotten and the English would unite in applause and admiration.[1]

The English public, however, did not share Buckingham's boundless confidence in himself. They saw only military failures and forced loans, threats to Parliaments and to Protestantism. Some ascribed Buckingham's unnatural influence over his master to witchcraft; his personal astrologer was lynched in a London street. In fact the duke's ascendancy was simply that of a strong personality over a weak one: he was an adored surrogate elder brother. His death left a void in Charles's life which was to be filled – but only in part – by his wife. His marriage to Henrietta Maria, daughter to Henry IV of France, was (like most royal marriages) concluded for reasons of state. Henrietta proved childish and petulant, making no effort to hide her contempt for the English and their Protestantism. Buckingham, fearful of losing his hold over the king, did all he could to sow discord between the king and queen. Once he was dead, however, mutual affection grew. Henrietta was soon pregnant; she miscarried, but a second pregnancy had a happier outcome. On 29 May 1630 she gave birth to a son, christened Charles.

He was a large baby and as an adult stood over six feet – noticeably tall by seventeenth-century standards. Neither of his parents was tall: Charles's growth had been stunted by rickets, Henrietta was short and very thin. The young prince probably owed his robust physique to his grandparents. Henry IV, while of modest height, was immensely energetic; his wife, Marie de Médicis, was an ample lady, chosen by her husband as a 'good breeder'. James I, until he was overcome by drink and senility, was physically very active and hunted with a recklessness far removed from his wonted caution. Apart from his size, what people most remarked on was the baby's dark complexion. He was far more Latin than Anglo-Saxon in appearance – another legacy, perhaps, from Marie de Médicis. He was under no illusion that he was handsome, but compensated for his lack of looks by his bearing, his charm and his intelligence. It is tempting to suggest that he derived the last of these from his grandfathers. James was a scholar-king – if he had not been a king he would have liked to be an academic – and wrote books of political philosophy and on subjects ranging from witchcraft to the evils of tobacco. Henry, by contrast, was a graduate of the university of life, a soldier moulded by experience into a shrewd judge of men; he also shared his grandson's inordinate love of women. Young Charles would, one imagines, have got on well with Henry (who had been assassinated twenty years before Charles was born). They shared the same relentless energy, the same concern for the practical and the mechanical, the same fondness for physical contact and for children, the same easy informality and dislike of paperwork. With his father, Charles had less in common. Charles I was obsessively formal and prim to the point of prudery; he derived deep spiritual satisfaction from religious worship. Shyness and a stammer made communication difficult for him and created an impression of coldness and aloofness. Lacking natural authority, he placed excessive stress on his authority as king. Intellectually unable to cope with complex problems, he took refuge in routine and delegation. In short, father and son had little in common, except perhaps for a love of art, especially Italian painting.

Despite their differences, a real bond of affection developed between them. The family steadily grew: by the time Charles was ten he had two brothers, James Duke of York and Henry Duke of Gloucester, and two sisters, Mary and Elizabeth; another sister, Henriette, was born in 1644. Alongside the royal children were Buckingham's, whom Charles brought up as his own. The elder son, George, the second duke, inherited much of his father's charisma and waywardness, but not his capacity for application to business. Their common upbringing gave the younger Buckingham a special relationship with Charles; his caprices and vendettas were to add an element of unpredictability to Restoration politics. Such problems, however, lay far in the future. Charles and his siblings spent their early years in a large, loving family in a court insulated from the harsh realities of life outside. The young Charles was not overburdened with studying. His governor, the Earl of Newcastle, was later to blame the civil wars on too much education, which (he claimed) gave the lower orders ideas above their station.[2] Newcastle laid much stress on gentlemanly accomplishments, such as horsemanship and fencing. Charles became an excellent dancer and no mean tennis player; he also acquired an abiding enthusiasm for music. He did not heed all of the earl's advice – his claims that ceremony was politically useful fell on deaf ears – but in general Charles must have found his attitude congenial.[3]

Responsibility for the bookish side of Charles's education fell to his tutors: first Brian Duppa, then John Earle, both of whom later became bishops. They eschewed the then fashionable practice of trying to beat learning and piety into their charge, seeking instead to engage his interest and to set him an example of Christian conduct. Their success was limited. Charles was always lazy. He displayed considerable intellectual curiosity and in later life read widely (if not deeply), but when young he showed little interest in books. With the help of a retentive memory he acquired a smattering of knowledge on many subjects. Largely ignorant of Latin and Greek, he learned in exile to speak fluent French and to understand Italian.[4] He was more interested in science – anatomy, chemistry, 'the easier mechanical mathematics' and especially shipbuilding and navigation. His tutors' hopes of leading him to piety bore little fruit. True, he later showed a knowledge of the Bible which some found surprising and proved an astute and severe critic of court preaching (which casts doubt on his jocular claim that he habitually slept through sermons). On the other hand he had little time for formal worship and his attitude towards the clergy was ambivalent. He expected them to eschew politics, to maintain their dignity and to set a moral example to the lower orders – he even disapproved of bishops marrying; but however well they conducted themselves, he had no intention of letting them influence his actions.[5] His conception of morality owed little to any Church, but something to natural justice and basic Christian precepts. The Scottish historian and divine, Gilbert Burnet, who often talked with him of religion, wrote that Charles believed that God would never damn a man for allowing himself a little pleasure: 'He thinks to be wicked and to design mischief is the only thing that God hates and ... he was sure he was not guilty of that.' As Charles wrote to his sister: 'I am one of those bigots who think that malice is a much greater sin than a poor frailty of nature.'[6] Whatever his personal views on religion and morality, Charles saw organized religion in political terms. Newcastle had stressed that Churches were useful for teaching subjects the duty of obedience and Charles thought that 'an implicitness in religion is necessary for the safety of government and he looks upon all inquisitiveness into those things as mischievous to the state'. Once 'common and ignorant people' began to read the Bible, they started to question all types of authority.[7]

Such attitudes doubtless owed much to the experience of civil war, which was soon to disrupt his education; like Henry IV he learned more from experience than from his tutors and governor. If these taught him anything, the tutors' piety may have nourished an appreciation of human goodness, but their most lasting legacy was not academic. An aristocrat's education was intended to furnish him with the attributes of a gentleman – above all, the politeness which men of birth were expected to display towards all ranks of society. Even his critics admitted that Charles was 'the civillest and best bred man in the world', conscious both of his rank and of the conduct expected of a gentleman and a king.[8]

As the 1630s neared their end, the peace of the royal family was threatened by ominous developments to the north. The Scots rebelled against Charles I's demand that they adopt an English prayer book. The prospect that he would be forced to call Parliament triggered an explosion of complaint. For fifteen years many of his subjects had felt that his regime threatened their liberty, property and religion: now they hoped for redress. The Parliament that assembled at Westminster at the end of 1640 focused its attention on the Earl of Strafford, who was accused of advising Charles to act violently and to rule arbitrarily. The Commons' response was no less arbitrary: an Act stating that the earl was guilty of treason and should suffer accordingly. Huge crowds gathered around Whitehall Palace, calling on the king to sign the death warrant. Inside panic reigned, especially among the Catholics of the queen's household. Fearing for his family Charles signed, an action he was later bitterly to regret. He sent Prince Charles to Parliament to plead for a stay of execution, but the Houses were implacable. Strafford was beheaded on Tower Hill, before a crowd of two hundred thousand people.

The sacrifice of Strafford increased the king's determination not to come to terms with Parliament. He made concession after concession, biding his time until he could regain by force the powers that he had lost. When he finally made his move, on 4 January 1642, it was a fiasco. He came to

Westminster to arrest five leading MPs, but they had been forewarned and Charles retreated from the Commons with cries of 'Privilege of Parliament!' ringing in his ears. With London in an uproar, he and his family slunk away to Hampton Court: the king was not to see his capital again until he returned as a prisoner in 1648. His son left London, as a fugitive, a boy of eleven; he was to return in triumph, as king, on his thirtieth birthday.

For eighteen years, as boy and man, Charles II was doomed to wander. He experienced the horrors of civil war and of his father's execution, the privations of exile, flattery and falsehood, deceit and disillusionment. He was expected to lead, to assert his authority over adults decades older than himself. Wily foreign powers, capricious Cavaliers and his own mother all tried to use him for their own ends. Again and again, hopes of help from the continent or Royalist risings at home proved illusory. Yet all was not gloom and despair. Being footloose conferred a certain freedom. From the age of eighteen Charles was largely freed from the control of his parents, and so from their decorum and straitlaced views of morality. With his young companions, he could dance and sing, drink and make love. It seems that his first lover, at the age of fifteen, was his former nurse, Mrs Wyndham.[9] There were to be many others, including a lady with a chequered past called Lucy Walter, who in April 1649 bore him a son, James, who was later to be created Duke of Monmouth. Lucy was not only promiscuous but evil-tempered and spiteful. As she drifted from lover to lover, she refused to hand the boy over to his father, while leaving him in no doubt that he was a king's son. She claimed that Charles had married her, but the claim seems to have rested on nothing more than her bare assertion (and the later wishful thinking of Monmouth's supporters). As the relationship during which Monmouth was conceived lasted only a week, the claim seems improbable; and Charles, for all his fondness for the boy, never wavered in his denial that he had married Lucy. Charles gained custody of his son only in 1658, by the drastic expedient of having him kidnapped. He was taken to the French court and taught, belatedly, to read and write. His mother died (some said of venereal disease) later the same year.[10]

Some months after the start of the civil war, the Royalists made their headquarters at Oxford. Young Charles accompanied his father on visits to the various armies, but early in 1645 the king sent him to command his armies in the west. By now the royal family was widely scattered: Henrietta Maria and Henriette in France; Mary, now married to William II, Prince of Orange, in the Dutch Republic; James at Oxford; Henry and Elizabeth in London. Charles was sent to the west partly to reduce the danger of the whole family's being captured at once, partly in the hope that he could impose his authority on the king's feuding commanders. But Charles was too young, the feuds were too bitter and to make matters worse the king sometimes overrode orders from the Prince of Wales and his council. As the Royalists' prospects worsened, the king became concerned that his son should escape from England while he still could. He ordered him to join his mother in France and to obey her in all things, except those relating to religion. On 2 March 1646, with the Royalists on the verge of defeat, Charles sailed for the Scilly Islands, whence he made his way, via Jersey, to France.

By now Charles had acquired a counsellor who was to guide him for over two decades. Edward Hyde was twenty years Charles's senior. Prim, serious and stolidly committed to the Church of England, he never hid his disapproval of Charles's frivolity and casual indifference to conventional morality. Hyde was a lawyer who had in 1641 denounced Charles I's record of misgovernment, but had then come to see the innovations and aggression of the Parliamentary leaders as posing a far greater threat to the traditional constitution. By early 1642 he was one of the king's leading advisers, urging him to stand by the constitution and the Church and so win the support of the moderate, conservative men who made up the bulk of the political nation. Such counsels appealed to Charles I: he had an instinctive respect for the law (even if he often flouted its spirit) and a deep attachment to the Church. But other, less prudent counsels also appealed to him. The queen and her circle argued that such a timid, temporizing approach would achieve nothing: Charles should gather men and money wherever he could and crush his enemies. The king's most – indeed only – loyal subjects were, they claimed, the Catholics and the only foreign powers that were likely to help him were Catholic, so Charles would be wise to abandon his support for the Church and grant toleration to Catholics. This advice, too, appealed to Charles. He saw Puritans as seditious and thought far too many members of the Church of England were tainted with Puritanism, whereas the Catholics (though theologically wrong) were at least good subjects. He felt angry and humiliated at being forced to make concessions to Parliament, and above all by the sacrifice of Strafford. Besides, as a weak, vacillating man who was still very conscious of his kingly dignity, he derived a delicious frisson from the thought of asserting himself against his enemies.

Throughout the first civil war, Hyde tried to persuade Charles I to stick to traditional ways of doing things and not to compromise his credibility as head of the Church of England. The exigencies of war, however, made it difficult to adhere at all times to the letter of the law and Charles was often seduced by the prospect of Catholic military aid. With the war lost, the issues had not changed: Hyde argued that any hope of negotiating a reasonable settlement with Parliament would be ruined if the king abandoned the Church. The queen responded that it was futile for Charles to try to conciliate his subjects – they would strip him of all his authority and still demand more – so his only hope was either to enlist foreign Catholic aid or else to come to terms with the Presbyterian Scots.

Well aware of the queen's hostility towards him, Hyde remained at Jersey while Prince Charles went to Paris. There Duppa and Earle continued his education: his mathematics tutor was Thomas Hobbes. Back in England, his father refused to make the concessions which Parliament demanded and was pleased to find that the sympathies of his people, who were weary of war and war taxation, were swinging his way. Another development was more ominous: the New Model Army, which had made Parliament's victory possible, now demanded a say in any settlement. More radical than Parliament, in politics and religion, it was quite prepared to use force to achieve its ends. Widespread resentment of Parliament and army burst out in a series of revolts in the summer of 1648; the Scots signed a secret treaty with the king and invaded England. Part of the Parliamentary fleet mutinied and sailed to Helvoetsluys; Charles rushed to the Dutch Republic to lead it against his father's enemies. He found his brother James (newly escaped from England and nominally lord admiral) eager to take command, but Charles invoked his seniority and insisted that he should do so. When the fleet eventually put to sea its hopes were soon dashed by news of the crushing of the rebellions and Cromwell's victory over the Scots at Preston. Divided and disconsolate the fleet limped back to port.

The second civil war sealed the king's fate. Many in the army had seen the first civil war as a conclusive indication that God had 'witnessed' against the king. For him to defy God's verdict and to embroil the nation in further bloodshed seemed little short of blasphemy. It took the army a while to defeat the Scots and to mop up the remaining Royalist resistance. Charles and James could only watch and wait (when they were not laid low by smallpox). William and the Dutch soon became weary of them. Though almost penniless, they expected to be treated like royalty, while making little effort to conceal their contempt for their hosts. (Mary shared their attitude: after six years she had yet to learn Dutch.) James and his followers were persuaded to leave for Paris, but Charles and his entourage remained: they squabbled about who was to blame for past failures while waiting for the next grim piece of news from home. In December Colonel Pride purged Parliament of all those who wished to continue to negotiate with the king. Charles I was brought to London for trial and finally, on 5 February 1649, came the news that he had been executed outside his own palace of Whitehall.[11]

To Charles, his father's death came as no great surprise, although he was amazed that it had been done so openly, in the light of the sun.[12] As all commissions ceased with the king's death, he was besieged by aspirants to offices which might now involve few duties and fewer rewards, but promised their holders power and fortune if Charles were ever restored; others begged promises of honours and pensions. As if this were not enough, he now became the focus of the policy debates and personal rivalries which had long bedevilled the Stuart cause. His mother begged him to come to France and to grant no places until he had seen her: she wished to manage the son as she had tried to manage the father, and her favourite Henry, Lord Jermyn declared that Charles would be ruined if he gave any office to Hyde. Not all was gloom, however. The trusty Marquis of Ormond had kept the Royalist cause alive in Ireland and urged Charles to come and lead his forces; the Scots Presbyterians hoped to use Charles (who was now their king) to rally support against the English assault that was bound to follow their defeat at Preston. Hyde (long Ormond's political ally) urged Charles to go to Ireland, not least because the Scots were certain to demand that he should endorse Presbyterianism. The queen and Jermyn, who hated Hyde and had no affection for the Church of England, urged Charles to come to terms with the Scots. William and the Dutch agreed: they much preferred the Calvinist Scots to the Catholic Irish. Even so, Charles was about to leave for Ireland when he was persuaded to go first to the French court.[13]

His decision was a severe defeat for Hyde: rather than face the queen, he left for Madrid to try to win Spanish support. As for Charles, the initial joy of his reunion with his mother soon passed. She complained that he had appointed councillors without consulting her; the more she interrogated him about his plans the more reserved he became. Charles felt so uncomfortable that, even after Ormond had been defeated, he had no wish to remain in France. The French were by no means eager that he should stay: as France became embroiled in the Fronde, a bloody civil war, the young Louis XIV and his mother were forced to flee from Paris. They had no money to spare for Charles and his dissolute hangers-on, nor did they wish to risk the hostility of England's new rulers. Charles began to fear that they would recognize the republican regime: as he did not want to go to Scotland, he and James set out for Jersey, almost the last Royalist stronghold.[14]

Flight to Jersey merely delayed the need to decide the next move. With Hyde away there were few to counter the arguments that Charles's fortunes could be advanced only by the Scots and by the Catholic powers and that concessions to Presbyterians and Catholics were a necessary – some would say a small – price to pay for their aid.[15] As the Marquis of Montrose struggled to keep alive the Royalist cause in Scotland against the Presbyterian Covenanters, Charles continued to assure him of his support, but his resolution was weakening. He began to negotiate with the Covenanters' representatives. Both the queen's servants and William II urged him to agree to their demands, which included the imposition of Presbyterianism in all three of his kingdoms. Charles's father had often exhorted him never to abandon the Church of England, and Hyde, just as often, had warned him that if he did so he would never return to England.[16] Such were the arguments of conscience; but on the other hand there seemed no other practical means of bringing about his restoration. Negotiations began at Breda in January 1650. Charles did not succumb easily. He refused to promise to change the religion of England and Ireland without the approval of their Parliaments, but (in effect) he accepted the Covenanters' demands as far as Scotland was concerned. Even the queen was reported to be appalled at some of the promises he made, including one to encourage his family to subscribe the Covenant, the founding document of Scots Presbyterianism: this, she argued, could damage his credit with Catholic princes. Some of her servants, however, were delighted, claiming that Hyde's cronies had been against the deal only because the queen promoted it. A by-product of the agreement was that Montrose was left to his fate; the reward for his loyalty to the Stuarts was execution at Edinburgh.[17]

If Charles thought his humiliations were over, he was wrong. Once the Scots had him in their hands they increased their demands: he was to denounce the sins of his parents and swear to impose the Covenant on England. Buckingham, who had inherited his father's flexible attitude towards promises, urged Charles to comply: once he had secured Scotland he could go on his own sweet way.[18] But Charles found little that was sweet in Scotland, as he was forced to sit through interminable sermons: their hypocrisy, he wrote, served only to confirm his attachment to the Church of England.[19] Militarily, too, the Scots were a disappointment. The Presbyterian clergy ascribed their crushing defeat by Cromwell at Dunbar on 3 September to God's anger that they had been so lenient towards Charles. Their remedy was a further purge of 'undesirables' from his household. After an abortive attempt at flight, Charles resolved to make the best of his situation. His coronation enhanced his personal standing and he began to rally support against the English army, despite the clergy's irritating insistence on valuing religious orthodoxy above military competence. As 1651 wore on, however, it was the king who played the dominant role in the war effort. Painstakingly, he built up an army with which to march into England and recover his own.

It was not to be. The Scots soldiers' enthusiasm waned the further they advanced into England and they deserted in droves. The English Royalists were cowed and under strict surveillance. Charles's problems were compounded by Buckingham who, despite minimal military experience, demanded to be made commander in chief. When Charles refused, the duke sulked, refusing either to change his linen or to attend council meetings.[20] Tired and dispirited, the army trudged south until it was cut to pieces outside Worcester on 3 September. Charles did his utmost to rally his forces, but the enemy were greatly superior in numbers and firepower. On the run with a price on his head, Charles had to rely on his wits and his friends and came into closer contact with ordinary people than most of his forebears ever had. In retrospect his six weeks on the road seemed a great adventure, a source of endless stories with which to bore his courtiers. At the time it must have seemed far less pleasant. His size and complexion made disguise difficult, while his companion, Lord Wilmot, disdained any disguise more elaborate than a hawk on his wrist. The king evaded capture thanks mainly to a group of Catholic gentry and their servants, who were used to conveying priests secretly from one house to another. Their loyalty made a deep impression on him: he assured one of the priests, Father Huddleston, that if he were ever restored he would allow toleration for Catholics. In mid-October he reached France, deeply disillusioned with the Scots in general and the Covenanters in particular.

He found the exiled court as divided as ever. His mother continued to urge him to pin his hopes on Catholic help. She had converted Henriette in 1650 and in January 1651 the French queen mother forbade Protestant worship at Henrietta Maria's court.[21] His brother James had left France, persuaded by his servants that Charles's cause was doomed and so that he (James) should carve himself out a career as a professional soldier. Nobody, however, seemed eager to employ a seventeen-year-old with no experience, even if he was a king's son. Bored and short of money, only fear of loss of face prevented James from responding to his brother's orders and his mother's entreaties and returning to Paris. The deadlock was broken by the queen: with a rare display of tact she sent Hyde, newly returned from Spain, to persuade him to return. Charles dismissed those who had advised James to leave Paris and told him to pay more heed to wiser heads, like Ormond and Sir Edward Nicholas, Charles I's secretary of state. Meanwhile, the queen starved James of money in an effort to bend him to her will.[22]

With the royal family together once more, the old struggle resumed between Hyde and Ormond on one hand and the queen and Jermyn's faction (known as 'the Louvre') on the other. The queen had the advantage that Charles could deal with the French court only through her, so he felt impelled to include Jermyn in his small privy council, along with Wilmot, Hyde and Ormond. Nicholas, more sensitive than others to the queen's hostility, stayed away from Paris.[23] Wild projects abounded. Charles talked of raising an army in Germany or sending mercenaries to Ireland. There were moves to convert him to Catholicism: he himself hinted to the pope that he might turn if the terms were right. Buckingham talked of marrying Mary, now a widow; the queen told her that she would tear her in pieces if she consented. Nicholas remarked, with some understatement, that Buckingham was not short of wit, but lacked ballast.[24] By February 1652 Charles and Hyde, tired of the bickering and penury, were eager to leave France, but lacked the necessary means. With the Fronde not yet over, money was far from plentiful at the French court, but the queen made sure that most of what she obtained went to Jermyn and herself, not to Charles. Some feared that this financial pressure would break his resistance. The queen pressed him to turn Catholic, Jermyn urged him to attend the Huguenot church at Charenton to woo the Presbyterians. Both insisted that potential supporters were repelled by Hyde's intransigent Anglicanism.[25]

For Hyde, these were gloomy times. He bemoaned:

the general corruption and licence of the court and indeed of our nation, who ... have shaken off all those obligations and respects they have formerly been liable to and every man takes himself to be a competent surveyor and censurer of all persons and actions and every man assumes that nothing is done because he knows not what is done.

Nothing, he concluded, could reform Charles while he remained with the queen.[26] In December 1652, ominously, the French court established diplomatic relations with the English Republic, but still Hyde could see no prospect of leaving: Charles had no money and nowhere to go. Those around Mary made it clear that he would not be welcome in the Netherlands, even as a volunteer on the Dutch fleet.[27] The only positive reason for staying was the arrival of Henry, whom Mary reluctantly sent to Paris at their mother's insistence. Both Charles and Mary feared that, having failed with his two older brothers, the queen might try to convert Henry to Catholicism. All were delighted with him: 'the finest youth and of the most manly understanding that I have ever known', wrote Hyde with uncharacteristic enthusiasm. His presence brought some much needed joy to an embittered court.[28]

Throughout 1653 the same themes recurred in Hyde's correspondence: factionalism, debt, disorder. He himself had to fend off accusations of treachery and was accused of denigrating Charles behind his back, saying that he devoted too little attention to business. (Charles's characteristic response was that Hyde often said the same to his face and that he did not mind.)[29] With the Fronde over, the French queen mother's chief adviser, Cardinal Mazarin, could concentrate on the long-running war against Spain. Whatever his personal feelings, diplomatic need drove him to seek a close understanding with Cromwell, who was declared Lord Protector at the end of the year. At first he found Charles's presence useful – Mazarin could threaten to take up his cause – but as agreement grew near, Charles's usefulness ended. When, early in 1654, Charles announced his wish to leave for Germany, the Cardinal was happy to facilitate his departure; Charles was granted a regular allowance which, for once, was not to be paid through the queen. Mazarin delayed his departure until agreement with Cromwell was certain, but on 30 June Charles left Paris.[30]

He had no clear idea where he would go: he just wished to get away from France. He met Mary at Spa, then moved to Aachen, where Nicholas joined him and resumed his duties as secretary. At last he had a regular income, carefully managed by Stephen Fox. As winter approached, Mary returned to Holland and Charles moved to Cologne. Although its prince was a Catholic archbishop, the magistrates allowed Charles a Protestant chapel. Hyde wrote later that Charles spent his time walking, riding and learning French and Italian. Cromwell's agents wrote of drinking, dancing and wenching.[31] Charles was never a heavy drinker, except perhaps in old age, but he enjoyed wine and sometimes got drunk 'in a frolic'. Some of his courtiers, however, were reported to be mad with wine.[32] It was also noted, with disapproval, that Charles attended Catholic churches and met the papal nuncio.[33]

It seems likely that such actions indicated only that Charles neglected no possible source of assistance, not that he inclined to Catholicism; much the same could be said of a planned approach to the English Catholics.[34] His true position was made clear by his mother's attempt to convert Henry to Catholicism. Charles had let her persuade him to leave Henry in Paris to complete his education, but he had made her promise she would not attempt to convert him; he also warned James to be on his guard against any such attempt.[35] Henrietta Maria's attitude towards promises proved as cavalier as Buckingham's. She told Henry that the Church would offer him a brilliant career and that Charles would not really object to his conversion – if he objected, why had he left Henry in France? Indeed, to convert would help his brother by winning the support of Catholic princes. Brushing aside the timid remonstrations of Henry's tutor, she enlisted the Abbé Walter Montagu (himself a convert) to press him to enter the Jesuit college at Pontoise. Well aware of Charles's likely reaction, she had the Cologne mail searched at the post office.[36] The news still got through and Charles reacted vigorously: Hyde declared that he had never seen him so troubled. He wrote to his mother that he could only assume that she had no wish to see him restored. It was not up to Montagu, he declared, to decide how far he should be obeyed and he reminded her of the late king's injunction to his children never to desert the Church of England. He ordered Henry not to enter the college and sent Ormond to bring him to Cologne. The queen placed every possible obstacle in Ormond's way, but at last she had to let Henry go, refusing him her blessing when he left.[37]

Charles's resolute action on this occasion was at best an exercise in damage limitation: it did nothing to win him his throne. Worcester had ended serious resistance to the New Model within the British Isles. Disaffection remained, but lacked unity or a focus and few would risk a rising without solid assurances of foreign military aid. But where could such aid come from? Mazarin busily sought Cromwell's friendship. Any hope of help from the Dutch Republic had ended with the premature death of William II in 1650, in the midst of a furious power struggle. Traditionally the Princes of Orange had been the first servants of the republic, but William had wished to become, in effect, a king. His efforts were stubbornly opposed by the 'regents', the rulers of the great trading cities of Holland. These wished to preserve the old federal constitution, in which the rich cities, as the main payers of taxation, exercised a dominant influence. William's death gave them a chance to destroy the power of the House of Orange; neither Mary nor her infant son, William III, was in any position to stop them – or to help Charles. He and his followers had, indeed, done little to endear themselves to the Dutch in 1648–9 and the republic's new rulers, like Mazarin, were eager to be on good terms with the English Republic. The third major power in western Europe was Spain, but the Spaniards, having finally conceded Dutch independence in 1648, were fully stretched defending the Southern Netherlands against France. After decades of war, the strain of maintaining their great empire, in Europe and the Americas, was proving too much. With a falling population and a stagnant economy, the Spaniards were finding it more and more difficult to transport men and money to Flanders and were beginning to think of cutting their losses and concentrating their efforts in the Mediterranean and the New World. In principle, they might be willing to help Charles, especially when Cromwell attacked their American possessions. Whether they could translate good intentions into practical aid was another matter. An invasion would require men, money and a fleet capable of taking on that of the Protectorate; and these the Spaniards did not possess.

In these circumstances, the schemes for Royalist risings in the 1650s tended to be over-optimistic. To make matters worse those who conspired against Cromwell were dogged by the feuding that seemed inseparable from Royalism. Men talked in their cups and their intrigues were infiltrated by the agents of Cromwell's spymaster, Thurloe. Again and again, hopes were dashed and Charles's court returned to its drinking and dancing. After the pressure that she had put on Henry, Charles refused to be reconciled to his mother. Her court became a haven for those expelled from Charles's, while Jermyn was seen as an agent of Mazarin.[38] As relations worsened, Charles pressed James (now serving with the French army) to join him at Cologne. James should have been expelled from France under Mazarin's treaty with Cromwell, concluded in October 1655, but he kept finding pretexts to stay. He found the prospect of further action under the great general Turenne far more alluring than an uncertain future elsewhere. As the Spaniards began to respond to his overtures, Charles moved to Brussels and his summonses to James became more insistent. In June 1656 the Spaniards agreed that Charles should raise four foot regiments, to serve with the Spanish army. They hoped (and Mazarin feared) that British and Irish officers and soldiers would defect from the French army to serve under Charles. James still dragged his feet: not until September did he join his brothers at Bruges.[39]

James's arrival added to the factional divisions at court. As Hyde spoke only English, negotiations with the Spanish authorities were conducted by the Earl of Bristol, whom Charles appointed secretary of state (the office he had held under Charles I) in 1656. Restlessly ambitious and impulsive, he was never an easy colleague, especially for the cautious, steady Hyde, with whom he had a history of disagreement going back to 1641. Bristol blamed James's tardy departure from France on some of his servants who were known to be associated with the queen and Jermyn: Sir John Berkeley, Charles Berkeley and Henry Jermyn the younger. Sir John, James's governor, was seen in particular as exercising an undue influence over his charge. When Bristol pressed James to dismiss Sir John, James refused: to dismiss a man whom he regarded as innocent of any crime would (he thought) be dishonourable; besides, he feared that if he gave in Charles would seek to choose all his servants for him. (He had already been forced to employ Charles's friend, Sir Henry Bennet, as his secretary.) When Charles insisted that Berkeley should go, James left too, together with Charles Berkeley and Jermyn. Charles quickly saw that he had pushed his brother too far. Faced with the prospect that he might set up as his rival, Charles allowed him to return on his own terms; Bennet was removed from James's service and appointed ambassador to Spain. Having the Berkeleys at court was a small price to pay for the unity of the royal family.[40]

Through 1657 and 1658 the prospects for Charles's restoration were no brighter. Glimmers of hope were quickly extinguished. Spanish invasion plans were thwarted by an English naval blockade; Cromwell's death did not lead to the collapse of the Protectorate. Bored with Bruges, Charles insisted on serving with the Spanish forces, alongside his brothers, and became increasingly vexed by the 'affronts' and 'scurvy usage' he suffered at the Spaniards' hands. He took part in the siege of Mardyke, which fell to Spain in October 1657, but this success was overshadowed by the fall of Dunkirk to an Anglo-French force in 1658, which gave Cromwell a foothold on the continent and strengthened his grip on the Channel.[41] English seapower made it difficult to transport money from Spain, but the English court preferred to blame shortages on the Spaniards' ill-will.[42] There were still proposals for Charles to seek Catholic or Presbyterian help and even renewed talk of Gloucester's conversion. Charles secretly assured the King of Spain and the pope of his goodwill towards Catholics, but carefully sidestepped talk of his conversion. The main thrust of his strategy was demonstrated by his appointing Hyde lord chancellor in January 1658.[43]

For much of 1659 things seemed no better. Bristol showed his lack of confidence in Charles's prospects by converting to Catholicism, apparently convinced that this would improve his chances of office; James considered the post of High Admiral of Spain. The Spanish authorities in Brussels scaled down their assistance as Madrid became convinced that Charles's condition was hopeless: Bennet urged his master to come and plead his case in person. As his relations with Spain cooled, there were hopes of reconciliation with France but Mazarin disapproved of Charles's favour towards the old Frondeur, Cardinal de Retz.[44] Ever more bizarre schemes were hatched involving, among others, the Jesuit Peter Talbot, the former Leveller John Wildman and Buckingham, who had made his peace with the regime to the point of marrying the daughter of Fairfax, formerly commander of the New Model. Talbot was expelled from the Society, but continued to shuttle between Madrid, Paris and England.[45] The rift between Richard Cromwell, Oliver's successor, and the army raised Royalist hopes. Charles travelled to Calais to await the call, but a rising led by Sir George Booth was put down and Charles switched his attention to the negotiations which were about to bring the long Franco-Spanish war to an end. He made his way to Fuentarabia, hoping to enlist the support of one side or the other. Mazarin assured him of his good intentions but was wary of offending the English government. The Spaniards were still at war with England, but were reluctant to waste scarce resources on Charles, so he travelled back to Brussels. En route, he visited his mother incognito; briefly the unkindness between them was forgotten and he created Jermyn Earl of St Albans.[46]

From Paris, Charles made his way disconsolately back to Brussels, but for once his position was less gloomy than it seemed. Ever since Pride's Purge and the king's execution, the republic and Protectorate had been militarily strong but politically weak. England's government depended, more than that of most states, on the co-operation (or at least acquiescence) of the governed, in administration, law enforcement and taxation. To secure that acquiescence, it was necessary to secure at least the appearance of consent to taxation and legislation: hence Oliver's repeated attempts to work with Parliaments. His need to win consent for taxation was all the greater because he inherited huge debts from the Long Parliament, which his own wars and the continuing cost of the army did nothing to reduce. The first Protectorate Parliament voted him taxes, but these were due to expire at the end of 1659. Most of his attempts to work with Parliament (especially the last) ended in failure, but the very fact that he tried helped win a measure of acceptance for his rule. He had also gone as far as he could to reconcile the interests of civilians and military. Most Parliamentarians had fought against Charles I, not to destroy the monarchy, but to make him agree to safeguards against a repeat of the misgovernment of the 1630s. His refusal to make concessions perplexed and embarrassed them, but they continued to negotiate, hoping he would, in the end, see reason. Those who wished to continue negotiations came to be known as Presbyterians, as they mostly stood not only for limited monarchy, but also for a broadly uniform national Church with a liturgy plainer and more Protestant than that of the old Church of England. The Presbyterians had no sympathy for the new sects (Quakers, Baptists, Independents) who emerged in the 1640s and 1650s and challenged the whole traditional notion of a Church as embracing all of the community. These sects often supported the army, but they made up only a small part of the population, they were divided among themselves and their members were mostly from outside the old ruling elite, so lacked social and political weight. The Presbyterians were both more numerous and of higher status: if Oliver were ever to establish a viable basis of support, he would have to win many of them over. But they had been appalled by Pride's Purge and the king's execution and they hated the army and the sects. To win their support he would have to abandon all that the army had fought for – religious liberty, the republic, its very existence – and this he was not prepared to do. Forced to choose between the Presbyterians and the army, Oliver chose the army.

By contrast, his son Richard had no military background. When he called a Parliament early in 1659 many hoped that he would bring the army under civilian control, but the army leaders would have none of it. Their dismissal of Richard and his Parliament, however, exposed the nakedness of military rule. The number of soldiers in England doubled between April and September and the army leaders cast around desperately for a body that would give their regime even the flimsiest trappings of constitutional legitimacy. They revived the Rump Parliament, created by the exclusion of so many MPs in Pride's Purge. Oliver had found it dilatory and obstreperous, so had dissolved it in 1653; those who revived it found it more intractable than ever. As the regime's debts mounted, exacerbated by the war with Spain, the taxes voted earlier were about to expire and there were ominous signs that taxpayers were refusing to pay.[47] The army was still strong enough to put down Booth's rising, but it could not coerce a whole nation, especially as the soldiers were becoming demoralized by civilian hostility.

Through all its troubles, the army had remained united, thanks in large part to Oliver. Now a serious rift developed. George Monk, who commanded the army in Scotland, was a gruff professional soldier who had once served in the Royalist army but had been won over by Oliver. Now that Oliver was dead, Monk's loyalty to the Protectorate was dissolved and he began to consider what was best for the nation and for himself. He resented the English high command's attempts to interfere in appointments in his army and was alarmed at the regime's increasing reliance on Quakers and other sectaries. He received Royalist approaches cautiously: he was aware of the plans for Booth's rising and sympathized with its ostensible goal of a free Parliament (which would probably restore the king). Booth was defeated before Monk could declare himself, but he had already sounded out many of his officers and now knew which he could rely on.[48] Not long after, the army expelled the Rump (again) for trying to assert its control over military affairs. By now, however, it was proving easier to expel Parliaments than to replace them. An elected body was out of the question, as that would disband the army and recall the king. Some talked of a senate composed of men of impeccable republican virtue, but such men were few and it was very doubtful whether people would pay taxes 'voted' by such a body. Indecision reigned and the French ambassador, Bordeaux, wrote in October that there was now no government in England.[49]

The expulsion of the Rump gave Monk a plausible cause – the restoration of a 'lawful' Parliament – while a commission sent to him secretly by the Rump's executive organ, the council of state, gave him a pretext to act independently of the English high command. His stated aims, apart from the recall of Parliament – he was at first somewhat evasive as to *which* Parliament – included the re-establishment of a godly learned ministry (in other words, a Presbyterian Church system) and the disbanding of the militia of sectaries lately raised by the army. He explicitly declared against the restoration of either the king or the House of Lords.[50] He wrote to the great Independent pastor John Owen that it was essential to free England from the tyranny of a 'sword government' and that the only sure foundation of a free state could be a Parliament.[51] To win the time needed to remove unreliable officers, he opened negotiations with the English army leaders.

Charles's agents had no idea what to make of Monk. Some feared that he would fall in with the Presbyterians and restore Charles only on the most stringent conditions, similar to those offered to Charles I in 1648 on the Isle of Wight; these included a Church without bishops, to which Hyde said Charles could never agree. Other Royalists argued that Charles should approach Lambert, the most able and ambitious of the generals; some talked of marrying James to Lambert's daughter.[52] What Monk's true intentions were we shall never know. A man of few words, he would chew his tobacco, spit and look profound. Later his eulogists claimed that he had decided from the outset to restore the king. It could be true. For a man with his conservative instincts, the confusion of late 1659 must have seemed intolerable. They also claimed that if he had declared for Charles too early he would have ruined any chance of his restoration. But the fact that he took so long to declare himself creates uncertainty; besides, *if* he intended to restore the monarchy, on what terms did he intend to do so? There is substantial evidence that he did indeed lean towards the conditions set out at the Isle of Wight. After 1660 almost everyone agreed that Monk was no genius: Pepys called him 'this blockheaded duke', others complained that he was ruled by his wife. He was malleable: 'importunity and the last tale' weighed heavily with him. He did have certain advantages: a prodigious capacity for drink and ability to keep his own counsel.[53] He also knew his officers well and looked after his soldiers, ensuring that they received their pay: those he trusted rarely let him down. Faced with the complex circumstances of the winter of 1659–60, it seems most likely that Monk kept his options open and waited on events. Like any professional soldier, he was keen to end up on the winning side.

In December 1659 the army succumbed to what would now be called 'people power'. As law enforcement and tax collection ground to a halt – it was claimed that no judges were working – calls for a free Parliament became increasingly insistent. Some wanted fresh elections, others Richard's Parliament or the Long Parliament as it had been before Pride's Purge, with a Presbyterian majority. Londoners drew up a petition for a Parliament; the soldiers tried to suppress it and in the ensuing clashes at least two people were killed.[54] Popular hatred of the army was taking its toll. As the cavalry paraded in their armour, apprentices mockingly called them lobsters. 'The soldiers here', it was noted, 'are so vilified, scorned and hissed that they are ashamed to march.' Sixty soldiers 'laid down their arms till they be satisfied for what and whom they engage'. Three troops of horse called for the restoration of Richard's Parliament. The garrison at Portsmouth declared for a free Parliament, as did part of the fleet, under Sir John Lawson, which blockaded the Thames estuary. With their pay up to nineteen months in arrears, bewildered by repeated politically motivated purges of officers, the soldiers' patience was wearing thin.[55] Conscious that they were losing the support of both common soldiers and junior officers, the high command retreated, weeping and praying. Fleetwood remarked plaintively that to agree to a free Parliament would lead to the return of the king (which, as Bordeaux remarked, was what most people wanted). The army leaders promised that a new Parliament would meet in February and appointed 'conservators' to draw up stringent restrictions designed to ensure that it would neither harm the army nor abandon the republic. This, however, was to concede too little too late. Monk had now declared explicitly for the Rump, so the army leaders recalled it: it reconvened in triumph on 26 December, while General Fleetwood moaned that God had spat in his face.[56]

For the army the Rump was a lesser evil – just – than a free Parliament: at least they knew its composition. Soldiers cheered the members as they returned: civilians were less enthusiastic. In the London common council elections, the army's main civilian allies, the sectaries, were crushingly defeated. The new common council began to change the officers of the trained bands (the City militia), replacing Baptists and Quakers with (it was said) Royalists, while insistently calling for a free Parliament.[57] The Rump, however, claimed (as it had since Pride's Purge) to be the sole legitimate Parliament, the lineal heir of the Long Parliament called by Charles I in 1640. It haughtily rejected calls to restore the 'secluded MPs' ousted in 1648: when some of them tried to claim their seats they were turned away. The Rump also hastened to renew its quarrel with the army. Seven commissioners were appointed to command all forces (including the militia) with power to disband any which had been raised without the Rump's approval. (Monk's own regiments were exempted from the commissioners' authority.) For the moment, the army was too demoralized to resist, but this eagerness to reopen old wounds (and its manifest unpopularity) did not augur well for the new regime. Everything depended on Monk. After weeks of careful preparations and changes in the officer corps he was ready to move. On 1 January 1660 his army crossed the Tweed and marched into England.[58]

The Promised Land

The new year dawned with the Rump's arrogance at its zenith and the army's morale at its nadir. The former voted that the 'secluded' MPs had been duly expelled and that elections should be held to fill their places; those elected were to renounce the House of Stuart.[1] The Rump also ordered the sale of the estates of those involved in Booth's rising, ordered the army's leaders to their homes in the country and then began to remove all officers commissioned since its expulsion in October. Petitions for a free Parliament were received rudely.[2] Yet the Rump's position was much weaker than such conduct would suggest. Members of the new council of state were required formally to renounce the Stuarts: fewer than half did so. The latest changes in the officer corps still further eroded the soldiers' loyalty – there were many reports that they said they did not care whom they served so long as they were paid. Even when the Rump voted money for them, discontent continued.[3] The soldiers could not be unaware of the intensity of civilian hostility towards the army and the Rump: boys in London cried 'kiss my Parliament' instead of 'kiss my arse' and soldiers bawled for a free Parliament as well as for money. Despite the timorousness of their leaders, London's citizens continued to demand a free Parliament; petitions to that end circulated all over the country. Resistance to taxation continued. There was a huge gap between the Rump's posturing and its ability to get things done.[4]

The Rump possessed one trump card: Monk. If he adhered to his stated position, that the Rump's was the only legitimate authority, nobody could seriously challenge it. It quickly sent two of its members, Scot and Robinson, to watch him every hour of the day and to try to isolate him from other influences, including the delegations bearing petitions for a free Parliament. Monk said little; those who dealt with him sensed that he had no clearly formulated plans and was open to the influence of those around him, especially his wife and kinsmen (Thomas Clarges, William Morrice and John Clobery).[5] He declared publicly for the Rump, but would not abjure the king and assured Clobery privately that he did not support the Rump.[6]

Events soon forced him to declare himself. On 8 February it was reported that the London common council had resolved to pay no more taxes until the secluded MPs were allowed to return to the Commons. (In fact, it had merely received favourably a petition to that effect.) Next day the Rump voted that the common council should be 'discontinued'; the council of state told Monk to arrest some leading councilmen, to take down the City's gates and to remove the posts and chains which could be used to close the streets to cavalry. Monk replied that he was sure that the City would agree to pay its taxes, adding that if the Rump hastened preparations for a new Parliament it would greatly contribute to the public peace. The Rump was adamant and next day Monk reluctantly carried out its orders.[7]

The Rumpers were jubilant: the proud and truculent City had been humbled. In their jubilation, they overplayed their hand. Hitherto, they had endorsed all Monk's actions and voted him money; now that it seemed that he would obey even unpalatable commands, there seemed no further need to do so. On 11 February it was resolved to set up a new commission to direct the army, consisting of Monk and four hardline Rumpers. There was to be a quorum of three, so that Monk could always be outvoted; he was not even to be one of the quorum.[8] It was a fatal error. Monk was already upset about the order to pull down the gates; many officers had threatened to resign in protest. Now effective command of the army was to be put in the hands of a vindictive clique. Already sure of the co-operation of the governor of the Tower, Monk marched into the City. He sent a long letter to the Speaker, upbraiding the Rump for betraying the Parliamentary cause. He ordered it to issue writs for fresh elections and then to prepare to dissolve itself.[9]

The reason for Monk's change of heart remains a matter for conjecture. Bordeaux wrote that he was furious that he had been deprived of command of the army. Others thought that he had been persuaded by his officers, or had cunningly encouraged the Rump to overreach itself. Whatever his motives, the Londoners' reaction was one of amazement and joy. Pepys could see thirty-one bonfires at one time; the soldiers, recently so despised, were plied with endless food and drink and many were drunk from morning till night. Monk's letter stated that nobody should be eligible for election who had been in arms against Parliament (or who had been 'disaffected' towards it); the strength of public feeling was such that the elections were likely to produce a Parliament that would recall the king, albeit on terms.[10]

The Rump did not accept defeat graciously. The following week it drew up electoral qualifications so rigorous as to disenfranchise the great majority of the population; it also wished to hold elections only for those constituencies whose MPs were secluded or dead: existing MPs were to keep their seats. Monk had, it is true, talked of 'filling up your number', but he had linked this to a demand for a speedy dissolution.[11] The Rump's intransigence led Monk to consider another option. Some of the secluded MPs were invited to put their case before Monk and his officers and the Rumpers were invited to reply. The former assured Monk that, if reinstated, they would quickly dissolve themselves and hold elections; they would also vote money for the arrears of the army and navy. The Rumpers, by contrast, rejected proposals to change the membership of the council of state. The outcome of these discussions was seen on 21 February: a group of MPs, who had not sat since Pride's Purge, came to Westminster with a military escort and took their seats. Monk told the enlarged assembly to provide for the armies and for a new Parliament, to meet on 20 April. He called for an ordered national Church, with some provision for 'tender consciences', and insisted that England should remain a republic, without a king or House of Lords. The House aborted the Rump's preparations for elections and appointed a new council of state; Monk was made commander in chief of the land forces of England, Scotland and Ireland. London's gates were to be restored at public expense.[12]

Reactions to these developments varied. Most thought that Monk wished to maintain the republic and to establish a moderate Presbyterian Church, but he also indicated that he would comply with the wishes of a free Parliament.[13] His caution owed much to the need to assure the army of his continued commitment to 'our cause' and 'a free state'. A letter signed by Monk and twenty-six senior officers stressed their wish for a 'full representative', but also the need to impose qualifications on its members 'for the establishing this commonwealth upon the foundations of justice and true freedom'. They talked of God's Providence and expressed confidence that the new Parliament would not rescind sales of royal and episcopal lands or interfere with the disposition of lands in Ireland, both matters of great concern to the soldiery. Despite its conciliatory tone, however, the letter made it clear that Monk expected the soldiers to acquiesce in what he had done. Those officers who expressed dissatisfaction were cashiered.[14]

The task of placating the army was made no easier by the conduct of Parliament. Its proposed qualifications for MPs would have excluded not only active Royalists (which Monk had stipulated) but also sectaries, who denied 'magistracy and ministry' to be 'ordinances of God'.[15] It also sought to establish a statutory basis for a Presbyterian national Church, which was to use the Scottish service book (the Directory); its clergy, supported by tithes, were to subscribe a single confession of faith. Such a scheme had been conceived in 1646–8, but aborted by the rise of the New Model. Its reintroduction would be most unwelcome to the sectaries inside and outside the army.[16] Parliament also sought to re-establish the militia, under the command of the county gentry, as a counterweight to the army. Monk opposed sweeping changes in the London lieutenancy, which directed the trained bands, until it was made clear to him that if he did not agree the City would advance no money for the soldiers' pay; the new lieutenancy promptly disarmed the London Baptists. As a conciliatory gesture, Monk was appointed overall commander of the militia, but a move to exclude from the militia all who had not been actively engaged against Charles I was laid aside and all army officers were ordered back to their regiments.[17]

By now it was clear that, with the return of the secluded MPs, Parliament was much as it had been on the eve of Pride's Purge, dominated by Presbyterians who wanted a settlement based on limited monarchy and a moderately Puritan national Church. It framed a new oath for councillors of state, requiring them, not to abjure the king, but merely to do their duty. On the other hand, it ordered that the Covenant, which spoke of serving Parliament and king, should be displayed in every parish church. Pepys noted that many openly drank the king's health, but most MPs were more circumspect. When William Prynne proposed settling the ancient government of king, Lords and Commons, Arthur Annesley declared that it was a weighty matter and they had much else to do, so it was laid aside. His caution reflected continuing anxiety about the army.[18] On 7 March a meeting of officers declared against government by a single person, whether king or Protector; Monk told them not to meddle with affairs of state. Other officers pressed Parliament to reverse the changes in the militia and to guarantee them an indemnity for their past actions and confirmation of their purchases of crown and Church lands. Parliament rejected the first request; its response to the others was non-committal, but it was significant that some officers now seemed prepared to submit to Parliament, to sacrifice their political ideals in return for securing their personal safety and material interests; indeed, Parliament's refusal to meet similar demands had triggered the army's move into politics in 1647. As one of this group of officers was Clobery, they may have reflected Monk's views – suspicious of the new militia, but anxious to secure the best possible deal for the soldiers.[19]

Monk's letter to the army after restoring the secluded MPs had been apologetic in tone; his response to the officers' denunciation of a 'single person' was noticeably more resolute. He had long declared that the army should answer to Parliament; now he saw it as owing its allegiance not to the Rump, or the restored Long Parliament, but to the Parliament soon to be elected. His firmness reflected a growing confidence that the army would obey him. On 16 March the Act of Dissolution brought the Long Parliament to an end. Since it had first met in 1640, many of its members had died or been expelled, two parts of the trinity of king, Lords and Commons had been removed and the third had undergone purges and forcible expulsions. It had, however, continued to claim a measure of legitimacy and by an Act of 1641 it could not be dissolved without its own consent. Its dissolution cleared the way for a settlement more acceptable to the nation than any of the regimes since Pride's Purge – or even since 1642. It seemed clear that the settlement would be based on monarchy – but what sort of monarchy? The electoral qualifications enacted by the expiring Long Parliament were designed to produce a Presbyterian House of Commons, which would restore the monarchy, but with stringent restrictions; and many suspected that Monk favoured such restrictions. The conditions upon which Charles would return were to be determined by a complex interplay of forces, including Monk and the army, Presbyterian politicians and Royalist agents, the French and Spanish governments and Charles himself. Still more important, however, was the battle for the hearts and minds of the electorate and of the inhabitants of London. 'People power' had demoralized the old army leadership and defeated the Rump; and 'people power' was to bring Charles home without preconditions.

While these momentous events unfolded, Charles could do little more than watch, wait and try to do nothing to harm his prospects. He assured the City of his goodwill and stated that he would rebuff none of those willing to serve him, even if they could not agree among themselves. Distance could impede understanding. Charles was unhappy at the return of the secluded MPs, many of whom had proposed restrictions on the monarchy in 1648; Hyde could not see why the restored Long Parliament did not resume negotiations on the basis of the 1648 proposals.[20] At first the French and Spaniards, while basically sympathetic to Charles's cause, were reluctant to offend the English government, but as Charles's prospects improved they came to regard him not as an embarrassment but as a potential asset which they wished to control. Charles, for his part, placed little reliance on the Spanish authorities in Brussels, who still hoped to engineer his restoration by means of negotiations with the Levellers. On the other hand, he tried to persuade Mazarin to order Bordeaux to be active on his behalf and as late as 24 March he wrote that France was the fittest place from which to negotiate for his return.[21] Soon after, Monk sent over Sir John Grenville and John Mordaunt, who advised Charles to leave Brussels for Breda, in the Dutch Republic. Hearing that the Spaniards intended to hinder his departure, he slipped away and reached Breda on 4 April.[22]

At Breda, an Orangist city, well away from the Hague, Charles was a freer agent than he could have been in Brussels or Paris. Those around the queen still argued that Charles could be restored only through negotiations with the Presbyterians, who, they hoped, would insist on Hyde's exclusion from power. Jermyn argued that Charles should accept any conditions that he could get, even if they drastically weakened the monarchy: he could always renounce them later. The queen had severe qualms about this, but Jermyn and Montagu persuaded Mazarin that theirs was the only feasible strategy and Bordeaux was ordered to support the Presbyterians and proposals for a conditional restoration.[23] Such a strategy, however, was both warped by factional animosities and increasingly out of date. Back in January Mordaunt had argued that Charles should concede some of the Presbyterians' demands (notably a confirmation of land sales) and Allen Brodrick advised him to grant a general indemnity. Mordaunt also stressed the need to win over Cromwell's old antagonist, the Earl of Manchester, who wished to be lord treasurer.[24] Before they disbanded, the members of the Long Parliament tried to guarantee that the new House of Commons would be overwhelmingly Presbyterian. Monk, through Grenville and Mordaunt, urged Charles to promise a confirmation of land sales, an indemnity and a general liberty of conscience. Charles did not relish such proposals, especially the suggestion that he pardon his father's murderers, but he realized that it would be impolitic to reject them, so replied that these were complex matters, best referred to Parliament. Everything, therefore, hinged on the forthcoming elections.[25]

Once again, it was the people (or at least the electorate) who gave new momentum to the moves for Charles's restoration. Those who had been active Royalists in the civil wars were mostly deterred from standing by the recent Act, but many others with Royalist backgrounds were not; the provision that Royalists could not vote was everywhere ignored. In the counties, where the franchise was broadest, most of those chosen were identified as Royalists, or else Presbyterians believed to favour an unconditional restoration. In Worcestershire two 'arrant Cavaliers by generation and education' defeated the great Presbyterian ironmaster, Thomas Foley, despite all the efforts of the Presbyterian clergy and the military. In Cambridge a knight and a baronet were defeated by two obscure gentlemen because they would not pledge themselves to support an unconditional restoration in Church and state.[26] The few radicals who were returned were mostly chosen in small boroughs: the regicide Edmund Ludlow owned the manor containing the Wiltshire borough of Hindon (twenty-six voters); Luke Robinson owed his election at Scarborough to the backing of the popular admiral, Sir John Lawson. (It should be added that Ludlow was unseated on petition and Robinson emotionally recanted his republican views.)[27] Overall, the election produced a House of Commons fairly evenly divided, between those of Royalist and Parliamentarian backgrounds and between those of Anglican and Presbyterian views on religion.

The elections took place over a period of three weeks, during which the complexion of the Commons became increasingly apparent. The Royalists grew in confidence, the Presbyterians were driven on to the defensive. The council of state appointed by the expiring Long Parliament began to shift its ground. It had been expected to present Charles with proposals based on those of the 'treaty of Newport' in 1648. These included demands that Charles should share his direction of the government (notably his choice of ministers and command of the armed forces) with Parliament; that he should agree to abolish bishops and establish Presbyterianism; and that active Royalists be excluded from public life, which would give the Presbyterians a monopoly of office (and exclude Hyde from power). To this would now be added a general indemnity – all who had fought against Charles I were legally guilty of treason – and a confirmation of the sales of lands confiscated from the crown and Church. The Presbyterian peers also hoped to exclude from the Lords all peers created since 1642.[28]

The proposals about the indemnity and confirmation of sales (which, unlike the others, did not materially affect the king's prerogative) were sent to Charles in late March. At that time, it still seemed that Monk would join with the council of state to press for something like the 1648 conditions, but by mid-April he was apparently changing his tune. He did not discourage Royalists from voting in the elections, dealt more openly with Charles's emissaries and urged the council of state to refer everything to Parliament. There were two probable reasons for his change of attitude. First, the electors were making clear their hostility to preconditions for Charles's return. Second, he had secured a promise from all the officers in the army to acquiesce in whatever Parliament should decide. As purges of the army and navy continued, their political complexion changed: soldiers in Hyde Park cried, 'God bless king and Parliament!'[29] Meanwhile, the Presbyterians' confidence sagged. Some concentrated on the call for an indemnity, others disguised their unease with loud talk and strident demands. Demoralization bred division and fears grew that councillors would break ranks and make individual deals with the king. Thurloe told Bordeaux that the council hoped to negotiate terms before Parliament met, but time was running out. By 14 April the Presbyterians despaired of a majority in the Commons and pinned their hopes on the Lords, where the fourteen peers who had sat in 1648 hoped to set themselves up as a 'noble Rump' and block unacceptable bills sent up by the Commons.[30]

Charles, meanwhile, cautiously reacted to events, writing to those who might be able to serve him and receiving graciously all who came over from England. To please Monk, he promised the second secretaryship, vacant since Bristol's conversion, to Morrice. He also urged his supporters to renounce all thoughts of revenge.[31] In response to Monk's approach through Grenville and Mordaunt, a declaration was drafted (in large part by Hyde) to be delivered to the new Parliament. Dated 4 April, at Breda, it referred the contentious issues of the indemnity, Church settlement and land sales to Parliament. Charles assured the soldiers that they would be paid in full and that, if they wished, he would take them into his service. While on some points he expressed a preference – for example, for a measure of 'liberty to tender consciences' – he made it clear that he would act only in conjunction with Parliament. His aim, he said, was to bring discord to an end and establish peace and unity.[32]

In many ways, what the declaration did not say was as important as what it did: there was no mention of the king's prerogatives, or of the 1648 demands. Instead, it concentrated on reassuring those who had fought against Charles I or served the regimes of the 1650s that they would not lose their lives, lands or religious liberty if Charles returned. As the political balance in the new Parliament became clear, former Parliamentarians could be confident that it would not become a vehicle of Cavalier vengeance and so would be willing to follow Monk's advice and leave it to Parliament to lay down the ground rules of the restored monarchy. Those who harboured hopes of office, moreover, could now seek the king's favour without anxiety.

Hyde claimed later that there were parts of the declaration that he disliked,[33] but its reception vindicated his insistence that Charles should sacrifice neither prerogative nor Church, but trust in the loyalty and good sense of the bulk of his people. Now, as the iron grip of the New Model relaxed, that loyalty and good sense could express themselves. This became clear when Parliament (called a 'Convention', as it had not been called by a king) met on 25 April. Much clearly depended on Monk, who (along with Morrice) tried at first to persuade both Parliament and king to agree that the latter should return on conditions. At the least, Monk insisted on the points that he had put to Charles a month earlier – an indemnity and a guarantee of land sales, which (it could be argued) were vital, to bring the army to acquiesce in the king's return. It seems possible, however, that (like the Presbyterians) Monk wished to impose more stringent conditions – possible, but not certain, because his conduct was far from consistent. He was easily influenced by those about him, who proffered diverging advice, and it is by no means clear that he ever fully thought through what he intended to do. As the mood of the Commons became clearer and some Presbyterians, judging Charles's return to be inevitable, rushed to seek his favour, Monk edged towards a restoration without preconditions. Later, he naturally claimed that this had been his aim all the time, but there is considerable evidence that he would rather it had been otherwise.

When the Convention met, Monk helped to hurry through the election of a Presbyterian as Speaker of the Commons, in a thin House. He supported proposals to inspect MPs' qualifications, with a view to excluding those of Royalist backgrounds, and to deny peers created since 1642 the right to sit in the Lords. He declared that the army expected these Royalists to be excluded, but later changed his mind.[34] While he refused, in the end, to allow the Presbyterians to determine the Houses' composition, he hesitated to espouse the king's cause. Not until 1 May would he allow Grenville to present the king's declaration and letter to the Commons. His pretext was the need to allow time for recently elected MPs to arrive, but his later conduct suggests another motive. After the House had stood, bareheaded, to hear the declaration, Morrice told MPs that Charles would not keep his throne long unless he came in by some 'convenient agreement'. The king's letter, he claimed, suggested that he was willing to accept terms and called for a bill to be prepared to that effect. On the 5th Morrice advised Charles to let the House know that he would agree to such 'necessary things' as should be proposed to him. This would 'make your empire more safe by being less absolute' and would lay to rest any lingering 'ill-humours' among the army and people.[35]

In the first week of May, various restrictions were proposed in the Commons. Monk assured his Royalist friends he was entirely the king's, but that he had given his word that he would see the soldiers' land purchases confirmed.[36] In fact, he and the Presbyterians pressed for much more. Bills confirming the legality of the Convention and of the judicial decisions of the past eighteen years won wide support and were later to receive the royal assent. There were also others: to confirm land sales; for an indemnity; to allow freedom of worship, until religion could be settled by a national synod; and to confirm the abolition (in 1645) of the Court of Wards. All of these were included in a package of reforms proposed by Monk, together with his appointment for life as lord general, the annulment of all grants under the Great Seal since 1642 (which would include peerage creations) and a promise by Charles to approve such Acts and ordinances passed without the royal assent (since the end of 1641) as the Convention should present to him.[37] There were also proposals, originating in the Lords, that the king's powers of appointment should be restricted and that a committee of both Houses, with powers similar to those of the council of state, should direct the government.[38] These last proposals, rejected in the Commons, showed the Presbyterian peers' eagerness to secure office and to deny Hyde the chancellorship; to the latter end, they proposed that the Great Seal be entrusted to commissioners, of whom Manchester was to be one. There were also strenuous attempts to prejudice Monk (and his wife) against Hyde, equally strenuously countered by Hyde's supporters.[39]

For all their efforts, time was not on the side of Monk and the Presbyterians. As it became clear that the Commons wanted Charles back without conditions, Monk bowed to the inevitable. On the 5th, despite all Morrice's arguments, Monk agreed that it should be proposed that Charles be invited home. He still insisted that the soldiers should, at the very least, be granted long leases at moderate rents of the crown and Church lands they had bought: after his promises to them, he could do no less. Since the Declaration of Breda, however, the onus for making good that promise now lay not on the king but on Parliament and so posed no obstacle to Charles's return. On the 8th the Commons resolved that Charles should be proclaimed king and invited to return as soon as possible. Further proposals were advanced for bills to be presented to him on his return, but now that the invitation had been issued, there was little enthusiasm for preconditions.[40]

Charles must have observed these developments with a mixture of joy and trepidation. Hyde had made it clear in April that Charles put all his trust in Monk – he had little option – but the reports he received (and Morrice's letter of 5 May) must have made him anxious. On the 10th Charles wrote to Monk, praising the general's discretion and intimating that it would be easier to find ways of removing anxieties once Charles was in England. He also remarked that some needed to be subdued by force rather than wooed by kindness. To Morrice, he stressed that the Royalists in the Commons had renounced vengeance and argued that it would be unreasonable to take advantage of their restraint by advancing 'inconvenient' demands. In both letters, there was just the hint of a threat and he reminded Monk that both he and the army had promised to submit to the will of Parliament.[41] Underlying the polite phrases was a clear message: Charles would not agree to preconditions. His information, or his instincts, suggested that Monk would not stand out against the wishes of the greater part of the Commons and of the nation, and he was right. By the time his letter arrived the Commons had resolved that no bills should be presented to him before his arrival in England. The Commons prepared an indemnity bill and agreed (largely at Monk's urging) to exclude only seven of the regicides from pardon. They also, however, ordered that all who had sentenced the late king to death should be arrested and there matters rested until his son returned.[42]

The sudden turn in Charles's fortunes was not universally appreciated, or welcomed. Even in early May the Spaniards still claimed that they could restore him with Leveller help. Edmund Ludlow wondered how God could have turned against His people to the point of allowing 'the worm' to return. The 'queen's party' denounced the Presbyterians for losing heart and rushing to make their peace with the king. They (and Mazarin) also blamed the queen for not ensuring that a reliable person was at Charles's side to counter Hyde's malign influence; when she sent St Albans to England at the end of May it was far too late.[43] For Charles and his brothers, by contrast, these were heady days. The States General, which had more than once in the past denied them entry into the republic, wined and dined them sumptuously at the Hague. Charles was still short of money and shabbily dressed, but gold flowed in from Parliament and well-wishers. Setting sail on the *Naseby* (hastily renamed the *Royal Charles*), on 25 May he landed at Dover. He refused to set foot on English soil until Monk was there to greet him and, having done so, did all that was expected of him. He fell on his knees and thanked God, then rose up, embraced the general and called him 'Father'. He assured the Speaker of the Commons that he would uphold the laws and the Protestant religion. When the Mayor of Dover presented him with a Bible, Charles declared that he loved it above all books in the world.[44]

In the next few days, the royal brothers were dazed by all the bells, bonfires and cheering crowds. At Canterbury, Charles attended a service in the battered cathedral, in which the Book of Common Prayer (banned since 1645) was used. Monk gave Charles a long list of those he said should be appointed to offices as 'acceptable to the people'; Charles put it in his pocket, mumbling that he would always be ready to receive Monk's advice. Morrice, now Sir William, entered upon his duties as secretary; he told the king that Monk had promised these people that he would do what he could for them and that it would perhaps be wise to grant what they asked. Charles, tactfully, said nothing.[45] Escorted by many volunteer troops of cavalry, he made his stately way to London, completing his journey on the 29th, his birthday. The diarist John Evelyn watched his entry:

with a triumph of above two hundred thousand horse and foot, brandishing their swords and shouting with unexpressable joy; the ways strewed with flowers, the bells ringing, the streets hung with tapestry, fountains running with wine; the Mayor, aldermen and all the companies in their liveries, chains of gold, banners; lords and nobles, cloth of silver, gold and velvet everybody clad in; the windows and balconies all set with ladies; trumpets, music and myriads of people flocking the streets and ways as far as Rochester, so as they were seven hours in passing the City, even from two in the afternoon till nine at night. I stood in the Strand and beheld it and blessed God. And all this without one drop of blood.[46]

When he entered his capital Charles was in his prime: tall and vigorous, with only his greying hair hinting at advancing age and the privations of exile. As he freely admitted, he was no beauty, but the lines of his face had not yet been distorted by sagging jowls. He dressed plainly and his pleasures were often simple – fishing, boating, riding, tennis and above all walking (for several hours each day). As patron of the Royal Society he was much more than a figurehead: his scientific activities included dissections and chemical experiments in his own laboratory. He leaned more towards the practical than the theoretical, talking at length with the craftsmen who worked on his palaces and showing an especial interest in shipbuilding. In general, he disliked sitting still: only late in life did he begin to read regularly. He believed that vigorous exercise was good for his health, trusting more in that (and a moderate diet) than in the ministrations of his doctors, except on the rare occasions when he was seriously ill.[47]

Given his simple and active tastes, he not surprisingly eschewed the elaborate and static formality which was the norm in continental courts and which reached its apogee at Louis XIV's Versailles. Charles spoke contemptuously of the King of Spain, who 'will not piss but another must hold the chamber pot'.[48] His court was as domestic as the scale of his palaces allowed – Whitehall, in particular, was a labyrinth of chambers and corridors. He loved to escape from the smoke and disease of London to Windsor or Newmarket, where affairs of state counted for less than the prowess of horses and hounds and he was under no pressure to act the part of a king. Even at Whitehall, he dined in conditions that Pepys thought squalid and his beloved spaniels were everywhere, especially in the royal bedchamber, where before a roaring fire and amid a confused cacophony of chiming clocks, the bitches were allowed 'to puppy and give suck, which rendered it very offensive and indeed made the whole court nasty and stinking'.[49] Above all else, Charles loved 'sauntering and talking': a good listener himself, he was always looking for a new audience for his favourite stories, especially those about his adventures after Worcester. He talked more like a gentleman than a learned pedant, thought the Earl of Ailesbury. He was unfailingly courteous, doffing his hat to people of all ranks in the galleries at Whitehall and receiving suitors and ambassadors with his hat on, so that they (according to established convention) could keep theirs on too.[50]

Charles, in short, was in many respects 'a very honest gentleman': affable and courteous, without vanity or jealousy and so not susceptible to flattery. Sometimes, however, his inclination towards the leisured lifestyle of a country squire came into conflict with his responsibilities as king. He found it difficult to look and act like a king, to maintain his dignity and keep his distance; too often he would let 'all distinction and ceremony fall to the ground as useless and foppish'.[51] He was a poor public speaker and did not mind being told his faults in private, provided this was done in a witty or gentlemanly manner. He also, however, had a fiery temper and could, if he chose, put on 'an awful majesty'.[52] Indeed, if he did not 'act that part of a king', this was largely because he was so conscious of his rank that he felt no need to do so; when he felt that his rank was being impugned (in protocol disputes, or when Dutch ships refused to salute the English flag) he vigorously defended his dignity. By avoiding a formal routine, he gained a greater flexibility in the conduct of business than Louis XIV enjoyed. He talked with foreign ambassadors in his wife's bedchamber; politicians out of favour could gain access via the backstairs. He did not neglect routine altogether – he would usually be in the queen's apartments around seven in the evening – but such routines could not be relied on: in 1668 the public entry of the Venetian ambassador had to be postponed when Charles suddenly left town and in 1671 a visit to Plymouth was marred (from the corporation's point of view) by his arriving before they were ready and leaving before they could kiss his hand.[53]

Although Charles was deeply conscious of his status and (thanks to his informal style) worked harder than his relaxed manner might suggest, it is still hard to avoid the impression that he did not take the business of governing entirely seriously, especially in the 1660s. In exile, he had at times seemed unconcerned about being restored; once installed as king, he was determined to enjoy life to the full. He disliked paperwork and often forgot to send letters which he had promised.[54] He attended the privy council regularly, but gave little direction to its proceedings. Easily bored, he passed the time exchanging notes with Hyde. The council did not usually discuss the matters which most interested him – the traditional preserves of monarchs, diplomacy and war. Charles talked at length with foreign ambassadors. His army was too small to be an effective instrument of policy, but he devoted a great deal of time to the navy, particularly the deployment of ships and the appointment of officers. He showed little interest in other areas of administration. Ministers had to keep their business brief, or Charles would lose interest; suitors could find themselves repeatedly interrupted. Lord Treasurer Southampton had to beg Charles to devote just one hour to the consideration of his revenue. Pepys deplored his lack of attention at council meetings: he fiddled with his dogs or his codpiece and his comments were often vapid or irrelevant.[55] His ministers had to 'administer business to him as doctors do physic, wrap it up in something to make it less unpleasant'. One French ambassador, Courtin, learned that by talking of women he could slide the conversation around to other matters. Another remarked that although Charles divided his time between pleasure and business, he applied himself far more to the former.[56]

But did this matter? No king could do everything himself: kingship was a matter of delegation, but with the king making the major decisions. Effective delegation, however, required, first, choosing competent ministers and, second, a willingness to follow their advice and to back them up when necessary. Charles was certainly capable of recognizing talent. Hyde (soon to be created Earl of Clarendon) was a diligent administrator and many of Charles's other ministers (including Shaftesbury, Danby and Clarendon's son Rochester) were men of great ability. Others were less distinguished. Hyde's old friend Southampton was incapable either of managing the treasury or of persuading the king to look seriously at his finances. Conway, who as secretary of state shared the responsibility for foreign affairs, had never heard of the circles of Germany.[57] But the most extraordinary of Charles's advisers was Buckingham. He held no ministerial office but at times exercised a substantial influence on domestic and foreign policy. His character was immortalized by Dryden:

> A man so various that he seem'd to be
> Not one but all mankind's epitome.
> Stiff in opinions, always in the wrong,
> Was everything by starts and nothing long:
> But in the course of one revolving moon
> Was chemist, fiddler, statesman and buffoon.

Dryden's view might be dismissed as the product of Tory bias, but it was largely shared by the Whiggish Burnet. Usually Burnet tried to find something positive to say in even the most hostile of character sketches – but not in Buckingham's case:

He was never true either to things or persons, but forsakes every man and departs from every maxim, sometimes out of levity and an unsettledness of fancy and sometimes out [of] downright falsehood; he could never fix himself to business but has a perpetual unsteadiness about him. He is revengeful to all degrees and is, I think, one of the worst men alive, both as to his personal deportment and as to the public.[58]

Buckingham's influence upon Charles rested in part on sheer force of personality – what Pepys called 'briskness' – and partly on his ability to exploit Charles's love of pleasure. By keeping Charles amused with wine, women and wit, Buckingham could separate him from his graver counsellors and insinuate his own prejudices and projects.[59] He was often banished from court and even sent to the Tower for his outrageous behaviour, but as a rule Charles quickly forgave him, as he found his jests and company irresistible. As a result, foreign ambassadors had to take the duke seriously, although they found it hard to deal with a man who would carouse all night and sleep all day. As for his advice, it was neither consistent nor disinterested. The dreams of military glory to which he had given voice on the eve of the battle of Worcester resurfaced in 1670–3 and he reacted just as petulantly when his claims were rebuffed. An old courtier, Lord Crofts, remarked that if the duke ever applied himself he could have had all Charles's favour, but he always wished to be popular, to please the people as well as the king. His acerbic wit made him many enemies – few were challenged to so many duels (and fought so few of them) – and he used his credit with the king to pursue his vendettas. Sir William Coventry was one of the few administrators respected by Pepys for both ability and integrity and was a leading figure on the treasury commission which tried to bring order to Charles's finances after Southampton's death. He soon fell foul of Buckingham. Knowing that Coventry had recently acquired a circular desk, Buckingham wrote a play in which two buffoons sat in the middle of similar desks, prattling foolishly. Coventry, never renowned for his sense of humour, sent the duke a challenge. Charles dismissed him from his offices, thus sacrificing a servant who was industrious and disinterested (if abrasive) to a companion who was neither.[60]

If choosing well was one necessary aspect of delegation, the other was to trust in and support those chosen. Trust, however, did not come easily to Charles. For almost as long as he could remember, he had been used and betrayed by those close to him (not least his mother), beset by spies and surrounded by intrigues and feuds. Such experiences bred a cynical view of human nature, as essentially self-interested, so he placed unstinting trust in no one. Instead, he resorted to the time-honoured strategy of balancing one minister against another. The Marquis of Halifax later wrote:

He had backstairs to convey informations to him, as well as for other uses; and though such informations are sometimes dangerous (especially to a prince that will not take the pains necessary to digest them) yet in the main that humour of hearing everybody against anybody kept those about him in more awe than they would have been without it.[61]

That, certainly, was what Charles believed. He claimed that he showed favour to both Buckingham and Arlington (the former Sir Henry Bennet), knowing that they loathed each other, but that he would never abandon himself to their caprices. As Coventry's case shows, such claims are open to question and Halifax himself was to complain bitterly of Charles's inconstancy.[62] What made things worse, from the ministers' point of view, was that their influence on Charles was often less than that of the companions of his pleasures. Having reached a decision in council, he allowed those who waited upon him 'to examine and censure what was resolved; an infirmity', wrote Clarendon feelingly, 'that brought him many troubles and exposed his ministers to ruin'.[63] As a result, the body servants, the wits and the women (the 'little people', Clarendon called them) exercised real political influence. Charles might try to convince himself that he was in overall control and that he could separate business from pleasure: jests were one thing, matters of state another. Clarendon wrote that Charles 'did not in his nature love a busy woman and had an aversion from speaking with any woman, or hearing them speak, of any business, but to that purpose he thought them all made for; however,' he added, 'they broke in afterwards upon him to all other purposes'. Pepys noted that Charles was a slave to women and could not control himself in their presence. Clarendon blamed his downfall on one mistress, the Countess of Castlemaine, and another, the Duchess of Portsmouth, was one of the leading political figures of the latter years of the reign.[64]

Charles's ruthless sacrifice of Clarendon, after twenty-five years' loyal service, showed how little he could be relied on: many remarked that he forgot his friends as easily as he forgave his enemies.[65] Halifax might claim that 'he tied himself no more to them [his ministers] than they did to him, which implied a sufficient liberty on both sides'.[66] Maybe so, but where there was no trust there could be no loyalty. Unable to rely on the king, ministers lived in constant fear of attack from court or Commons; they also had to devote time and effort to managing the king and the courtiers and to fighting off potential rivals.[67] Under Charles II, a minister's lot was not a happy one.

Kings needed to be able to delegate; but they also had to make decisions. Effective decision-making requires both adequate information and a measure of consistency. Charles's lack of application created a risk that he would base decisions on insufficient knowledge. Moreover, he came to the throne not only with minimal experience of government but in many respects as a stranger in a strange land: he wrote shortly before his return that he did not *know* most of those with whom he had to deal.[68] To this should be added the fact that the quantity and quality of information available to early modern governments were vastly inferior to those of the present day. The civil service was tiny and the science of statistics, upon which rational decision-making so often depends, was only just beginning to be applied to the practicalities of government. Charles's ministers had only a hazy idea of the population of his kingdoms, the basic outlines of their economies and the relative numerical strengths of the various religious denominations. Understanding of the king's finances, for which the relevant information did exist, was hampered by the exchequer's antiquated and eccentric system of accounts. On top of all this, the quality of information available to Charles was further reduced by his habit of heeding the views of those he liked at least as much as those of his experienced officials.

If his information was deficient, his capacity for making decisions was still more so. Almost everyone agreed that Charles had the intelligence to understand the problems that faced him, but that he was not good at making decisions. Sometimes, he just could not be bothered or shied away from depressing realities, especially in matters of money: the way to succeed with Charles was to make him believe things were better than they were. He seems to have found finance not only boring but vulgar: he was 'of so generous a nature as not to love the discourse or dispute of money matters'. He rarely appreciated the value of money, especially if he could not see it.[69] It is, however, important to distinguish between public and private money. It was never easy to focus his attention on the crown's revenues or accounts, but when it came to his personal finances he was much more careful. He resented losing small sums at tennis and complained when his mistresses lost money at cards; and yet he provided for them lavishly from the public purse. He valued a few hundred pounds in the privy purse more than many thousands in the exchequer and in his last years amassed a nest-egg which was worth close on £100,000 when he died. It may be that he simply could not distinguish between different orders of magnitude, but it is also possible that he treasured the illusion of independence that came from a private fund of his own.[70]

Quite apart from his indolence and reluctance to face financial reality, Charles was congenitally indecisive. The sharp intelligence which enabled him swiftly to understand a problem also showed him the snags inherent in any course of action. He disliked being troubled with 'the intricacy of affairs' and recoiled from bold (and irrevocable) decisions.[71] Unwilling to trust fully in his own judgement, he sought the advice of others; he might be persuaded for a while, only to have his mind changed by other arguments. Despite his innate mistrust he was easily led – and misled; while quick to spot the follies and errors of others, he was curiously blind to his own.[72] Perhaps more to the point was the fact that Charles found decisions difficult. He tended to see both sides of a question and to be swept along (for the time being) by others more strongwilled than himself. Hyde, it was said, would get Charles among his papers, reading and commenting on one letter after another. As Charles did not like to be 'overpressed with such knotty and intricate things' and longed to be off to his pleasures, Hyde was able to lead the king to the resolutions he wanted.[73] Others managed the king differently – Buckingham, as we have seen, used revelry and raillery – but the important point was that he could be managed. His was not a strong personality and he found it hard to resist importunity. Weakness or politeness made him reluctant to say no, so he made promises which he knew his ministers would not allow him to keep.[74] Perhaps for this reason he disliked being reminded of what he had said the day before, which made it extraordinarily difficult to tie him to a consistent line of policy.[75] Ministers complained of the difficulty of bringing him to a resolution; but he could also be rushed into decisions which he later regretted.[76]

That, at least, was how it seemed to contemporaries: but was Charles perhaps cleverer than they thought? Behind the mask of affable inconsistency, was he playing a subtle game, keeping his courtiers and ministers guessing, while he alone really knew what was going on? Clearly, he was adept at dissimulation: like a spy or a riverboat gambler, deceit for Charles became second nature. But could dissimulation alone be an effective basis for government? People could become used to it, charm could wear thin.[77] To test the hypothesis that Charles was the arch-manipulator, always in control, one needs to look at what he did, not at what he said. One needs to deduce the assumptions upon which he acted, his perception of his political world and of the problems that faced him. If those assumptions and perceptions seem, with hindsight, inaccurate or incongruous, they may still have significantly influenced his actions. Given his ability to hide his true feelings, no one will ever be entirely sure about his motives or intentions: probably he was not sure himself. My impression is that he was intelligent but irresolute; he found it easier to perceive problems than to resolve them by a positive decision. He was pulled this way and that by the advice and insinuations of those around him, by conflicting policy considerations and by tensions between his personal and official capacities, between the man and the king. He was a warm, emotional human being, affectionate and tactile, easily moved to love or anger, easily appeased. He was 'an easy generous lover, a civil obliging husband, a friendly brother, an indulgent father and a good natured master' – but not 'a firm and grateful friend'.[78] To see only the king, to the exclusion of the man, would be rather like seeing *Hamlet* purely as a political play.

In order to assess Charles's priorities in 1660, we need to consider his perception of his kingdoms. The past twenty years had seen civil wars, his father's execution and the abolition of the House of Lords. For eleven years, the army had raised up and cast down one Parliament after another. In the localities the old ruling families had been pushed out of office or subjected to the direction of low-born soldiers, like Colonel Pride, the drayman, and Colonel Hewson, the cobbler. The Church of England had been overthrown, bishops abolished and use of the Prayer Book forbidden. Into the vacuum thus created had rushed strange new sects, each demanding the right to worship as it chose; their leaders were not learned, ordained clergymen but 'rude mechanics' and even women. They were as abhorrent to old-style Puritans (or Presbyterians) as they were to adherents of the pre-civil-war Church. Everywhere comfortable ordered certainties seemed to be dissolving: the world was being turned upside down.

As these developments unfolded, Charles must have been far more conscious of the extent of the damage sustained by the old order than of the fact that much of what happened violated the deepest principles of those involved. Most Parliamentarians took up arms for negative reasons, to prevent the changes which seemed to be threatened by Charles I, not to build a New Jerusalem. England's government rested much more than most on the co-operation and consent of the governed, from MPs at Westminster down to constables and overseers of the poor in the villages. Law enforcement depended on the participation of private citizens, as magistrates and jurors, in cases ranging from murder and rape at county assizes down to boundary disputes and nuisances in manorial courts. This permeation through society of legal knowledge and legal values ensured that England's was, by the standards of the time, an unusually law-abiding society: even rioters were quite convinced that the law was on their side. The practical fact of popular participation in government was mirrored in theories of the constitution, which stressed mutuality, co-operation and consent. Add to this that the nobility had largely lost its military power – indeed, English society was probably the least martial in western Europe – and it would seem that civil war was profoundly unlikely. Yet there was another side to this picture. Habits of co-operation and consent invited discussion of the terms upon which they were exercised. The deep sense of legality created expectations that the conduct of government would meet certain standards of justice and equity. The relatively wide dissemination of political and parliamentary news, especially in London, created an informed public opinion. Any serious deviation from expected standards of fair dealing would provoke, not a rebellion, but serious disquiet in the body through which the English had come to deal with their king – Parliament.

It is worth stressing that the armed resistance which forced Charles I to call the Long Parliament came not from England but from Scotland. When Parliament began to arm late in 1641, it did so in response to the perceived threat that the king would resort to force: talk of self-defence was more than empty rhetoric. If Parliament failed to come to terms with the king, it was not for want of trying; it did, however, open the way for others who sought more radical solutions. The collapse of the army's power in 1659–60, however, allowed the nation's overwhelming attachment to monarchy to reassert itself and Charles returned on a wave of popular acclaim.

That, at least, is how historians can see the situation, with the benefit of both hindsight and a wide range of information not available to Charles II. He, by contrast, grew up within a politically enclosed environment, surrounded first by the Royalist high command, then by squabbling exiles. The information that he received was often distorted by factional bias or wishful thinking and was filtered or 'interpreted' by those around him. He was naturally more struck by the visible defiance of Parliament and visible radicalism of soldiers and sectaries than by the stolid law-abiding conservatism of the bulk of the nation, in which Hyde put so much faith. In retrospect, it must have seemed that by resisting the king Parliament had unleashed forces of republicanism and regicide which it could not control. Experience of Scotland convinced Charles that Presbyterianism was hostile to monarchy; experience of England in the 1640s must have left him with a similar view of Parliaments and of his subjects in general. He was probably only half joking when he said, on his return to London, 'that he doubted it had been his own fault that he had been absent so long, for he saw nobody that did not protest he had ever wished for his return'.[79]

This distrust of his people suggested two possible strategies. Either he could try to conciliate them, or he could try to build up his power so that he was no longer dependent on their goodwill. The former would suit Charles's indolence and caution and seemed appropriate to his uncertainty about how the nation would react to having a king again. The second option, of moving towards an 'absolute' monarchy like that of France, also appealed to him. He declared that he did not think he was a king while Parliament could examine his actions, ministers and accounts, and some of his advisers dangled before him the prospect of much greater power.[80] Some historians, too, see 'absolutism' as the natural line of development for the later Stuart monarchy.[81] This view, it seems to me, is seriously flawed. Absolutism developed on the continent as kings struggled with the problems of provincial diversity and of the dispersal of political power (to towns, groups of officials and the like) which impeded the mobilization of men and money for war. England, however, was far more uniform institutionally than France or Spain and already possessed (as they did not) a means of mobilizing consent at a national level. Moreover, in the 1640s Parliament had constructively tackled the practical problems of making war, creating a fiscal system which tapped the nation's wealth far more efficiently than any which had previously existed in England (or indeed in most states in Europe). Parliament had also built the navy into a formidable force: it contained three times as many ships in 1664 as in 1642 and if the number remained much the same for the rest of the reign, the proportion of larger ships grew substantially. It also created England's first professional army: if much of it was disbanded in 1660, there remained in being the foundations of a 'fiscal-military state'.[82] For its full potential to be realized, kings needed the co-operation of Parliament, which alone could vote (and so legitimate) the large taxes which an effective war effort required. Thus on the continent the needs of war tended to lead to the obliteration of traditional liberties and the denial of consent; in England, by contrast, the needs of war reinforced the king's dependence on his people's co-operation.

It would seem, then, that the main stimulus to the development of western European absolutism (the need to raise money for war) was lacking in England. There were fears that Charles would try (like Cromwell) to impose military rule, or to undermine Parliament's independence through bribery or electoral chicanery, thus detaching the appearance of consent from the reality. Charles sometimes made tetchy remarks about Parliaments, but there is no evidence that he intended to do without them: as he once remarked, a king who was not slave to five hundred kings was great enough. Burnet remarked that Charles may have liked the idea of absolutism, but lacked the energy (and maybe the courage) to put his ideas into practice.[83] His instincts inclined him to conciliation, not confrontation, but that did not ensure an easy reign. The surviving radicals of the 1650s might be a small minority, but some still hoped to overturn the restored monarchy: this ensured some anxious years for the new regime. Moreover, policies which were intended to be conciliatory could turn out to be provocative, simply because Charles and his advisers had misjudged public, and Parliamentary, opinion. His years of exile had given Charles a distorted impression of the balance of political and religious forces within England: he overestimated the strength of Dissent and so made concessions to Dissenters which infuriated the Anglican majority. Finally, he had to contend with an informed and politically sophisticated public opinion. The country squires who served as JPs and MPs; the London plutocrats upon whom the crown depended for loans; the provincial lawyers and merchants who ran municipal government; the yeomen and citizens who voted in elections and who, if they took to the streets, could severely embarrass a government with limited powers of coercion: all of these had expectations of Charles II. They expected his government to be competent, fair and reasonably free of corruption; and they expected it to pursue policies of which the public broadly approved. How far Charles would match up to these expectations remained to be seen.

The King Restored

Inevitably the euphoria which greeted Charles's return did not last long. There were too many conflicting expectations and the divisions of the previous twenty years could not be conjured away, as if by magic, by the king's return. Many Royalists had suffered huge losses. They had brought their gold and silver to aid the war effort, their lands had been confiscated and many had had their homes plundered. But others had claims on the king's gratitude. Some of the exiles had secured promises of favours which, at the time, had seemed hypothetical but could now be cashed. Presbyterian politicians and army and navy officers had rushed to Holland to assure the king of their loyalty and to persuade him of their usefulness. Their cause was most vehemently pleaded by Monk, but Hyde agreed that many Presbyterians had performed services worthy of reward, while too many Royalists were dissolute and vindictive.[1] By the time Charles returned, so many places and favours had been promised to exiles or Presbyterians that there was little left for the Royalists and Charles could not afford to reward them from his own pocket. He inherited heavy debts from the previous regimes and his own revenues were settled slowly and at first proved insufficient. Moreover, in soliciting for favours impoverished Royalists found themselves at a disadvantage, as they could not afford the fees and douceurs demanded by those in power at court, from Lord Chancellor Hyde downwards; many Presbyterians, however, could. Even before the end of June, old Cavaliers complained bitterly that Charles had forgotten his father's friends and sought only to reward his enemies.[2]

The dominant figure at court was Hyde. Monk enjoyed great prestige as the military strongman who had brought about the Restoration, and was laden with honours and rewards, but he had little talent for politics or administration. His endless importunities eroded his credit and he was appointed Lord Lieutenant of Ireland to get him out of the way.[3] By contrast, Charles saw Hyde as the master strategist who had made his return possible and found him a willing administrative workhorse, who also had the strength of character (which Charles had not) to say no to suitors; this had the added benefit that those who were disappointed blamed Hyde, not Charles. However, although Charles appreciated Hyde's usefulness, the two did not always see eye to eye. More than twenty years older than his master, Hyde was solemn, ponderous and censorious. Borne up (some would have said puffed up) by confidence in his own rectitude, he scorned the odium which his conduct aroused. He had little sense of fun and strongly disapproved of Charles's obvious determination to enjoy himself after the enforced austerity of exile. He bemoaned Charles's fondness for lewd and irreverent companions, his refusal to apply himself to the business of government or, indeed, to take anything entirely seriously. To Hyde this was just one more symptom of the way in which the civil wars had destroyed the old values – friendship, honour, respect for one's elders. He wistfully told Parliament that he hoped the nation would return to 'its old good manners, its old good humour and its old good nature'.[4]

Both the chancellor's age and his training as a lawyer encouraged him to revere the old ways and the old constitution, with its ideal of a balance between the king's powers and the subject's rights. He thought that the king should govern, as in the past, in consultation with his privy council. In fact, as this proved too unwieldy to handle the mass of business which came before it, much was delegated to specialist committees, such as those for the plantations and for Ireland. Besides, it was impossible to maintain secrecy in a body of around forty, so a small, select 'committee for foreign affairs' was created. The brutal fact was that, despite Hyde's reverence, the privy council had long ago proved unable to co-ordinate government, especially in wartime. Similarly, the traditional great offices, such as lord treasurer or lord admiral, could prove too burdensome for one man. Charles at times recognized this; following the example of the regimes of the 1640s and 1650s, he appointed commissions to perform the functions of such offices. Hyde denounced such practices as fitter for a republic than for a monarchy. He had no time for novelty or for foreign models: in his long exile he had failed to learn enough French or Spanish to carry on a conversation or write a letter. Charles, to Hyde's disgust, positively approved of innovation.[5]

This does not, however, mean that Charles's constitutional views differed fundamentally from Hyde's. He showed little inclination to embark on radical changes, nor is there any sign that he had any clear-cut strategy at all: he simply wished to enjoy his own. Given the suddenness of his return and his lack of familiarity with English institutions and politicians, it would have been amazing if he *had* come over with a blueprint for change. Less than confident of the strength of his position, his instinct was to feel his way. Later he was persuaded that Hyde had missed out (perhaps deliberately) on a great chance to secure both a large standing army and a much enhanced revenue.[6] Bristol claimed as early as July 1660 that the monarchy could have been made much stronger had Charles exploited the torrent of affection in his favour.[7] But such claims were usually made by Hyde's enemies: a close examination of the Convention's conduct between June and December 1660 suggests, not that ministers wilfully or negligently missed chances to strengthen the king's position, but rather that they liquidated the legacies of the Interregnum with skill and determination; where issues could not be resolved to Charles's advantage, they reserved his position. Hyde's caution complemented Charles's inclination to avoid irrevocable commitments and keep his options open. Hyde wrote that some 'are impatient to have all done at once, but I think it must be done by degrees'. There is no sign in 1660 that Charles was dissatisfied with Hyde; on the contrary, despite their differences of age and temperament, Charles valued the chancellor's services and apparently felt considerable affection for him. The notes that passed between them at council show, if not the relaxed intimacy of Charles's dealings with close friends like Bennet or Charles Berkeley, at least a familiarity born of long collaboration. Hyde later wrote that Charles's confidence in him rested more on respect for his industry than on 'any violence of affection, which was not so fixed in his nature as to be like to transport him to any one person'.[8] Such a comment perhaps reflects Hyde's later sense of betrayal rather than Charles's conduct towards him in 1660. Then his credit was widely seen as unshakeable, a view illustrated by the furore surrounding his daughter Anne's marriage to the Duke of York.

When James returned to England, Anne was already carrying his child. On 3 September the two were married (with Charles's permission) so secretly that even Hyde was not informed. He was naturally deeply embarrassed when the news leaked out; his enemies gleefully blackened the bride's character and stressed to both Charles and James the dangers and indignity of such a misalliance. The duke's servants claimed to have enjoyed Anne's favours in a variety of improbable locations; St Albans and Lord John Berkeley urged Charles to have the marriage annulled. Soon after, the queen arrived to add her voice to the clamour. James was badly shaken by the onslaught: he disowned his wife, then changed his mind when she gave birth to his daughter. Charles was much more resolute. He could see no lawful way to break the marriage, except by Act of Parliament, and he would never allow Parliament to adjudicate on royal marriages or the succession: that in his view would destroy the essence of hereditary monarchy – God alone should determine the succession. He may also have thought it unjust to dissolve a marriage entered into by consenting adults, with his permission: while he often behaved deviously, he possessed an innate sense of justice and told his brother he would not allow him to break the laws of God and man. It was quite clear to him that Hyde had known nothing of the marriage until it was concluded, so that complaints of the chancellor's presumption in marrying his daughter into the royal family were simply malicious. Charles showed his contempt for such gossip by offering to make Hyde a duke; Hyde declined, fearing the envy that the honour would arouse. He contented himself with the title of Baron Hyde and was created Earl of Clarendon in 1661. Finally, family tensions may have stiffened Charles's resolution. He regarded his stolid brother as a bit of a fool and probably enjoyed his discomfiture: some claimed that Charles thought that their mother had always preferred James. Besides, Charles was determined not to allow his mother to dictate to him. She and her servants complained that Charles showed more concern for a mere commoner than for his own mother; Charles in return made it clear that her claims to revenues from England would be settled only if she did his bidding. Reluctantly she bowed to the inevitable, speaking to Hyde with at least a pretence of politeness: the stiffness on both sides greatly amused the king. Her discomfiture did not end there. Mazarin told her firmly that her stubbornness was holding up an Anglo-French rapprochement; she gritted her teeth, received her new daughter-in-law and gave her her blessing.[9]

By now it was clear that she would never regain the political influence that she had enjoyed with Charles I. Faced with the prospect of losing her revenues, she assured her son that she had no intention of interfering in his affairs: she would simply make suggestions. Charles, however, refused to listen to them, turning his back and whistling when she tried to talk about public affairs. The queen became bored and miserable, complaining that she knew no one and that no one told her anything: only the need to settle her revenues kept her in England. To compound her miseries, Henry died in September and Mary (of smallpox) in December: only three of her children – Charles, James and Henriette – now survived. Charles, too, was deeply distressed by their deaths; his mother, with more than a hint of self-pity, exclaimed that she was used to finding sorrow in England and did not conceal her impatience to take Henriette back to France.[10]

One reason why Hyde's credit seemed unshakeable can be found in the success of the Convention. Charles had returned without preconditions mainly because the Declaration of Breda had referred to Parliament the matters which were likely to prove most immediately contentious – the indemnity, sales of royal and Church lands, liberty to tender consciences. These issues, weighty though they were, had mostly emerged since 1642: to settle them would not resolve the problems which had brought about the civil war. Central to these was the nature of royal power. Traditionally, the king had possessed a wide range of powers and a certain discretion about the way he used them. He was expected to observe the law, but the law was often open to abuse or differences of interpretation; besides, it had long been accepted that he could override normal legal procedures and rights if the national interest required it. Apart from his powers, the king also had various sources of revenue over and above those granted by Parliament. Charles I repeatedly twisted and stretched his legal powers, usually in order to raise money, to a point when his subjects no longer felt their liberty and property were safe. In 1641, therefore, the Long Parliament stripped him of most of his non-Parliamentary revenues and sought to restrict his powers. Charles I refused to give up control of either the armed forces or his choice of ministers so the Long Parliament proceeded without him. It passed an ordinance taking over control of the militia, followed by others which abolished the Court of Wards, episcopacy and the Prayer Book. Later Parliaments passed a wide range of legislation, ranging from the first Navigation Act (designed to give England a monopoly of trade with its colonies) to an Act imposing the death penalty for adultery.

The legal and constitutional legacy of the 1640s and 1650s was both complex and contentious. Two early measures resolved potentially awkward problems. On his return, Charles gave his assent to a bill declaring the Convention a lawful Parliament, even though it had not been summoned by a king. Three months later, the Act to confirm judicial proceedings ensured that verdicts reached in the past twenty years could not be challenged by disgruntled litigants.[11] These apart, the most pressing issue was the indemnity. Many could not feel secure while there remained a possibility that they could be prosecuted for their past actions. The Declaration of Breda promised a free pardon to all who accepted it within forty days and promised to be good subjects in future. Charles referred to Parliament the question of who was to be excluded from the benefits of this pardon, expressing the pious hope that all divisions and discords would be forgotten. His plea fell on deaf ears. The Commons were already debating the steps to be taken against those responsible for Charles I's death. They resolved that all who had handled any public moneys since 1642 should be called to account. They asked the king to order that all those in public office should take the oaths of allegiance and supremacy, as the law required; the Commons issued a similar order relating to the army and navy. (The oath of supremacy, recognizing the king as head of the Church of England, would be especially unpalatable to sectaries.) Soon after, the House asked Charles to issue a proclamation condemning Milton's political writings.[12]

Meanwhile, MPs plunged eagerly into the ghoulish business of deciding who should be left out of the general pardon. It seemed clear from the outset that the regicides (those who had condemned the king to death) would be excluded and on 6 June Charles issued a proclamation ordering them to give themselves up. Many MPs wanted the exclusions to be much more sweeping. One:

moved against those that petitioned against the king, or sat in Parliament between '48 and '49 and the high court of justice men and the contrivers of the Instrument [of Government] and the imposers of taxes under Oliver and major-generals and decimators and though he never pressed for the death of any, yet to secure the future peace of the realm he could not be silent.[13]

The debates in both Houses were long and ugly. MPs sought to protect their friends and destroy their enemies and the past was raked up angrily and often. There were two main points at issue. First, while it was accepted that all the regicides were to suffer in some way, how many were to lose both life and estate and how many were to suffer lesser punishments? Were those who had surrendered themselves in obedience to the king's proclamation to be treated more favourably than those who had not? Second, how many non-regicides were to be excluded (at least in part) from the benefits of the pardon? In the end, after almost three months of argument, the bill of oblivion was passed. It granted a pardon for all offences connected with the wars. For three years, anyone who indulged in recrimination about what had passed was to be liable to a fine. Thirty of the regicides were wholly excluded from pardon so that, if convicted of treason, they were to suffer the full penalties. The nineteen who had surrendered were also excluded, but if they were convicted the sentence could be carried out only after the passage of a special Act of Parliament. For those regicides who were no longer alive the question of the death penalty did not apply, but three (Cromwell, Ireton and Bradshaw) were wholly excluded from pardon; the rest were to forfeit their estates. Others who had helped bring about the king's death but had not sat as judges, or who had sat on the 'high courts of justice' which sentenced prominent Royalists to death, were to be liable (if convicted) to various penalties not extending to life; others were debarred from public office. Finally, John Lambert and Sir Henry Vane were wholly excluded from pardon, but the Commons undertook to petition the king on their behalf.[14]

Outwardly, except towards the regicides, Charles's attitude was one of forgiveness. To expedite the bill, he told the Lords on 27 July that he had never thought of excepting any but 'the immediate murderers of my father'. Hyde, however, made it clear that Charles expected the punishment to extend to all the regicides: the proclamation calling on them to surrender was not a promise of pardon. Moreover, Charles urged the Lords to take steps to guard against those 'of such dangerous and obstinate principles that the peace of the kingdom cannot be preserved whilst they have liberty in it'. (He later made it clear to the Commons that he was referring especially to Vane, Lambert, Heselrig and Axtell: all four were duly excluded from pardon.)[15] Clearly, Charles's eagerness that the bill should pass, even if this meant abandoning moneys which might be due to the crown, reflected less an inclination to mercy than a belief that its passage was politically essential. Until the soldiers and sailors had been assured of immunity from prosecution it would be impossible to disband them. Besides, the City made it clear that it would be reluctant to advance the necessary cash (on the security of taxes voted, but not yet collected) until the bill passed.[16] After he had assented to the bill, Charles's tone changed. In future, he told the Houses, 'the same discretion and conscience which disposed me to ... clemency ... will oblige me to all rigour and severity, how contrary soever it be to my nature, towards those who will not now acquiesce, but continue to manifest their sedition and dislike of the government, either in action or words'.[17] The last months of 1660 saw a series of treason trials, intended as much to emphasize to the public the sinfulness of rebellion as to punish the guilty. One after another, the regicides suffered the gruesome penalties for treason, until the inhabitants of the area around Charing Cross complained that the smell of burned bowels was putrefying the air.

Still, the thirst for vengeance was not slaked. The queen sent to the Houses, calling for justice against all those involved in her husband's death. The Commons ordered that the corpses of Cromwell, Ireton and Bradshaw be exhumed and displayed, as an awful warning of the consequences of rebellion.[18] Those regicides who escaped death were condemned by the next Parliament to suffer imprisonment and loss of property and to be paraded around London, like circus freaks, once a year. Lambert and Vane were tried for treason, although neither had been a regicide. Lambert threw himself on the mercy of the court and was condemned to life imprisonment, in which he quietly lost his mind. Vane, the most unbending of republicans, scorned to renounce his principles. Charles was furious at his defiance: 'if he has given new occasion to be hanged, certainly he is too dangerous a man to let live, if we can honestly put him out of the way'. When Vane was executed, on 14 June 1662, trumpeters were ordered to drown the speech he tried to deliver, but nothing could efface the courage which he displayed.[19]

Obviously, no Act of Parliament could wipe out the memories of twenty years of civil strife. In 1670 it was noted that of three hundred horsemen who greeted Ormond in Staffordshire, there was not one Roundhead.[20] There were many scores to be paid off. Clergymen and town councillors ousted during the previous twenty years secured orders for their reinstatement. Militia officers harassed those they chose to regard as disaffected; the persecution of Quakers and sectaries began before new laws were enacted against them. Many who had collected the revenues of the recent regimes were now required to account for their arrears. Yet while the past conduct of Parliamentarians and Puritans made them conspicuous and liable to harassment, they were at least immune from prosecution for treason and for other actions committed in time and place of war.

If the mildness of the Act of Indemnity annoyed vindictive Royalists, they were no better pleased by the steps taken to settle the question of land sales. These were of three types: the lands of bishops and deans and chapters, sold after the abolition of episcopacy; the lands of Royalists and Catholics, first 'sequestered' and managed for the state's benefit, then sold; and crown lands, sold after the abolition of the monarchy. For the regimes of the late 1640s and 1650s, such sales had been politically preferable to taxation. However, the lands had fetched only modest prices: they were sold quickly and potential purchasers feared that they might be reconfiscated if the monarchy and bishops were ever restored. Prices averaged (in real terms) about ten years' rent: in more stable times, purchasers would expect to pay twice that. Even so, the total value of sales up to 1653 has been estimated at £6,000,000.[21] The purchasers included, first, officers and soldiers; second, Presbyterian politicians and businessmen; and third, tenants who had seized the chance to own the land they had formerly rented.

As Charles could not afford to alienate the first two of these groups, the Declaration of Breda referred the issue to Parliament. It seemed likely that a system could be found to balance the interests of the old and new proprietors; Monk had proposed in May that purchasers should be confirmed in possession, but should pay a rent to the old proprietors.[22] Two abortive bills were brought forward to that effect. It became clear, however, that it would be impossible to lay down viable general rules: the conditions of sale had been too diverse. Justice could best be done by treating each case on its merits. In the absence of legislation, royal and ecclesiastical officials began to take possession of crown and Church lands and to grant new leases, where necessary negotiating terms with the purchasers which provided for a measure of compensation. (Some of the largest purchasers had lost all claim to their lands as they were excluded from the Act of Indemnity.) Before long, Charles set up a commission to determine this compensation. He did so on his own authority, but in so doing he followed the expressed wishes of the Commons.[23] The commission fixed compensation at levels which seem to have been regarded as reasonable: there were few complaints. Tenants who had purchased were mostly content to revert to leasing, provided the rent was fair. As for the Royalists and Catholics whose lands had been confiscated, most had either recovered them already through third parties or did so through litigation after the king's return. The only group who secured no redress were those forced to sell land to pay fines or other debts; it was these who had most reason to complain that the Restoration meant indemnity for the king's enemies and oblivion for his friends. In general, however, a potentially divisive problem was resolved with surprisingly little lasting rancour.

A third major legacy of the Interregnum was the problem of the army. Here Charles could do little. The Convention, perhaps by virtue of the 1642 Militia Ordinance, arrogated to itself the right to pay off most of the army and much of the navy. Although Charles had commissioned Monk captain-general, Parliament acted as if it had the sole direction of the armed forces; as it alone could raise money, Charles could do nothing about it.[24] He had offered to take the officers and soldiers of the New Model into his service, but the Commons had no wish to allow him an army for which there seemed no immediate use abroad and which could prove a threat to liberty at home. They resolved that garrisons should be reduced to the level of 1637: any additional forces should be maintained at the king's expense. The commissioners appointed to pay off the army, obsessed by the need to avoid wasting public money, proceeded with caution that probably cost the taxpayer more than it saved. Charles and Monk fretted that the army's 'infant loyalty' might be overborne by impatience.[25] In fact, the disbandment proceeded without a serious hitch. Learning from the mistakes of 1647, the Convention made sure that the soldiers received their arrears in full, as well as their indemnity; steps were also taken to make it easier for them to re-enter civilian life. Besides, after the confusions of the last two years, many soldiers must have lost whatever enthusiasm they had once possessed for the 'Good Old Cause'.[26]

The Commons' efforts to determine the future balance of the constitution were less successful. A bill to preserve the privileges of Parliament and confirm the fundamental laws was introduced, receiving its second reading the day Charles returned to London. It received its third reading on 3 July and was sent up to the Lords.[27] There it stuck: despite many reminders from the Commons, it never emerged from committee.[28] The Lords were normally more amenable than the Commons to the king's will, so it seems plausible that their inaction reflected his dislike of the bill, a supposition supported by its contents. It set out a list of 'fundamental laws' to be confirmed, including not only Magna Carta, the Petition of Right and much of the legislation of 1641, but also 'all other statutes formerly made and unrepealed for the defence and preservation of the rights and privileges of Parliaments and their members, the lives, liberties, freeholds and properties of the subjects, against arbitrary and illegal taxes'. The bill was loosely drafted: while the use of the word 'statutes' might imply that it referred only to Acts that had received the royal assent, this was far from explicit. (Monk had earlier proposed that Charles should confirm such Acts of the Long Parliament as should be presented to him.) The bill did nothing to secure or define the king's position. Had the Lords rejected it, they might have provoked a row between the Houses which could have jeopardized the indemnity and the paying off of the army. It could also have provoked the Commons into producing other bills more explicitly designed to curb the king's powers. It must therefore have seemed wiser to allow the bill to remain in limbo, in committee, until it died a natural death at the end of the Convention.[29]

Two of the issues which the Declaration of Breda referred to Parliament – the indemnity and land sales – were either completely or nearly resolved when the Convention began its summer recess on 13 September. The third proved more intractable. The Declaration expressed a hope that divisions of religion could be overcome in time and promised 'a liberty to tender consciences and that no man shall be disquieted or called in question for differences of opinion in matter of religion which do not disturb the peace of the kingdom'. Charles would, he declared, be ready to assent to any suitable bill to grant such liberty.[30] This promise addressed only one of several religious problems needing resolution in 1660 and offered a solution which would be welcomed by only a small, if vocal, section of the population. It was doubtless aimed at the army, where the proportion of sectaries was exceptionally high, but it also reassured Presbyterians (and others) that Charles would not unilaterally impose upon them an ecclesiastical regime of his own choosing. There could be little doubt that some sort of national Church would now be re-established; but what sort of Church would it be? and how much liberty would be allowed to those who wished to remain outside it?

Through Elizabeth's reign and much of James I's the Church of England and the Book of Common Prayer proved broadly acceptable to English Protestants. Some, usually called Puritans, bemoaned the retention of 'Popish' ceremonies, like the sign of the cross in baptism. They complained that the wearing of vestments made Protestant clergymen look like Catholic priests and that the set forms of service in the Prayer Book were reminiscent of Catholic practice. They argued that ministers should be free to pray as the spirit moved them and that the sermon, not holy communion, should be the centrepiece of the service. Deeply conscious of human sinfulness, Puritans called for more rigorous control over public and private morality: drunkenness and fornication should be punished and the sabbath kept holy. At the heart of Calvinist theology, which few in the Church challenged before the 1620s, lay the concept of predestination: God had decreed, since the beginning of time, who was to be saved and who damned. To this potentially dispiriting message, Puritan pastors added the gloss that (while nobody could be certain of God's intentions) it was probable that those He had chosen would show it by leading virtuous lives. Those who saw themselves as godly tended to distance themselves from the ungodly, holding private prayer meetings as well as attending public services. Moreover, where Puritans' social rank qualified them for public office, they used the power of that office to repress what they regarded as sin.

Puritan criticisms of the Church have sometimes been seen as expressions of 'popular' protest against an institution used by the elite as an instrument of social control: by discouraging people from thinking for themselves and feeding them hopes of happiness in the next world, it sought to make them content with their lowly condition in this one. Many historians have also taken at face value Puritan denunciations of 'scandalous' ministers, who set a poor moral example, and of 'dumb dogs', who merely read the Prayer Book and did not instruct the people. Such views should not be accepted without qualification. The conviction that they should obey God rather than man nerved Puritans to defy authority, but this same conviction drove them to seek to impose their views on those who, they thought, contravened the Word of God. Diversions which to most people seemed harmless – singing, dancing, Sunday games – were denounced by Puritans as abominations in the sight of the Lord. Similarly, when Puritans complained that, for many, religious worship went no further than outward observance, they judged them by standards which were perhaps unreasonably high. The rapt attention with which Puritans followed sermons could not be matched by those who lacked their dedication, especially among the illiterate rural poor: a minister who concentrated on the familiar words of the set services and kept his sermons short and simple might instruct his flock more effectively than one who preached at length about Old Testament characters with strange-sounding names. Moreover, a minister who had a drink with his parishioners after service, or who patronized Sunday cricket, might wield a greater influence over them than one who denounced such practices as sinful.

By the 1620s, within what might outwardly seem a broadly homogeneous Church, there had developed a divide between Puritan and non-Puritan that was more cultural than theological: for Puritans, rigorous obedience to God's word was more important than living in peace with their neighbours. They were not a majority – indeed, they took pride in how few 'the godly' really were – nor were they confined to a single social group: Puritanism was a matter of temperament rather than status. The stress on the Word meant that Puritans were likely to be literate, but literacy was not essential and some even among the very poor were able to read the Bible. Religious (and political) divisions ran vertically through all social strata in the seventeeth century. Puritans created an impression of dissatisfaction that was out of all proportion to their numbers, partly because in any society the dissatisfied make more noise than the satisfied, partly because keeping silent did not come naturally to them.[31]

Until the 1620s Puritanism posed only a limited threat to the Church's stability. Few ministers or laymen found the demand to conform so constricting as to be intolerable. With the rise of the so-called Arminians, led by Archbishop Laud, the official practice of the Church became (in Puritan eyes) almost indistinguishable from Catholicism. Church interiors were embellished and reorganized, so that instead of a communion table in the body of the church there was to be an altar, railed off, at the east end; people were to receive communion not seated, but kneeling. The greater stress on the sacerdotal role of the clergy was part of a larger attempt to reverse the erosion, since the Reformation, of their authority over the laity. The bishops became less and less tolerant of deviations from what they regarded as the official form of service. Their definition of 'Puritan' widened to embrace not only those who refused to wear a surplice or to bow at the name of Jesus but also many who had no quarrel with the Prayer Book, but disliked innovations which they regarded either as 'Popish' or as fussy, unnecessary and expensive.

Laud's ecclesiastical changes provoked a level of dissatisfaction with the Church that would have seemed inconceivable twenty years earlier. Some could stand it no longer and emigrated to the New World; most stayed, awaiting a chance to put things right. Many believed that Laud was bent on creating a Church that was Catholic in all but name and this belief was greatly to damage the cause of Laud's patron, Charles I. Anti-Popery was a central feature of English Protestantism. It rested on a view of Catholicism as not only theologically wrong, but also intellectually stultifying (the priests kept the laity ignorant and tried to stop them thinking for themselves) and morally depraved (priests would absolve people from any sin for a few 'hail Marys' – or for money). 'Popery' was thus not just another religion, but the quintessence of evil and degeneracy. Its political manifestation was absolute monarchy, which (like the Catholic Church) was founded on repression and on keeping the people slavishly ignorant. English Protestants saw their world in terms of apocalyptic struggles between God and Satan, good and evil. The millenarian prophecies of Daniel and Revelation led many (and not just zealous Puritans) to believe that the world was entering the last stage of its history, in which the forces of Christ would triumph over those of Antichrist, followed by the rule of the saints, the Second Coming and the Day of Judgement. They were doubly inclined to do so at a time of wars (the Thirty Years War, the Dutch Revolt) which could be seen as religious and in which the Protestants spent much of the time on the defensive. In such circumstances, it was natural to link the promotion of Laudianism with the perceived threat of absolutism, especially as the Laudian clergy explicitly exalted royal power. In 1605 the Gunpowder Plotters had tried to blow up both king and Parliament;

by 1640 the 'Papists' around Charles I were seen as plotting against Parliament.[32]

The use of anti-Popish rhetoric against Charles I in the 1640s may seem odd or unfair: he clearly was not a Catholic and it would be easy to see the rhetoric as mere rabble-rousing. Certainly, for John Pym and his allies it was tactically convenient to argue that on every issue there was a 'Protestant' position (theirs) and a 'Popish' one. It may also seem odd to blame (say) the decay of trade on the Papists. Against this it should be noted that people have always been inclined to think and argue in terms of polar opposites; that 'Popery' was much more than Catholicism, carrying resonances of violence, tyranny and moral turpitude; and that in 1640–2 there was strong evidence that Charles *was* planning to use violence against his subjects and was actively seeking Catholic help. As he came to see more and more of his Protestant subjects as 'Puritans' (and thus disaffected), so he came to value the Catholics' loyalty. If they were few in England, they were more numerous in his other kingdoms: Scotland and (above all) Ireland; he also hoped for help from continental Catholic powers.[33]

With Charles and his bishops widely seen as at best half-hearted Protestants, the Puritan minority seized its chance to demand that the Church be cleansed of all vestiges of 'Popery' and claimed that the only sure way to prevent a resurgence of Laudianism was to abolish bishops. Many who called for such changes had no wish to abandon the tradition of a national Church, with a qualified, ordained minister in each parish, paid for by tithes; nor were they against a standard form of service, provided the practices they disliked were removed. They fully supported the principle that all should attend their parish church and wished to increase the minister's powers to impose moral discipline, which would be ineffectual if Church membership ceased to be compulsory and excommunication carried no stigma or civil disabilities. Moderate 'Church-Puritans' of this type were usually called Presbyterians, which was in some ways misleading. They were opposed not to episcopacy but to 'prelacy' – the domineering rule of Laud. They found themselves committed to a Church without bishops because that was the price exacted by the Scots for a military alliance (the Solemn League and Covenant) in 1643. Most had few objections to Archbishop Ussher's scheme of 'limited episcopacy', whereby bishops would govern their dioceses in association with representatives of the parish clergy. Even Richard Baxter, that most punctilious of Presbyterian divines, reached agreement with Ussher in a mere half-hour.[34]

If the Presbyterians wanted a Puritan national Church, others took the logic of predestination much further. The collapse of episcopal authority in 1640 created a power vacuum in the Church, while the overthrow of the Laudian 'Antichrist' stimulated apocalyptic hopes of a new godly order.

Now, some argued, was the time for God's elect to come forward, to prepare the way for Christ's coming; they should also distance themselves from the ungodly multitude, in anticipation of the Day of Judgment. Many who thought that way were conventional Calvinists, for whom the duty to separate was all that divided them from Presbyterians. For these 'Independents' a Church should be a voluntary association of true believers – 'visible saints' – not saints and sinners mixed 'promiscuously' together. Others diverged further. Some congregations were led not by trained clergymen but by working men or even women. Baptists argued that if a Church should consist only of visible saints it was ridiculous to admit people to it (by baptism) as infants. The Quakers abandoned not only a professional ministry and set form of worship, but even the primacy of Scripture. Protestants had always claimed that true believers could approach God's truth through the Bible; the Quakers claimed to do so by divine inspiration, the inner light. It seemed as if what Catholic writers had long predicted was coming to pass: if one allowed everyone to interpret the Bible for themself, one would end up with as many Churches as people.

This did not happen: even the Quakers survived as a coherent denomination, thanks to George Fox's insistence that they develop a strong organization and sense of identity. Even so, between 1640 and 1660 English Protestantism underwent enormous (and, many thought, appalling) changes. Bishops were swept away, along with the Prayer Book and such 'Popish' festivals as Christmas. Only when these were removed did the strength of popular attachment to the Church become apparent; but for the moment those who loved the old ways had little influence. Parliament's attempt to establish a new 'Presbyterian' system was thwarted by the army. Cromwell retained the shell of a national Church – each parish still had a minister, maintained from tithes – but ministers were not required to use a particular service-book or subscribe a confession of faith; it was enough that they should be 'called' by their parishioners and be of adequate education and unblemished character. The parish clergy were now a motley collection of Presbyterians, Independents and Anglicans prepared to serve in a Church without bishops: 'prelatists' and Catholics were excluded. Meanwhile, the enforcement of church attendance was abandoned; those who disliked what was on offer in their parish church could go elsewhere – to Baptist or Quaker meetings, for example. Cromwell sincerely hoped to create a more godly society, but by dismantling the old machinery of ecclesiastical compulsion he made the task infinitely more difficult. Presbyterians bemoaned the absence of 'parish discipline' and seized on reports of the alleged antics of the Ranters and other fringe groups to argue that without that discipline the whole moral order would collapse.

The impact of the new sects was not confined to the ecclesiastical sphere.

The belief that one should obey God rather than man was always potentially subversive and had encouraged the development of theories of a right to resist a tyrant. A strong belief in God's Providence led to a conviction that the New Model was His chosen instrument and that Charles's defeat in two civil wars showed that God had witnessed against him: his crimes could be expiated only by his death. Moreover, by setting the elite of the spirit above the elite of earthly society, the sects threatened to turn the world upside down. By founding their own Churches and choosing their own leaders (most of whom had not enjoyed the university education which provided a common intellectual foundation for ordained clergymen and members of the gentry) the sects undermined the Church's effectiveness as a means of maintaining hierarchy and social discipline. Quakers especially, fortified by the inner light, saw no need to show conventional marks of respect (such as doffing of hats) to gentlemen or magistrates; nor did they regard clergymen as possessing a right to preach. Their refusal to swear oaths threatened to dissolve the bonds of civil society: without invoking supernatural sanctions, would men keep their bargains or tell the truth in court? Small wonder that some of the more paranoid Presbyterians saw Quakerism as created by Jesuits, to divide Protestantism from within.

Most of these extraordinary developments occurred while Charles was in exile, so his perception of the balance of religious forces in 1660 was bound to be somewhat awry. From Paris or Brussels, the sectaries' strength within the army was much more apparent than their comparative weakness outside it. Moreover, he had come increasingly to pin his hopes on the Presbyterians, as the Royalists' attempts to bring him back proved inept and ineffectual. The Presbyterians had the great advantage over the Royalists that they were not formally excluded from public life in the 1650s and so were much more visible than the more numerous adherents of the old Church upon whom Hyde pinned his hopes. As Charles's restoration began to seem likely, Presbyterian politicians and divines naturally exaggerated their numerical strength and social and economic importance in order to convince him that they would have to be accommodated in any settlement.

But what sort of settlement? The sectaries – Independents, Baptists and Quakers – wished to be left alone. The Presbyterians wanted an effective national Church. Most had no objection to the restoration of bishops, provided their powers were limited, and were prepared to use a modified version of the Prayer Book. They had no wish to allow toleration to the sects (especially the Quakers) or to Roman Catholics. There were thus several possibilities. The Church might be restored as it had been in 1640, or its worship and government might be modified to accommodate (or 'comprehend') the Presbyterians. In either case, the main point at issue would be the nature of the liturgy and discipline to which all the parish clergy would be required to conform. If the Church was restored unchanged, many Presbyterians would refuse to conform, thus increasing the number of nonconformists outside the Church. This might strengthen the case for a toleration (or indulgence) for 'tender consciences'. If not, the authorities would be faced with a serious problem of Dissent.

In a western world whose priorities are increasingly secular, many find it hard to understand the religious intolerance of the seventeenth century, but it is important to try to do so. For both Presbyterians and Anglicans[35] not only was religious truth indivisible but a coercive Church seemed essential to impose Christian standards of conduct on an inherently sinful population. For many Anglicans, moreover, the Church of England was much more than just one Church among many: it claimed a continuous visible existence to match that of the Roman Church and so had an equal right to call itself a true Church. Thanks largely to Rome's baleful influence, the English Church had become corrupted in the middle ages, but (unlike Rome) it had expunged these corruptions at the Reformation; whereas Rome stressed its unbroken succession of popes, the Church of England claimed an unbroken succession of bishops. This stress on continuity led many Anglicans to distance themselves from non-episcopal Protestant Churches on the continent, with which those of more Puritan inclinations had a strong sense of solidarity.

As, for many Anglicans, the nature of Church government was divinely ordained, so obedience to the king (as head of the Church) and bishops was a Christian duty: the ceremonies enjoined by authority were obligatory and separation from the Church could never be justified. Similarly, the Church taught, both before and after the civil wars, that to resist royal authority was a sin. (The Church did not require unqualified obedience: those who could not in conscience obey the king's commands should follow the example of the early Christians and submit passively to whatever punishment he might impose.) Churchmen saw a direct link between ecclesiastical disobedience and political resistance: Puritan defiance of the Church had led to the civil war and the king's execution. The Declaration of Breda talked of 'tender consciences' and of differences of opinion in religion 'which do not disturb the peace of the kingdom'. To churchmen, talk of tender consciences was hypocritical: nonconformity sprang from spiritual pride, not conscience, and recent history suggested that it certainly disturbed the peace of the kingdom. Mildness, they argued, would merely encourage further defiance: they needed, for their own good, to be subjected to the wholesome discipline of the Church.

Charles agreed that Dissent was politically and socially subversive. He lamented the rise of the sects, 'each interpreting [Scripture] according to their vile notions and to accomplish their horrid wickednesses'.[36] For a while he found the Quakers' antics amusing, but soon he came to see them as posing as much of a threat to his authority as the other sectaries. Since the Reformation, he argued, ordinary people had claimed a liberty to enquire into matters of religion, which led them to question matters of state: government was safer when authority was accepted as infallible and the people's faith and submission were implicit. He spoke contemptuously of the divisions of Protestantism and wondered why Anglicans condemned Dissenters for separating from the Church when the Church itself had separated from Rome.[37] This is not to suggest that he had a principled commitment to Catholicism, although he may have felt that the Roman Church had the best claim to authority and clearly approved of its stress on obedience: he had been greatly struck by the Catholics' loyalty in the civil wars. The Earl of Mulgrave saw him as a deist, made cynical by his ability to see through the 'specious pretences' of all denominations.[38] His religious policies, indeed, were determined by political considerations. Experience of Scotland convinced him that Presbyterianism was no religion for gentlemen and certainly not one for kings: it was worse than Popery, in that it could make all things legal and encouraged the clergy to try to direct the state.[39]

Charles thus shared the Anglicans' distaste for Presbyterians and sectaries – indeed, his biggest criticism of the Anglican clergy was that they failed to root out Dissent – but he lacked an emotional and spiritual commitment to the Church. His religious policies were determined by his perception of the strength of the various denominations: despite his contempt for the Presbyterians, he had no wish to be thought their enemy as he knew the harm they could do him.[40] The Presbyterians claimed that they and the other nonconformists comprised over half the population and controlled most of the nation's trade, industry and ready money. Lacking detailed statistics, Charles saw no reason to challenge these claims, especially as Dissenters were clearly very numerous in London. Only with the so-called Compton Census of 1676 did it become clear that in the nation as a whole Dissenters were a small minority; thereafter, Charles's inclination to tolerate Dissent diminished markedly.

In 1660, however, Charles was still feeling his way. He saw clearly the advantages of a single episcopal Church, under royal control, to teach the people their duties, but the belief that he needed to appease Presbyterian plutocrats and the sectaries in the army led him to support a measure of both comprehension and indulgence. Hyde's attitude is difficult to pin down. His commitment to the Church and to episcopacy was much stronger than Charles's and he had always advised his master to rely on the support of the Anglican majority. In the autumn of 1659 he had expressed deep concern that the few surviving bishops would soon die:[41] if they did not consecrate new bishops, the thread of continuity would be broken. In 1660, as Charles's return became increasingly likely, Hyde opened negotiations with lay and clerical Presbyterians through his friend George Morley, soon to be created Bishop of Worcester. While he would not commit Charles too far, Morley stressed his goodwill and found them inclined to accept a modified episcopacy.[42]

Meanwhile, the Convention's first moves to settle religion are obscure. Monk's paper, circulated in early May, proposed that 'the exercise of the Protestant religion and ministry shall continue as now', until settled by an assembly of divines and by Parliament. On the 8th the Commons announced that they were preparing a bill to secure the Protestant religion and settle a learned and pious ministry, with 'a due care of tender consciences'.[43] The 'bill of religion' (or bill to settle ministers) was brought in next day. It seems to have been promoted by Presbyterians and to have been intended, first, to confirm existing incumbents in their livings and, second, to preserve the existing latitude of practice until the synod could meet. By the time Charles returned, however, these issues had become separated, as we shall see.[44]

As May wore on the Presbyterians found, in religion as in politics, that their bargaining position was becoming weaker. The Royalist MPs were strong enough to block attempts to impose preconditions on the king and many Presbyterian politicians sought to come to terms with him. These tried to persuade Charles of the Presbyterian clergy's moderation (and influence), but Charles (while receiving them graciously) would not be hurried into concessions which might prove unnecessary: he had, he said, referred such matters to Parliament and insisted that he should be free to use the Prayer Book in his chapel.[45]

Once Charles had returned, the most immediate problem was that of the parish clergy. Many ousted in the 1640s as 'scandalous' (which often meant Laudian or Royalist) demanded reinstatement; their replacements (mostly Presbyterians or Anglicans who had conformed to the new order) sought to be confirmed in possession. Charles had no wish to take sides. Following a similar order by the Commons, Charles issued a proclamation on 1 June to the effect that no incumbent should be removed except by due process of law or by order of Parliament. In the following weeks, a bill to confirm ministers in their livings slowly made its way through the two Houses. The Presbyterians were forced to concede that those removed for loyalty alone, who were not otherwise 'scandalous', should be restored. On the other hand, Anglican attempts to force all incumbents to subscribe the Thirty-nine Articles and to submit to reordination by bishops (if they had not been episcopally ordained) was rejected. The Act, as it finally passed in September, led to the ejection of maybe 700 ministers: these included those whose views were most radical, but the main criteria for ejection were legal and were apparently generally regarded as fair, since the ejections provoked little disturbance.[46]

As Dr Ian Green has remarked, the most striking feature of the Act was not that it removed a few hundred ministers but that it confirmed in their livings several thousands more, who had served during the 1640s and 1650s. Men of this type also made up the majority of those appointed to livings by the king during 1660: Charles's Church patronage showed no evidence of an Anglican (or anti-Presbyterian) bias and the same is true of Charles's stance on the Church's government and liturgy.[47] Quite apart from his own uncertainty about the balance of religious forces, it is worth noting that, with the possible exception of Hyde, few of those around him were committed Anglicans.[48] His privy council included Presbyterians like Manchester, Annesley and Holles and he was persuaded to appoint ten or twelve Presbyterian chaplains; although he rarely heard them preach, it did give Baxter and his colleagues access to his person. At Manchester's suggestion, Charles called these chaplains to an informal meeting, at which Baxter claimed that the Presbyterians were loyal and peaceable and that some changes in the Church's liturgy and government would unite them in love and obedience to the crown; he also warned that to replace godly pastors with scandalous clerics would cause great disruption and distress. Charles declared that he would do all he could to bring his people together, but that there had to be concessions by both sides. He asked the ministers to draw up proposals about Church government, which seemed the main point at issue, and told the episcopalians to do the same. Throughout he stressed his wish to keep the discussions as informal and discreet as possible.[49]

While the ministers prepared their arguments, the Commons discussed the bill to settle religion. The motion that all ministers should subscribe the Thirty-nine Articles opened up a debate on the nature of the Church. Some disliked talk of tender consciences, others claimed that there was no need to legislate: 'Sir Heneage Finch said ... the religion of our church is not to seek, but we have enjoyed it long and therefore now should not be to enquire for it ... there was no law to alter the government by church and bishops.'[50] On the other side, Presbyterian MPs complained of the 'boundless' power claimed by bishops and called for a 'circumscribed' episcopacy, as consonant with 'the king's present inclinations and endeavours': one, indeed, gave the current consultations as a reason for laying the matter aside. As the debate became heated, Presbyterians associated with the court (such as Annesley and Ashley Cooper) moved that they should adjourn. At last, it was agreed to postpone further discussion until October and that the king should be asked to call an assembly of divines to settle the future shape of the Church.[51]

The Commons' decision left the initiative with the king. Some thought that he was determined to restore episcopacy: a warrant dated 20 July talked of 'the next bishop' of Durham.[52] What was at issue, however, was less the restoration of episcopacy than its form: given the preponderance of Presbyterians and Commonwealth conformists among the parish clergy, an assembly of divines was unlikely to support the restoration of full-blown Anglicanism. Charles's own intentions remained obscure, perhaps even to himself. One possible clue can be found in an exchange of letters between Abbé Montagu and Richard Bellings, an Irish Catholic who acted as secretary and interpreter to Hyde. Copies of this correspondence survive in Hyde's papers, but neither Montagu nor Bellings knew that Hyde was aware of it: the letters were presumably opened, deciphered and copied at the post office, and sent on.[53] On 15 August Montagu wrote that it was in Charles's interest to delay the settlement of episcopacy (which Hyde was pressing for), as once bishops had been settled they would be less likely to yield to the king's will.[54] Bellings's reply, dated the 23rd, is worth quoting at length, despite the problems created by inept coding or decoding:

The king bids me tell you that as far as he durst he still opposed that establishment of bishops and appears si [so] cool in so important a business that his friends were [mu]ch unsatisfied; with lord [?] of late he has expressed more warmth, not upon that score th[e]y imagine, but at an offer that Scotland absolutely refused to admit of an episcopacy; that England begins to speak the same language; that London is drawing up of a petition to resettle government of a Presbytery. He thought it absolutely necessary to countenance [tho?]se who can't take root to oppose the other faction that would presently overrun all and prove a much greater obstacle to his designs than a settled hated episcopacy.

In the mean time Lord Hyde is reconci[li]ng all differences and has written a treaty which the king calls a strange tipotae[??]. If you can propose any expedient that embroiling episcopacy will not advance Presbytery, it will be most welcome.[55]

Four days later Bellings wrote that Charles was far more concerned about the possibility of marrying Mazarin's niece than about bishops, 'for money and a wife are the things he most wants. As for episcopacy, you know it is his religion to promote it, but you need not fear he will proceed so rashly as to venture his crowns.'[56] Dr Green speculates that Charles may have been reluctant to create an over-strong episcopate as that could make it harder to grant liberty to Catholics. Montagu's letter would seem to support such a view, but others believed that the Catholics' interests would best be served by a strongly episcopal (in other words narrowly Anglican) Church, which would strengthen the case for granting indulgence to those remaining outside it.[57] More plausible is the suggestion that he sought a rough balance between Anglican and Presbyterian, with a view to playing one off against the other and keeping his options open until he better understood the balance of religious forces. (Alternatively, he may just have been avoiding any irrevocable decision.) Bellings's letter of 23 August would suggest that Charles was more likely to support the episcopal party if it was weak than if it was strong. His first episcopal appointment (translating Duppa to Winchester) came just five days later. Seven more appointments or promotions followed in September and seven more between 3 and 20 October. Among those offered bishoprics were Baxter and two other Presbyterians, one of whom accepted. Those appointed represented a wide spectrum of opinion and some (notably Monk's brother) were chosen for reasons which had little to do with ecclesiastical distinction. Few were renowned as scholars, or had played a conspicuous role under Laud. Only one, John Cosin, protested openly against a proposal that they should share their authority with the parish clergy. If Charles was seeking a bench of bishops prepared to obey his will and to accept a measure of comprehension, he was going about it the right way.[58]

Charles may have been encouraged to move towards comprehension by the corporation of London's reluctance to advance money: some said the citizens resented his failure to stand by his assurances to the Presbyterians.[59] Soon after, Hyde produced a draft declaration on ecclesiastical matters. This was intended to set the agenda for a synod and may have been the 'treaty' to which Bellings referred. It stressed Charles's zeal for Protestantism, despite the unkindness of many Protestants towards him and the kindness of Catholics. His main goal was to combine a 'union of affections' with submission to authority. He praised episcopacy as 'the best means to contain the minds of men within the rules of government'; it was also as ancient a part of the constitution as Christian monarchy itself. He also stressed that in the early Church the ecclesiastical power had been subordinated to the civil, an implied criticism of both Scots Presbyterians and those Laudians who claimed that episcopacy was of divine ordination (and so, by implication, not subject to the crown). Bishops, he suggested, should share their power with presbyters. The liturgy of the Church was the best Charles had seen (he used it in his own chapel), but it included some archaisms and could surely be improved. Ceremonies served a valid purpose but Charles would allow some divines with genuine scruples to omit some of them.[60]

For the Presbyterian ministers, this was a step in the right direction, but not nearly far enough. With a fine lack of tact, both they and the London common council planned petitions in favour of the Covenant, the former complaining that Charles had broken his promise to adhere to it; both then thought better of it.[61] Instead, Baxter and his colleagues concentrated on Hyde's draft. They bemoaned the lack of provision for parish discipline and the excessive powers still to be allowed to bishops and complained that JPs were harassing ministers who would not use the Prayer Book. On Hyde's advice, they scaled down their response, focusing on the bishops' powers, kneeling at communion and the composition of the body that was to revise the liturgy. By now the Indemnity Act and the Act to settle ministers had been passed and the Convention had been adjourned. In his closing speech, Hyde had complained of seditious sermons against 'Popery' and evil counsellors and told the Houses that Charles would soon issue a declaration giving liberty to tender consciences, which he hoped would bring a measure of uniformity and unity. The king, he added, had confirmed in their livings all who had asked for it, even though (he added somewhat gratuitously) some had been thoroughly unworthy of such favour.[62]

Hyde's conduct at this time is not easy to reconcile with his later reputation as a staunch defender of the Church. His commitment to episcopacy was never in doubt but, as his draft declaration made clear, he believed that the bishops should be subordinated to the crown. He himself seems to have seen the essentials of Christian belief as relatively simple; provided these were respected, particular forms were a matter of convenience. Limited alterations, to bring in the Presbyterians, would be acceptable, but disagreements about worship or Church government could never justify challenges to legitimate royal authority. Moreover, once Parliament had passed laws to settle the Church, to refuse to respect those laws was seditious and immoral. Hyde was no revanchiste Anglican, but he believed that the law should be obeyed.[63]

If Hyde was prepared to countenance a measure of comprehension, that did not mean that his views were the same as Charles's. On several occasions, he showed signs of an emotional commitment to the Church which his master lacked: in the remarks in the draft declaration about the excellence of episcopacy and the liturgy, in his aside to Parliament about unworthy ministers; he was also to be excluded from the meeting which produced the final declaration. Whatever his feelings, however, he was dependent on the king's favour, especially as (since his daughter's marriage) the queen's cronies were baying for his blood.[64] On 22 October Charles and a group of councillors, Anglican and Presbyterian, came to Hyde's residence, Worcester House. Hyde read his draft and there was a long debate. At one point Hyde produced a paper from Independents and Baptists asking that liberty should be allowed to 'others', provided they did not disturb the peace. Baxter opposed this vehemently, claiming it could be used to allow liberty to Catholics. As the meeting broke up in some disorder, on the news that Anne Hyde had gone into labour, Charles declared which parts of the draft he wished to retain and told two Anglican and two Presbyterian divines to draft the alterations that were to be made. In case of disagreement, two Presbyterians (Holles and Annesley) were to adjudicate.[65]

Baxter came away full of pessimism, but he was never inclined to settle for anything less than perfection (which may explain why he, as well as

Hyde, was excluded from the final discussions). On the Anglican side Morley was eager to secure a speedy agreement, so that Protestants should be united against the Papists before the queen arrived. When the Worcester House Declaration was issued on the 25th Baxter was pleasantly surprised. It stressed the need for a single Protestant Church to guard against Popery and for the submission of the spiritual to the civil power. Bishops were to exercise spiritual jurisdiction only with the advice of presbyters and were to be assisted by suffragans in the government of their dioceses. Ministers were to have greater powers to exclude errant parishioners from communion. The Prayer Book was to be revised by an 'equal number of learned divines of both persuasions', pending which ministers could omit those items they disliked. Baxter told Hyde that if the liturgy were duly reformed and the Declaration confirmed by Act of Parliament, it could help to achieve the concord which the king sought.[66] Charles, however, had no wish that his Declaration should be confirmed. He had taken the matter into his own hands and, when Parliament reconvened and such a bill was brought in, it was reported that, if it passed, he would veto it. He did not have to: it was rejected on the second reading, Independents joining with Cavaliers to throw it out.[67]

Nicholas wrote smugly that the bill had failed largely because of the violence of those who promoted it, but its rejection alarmed the Presbyterians: Baxter and Edmund Calamy turned down the bishoprics which Charles had offered them. Charles, on the other hand, was happy to have kept his options open until he could see which way public opinion was moving; if he chose to amend the terms of the Declaration, he would be quite free to do so. As Andrew Marvell remarked, the Presbyterians had now to rely on the goodness of the king who 'hath hitherto been more ready to give than to receive'.[68] He had also kept open the option of allowing liberty to those determined to remain outside the Church, including the Catholics, whom he regarded as loyal, despite claims that some had collaborated with Cromwell. Most MPs, however, regarded Catholics as quite unworthy of indulgence: Catholic recusancy and other religious offences were excluded from the general pardon, for which Montagu typically (and almost certainly unfairly) blamed Hyde.[69] Charles had made his feelings clear on 22 October: when Baxter inveighed against liberty to Catholics, Charles replied that there were already laws enough against them; the irrepressible Baxter replied that the crucial question was whether those laws were enforced. He was right: as Charles explained to Montagu, the best the Catholics could hope for was liberty by connivance.[70] This might seem an admission of defeat, but only if one believes that securing liberty for Catholics was one of Charles's prime objectives: as we have seen, there is little hard evidence that this was so. Indeed, as the year neared its end he could be well pleased that, on the tricky issue of the religious settlement, he retained the initiative.

While the bill for confirming the fundamental laws remained stuck in committee in the Lords, the Commons showed little eagerness further to define the king's powers. His supporters, for their part, argued that those powers were his by prescription and had never lawfully been taken away. Such an assumption underlay the king's conduct towards the militia. The royal right to direct the militia had, in fact, been open to question in 1641: its basis in statute had been destroyed when the relevant Act was repealed in 1604, but Charles I's lawyers claimed that it was fully established by the Statute of Winchester of 1285 and that Parliament's Militia Ordinance of 1642 was invalid, as it had not received the royal assent. On 7 June Charles II's privy council ordered the attorney-general to prepare commissions for the militia in the traditional form: with the loyalty of army and people uncertain, the council felt the need for some sort of military force under royal control. By July the new lords lieutenant were preparing their lists of deputies, but the process took weeks and even months. Many of the deputies were totally inexperienced and some doubted whether they could legally act at all: at the end of October the Staffordshire militia was said to be in great disorder. Perhaps because of these problems, some lords lieutenant also enrolled bodies of gentlemen volunteers, to guard against the danger of disaffection.[71]

The commissioning of deputy lieutenants was part of a general overhaul of local government. In the counties well over half of the JPs were replaced. Not all non-Royalists were removed: it was necessary to maintain a measure of administrative continuity and to avoid perpetuating old divisions. In corporate towns, which chose their own magistrates, Charles moved cautiously, encouraging the reinstatement of those removed for their loyalty to his father. The installation of Royalists in local offices took time, not least because Charles and Hyde lacked knowledge of the county gentry and had to rely on others' advice: Devon (where Albemarle was lord lieutenant) had an unusually high proportion of Parliamentarian deputies.[72] In most counties it was probably well into the autumn before the militia was fully settled, by which time the Act of Indemnity had passed and the disbandment of the army was well under way. On 1 October, lords lieutenant were ordered to seize the arms of the disaffected and use them to arm the militia.[73] Now that they were authorized to use force against their former enemies, many Cavaliers were quick to do so: complaints flooded in, especially from the Earl of Derby's lieutenancies of Lancashire and Cheshire. When the Commons reconvened in November, the question of the militia was raised on the first day. Although some claimed that the king already enjoyed full power over

the militia, it was resolved to bring in a bill to define his authority. Presbyterian MPs took the lead in calling for the bill, but changed their tune
when they saw its provisions. One claimed that it contained 'arbitrary'
clauses from a bill of 1656, to confirm the powers of Cromwell's major-
generals. Lawyers like Sir Heneage Finch were dismayed at the provisions
for martial law. Enthusiasm evaporated and the bill was allowed to lapse:
Marvell wrote, again, that it would be wisest to trust in the king's goodness.[74]

Despite the failure of the militia bill, by the end of 1660 a civilian militia
was more or less in place and the New Model had mostly been disbanded.
This was not entirely what Charles had wanted. In June a plan to raise a
body of 1,200 horseguards was first scaled down and then abandoned. In
December the government renewed its claim that Charles needed guards,
using as a pretext an alleged plot led by one White, which Montagu thought
was far less serious than ministers made out. The Commons, however, had
taken good care to keep the disbanding of the New Model in their own
hands and refused to vote him any money to raise additional troops: if he
wished to do so, he would have to pay them out of his existing revenues.
Charles had, in fact, commissioned a new regiment in November and more
were to be raised after Venner's rising in January 1661. In general, however,
it seemed clear that the militia was to be the main military force of the new
regime and Hyde argued that its re-establishment showed that Charles was
eager to return to the traditional form of government.[75]

If the Convention reached no resolution on the king's military powers,
on the question of the royal revenue it made important and far-reaching
decisions. Until 1641 the revenue had come in part from Parliamentary
grants (customs duties, temporary 'subsidies' on land) and in part from a
motley collection of feudal and property rights and powers of economic
regulation. Charles I's misuse of these sources led to their being drastically
limited by the legislation of 1641, to which he had given his assent. By law,
the king could now raise revenue only in ways approved by Parliament and
Charles II was never to resort to the dishonest and dubiously legal methods
of his father. As his personal revenues were clearly insufficient to meet the
normal peacetime costs of government, the Commons had a choice. Either
they could vote him less than he needed (or vote him his revenues for a
limited time); or they could maintain the ancient principle that he should
'live of his own' by voting him a sufficient revenue for life. If they took the
former path, they would be able to use their power to grant or withhold
money to extort concessions, to influence policy and appointments and to
impose upon him their interpretation of his powers. If they chose the second
option, they would hand over to him responsibility for directing government
and renounce the possibility of influencing government on a day-to-day
basis.

Even before Charles returned, the Commons made it clear that they intended to provide him with some independent revenues. When a bill was brought in to take away the Court of Wards, the House agreed that Charles should receive £100,000 a year in compensation for the consequent loss of revenue. On 19 June they resolved to grant him the customs (tonnage and poundage) for life and to revise the rates on particular commodities: Charles I had been denied such a grant at his accession.[76] A committee was set up to consider the annual cost of government; it came up with a figure of £1,200,000, which was accepted without a division.[77] The House then calculated how much would be raised by the customs (and other sources) and how much more would be needed. On 21 November it voted that half the excise (hitherto continued on a temporary basis) should be granted to the crown in perpetuity, in compensation for the abolition of the Court of Wards. Six days later it added the other half, this time for Charles's life, 'in full of' the £1,200,000.[78]

The debates on the revenue suggest that many MPs were confused, unfamiliar with the technicalities of taxation. Charles's financial advisers were equally inexperienced, which may explain why they failed to notice that the House's figures, which purported to show that these revenues would bring in £1,200,000, counted the compensation for the Court of Wards twice. Charles and his court, however, were delighted: Montagu wrote that the excise would carry the revenue above the stated figure.[79] Only later did such flaws, and the over-optimism of some of the estimates, become apparent: it was years before the ordinary revenue reached £1,200,000. Considered in a wider perspective, however, the revenue settlement was very advantageous to the king. First, the Commons granted, not a fixed sum, but a variety of revenues for him to exploit as best he could. In the short term, the yields fell well short of the Commons' estimates, but by the end of the reign (thanks to increased trade and better management) the ordinary revenue was around £1,400,000 and Charles was able to rule without calling Parliament.[80]

A second advantage concerned not so much the content of the settlement as the attitudes which underlay it. The Convention was not a predominantly Royalist body, but the settlement made it clear that its members wanted Charles to govern. The Long Parliament had taken on the executive responsibilities hitherto exercised by the king – raising money and soldiers, directing foreign policy – not because it wanted to, but because the need to fight the civil war left it no option. Some MPs revelled in their new role; most did not. Attendance at committees was low; most were dominated by the few who were truly zealous for the war effort or who enjoyed administration. They did their job well, but most of their colleagues found that drudging over reports and accounts was not for them. They had sought election in order to serve their locality, to enhance their own standing and to strengthen their hand when seeking favours. They were unpaid and did not think of themselves as professional MPs. No Parliament had ever sat so long or so often and many sneaked off into the country whenever they could. The Restoration offered such men a chance to return to normal. They could hand back to the king the responsibility for governing, while reserving for themselves the less demanding tasks of complaining and criticizing if they did not like the way he governed. The Convention reserved to itself only one major executive task – paying off the New Model; its successor abandoned Parliament's recently assumed executive role altogether.[81]

The willingness to allow Charles to govern reflected a broader concern to return to the old constitutional balance between the powers of the king and the rights of his people. Charles I's conduct had upset that balance and the civil war stimulated the development of political ideas in which the rights of the people were emphasized at the expense of those of the crown. Many Parliamentarians, however, hesitated to base Parliament's right to resist the king on its representing the people: what if the people sought to dictate to Parliament? The emergence of a genuinely democratic movement, the Levellers, and the upheavals of Pride's Purge and after provoked a conservative and authoritarian backlash. The old balance had been tipped too far towards the people: the world was being turned upside down. To reestablish social hierarchy and subordination it was necessary to re-establish the old political and ecclesiastical order, with a king at their head. The gentry had no wish for the king's power to be unlimited: they remembered how their liberty, property and religion had been threatened by Charles I's misgovernment. However, at this stage the more immediate threat to their interests seemed to come not from the king but from revolution from below. To guard against republicans and radicals, they needed an effective king.

The effectiveness of any pre-modern government depended not only on its powers of coercion but also on the willingness of subjects to obey. The strength which came from this willingness could not be quantified, like money or soldiers, but was none the less real. Hyde instinctively understood this; Charles, in so many respects a foreigner, did not, but for the moment wisely followed the chancellor. Both Hyde and the Commons pointedly used the rhetoric of mutual trust and affection. The Commons explicitly refrained from insisting on redress of grievances before granting supply; the king responded by hastening to comply with their wishes.[82] All in all, Charles must have been well satisfied with the Convention. His decision, in November, to dissolve it came as no great surprise. Despite the Act declaring it a true Parliament, a new one, elected at a king's command, would be seen as more unequivocally legal; it would also be more Royalist.[83] Attempts to debar Royalists from voting in April had had some effect and the Royalists' electoral prospects would also be helped by the fact that they now dominated county government and the militia. Some Presbyterian MPs, aware of this, tried to delay the revenue bills in order to prolong the Convention, but to no avail.[84] As it neared its end, ministers could look back with satisfaction at having resolved some contentious issues (land sales, indemnity) and at having kept others from being resolved unsatisfactorily (militia, Church). Above all, Charles had avoided any new restrictions on the prerogative and had in principle been granted an independent revenue for life. Whatever the personal tragedies of its last months, politically 1660 had indeed, for Charles, been an *annus mirabilis*.

'Dunkirk and a Barren Queen'

At the end of 1660 Hyde's credit with the king seemed impregnable. He had survived the scandal of his daughter's marriage and the Convention had done much to secure the newly restored monarchy. His policy of studious moderation and constitutional conservatism did not please everybody – no policy could have done that – but it seemed likely to ensure a return to peace and normality. His political dominance was to last for almost another eighteen months, during which time most of the remaining elements of the Restoration settlement were put in place. Although not without its alarums and controversies, it was generally a period in which crown and Parliament worked together and court factionalism did not seriously disrupt decision-making.

In the summer of 1662 all that changed. A serious rival emerged in the person of Bennet, who had returned from the Madrid embassy in April 1661, the same month that Hyde became Earl of Clarendon. The enmity that developed between the two men owed much to the chancellor's jealousy and suspicion of the younger man, whose affability and ingratiating charm offered (from the king's point of view) a pleasing change from Clarendon's unremitting seriousness. Bennet was aided and abetted by Hyde's old enemy Bristol: although debarred from office as a Catholic, the earl was an energetic intriguer at court and a vigorous orator in the Lords. For some time, Bennet and Bristol made little impression on Clarendon's position, which rested on the solid foundations of the king's favour and the Commons' respect. Suddenly he lost both. First the king's marriage (for which Clarendon was in large part responsible) turned out to be disastrous, personally and politically, bringing less profit than expected and threatening to commit Charles to heavy expenditure. Then Clarendon's plan to sell Dunkirk to the French proved bitterly unpopular and failed to lead to the anticipated improvement in Anglo-French relations. The chancellor, intermittently prostrated by gout and with his credit badly shaken, was unable to prevent Charles from adopting policies which provoked the Commons to an anger reminiscent of the Long Parliament. As Charles failed to control the feuds at court, factious politicians incited the Commons to investigate the alleged misdeeds of those in office, in the hope of driving them out and taking their places. The more intemperate the Commons became, the more Charles subsided into lethargy and lust and his popularity sank. By the spring of 1663 he was complaining that few peers or knights attended him at Windsor and Pepys noted that only a few poor people bothered to attend church to celebrate his birthday, the occasion of so much rejoicing only three years before.[1] In the end Charles was saved from his weakness and folly by Bristol's recklessness: impatient to bring Clarendon down, he launched an impeachment which so offended the king that he resolved to bring some order to his affairs.

In the last weeks of 1660 cracks appeared in the façade of moderation which Charles's government had maintained hitherto. Vengeful Royalist magistrates and militia officers harassed Parliamentarians and sectaries; Charles, while stressing that the Act of Indemnity had to remain inviolate, insisted that there could be no indulgence towards those who after its passage continued to act on factious principles. On 4 January 1661 the council ordered lords lieutenant to disarm such persons (and sectaries). Three days later the need for vigilance was underlined by Venner's rising: although less than forty people were involved, it took the London authorities three days to suppress them.[2] Not unnaturally, the government assumed that this little group of men would not have fought so ferociously unless they had been confident of assistance from others (apart from God), and it searched frantically for evidence of a nationwide conspiracy. While it could unearth little hard evidence, the scraps of information which it acquired were fleshed out by the over-anxious imaginations of men who could not believe that the radicals who had dominated the army and the nation would now quietly disappear from the political scene. To a surprising extent, however, that is what happened. Some did continue to uphold the 'Good Old Cause', but most of what the government saw as political disaffection could be more accurately described as religious nonconformity – not that contemporaries were inclined to distinguish between the two. The lack of republican activism after 1660 might seem strange, but doctrinaire republicans had never been numerous and many with such sympathies, conditioned to see earthly events as the workings of God's Providence, reacted to the Restoration with either perplexity or fatalism.[3]

That said, it should be stressed that until 1667 (and to some extent later) the state papers contain many reports of plots, conspiracies and religious disaffection. Many came from local officials, but others were provided by spies who sought to earn their money by making the most of whatever information they had.[4] Often there were suspicions that the government exaggerated the danger of revolt to provide a pretext to raise troops or to seek money from Parliament,[5] but there seems little doubt that ministers were genuinely anxious.[6] They were acutely conscious that the state lacked coercive power. The disbanding of the New Model left Charles with few soldiers apart from those at Dunkirk. The militia's legal status was still uncertain and some of its members doubted whether they could legally act, or arrest suspicious persons or Dissenters.[7] In response to Venner's rising, the council ordered that more guards should be raised, even though there was no money to pay for them. It also ordered that inland garrisons should be suppressed and their fortifications razed, but it is not clear whether its aim was to save money, which could be spent on more soldiers, or to prevent these forts being seized by dissidents.[8] Similar orders, issued in 1662, would suggest that little was actually done.[9]

To settle the militia, and much else, a new Parliament was needed and elections were held in the spring of 1661. As many had predicted, men of Cavalier backgrounds fared better than they had in 1660. The House of Commons which met on 8 May was, if anything, to prove too ebulliently Royalist and Anglican for the king's taste. While stressing to the Houses the need to pull up 'rebellious' principles by the roots and that plotters and seditious preachers deserved no indulgence, both king and chancellor insisted that the Convention's legislation – above all the Act of Indemnity – had to be confirmed. Many MPs were far from eager to comply. A bill was brought in to give an indemnity to 'the king's faithful subjects' and to restore the estates taken from them, which would have overturned much of what the Convention had done. Charles had to make it very clear (not least to his own servants) that he was honour bound to preserve the Act of Indemnity in its entirety. On 22 June, after another pointed reminder from the king, the Commons agreed that the bill of confirmation should pass.[10] They gave vent to their frustrations in a bill for the execution of the nineteen regicides who had escaped death the previous year. Much to the relief of the king (who declared himself weary of hanging) the bill stuck in the Lords.[11]

Other legislation proved less contentious. The Act for the Safety and Preservation of the King's Person and Government resolved the question of the legality of the Long Parliament's legislation: all bills which had not received the royal assent were declared null and void. Thus the reforming Acts of 1641 were to stand; the Militia Ordinance and subsequent legislation were not. This did not preclude further legislation to amend that of 1640–2: acts against ecclesiastical courts and excluding bishops from the Lords were repealed. It seems likely that Charles and his advisers would have liked further changes. In both 1662 and 1663 the Lords proposed to repeal all the Acts of the Long Parliament and appointed committees to consider which should then be re-enacted; among other points, they discussed the terms upon which a court similar to Star Chamber could be established. Both Houses also considered repealing the 1641 Triennial Act, which bound the king to call Parliament at least once every three years for at least fifty days.[12]

Apart from re-establishing the king's prerogatives, much of the legislation of 1661–2 reflected fear of revolution from below. The Act for the Preservation of the King's Person also made it an offence to call him a Papist – an indication of the effectiveness of anti-Popery in the 1640s – and declared 'that the oath usually called the Solemn League and Covenant was in itself an unlawful oath, and imposed upon the subjects of this realm against the fundamental laws and liberties of this kingdom'. Remembering how crowds had hustled and intimidated members of both Houses on pretence of presenting petitions, the Act against Tumultuous Petitioning forbade the collection of more than twenty signatures without the permission of three JPs or some similar authority; no petition was to be presented by more than ten persons. The concern to curb popular political activity also underlay the 1662 Licensing Act. Before 1640 press censorship had rested on the royal prerogative. All published works had to be licensed by a secretary of state, bishop or equivalent figure; publication of unlicensed works could bring serious penalties including mutilation – the combative William Prynne had had his ears cropped twice – imprisonment, heavy fines and the destruction of presses and type. The explosion of political publishing after censorship collapsed in 1640 made possible an unprecedented growth of popular political awareness; Charles seems to have taken a personal interest in reversing this process by means of a bill to put the licensing system on a statutory basis. Not only did the bill originate in the Lords – usually a sign of government initiative – but Charles twice urged the Commons to hasten its passage. The Commons clearly had reservations about it, as the Act was to be in force for only two years. Later it was extended for short periods and then until the end of the first session of the next Parliament, which (as it turned out) was not to be until May 1679.[13]

The concern with disaffection did not end there. The problem was greatest in towns, with their concentrations of population and higher than average levels of literacy and political consciousness; Dissent, too, was especially prevalent in towns. Whereas country-dwellers were often seen as economically subordinate and socially subservient to the landowners, townspeople were more independent, and so interconnected by trade and business that few exercised unequivocal authority over others. In addition, a sense of neighbourliness – or community pride – could lead rulers and ruled to unite against outside interference.[14] On top of this, most towns were to some extent self-governing. In the shires the king entrusted law enforcement and administration to JPs whom he appointed and whom he could remove. Most towns of any size had received royal charters under which the king delegated many or all of the functions of county JPs to members of an elected corporation. The 'election' might be little more than thinly disguised co-option, but those chosen were neither appointed nor removable by the crown.

In normal times, such a process of delegation ensured that the towns were run (at no cost to the crown) by men of local standing and local knowledge who, being wealthy, had a vested interest in maintaining law and order. The early 1660s were not a normal time: the air was full of rumours of revolt and town government was still run mainly by men who had gained office in the 1640s and 1650s. Although many corporations celebrated the Restoration and sent the king lavish gifts, the niggling suspicion remained that their commitment to the monarchy (and the Church) left much to be desired; they certainly could not be trusted to suppress religious dissent. Where they had received new charters since 1640, the price for renewing those charters could be the removal of 'disaffected' councillors. The renewal of charters was, however, a slow process: each had to be carefully checked by the crown's law officers and the Commons soon made it clear that they disapproved of any wholesale tampering with charters or with the principle of municipal self-government: more than four-fifths of MPs sat for borough constituencies. Some in the government clearly wished the king to gain much more sweeping powers to intervene in municipal affairs and to enhance the element of oligarchy in both municipal and Parliamentary elections: a warrant dated 7 May makes this clear. Soon after, a bill to purge all disaffected members of corporations was introduced in the Commons, probably by Cavaliers angry at being asked to confirm the Act of Indemnity. The Lords added amendments which effectively recast the bill: all charters were to be renewed by June 1662; the king was to appoint all recorders and town clerks; county JPs were also to act as JPs in boroughs. The Commons rejected these changes, first because they would allow wide-ranging government interference in municipal affairs, and second because the original crux of their bill – the purge of the disaffected – had been removed.[15]

The Houses remained deadlocked until December, when a revised bill (drafted by the attorney-general) quickly passed. It was far closer to the Commons' original bill than to the Lords' amendments: its main provision was for a purge by commissioners, with powers which were to last until March 1663, appointed by the king. Members of corporations were to take the oaths of allegiance and supremacy and were formally to repudiate the Covenant and renounce the principle of resistance to the crown; they were also to take communion according to the Anglican rite at least once a year. Even those who met these requirements could still be removed if the commissioners judged them to be disaffected. The commissioners could fill vacancies as they chose. The result, as the Commons intended, was a massive change in the personnel of municipal government, but with no extension of royal interference in the towns' affairs. The crown's powers were, in fact, to be extended but in a slow and piecemeal way: as new charters were issued, they stipulated that no one could serve as recorder or town clerk unless their election had been approved by the king. Such intervention, however, was much less extensive than that envisaged in either the warrant of 7 May or the Lords' amendments to the corporation bill, nor is it at all clear that Charles and his advisers saw the Corporation Act as a defeat. It is doubtful whether they had a coherent policy towards the towns, other than a feeling that they were potentially dangerous and needed to be watched. The Corporation Act offered a means of neutralizing that danger and Charles was apparently content to let it pass in the form the Commons wanted. Only time was to show that the removal of the 'disaffected' from town governments was to be merely temporary.

The history of the corporation bill makes it clear that, while eager to guard against revolution from below, MPs had no wish to extend royal power to a point where it could threaten liberty and property. They showed a similar wariness in response to attempts to strengthen the crown's military resources. They declared that the king alone should direct the militia and armed forces, thus resolving in his favour one of the key constitutional disputes of the civil war.[16] The right of command, however, was of limited use while the army was so small and the king's legal right to raise men and money for the militia remained questionable. As far as the army was concerned, there was no legal barrier to his raising more regiments, but his finances would not allow it. His ministers tried in vain to persuade the Commons to fund a standing force. In December 1661 the House was told of an alleged Roundhead plot in Lancashire – Pepys, for one, was sceptical. Clarendon proposed that a committee should sit during the Christmas recess to investigate it and suggested that a standing force should be raised, if only temporarily, to relieve the burden on the militia.[17] The committee achieved nothing: in early January Clarendon referred the matter back to the House and spoke of imaginary jealousies: Charles, he said, had no intention of raising a standing army. A proposal that the militia should be reconstituted as a more permanent and professional body was also dropped.[18] On the other hand, the Second Militia Act (1662) at last put the militia on an unequivocal statutory basis and laid down who was to be obliged to serve and to contribute to the militia rate. It contained two novel elements. First, the king was empowered to levy up to £70,000 a year (on top of the militia rate) for three years, which would enable him to deploy it more extensively: as with the Licensing Act and the appointment of the Corporation Act commissioners, Parliament here gave Charles more extensive powers to deal with disaffection – but only for a limited period. Second, all who served in the militia were to take the oaths of allegiance and supremacy and declare that it was unlawful to take up arms 'upon any pretence whatsoever' against the king or those commissioned by him. Some lawyers (including strong Royalists) thought the latter declaration dangerously sweeping. On the other hand, effective direction of the militia was to be in the hands not of the king but of the lords lieutenant and their deputies.[19]

Another area in which the Commons proved unwilling to trust the king too far was the revenue. By early 1661 the court's initial glee about the revenues voted by the Convention had worn off. Charles talked of the gulf between his income and his necessary expenditure: beggary, he said, was worse for kings than for ordinary men. He talked boldly of putting his finances in order bit by bit, so that in a few years he would be one of the most powerful princes in Europe. That, alas, was merely talk: he lacked the necessary willpower and it was becoming apparent that the Convention's estimates of yield had been over-optimistic. As debts mounted something had to be done. Hyde claimed in April that Charles would not press Parliament for money, as other matters took precedence; three weeks later, when Parliament met, he was quick to ask for supply.[20] The Commons responded with a benevolence or free gift but this, and the eighteen months' assessment (worth over £1,000,000) which they voted in December, did not get to the root of the problem. The revenues which were supposed to support the normal expenses of government were yielding £250,000 to £300,000 less than the Convention's estimate. On 30 May the Commons voted 'to settle a full, constant and standing revenue for the time to come',[21] but failed to match their deeds to their words. While broadly accepting the Treasury spokesmen's figures, the Commons first considered how to improve the yields of existing revenues. After protracted enquiries into the excise, it was resolved not to extend it to all beer and ale but to impose a hearth tax, on the principle that the number of hearths in a person's dwelling gave a rough indication of their wealth. The bill's sponsors claimed that it would yield close to £1,000,000 a year; in fact it at first produced less than £200,000 and proved bitterly unpopular and difficult to collect.[22]

Various reasons may be advanced for the Commons' failure to provide more amply for the king. Both Clarendon and Southampton alleged that the court chose not to press too hard for money.[23] Clarendon also claimed that MPs suffered from a measure of wilful ignorance. Numeracy was generally not their strong point and reports of their discussions often contain wildly diverging figures. Parliaments, he wrote, 'seldom make their computations right, but reckon what they give to be much more than is ever received and what they are to pay to be as much less than in truth they owe'. Southampton's secretary, Sir Philip Warwick, recalled that when he laid figures before a committee of the Commons, MPs were reluctant to examine them fully or to believe that all the expenditure was necessary.[24] But beneath this real or feigned lack of fiscal understanding lay the more fundamental point that, while MPs were dissatisfied with major elements of royal policy, they would not surrender the bargaining power given them by the king's financial weakness. They knew that a poor king would not be able to afford a standing army; the Lords' amendments to the corporation bill upset many MPs; but the most crucial source of dissatisfaction, which provoked the most explicit threats to hold up money, was religion.[25]

The Act for the Security of the King's Person, by sweeping away all legislation which had not received the royal assent, in law restored the Church as it had existed before the civil war (except for the Church courts). The Act of Uniformity of 1559 required that the Prayer Book be used in parish churches and imposed penalties for absence from church; an Act of 1593 laid down draconian penalties for attending unauthorized religious meetings (or conventicles). Even before the Cavalier Parliament met, some had claimed that this old legislation was still in force; the privy council, however, preferred to proceed against conventicles under the laws against riotous and unlawful assemblies.[26] Once the Cavalier Parliament had restored the old legal foundation of the Church, however, it did not follow that it would remain unchanged. The Worcester House Declaration suggested that Charles was prepared to contemplate changes; what would be Parliament's response?

We have seen that in 1660 Charles judged it politically expedient to comprehend at least some of the Presbyterians within the Church. He had shown no eagerness to replace Presbyterian parish clergymen with Anglicans or to restore the machinery of ecclesiastical administration. On the other hand, Venner's rising and reports of conspiracies led him to command that sectaries should be prosecuted as a danger to public order. He and Hyde still paid lip-service to the idea of 'tender consciences': indeed, Charles ordered that Quakers imprisoned only for scruples of conscience should be released.[27] Such a distinction would mean little in practice: most officials automatically equated religious dissent with political disaffection. Thus Charles had, in effect, abandoned all thoughts of indulgence for Dissenters (though not, as we shall see, for Catholics). He may well have felt that, with the army disbanded, he no longer needed to pander to the sectaries. He was still, however, determined to secure a measure of comprehension and fought a long, losing battle to prevent the Cavalier Parliament from re-establishing an unbendingly Anglican Church.

The mood of the new House of Commons soon became clear. The House ordered that all members take communion according to the Anglican rite and that the Covenant be burned by the common hangman. A Congregationalist MP who refused to receive communion was suspended; others with similar sympathies, realizing that they were heavily outnumbered, kept quiet.[28] The legislation of 1641–2 abolishing Church courts and excluding the bishops from the Lords was repealed and a bill was brought in against Quaker meetings. The House also brought in a bill to restore advowsons (rights to nominate parish clergymen) and impropriated tithes (those collected by laymen) which had been confiscated during the civil wars. The income from the latter had mostly been used to augment clerical stipends, but MPs were clearly determined to enable Cavalier landowners to recoup at least some of their losses, even if this was to be at the expense of the Church; a Lords' amendment to reserve one-third of the value to the Church was defeated. The bill eventually passed in 1662 and showed that MPs were determined to restore not only the old Church but also lay domination over the clergy.[29]

None of this legislation was unacceptable to the king: the real sources of contention were to be the Church's future government and above all its liturgy. Were changes to be made to enable conscientious Presbyterian ministers to remain within the Church? Or was the old liturgy to be retained in its entirety and were the clergy to be required to endorse every detail? It has been suggested that the Commons' rigour reflected the views, not of the majority of MPs, but of a militantly Anglican minority, who played on the fears and anxieties of their less committed fellows. This could well be true: it would certainly be naive to suggest that debates on religion were innocent of political considerations. On the other hand, the sullen resistance to the prohibition of Anglican practices in the 1640s and 1650s and the spontaneous revival of Prayer Book services in so many parishes would suggest that Anglicanism had deep roots in the affections of people of all ranks.[30] The fact that many JPs were to prove reluctant to persecute Dissenters is not conclusive evidence of limited support for the Church. It could be that they regarded the laws against nonconformists (like those against Catholics) as necessary for the public safety, but in normal circumstances saw no great need to enforce them.[31]

Whatever the relative strength of the differing shades of opinion within the Commons, there can be no doubt that the House insisted on the full restoration of the old order. Seeing this, Charles tried to change the forum of religious debate. First, he summoned the promised assembly of divines, the Savoy Conference, but this failed to reach agreement. Baxter, as always, proved unable to decide on his priorities and tired himself and others with his verbosity; his colleagues, pessimistic about the outcome, attended only sporadically. Confident of the Commons' support, the bishops accused the Presbyterians of being unwilling to bow to authority, and insisted that the onus was on them to show that the practices they complained of (such as kneeling at communion) were unlawful and unscriptural.[32] Meanwhile, Charles summoned Convocation, the clergy's representative assembly, which traditionally met at the same time as Parliament. He had delayed his summons in the hope that the Savoy Conference would produce definite proposals and ordered the attorney-general to omit the usual stipulation that Convocation should agree nothing contrary to the established law and liturgy of the Church. If he had hoped for a strong Presbyterian presence in Convocation, the elections were to disappoint him. Its first session achieved little of moment, but by the time it reconvened in November it was clear that the Savoy Conference had failed. Charles therefore handed to Convocation the task of reviewing the Prayer Book; within a month it had completed its task, deciding that few changes were necessary. By February the revised Book had been approved by the privy council, where Charles was careful to give its critics every opportunity to express their views.[33]

By the time Charles referred the Prayer Book to Convocation, it was clear that the Commons would not agree to the alterations which the Presbyterians demanded. On 25 June they had resolved to bring in a 'compendious bill' to ensure 'effectual conformity' to the Church's liturgy. It had passed the Commons before the autumn recess and, when Parliament reconvened, Charles saw no point in opposing it openly. Religion, he told the Houses, was too hard a matter for him and he would leave it to them; there were also signs that his earlier favour towards Presbyterians was diminishing.[34] The Commons responded to his invitation by discussing the Convention's Act confirming ministers in their livings, which had yet to be confirmed by the new Parliament. As with the Indemnity Act, 'amendments' were proposed which would effectively have nullified the original Act. Most of these amendments were approved by the Commons, but rejected in the Lords, after a bitter debate in which Clarendon persuaded seven bishops and the Duke of York to oppose them. In an angry exchange, Charles told some members of the Commons that he had promised at Breda to confirm ministers in their livings. (There was no mention of this in the Declaration, but he may have given such assurances informally.) When the MPs said that the Commons might not pass 'the bill intended for the enlarging of his revenue' if Charles insisted that the ministers should be confirmed, he reportedly replied that 'he would trust God Almighty's Providence rather than break his word'.[35]

In taking this stand, Charles may indeed have been concerned for his honour, but he also knew that if the ministers were not confirmed in their livings many would be ousted, swelling the number of Dissenters. The Commons dropped their amendments and the Act was confirmed – but then many of the same provisions were added to the uniformity bill, notably the requirement that all incumbents should have received episcopal (rather than

Presbyterian) ordination and should abjure the Covenant. Faced once more with the prospect of mass expulsions from the Church, Charles struggled to temper the Commons' rigour. Clarendon promoted a proviso to allow the king to dispense peaceable individuals from the need to wear the surplice or use the sign of the cross in baptism. The proviso's tone was defensive, almost plaintive. Some claimed that it was a response to Presbyterian offers of money; Bristol opposed it violently, claiming (untruly) that Charles knew nothing of it. Despite his opposition, and that of some of the bishops, the Lords approved the proviso, but it was then summarily rejected by the Commons. Faced with the Lower House's intransigence, the peers abandoned, one by one, their attempts to mitigate the severity of the bill; it passed in the form that the Commons wanted. Charles did not accept defeat graciously. In May, at the start of a nine months' prorogation, Clarendon told the House that Charles, with his great experience of mankind, was better equipped than anyone to distinguish between tenderness of conscience and pride of conscience. In fact, the king's plans for comprehension had been comprehensively rejected and the scope left for flexibility or manoeuvre was legally nil.[36]

The extent of his defeat soon became apparent. Existing incumbents had until 24 August to declare their unfeigned assent and consent to the Prayer Book and all that it contained. Four days after the deadline, a group of Presbyterians petitioned to be dispensed from this requirement. They had been encouraged to do this from within the court, but their proposal was vigorously opposed by Gilbert Sheldon, Bishop of London; after consulting Chief Justice Bridgeman and the attorney-general, the privy council decided that the law should take its course. Not merely were the petitioners disappointed, but many Presbyterians failed to conform in the hope of a last-minute reprieve from the king. As a result, the expulsions which followed were probably more numerous than they might otherwise have been.[37] Maybe 1,800 ministers, around a fifth of the total, were ejected from their livings, but despite the threats of some, and the fears of others, the ejections passed off peacefully.[38]

For Charles the ejections compounded a dispiriting defeat. Together with the hostility aroused by the hearth tax, they exacerbated the government's fears of disaffection and disorder. Clarendon's views are harder to gauge. Outwardly he supported the king's policy of moderation and comprehension, marshalling the opposition to the Commons' amendments to the Act for the Confirmation of Ministers and promoting the proviso to allow the king a limited power to dispense with the requirements of the Act of Uniformity. On 1 September 1662, however, he wrote to Ormond:

The very severe execution of the Act of Uniformity which is resolved on may, I fear, add more fuel to the matter that was before combustible enough. But we are in and must proceed with steadiness and so must you [in Ireland] and I wish I were as confident that we shall do so as that you will.[39]

One cannot tell, however, if he held such opinions earlier: he may simply have accepted the Act as a *fait accompli,* which (at the time) even Bennet professed to do.[40] As for Charles, whatever his private opinions, he was unwilling to go against the council's advice and the ejections were allowed to proceed.

Charles's plans for comprehension may not greatly have strained Clarendon's conscience; those for the Catholics must have proved more problematical. Following a number of petitions, the Lords appointed a committee in July 1661 to consider how far the burden imposed on Catholics by the penal laws could safely be alleviated. It recommended that priests (apart from Jesuits) should be allowed to remain in England, provided they registered with a secretary of state. Some of the more draconian penalties for absence from church and refusal of the oath of allegiance should be abolished, as should the prohibition on sending children to the English Catholic colleges on the continent. Catholics were to take 'an oath of allegiance', which implied that the existing oath (unacceptable to most Catholics, as it described certain powers claimed by the pope as 'impious, damnable and heretical') was to be amended. The committee proposed that a bill to this effect should include in its preamble a statement that the king wished to protect those Catholics who were loyal and peaceable and dissociated themselves from those who cherished the 'Inquisition and suchlike cruel laws'. The proposed changes would leave in place the laws excluding Catholics from civil and military office. The committee stressed the need to guard against 'the growth and encroachment of Popery or any other sectaries' and exhorted the bishops to ensure that the young were fully instructed in the ways of the Church of England.[41]

The committee's recommendations included many points raised in the Catholics' petitions, which argued that (unlike the sectaries) Catholics posed no threat to the crown. Leading Catholics had also discussed possible modifications to the oath of allegiance.[42] The provision against the Jesuits had been included in the House's instructions to the committee and may have been inspired by a strongly anti-Jesuit element among the Catholic clergy. Alternatively it may reflect an attempt to discriminate between the 'loyal' and the 'disloyal' which was to run through both Charles's treatment of English sectaries and Ormond's policy towards Irish Catholics.[43] There can be no doubt of Charles's broad support for the committee's proposals: a draft oath of allegiance, 'framed by the king himself', may date from this time.[44] The proposed changes, however, never materialized. After the autumn recess the bishops returned to the House and the matter was not pursued.

The court Catholics were bitter that a project into which they had put so much effort had come to naught. Some (notably Bristol) accused Clarendon of opposing the bill 'underhand' and there were reports that he was severely reprimanded by the king.[45] The accusation was probably unfounded, but such trivial considerations never bothered Bristol and the chancellor's credit with his master was badly shaken. The major influence on the king's policy towards the Catholics was not Bristol, however, but Charles's kinsman, Louis Stuart, Sieur d'Aubigny. French by upbringing, he was far more urbane and polished than Charles's other courtiers and single-mindedly used his considerable political finesse to promote his own elevation to the cardinalate. Unfortunately, the French regarded him with suspicion as a former associate of de Retz, while the Vatican suspected him of Jansenism.[46] Nevertheless, he claimed that his promotion would benefit the English Catholics: the secular clergy (those not in 'regular' orders, such as Benedictines or Jesuits) had lacked a head since Bishop Richard Smith left England in 1631. Charles at first feared that for the pope to appoint a Catholic bishop might weaken his own claim to supremacy over the English Church, but late in 1662 he sent Bellings to Rome to press the pope to make d'Aubigny both a bishop and a cardinal. The Vatican, however, sought a wide range of assurances on behalf of both d'Aubigny and the English Catholics. By May 1663 Bellings was back in London with 'less than a promise', at which Charles was deeply offended. When the Brussels internuncio came to court in 1664 he was told that Charles would one day avenge this 'slight' and that he planned to appoint Catholic bishops in Ireland and at Tangier who would swear not to recognize the pope's authority. In 1665 Charles's sustained pressure finally told: the pope agreed to the promotion, but d'Aubigny died before the news could reach him.[47]

The moves on behalf of d'Aubigny posed no direct threat to Clarendon: he was fully aware of them – indeed, Bellings was his secretary – and yet there is good reason to doubt the Venetian envoy's claim that both king and chancellor ardently wished for d'Aubigny's elevation.[48] Clarendon, while no bigoted anti-Papist, did not fully share Charles's sympathy for the Catholics' plight, so was vulnerable to attack from those who did. By the spring of 1662 Bristol was openly hostile, as shown by their confrontation over the proviso to the uniformity bill. On that occasion, Clarendon was supporting the king's policy of comprehension, while Bristol sought to promote indulgence for both Dissenters and Catholics.[49] If, however, the chancellor failed to support the policies Charles favoured, or failed to deliver the expected results, his position would become extremely vulnerable.

*

Thus far we have concentrated almost exclusively on England's domestic affairs, but most princes saw diplomacy (and its natural extension war) as their most important responsibility. Foreign policy decisions were seldom straightforward. They were influenced by a complex of factors, involving both the internal affairs of states and their interrelationship, so that it was seldom possible to isolate one issue or area from others. Much depended on each protagonist's perception of the others' motives or intentions and different policy considerations – profit and principle, power and honour – could pull against one another. In short, foreign policy decisions were often based on inadequate information and unfounded assumptions and, thanks to the slowness of communications, were frequently overtaken by events. It would thus be unrealistic to expect any seventeenth-century ruler to pursue consistent, coherent and fully thought-out policies. Even Louis XIV, a model of diligence and a great believer in order and method, could spend months or even years teetering in indecision between incompatible lines of policy; he could also make catastrophic errors because he had misread the minds of others. Historians, thanks to their access to diplomatic correspondence, are often better informed than those involved at the time, but in analysing the latter's conduct it is necessary to bear in mind their perceptions and misconceptions as well as objective fact.

In the second half of the seventeenth century, the issue which dominated European affairs was the Spanish succession. The Spanish crown had built up a huge multinational empire, including the Netherlands, Portugal, Milan, Naples, Sicily and Franche Comté, not to mention vast areas of the New World. Controlling this empire imposed unbearable strains on a primitive economy, strains made worse by long, vulnerable lines of communication. By 1660 there were signs that the empire was breaking up. After eighty years of war, the Northern Netherlands had won independence, as the Dutch Republic, and Portugal was in revolt. The concession of Dutch independence was a confession of exhaustion: it was becoming impossible to raise enough men and money to continue the struggle. Even Portugal – poorer, weaker and much closer to home – proved a stubborn adversary. Spain's economy was increasingly run by foreigners (above all Dutch and French), who possessed the capital and expertise that the Spanish lacked. Already in the 1660s there were signs that the Spanish court was coming to terms with economic and military reality and was considering exchanging the Spanish Netherlands and its other northern possessions – distant, costly and culturally alien – in order to concentrate its resources on the Mediterranean and the New World. It was not, however, an easy decision, as to pull out would involve a grave loss of face and a blow to national pride.[50]

To these long-term causes of the decline of the Spanish system should be added the more random, but no less important, factor of biology. King

Philip IV, who died in 1665, had only one son, a sad example of the genetic consequences of the Habsburg dynasty's habit of marrying within itself. The family's jutting jaw was in his case so prominent that his two sets of teeth did not meet; he was also mentally retarded. When he succeeded his father, as Carlos II, nobody expected him to live for long: in fact, he confounded expectations by surviving until 1700. Equally confident predictions that he would leave no heirs mercifully proved correct. Thus for the best part of four decades European rulers speculated on the eventual fate of the Spanish lands: Charles II was just one of many to look forward greedily to their eventual dismemberment.

Others had a more direct interest. Philip IV's younger daughter had carried on the family tradition by marrying her Habsburg cousin, the Emperor Leopold I; the elder, Maria Teresa, married Louis XIV of France. Louis was eight years Charles's junior and it caused considerable surprise when, soon after Mazarin's death in 1661, he announced that he would take over the direction of government himself. Unlike Charles, however, he had received an exhaustive training in kingship from the cardinal. He brought to the task a dogged sense of purpose, making up in assiduity what he lacked in intuition. Always careful to base decisions on full information – ambassadors who sent terse dispatches were told to write more – he sought to analyse that information methodically and logically, in an effort to understand the interests of other rulers and to anticipate their conduct. He showed a similar attention to detail in organizing and equipping his armed forces: by the end of the 1660s France was the supreme military power in Europe and its navy, once negligible, was coming to rival those of the Dutch Republic and England.

Power, for Louis, was never an end in itself. He aimed to promote *la gloire*, the prestige of both the House of Bourbon and himself. He built Versailles as a monument to his greatness and created a court ceremonial geared to the glorification of the king. In an age punctilious about honour and precedence, he took such matters more to heart than anyone. When he heard that the Spaniards had worsted the French in a bloody contest for precedence in London, Louis (renowned for his self-control) was so angry that he could hardly speak. His policies were also, however, influenced by solid geopolitical considerations. France was surrounded by Habsburg territories: apart from those of Spain (the Southern Netherlands, Franche Comté, Milan and Spain itself) the emperor (whose main lands lay in Austria-Hungary) possessed extensive, if ambiguous, rights in Alsace and claimed suzerainty over most of Germany. As recently as 1636 Spanish troops had swept through Northern France to within eighty miles of Paris. Louis believed that France needed more defensible frontiers to the north and east, which meant either conquering new territory or rationalizing existing frontiers to remove salients, enclaves and ambiguities, at least on the French side: he had no objection to any that remained in others' territories, as those could serve as a pretext for future acquisitions. His ambitions did not stop there. At the time of her marriage Maria Teresa had renounced all claim to the Spanish inheritance, but Mazarin had cunningly insisted that the renunciation should be conditional on the payment of her dowry. The Spaniards, strapped for cash, failed to complete the payments, so Louis became convinced that the whole Spanish inheritance would come to him, by right, when Carlos died. He was not, however, inclined to wait that long. He claimed that substantial areas in the Spanish Netherlands fell to him when Philip IV died, on the pretext that local custom gave the daughter of a first marriage (Maria Teresa) a claim superior to that of the son of a second (Carlos). He pursued these claims with ruthless determination and an utter conviction of his own rectitude: he persuaded himself without difficulty that what others saw as naked acquisitiveness was a matter of undeniable right.

This combination of arrogance, self-righteousness and iron resolve did not make Louis easy to deal with. Charles, who had known him as a teenager, took some time to take him seriously and to come to terms with the way he squeezed every ounce of advantage from every negotiation. Unlike Charles, Louis understood the value of money and haggled like a miser over what, for him, were paltry sums. He talked much of honour and justice while behaving in ways which many regarded as devious. He was quick to take offence and showed a sadistic pleasure in humiliating his enemies – or those who had merely offended him. As a result Charles's attempts to establish a good understanding between them were dogged by rows, to which the incompetence and incomprehension of Charles and his advisers made no small contribution.

Louis' territorial ambitions would not go unopposed. Under Cromwell Europeans realized that England could no longer be dismissed as militarily negligible: the New Model helped the French against Spain and in return received Dunkirk. Although the army was disbanded in 1660, the navy was to remain very much larger than it had been under Charles I. Louis, however, remarked in 1662 that he did not regard England as posing a threat to his interests;[51] the Dutch were another matter. Although the republic's population was tiny compared with that of France or Spain, it had emerged as a great power. It owed that power to trade, to carrying and handling the goods of others. Far-flung commercial interests made necessary (and paid for) a powerful navy; the long struggle for independence led to the creation of a large army.

The Dutch state was singular not only in being founded on trade, but also in being a federal republic in a world of monarchies. Consisting of seven of the seventeen Netherlandish provinces formerly ruled by Spain, its constitution maintained long traditions of local autonomy. Each province had an assembly (or 'states') representing, in varying proportions, nobles and towns, and on many issues decisions were supposed to be unanimous. Somehow, the disparate provinces had worked together to fight Spain, thanks to the efforts of the States General and the Princes of Orange. In the former, major decisions could be vetoed by any province or great town, but agreement often proved possible, partly because the very nature of the constitution encouraged bargaining and compromise, partly because of the overwhelming economic power of the great cities of the province of Holland, which alone provided 60 per cent of the federal revenue: almost half of that came from Amsterdam. This gave the province (and its grand pensionary, Jan de Witt) a disproportionate influence in the debates and resolutions of the States General.

Collective leadership served to preserve provincial and municipal liberties, but posed problems. The need to secure agreement encouraged the bending and breaking of constitutional rules and led to unedifying wrangles. Security was lamentable: even the most secret resolutions were quickly leaked to foreign ambassadors. However, the need for secret and swift decisions, in diplomacy and war, encouraged the Dutch to look to their leading noble family. The House of Orange had extensive lands in Germany as well as the Netherlands and took its title from a small principality on the Rhône. Its head was usually elected 'stadhouder' (lieutenant) of five provinces (the others being held by a cousin); he was also usually appointed captain- and admiral-general of the republic's forces. Their quasi-royal status, and the tensions between the princes' insistence on quick decisions and the provinces' dogged defence of local autonomy, nourished fears that they might try to set up an Orange monarchy, modelled on that of the Bourbons. These fears reached a peak in 1650, when William II imprisoned leaders of the republican (or 'States') party and attempted a military coup against Amsterdam. His untimely death gave de Witt and the States party a perfect opportunity to ensure that such a thing could never happen again and that William's son, William III, would never wield the powers enjoyed by his forebears.

Charles II was thus faced with three very different neighbours: Spain, whose empire was crumbling; France, with a young and ambitious king; and the Dutch Republic, commercially formidable but politically divided. Later generations saw the containment of France as the natural priority of England and the other European powers, but such a view owed much to accumulated experience of Louis XIV. From Charles's perspective, in the early 1660s, the picture was far less clear-cut: different considerations could pull him different ways. As much of his revenue came from taxes on trade and consumption and as the London merchant community was his main source of loans, he might be expected to encourage commercial and colonial expansion. The need to secure taxes from Parliament, both for war and to make good the shortfall on his ordinary revenue, might lead him to be swayed by public opinion, in a way that Louis XIV rarely was. The lust for glory, to which he was not immune, might lead him to hanker after territorial acquisitions, in Europe or elsewhere. Concern for his honour might embroil him in protocol or precedence disputes. Fear of rebellion might lead him to seek a foreign ally with a powerful army. Or he might be swayed by personal prejudices – fondness for France, dislike of the Dutch, scorn for the Spaniards. The interplay between such considerations ensured that Charles's foreign policy showed little of the rigorous – sometimes over-rigid – consistency to which Louis aspired. Moreover, he suffered initially from inexperience: begging for aid around the courts of Europe raised problems far less complex than those of conducting the foreign and commercial policies of a major state. Charles and his advisers took time to learn the skills of diplomacy – the hints and insinuations, the careful choice of words to avoid irrevocable commitment, the ability to extract the maximum advantage from a particular situation. It took time, too, to accumulate the information which effective policy-making required. England's diplomatic service had always been skeletal and underfunded; many ambassadors treated their papers as their personal property, so documentation from the past was far more patchy than in France or Spain, a problem exacerbated by the disruption of the Interregnum. At times ministers could not find the treaties that were to serve as the basis for negotiations and it was only gradually that the new regime established more regular methods of record-keeping.[52]

Perhaps the most consistent element in Charles's foreign policy was his admiration for France: its culture, its aristocratic society, its government. From slightly amused condescension, his attitude towards Louis quickly became one of respect: again and again, year after year, he declared that he wanted a personal friendship and a political liaison with his French cousin. There was more to this than mere personal predilection. Louis had a large army and Charles more than once asked him for promises of military help in case of need. France, at first, offered much less stern commercial and colonial competition than the Dutch. Moreover, Charles never regarded the prospect of French expansion into the Netherlands as a threat to England: indeed, he hoped to profit from it, in the form of either Flemish and Dutch towns, or colonies and trading rights in Spanish America. He saw the Spaniards as pathetic, unable even to protect themselves, so he waited, like a hyena, to pick off scraps of carrion from the carcase of the Spanish empire after the French lion had had his fill.

By contrast, Charles regarded the Dutch with patrician dislike heightened by a sense of family grievance. It seemed an inversion of the natural order for grubby bourgeois to rule over noblemen and deny princes their hereditary rights: it raised unpleasant echoes of his own experience in the Interregnum – and to add insult to injury, the Dutch (like Cromwell) were so damnably successful. Translated into practical policies, his prejudices focused, first, on rivalry for trade and empire and, second, on the advancement of his nephew.

Dutch prosperity rested partly on their carrying the products of other nations more efficiently and cheaply than anyone else and partly on their possessing the naval might to protect their own trade and colonies and to harass those of others. Only with the great expansion of her fleet from the late 1640s could England begin to offer a serious challenge. The Navigation Acts sought to give England a monopoly of trade with her colonies (including Ireland) and to ensure that all goods brought into England were carried either in English ships or in those of the country of origin: the Dutch, Europe's great middlemen, would be excluded. Charles made little contribution to these Acts: the first had been enacted in 1651 and he apparently did not see that of 1660 until it had passed both Houses.[53] Even so, so much of his revenue depended on trade that he had every incentive to make sure that the Acts were enforced.

Charles's attitude towards William was determined by a mixture of family and political considerations. He had been very fond of his sister and resented the way that the States party had, in his opinion, mistreated her and her son. Once his hostility to the republic grew, however, Charles saw the promotion of William's interests as a means of destabilizing the Dutch regime. The States party's strength lay among the great merchant oligarchs (the 'regents') of Holland and Zeeland. The eastern provinces, by contrast, were mainly agricultural, dominated by the landed nobility who mostly supported the House of Orange, not only as fellow aristocrats but also as military leaders – the nobility's traditional *métier* was war. Even in the cities, there was much support for the Orangist cause among the poor, encouraged by preachers of the Dutch Reformed Church, who bitterly condemned the regents' religious tolerance: persecution was bad for business, toleration attracted immigrants of all religions, or none. In pushing for William to be appointed stadhouder and captain-general, therefore, Charles deliberately sought to reopen old wounds and, by unleashing the popular Orangism of the cities, to overturn the power of the regents. It was a dangerous game and rested on the assumption that William, twenty years Charles's junior, would prove an obedient puppet: experience was to show that this assumption was unfounded.

In his efforts to advance William, Charles sought to enlist the aid of Louis XIV. Louis, however, saw Orange as a nest of Huguenots and rebels: in 1661 he removed the governor appointed by William's guardian and had the walls razed. More fundamentally, he had no wish to overthrow the States party. For decades France had assisted the Dutch rebels against Spain and now Louis saw a regime dominated by a military nobility as far more dangerous than one preoccupied with trade. True, his long-term concern to build up France's trade and colonies and his ambitions in the Spanish Netherlands were likely eventually to lead to conflict with the Dutch, but for the moment Louis' first priorities were to rebuild his finances after the long war with Spain, and then to expand his army and navy. De Witt, worried by Louis' growing might and by Charles's support for William, was prepared to be conciliatory. He proposed various schemes for a barrier between France and the republic, including one for an independent federal republic in the Southern Netherlands, divided (like Switzerland) into cantons. Louis listened politely and discussed the details at great length, but would not commit himself: he had no wish to agree to the cantonment scheme, but nor did he wish to antagonize de Witt and the Dutch.[54]

At the Restoration Charles inherited Cromwell's war with Spain, which had brought England Dunkirk and Jamaica, but also a massive increase in the government's debts. Both sides soon proclaimed peace, rather nebulously, but no treaty was signed. Charles had been inclined to agree terms, but the Spaniards insisted that these should be on the basis of the treaty of 1630, a time when Spain had been far more formidable and England far weaker. The Spaniards proposed that England should hand back Dunkirk and Jamaica, promise not to assist Spain's enemies (especially Portugal) and refrain from privateering or other potentially hostile acts in the New World. Bennet, Charles's ambassador, agreed in principle to such terms as the basis of a new treaty, but this was quickly disavowed: sporadic fighting continued 'beyond the line' for most of the 1660s.[55] Yet if relations with Spain were bad, those with France were initially worse. Charles's irritation at his earlier expulsion was compounded by the efforts of Mazarin and Henrietta Maria to control the negotiations for his restoration: they repeatedly urged him to come to France, while Bordeaux supported the efforts of the queen's Presbyterian allies to lay down conditions for Charles's return. The ambassador blamed Hyde for persuading Charles to go to Breda (rather than Paris) – all, naturally, because Hyde hated the queen – and complained that some Presbyterians made their peace with the king, putting their interests before those of the people.[56] When Charles returned, Thurloe informed him of Bordeaux's activities: he was also accused of urging Monk to make himself Protector. The ambassador protested his innocence, claiming that Charles did not believe the charges against him, but that he was overborne by Hyde and Ormond. Even Bristol, however, wrote to the French secretary of state, Hugues de Lionne, that Charles could not in honour receive a man who had been ambassador to the republic. After all his bluster, Bordeaux had no choice but to go.[57]

After Bordeaux's expulsion, Mazarin would not send another ambassador – that was a point of honour – but tried to heal the breach. Bordeaux had probably acted either on his own initiative or on the queen's advice – Mazarin had been away from Paris and his orders had been non-committal.[58] When he heard of the Restoration he wrote, pragmatically, that Bordeaux should work with Hyde, the man in favour, and that the queen should go to England, to remove misunderstandings. The betrothal of Henriette to Louis' brother should also have eased tension between the two kingdoms, although it could perhaps have been predicted that the effeminate and spiteful 'Monsieur' would prove a far from ideal husband. When the queen eventually arrived in England, her determination to break James's marriage further estranged her from Charles. To reduce the damage she had done, Mazarin wrote Charles a letter (which he showed to Hyde and Ormond) which was full of assurances of friendship and of his esteem for the two councillors. At his command, the queen swallowed her pride and received her daughter-in-law. Charles and Ormond sent the cardinal fulsome letters and Charles prepared to reopen diplomatic relations by sending St Albans as ambassador to Paris.[59]

Late in January 1661 Charles had a long talk with Bartet, the French chargé d'affaires. He spoke of the need to put his finances in order and asked if he and Louis could together find a use for the fleet, then lying idle. The Dutch, he declared, were scoundrels, no better than common sailors, while the Spaniards had no sense and no money. St Albans's instructions, drawn up at about the same time, stressed Charles's desire for a close liaison with France and the same theme recurred endlessly in his conversations with successive French ambassadors. Early in 1662 he talked with the Comte d'Estrades of Philip IV's illness and exclaimed that he looked forward to the day when he would no longer be weak and useless and could join with Louis against their common enemies.[60] The path to such a liaison proved far from smooth, however. Channels of communication were often interrupted. Mazarin died in March 1661; the direction of negotiations passed to the finance minister, Fouquet, who in August was dismissed and disgraced. D'Estrades had arrived in London in July, the first full ambassador there for almost a year, only to withdraw in October after being worsted in his battle for precedence with Watteville, his Spanish counterpart. Louis graciously absolved Charles from blame for the fracas, but d'Estrades returned only in August 1662 and was soon superseded by Cominges, whom both Charles and Clarendon disliked and distrusted.

On one issue the thawing of Anglo-French relations yielded quick results. One reason for the continuing friction between England and Spain was the

English government's support for Portugal's revolt against the Spanish crown. By 1660 the Portuguese were desperate for foreign aid, and the hand of the king's daughter, the Infanta Catherine, was one of the few assets which they could offer in return. The proposal that Charles should marry her was opposed by his mother, who put forward Mazarin's niece, the beautiful Hortense Mancini, and by Bristol, who touted the claims of the two Princesses of Parma. Mazarin, however, would not allow his niece to be considered, while the princesses were reported to be fat and ugly respectively. Spanish promises of a vast dowry for any princess other than Catherine were received at Charles's court with a derision that they probably deserved. Against this, the Portuguese offered a dowry of around £350,000, together with Tangier (from which, it was said, the English would be able to dominate the trade of the Mediterranean) and Bombay. The proposed match was eagerly supported by the French. Debarred by the Treaty of the Pyrenees from open hostilities against Spain, Mazarin and Louis saw the Anglo-Portuguese marriage treaty as a way of channelling indirect aid to Portugal and so keeping open a running sore that was sapping Spain's strength: that was why the cardinal refused to allow his niece's name to be put forward. The English privy council approved the Portuguese proposals in May 1661 but it was to be another year before the new queen arrived in England.[61]

The marriage negotiations proceeded smoothly because for once the aims of the English and French were compatible. The treaty offered Charles much-needed money and dreams of empire; it enabled Louis to continue, covertly, his struggle against the Habsburgs. On other matters, their interests diverged. There were niggles about honour and protocol. Charles demanded that Louis should concede to him all that Mazarin had conceded to Cromwell: a king could not be expected to settle for less than a usurper. The treaty with Cromwell had exempted English ships wishing to enter Bordeaux from the requirement to pay a duty and to unship their cannon, at Blaye. Louis claimed that this concession had been made in return for Cromwell's dropping the title 'king of France', to which he naturally laid no claim. The title dated back to the days when English kings had ruled large parts of France and had been retained as a slightly pathetic, but much prized, reminder of vanished empire. Charles refused to budge and the matter remained unresolved.[62] Louis, for his part, accused Charles of siding with Watteville in a dispute over precedence at the Venetian envoy's entry and initially blamed Charles for the mayhem at that of the Swedish ambassador.[63]

Although historians tend greatly to underestimate the importance of honour and protocol to seventeenth-century rulers, there were also more tangible sources of friction. St Albans was instructed to seek to renew old alliances and to form a new one, for mutual assistance (with both troops and money) against both foreign enemies and domestic insurrection.[64] Hyde, however, claimed that the danger of revolt was far greater in France than in England: any help from France should be in money, as to bring foreign troops into England would be counter-productive.[65] Charles may have thought differently. In June St Albans proposed that each king should promise to support the other with up to 3,000,000 *livres tournois* (about £225,000) or the equivalent in men and ships.[66] The French comments on this proposal suggest that they saw the question of mutual assistance as less important than St Albans's call for a general league against all and sundry, which Louis' advisers saw as being aimed mainly against the Dutch. Louis had no objection to the English and Dutch being on bad terms – far better that than that they should join against France – but he had no desire to betray or ruin his Dutch allies, nor did he wish to strengthen Charles's influence in the republic by enhancing William's power.[67] Both Charles and Clarendon, by contrast, expressed great hostility to the Dutch: the latter wrote of the need to curb their 'insolence' and claimed that the English nation was mad for war against them. Charles described them as proud and deceitful and urged Louis to espouse William's interests as a means of bringing the republic to see reason. Later he remarked plaintively that he could not understand how Louis could value the friendship of the Dutch more highly than his own.[68]

But Louis did: indeed, Charles's and Clarendon's diatribes against the Dutch reflected a deep unease about the negotiations, in 1661–2, for the renewal of France's treaties with the republic.[69] Aware of their anxieties, d'Estrades persuaded the great general Turenne (for whom Charles had deep respect) to write that he, Lionne and Chancellor Le Tellier agreed that it was necessary for France to be on good terms with the Dutch, but that this did not imply that Louis intended to attack England.[70] He did not mention that there were two areas where French and Dutch interests coincided. First, the English crown claimed sovereignty over the Narrow Seas and tried either to force the Dutch to buy licences to fish there or to limit the areas where they could do so. The Dutch had long opposed this, taking their stand on the principle of the freedom of the seas, while a recent claim by the Commons that the English should enjoy exclusive fishing rights within ten leagues of the coast threatened French as well as Dutch interests. Friction was increased by the arrest of French fishing-boats, which Clarendon blamed on over-zealous admiralty officials. Louis responded by renewing the order that English ships should unload their cannon at Blaye. Faced with the possible ruin of the lucrative Bordeaux trade, Charles backed down. He ordered that French fishermen should not be molested and his ambassador at the Hague, Sir George Downing, declared that the Dutch could trade and fish with the same freedom as in the past.[71] The Dutch, however, insisted that the renewal of their treaties with France should include a specific guarantee of free access to the North Sea fishing grounds. Louis was reluctant but the Dutch threatened to break off negotiations if he refused. At last he complied, insisting that Charles should accept that he did so only in order to prevent the Dutch joining with Spain, which would have meant the ruin of Portugal. His reasons, he added with characteristic self-righteousness, were so unimpeachable that if Charles refused to accept them he would be either unreasonable or malevolent.[72]

The second point upon which the French and Dutch differed from the English was the flag. From English claims to sovereignty of the seas derived claims that foreign ships should salute those of England, although there were disputes about the extent of the area within which the obligation applied. In December 1661 Louis ordered his admirals to ensure that all foreign ships should dip their flags to those of France. Charles was indignant. England's right to the salute had never been questioned: it was 'la plus belle marque de la royauté' and he was honour bound to maintain it. When d'Estrades warned him not to forfeit Louis' goodwill, Charles replied that he would not lack friends; Clarendon asserted that Parliament and people would be squarely behind the king. D'Estrades warned Turenne that Louis could not afford to antagonize Charles on both this question and that of the fishing. Louis expressed indignation at some of Clarendon's remarks and claimed that Walter Montagu had assured him that Charles did not want a confrontation; but he was clearly shaken. Lionne wrote that his ministers had had to beg him, on their knees, not to show his resentment, but when Charles proposed a compromise – that neither English nor French should salute the other south of Cape Finisterre – Louis promptly agreed, hoping to extend the principle to the Narrow Seas in due course. The matter was not settled, but at least it had been shelved for the moment.[73]

One final recurrent problem undermined Charles's hopes of a close liaison with Louis – money. In April 1661 Hyde asked if Louis would lend Charles £50,000 for ten or twelve months. Louis agreed, for which Charles thanked him warmly, but declared that he would take up the offer only if he had to.[74] A few months later, after the marriage terms had been agreed, d'Estrades was asked if Louis would provide money to enable Charles to help the Portuguese; Mazarin, he was told, had promised such assistance to the Portuguese ambassador in Paris. Fouquet agreed to supply between 1,800,000 and 2,400,000 *livres* (£135,000–£180,000) over two or three years.[75] By then, however, Fouquet's days in power were numbered and Louis denied that he was obliged to pay anything to succour the Portuguese. Later he shifted his ground, acknowledging that he had led Charles to expect 1,800,000 *livres*, but as a loan, not as a gift. Clarendon replied that without a gift of 2,000,000 *livres* at once, no aid could be sent to Portugal.[76] Louis sent over 600,000 *livres* in January 1662; he later claimed that none of this reached the Portuguese and that in future he would find a way to send money direct to Lisbon. He also claimed that Charles and Clarendon had promised to send to Portugal each year a sum three times that paid by Louis, a claim which both flatly denied.[77]

In rejecting Charles's requests for money, Louis argued that under the terms of the Treaty of the Pyrenees France could send no direct aid to Portugal. Such scruples of honour made no impression on Charles, who assumed that a breach between France and Spain was only a matter of time. In an attempt to stir Louis to action, he dropped hints of approaches from Spain, although the fact that there had been no Spanish ambassador in London since Watteville's expulsion reduced the credibility of such insinuations; moreover, Anglo-Spanish relations were far from cordial, thanks to English aid to Portugal and clashes in the Caribbean.[78] In July 1662 Charles mounted a new initiative. He sent Bellings to Paris and d'Estrades (now appointed ambassador at the Hague) passed through London en route to his new posting.[79] His mission was to negotiate the sale of Dunkirk. Both Charles and Clarendon had sometimes stressed its usefulness – the latter in a speech to Parliament as recently as May[80] – and the Convention had brought in a bill to annex it to the English crown. As a 'frontier' port, its inhabitants had a tradition of sturdy independence and Dunkirk privateers were feared by merchants of most nations: so long as it remained under English rule, English merchantmen would be safe. On the other hand, it was a heavy drain on Charles's financial resources. Its sale allowed Louis to contribute to the relief of Portugal without formally contravening the Treaty of the Pyrenees: indeed, Charles and Clarendon told him that if he did not purchase the town they would be unable to do anything for the Portuguese. After much hard bargaining Louis agreed to pay 5,000,000 *livres* (about £375,000); much more (he remarked sanctimoniously) than the town was worth. There were unseemly wrangles about the way in which the money was to be paid. At one point d'Estrades threatened to leave (although he wrote privately that Louis was behaving unreasonably); Charles talked wildly of great offers from Spain; Southampton, more prosaically, asked what security they would have that the money would be paid: Charles replied that he would trust in Louis' word.[81] Many councillors attacked the agreement: indeed, only Clarendon's determination kept Charles from reneging on it. Instead, he assured doubters that he would trust in Louis' promise to continue to provide for Portugal. Worried about public reaction, Charles and Clarendon claimed that the initiative had come from Louis and asked if the French king would come to their aid if the sale led to serious disorder. D'Estrades offered some general assurances, but privately Louis insisted that he would do no such thing.[82]

Neither Charles nor Clarendon had much experience of foreign policy compared with de Witt or even the much younger Louis, who had been well schooled by Mazarin. Charles set out with naive hopes of helping the Portuguese win their independence and joining with Louis, as one king with another, to humble the Dutch republicans and raise William to the offices to which his birth entitled him. Charles's gushing enthusiasm, as reported by Bartet or d'Estrades, should not perhaps always be taken at face value, but it is clear that he was genuinely hurt by Louis' renewing his treaties with the Dutch – preferring de Witt to him – and by his ungentlemanly failure to abide by what Charles had seen as a promise to give money. He tended to see hints and insinuations as promises, although his own attitude towards promises and treaty obligations could prove alarmingly casual. In later years Charles and Clarendon spoke of Louis' closing with the Dutch as a betrayal, as Louis had agreed to conclude nothing without consulting them. Charles especially resented the guarantee of the fishing, as Fouquet had assured him that that would not be mentioned.[83] Charles was learning the hard way that carefully phrased verbal assurances were worth nothing, and there were further hard lessons in store. As we have seen, d'Estrades regarded some of Louis' stipulations about Dunkirk as unreasonable, and so made promises to Clarendon of which Louis was never informed.[84] These apparently included assurances of continued French financial aid to Portugal, which was to become a major source of contention in 1663-4.

The question of aid to Portugal brings us back to that of the king's marriage. The terms had been agreed at a time when the revenue had not been settled and when it would have been impossible to foresee the extent to which it would prove insufficient. The much vaunted dowry proved a disappointment. More than half of the £350,000 was paid in 1662-3, but then payments stopped for five years, after which further sums trickled in, which by 1680 had raised the total to £243,000. As Bombay was not handed over until 1665, as Tangier's upkeep cost £55,000 a year and as the relief of Portugal involved an ongoing (if not enormously large) financial commitment, the marriage proved much less advantageous than had seemed likely.[85] Those who had opposed the marriage, or who were at odds with its architect, Clarendon, eagerly pointed out these disadvantages, but its success or failure ultimately hinged on Charles's relationship with his new queen.

Within a week of Charles's return, his mother was sounding him about a possible marriage partner and was delighted that he declared himself willing to marry a Catholic. Abbé Montagu's letters spoke excitedly (if obscurely) of 'our grand design', which seemed to consist of an Anglo-French accord, a payment of money by Mazarin, Charles's marriage to Hortense Mancini and an easing of the burdens on Catholics in England.[86] Whatever its precise form, the design came to nothing, except perhaps for Henriette's marriage, but it became clear that Charles's preference for a Catholic stemmed largely from his dislike of women from the cold countries of Europe; he much preferred the 'manners' of France. He also insisted that his wife would have to be beautiful, as he wished to love her and live well with her – not always a major consideration in an age when royal marriages were determined by dynastic and political considerations. Bartet thought that he was trying to find reasons not to marry Catherine, but his reticence probably owed much to the efforts of Watteville and Bristol to persuade him to marry another. Some claimed that Hyde arranged the match for his own advantage, claims which were repeated when Catherine failed to bear children. The chancellor's enemies then argued that he had chosen a queen who he knew would prove barren, so that James (and eventually Clarendon's grandchildren) would succeed to the throne.[87]

Such allegations were almost certainly unfounded. The queen was to miscarry in 1666, 1668 and (probably) 1669. The most promising pregnancy, that of 1668, ended when a pet fox jumped on to her bed and startled her: on such trivial incidents can the fate of kingdoms turn. Besides, it is extremely improbable that Clarendon (who had not even known of his own daughter's marriage) could have been able to predict whether Catherine could have children; his preference for the Portuguese marriage could be explained quite sufficiently by the financial and other advantages that it offered. Nevertheless, in some respects Catherine was not the ideal bride for Charles. She had had a sheltered and devout upbringing; he had enjoyed an unusual degree of freedom and had developed habits of cynicism and self-indulgence. 'He delivered himself up to a most enormous course of vice, without any sort of restraint,' wrote Burnet primly, 'and it was believed that the nearest relation in blood, even that of a daughter, made no difference to his esteem, who allowed of all appetites to all women; and even a modest whore was unacceptable to him, for studied brutalities were the only things that recommended women long to him.' The allegations of incest, whether with his sister Henriette (implausible) or his daughter Lady Sussex (less so), are less well attested than his obsessive pursuit of physical gratification. It became a matter of common gossip: Pepys heard 'that he is at the command of any woman like a slave ... yet cannot command himself in the presence of a woman he likes'. 'The king doth spend most of his time in feeling and kissing them naked all over their bodies in bed – and contents himself, without doing the other thing, but as he finds himself inclined; but this lechery will never leave him.' John Wilmot, Earl of Rochester, agreed that he was dominated and manipulated by women:

> Restless he rolls from whore to whore,
> A merry monarch, scandalous and poor.

Another courtier-poet, the Earl of Dorset, thought an ability to swear, drink and talk bawdy were necessary qualities for a royal mistress, while Rochester advised Nell Gwynn 'with hand, body, head, heart and all the faculties you have contribute to his pleasure all you can and comply with his desires'.[88]

As royal courts took their character from kings, so Charles's attracted a motley collection of rakes, debauchees, drunkards and whores. Rochester, who died of alcohol abuse and syphilis at the age of thirty-three, was an extreme example of a recognizable type: self-indulgent to the point of self-destruction, brilliant, witty, crude, violent and unpredictable. Confident in the authority conferred by his aristocratic birth, he set himself up as patron of the arts and critic. His love poetry was utterly unromantic, relentlessly cynical about human conduct, but also tinged with a certain disgust at the brutishness of mankind. Like Buckingham (with whom he had much in common), Rochester was occasionally banished from court for outraging even Charles's lax standards, but the king soon missed his raillery and bawdy and allowed him back. Like Buckingham (but unlike the king) Rochester was bisexual and both the discussion and the practice of sodomy were apparently common at court. Like Buckingham and some other rakes, he repented of his vices in later life and underwent a much publicized conversion at the hands of Burnet; Buckingham's interest in religion, never entirely absent, became much more marked in his old age. Charles, however, showed no such change of heart; if his sexual prowess diminished in his last years, his love of women and of bawdy did not.[89]

The women of Charles's court, if one believes the gossip and the lampoons, were no better than the men:

> No ways to vice does this our age produce
> But women with less shame than men do use;
> They'll play, they'll drink, talk filth'ly and profane
> With more extravagance than any man.

Such vices were not confined to actresses: the wives and daughters of the court nobility conceded nothing in drunkenness and promiscuity to their social inferiors, and their genitalia were discussed as freely as the king's sexual antics.[90] Among these ladies, none was more voracious than the king's mistress at the time of his marriage, Barbara Palmer, Countess of Castlemaine:

> Cloy'd with the choicest banquets of delight,
> She'll still drudge on in tasteless vice,
> As if she sinn'd for exercise.

Married to an ineffectual Catholic, whom Charles raised to the peerage to give her a title, she had been the king's mistress before the Restoration and bore him a child a year between 1661 and 1665. Although Charles was said to prefer women who made his life easy, Barbara was grasping and strong-minded, with a ferocious temper; she took many other lovers (including John Churchill) and bullied Charles unmercifully. She was not a woman to let the mere fact of Charles's being married change their relationship.[91]

It may seem unnecessarily prurient to dwell on the sexual mores of Charles and his court, but such matters were important. First, in hereditary monarchies the transmission of the crown depended on the ability to sire and conceive children and even royal bastards often wielded considerable power. Second, Charles's airy claims that his mistresses, and those who procured them, did not influence him were palpable nonsense, so that their role has to form part of any political study. Third, the court's frenetic indulgence seriously damaged the king's image. If it was not necessary to raise ceremonial to an art form, as at Versailles or Madrid, kings still needed to maintain a certain dignity and to avoid outraging the public's sense of decency. Samuel Pepys was no prude, but he was shocked by what he heard and saw. The discourse of the king's companions, he heard, 'is so base and sordid that it makes the ears of the very gentlemen of the backstairs ... to tingle'. Pepys himself was repelled by the glee with which Charles watched geese mating in the park. As he noted in his diary, it was necessary to have 'at least a show of religion in the government, and sobriety ... it is so fixed in the nature of the common Englishman that it will not out of him'.[92]

Into this court, which must have seemed like a cross between a brothel and a beargarden, came Charles's new queen. Brought up by her pious mother, unable to speak English or French, she was thrust (still queasy after a long and uncomfortable voyage) into an alien and barbarous environment. Charles at first seemed kind, expressing himself well pleased with his bride and refusing to be ruffled by her scruples about the marriage service.[93] The outlandish fashions of the Portuguese ladies with their 'monstrous fardingales' attracted much ribald amusement and they were generally thought old and ugly. Evelyn thought the queen the handsomest of an uninspiring bunch – 'though low of stature, pretty shaped, languishing and excellent eyes, her teeth wronging her mouth by sticking a little too far out, for the rest sweet and lovely enough'. Her coiffure, however, with hair swept to the side, was widely ridiculed: 'Gentlemen,' Charles is said to have remarked, 'you have brought me a bat.'[94]

Charles's kindness did not last long. The queen was not inspiring company: she was constantly unwell, unable to adapt to the climate or the food, and was frightened and repelled by the confusion of the court. Her ladies urged her to dress and to conduct herself in the Portuguese fashion; only when she saw that Charles was angry did she agree to wear the clothes he had brought for her. Charles soon returned to London and stood godfather to Castlemaine's latest child. Egged on by courtiers who urged him to follow the example of his grandfather, Henry IV, and be open in his amours, he resolved to make his mistress a lady of the queen's bedchamber. The queen would not agree – very reasonably, thought Henriette – but gradually her resistance was overcome.[95] Charles began to complain about the delay in paying her dowry and threatened to send her Portuguese ladies home. He withdrew the threat when she allowed Castlemaine to kiss her hand and attend her. For a while her credit rose, when it was believed that she was pregnant; when it became clear that she was not, there were rumours that she could not conceive. She was civil to Castlemaine, persuading herself, perhaps, that she and the king were just good friends.[96] Then, at the end of August, Charles ordered her to send the Portuguese away and admit Castlemaine to her bedchamber. He told Clarendon that he was obliged to insist on the latter to maintain his own honour and to redeem Castlemaine's reputation; he would never, he promised, seek to impose a servant on his wife in the future. The queen submitted meekly, probably on Clarendon's advice, whereupon she was allowed to keep one Portuguese lady. Castlemaine ranted that even one was too many; as that lady cooked the queen's food, she became convinced that Castlemaine wished to have her poisoned. When one of her priests talked of the king's being 'enchanted' by his mistress, the queen understood this as meaning that she had bewitched him. By the end of September, courtiers avoided the queen, the king ignored her and the queen mother treated her with contempt and courted Castlemaine, as the woman in favour. News of Spanish military successes against Portugal added to the poor queen's gloom. Isolated and miserable, she fell ill once more.[97]

Charles's cruelty and spite towards his wife, so foreign to his normal good nature, owed little to the queen's flaws of character. True, she was sometimes tactless (as when she told Charles that Castlemaine had bewitched him) and she could be stubborn about small things. The main reason for Charles's harshness, however, was the malign influence of Castlemaine, who also did much to turn the king against Clarendon. She declared that she hoped to see the chancellor's head on a stake: 'there is no limits to her power nor to his fondness,' wrote the courtier Daniel O'Neill; 'it's happy her parts do not answer either, else she would make mad work'. Charles told the chancellor that, if anyone opposed his making Castlemaine a lady of the bedchamber, 'I will be his enemy to the last moment of my life.'[98] Clarendon was in no position to argue. Bristol revived the accusation that the chancellor had deliberately failed to maximize the revenue at the Restoration and it was noted that he and Bennet rose in favour as Charles became more besotted with Castlemaine. Both Bristol and Castlemaine argued that some relaxation of the Act of Uniformity was necessary to prevent a major rising. When Charles was persuaded not to agree to such a relaxation – Clarendon, Nicholas and even Bennet argued that it was unnecessary and undesirable –

Castlemaine was livid.[99] Clarendon felt thoroughly insecure, buoyed up one day by a long friendly conversation with his master, cast down in gloom the next. He wrote sadly to Ormond, 'The worst is the king is as discomposed as ever, and looks as little after his business, which breaks my heart and makes me and other of your friends weary of our lives. He seeks for his satisfaction in other companies, which do not love him so well as you and I do.'[100] The queen mother, who had been civil towards the chancellor, now added her voice to those of his enemies.[101] In October Nicholas was eased out of the secretaryship into lucrative retirement; Bennet took over his office and his lodgings and had a door made to give him direct access to the king's apartments. Charles Berkeley, rapidly emerging as Charles's prime favourite (and regard by Pepys as very vicious), took over the profitable and influential post of keeper of the privy purse. Everywhere, it seemed, Clarendon's enemies were installing themselves close to the king.[102]

As 1662 neared its end, Clarendon seemed doomed. There were rumours that Charles might legitimate his eldest son, created Duke of Monmouth in February 1663, and so cut James (and Clarendon's daughter) out of the succession. Charles ceased to visit Worcester House: instead he summoned the chancellor to Somerset House, home of the queen mother and centre of the anti-Clarendon faction. Bennet took over much of the direction of foreign policy, leaving Clarendon to concentrate on his work as chancellor. Charles's kindness towards his old servant was not wholly extinguished, however: when he succumbed to his usual winter gout, Charles was visibly concerned.[103] Meanwhile, the government's fears of plots and risings were sharpened by the outcry against the sale of Dunkirk. Several hundred 'fanatics' were arrested in October, but (to Bennet's disappointment) they would not reveal the names of those of higher rank, who (he assumed) had set them on. Nevertheless, he and Charles thought it necessary to hang half a dozen of them, to discourage others from plotting and to convince a sceptical public that there had indeed been a design against the state.[104]

It was in this atmosphere, heavy with fear of disaffection, that Bennet drafted a declaration on religion. Its tone was defensive, stressing that Charles had no wish to overturn the Act of Indemnity or to introduce a military form of government. He had assented to the Act of Uniformity, which had secured the Protestant religion, but wished to find a way, through Parliament, to relieve peaceable persons who 'through scruple and tenderness of misguided conscience' felt unable to comply with its provisions. As for the Catholics, he deplored the use of anti-Popish slurs against his father and himself and stressed the loyalty of many Catholics in the civil wars: he hoped that these might find a place in any Act of Parliament for the relief of tender consciences.[105]

The declaration reflected a long-standing hostility within the court to the unbending Anglicanism of the Commons. Some, like Ashley Cooper (now Lord Ashley) and Buckingham, sympathized with the ejected ministers and the sectaries and claimed that the autumn's disturbances showed a need for flexibility. Such thinking underlay the king's directions to preachers, designed to inhibit overzealous clerics from preaching provocatively. More influential – and, many thought, more sinister – were the Catholics, led by Bristol and the queen mother and warmly supported by Castlemaine. Sheldon was sufficiently conscious of their power to warn Cosin against undue severity against Catholics (although he stressed that this did not mean that nothing was to be done against them). Bristol was generally seen as the leading proponent of liberty of conscience and (although he denied it) as the moving spirit behind the declaration. Many, noting the kind words about the Catholics, thought that its main purpose was to favour them and indeed the declaration marked a change in Charles's priorities. Through most of 1661–2 his main concern had been to reduce the rigour of the uniformity bill and so prevent the expulsion of Presbyterian ministers from the Church. He now reverted to the view expressed in the Declaration of Breda, that a measure of freedom of worship should be allowed to peaceable persons with tender consciences, which implied sectaries (and even Catholics) as well as Presbyterians. In other words, he now expressed support for indulgence, as well as (or even instead of) comprehension.[106]

There can be little doubt that (as Bennet and Bristol stressed) the declaration reflected Charles's own views. His support for indulgence to Dissenters was qualified by the insistence that they should worship 'modestly and without scandal' and he urged Dissenting leaders to meet in moderate numbers and to teach nothing offensive to the state: clearly considerations of public order were uppermost in his mind. Clarendon's attitude towards the declaration was far more equivocal. Bennet alleged that he had approved it in every detail, but Clarendon wrote that he had objected to some parts of it: when Bennet stressed that Charles wished to publish it, the chancellor remarked gnomically that declarations were a ticklish commodity and that it was vital that it should do no harm. He may, like Sheldon, have felt confident that the Commons would insist on upholding the Act of Uniformity.[107] Politically he was in no position to make his feelings clear and his gout offered a pretext not to attend Parliament. (This did not prevent Cominges from reporting – doubtless from Bristol – that Clarendon was the leader of the 'party of uniformity'.) When Parliament met, Charles made a short and (Pepys thought) not very obliging speech in support of the declaration. The Lords responded with a bill to allow the king to dispense with the Act of Uniformity (which could benefit Presbyterians, but not sectaries) and made it clear that no liberty could be allowed to Catholics.[108] The court expected a more favourable response from the Commons, but (as so often) ministers

had sadly misjudged the mood of the House. Without waiting for the Lords
to complete their bill, the Commons resolved to set out the reasons why no
indulgence should be allowed to any Dissenters. The old Cavalier Henry
Coventry wrote smugly that Charles should learn from this that his own
party wished to serve him against the Presbyterians and Papists. When
Clarendon at last struggled from his sickbed, he persuaded the Lords to
shelve the matter, thus sparing the king the humiliation of defeat.[109]

The Commons had not finished with the matter. Incensed by what they
saw as the insolence of the 'Popish party' (and, some thought, egged on by
the bishops) they brought in a bill against the growth of Popery and
asked Charles to issue a proclamation banishing priests from the kingdom.
Clarendon tried to restrain their fury by reviving in the Lords the proposal
of 1661 that only the Jesuits should be banished and that a register should
be kept of other priests. The peers, however, resolved to concur with the
Commons.[110] King and chancellor continued to stress the Catholics' loyalty,
and their kindness during the years of exile, but as the Commons were
adamant Charles declared that the priests had abused his good nature and
agreed to issue the proclamation. Many, however, found it defective as it
did not extend to native-born priests in the households of the two queens,
for which Clarendon was blamed. The chancellor probably had no enthusiasm for his allotted role as defender of the Catholics, but knew that any hint
he gave of hostility towards them would be ruthlessly exploited by Bristol
and his other enemies. As for Charles, he now realized that the best the
Catholics could hope for was the quiet non-enforcement of the existing
laws.[111]

If Clarendon's conduct on matters of religion damaged his credit with
the Commons, it improved his standing with the king, who again visited
Worcester House and conferred at length with the chancellor. Soon after,
he was reconciled to the queen mother; alarmed, Bristol, Ashley and Bennet
claimed that Clarendon was responsible for the failure of the declaration and
insinuated that his alliance with the Duke of York posed a threat to the
king.[112] Meanwhile, their cronies in the Commons launched an investigation
into the sale of offices. Backbenchers were easily aroused by a whiff of
corruption. Many also resented the favour shown to Presbyterians in 1660
and saw the investigation as a way of opening up vacancies for old Cavaliers:
on 5 May a bill was brought in to ensure that offices should be granted only
to loyal subjects who conformed to the Church. These proceedings posed a
particular threat to Clarendon, Southampton and York: the chancery, the
treasury and the admiralty all contained many lucrative places. York's
position was also threatened by Charles's fondness for Monmouth.[113] The
Commons showed similar ill-temper when considering the revenue. Charles
was confident that close inspection would reveal that it was insufficient to

cover the cost of government, but the work proceeded slowly. MPs clearly suspected that the revenue had been mismanaged and there were ominous moves to tie specific items of expenditure to particular branches, which would have destroyed the king's traditional freedom to manage his revenues as he saw fit.[114] Bennet petulantly blamed intransigent Churchmen for these difficulties, but the real reason was simpler, if from his point of view less palatable: a House which (as Bennet recognized) was loyal and well meaning had lost faith in the king's administration.[115]

This loss of faith was not unreasonable. As O'Neill wrote, the enmity between Clarendon and Bennet paralysed the government and 'notwithstanding all the disorders and distempers in court and Parliament, [the] king regards nothing but Castlemaine and all time is spent in her nursery. God help us.' Henry Coventry complained, 'I can neither tell you what the House intends nor what we at Whitehall wish they would.' 'The truth is', wrote O'Neill, 'the disputes of the court raised these spirits and their reconciliations cannot allay them; nor do I believe any other charm will but that I despair of, which is His Majesty's changing his present manner of living and strongly applying his thoughts to his business, which is governed little to the satisfaction of those that wish well to him or the peace of the kingdom.'[116] There seemed little chance that O'Neill's hopes would be fulfilled, until the feuds at court reached a point where Charles was forced to take action.

Early in June St Albans (so often the peacemaker) arranged yet another reconciliation between Clarendon and Bennet; this time, however, Bennet severed his links with Bristol, who set out to gain revenge. The method he chose was to seek to undermine Bennet's credit with the king by showing that he, Bristol, could succeed where Bennet had failed, in managing the Commons. He told the king that the Commons would never be amenable while he retained his present councillors and that his ally Sir Richard Temple undertook to get whatever measures Charles chose through the Commons, above all an enhanced revenue. Charles, however, had little faith in Temple, who for some time had opposed his measures in Parliament, in the hope that the king would buy him off with a substantial office. Perhaps on the advice of Henry Coventry, Charles sent word to the Commons of the proposed undertaking and forbade Bristol to come to court. Castlemaine was in no position to help him: faced with a serious rival in the person of Frances Stuart, she had left the court in a huff.[117]

Having incensed both king and Commons, Bristol resorted to desperate measures. On 1 July he appeared before the Commons. In a long and histrionic speech, he persuaded the House that there had been no 'undertaking' and bitterly attacked the king's ministers: he might be a Catholic, he declared, but he had never sought a cardinal's hat for an English subject.[118]

When he eventually showed Charles a copy of his speech, Charles accused him of trying to overturn the government in the hope of profiting from the ensuing chaos. He would not allow Bristol to accuse the chancellor of treason, to which the earl responded with wild threats of what he might do. As there was only one other person present at the interview (ironically, d'Aubigny) Charles was unable to prosecute the earl for his insolence and had to be content with banishing him from his presence. Having tried in vain to beg the king's forgiveness, Bristol, at his wits' end, presented his charges to the Lords. Charles would happily have had them rejected out of hand, but Clarendon insisted that they be fully investigated, to make his innocence clear to all. The charges were referred to the judges, who declared that they did not amount to treason. Charles sent word that he knew the accusations to be unfounded, but Bristol claimed that he could prove them, given time: Clarendon urged that he should be given the opportunity to do so.[119]

The chancellor's determination to prove his innocence did not please the king, who saw the charges as a 'libel' which could do him serious political damage: the revelation that he had asked the pope to make d'Aubigny a cardinal greatly perturbed the Commons. MPs were already displeased that the Lords had not passed their bills against conventicles and the growth of Popery; they asked the king to put into effect the laws against all kinds of nonconformity, which he agreed to do. On 27 July Parliament rose, after a generally sterile and acrimonious session. The vote of taxation, in the old form of subsidies, proved to be worth little, but on the credit side the Commons had passed another Militia Act, allowing each unit to be kept on foot for up to fourteen days, which made it possible to sustain a guard for most of the year.[120] Moreover, the flames of faction, which Charles had allowed to rage unchecked, had largely burned themselves out. Bristol's political credibility had been destroyed – Charles ordered his arrest on 4 August – and his attempts to pose as a martyr for the people's cause merely increased the king's animus against him. Castlemaine's loss of favour was more temporary, but the rise of Frances Stuart meant that she would never again dominate the king as she had recently done. On the other hand, Clarendon's credit was greatly revived: Charles had an innate sense of justice and on this occasion had been accused along with the chancellor. As for the queen, she had learned English and showed no resentment of Castlemaine or Stuart: she even took the former with her to Tunbridge Wells. Charles now seemed kinder towards her; only her failure to conceive (the reason for her taking the waters) cast a shadow over their relationship.[121]

It seemed, in the autumn of 1663, that Charles had learned from his mistakes. He now realized that in diplomacy it was vital to define carefully what was being discussed and agreed: casual assurances between gentlemen counted for nothing. He had seen the effects of unchecked factionalism and of allowing himself to be dominated by a woman: whether he had the strength of character to apply those lessons remained to be seen. He had learned that the Commons were both unswervingly Anglican and deeply suspicious of corruption and mismanagement, while information from the provinces reminded him of the danger from political and religious disaffection. Finally, Southampton made it clear that, as revenue fell well short of expenditure, Charles would have to reduce the latter. For a while, he seemed determined to do so, although courtiers like O'Neill denounced the proposed economies as shameful.[122] It was not, however, in Charles's nature to pursue for long policies which were unpleasant in themselves or unpopular among those close to him. The habits which had brought so much trouble in 1662–3 were to creep back. Charles was once more to allow expenditure greatly to exceed income and to tolerate – indeed encourage – bitter faction-fighting in his court. For the moment, however, he enjoyed the calm before the storm, a calm that was to be shattered by the guns of war.

5

Sword and Fire

After rousing himself to meet Bristol's challenge, Charles soon relapsed into lethargy and lust, kissing and fondling Frances Stuart in public. She refused to become his mistress, however; not until 1666 was it reported that she had succumbed and even then it is uncertain whether the reports were true. He still supped with Castlemaine and acknowledged as his the children she bore (although others had their doubts). He adored his offspring and would visit Castlemaine's nursery at all hours to cuddle them. If his passion for their mother was now less ardent, he was still fond of her and her influence remained considerable. Their quarrels were as dramatic as ever: she would storm away from court and threaten to publish his letters; he would send her away in a fury, but she would soon return and the two would be as close as ever. He was always ready to punish those who insulted her and, though the treasury might be empty, he found tens of thousands of pounds to enable her and Frances to indulge their fancies and pay their debts. Whereas Frances was sweet and simple, Castlemaine was very much a political animal: her supper-table was thronged with courtiers, councillors and others who sought informal access to the king.[1]

The queen bore Charles's infidelities as patiently as she could. She tried hard to improve her English and to be affectionate and debonaire, but could not compete with Stuart's ravishing good looks or Castlemaine's force of personality. Charles was not consistently unkind – consistency, indeed, was never one of his virtues. When it seemed that she might die of spotted fever late in 1663, Charles showed every sign of distress. As she began to recover, she suffered bouts of delirium in which she believed that she had three children. Charles humoured her, displaying every outward kindness – then went to sup with Castlemaine.[2] The queen cannot have been unaware that many at court would have been happy if she had died and there was much talk of who the next wife should be. As she showed in her delirium, she was intensely conscious of her failure to bear children and the fact that Charles slept with her infrequently did not improve her chances of conceiving. When she miscarried early in 1666, Charles allowed himself to be persuaded, despite the assurances of her doctors, that it had been a phantom pregnancy and there was once more speculation that he might legitimate Monmouth.[3]

Charles's obsession with women was but one aspect of his habit of putting pleasure before business. His old friends and conscientious servants pressed him to apply himself, but were outmanoeuvred by 'this little sort of people', who enjoyed 'those evening opportunities and familiarities' – men like Edward Proger, Bab May, Charles Berkeley and (intermittently) Buckingham. These were 'too much companions of his pleasure to be at leisure to drudge in the matters of state'.[4] Even Bennet, for all his diplomatic experience, was dilatory and often careless – witness his assurance to the Spaniards in 1660 that England would renew the treaty of 1630. Denzil, Lord Holles, the ambassador to Paris, was driven to distraction by Bennet's slowness in gathering information and formulating instructions. At one point, having been driven to feign illness to excuse his inaction, Holles asked plaintively how long he would have to remain sick. He also complained that the letters he received were wrongly ciphered and explained repeatedly, but unavailingly, how to seal packets so that they could not be opened and resealed at the French post office. Some of his letters with long passages in cipher remained undeciphered.[5] The administrative insufficiency of the men of pleasure led Charles to rely, as always, on the old workhorse Clarendon, but he was getting old: each winter he was laid low by gout for weeks on end. He was also set in his ways, reacting with outrage to anything which smacked of novelty, and his knowledge of foreign and commercial affairs was limited. His old friend Southampton was less than dynamic, content to let matters drift, so long as he could draw his salary and enjoy an occasional game of cards. He too had no time for the innovation which changing circumstances (and the needs of war) made necessary and his accounting methods left the treasury dangerously vulnerable to Parliamentary criticism.[6]

Whatever the inadequacies of his servants, the final responsibility for the conduct of government lay with the king. Southampton complained that Charles would not take the time to understand the state of his revenue – perhaps he did not want to – and repeatedly overrode the treasurer's objections to grants and pensions.[7] He listened to extracts from ambassadors' dispatches and left it to the secretaries to reply, rarely bothering to check what they had written. Even when he could be brought to apply himself, he was rarely decisive. Pepys was told that 'nobody almost understands or judges of business better than the king, if he would not be guilty of his father's fault, to be doubtful of himself and easily be removed from his own opinion'.[8] Time after time, he changed his mind on taking further advice or in the face of importunity or ridicule. This, and his forgiving nature, led some to act first and secure the king's approval later. At bottom Charles disliked hard decisions: he wanted everyone to be happy, but could never satisfy the ambition and avarice of those around him.[9]

Clarendon's pre-eminence ensured that much of the faction-fighting at court would focus on him. For a while, his enemies hoped to revive Bristol's accusations, but Charles for once remained firm, ordering that the fugitive earl should be prosecuted as a Popish recusant. Bristol responded by conforming to the Church of England and sent a priest to Lisbon to find evidence that Catherine had been known to be barren; Charles promptly had the priest imprisoned.[10] As the next session of Parliament approached, Bristol's friends and relations lobbied MPs and begged that he should be allowed to come to court; Charles renewed the order to arrest him, saying that the world would see whether he or Bristol was king.[11] Undeterred, the earl declared his intention to take his seat in the Lords and begged the peers to mediate between the king and himself; he also pleaded with Charles to allow him a hearing, but added that if Charles refused he would have no choice but to put the matter before Parliament.[12] The Lords refused to receive his message and Charles posted guards around Westminster with strict orders to arrest the earl and take him to the Tower; the fact that he had disseminated papers asserting his innocence added to the king's anger. Bristol's friends at court, not least the ladies, pleaded his cause, but to no avail: Charles, James and Clarendon had never been so united.[13] Reluctantly, the earl went back into hiding. Later in the year he returned to London, despite the fact that Charles had refused him permission to do so, and stayed for a while with Buckingham. By the summer of 1665 he was seeing Charles secretly, but not until 1667 did he re-emerge into the public eye. In the meantime his former allies, Ashley, Lauderdale, Charles Berkeley and Buckingham, continued the campaign against the chancellor, using methods more subtle and insidious than a frontal attack in Parliament.[14]

Clarendon's enemies were a motley crew. Buckingham and Berkeley (soon created Viscount Fitzharding and then Earl of Falmouth) were courtiers and companions of pleasure. The former owed his influence to his dominating personality and coruscating wit; unlike his father, he had no aptitude for administration, which required a diligence and regularity of which he was incapable.[15] Falmouth, by contrast, was 'soft and agreeable', generous and noble. Lacking Buckingham's vindictiveness, he was at times prepared (at Charles's command) to live on amicable terms with Clarendon. While determined to accumulate riches, he knew that he lacked the ability to direct great affairs of state and was happy to take the advice of men abler than himself.[16]

Ashley and Lauderdale, on the other hand, were experienced administrators with chequered political pasts. Ashley had (at different times) supported both sides in the civil wars and had served in Parliament and on the council of state in the 1650s. He had made his peace with Charles in 1660 and later made sweeping (and perhaps exaggerated) claims about his contribution to the Restoration. His interests ranged from colonial administration to law and finance and his ready wit and drollery served him well at court. He was a persuasive speaker, but some found him superficial and inconstant, a charge which (while understandable) was perhaps unfair. If his religious convictions were probably minimal, he (like Buckingham) consistently advocated toleration for Dissenters, on the grounds of natural justice and economic utility (to which should be added, in each case, a dislike of clerical authority or 'priestcraft'). It can also be argued that Ashley was firmly committed to the traditional constitution and to liberty under the law. Unlike Buckingham and Lauderdale, he could never be seen as a proponent of absolutism and in his last years he dabbled in radical politics as the (much respected) patron of John Locke.[17]

Lauderdale was an even more complex character. Coarse in appearance, with a large frame, wild red hair and a tongue too large for his mouth, he possessed a shrewd mind and a wide range of leaning (including a knowledge of Hebrew). Candid and hot-headed, he gradually learned the dissimulation required for success at court. Charles did not find him personally congenial: he disliked the way that he helped himself to the royal snuff and cured him of the habit of inviting himself to dinner by serving him horse urine instead of syllabub. Despite Lauderdale's Presbyterianism and record of opposition to the late king, Charles was persuaded to put him in charge of Scottish affairs, which he managed brutally but effectively for almost twenty years. Charles had little interest in, or understanding of, Scotland. He applauded Lauderdale's ability to push measures through the Scots Parliament (always less independent than England's) but in general his main concern was to keep Scotland quiet: his faith in Lauderdale wavered only when he provoked what seemed a dangerous amount of opposition. Well aware of this, Lauderdale was careful to make frequent visits to court, to put his viewpoint and to counter the claims of his enemies, and to install reliable agents close to the king while he was away in Scotland. The politics of England and Scotland were never wholly separate. Some issues, like that of religious dissent, were common to both, while others (notably trade) could set one against the other. Lauderdale was thus drawn into the intrigues and manoeuvrings of Charles's court, where he became one of the most formidable advocates of ruthless and even absolutist measures.[18]

With so many enemies, Clarendon was soon on the defensive. His cause was not helped by his ill-health, his arrogance (he expected the king to 'trot' to him) and his tedious insistence on lecturing Charles about his moral and other failings. Remorselessly the men of pleasure mocked and mimicked him; at times, Charles joined in. The king's visits became less frequent and the range of issues on which Clarendon was consulted became narrower. Some thought that Charles was maintaining a balance between Clarendon's supporters and opponents, but the uncertainty – he was treated kindly one week, slighted the next – took its toll. By May 1665 he was talking of retiring and soon after he resumed writing his history, which he had laid aside in 1660: clearly he felt a renewed need for self-justification.[19] By that time he had an added reason for anxiety: he feared the consequences of the decision, taken against his advice, to make war on the Dutch.

Before examining the reasons for the war, it is necessary to consider the state of affairs at home. The spectre of disaffection continued to haunt the king's ministers. In October 1663 local officials uncovered plans for a rising in Yorkshire, Durham and Westmorland. This time there can be no doubt that a rising was intended, as a protest against high taxes and religious persecution, but the would-be insurgents were few in number. Nevertheless, the authorities mounted a series of well-publicized trials, which led to twenty-four executions: an example had to be made. Although there was to be no further rising until late 1666 (when a revolt in Scotland was quickly crushed) the government remained nervous; its fears were fed by alarmist reports from the localities – and from Louis XIV.[20]

In its anxiety the government sometimes overstepped the strict bounds of law. Charles's attitude to such matters tended to be casual. He expressed irritation when told that it would not be possible to pass a special Scottish Act of Parliament for Monmouth's benefit. He also supported a proposed bill concerning Irish land even though it had not, as the law required, been approved by the English privy council. In fact the bill was dropped, and Charles's high-handedness probably owed more to incomprehension than to authoritarianism.[21] He urged severity against those who deserved it (such as those implicated in the Yorkshire plot) and lamented that he was unable to prosecute Bristol for the threats he had uttered; in other words, he became annoyed when the strict requirements of law did not seem congruent with his sense of justice. Usually, however, those who infringed individuals' legal rights were not the king's ministers but over-zealous JPs who locked up 'suspicious' persons first and asked questions later.[22] With the lapsing of the three-year limit set by the Act of Indemnity, it became possible to discriminate openly against those who had fought against Charles I. Following the abortive rising of 1663 the 'well affected' of County Durham formed an association to keep the peace and parish ministers drew up lists of those who had been in arms for Parliament.[23]

Fearful of disorder, Charles considered raising additional regular forces. In 1665 there were reports of a plan for the Duke of York to raise an army in the north, independent of Albemarle (who, as lord general, had overall command of the army); Albemarle (it was said) found out about the plan and it was dropped. The chief obstacle to enlarging the army, however, was lack of money: in 1663 talk of raising new regiments came to nothing. Three were raised in 1666, possibly using commissions issued in 1662. The king ordered that any money remaining from the £70,000 a year raised for the militia over the past three years should go towards their maintenance, as it was 'properly to be used for the defence of the kingdom'. The regiments were soon disbanded, essentially because the king could not afford to keep them.[24] Charles was thus forced to rely on the militia, to guard against disorder and to watch the coasts. He ordered that the £70,000 should be raised in 1666, despite the fact that under the 1662 Act it should have been levied for three years only. There were apparently no protests, presumably because the danger of invasion was all too obvious.[25] In Stuart England ideas of 'legality' were somewhat subjective: actions which were not strictly legal could be tolerated if they were perceived as being in the public interest.

Fear of rebellion also influenced Parliament. In March 1664 Charles claimed that the plotters in the north had alleged that, under the 1641 Triennial Act, the Cavalier Parliament was dissolved and that they should choose new members. In fact, the Act had stated that Parliament should meet at least once every three years for a minimum of fifty days and had laid down elaborate procedures for holding elections if the king failed to issue the necessary writs. Charles reminded MPs that the Act had been 'passed in a time very uncareful for the dignity of the crown or the security of the people'. He was well aware, he said, that the crown could not be happy without frequent Parliaments, but he 'would never suffer a Parliament to come together by the means prescribed in that bill'. Within a week the Commons had passed a new triennial bill, repealing the 1641 Act. It stated that there should be a Parliament at least every three years, but laid down no minimum duration and no mechanism for ensuring that it should actually meet.[26]

Fear of disorder also underlay two other measures. The Conventicle Act of 1664 forbade meetings of five persons or more 'under colour or pretence of any exercise of religion'; penalties ranged from a £5 fine for the first offence to transportation to the colonies for the third. The Five Mile Act of 1665 forbade preachers and teachers who refused the oaths and declaration required under the Act of Uniformity to come within five miles of any corporate town or of any parish where they had taught. The Act also required that parish incumbents should subscribe the renunciation of resistance in the Corporation and Militia Acts and declare 'I will not at any time endeavour any alteration of government either in Church or state.'[27] This declaration became known as the 'Oxford oath' – Parliament met at Oxford because of the plague in London – and was widely criticized in the Lords. Southampton and others complained that it would preclude even peaceful and necessary reforms in the Church, but the oath's supporters argued that without it neither crown nor Church could be secure. An attempt in the Commons to impose the oath on the entire population was defeated by only six votes.[28]

The passage of the Conventicle and Five Mile Acts showed that Charles had, for the moment, lost interest in comprehension and indulgence. It is surely no coincidence that Clarendon's stance now became far less equivocal: he called for the rigorous execution of the laws against Dissent, while still insisting that peaceable former Parliamentarians should be left alone.[29] Charles now saw severity, not conciliation, as the best means of keeping the Dissenters quiet: it was wise to have strong laws in force against them, even if they were not always enforced. The Church now seemed to offer the soundest basis of support in a land apparently riddled with disaffection. This perception, together with his natural indolence and shortage of money, militated, at home, against the pursuit of ambitious policies; he and his ministers just reacted to events. Foreign affairs were quite another matter and it is to these that we must now turn.

England's commercial rivalry with the Dutch was decades old, but grew in intensity from the 1650s. On one hand, the English became noticeably more assertive, with the Navigation Acts and the expansion of the navy. On the other, the weakness of Spain created vast new oppportunities. The trade of the Spanish empire – including that of Spain herself – was dominated by foreigners (above all, the Dutch). Dependence on foreign enterprise and markets was exacerbated by the Spanish government's habit of mortgaging sectors of the economy to foreign financiers in order to raise money for war. Moreover, the Treaty of Munster, in 1648, granted the Dutch a monopoly of the trade between the East Indies and Spain. Trade with Spanish America was, in theory, closed to all but Castilians; in practice, the Dutch controlled much of it and hoped before long to gain formal access with the grant of the *asiento*, the contract for the supply of slaves, which would open the way for all sorts of other trades, licit and illicit. In practice, Spain lacked the naval power to keep out other nations' ships. Dutch and English privateers carried on a vigorous trade with the Spanish colonists, which sometimes degenerated into plunder and piracy. In these activities Jamaica, recently captured from Spain, provided a valuable base: it was from there that Sir Christopher Myngs sailed to sack Santiago de Cuba in 1662.[30]

Within Europe commercial treaties and international law imposed some constraints on the conduct of trade, though rules were often honoured as much in the breach as in the observance. Elsewhere the law of the jungle prevailed. Actions like the sack of Santiago or the so-called 'massacre' of English traders by the Dutch at Amboyna in 1623 might merit compensation but did not inevitably lead to war between the mother countries: there was no peace 'beyond the line'. By the 1660s the Dutch, with a canny mixture of business acumen and brute force, had built up a commercial pre-eminence in which some (especially in England) detected a design to establish 'universal dominion'. The English complained of their 'unfair' trading practices, bribing foreign princes to secure monopolies and firing on Africans or Indians who dared to trade with the English. (The English, of course, used similar methods whenever they could.) Those in authority in distant lands often ignored orders from the government back home, which in turn tacitly condoned their conduct. Thus in 1654 the Dutch agreed to cede to England the island of Pula Run in the East Indies, but still had not handed it over ten years later.

By 1660 decades of Anglo-Dutch rivalry had created a catalogue of grievances on both sides. The Dutch denounced the Navigation Acts and English claims to sovereignty over the Narrow Seas, which led to disputes over fishing rights and the flag. The English complained of Dutch attempts to shut them out of the East Indies (despite their talk, elsewhere, of 'the freedom of the seas') and of their failure to hand over Pula Run or to pay compensation for two merchant ships seized in 1643. A treaty between the two countries in 1662 left these issues unresolved: indeed, that of the fishing was made more contentious by France's guarantee of freedom to fish in the North Sea. The sense of hostility was sustained by the conduct of Charles's ambassador at the Hague. Sir George Downing was well aware of the importance of colonies, having been raised in New England (and educated at Harvard). A Cromwellian who came over to the king in 1660, his hatred of the Dutch was matched only by his contempt. Reason, he believed, counted for nothing with them: they would respond only to force and, despite their bluster, in the final analysis they would not fight, having learned their lesson in the First Dutch War (1652–4). He therefore kept finding new matter for complaint – for example, the fact that some of the regicides had taken refuge in the republic. He also hoped to undermine de Witt by promoting the cause of the young Prince of Orange.

Downing's confrontational approach, fully supported by Charles, carried with it the risk of war, and Charles was eager to ensure that, if war came, he would have allies. As we have seen, he was bitterly disappointed that Louis chose to renew his treaties with the Dutch and their relationship did not improve after 1662. The two kings continued to argue about the money which Charles claimed had been promised him in 1661 and about the relief of Portugal. Louis claimed that Charles had promised that most of the money he received for Dunkirk was to go towards the Portuguese war effort and that he would contribute three times as much as Louis did; Charles vigorously denied both claims.[31] It is uncertain which king was in the right.

Thomas Osborne, Earl of Danby (from the studio of Lely), a hard and abrasive politician, he tried desperately in the 1670s to persuade the King to tailor his policies to meet Parliament's expectations.

James, Duke of York: a sketch by Lely. What he lacked in quickness and wit, he made up in dogged loyalty and single-minded determination (or purblind stubbornness). Identified by Charles, in the 1670s, as the main source of his problems.

Henrietta d'Orléans ('Madame'), by Pierre Mignard: Charles's beloved sister played a vital role as a channel of communication in the negotiations leading to the Secret Treaty of Dover.

Whitehall Palace, a labyrinth of corridors and apartments: Charles never liked it, partly because the air was bad, but also because of its association with his father's execution.

Winchester Palace: Charles's comparatively modest answer to Versailles gave him great pleasure in his last years and was not quite complete when he died.

George Monck, Duke of Albemarle, by Lely: a bluff, shrewd career soldier, his knowledge of (and prestige within) the army helped him to act as the architect of the Restoration.

Barbara, Countess of Castlemaine (later Duchess of Cleveland), by Lely, a woman with a strong personality, a ferocious temper and a vigorous interest in politics.

Louise de Quérouaille, Duchess of Portsmouth, by Henri Gascard: sweet, calm and demure, she made a soothing change from Castlemaine. If she eventually played an even more significant political role, it was because Charles wished her to do so and sought her advice.

A horserace at Windsor in 1684: Charles loved to
get away from London and Whitehall to Windsor
or Newmarket, where the talk was of horses and
hounds and he could conduct himself as if he were
an ordinary country gentleman.

Bust of Charles by Honoré Pelle.

D'Estrades wrote that Charles said that he would use the Dunkirk money for Portugal,[32] but he may have read more into Charles's words than Charles had intended. It is also possible that Charles had no compunction about reneging on his assurances because he believed that Louis had reneged on his promise to pay the 2,400,000 *livres*.

The prospects for repairing the damage caused by these mis-understandings (if such they were) were not improved by the conduct of d'Estrades' successor, Cominges, whom Clarendon found difficult and odd, 'hypochondriac' by nature and unable to sleep without opium. He refused to make a formal entry, because Charles, following the recent fracas, had forbidden ambassadors to use coaches on such occasions. Charles hastily sent an envoy to Louis to explain his reasons: his only concern was to maintain public order, he insisted, and he would, where possible, give the French ambassador precedence over the Spanish. The French king was mollified, but new sources of friction soon appeared.[33] Charles still said he wanted a treaty of union, but seemed in no hurry to begin negotiations, arguing first that Cominges should make his formal entry and then that the French should make the first proposals. (He may just have sought to delay serious discussions until after the current session of Parliament.) Charles complained of Cominges' lack of urgency, while Clarendon sounded d'Estrades about the possibility of his returning to London. To break the deadlock, Charles sent Holles as ambassador to Paris, while Louis sent the experienced Huguenot diplomat, Ruvigny, as special envoy to London.[34]

Louis' decision to send Ruvigny owed much to rumours of a rap-prochement between England and Spain. A mysterious agent called Moledy, who was probably Irish, had brought overtures from Madrid, which some thought included proposals for an alliance; Charles and Clarendon spoke of great offers from Spain. Louis was quick to connect Moledy's mission with Bennet's appointment as secretary. The former ambassador to Madrid was regarded as pro-Spanish and it is perhaps no coincidence that after his appointment the conduct of England's relations with France became more lethargic and more subject to disputes about protocol. It was probably to take matters out of Bennet's hands that Clarendon secured the appointment of his friend Holles to the Paris embassy. In fact, there was no substance to the rumours of an Anglo-Spanish alliance: Charles had nothing but contempt for Spain's weakness and he still wanted a close liaison with France. On the other hand, it did no harm to let Louis believe that Charles had other suitors and Bennet had proposed in September 1662 that Charles should mediate between Spain and Portugal. A year later Charles decided to send Sir Richard Fanshawe to Madrid, with instructions to try to end the war and to threaten the Portuguese with the loss of English aid if they refused to co-operate. He was to ask that English merchants should be able to trade in

Spain on terms at least as favourable as those enjoyed by the French and Dutch; it was also suggested that England should take over the Spanish wool trade.[35]

These instructions suggest that Charles's ministers had an exaggerated perception of Spain's weakness and believed that Madrid would pay almost any price for England's friendship. They also show that Charles had lost all enthusiasm for aiding Portugal. Few of the advantages for which he had hoped from the marriage treaty had materialized. Much of the dowry remained unpaid, Bombay had not been handed over and he was less than enamoured of the queen. Moreover, the alliance had produced unforeseen disadvantages. Spain had retaliated by harassing English ships, claiming that they were carrying 'contraband' to Portugal, arresting English merchants and confiscating their goods. Tangier proved difficult and expensive to secure, especially as Spain encouraged the local Moors to attack it. The Spaniards even fomented conspiracies among disaffected radicals in England. While the Spaniards, despite their weakness, proved well able to harm the English, the Portuguese proved expensive and unreliable allies. English troops in the Portuguese service were badly paid and badly treated; many defected to Spain. Most galling of all, in 1661 Portugal signed a treaty giving the Dutch the same trading rights as the English in the Portuguese empire, while their treaty with Charles obliged him to aid Portugal in case of a renewed war with the Dutch: in other words, England might be called upon to defend Portuguese possessions against the all-pervasive Dutch. In these circumstances, the haggling with Louis about money must have seemed the last straw. Charles still paid lip-service to his obligations to Portugal, but had no intention of throwing good money after bad: if Louis wanted Portuguese resistance to continue, he would have to pay for it himself.[36]

In these circumstances, Charles's approach to the negotiations with France was uncompromising. He would accept no less than had been conceded to Cromwell: he expected that Louis should abandon his claim that cannon should be unshipped at Blaye and insisted on being accorded the title of King of France. Louis demanded that his subjects should have the same legal rights in England as the English and that Charles should hand over tracts of land in Canada long claimed by France.[37] With such firmness on both sides, progress was slow; the English found pretexts for delay and new sources of friction appeared. The English claimed that the French could not fish off the English coasts without passes, on pain of having their nets seized. Louis as yet lacked the naval power to rebut these claims, so sought the support of the Dutch in defence of 'the freedom of the seas'.[38] Holles was ordered to press for the restitution of Orange or at least that William should have the right to appoint the governor; Louis' refusal (which Cominges thought unreasonable) effectively denied William's sovereignty over the principality. Charles was also deeply offended that d'Estrades' coach refused to give precedence to William's at the Hague.[39]

This was not the only protocol dispute to sour Anglo-French relations. Cominges was appeased only with difficulty when, arriving late and unexpectedly at the lord mayor's feast, few of the privy councillors present rose to greet him.[40] Far more intractable was the problem of Holles's formal entry. Although the ambassador could be prickly and hot-tempered, the question of whether he should allow his coach to be preceded by those of the French princes of the blood was first raised by Bennet, acting (he claimed) on information from Downing. Holles feigned illness while awaiting further instructions. It transpired that the French had changed the rules of precedence after the recent climbdown by Spain. Charles refused point-blank to abandon any right enjoyed by his predecessors, but (despite Holles's pleas) Bennet was infuriatingly slow to seek out the two surviving pre-war ambassadors, who alone could provide the information which Holles needed to counter French claims that they had a century of precedents on their side.[41] Holles offered to waive his entry, but Louis insisted that it should go ahead, in the form prescribed by the French. Charles would not agree. As he wrote to his sister (known, since her marriage, as 'Madame'), 'There is nobody desires more to have a strict friendship with the king of France than I do, but I will never buy it upon dishonourable terms'; if Louis did not want his friendship, others did.[42] Cominges thought Charles seemed more amenable than his ministers, especially Clarendon (whose dislike the ambassador clearly reciprocated), but as Bennet slowly gathered evidence to support the English case, even Lionne conceded (privately) that not all the precedents were on France's side. At last, in March 1664, four months after the dispute started, Holles had his first audience with the king; at Madame's suggestion none of the princes was present.[43] Louis' decision to allow the audience owed much to the fact that Parliament was soon to meet: Cominges wrote of growing popular hostility to France and of talk that Louis aimed at universal dominion.[44] Louis showed his displeasure at having backed down by subjecting the hapless ambassador to a series of petty humiliations, receiving him so aloofly that his compliments were made to seem like homage. Holles's patience snapped: he now reacted so angrily to every affront, real or imagined, that Charles and Bennet had to tell him to calm down and concentrate on the matter in hand. Holles, for his part, begged to be recalled, but it was not until the spring of 1666 that he finally left for home.[45]

With so many sources of friction, the negotiations conducted by Holles in Paris and Cominges in London proceeded at a snail's pace. Cominges blamed the sloth, factionalism or Spanish sympathies of Charles's councillors, Louis complained that Holles was too quick to take offence, but at bottom neither was really eager to reach agreement. There was little that Louis really wanted from Charles: he certainly did not need a close alliance with him. Charles, for his part, was no longer willing to prop up the Portuguese war effort in order to enable Louis, underhand, to weaken Spain; nor was he willing to compromise England's commercial and colonial interests, especially in the face of ominous signs of French interest in the East Indies. He found Louis' attitude towards precedence arrogant and unreasonable. Worst of all, Louis clearly preferred the friendship of the Dutch to his own, and this at a time when Anglo-Dutch relations were deteriorating sharply.[46]

By early 1664 many at court and in the City were eager for war. Charles complained formally to the States General that papers insulting his brother had been stuck up in several towns and demanded that the culprits be punished.[47] A Commons committee invited merchants to bring in their grievances, especially those involving the Dutch. The most active members of the committee were not merchants, but men closely associated with the court. The response from the trading companies was mixed. Many of their complaints did not relate to the Dutch at all; some (including the Levant Company) feared that their trade would be ruined by a war. Only the Royal Africa Company was unequivocally anti-Dutch. This had been established partly to trade in slaves from West Africa, but more to find a pretext for a quarrel. On 21 April the committee reported that the violent and unfair practices of the Dutch constituted the greatest obstruction to trade and urged that the king be asked to seek redress. The House concurred, adding that they would 'with their lives and fortunes assist His Majesty against all opposition whatsoever'.[48]

The Commons' resolution was greeted in London with wild enthusiasm; seamen, transported with animosity, hope and drink, called loudly for war; but the strongest pressure for war came from a faction within the court, headed by the governor of the Royal Africa Company, James Duke of York. In the 1650s he had seemed destined for a military career; now, as lord admiral, he craved action and glory. The court's bellicosity owed much to an eagerness to reassert English claims to sovereignty over the Narrow Seas and to vindicate the nation's honour. Some hoped to make fat profits from prizes (captured Dutch merchant ships) – the Elizabethan belief that a maritime war could pay for itself died hard – while others saw war as a useful pretext to secure money from Parliament: William Coventry had to explain to Fitzharding that a Dutch War was most unlikely to yield a surplus.[49] Charles was more hesitant, fearing the political consequences of an unsuccessful war, but he put on a brave face, trusting in Downing's assurances that the Dutch had no stomach for a fight.[50] By September he was committed to action. For some years trading rivalries in West Africa had teetered on the verge of open violence. Early in 1664 Robert Holmes captured most of the Gold Coast; the Dutch sent Admiral de Ruyter from the Mediterranean to retake what had been lost. Charles, meanwhile, ordered another expedition to Guinea, denounced the sending of the Dutch fleet as a declaration of war and airily rebuffed de Witt's demand that the English should restore all they had taken.[51]

Charles's firm stance contained an element of bluff. Apart from Clarendon and Southampton – both old and cautious – he was almost alone in not being mad for war; Cominges wrote that it was almost as if he was mediating between his subjects and the Dutch. When Louis offered his mediation, Charles listened politely, but declared that he had gone too far to draw back without a loss of honour. Louis' offer was far from disinterested: he feared that a war in Africa could spread to Europe, in which case he would be obliged, under the 1662 treaty, to side with the Dutch and so would have to postpone his designs in Flanders.[52] Charles sent Fitzharding to assure Louis of his friendship and to offer a treaty of mutual defence, which would, in effect, supersede Louis' treaty with the Dutch.[53] Fitzharding's main task, however, was to discover whether Louis would stand by his obligations to the Dutch. Charles thought it strange that he should do so; when Louis insisted that he had given his word, Charles argued that he was not obliged to keep it because the Dutch were the aggressors; at the very least, Louis could act covertly against the Dutch, much as he had assisted the Portuguese. All these arguments – and Charles's hints that he might join with Spain – had no effect; Louis, however reluctantly, was determined to keep his word.[54]

Among Charles's manifold anxieties, one at least – the fear of being committed to war without having the money to pay for it – proved unfounded. Parliament voted £2,500,000, many times greater than its largest grant under the early Stuarts. Few at court heeded the warnings of wiser heads, like Southampton and William Coventry, that it might not be enough: a huge and expensive backlog of naval maintenance would eat up much of the grant before the court could even begin to prepare for war.[55] After such a grant Louis' attempts to mediate stood little chance; he also became increasingly annoyed by English seizures of French ships.[56] The commissioners appointed to adjudge whether these ships were lawful 'prizes' were both exceedingly rapacious and inclined to regard all foreigners as suspect and all goods as contraband: the presence of even three Dutch sailors on a ship was taken as proof that the ship was Dutch.[57] Charles, meanwhile, renewed his complaints that Louis had, in 1662, broken his promise not to conclude a separate deal with the Dutch and continued to grumble that Cominges misrepresented him.[58] He also, however, pressed Louis to conclude the Holles treaty and offered to help Louis' designs in Flanders if the French king would assist him at sea. William Coventry, at about this time, produced a paper in which he argued that, if Charles and Louis joined against the Dutch, Louis could make himself master of Flanders, while Charles could secure some coastal towns and make himself master of the world's trade.[59]

Such airy visions were far removed from the realities of early 1665. Far from caving in, the Dutch prepared vigorously for war. Hopes that the profits from prizes would meet much of the cost of the war were dashed when the States General ordered a cessation of trade. Thwarted, the English stepped up their depredations on the French, now seen as favouring the Dutch.[60] In a desperate attempt to avoid being drawn into the war, Louis sent his uncle, the Duc de Verneuil, and Honoré de Courtin to join Cominges. He did not, he told them, wish either the English or the Dutch to become all-powerful at sea, nor did he wish to drive England into the arms of Spain. Convinced that Charles did not really want war, Louis ordered the three ambassadors to stress how difficult it would be to defeat the Dutch and to press him to accept Louis' mediation; he was in no doubt, he added, that within Europe England was the aggressor. If the current dispute could be resolved, however, he would welcome a close union with Charles.[61]

The ambassadors remained in England from April to December. Again and again they put forward proposals which Louis thought eminently reasonable; Charles responded that Louis was asking him to make concessions that would wound his honour and reputation, while the proposed 'concessions' by the Dutch amounted merely to the restitution of what should have been his by right. He and Clarendon again complained of the 1662 treaty and intimated that they did not believe that it obliged Louis to break with England: Charles still found it hard to believe that Louis preferred the Dutch to him. While insisting that the ambassadors put their proposals in writing – itself a sign of distrust born of bitter experience – Charles still talked of his hopes of a closer union with France.[62] His enthusiasm for the war effort varied with the fortunes of war. At times he claimed that he had been swept along by the bellicosity of court and Parliament, but he insisted that he could not make peace on terms which Parliament would find unsatisfactory. He asked particularly that the Dutch should pay reparations (thus admitting that they were the aggressors) and that Louis should help to install William as stadhouder and captain-general, a demand which Louis dismissed as unrealistic. Still more unrealistic was Holles's demand for a cautionary town, as security for the implementation of what was to be agreed.[63]

In the first major engagement of the war, York won a striking victory off Lowestoft on 3 June. Five thousand Dutch sailors were killed and over twenty ships sunk or captured. For Charles, the joy of victory was tempered by grief: Falmouth was killed, struck on the head by a cannonball, thus (as Marvell cruelly remarked) proving for the first and only time that he had brains.[64] The victory was not followed up: after a battle on that scale, the fleet had to return to port to refit and revictual. The fact that the Dutch had not been swept from the seas, however, highlighted a strategic dilemma. With the entire fleet brought together to seek out and destroy the Dutch fleet, English merchant shipping was left unprotected, especially in the Mediterranean. Such a strategy rested on the assumption that merchant losses could be offset by a crushing victory, which, as time went on, came to seem increasingly unlikely. The alternative strategy was to attack Dutch trade. This had the attraction of being profitable, not least for individual captains: indeed, York justified the attempt to seize the Dutch Smyrna fleet in the neutral port of Bergen purely in terms of the profit it would bring. On the other hand, a war on trade involved dividing the fleet into smaller units, which would make it more risky to engage the Dutch battle fleet. For the time being, however, Charles remained optimistic. He was persuaded that the Dutch would now agree terms and recalled York from the fleet.[65] Without his restraining influence, the feuding and indiscipline of the officers became worse and private interests prevailed over public. Naval officers, from admirals downwards, helped themselves to prize goods. Courtiers and noblemen, led by Albemarle and Ashley, fitted out privateers to prey on 'enemy' shipping: as the profits were high and the risks few, seamen transferred to the privateers, leaving the king's ships undermanned.[66]

Faced with these problems, Charles betook himself to his pleasures once more and the management of his finances went from bad to worse. It was difficult enough to monitor spending in peacetime; Southampton clearly lacked the energy to do so and even officials who were well meaning and honest, such as Sir George Carteret, treasurer of the navy, did not always keep methodical accounts. Ashley persuaded Charles that, as treasurer of the prize money, he should account directly to the king and pay out money as he ordered, thus bypassing the exchequer's accounting procedures. This expedient appealed to Charles's love of having money of his own, but was wide open to abuse. Southampton opposed it, but to no avail. His credit with the king was diminishing: there were proposals that the treasury should be put into commission, but the old earl would not resign and Charles would not dismiss him. Southampton also deeply resented an expedient proposed by Downing to strengthen the king's credit. In 1665 the Act to raise another £1,250,000 for the war included provisions that the entire sum was to be appropriated to the war and that loans raised on the security of this tax should be repaid in strict chronological order. Clarendon and Southampton denounced these as dangerous innovations, which would destroy the lord treasurer's authority; but they were to be an important component of the system of 'treasury control' introduced after Southampton's death, a system which was to bring much greater order to the royal finances.[67]

Thus the great grant of £2,500,000 melted away, while Charles's ordinary revenue fell as trade was disrupted by the war and the plague. In July the court left London to escape the infection, thus further dislocating an already overstretched administration. It settled at Salisbury: 'a fine place', said Charles, 'if it could afford meat, drink or lodging'. He wanted to move to Wilton, but abandoned the idea when Castlemaine refused to go.[68] In the autumn Parliament met at Oxford. Clarendon laid aside his reservations about the war and made a bellicose speech, which hinted at the possibility of a breach with France. The Houses responded with a great hum and voted £1,250,000.[69] This grant killed any lingering hopes that the French mediation might succeed and the ambassadors prepared to return home. In other respects, the session proved less satisfactory. MPs complained of the decay of rents, which many blamed on imports of cheap Irish cattle. A bill to ban such imports passed the Commons, but failed in the Lords, supposedly for lack of time, but Charles had also lobbied hard against it. This was, however, an emotive issue which was bound to resurface next time he wanted money.[70] There were also many complaints about the conduct of the war. Albemarle denounced the Earl of Sandwich for bringing the fleet into port too soon: Dutch ships had appeared off the coast, provoking something close to panic. Sandwich was already vulnerable, having allowed his officers to help themselves to goods from a rich Dutch prize. The fact that Charles retrospectively approved his conduct did nothing to dispel the impression that many in high places put private profit before public service, while the rest of the nation suffered the burdens of high taxes, economic depression and plague. Sandwich's appointment as ambassador to Madrid did little to assuage public anger. Unless the conduct of the war improved markedly, in the next session Parliament was unlikely to prove so generous.[71]

The new year dawned with little cause for optimism. France was about to enter the war: as it turned out Louis' naval assistance to the Dutch proved little more than a gesture, but his troops took St Kitts and French privateers harassed English trade. Charles felt impelled to divide his battle fleet: part was to cruise off Plymouth to watch for the French, which left the main body less well able to contend with the Dutch. Moreover, Louis acted swiftly to oppose the forces of the Bishop of Münster, Charles's only ally. Fanshawe and Sandwich painstakingly negotiated a series of treaties which were to regulate Anglo-Spanish commercial and colonial relations for many years to come and to pave the way for Portuguese independence, thus relieving Charles of one drain on his finances. The first of these treaties was not, however, completed until 1667. In the meantime, as Bennet (now Lord Arlington) remarked, they had lost France without gaining Spain. This, and the lack of money, made the court secretly long for peace – but since Parliament's last grant any overt move in that direction was unthinkable.

Coventry (now Sir William) told Pepys that the war had been a mistake: the best they could hope for was a peace that was less than disastrous. But the war had to go on. Albemarle was given command of the fleet: he was vigorous enough but many doubted his grasp of matters nautical. He soon had to share his command with Charles's cousin, Prince Rupert. Once a dashing cavalry commander, Rupert was now older and more cantankerous, but he did possess naval experience thanks to years of privateering (or rather piracy) in the 1650s.[72] Money was short: circulars were sent to mayors, deputy lieutenants and the clergy, urging them to encourage people to lend on the security of the recent Parliamentary grant.[73] The court's return to London in February did something to raise morale, but war weariness was growing and the government's incompetence made Pepys fearful of both the outcome of the coming campaign and Parliament's mood when it next met.[74]

His forebodings were fulfilled when the reduced English fleet met that of the Dutch in early June. The Four Days' Battle was bloody but inconclusive. Charles hailed it as a victory; Albemarle claimed that he had taught the Dutch a lesson; most Londoners regarded it as a defeat.[75] In the weeks that followed, fears of a Dutch or French invasion mounted and Charles mobilized the limited forces at his disposal. Few would advance money; the government remained desperately short of ready cash; seamen's wives clamoured for their pay. Pepys, fearing riots and insurrections, withdrew his money from his banker. Nothing could save England, he wrote, but Charles's applying himself to his business; until he did so, no one would be called to account for their conduct.[76] His anxiety was relieved by a striking victory over the Dutch on 25 July. Buckingham urged the king to seize the chance to attack the French fleet, then on a courtesy visit to Lisbon: Charles (he argued) owed the king of Portugal nothing and, once deprived of the prospect of French help, the Dutch would soon come to terms.[77] Charles wisely ignored his advice, but the public mood was more hostile to France than to the Dutch, especially after the Great Fire of London in September. Amid the smoke, the stench and the panic Charles showed a rare vigour, limiting the damage by having houses blown up or pulled down to stop the blaze from spreading. His authority, and that of his brother, was vital: the lord mayor, for all his efforts, could not get himself obeyed and most citizens were more concerned to save their belongings than to fight the fire. The royal brothers worked tirelessly, handling buckets and water engines, and Charles gave orders to have bread and cheese provided for the poor – no small problem, since many bakers' shops had been destroyed.[78]

Despite his outward resolution, Charles (and his ministers) feared that the Fire could lead to serious disorders. Albemarle, still regarded as a strongman and well respected in the City, was hastily summoned from Portsmouth. The precaution proved unnecessary. Public anger was turned not against the court but against conspirators: some blamed the fanatics, others the Papists or the French. Fears of Popery swept the provinces, foreigners were attacked in the streets of London.[79] A crazy Frenchman confessed to starting the Fire, but many, on reflection, came to doubt that it had been a case of arson: tenants had a vested interest in establishing that it had not been an accident, as in that case they were not liable to meet the cost of repairs.[80] Yet even if the government, for once, was not blamed, the Fire still created a mood of despondency, and trade (and the revenue) were bound to be further disrupted. The earlier causes for complaint had not gone away and it was reported that tactless courtiers rejoiced at the Fire, claiming that the City would now be less able to resist the king's will.[81] It was in this unpromising atmosphere that Parliament reconvened on 18 September.

6

Retribution

By the time Parliament met, the patriotic exuberance of 1664 had long since evaporated. Sanguine expectations of easy victories and rich pickings had given way to recrimination. Those of a religious cast of mind saw the scourges of plague and fire as evidence of divine disapproval; others more prosaically bemoaned the mismanagement of the war effort, the interruption of trade and the decay of rents. Enquiries into the Fire raised once again the spectre of Popery; the raising of forces for the war revived that of absolutism. This last anxiety was not, indeed, wholly fanciful: some suggested that the king should threaten or coerce Parliament or raise money without its consent. Underlying and linking all these fears and resentments was a sense that the core of the government was rotten – an unconcerned king in a corrupt and vicious court.[1]

Lack of leadership, indeed, was all too obvious. In the fleet Albemarle and Rupert bickered while indiscipline raged all around them. In the revenue Southampton's limitations were cruelly exposed by the added demands of war. Clarendon, as rapacious and reactionary as ever, went on his ponderous way, reminding all and sundry that he had not wanted the war, so he could not be blamed if it was going badly. Serious administrators like Pepys or Sir William Coventry complained endlessly of Charles's failure to exert his authority, but Charles had other things on his mind. Frances Stuart, tired of rebuffing his advances, took refuge in marriage to the bibulous but inoffensive Duke of Richmond. Her withdrawal from court greatly displeased the king: some thought he had intended to divorce the queen and marry Frances. Castlemaine, meanwhile, continued to bully and berate the hapless monarch. Many thought that he had tired of her and would gladly be rid of her, 'but he is so weak in his passion that he dare not do it'.[2] Baulked of his hopes of Frances, Charles took other lovers; Castlemaine responded in kind, but still claimed that her children were Charles's and continued to make political capital out of her influence over him.[3]

The Countess found a powerful ally in her kinsman, Buckingham.

Hitherto his political role had been limited. He had made clear his hostility
to Clarendon and support for Bristol, so when he came to the fleet as a
volunteer York would not admit him to the council of war; Buckingham
went home in a huff.[4] Late in 1666 he left the court after quarrelling with
Castlemaine and began to pose as a champion of clean government and the
rights of the subject. His call for a bill to make the embezzlement of the
public revenue a capital offence was seen by some as a joke, but he carried
on his vendetta against Clarendon in deadly earnest and with a determination
of which many had thought him incapable.[5] Along with some members of
the Commons, he called for a rigorous investigation into the conduct of the
war and the management of the revenue. Backbenchers were always inclined
to be resentful of failure and suspicious of those in power, but Buckingham
and his allies were more interested in office for themselves than in more
effective government. They insinuated to Charles that the Commons would
become much more amenable once Clarendon and his friends had been
removed: Buckingham, indeed, claimed that he and his cronies could manage
Parliament far more effectively than either Clarendon or Arlington. Experience was to show that Buckingham was much better at raising discontents
than at allaying them; for a while, however, Charles allowed himself to be
persuaded that the mercurial duke could do as he promised. As a result, the
power struggles and animosities of the court spilled over into Parliament
and greatly exacerbated the inevitable political crisis.

At the start of the session Charles made a 'pathetical' speech, stressing his
reluctance to burden his people further but insisting that more money was
needed for the war. The Commons accepted with alacrity the king's offer to
produce accounts to show that previous grants had been well managed. They
also showed their ongoing support for the war by voting another £1,800,000,
but found it hard to agree how the money should be raised. The differences
on this question owed something to politics and something to economic
interest. The 'court party' called for a general excise; their opponents
(described as 'Presbyterians' or 'patriots') supported a land tax, on the
grounds that that would be granted for a finite period and was much less
likely than an excise to become perpetual; some thought that the calls for
an excise suggested that Charles wished to rule without Parliaments.[6] Others
argued in different terms. Landowners, badly hit by the decay of rents, were
reluctant to burden land further. Some claimed that the bankers had grown
rich by lending money for the war and should be forced to disgorge some
of their ill-gotten gains: some even talked of forced loans, at which the
bankers declared that they would advance no more money.[7] There was also
talk of Parliament's 'buying back' the hearth tax for the equivalent of eight
years' yield, but no one could agree on how the money was to be raised:

again MPs showed that they were wary of creating any further perpetual taxes and Charles killed off the project by declaring that he would never give up the hearth money. At last, the House agreed to raise the bulk of the £1,800,000 by an eleven months' assessment, starting in January 1668, the remainder coming from a poll tax. This was to be in part a tax on people, graduated according to status, but it also tried to tax forms of property unaffected by existing taxes, including ready cash and the profits of government office.[8]

If the debates on supply were both ill-tempered and confused, this owed much to the lack of discipline among the king's supporters. On one occasion, two of them babbled drunkenly for half an hour, despite all attempts to silence them; but the problem went deeper. Arlington had tried to create a system of management based on rewards (or promises), canvassing and kind words from the king, but Arlington was now in the Lords and his contact with the Lower House was limited. Instead of rewarding loyalty, his habit of 'taking off' able critics of the court merely encouraged MPs to be fractious.[9] Much might still have been achieved had government spokesmen given a clear lead, but they did not: 'We are not directed as formerly and, being left to the accident of wind and tide in a popular assembly, drive at random.'[10] Thus indecision about the manner of raising supply – the court first opposed, then supported a land tax – led to unnecessary delays and allowed its opponents ample time to raise other grievances.[11]

By contrast, the court's critics had a clear idea of what they wanted: a full investigation into past misdeeds and especially the mismanagement of money. The House found the accounts produced by the treasury intricate and confusing and appointed a sub-committee to probe the matter further. Charles feared that the results of this scrutiny could prove embarrassing, but the House declared itself sufficiently satisfied to agree to vote the £1,800,000.[12] At this point, the issue of imports of Irish cattle reared its ugly head once more. These were especially resented by the over-represented (and mainly pastoral) western counties, but their resentment was exploited by others with more dubious motives. Buckingham, Ashley and Lauderdale hoped to oust Clarendon's ally Ormond from the lord lieutenancy of Ireland: it was said that they wanted Monmouth to succeed him, although Clarendon declared imperiously that they lacked the wit to carry through such a design. It was also suspected that Ashley and Lauderdale had a project to monopolize the Anglo-Scottish cattle trade, which would naturally be boosted by the ending of Irish competition.[13] With the reopening of this emotive issue, the Commons' mood changed. Some MPs denounced Irish cattle as the source of all their woes, in terms reminiscent of 1641: there was even talk of Popish plots. In the Lords the anti-Irish rhetoric of Buckingham and Ashley infuriated those, like Ormond's son Ossory, with Irish connections.[14] The bill to ban imports sailed through the Commons, but made slow progress in the Lords and passed in November only with an important amendment. The Commons had described Irish cattle imports as a 'nuisance' in order to prevent Charles from using his power to dispense with the penalties of regulatory statutes in particular cases. The Lords removed the word 'nuisance'; the Commons insisted that it should remain and threw out a proposal to allow twenty thousand cattle to be brought over for the poor of London. With the Houses deadlocked, Charles and Arlington feared that the Commons might either abandon the assessment bill or tack the cattle bill to it; the latter would thus become part of a money bill, which the Lords could accept or reject, but not amend. Desperate for money and against the advice of a majority of his councillors, Charles made it clear that he wished the Lords to pass the bill in the form the Commons wanted. Many peers absented themselves or protested, but the bill passed on 14 January 1667.[15]

The rancour aroused by the issue of Irish cattle enabled the court's opponents to broaden their attack. They began to express dissatisfaction with the accounts they had been shown and claimed that a more rigorous scrutiny was needed. A move to bring in a bill to set up an accounts committee narrowly failed, largely because of uncertainty whether the Commons could empower such a committee to examine people on oath. Instead the House resolved to ask the Lords, who undoubtedly possessed such a power, to set up a joint commission.[16] The Lords hesitated to concur, so the Commons proposed to tack a proviso setting up such a commission to the poll bill. The court scoured the playhouses and brothels, but failed to muster enough MPs to have the proposal rejected in committee.[17] When the committee reported to the House, however, the court repaired the damage. The House decided that the commission should be established by a separate bill, which meant that the Lords could feel free to amend or reject it without jeopardizing supply. The Lords, indeed, denounced the proposed commission as infringing the king's prerogative right to manage his own finances and resolved to petition him to appoint a commission to perform the same function. Charles duly issued such a commission and nominated most of those named by the Commons, but he pointedly omitted (among others) Buckingham. The idea was Clarendon's; the Commons angrily denounced the commission as unParliamentary and members of the Lower House refused to serve on it. Arlington feared that the Commons might tack the accounts bill to the assessment or poll bill, but it remained with the Lords until early February. By the time it was sent down, with amendments, the Commons had lost much of their enthusiasm (or anger). Their discussions proceeded slowly and reached no conclusion before the prorogation.[18]

Having revived the Commons' interest in mismanagement, the 'patriots' extended their attack. Alarmed by the Fire and the threat of a French invasion, the Commons called for the enforcement of the laws against Popery and a ban on imports from France: Charles promptly complied on both points. Although the French and Papists were both 'alien', the recrudescence of anti-Popery raised nasty echoes of 1641.[19] Two other grievances struck directly at the court. The Canary Company, established by royal charter in 1665, was denounced as a monopoly, a view with which Allan Brodrick, though a courtier, tended to agree. Lord Mordaunt, constable of Windsor Castle, was impeached for a variety of alleged oppressions.[20] Such issues helped sustain a sense of resentment against a regime which seemed inclined to put private profit before the public good and to misuse its authority: there was also a proposal for a bill to regulate and discipline the army. Much of the anger focused on Clarendon, whose haughtiness and rapacity had made him many enemies. He was blamed for the Lords' rejection of the word 'nuisance' in the cattle bill and for the king's accounts commission. As rumours multiplied that the chancellor would be impeached, it was reported that he advocated the dissolution of this 'insolent' Parliament.[21]

For all the sound and fury that they raised in Parliament, the patriots achieved little. Charles assented to the Irish cattle bill, but the accounts bill and the attacks on the Canary Company and Mordaunt proved abortive. Above all, the patriots failed to link redress of grievances to supply: on 25 January the Commons resolved to let the assessment bill go up to the Lords before other issues had been settled.[22] However angry MPs might be, and however anxious Charles and Arlington sometimes were,[23] the Commons accepted that the war had to go on. Even so, the assessment (worth over £1,250,000) was not to start for almost another year: in the meantime, the government would have to try to borrow on the security of what was to be collected. Some at court hoped that a quick peace would leave the king with enough revenue to do without Parliament for a while, but such hopes were crassly naive. The poll tax proved (as Pepys predicted) far too complex to yield its full potential: he himself was taxed on neither his capital nor the profits of his offices. Wiser heads worried that the anger shown by the Commons did not augur well for the future: the next session was unlikely to go any better, especially if the war went badly, and the court's recent Parliamentary management did not inspire confidence. The real problem, however, lay in Charles's continuing failure to impose his authority on his courtiers and councillors. All too often those who talked most loudly of grievances were his own servants. As Brodrick remarked, Buckingham had felt free to behave as he had 'knowing the infinite good nature of His Majesty to pardon such offenders'.[24]

Even Charles's patience had its limits, however. Such was Buckingham's popularity that Charles did not dare to move against him during the session, but after the prorogation he acted swiftly. Arlington gathered information about the duke's dealings among the seamen (who had recently rioted in protest against their lack of pay) and Dissenters. He found that Buckingham had hired an astrologer to cast the king's horoscope, which could be construed as treason (compassing or imagining the king's death). It was widely believed, however, that his real offence was to have exposed the misdeeds of those in power (and to have opposed Popery); Charles, for his part, claimed that, had the duke not opposed the granting of money, the Dutch would have come to terms.[25] Orders were given to seize him, but he proved elusive. His friends tried in vain to persuade the king to allow him to return to court, so at last, in June, he surrendered himself and travelled in state to the Tower, revelling in his role as martyr for the liberties of the people.[26]

Louis XIV had entered the war reluctantly. He had little fondness for his Dutch allies and, now that Philip IV was dead, he was impatient to pursue his designs in the Spanish Netherlands. As the 1666 campaign neared its end, he sounded Charles about the terms upon which he would be willing to make peace. Charles replied that he would prefer to reach agreement with Louis before approaching the Dutch. In January 1667 he sent St Albans to Paris to propose that both English and Dutch should keep what they had taken and that the previous treaty between them (that of 1662) should be fully observed. Regulations should be agreed between the two states to prevent clashes outside Europe. St Albans was also to demand at least £200,000 in war damages and to press Louis to hand back St Kitts and to take up William's interests. Charles, for his part, would commit himself only to remain neutral in any future war between France and Spain. Shortly after the prorogation, Charles accepted in principle a French proposal that he should write a letter, to be kept by his mother, promising to make no league contrary to Louis' interests in the coming twelve months. During that time he was to negotiate the close alliance with Louis of which he had spoken so often. Arlington saw this as evidence that Louis wished to secure Charles's friendship and then break with Spain.[27] The French seemed delighted at Charles's move. Lionne told St Albans that peace was as good as made; privately he rejoiced that it now seemed that Charles had, after all, concluded no agreement with Spain. Louis was less sanguine. He could not understand why Charles had taken three months to respond to his overtures – clearly he thought the recent session of Parliament an insufficient reason for the delay. Louis also disliked the way Charles had ignored his insistence that the Danes be included in any settlement and his attempts to sow dissension in the republic. Convinced that the people there were mad for peace and for William's elevation to office, Charles urged that any peace conference should be held at the Hague, where the Dutch negotiators could be subjected to popular pressure. A further complication was the vexed question of Pula

Run: Charles demanded that it be handed over, as the 1662 treaty required, but it was far from clear who now held it.[28]

When Clarendon and Arlington heard that Louis refused to insist either that negotiations should take place at the Hague or that the Dutch should hand over Pula Run, they complained that he talked of peace but would do nothing to bring it about. Lionne, for his part, was convinced that the English had no intention of coming to terms before the end of that summer's campaign.[29] Lionne mollified them somewhat by saying that he had not realized that the Dutch had ever promised to restore Pula Run. Charles then agreed to drop his insistence on the Hague, substituting Breda, which the Dutch would find much more acceptable. Louis responded by agreeing to press for the restitution of Pula Run, but intimated that Charles would be wiser to cut his losses and take what terms he could. Meanwhile, St Albans had not yet handed over to the queen mother the letter promising that Charles would conclude no more leagues for a year.[30] His failure to do so increased French fears that Sandwich's negotiations in Madrid involved more than a simple commercial treaty. They also heard (correctly) that Charles was seeking to use the emperor's envoy, Baron de Lisola, as an intermediary between himself and de Witt: Charles had even told Lisola that St Albans had no power to negotiate.[31] Gradually the obstacles to an understanding were removed. Charles's ministers convinced the French that all negotiations would break down unless the Dutch gave up Pula Run. St Albans at last handed over the letter and in April even Louis wrote that agreement was imminent. New snags soon appeared, however. The English demanded compensation, as agreed in 1662, for the *Bonaventure* and *Bona Esperanza*, seized by the Dutch in 1643 and valued by the English at £100,000. At the end of May, de Witt decided that the time for negotiation had passed and the Dutch fleet put to sea.[32]

Clarendon was in despair. Louis had promised to secure honourable terms, he wailed, but had merely advised Charles to accept every insolent demand that the Dutch chose to make. The French complained that the English had wrecked the negotiations by insisting on trifles. Privately, in view of Charles's dealings with Lisola, they must have wondered if he could ever be trusted.[33] Charles's government now faced a campaign for which it was anything but prepared.[34] Lack of money, and over-reliance on French help at the negotiating table, had led him to keep his great ships in harbour and to send out a squadron of smaller third-rates to patrol the coasts. The fortifications of the major southern and eastern ports were hastily reinforced and lords lieutenant were ordered to keep the militia in readiness.[35] Such measures were hardly indicative of confidence and those responsible for carrying them out were often highly pessimistic. Money was desperately short, signs of negligence abounded. Londoners called urgently for peace, yet feared that the terms would prove unsatisfactory. Only at court were people as merry as ever, confident that peace was certain.[36]

Such illusions did not last long. In late May the militia of the maritime counties was ordered to watch the coasts. The month's pay allowed under the Militia Acts had already been spent, however, and the additional £70,000 provided for under that of 1662 had been for three years only. The privy council declared that, in a national emergency, the militia was obliged to turn out if summoned and that the lords lieutenant were obliged to defray its cost: the council mentioned the money for ammunition and fines on defaulters. Not all deputies, however, were convinced that it would be legal to divert this money. On 11 June the council ordered the mobilization of all the militia horse and volunteer troops, with no mention of where the money was to come from, except an assurance that the king would burden the country no longer than was necessary.[37] His first priority, however, was to defend London and Chatham, where most of his great ships lay. As far as the latter was concerned, Albemarle declared himself satisfied with its defences, which included a boom across the mouth of the Medway, but others remarked that the fortifications of Gravesend and Sheerness were in poor condition. On 12 June the Dutch broke the boom, burned some of the great ships and carried off others in triumph, including the flagship, the *Royal Charles*.[38]

News that the Dutch were in the Thames estuary triggered a panic in London. Charles ordered the raising of twelve new foot regiments and many troops of horse, but he had no money to pay them and his prospects of finding any were not improved by a run on the banks.[39] As it became clear that the Dutch would not push on towards the capital, panic turned to fury: scapegoats would have to be found. People were reluctant to blame the still-popular Albemarle, so some denounced the king's master shipwright, Peter Pett, for failing to move the *Royal Charles* further upriver and out of danger. The thinking behind this did not impress Andrew Marvell:

> Pett, the sea-architect, in making ships
> Was the first cause of all these naval slips.
> Had he not built, none of these faults had been:
> If no creation, there had been no sin.[40]

Others spread the blame more widely. Brodrick wrote bitterly: 'In all places, the same face of supine security. Had the Dutch come on they had without resistance fired all the shipping to London Bridge.'[41] The Spanish ambassador wrote that everyone blamed Clarendon; some, however, blamed the king. Charles made some effort to rally the Londoners, but his leadership was far from inspiring.[42] Rumours circulated that he had been in Castlemaine's lodgings chasing a moth – or worse – as the Dutch carried off his ships:

> So our great prince, when the Dutch fleet arriv'd
> Saw his ships burn'd, and as they burn'd, he swiv'd.[43]

The Medway disaster unleashed a storm of pent-up dissatisfaction. The kindest critics spoke of gross negligence, others of corruption, treachery and betrayal by 'the Popish and profane party', opening the way for a French invasion. Some even blamed the bishops: Dissenters regained confidence and Oxbridge dons talked fearfully of liberty of conscience.[44] Charles, it would seem, saw matters differently. Four days before the Dutch broke the boom, talking to a rising politician, Sir Thomas Osborne, he bitterly denounced the conduct of Osborne's patron, Buckingham. The duke, he declared, had obstructed all his business in the last session of Parliament and was forever aspiring to be 'popular' – always a pejorative term in the mouths of Stuart kings. Charles claimed that calls for an accounts commission had been intended to foment distrust of his government and blamed the current danger of invasion on 'ill men' in Parliament and those seduced by them.[45] While it is always unwise to take Charles's statements wholly at face value, it seems likely that he really wanted to believe that criticisms of his government were unfounded and that those who complained were misled by factious rogues like Buckingham: he always preferred to think that all was well. It says little for his political sagacity, however, that he seems to have understood politics solely in terms of court faction. In these circumstances, Buckingham's attempts to make his peace with the king were predictably rebuffed and he began a brief but comfortable sojourn in the Tower. Equally predictably, some of his courtiers learned nothing from the Medway disaster: as the Dutch withdrew, they resumed their old bravado, calling the Dutch cowards.[46]

Faced with public clamour and plummeting credit, Charles decided to recall Parliament, although some doubted whether he could legally do so before the date in October to which it had been prorogued. Some councillors hoped that news of a peace could extricate Charles from his problems: he had already dropped his demand for compensation for the two ships. Others were simply terrified of what Parliament might do.[47] Pepys heard that James had urged his brother to raise money as he pleased and that Clarendon said that Elizabeth had done her business without Parliament in 1588. The earl admitted later that he may have mentioned that contributions had been levied locally during the civil wars. Money, indeed, remained the overwhelming problem. The king had no means of paying either the militia or the regular regiments which he had just raised. Lawyers and clergymen were urged to advance money, and lords lieutenant and their deputies were ordered to levy what was needed, all on the security of the eleven months' assessment, collection of which was to start in seven months' time. The response was cool. When the Earl of Lindsey summoned the JPs of Lincolnshire to consider how to meet the cost of the militia, few turned up and those who did said that the county had paid more than enough taxes already.[48]

Clarendon was against calling Parliament: he claimed that to do so would be illegal and that any money that it voted would come in too slowly to resolve the king's present problems. Despite his claims that he could not be blamed for the ill conduct of a war which he had opposed, he must also have feared that his days in power were numbered. Southampton had died in May, to be replaced by a group of younger commissioners, who were far from sharing the chancellor's horror of novelty. He wrote sadly to Ormond: 'I have lost a friend, a fast and certain friend, and whether my only friend or no you only know.'[49] He might be convinced that the failures of the war could not be laid at his door, but 'he is railed at with the same vehemence as if he alone had managed the affair'.[50] To anger at the mismanagement of the war was added alarm at the raising of the new regiments: a measure born of panic was widely perceived as part of a dastardly design 'to have a land army and so to make the government like that of France'. Pepys, however, was sceptical: 'our princes have not brains, or at least care and forecast enough, to do that'.[51] Panic and confusion reigned at Whitehall: Clarendon declared that he did not have a clue what was going on. Charles, meanwhile, seemed inclined to seek salvation in the form of Buckingham, the darling of the people. Summoned before the council, the duke behaved with unaccustomed submission, except towards Arlington, whom he blamed for his incarceration. Charles declared himself convinced of Buckingham's innocence, but forgiveness did not come quite so easily – memories of his conduct in the last session still clearly rankled – and he was returned to the Tower. By now Castlemaine had forgotten their quarrel and was pressing hard for his release: when Charles told her she was a meddlesome whore, she retorted that Buckingham was the best subject he had. Pepys heard that Buckingham had offered to join with Clarendon against Arlington, but had been rebuffed. If the story was true, Clarendon had been unwise. On 16 July the duke was released and kissed the king's hand.[52]

It was to take some time for Buckingham fully to regain Charles's favour. In the meantime, the government had other concerns. Amid the encircling gloom there now burned one glimmer of hope. Normally the Dutch triumph in the Medway would have been followed by fresh demands, but times were not normal. In May Louis had launched his long-planned assault on the Spanish Netherlands, claiming that, by local law, certain territories had 'devolved' to his wife on the death of her father. This had led de Witt to seek to knock England out of the war by attacking the Thames estuary: he cannot have expected it to prove so easy. Fortified by this success, he hastened to make peace. By the Treaty of Breda England gave up Pula Run and Surinam and abandoned most of her claims to territory in West Africa and for compensation for losses sustained before 1662. Disagreements about trading practices were referred to a future treaty. The Dutch refused to send home those who had sought refuge in the republic for conscience's sake. The English gained only the little-valued territories of New Amsterdam (renamed New York), New Jersey and Delaware. Shortly afterwards, de Witt dealt a serious blow to Charles's aspirations for William: he pushed through the States of Holland a 'Perpetual Edict', which invited William to serve on the council of state, but laid down that no Prince of Orange should ever combine the office of stadhouder of any province with that of captain-general of the union.[53]

As Clarendon admitted, the English were lucky to get off so lightly. Arlington had hoped that peace could be concluded before Parliament met, but on the appointed day, 25 July, the news had not arrived. The Speaker asked the Commons to adjourn for four days, but an obscure backbencher, Sir Thomas Tomkins, denounced the standing army and a call for its disbandment was carried without a dissenting voice. Sir William Coventry's assurances that it would indeed be disbanded were swept aside and the councillors in the House were deputed to carry the resolution to the king. By the time the House next met, news of the peace had arrived and Charles prorogued Parliament until October.[54]

This brief meeting of Parliament confirmed the court's worst fears: the old Cavaliers were as angry as anybody and many grumbled at having made the journey to London to so little purpose. Rumours persisted that the courtiers complained that Charles was allowing them to starve and that he should use the army to dispense with Parliament. All agreed, noted Pepys, that the king was governed by wine, women and rogues.[55] Desperately, ministers sought to restore the government's credibility. Arlington hoped that the labours of the treasury commission would show that Charles was putting his finances in order, but the commissioners found the position even worse than expected and there was much talk of retrenchment.[56] Public outrage demanded more – a visible change in the conduct of government. While Buckingham was portrayed as the nation's potential saviour, Clarendon was increasingly blamed for the government's failures.[57] His haughty demeanour – even towards his friends – did nothing to deflect criticism. He took refuge in 'the pride of a very good conscience'. He remained convinced that Charles still valued his 'honesty and good meanings' and that the current 'fumes' would soon disappear.[58] As Buckingham had not yet been able to re-establish himself at court, the assault on the chancellor was led by Arlington and by Castlemaine, who hectored the poor king almost out of his wits. Their task was made easier by the fact that for some days after the death of his wife, on 9 August, Clarendon stayed away from the council.

Seasoned observers judged that his days in power were numbered.[59]

One day in late August Charles told James that he had heard of a plan to impeach Clarendon when Parliament next met: for both the king's sake and his own, the chancellor should resign. On the 26th Clarendon told the king that he would not do so, as he had committed no crime; Charles replied that innocence had not saved Strafford in 1641, but declared that he would consider further. The next few days saw a furious struggle between the chancellor's supporters, led by York, and his enemies, who argued that for Charles to change his mind now would be weak and undignified: if Clarendon would not resign, Charles should disown him and leave him to his fate. At last, on the 30th, Charles sent Morrice to Worcester House for the seals. Castlemaine was exultant and Bab May threw himself on his knees, declaring that Charles was now truly king for the first time.[60]

Why did Charles finally decide to dismiss the chancellor? Doubtless, as he wrote to Ormond, he genuinely believed that Clarendon's 'behaviour and humour was grown so insupportable to myself, and to all the world also, that I could not longer endure it, and it was impossible for me to live with it and do those things with the Parliament that must be done or the government will be lost'. There were, however, other reasons. The argument that Parliament would demand Clarendon's removal probably originated with Arlington: it figures prominently in his letters. Sir William Coventry, who now resigned from York's service, believed that the chancellor was an insuperable obstacle to administrative regeneration and even to free discussion in the council. Last but not least, Castlemaine's nagging played an important role, as did the insinuations and raillery of the 'little people'.[61] The chancellor's removal was opposed by such powerful figures as York, Albemarle, Archbishop Sheldon and (some said) Buckingham, whose hatred was still focused on Arlington.[62] There may have been an additional factor. For some time Frances Stuart had sought Charles's permission to marry the Duke of Richmond. Charles threw every possible obstacle in her way, until at last she lost patience and eloped. Charles was bitter. On 26 August, the day of his interview with Clarendon, he wrote to Madame, 'how hard a thing 'tis to swallow an injury done by a person I had so much tenderness for.' (He originally wrote 'love' instead of 'tenderness'.) At the time she eloped Frances had been visiting Clarendon's son, Lord Cornbury, which led some to claim that the chancellor had organized the elopement in order to protect his grandchildren's claim to the throne.[63]

A few days after Clarendon's dismissal Charles had a long interview with Buckingham; by the end of September the duke had been restored to the privy council and to his offices, much to the alarm of Arlington and Coventry.[64] Meanwhile, at Arlington's instigation, Charles set out to appease Parliament. Orders were issued to enforce the laws against Catholicism.[65]

An investigation into 'prisoners of state' led to many being released.[66] There were also hints of a more flexible attitude towards Dissenters. Clarendon was now clearly seen as their enemy and his fall improved the prospects for comprehension and indulgence. The court, it was reported, was ready to sacrifice the clergy to propitiate the Commons and there were rumours of clandestine meetings with nonconformist ministers.[67] By September rumours of liberty of conscience were rife, amid hints that the government regarded the Dissenters' case as being very different from that of the Catholics.[68] By October a comprehension bill had been drafted, designed to accommodate within the Church some of those who had refused to conform in 1662. There were as yet no positive steps to offer indulgence to the sectaries.[69]

Many saw the hand of Buckingham behind these developments. 'Liberty of conscience' was also supported by Lord Keeper Bridgeman, who received the Great Seal after Clarendon's fall, and by Dr John Wilkins, scientist and polymath, soon to be appointed to the bishopric of Chester. All claimed that to alienate a body as rich and numerous as the Dissenters would be very dangerous.[70] Buckingham's first priority, however, was to destroy Clarendon, who still had powerful friends who might try to restore him to office. Besides, Buckingham had many clients, who coveted the offices of Clarendon's followers. As the weeks went by, Charles talked more and more bitterly of his old servant, of his overbearing manner and his refusal to lay down his offices voluntarily. By the end of September he had ordered that charges should be prepared against him, though these were reportedly to stop short of treason. Clarendon was sufficiently concerned to offer to withdraw from London during the coming session; he also left Worcester House, to defuse allegations that he was conspiring with York.[71]

Parliament met on 10 October. Charles admitted that there had been miscarriages in the past, but he had now changed his policies and was resolved to give all possible satisfaction; in return, he was sure that they would provide for his needs. Bridgeman added that the scrutiny of accounts was to be left entirely to Parliament. The Commons voted to draw up an address of thanks for the king's gracious speech.[72] Charles insisted that it should include thanks for removing the chancellor; he got his way, but many suspected that the Commons would not have mentioned the matter had he not insisted.[73] This vote was merely the preliminary to an impeachment. While the Commons investigated the miscarriages of the war, Buckingham and his friends added to the list of charges prepared earlier others which amounted to treason. On 22 October the Earl of Conway wrote that Clarendon was doomed to die and that Charles would be the chief witness against him; Buckingham ruled all, thanks to his assurances that he could bring Parliament to give money – and indeed to make England as strong as it had been under Cromwell.[74] Arlington and Coventry had no wish to see Buckingham become all-powerful and opposed the impeachment as much as they dared. Coventry's credit was shaken when he produced a letter from the ever-popular Albemarle stating that the Dutch ships in the Thames could do no harm, while Arlington was pressed by the king to make his peace with Buckingham. On 26 October the Commons appointed a committee to consider how to proceed on an impeachment on capital charges.[75]

By now Buckingham, and Bristol, had convinced Charles that only Clarendon's condemnation and death could appease the Commons. James naturally disagreed, but he too was vulnerable. There was renewed speculation that Charles might send the queen to a nunnery or legitimate Monmouth; Charles's anger at Frances's elopement doubtless fuelled such speculation. Charles was angry that James had refused to support the address of thanks for Clarendon's removal and Buckingham tried to persuade the king that Clarendon might induce James to lead a revolt. Indeed, Ruvigny, one of the best informed of French ambassadors, ascribed Charles's hostility towards Clarendon mainly to fear of James.[76]

On 26 October the Commons debated some of the charges against the former chancellor. His friends demanded that witnesses should testify before the House; his enemies argued that these might be tampered with – it was sufficient that they should appear at the trial. Most of the charges were thus allowed to go forward on the basis of 'common fame' or the assertions of individual MPs that they could be proved. Many also claimed that the House could define 'treason': there was no need to adhere to the existing statutory definition. Some even tried to rake up the old story that Hyde had corresponded with Cromwell.[77] The House as a whole, however, was wary of stretching the law. Only one charge, that of betraying the king's counsels to his enemies, was voted to be treason – if it could be proved. The Commons resolved that the sale of Dunkirk and the claim that Clarendon had advised Charles to rule by an army did not amount to treason and a charge relating to the king's marriage was dropped.[78]

On 13 November the charges were taken up to the Lords. There, in the highest court in the land, Clarendon could expect more impartial treatment. The Commons were angry that the peers refused to commit the former chancellor to gaol on the basis of unspecified charges of treason. Aware of the weakness of their case, and jealous of their privileges, the Commons asserted that there was no need to be specific. Driven on by Buckingham, Charles canvassed many peers to comply with the Commons and raged at those who refused to do so (especially the bishops); James was freed from the need to commit himself by an attack of smallpox. Despite all the king's efforts, the Lords stood firm.[79] Their firmness was increased by news that the Commons' only charge of treason was decidedly shaky: Lisola, who had claimed that he had proof that Clarendon had leaked secrets to Louis, refused to produce it.[80] It became clear that the impeachment would fail and there was talk of convening a court of the lord steward, the body which tried peers when Parliament was not in session. Unlike the House, this had no fixed membership and could be packed with Clarendon's enemies, and it was this prospect which led him to seek the king's permission to go abroad. Charles refused to give him a pass, but hinted that he would be wise to go without one, advice echoed by his younger son Lawrence, Ruvigny and York. On 30 November he fled, leaving a paper to justify his conduct.[81] Even his friends thought that the paper was ill advised. By fleeing he implicitly acknowledged a measure of guilt, but by insisting on justifying himself he impugned the justice of Parliament: the Lords ordered that the paper be burned by the common hangman. A proposal for a bill of attainder, declaring him guilty of treason, was dropped, but a bill of perpetual banishment quickly passed both Houses.[82]

The proceedings against Clarendon form a sordid tale, from which few emerge with credit. The promoters of the impeachment showed a cynical disregard for natural justice and the rules of evidence: most hoped to profit from the redistribution of offices which was expected to follow the chancellor's disgrace. Pepys's cousin Roger said he had never known what knavery was until he came into the Commons, 'where there is nothing done but by passion and faction and private interest'. Few in high places showed the moderation of Coventry, who thought that Clarendon was unfit for administration, but had no wish to harm him.[83] The vindictiveness of Buckingham and Bristol was entirely predictable: far less so was Charles's willingness to support them so wholeheartedly. Buckingham boasted, or so Pepys heard, that he could govern Charles as he pleased; others thought that the king was so besotted with the new Duchess of Richmond that he cared for nothing else. He assured Madame that he was fully in control and that his authority would not suffer by his endorsing these proceedings: few believed him.[84]

It soon became clear that Clarendon's disgrace would not prove the panacea that Charles had been led to expect. Hitherto preoccupied with the impeachment proceedings, the House now turned its attention to the royal accounts and the mismanagement of the war.[85] This gave Buckingham the opportunity to extend his assault to Clarendon's allies and followers. He argued that the Commons would never give money so long as Charles retained in office those denounced by Parliament. For some months there had been talk that Ormond might be impeached, for allegedly favouring the interests of the Irish Catholics against those of the Protestant settlers.[86] Charles's order to investigate the imprisonment of Quakers led to reports of an imminent grant of liberty of conscience, reports given credence by his coldness towards the bishops, who had supported Clarendon almost to a man. He removed Sheldon from the council and refused to hear him preach at court. The bishops of Winchester and Rochester were dismissed from their places at court, while the one bishop who had consistently opposed Clarendon, Croft of Hereford, was made dean of the chapel royal. Charles was also heard to say that, if the clergy had done their job better, the peace of the kingdom would not be disturbed by conventicles.[87]

Shortly before Christmas, Parliament was adjourned, until 6 February. There had as yet been no talk of supply: Buckingham argued that this showed how necessary it was to take steps to please the Commons. A few of Clarendon's friends were dismissed, but the furious competition for their places merely added to the general rancour. Buckingham continued to play on Charles's fears of his brother; York responded in the best way he could, with meekness and submission. The king's debts continued to mount, but Charles showed little concern.[88] Ruvigny remarked that it was just as well that Buckingham was so inconsistent and capricious: a more single-minded individual with a comparable influence over the king would have damaged his affairs even more. It seemed that his standing might be shaken when he fought a duel and killed the Earl of Shrewsbury, the husband of his mistress. Castlemaine, however, was now firmly on his side and Charles's resentment of such peccadilloes rarely lasted for long.[89]

Apart from sweeping changes in office, Buckingham claimed that Parliament also wanted liberty of conscience, and bills were drafted for both comprehension and indulgence. During discussions involving Baxter and other London Presbyterians, it was intimated (as in 1660) that such proposals might win more support if there was also some provision for Catholics; Baxter, with more restraint than usual, replied that he was concerned only for a comprehension on the lines set out in the Worcester House Declaration. As for indulgence, Wilkins and Bridgeman proposed that those unable to accept even a more comprehensive Church should be allowed to worship publicly, but only in licensed meeting houses; preachers were to avoid reflections on the government. Conventicles – in other words, unlicensed meetings – were to remain illegal and nonconformists were to continue to be ineligible for public office. By late January it was widely known that the council had approved the comprehension bill and Buckingham and his cronies expressed confidence that it would pass. They were wrong: as soon as the Commons met they passed a resolution designed 'to prevent the bringing in the bill of comprehension which will be brought in and countenanced by very great persons'.[90]

Charles ignored the rebuff. He commended both comprehension and indulgence to the two Houses; the Commons called for a proclamation to enforce the laws against conventicles. Buckingham's allies in the Commons continued to press the matter, but after a long debate on 11 March discussion was adjourned for a month (in other words, *sine die*). The House also asked to see the text of the proclamation against Papists and conventicles; many MPs found it too mild. On the 13th it was resolved to bring in a new bill against conventicles, the old Act being about to expire. This was not totally incompatible with the court's plans for comprehension and a limited indulgence, but MPs showed great hostility to both. It was resolved that, for the new poll tax, all who had not received communion in the past year should pay double (although this was later dropped). The conventicle bill passed the Commons only to fail in the Lords, as relations between the Houses were disrupted by disputes over jurisdiction in the case of *Skinner* v. *the East India Company*. An attempt to refer the issue of comprehension to the king was easily rejected. Moves by Buckingham's followers to attack the bishops or to order the sale of dean and chapter lands to raise money for the crown won minimal support.[91]

Many MPs must have wondered why Charles should have countenanced men who advocated measures such as these, which were not only unpopular but also seemed against his interests. The answer was that Charles badly misread the mood of the House. He suspected that criticism of mismanagement was a cover for an assault on the prerogative and was sufficiently worried to accept the argument that only sweeping concessions could propitiate the House. Sir Richard Temple and others promoted a triennial bill, which would have restricted the king's power to call and dismiss Parliaments as much as the 1641 Act had done: it would, for example, have allowed no prorogation for longer than eighteen months. The Commons were clearly hostile and it was withdrawn.[92] It was claimed that Temple and his friends had 'undertaken' to manage Parliament, claiming that they could secure money in return for measures, like the triennial bill, which they claimed would be popular among MPs. If so, they were spectacularly unsuccessful. Backbenchers were always wary of being manipulated and most had no wish to curb the king's powers. When one 'undertaker' talked of 'compelling the king' the House was outraged: he asked pardon, claiming that he had really said 'compelling the thing'.[93]

After the failure of the comprehension scheme and the triennial bill, the undertakers switched to disruptive opposition.[94] They urged the House not to vote money until the mismanagement of the war had been fully investigated. Their motives remain uncertain. It seems likely that, when pressing for comprehension, they genuinely misread the mood of the House.[95] Thereafter they probably set out to show that Arlington could not manage Parliament either; given the earl's habit of trying to buy off critics, they probably also wished to demonstrate their nuisance value: even factious opposition could be a paying proposition. Finally, some hoped that if Charles could be induced to dissolve Parliament, a new one would be less Royalist and less hostile to Dissent. How far they had thought through the implications of their conduct is questionable: Buckingham tended to act on impulse and think only later (if at all). Like many of the undertakers, he had little respect for the prerogative and he may have been carried away by an image of himself as the people's hero. Some claimed that he wished to set himself up as another Cromwell, a claim given credence by his patronage of former Cromwellians and even the old Leveller, John Wildman.[96]

As the session limped from February to May, measures for the king's supply were opposed by those who not only claimed to act in the king's name but derived much of their credit in Parliament from his favour. Most backbenchers were not eager to vote money, especially as Charles had deceived them the previous year, securing money and then failing to send out the fleet. There was much talk of embezzlement: some urged that those responsible should be forced to disgorge their ill-gotten gains. The ex-undertakers played on such feelings, but the House agreed to raise £300,000, provided none was raised by either a land tax or a home excise.[97] After much obstruction, a bill was passed imposing duties on imported wines and spirits: as these were to be paid by the retailer, they were in practice (if not in theory) excises.[98] In all this, Charles did little to give a lead or to protect his prerogatives: he endorsed Temple's and Osborne's proposal that any money voted should be put into the hands of persons named by the Commons. Later, two more former undertakers, Sir Robert Howard and Edward Seymour, proposed that Parliament should appropriate part of the customs to support the fleet; the proposal was rejected, as implying distrust of the king.[99]

It might seem that Charles ought to have placed more trust in the Commons as a whole than in those who claimed they could manage it for him. As one MP remarked after the vote for the conventicle bill: 'The King, if he pleases, may take a right measure of our temper by this and leave off crediting the undertakers, who persuade him that the generality of the kingdom and of our House too is inclined to a toleration.'[100] The king was not so pleased, preferring to blame the intrigues of Clarendon's followers, just as a year before he had blamed those of Buckingham. This was the view fed to him by Arlington, who had claimed that, once the chancellor's malign influence was removed, the Commons would become far more tractable; there is every indication that Charles believed him.[101] Such arguments also helped Arlington – and others – maintain the rift between Charles and James. Temple, meanwhile, claimed that the session had been a failure only because Charles had not given the undertakers wholehearted support – in other words, a monopoly of office and power. In fact, the undertakers had contributed nothing to the session's one small success – the money bill: as

Arlington remarked, their insistence on raising religious issues had hindered the granting of money and they had impeded the supply bill at every stage.[102]

The fact that Charles seems to have accepted the analyses of Arlington, and even Temple, does not say much for his political sagacity. Not only did he fail to recover the goodwill of a basically well-intentioned House of Commons, but he placed his trust in men who seemed bent on disrupting his government and reducing his prerogatives. The adjournment typified much of what had gone before: it came after an acrimonious debate over Skinner's case, eagerly exploited by Buckingham, who hoped to force a dissolution, and brought to an end a session that had been directionless and sterile.[103] Since Clarendon's fall, it would seem not only that Charles was not directing affairs, but that he did not grasp what was going on. Yet at the same time he was embarking on a major diplomatic initiative, with repercussions that would profoundly alter the course of his reign.

The Treaty of Dover

Charles had sought a closer understanding with Louis since 1661. He had assumed that he and Louis were natural allies against the feeble Spanish and devious Dutch. He had been unpleasantly surprised to find that his young French cousin was a hard and exacting negotiator, who put the interests of his state and dynasty before considerations of kinship. Charles had also discovered that those who negotiated casually, without fully defining their positions, were liable to be worsted by others who were more careful; those who took a cavalier attitude towards promises were soon distrusted. By the time of the Treaty of Breda, Charles could look back at six years of Anglo-French disputes and misunderstandings: France had even declared war on England. How Charles broke out of the cycle of failure and distrust is the major theme of 1667–70, years when English perceptions of France were changing markedly. In the early 1660s, while the French were not popular in England, the Dutch (or even the Spanish) were seen as the national enemy. While France was still weak at sea, the Dutch were England's greatest rivals for trade and empire. England's trade with Spain was large and profitable, but intermittent hostilities continued, especially 'beyond the line'. By 1667 the picture was changing. The French navy and merchant marine were growing fast, thanks to Jean-Baptiste Colbert. France came to be England's most formidable competitor for empire, concerned (like the English, but unlike the Dutch) to settle and plant as well as to trade, and interested in the same areas – North America, the Caribbean, India. A growing web of protective tariffs made it harder and harder for English manufacturers to compete in French markets, while England continued to import French goods, especially wines and brandies. By the end of the 1660s English merchants were convinced that their balance of trade with France, unlike that with Spain, was profoundly unfavourable.

In 1667, however, English concern focused not on trade and empire but on Louis' ambitions in the Low Countries. Having carefully built up his military machine he swept through the Spanish Netherlands in 1667 with ominous ease; the speed of his success led de Witt to conclude a hasty peace with England. Many informed Englishmen now feared that Louis, like Philip II of Spain, aimed at universal empire: having overrun the Spanish Netherlands, he would conquer the Dutch Republic and then it would be England's turn. Charles's conduct in the 1670s would suggest that, while he saw France as a serious competitor for trade and colonies, he did not believe that she posed a direct military threat to England: indeed, he hoped to profit from French aggression against the Spaniards and Dutch. For the moment, however, Charles was in no position to undertake any major foreign policy initiative. His domestic political position in the latter part of 1667 was very weak: after a conspicuously unsuccessful war, he was very conscious of the need to placate public opinion. This was one of the considerations which underlay his treaty with the Dutch in 1668, which (with the adherence of Sweden) became the Triple Alliance. The treaty aimed both to halt French expansion into the Low Countries and to force the Madrid government to cede what it had already lost. Charles still, however, hankered after a closer liaison with Louis: after two years of convoluted negotiations they signed a treaty in which Charles committed himself to make war on the Dutch and to declare himself a Catholic.

Charles's motives – particularly for linking his 'conversion' to the alliance against the Dutch – must remain a matter for conjecture. Evidence is sparse. Few of his advisers knew of his 'conversion' and so the others conducted discussions blissfully unaware that what they were discussing was irrelevant to the main negotiation. Ralph Montagu, Charles's ambassador in Paris (and no stranger to deviousness), knew nothing of Charles's promise; nor, until late in 1669, did Louis' ambassador in London, the acerbic Colbert de Croissy, who many thought owed his appointment to his more famous brother. As a result, routine diplomatic correspondence throws little direct light on these transactions. For much of the time the historian must make do with chance survivals, notably drafts and other papers collected by Sir Thomas (later Lord) Clifford[1] and some miscellaneous items in the French foreign office archives. The most important of these is the surviving correspondence between Charles and Madame.[2] Although Charles had never been able to spend much time with her, he felt closer to her than to anyone. Madame endured an existence beset by ill-health, penury and her husband's tantrums: he drove away her female confidantes and blamed her for Louis' refusal to grant the favours he demanded for his favourite, the Chevalier de Lorraine. To devote herself to the interests of her adored brother offered a rare opportunity for escape and fulfilment. The fact that Louis liked her company made it possible for her to act as a discreet and effective go-between.

Charles's correspondence with Madame offers perhaps the best insight we have into his intentions in these years, but as a source the letters have their limits. They are not very numerous and are unevenly spaced in time, which would suggest that some have not survived. Some are short – Charles was not a keen letter writer – and others are maddeningly allusive or refer Madame to the bearer for further details. However, with their help and that of other scraps of evidence it is possible to build up a plausible, but not conclusive, explanation of Charles's conduct at a time when, for once, he was not content to react to events but sought to develop policies of his own.

Within days of the signing of the Treaty of Breda, Louis completed his instructions to Ruvigny, who was to return to London as ambassador. After referring to Charles's unreasonable behaviour in the past, Louis stressed his wish to establish a close understanding. Ruvigny was to avoid discussing trade: instead he should remind Charles that he had spoken to d'Estrades of the possibility of, first, mutal aid in case of rebellion and, second, joining to profit at the expense of the Habsburgs, Louis in Europe and Charles in the Indies.[3] Ruvigny found Charles eager to join with France, but fearful of the reactions of Parliament and of his subjects. Ruvigny hinted that, if he did not quickly agree terms with Louis, the Dutch (and Spaniards) might do so, leaving England isolated. Charles was still hesitant, but Buckingham was not. A fledgling statesman, eager to spread his wings, the duke assured Ruvigny that the people would welcome a French alliance provided England was assured of a share of Louis' conquests.[4] Parliament, he added, would give generously to support a foreign policy that brought glory and profit: he himself would cure the Houses of their aversion to France. 'Do what you please on land', he told Ruvigny grandly, 'and leave us a free hand at sea.'[5]

Such talk, airy though it might be, was what Louis wanted to hear. He told Ruvigny to stress to Charles that French gains in the Low Countries would pose no threat to England: indeed, the more powerful Louis became, the more his power would deter Charles's subjects from rebelling. Louis was ready to offer ships and money to help Charles seize Spanish possessions in the New World in return for Charles's sending troops to Flanders; he also hinted that he might abandon his 1662 treaty with the Dutch. Ruvigny, meanwhile, reported that it was generally believed that Buckingham could do as he wished and was more prepared to trust him than the cautious Arlington, who had a Dutch wife and was widely suspected of being pro-Spanish.[6] Most of the committee of foreign affairs, however, inclined to Arlington's view that, given Parliament's current mood, it would be danger-ous to embark on an unpopular French alliance. The most that Charles was prepared to offer was a benevolent neutrality: he would undertake not to act against France for (say) a year. In addition, Arlington argued that only a commercial treaty, to remove merchants' grievances, could make a French alliance acceptable in England. Ruvigny, fortified by Buckingham's assurances, urged Charles to ignore the committee's advice, but Charles refused to do so.[7]

By the beginning of December the king had apparently changed his mind. Arlington and Buckingham now talked of an offensive and defensive alliance against the Dutch; on the 12th (the day Charles adjourned Parliament) Arlington produced a draft treaty. When Ruvigny mentioned Louis' 1662 treaty with the Dutch, Charles said he could not see how Louis could be bound by that any longer. On closer inspection, however, it became clear that Charles would commit himself only to do nothing to aid the Spanish authorities in Brussels during the coming year and to conclude no agreement with the States General without Louis' consent. Ruvigny suspected that the English proposals constituted a desperate attempt to prevent a Franco-Dutch agreement to partition the Spanish Netherlands; for all their talk, commercial considerations would prevent the English from breaking with Spain. The ambassador was therefore startled when Buckingham demanded that the English should receive Ostend and Nieuwpoort in return for their 'assistance'.[8] Louis found these proposals completely unacceptable. His first priority was to pursue his claims in the Spanish Netherlands: he was prepared to make war on the Dutch only if they broke the 1662 treaty by aiding Louis' enemies. On the other hand, his designs in the Low Countries could be seriously impeded if the English and Dutch joined against him, so Louis insisted that Charles should make no new agreement with the Dutch without his consent. He was, however, prepared to offer various inducements to encourage Charles to attack the Spaniards. If he did so in Europe, Louis would secure a maritime town for him; if in the West Indies, Louis would assist him with ships and a small quantity of money.[9] His offer to facilitate English expansion in the Caribbean was, however, less than ingenuous: at this time he was negotiating with the emperor a partition of the Spanish lands on the death of Carlos II, in which the West Indies were to be part of the emperor's share.[10]

The English response was dilatory and evasive. Arlington alleged that Clarendon had signed a secret agreement not to aid the enemies of the King of Spain; Buckingham claimed that he was not yet sufficiently well established on the council to ensure that the proposals were accepted. Ruvigny complained bitterly of the sloth of the English and of Buckingham's unreliability.[11] For once, however, the appearance of inactivity was misleading. De Witt had watched Louis' progress in Flanders with alarm. The Spaniards were incapable of defending themselves, the Dutch did not want a land war against a vastly superior military power and Charles's government was too divided and vacillating to take resolute action. From this position of weakness, de Witt had offered his scheme of 'cantonment', to create a buffer state between France and the republic. Louis responded by telling the Spaniards that he would either keep what he had taken or accept towns and territories of equivalent economic and strategic value. De Witt found neither of these options palatable, but calculated that if Louis resumed hostilities, he would take more towns and increase his demands. (He was not to know that Louis' relative moderation was a consequence of his negotiations with the emperor: under the proposed partition, the Spanish Netherlands were to go to France.) De Witt therefore urged Castel Rodrigo, the governor in Brussels, to accept one or other of the French 'equivalents', but Castel Rodrigo had orders from Madrid to cede nothing.[12]

De Witt thus faced two linked problems: stopping the French military juggernaut and persuading the Spaniards to accept reality. He eagerly sought English support: Charles, still preoccupied with Parliament, responded cautiously. By the end of December, however, his ambassador at Brussels, Sir William Temple, came home to find the court very dissatisfied with Louis' proposals. Temple and Arlington capitalized on this and persuaded Charles to join with the Dutch to force the Spanish to come to terms. It seems likely that they stressed past instances of Louis' 'bad faith' (notably his 1662 treaty with the Dutch and his declaring war in 1666) and held out the prospect that a Dutch alliance would be popular, in Parliament and in the nation at large; it would also prevent a new agreement between France and the States General. Charles may have hoped, too, that news of this alliance would encourage a counter-bid from France, but that was rendered far less likely by a secret article in the treaty. While the main purpose was to bring Spain to accept one of Louis' equivalents, it was also agreed that if he failed to abide by his offers, the signatories would force him to return all that he had taken since the Treaty of the Pyrenees in 1659. The Swedes joined the alliance soon after, and other princes, notably the emperor, were to be invited to adhere.[13]

Charles claimed (to the French) that the sole purpose of the alliance was to make the Spaniards see reason: it was not aimed against France. He assured Louis of his undying friendship and of his desire for a close liaison once peace had been concluded.[14] The French were unimpressed: Lionne remarked that it was less than a year since Charles had promised to make no liaisons without Louis' consent in the coming twelve months. If Charles had any proposals, he added, the French would listen; but they would never trust Arlington again. Lionne, indeed, had never trusted Charles and had long believed that the best France could hope for was England's neutrality. The more bellicose Turenne, however, believed that England could prove a valuable ally against Spain: whatever Charles's past record, Louis should continue to seek his friendship. For the moment, however, Charles seemed to offer little more than kind words. When he raised the question of the

1662 treaty yet again, Ruvigny replied with some irritation that after six months he had still received no serious proposals and that details of their negotiations had been published by Lisola; Arlington apologized for the leak.[15] Meanwhile, the hope that the alliance would induce the Commons to vote money proved largely unfounded: £300,000 would not solve the king's financial problems. On the other hand, when Seymour and Sir Richard Temple proposed that the House should demand to see the league (presumably with a view to embarrassing Arlington) they won little support: this, they were told, was a matter for the king alone.[16]

If the Commons' response to the Triple Alliance was muted, the treaty nevertheless achieved its desired effect. For a while it seemed possible that Louis' response would be an attack on England – Charles felt impelled to put out a larger than usual fleet – but in the end, after months of tense and complex negotiations, peace was signed in May at Aix-la-Chapelle. Louis gained Lille, Charleroi, Douai, Oudenarde and other towns; Franche Comté, which he had recently conquered, was restored to Spain. Many at Louis' court – notably the soldiers Turenne and Condé and the war minister Louvois – had wished to continue the war and saw the peace as humiliating. Louis, they claimed, had abandoned lands to which he had a just title – and which he had the power to take. They stressed the wealth of the cities of the Low Countries and that they had served as a base for discontented elements during the Fronde. While knowledge of Charles's perfidy rankled, especially after the leaking of the secret article, French resentment focused on the Dutch, and their lack of gratitude for French help in their long struggle against Spain. Louis was particularly incensed by medals which claimed for the Dutch credit for bringing peace to Europe. No sooner had the peace been signed than Louis and the 'hawks' at his court began to plot the downfall of the republic.[17]

On 9 May 1668 Parliament was adjourned until August. Further adjournments followed, and a prorogation, so that it did not reconvene until 19 October 1669. In the meantime, the factional disputes, which had done so much to disrupt the last sessions of Parliament, continued unabated. At their heart lay the rivalry between Arlington and Buckingham. The former was assiduous and supple: while he could be haughty to those who posed no threat to him, he was generally pleasant and ingratiating. He found allies where he could and shifted his ground when necessary, but he was always vulnerable because of his association with the government during the Dutch War. Over the years he had established his friends and clients in the administration, notably the up and coming Clifford: Pepys noted that no patron 'endeavours more to raise those that he takes into favour than my Lord Arlington'.[18] Buckingham had not been prominent in government before the autumn of 1667 and could establish his clients in office only by ousting those of Clarendon – and Arlington: hence his eagerness to make accusations of mismanagement. His favour with the king depended on wit and sheer force of personality: 'there is no way to rule the king but by briskness, which the Duke of Buckingham hath above all men'.[19] He encouraged Charles to indulge his love of pleasure; Charles protected him in his japes and vendettas. When Lady Shrewsbury sent her servants to beat up Thomas Killigrew, for casting aspersions on her honour, Buckingham ensured that they went unpunished. When a London magistrate committed one of the king's doctors to gaol, despite the king's command to the contrary, Buckingham had the doctor released and the magistrate sent to gaol, and ordered that the constables who arrested the doctor should be whipped. (Of the magistrate, Sir Edmund Berry Godfrey, we shall hear more later.)[20]

Much of Buckingham's animus against Arlington stemmed from his conviction that the latter had wished to have him hanged at the time of his incarceration in the Tower. This element of bloodfeud explains why the duke was prepared to ally with almost anyone – even York – against Arlington, and why the reconciliations which Charles tried to arrange never lasted long. It was fortunate for Arlington that, thanks to his irregular lifestyle, Buckingham's influence on affairs was intermittent. He had no aptitude for paperwork and wished to be both a good Royalist and popular with the people: indeed, his standing with the king owed much to the credit he was said to possess among 'the factious'. He would carry the king to debauches or monopolize his attention when hunting, but then would disappear for days on end or stay up all night and sleep all day. Charles told his sister that his ministers did only as he would have them do: few believed him. Pepys was told 'how the king is made a child of by Buckingham and Arlington'. With both exercising such a strong influence and neither able to establish an unchallenged ascendancy, Charles's government lacked direction and purpose. As a result, the long period between sessions of Parliament saw much infighting and little achievement, especially at home. Nevertheless, other influences (notably that of James) began to make themselves felt and by early 1670 were playing a considerable role in decision-making.[21]

Those most at risk from Buckingham's vindictiveness were James and the queen. One of the few things on which Buckingham and Arlington agreed was that Clarendon must never return. Although he had been banished, they feared that Charles might pardon him, out of kindness of heart or at the behest of Louis XIV. Both sought assurances from France that the former chancellor would spend the rest of his days in exile. Their fears were not unfounded: James pressed his brother to allow the earl to return, while Cornbury continued to assert his innocence. Charles responded that he would not resent any kindnesses shown to the old man, provided he remained in exile.[22] James's support for Clarendon (and fear of his vengeance should he ever become king) led Buckingham to play on Charles's fear of his brother's ambition and to try to destroy York's clientele, especially in the navy. Knowing that he could never compete with Buckingham's 'briskness', James sought to reassure his brother by a display of stolid obedience.[23] Having achieved little success in his efforts to induce the Commons to hound men out of office, Buckingham tried to secure the same ends by lobbying the king; failing that, he promoted investigations by privy council committees, or special commissions, whose membership and proceedings he and his allies could influence more directly. James, alarmed, took steps to remedy abuses in the navy office before others did it for him.[24] He was unable to prevent Anglesey's removal from his post as treasurer of the navy, which led to rumours that he too might be dismissed and the post of lord admiral be put into commission.[25] There was also renewed talk that Charles would legitimate Monmouth.[26]

James weathered the storm. In December 1668 Buckingham suddenly made him an offer of service and friendship. James scornfully rejected it, remarking that Buckingham had never kept his promises in the past. Pressed on the question of Monmouth, Charles declared that he regarded York as his heir and had total confidence in him. Some ascribed Buckingham's *volte face* to the growth of Arlington's credit with the king; it seems more likely that Charles at last resolved to rouse himself from his lethargy, in domestic as in foreign policy. The Archbishop of Canterbury, disgraced twelve months earlier, now reappeared at court.[27] York also had an improbable ally, in Castlemaine. Charles's unbridled passion was a thing of the past, but they remained good friends. Having driven out Clarendon, she applied herself to promote what she saw as Charles's best interests – as well as profiting to the utmost from the favour she enjoyed. She and James agreed in disliking any suggestion that Charles should divorce the queen, who was a far less serious rival to Castlemaine than a new and younger queen would be.[28] By early 1669 she was resisting attempts to remove Cornbury from office and she was given much of the credit for reconciling Charles and James. Charles still visited her regularly, to see the children, but the talk often turned to politics; when she fell ill, he insisted on treating her himself. In 1670 he created her Duchess of Cleveland, in her own right: no longer did her title depend on her husband.[29]

If Castlemaine's stock remained high, the queen's did not. In May 1668 she miscarried; this time even Charles believed that she had been pregnant, although he had earlier feared her incapable of conceiving.[30] Her pregnancy temporarily halted talk of a divorce. When she conceived again in 1669 Charles was assiduous in his attentions; when she miscarried he forbade anybody to suggest that she had been pregnant. With the king confused and irresolute, Buckingham again began to talk of divorce and Charles slept with his wife even more rarely than before.[31]

Buckingham's greatest success came not with James or the queen but with Ormond. Despite – or maybe because of – his great wealth and rank, Ormond did not affect the haughty superiority that had done so much to ruin Clarendon. His status, his easy dignity and a generation of service to the crown had made him the obvious man to be Lord Lieutenant of Ireland. Great though his credit was, however, he was not invulnerable. He was diligent and honest, but not the most efficient of administrators, particularly where money was concerned; he also had a principled objection to diverting money from the Irish revenue into the pockets of English courtiers and politicians. The land settlement over which he presided inevitably made him many enemies. So much land had passed from old Catholic to new Protestant proprietors that it would be impossible to satisfy them all without, as Ormond remarked, a new Ireland.[32] Under the Acts of Settlement and Explanation, some Catholics adjudged 'innocent' of involvement in the 1641 rebellion were able to recover their lands. This, and the fact that Ormond was compensated for some of the great losses he had incurred, opened the way for dissatisfied Protestant 'adventurers' to claim that Ormond was biased in favour of the Papists; he may also have stretched his legal powers when dealing with the 'disaffected' in Ireland in the early 1660s. Buckingham, naturally, was eager to take up the adventurers' cause.

In October 1667 Ormond's enemies began to make allegations of misgovernment in Ireland, but the Commons showed only limited interest.[33] Ormond was still worried: he came over to England in May 1668, but his position was much stronger than Clarendon's had been, faced with the combined hostility of Arlington and Buckingham. After an initial coolness, Arlington had established a close working friendship with Ormond, helped by the fact that Arlington and Ossory both married daughters of Lodewijk van Beverweert, a kinsman of the Prince of Orange. Clarendon's fall imposed a strain on their relationship: Arlington's letters became somewhat defensive, while Ormond felt it necessary to assure the secretary that he had no intention of pressing for Clarendon's return (or of joining with York).[34] Even so, the very fact that Buckingham was eager to remove Ormond would make Arlington equally eager to defend him, if he felt it politically safe to do so.

In mid-July Charles sent Buckingham and Osborne to Tunbridge Wells to speak with Bridgeman, who was about to issue a commission to enquire into the Irish revenue. Ormond thought that it was aimed at Anglesey, vice-treasurer and receiver-general from 1661 to 1667 and widely regarded as neither competent nor honest. Ormond was not, however, reassured by the news that the commissioners were mostly his personal enemies. He was especially concerned at the activities of the Earl of Orrery, an experienced and unscrupulous politician, who possessed the financial expertise that Ormond lacked.[35] This, and the addition of Osborne, made many suspect that Ormond was the real target, but in September the duke wrote smugly that his enemies had been unable to make good their charges: Charles had no reason to dismiss him, and he would not resign.[36]

Having failed to make a convincing case against Ormond's financial management, his enemies fell back on court intrigue. Osborne and Bridgeman tried to persuade Arlington to join Buckingham in pressing to remove the viceroy; they sweetened the pill by proposing that Ossory should be one of the lords justices who would take over from Ormond – government by commission again – but Ormond and Ossory refused to co-operate and so, after some hesitation, did Arlington. Like Clarendon, Ormond calculated that, if an old servant refused to resign, Charles would be very reluctant to dismiss him.[37] Orrery and his allies had one success: Charles suspended Anglesey, after a woefully inept performance before the commission of enquiry. Anglesey had recently become treasurer of the navy: he was replaced by Osborne and Sir Thomas Littleton, protégés respectively of Buckingham and Arlington: York, who was not consulted, was deeply hurt.[38] It seemed that Buckingham's power knew no bounds. Many thought that Ormond, and even York, would be dismissed. Arlington hinted to Ormond that he was too closely linked to 'men unsatisfied' – apparently York and Sheldon. There was talk of a dissolution and of a new, Presbyterian House of Commons, which would confiscate the Church's lands and solve all the crown's financial problems. Ormond's dismissal would thus be linked to Charles's abandoning the Church for the Dissenters – and their great patron Buckingham. Arlington, it was said, would go along with this, as he was not strong enough to stop it.[39]

Then, early in December, the atmosphere changed. Charles declared that he would neither dissolve Parliament nor legitimate Monmouth and had a long conference with Sheldon. Buckingham, sensing a change, sought to be reconciled to James, and was rebuffed. Talk of Ormond's dismissal receded: Charles assured him that he had full confidence in him.[40] Such assurances were worth little. On 14 February 1669 he told the committee for foreign affairs that he was removing Ormond from his post: this implied no reflection on the duke's thirty years of service and he would still admit him to his most secret affairs. His successor was not Orrery but Lord Robartes, a morose and difficult man, with Presbyterian inclinations. Ormond challenged the king to tell him to his face that he was sacked; Charles denied it, but later sent word that Ormond was indeed dismissed and that the king had not wished to quarrel with him.[41]

Much remains obscure about Ormond's removal. Sir Ellis Leighton, an associate of Buckingham's of doubtful veracity, claimed that Arlington had joined with the duke to ruin Ormond. Arlington suggested that the decision to dismiss the viceroy was a *fait accompli*: he urged Ormond to bow to the king's will with good grace. Croissy thought that Arlington seemed distressed, but that would not prove that he had not joined with Buckingham against Ormond.[42] Ormond, and others, blamed Buckingham and Orrery, but most (apart from Leighton) saw Robartes's appointment as a defeat for Buckingham: it may have been intended to placate Arlington.[43] Charles was reported to have been very troubled the night before the decision was announced, but Croissy ascribed this to an unrequited passion for one of Castlemaine's ladies.[44] It is possible that Charles believed that a new lord lieutenant would manage the revenue better and make Ireland a source of profit rather than loss. However, if Ormond had been removed for that reason, he would presumably have been removed the previous summer; the commission of enquiry had failed to pin anything on him and it would have been perfectly possible to reform the finances while he remained in overall charge.[45]

If the duke was not dismissed for financial reasons, was it part of a move towards a policy of toleration, designed to favour Dissent and Catholicism? If it was, it could be linked to Charles's statement on 25 January (to be more fully discussed below) that he intended to announce his conversion.[46] One problem with such an argument is that the motives behind that statement are far from clear. Neither York nor Madame saw Ormond's removal as necessary for the 'Catholic design' and Charles took pains to assure his sister that his favour for Ormond was undiminished.[47] The instructions drafted for Robartes – apparently after considerable controversy, but also after consultation with Ormond – not only praised the outgoing viceroy but also ordered his successor to pursue much the same policies; all members of the army were to take the oaths of allegiance and supremacy on pain of dismissal.[48] Another problem is that Charles's attitude towards Dissent was equivocal: he was far from committing himself to abandon the Church. In December he declared, with unusual firmness, that he had no intention of dissolving the present Parliament. A few days later, however, he decided to prorogue Parliament until 19 October: Buckingham's influence seemed as great as ever and he and Arlington went through one of their periodic reconciliations. The two did not agree on much, but they did agree that the Commons – any Commons – would demand the punishment of those seen as responsible for the misgovernment of recent years. Charles seems to have accepted this – and that those punished should include Anglesey and Ormond. He needed, he believed, to cleanse the government and to show that he would not tolerate incompetence or malversation.[49] It has been argued, very reasonably, that Charles would not have removed Ormond unless he stood to 'gain' by it.[50] One could see 'gain', however, in terms of damage limitation rather than positive advantage: he had dismissed Clarendon in the fond hope that this would placate the Commons and he may well have been persuaded that Ormond's removal would serve the same purpose. As it turned out, Buckingham and Orrery were to find that the great duke was now to deploy his formidable influence at Charles's court, rather than at a distance from Dublin.

If Ormond's dismissal had some of the marks of tragedy, Sir William Coventry's had all the trappings of farce. Charles found his talk of application and duty unpleasantly reminiscent of Clarendon; Buckingham despised his diligence and earnestness. Together with Sir Robert Howard, Buckingham wrote a play, *The Country Gentleman*, whose characters included Sir Cautious Trouble-all, a fussy and pretentious bureaucrat, who was clearly modelled on Coventry. Coventry sent the duke a message, which was seen as a challenge to a duel. Charles affected to be outraged by the challenge to a privy councillor; he may also not have understood why Coventry was so angry – he had seen a copy of the play, but with the offending scene removed. For Buckingham, Coventry's disgrace was a triumph, rendered all the sweeter by the fact that York had interceded in vain on the poor man's behalf. Others felt differently: at least fifty carriages a day carried well-wishers to visit the fallen minister.[51]

Moving from personalities to policies, three linked issues preoccupied Charles's government at home: the revenue, Parliament and religion. The supply voted in 1668 was at best a palliative: the crown's revenues remained insufficient to cover expenditure, thanks in part to the disruption caused by plague and the Fire and to the backlog of debt from the war. A scheme of retrenchment was drawn up and the treasury commission began to impose restraints on spending.[52] The crown had few saleable assets: there was talk of selling fee-farm rents, payable on land granted away in the past by the crown, but for now the project was shelved.[53] It was clear that any meaningful increase in revenue could come only from Parliament, which raised two questions. First, should the king keep the present Parliament or call another? Second, if the former, when should it meet?

In April 1668 it was reported that Arlington was urging Charles to dissolve Parliament, but that Albemarle had declared that he would leave England if he did so. There was little real debate about extending the adjournment from August to November – MPs never liked coming to town at harvest time – but in the interim Buckingham, Arlington and Lauderdale were reported to be pressing for a longer delay, Arlington because he feared to be charged with maladministration. Ormond smugly remarked that those who had encouraged the Commons to attack ministers were now reaping what they had sown.[54] Following a further adjournment, to 1 March, there was talk of a dissolution and of solving the crown's financial problems by the sale of dean and chapter lands, to which the present House of Commons would never agree. Buckingham, however, relished the idea of striking a blow at the clergy and it was reported that the Dissenters had promised to give great sums in return for freedom of worship.[55] Against Buckingham and Arlington, who favoured a dissolution, were ranged York, Albemarle, Sheldon and Bridgeman, who urged Charles to allow Parliament to meet at the appointed time. Weeks of furious intrigue ended in a compromise: Parliament was to be prorogued from 1 March until 19 October, thus aborting all the business left incomplete in May, including the conventicle bill and the disputes about Skinner's case. Thus the Cavalier House of Commons was preserved, but its reassembling was delayed for more than six months, which many saw as the first step towards a dissolution: the anxiety of the existing MPs was shown when two hundred appeared for the prorogation ceremony.[56] Despite continuing talk of the confiscation of dean and chapter lands, Charles had decided by May that Parliament should reconvene as scheduled. York had stressed the loyalty of the existing House and Bridgeman told the king (after he had made his decision) that he could answer for neither the king's powers nor the peace of the kingdom if Charles called a new Parliament. Arlington set out to win the support of those MPs most likely to make trouble, but it was clear that Charles was far from confident about the way the Commons would behave.[57]

The court's uncertainty was reflected in its ecclesiastical policy, or rather policies, as there were two basic alternatives. One was to persist with the line which the king had followed since 1663, upholding the Act of Uniformity and persecuting nonconformists. This policy, supported by York, Sheldon and Ormond, would be welcomed by the present House of Commons. The other policy, a combination of comprehension and indulgence, was espoused by Buckingham, Ashley, Lauderdale and maverick bishops like Croft and Wilkins. As the introduction of comprehension would require an Act of Parliament, until that body met debate centred on the extent to which the existing laws should be enforced. The advocates of the second policy talked of the Dissenters' great numbers and wealth and claimed that giving them satisfaction in religion would reduce them to political quiescence. In addition, it was claimed that religious liberalization would stimulate the economy, by encouraging immigration; it was sometimes linked to other proposed reforms, such as a land registry (to simplify sales and transfers) and a general naturalization, to make it easier for foreign craftsmen to settle in England. Such views were widely held on the committee of trade, which was dominated by supporters of liberty of conscience.[58]

Forced to choose between these alternatives Charles vacillated. He had endorsed the comprehension bill in February 1668, only to have it rejected out of hand by the Commons. The Conventicle Act of 1664 was to lapse at the end of the current session, which came with the prorogation of March 1669 (although some thought it had lapsed at the adjournment the previous May). Even before it expired nonconformists were confident that their friends in high places, notably Buckingham, would protect them.[59] In September orders were issued that nobody who failed to meet the requirements of the Corporation Act should be admitted to municipal office, but these seem to have had little effect.[60] In November some leading Presbyterians thanked the king for tacitly allowing them to meet and promised to be good and peaceable subjects. This was not spontaneous: Charles had let Dr Manton know, through the Presbyterian doctor and lobbyist Sir John Baber, that he would be glad to receive such an address. In a secret meeting, Charles told Manton that he would willingly try to secure comprehension, but that something had to be done for the public peace and in the meantime he wished them to avoid scandal. Their meetings were too 'numerous', which brought the law into disrepute and would make it difficult to bring his plans to fruition. Charles was particularly eager that persons of quality should give a lead, meeting either discreetly or not at all: he cared little about the poor and ignorant 'riffle-raffle', whose opinions and example counted for nothing. The address was duly presented, but the 'cabinet council' decided not to make it public.[61]

This episode might seem to suggest that Charles inclined towards comprehension, but his assurances of goodwill were studiously vague and his main concern was 'the public peace': he saw conventicles as a problem of order, not of conscience. The interview with Manton took place when Buckingham's influence was at its height and when there was much talk of using Church lands to solve the crown's financial problems. Rumours of the meeting leaked out and encouraged nonconformists to meet more openly, which was precisely what Charles did not want. On the other hand, although Charles's icy reserve towards Sheldon suddenly thawed, this led to no immediate measures against Dissent, apart from a firm order to suppress conventicles in Newcastle.[62] A flurry of nonconformist activity, following the lapsing of the Conventicle Act in March, brought the matter to the king's attention once more: the judges were ordered to proceed against unlicensed preachers under the Five Mile Act, which was still in force. Pepys noted that Charles was 'hot' against conventicles, but suspected that his attitude would change when Buckingham returned to court. This time, however, Charles was resolute and in April Croft resigned as dean of the chapel royal.[63]

On 15 April the committee for foreign affairs discussed conventicles. Bridgeman and Arlington doubted whether they were seditious; they claimed that the laws against them were adequate and that any new severity could drive the Dissenters to despair. Buckingham declared that these were trading people and that it was in the kingdom's interest to promote trade. Charles, however, complained that Dissenters bragged of his indulgence towards them. He wished JPs to enquire whether conventicles were becoming more numerous and why the laws were not being fully enforced. York, now a secret Catholic, declared that he wished all were of one religion, but, as they were not, the religion of the state should be supported. Ormond complained that there were meetings almost at the gates of Whitehall and that Dissenters had kept Charles out of his kingdom.[64] The upshot was that orders were issued to investigate complaints of scandalous meetings on the pretence of religion; if these endangered the peace, or affronted the established Church, they were to be suppressed and the preachers were to be prosecuted.[65] Among those arrested was Baxter, who was imprisoned for refusing the oath in the Five Mile Act. He found Orrery, Arlington and Buckingham sympathetic, but was told that Charles insisted that magistrates should do their duty and that the law should take its course.[66]

Having helped to persuade Charles that nonconformity threatened public order, Sheldon sought to press home his advantage. He ordered his bishops to gather information about the illegal meetings in their dioceses, including the numbers present and the names of the ringleaders. The bishops were to try to suppress them, where necessary seeking the help of the civil magistrate; if JPs failed to do their duty, the king was to be informed.[67] He asked the Bishop of London whether some people went to several conventicles, thus making nonconformists seem more numerous than they really were, and whether 'they might be easily suppressed ... the greatest part of them, as I hear, being women, children and inconsiderable persons'.[68] Well aware that Charles's attitude towards Dissent was determined mainly by considerations of order, Sheldon here sought to counter the claim that Dissenters were so numerous that any attempt to suppress them would lead to serious disorders; he was to apply the same approach more systematically in the Compton Census. A few weeks later Sheldon reiterated his orders and urged the bishops to come up for the next session of Parliament.[69]

These orders, from the king and the archbishop, led to a flurry of investigation and repression.[70] As there was some uncertainty as to which laws were in force, the judges were consulted; they declared that all assemblies that disturbed the peace were punishable under common law.[71] Orders were issued to suppress conventicles in a number of garrison towns.[72] A group of Dissenters, probably encouraged by Buckingham, presented a petition in which they threatened to take their skills abroad if persecution continued. Before it was presented Charles asked the council's advice. York told him that he should forbid all unlawful assemblies, adding waspishly that Buckingham was too busy attending conventicles to come to the council. Buckingham replied that the Presbyterians controlled the manufactures of the kingdom: if they were treated badly, the economy would be ruined. Charles silenced them both, commanding them to be friends, but York's viewpoint carried the day. A proclamation declared that conventicles had become more numerous, threatened the public peace and were to be suppressed.[73]

The impact of the proclamation varied. Some JPs responded vigorously, suppressing many conventicles; elsewhere (not least in London) little was done.[74] Sheldon was very conscious that the laws were inadequate: the Five Mile Act applied only to preachers, and JPs were clearly reluctant to proceed against meetings as seditious. He also complained that some had strange interpretations of the Act of Uniformity and he looked to Parliament, and fresh legislation, for a remedy. Some advocated using the recusancy laws, which required attendance at church, as the best means of bringing Dissenters to conform, but Charles did not agree: he was against forcing people to attend church against their consciences, but could not excuse those who attended unlawful meetings, which were (he thought) always dangerous to the government.[75] In dealing with Dissent, Charles's criteria were those, not of right and wrong, but of feasibility: *could* it be suppressed? In England, as in Scotland,[76] he vacillated for much of his reign between indulgence and repression. Late in 1669, as the meeting of Parliament grew near, he increasingly inclined towards the latter.

Charles's inclination towards repression was closely linked to his decision to retain the Cavalier House of Commons. The decision had been opposed by Buckingham and Arlington, who both feared attack and so were unlikely to offer firm or constructive leadership in the coming session. Buckingham, indeed, conscious that Ormond remained influential, renewed his efforts to discredit him; there were also moves to recall Robartes.[77] In this power vacuum it seemed that Charles might find a new chief minister in Orrery, especially as he had a reputation as a financial wizard: although some claimed that Charles devoted more attention to financial matters than to anything else, it is far from clear that he understood them. He was encouraged to look to Orrery by Castlemaine, who denounced Arlington as timid and pusillanimous, ready to sacrifice his master's interests to save himself; Buckingham, of course, could hardly be seen as a serious administrator.[78] As the new session drew near, Charles's affairs seemed in their usual disarray. Arlington and Buckingham were still at odds; the latter, indeed, was ill and two council meetings were held at his bedside. Clifford urged that the king's supporters in the Commons should press for a land tax, but he was opposed so vehemently by Buckingham and Orrery that Charles vetoed the proposal.[79] The long interval between sessions thus ended as it had begun, with the king's government paralysed by infighting and indecision. Nothing suggested that Charles was capable of formulating and pursuing decisive policies. And yet, at this very time, he embarked on a major new strategy in foreign policy which was to alter the course of his reign.

The Triple Alliance and the Treaty of Aix-la-Chapelle not only interrupted, but changed the content of, Charles's negotiations with Louis. Previously, three main points had been discussed: first, an offensive and defensive alliance against the Dutch; second, the acquisition of towns in the Southern Netherlands in return for English aid against Spain; and third, French help for the English in the Caribbean. Of these, the second was ruled out by England's commitment to the Treaty of Aix, while the third was rendered increasingly inappropriate, not only by Louis' secret promise that Spain's possessions in the New World should eventually go to the emperor, but also by improving Anglo-Spanish relations. The Treaty of Madrid, ratified by Spain in September 1667, resolved many commercial differences and was widely seen as 'the best peace that ever England had with them'; it was followed by a similarly advantageous colonial treaty in 1670. Meanwhile, Spain's recognition of Portuguese independence in 1668 freed Charles from an embarrassing obligation and removed an ongoing source of friction between England and Spain. The prospect of improved trade with the Spanish Netherlands was also one reason for Charles's agreeing to the Triple Alliance, as it gave England a vested interest in their preservation.[80]

As we have seen, Louis chose to pin most of the blame for the Triple Alliance on the Dutch – and on Arlington. Charles continued to claim that the Alliance was designed mainly to bring the Spanish to see reason. He (and James) still talked of his wish for a close understanding with Louis, as between one gentleman and another. Ruvigny, annoyed that his earlier proposals had been leaked, insisted that Charles should make the first move, but Louis was inclined to see Charles as sincere.[81] When Charles sent St Albans to Paris in June, he found a general disposition to join with England and was assured, in effect, that the French no longer considered themselves bound by their treaty with the Dutch. (No doubt they chose to interpret the Triple Alliance as a hostile act.) When St Albans tried to find out how much they were prepared to pay for Charles's friendship, however, they were less forthcoming.[82]

Despite these encouraging signs, Charles made no positive move: Ruvigny thought that Arlington had persuaded him that, as a matter of honour, he should not make the first proposals. Worried by rumours of a Franco-Dutch agreement to partition the Spanish Netherlands when Carlos died, Charles told Ruvigny that only mistrust prevented the conclusion of a full offensive and defensive league between Louis and himself.[83] In an effort to break the deadlock, Louis recalled Ruvigny and sent Croissy in his stead. Louis told the new ambassador that, as a first step to a full union, he wished Charles to agree that neither king should conclude any agreement without the other's approval. While Louis no longer felt himself bound by his treaty with the Dutch, he had been perturbed by Charles's failure to abide by the assurances he had given in the letter he had entrusted to his mother. Louis therefore needed an unequivocal promise that Charles would not embark on any negotiations with the Dutch, against whom Louis was ready to take any measures that Charles wanted; Croissy was not, however, to reveal this until he had received some positive proposals from Charles. If the English talked of a commercial treaty, Croissy was to hint that Louis might still heed Dutch proposals to partition the Spanish Netherlands. Louis saw Charles as potentially useful, but not as worthy of respect: he remarked that ladies loved adventurers and that he (Louis) was no less honest for not having been driven out of his kingdom.[84]

Croissy soon found, like his predecessors, that dealing with the English was frustrating. Charles was full of expressions of goodwill, but stressed that a French alliance would be very unpopular and that France should take steps to make it less so – first, by a commercial treaty, to remedy what were seen as unfair tariff policies and trading practices and, second, by halting Louis' naval shipbuilding programme, which threatened England's pre-eminence in the Narrow Seas. The French, with some plausibility, blamed Arlington for inducing Charles to make such stipulations, but Buckingham advanced similar arguments. Louis responded with a certain irritation, not least to Charles's claim that he should have accepted the terms proposed by the English in December, but he determined to plod on.[85] The negotiating process was not helped by a privy council order that Charles should discuss public affairs with ambassadors only if they sought a formal audience. Given Charles's penchant for discussing such matters in an informal setting (such as the queen's bedchamber) it could well be that this order was a ploy by those close to the king to play on his concern for honour and protocol in order to restrict the access he allowed to Croissy.[86] The ambassador now saw Charles far less frequently and much of Croissy's information about his intentions came second-hand, above all from Leighton. Charles appointed commissioners to work on a commercial treaty, but they showed little urgency – and Croissy even less. Buckingham talked of his zeal for union, but insisted that there were matters to settle at home first, above all the destruction of Ormond. He and Leighton also stressed that a closer union would be possible only if Clarendon remained in exile.[87]

It is difficult, as always, to assess Buckingham's motives. He may have supported a close link with France simply because Arlington was against it; Croissy thought he wanted war with the Dutch because he yearned for military glory; and he told the ambassador that a successful war would be popular with Parliament. Buckingham's immediate concern, however, was to destroy his rivals at court.[88] He sent Leighton to Paris with letters, from Charles and himself, to Madame, the queen mother and St Albans, stating that Charles wished them to esteem Buckingham: in other words, he hoped to use support from the French court to strengthen his position in Charles's. Louis regarded Buckingham as better intentioned than Arlington, but wished he would apply himself more.[89] Meanwhile, Croissy told Charles that Louis no longer felt bound by his treaty with the Dutch. He got the impression that Charles would be happy to damage Dutch trade, if that could be achieved without open war; Charles stressed the benefits of England's trade with Spain. In a rare private audience in November, Croissy assured him that Louis had no intention of breaking with Spain or of dragging him into a war against the Dutch; indeed, Louis accepted that Charles's first priority was to consolidate his position at home. Charles replied in generalities, but expressed resentment that a Dutch captain at Leghorn had flown a captured English flag below that of the States General: he expected satisfaction, he said, and talked of the need to punish those whose negligence had made possible the attack on the Medway.[90]

This was the first occasion on which Croissy reported Charles expressing hostility to the Dutch: earlier, when he had sounded Charles about William, he had expressed little interest.[91] By the spring of 1669, by contrast, Charles was to speak often of Dutch 'insults' and of the humiliation of the Medway disaster.[92] For the time being, however, his comments about the captain at Leghorn seemed no more than a momentary flash of anger; Charles talked far more of English worries about the growth of the French navy, and his courtiers were preoccupied by Buckingham's vendetta against Ormond. Buckingham, indeed, told Croissy that it would take a year or two to bring his plans to fruition, but added that France should allow the English commercial advantages in return for an alliance: if Louis would allow the English to become the greatest merchants, they would not object to his becoming the greatest conqueror.[93]

Thus far there had been no indication that Charles's objectives amounted to more than a vague desire for closer links with France and an equally vague feeling that his subjects needed to be reassured about the threats posed by France's growing commercial and naval power. Then on 14 December he sent Madame a cipher and told her that he would prorogue Parliament until October, by which time there would be fewer miscarriages to investigate. Around this time James, who was considering conversion to Catholicism, asked him 'if he continued in [the] same mind as to his religion'. Charles said he did and wanted nothing more than to be instructed; he would, he said, consult with Lord Arundell of Wardour (a Catholic), Arlington and Clifford.[94] On 25 January 1669, the feast of the conversion of St Paul, Charles held a private meeting at which these three, and James, were present.

He said it was distressing not to be able to profess the faith in which he believed. He asked their advice how best to settle the Catholic religion in his kingdoms and when he should declare himself a Catholic. There would be great difficulties, he knew, but he and James were in their prime: they should act now, not when they had grown old and feeble. With tears in his eyes, he urged them to act as wise men, and good Catholics, should. After much discussion, it was decided that the first step should be to establish a close liaison with France; Arundell was to be sent to conclude one.[95]

The above account is based on the memoirs which James wrote, on and off, for most of his life. They are inaccurate on some points: for example, they say that Croissy was to be informed of the secret at once, whereas he was told nearly a year later. There is no doubting the central fact, however: Charles now linked the proposed French alliance to the announcement of his conversion. But why? James clearly found the certainty and authority of Catholicism psychologically reassuring. He thought in terms of simple polar opposites – right and wrong, obedience and disobedience. Having decided that Rome was the one true Church, he saw no need to trouble his limited mind with awkward questions about life, death and salvation. He told Burnet that he could never match him in theological debate, but that did not matter so long as he knew where the ultimate truth lay.[96]

Charles was very different. Whereas James was racked with guilt by his inability to control his sexuality, Charles was a free spirit, who believed he was absolved from, or above, the constraints of conventional morality. Sceptical about received wisdom, he had a highly personal view of God, as a deity who had a special relationship with kings – and a special indulgence towards their weaknesses. Unlike James, he would find it far from easy to submit his conduct to the guidance of a priest and his judgement to that of the Church. And yet this is precisely what he declared he would do. The fact that he did not go through with it has naturally led historians to assume that he never intended to and to devise ingenious explanations for his conduct. His insincerity has been taken for granted: true, he reportedly had tears in his eyes, but he seems to have been able to summon tears at will. Some have seen his 'conversion' as a device to extract more money from Louis, although their negotiations had not yet progressed to the point of talking about money.[97] Others suggest that by giving precedence to the announcement of his conversion, which Louis could hardly oppose, Charles sought to seize control of the timing of the forthcoming war with the Dutch. Nothing explicit had yet been said about fighting the Dutch, however: indeed, Croissy had recently assured Charles that Louis had no intention of dragging him into such a war.[98] Alternatively, the issue of conscience may have been raised in order to overcome Arlington's hostility to the French alliance. It is certainly not easy to explain why Arlington and Clifford, neither of them Catholics at this stage, should have been summoned to the conference on 25 January. Even so, Arlington was always inclined to yield to *force majeure* (as he did over Ormond's dismissal) and it seems probable that, if Charles had asserted himself, he would have fallen into line.[99] Perhaps the most plausible argument is that the 'conversion' was a gesture of good faith, an attempt to cut through the miasma of distrust that had bedevilled Anglo–French relations since 1660. In telling Louis of his intended declaration, Charles entrusted him with a secret so compromising that to reveal it would ruin him – a gesture of trust if ever there was one.[100]

All these explanations rest on the assumption that Charles was capable of formulating sophisticated long-term strategies. Devious and duplicitous he could certainly be, not least in denying responsibility for actions for which he was likely to be reproached: note his refusal to admit to Ormond's face that he had dismissed him. Since Clarendon's fall, policies and politics had been tossed hither and thither on the winds and tides of faction. One week Buckingham and Arlington were enemies, the next they were friends; one week Ormond and York seemed doomed, the next they were basking in the king's favour. If one accepts that Charles's 'conversion' (or 'Catholicity') was not likely to have been part of a grand strategy, the most plausible explanations of those advanced hitherto are those about bringing Arlington into line or winning Louis' trust; but there is another possibility. The fact that Charles never announced his conversion is not proof that he never intended to do so. Because he was so often duplicitous it does not follow that he was never sincere. Let us therefore look more closely at the circumstances of December 1668.

The date of James's conversion is uncertain, but his conversation with Charles in December suggests that he was already leaning towards Catholicism, even if he had not fully made up his mind. One important influence on his decision was the conversion of his former mentor, Turenne, news of which arrived in October. Charles, too, had great respect for Turenne; James told Pepys that the great general's credit was now likely to outweigh that of Colbert, inclining Louis towards conquests on land rather than the promotion of trade.[101] If this were to happen, it would reduce the threat from French commercial competition and make a Franco–Dutch war more likely. Madame saw Turenne (but not Colbert) as firmly in favour of an English alliance.[102] An additional factor was the sudden revival of James's fortunes. In November Buckingham had seemed set to turn Charles against him and even to cut him out of the succession; by early December James was able to dismiss imperiously Buckingham's proffers of friendship.[103] Was it mere coincidence that it was now that Charles sent a cipher to Madame and declared his willingness to receive instruction? He was always inclined to be swept along by those with stronger personalities. James was not normally dynamic and since Clarendon's fall he had usually been on the defensive: Now, for once, he had something positive to offer: conversion to a religion which Charles found congenial and which, to judge from Turenne's conversion, was very much in the ascendant. Religious enthusiasm may well have enabled James, for once, to show the sort of 'briskness' for which he was not usually renowned. This is not to suggest that other considerations were necessarily absent. Charles may also have seen his declaration as a way of bringing Arlington to heel or of convincing Louis of his good faith. This conjunction of circumstances did not last for long, however: nothing did at Charles's court. Within weeks Ormond was dismissed and James's fortunes suffered a severe setback, but Charles had committed himself too far – above all to Louis – to draw back. 'Catholicity' may have been born of a short-lived burst of enthusiasm, but Charles had to live with his commitment even after that enthusiasm had cooled, to make the most of the advantages it offered and minimize the disadvantages. If in so doing he showed a certain cynicism, it does not follow that he was insincere from the outset: circumstances alter cases.

Some days after the meeting on 25 January Charles wrote to Louis of his desire for a personal union: the only obstacle he could foresee was English anxiety about French seapower. He told Madame that he had not yet decided how to proceed, but that he wished all negotiations to pass through her.[104] There were two probable reasons for this. First, while Charles had expressed no dissatisfaction with Croissy, his kinship with Colbert made it most unlikely that he would prove flexible on naval or commercial issues. Second, Charles needed to find a way to emancipate himself from Buckingham. Although the latter's first priority was to ruin Ormond, he would not tolerate any rivals in the conduct of foreign affairs, especially Anglo-French relations. He complained bitterly that Croissy preferred to deal with Arlington (who at least worked regular hours), and Madame had to keep assuring him that the French relied on him alone. Such deceit was necessary because Charles lacked the strength of character to impose his will on the wayward duke. Arlington, however, could be led, which was why he was present at the meeting on 25 January that advised Charles to make the overtures to Louis which he had already started anyway. Meanwhile, Buckingham negotiated with Croissy, both of them believing that theirs were the substantive discussions.[105]

To break the stalemate, more was needed than assurances of goodwill. Arlington and Buckingham talked of the need for a commercial treaty (although the former was inexplicably slow to produce a draft) and Charles complained that the French had not yet, as promised, evacuated the English part of St Kitts. The latter point featured prominently in Montagu's instructions; he was also to insist on enjoying all the rights of precedence due to the king's ambassador in Paris.[106] Meanwhile, Louis, who regarded Arlington as hostile and Buckingham as unreliable, decided he needed a direct personal channel of communication with Charles. Madame was willing, but was ruled out by pregnancy and a jealous husband, so he fixed upon the Abbé Pregnani, whose astrological skills had recently impressed Monmouth. Charles had some interest in both astrology and physiognomy: the fact that the abbé also dabbled in chemistry was an added attraction, but his mission was not a success. Buckingham viewed him with intense suspicion and his attempts to use his skills to pick winners at Newmarket ended in humiliating failure (and, for Monmouth, financial loss). Charles spoke to him only of trivial things (he rarely dealt with business at Newmarket) and an attempt to focus his mind by casting a horoscope presaging his imminent ruin left the king unimpressed.[107]

While Pregnani was showing his ineptitude as a tipster, the kings' accredited ambassadors went through the usual diplomatic motions. Montagu quibbled about protocol (and found Louis more flexible than Holles had); Croissy discussed with Buckingham whether, in a future war with the Spanish or Dutch, England should seek gains on land or be content with supremacy at sea. Neither knew that the real negotiations were taking place elsewhere.[108] In March Charles sent Arundell to inform Louis of his intention to declare himself a Catholic.[109] He now began to declare his hostility to the Dutch: insolent rogues, who claimed to be the arbiters of Europe. On 6 June he wrote to Madame that they had used both Louis and himself scurvily; next day he wrote for the first time of breaking with the Dutch (as distinct from joining with France) and sent word to Louis that he would be ready to commence hostilities in eight or ten months.[110]

Towards the end of June Arundell at last brought Louis' response to Charles's overtures. It focused on four points. First, Charles had sought an offensive and defensive league against all other powers. Louis had at first inclined towards a defensive alliance only, which would not contravene existing treaties. Lionne, especially, doubted the usefulness of the English as war allies: he urged Louis to keep Charles neutral and wait for Carlos to die. Besides, offensive leagues should be specific, not general: if not, one partner might drag the other into a war which it did not want. On reflection, however, Louis declared that he would abandon his treaty with the Dutch (1662) if Charles abandoned his (1668). Second, Louis agreed in principle to provide men and money to support Charles's declaration, but advised him to delay: it might provoke great disorders in England, which could be exploited by foreign powers. It would be wiser first to find a pretext to raise an army, such as a war with the Dutch. Charles would then be far better able to deal with any opposition to his declaration. In order to encourage Charles to accept this order of priorities, Louis offered 1,200,000 *livres* and

4,000 men if Charles announced his conversion first and more if he made war first. Third, Charles had stipulated that he would agree to nothing that would involve his breaking the Triple Alliance. After some reservations, Louis agreed, provided it was accepted that the stipulation applied only to guaranteeing the Treaty of Aix-la-Chapelle and would not prevent Louis from pursuing any claims which might fall to him in future. Finally, Charles wished Louis to promise to build no more warships. At first Louis rejected this out of hand, but on reflection he agreed to suspend construction for one year.[111]

Charles's proposals combined two contradictory elements. For the most part they continued his long-standing efforts to forge an alliance with Louis and to separate France from the Dutch. At the same time they sought to safeguard English interests against possible threats from France, by maintaining England's naval superiority and preserving what remained of the Spanish Netherlands; if a commercial treaty could be concluded as well, so much the better. The one discordant element was Catholicity: as Louis remarked, it was likely to provoke a reaction which could paralyse England as an international force. Charles tried to reassure those who expressed such concerns – first Madame and Louis, later Croissy. He was fortifying the major ports, he said, and employing reliable governors; he was taking no less care of Ireland and Scotland. Opposition could be reduced if the pope agreed to modify certain aspects of Catholic practice which were particularly disliked in England and to promise that the Church would not try to take back the monastic lands confiscated by Henry VIII. The Dissenters, he declared, hated the Church far more than they hated the Catholics, so could be won over by a grant of toleration.[112] It is hard to take such statements seriously. His army was small and he made no move to enlarge it in 1669, or to change the officer corps.[113] Almost all the inland garrisons had been shut down in the early 1660s – the major exceptions being York and Chepstow – and, of the coastal forts, substantial sums were spent only on Sheerness, Portsmouth and Plymouth; Gravesend had been refortified in 1667–8. Many of the remaining forts were ruinous and the purpose of the new works was clearly to defend the coasts and more particularly the fleet: Charles could not forget the Medway. In short, Charles's military preparations were geared to foreign war, not to maintaining order at home.[114] The one apparent gain was an Act passed by the Scottish Parliament allowing for the militia to be used outside that kingdom, but this merely re-enacted an Act of 1663, passed after the disbanding of the standing army.[115] As for Ireland, Charles told Croissy that Ormond, who still had great credit there, would be loyal and that Orrery (a Presbyterian) was a Catholic at heart. Although Charles talked of toleration for Dissenters, he moved away from both comprehension and indulgence in the course of 1669; his brother denounced Dissenters as enemies to monarchy and declared that only Anglicans could be trusted.[116]

It seems clear that by June 1669, or at the latest by the end of the year, Charles and his most confidential advisers had abandoned Catholicity: the only exceptions were York, who longed to announce his conversion, and Clifford, who drew up plans for military preparations and proposals to be sent to the pope, both of which had only the most tenuous connection with reality.[117] As he could not admit that he had lost interest, Charles advanced various pretexts for delaying his declaration, which Louis was happy to accept. Catholicity still offered the prospect of a modest additional subsidy and, by insisting that it was his first priority, Charles could control the timing of the war against the Dutch, which was now his primary concern. In August he intimated to Louis that he might be prepared to delay his declaration until after such a war had started; he would, however, need money to start the war – maybe £1,000,000 – so it might be better to make his declaration first. He now abandoned two of his earlier stipulations. He declared that he would gladly support any new claims to Spanish territory which Louis might have and dropped his demand that Louis should stop building warships. Charles was clearly concerned about both the size of the French navy and the greater speed and manoeuvrability of French warships, but he failed to insist that Louis should either cut back on his shipbuilding programme or complete the commercial treaty. It would therefore be difficult to argue that the defence of England's maritime interests was his first priority.[118]

From now on, the broad outlines of the negotiations remained unchanged. While Charles talked of his impatience to announce his conversion, and Louis promised men and money to support it, attention shifted to military aggression, against Spain as well as Holland, and the terms on which the English were to assist the French. In September Madame urged Charles to put the war first and advised him to demand 'the most important maritime towns, whose commerce will depend entirely on the laws which you choose to impose upon them for the benefit of your kingdom and yourself'. Louis had talked of England's gaining such towns back in 1667, as an inducement to assist him against Spain and it seems likely that he had authorized Madame's suggestion: whereas he had earlier been content that England should make gains in the New World, leaving him a free hand in Europe, he had since changed his mind.[119] Madame was surprised by the alacrity with which Charles took up the idea of assisting Louis against Spain. Later, he also began to press for maritime towns, but as yet he talked more generally, of the need to agree upon the division of what was to be conquered from the Dutch. Louis was impatient to conclude and insisted that Croissy should at last be fully informed of the negotiations. In a long interview, Charles regaled the ambassador with an account of his plans for Catholicism which must have stretched even his powers of dissimulation: he declared, for instance, that Buckingham had no religion, but inclined more to Catholicism than to any other.[120]

In early December Croissy was presented with a draft treaty. The first article dealt with Catholicity: Louis was to pay £200,000 towards Charles's preparations, with the promise of further aid, in men and money, should his subjects rebel. The main thrust of the proposals, however, lay elsewhere. Charles undertook to assist Louis, at Louis' expense, to secure from Spain any new rights which might fall due to him; Charles was to receive in return Minorca and Ostend, which Louis was to try to obtain for him; the French were also to help Charles to seize all Spain's possessions in the New World. The two kings were to make war on the Dutch. As the main war effort was to be at sea, Louis was to pay £800,000 a year[121] towards Charles's naval expenditure, while Charles was to contribute 6,000 men to the French army. As his share of the conquests from the Dutch, Charles was to receive Walcheren, Sluys, Cadzand and the adjacent country.[122] As William was likely to suffer losses in this share-out of conquests, the two kings should try to ensure that he derived some benefit from the war; it was later suggested that he should receive Flushing. Such a commitment would strengthen the Orangists and sow dissension among the Dutch people. As for timing, Louis was to decide when to begin the war and Charles was to fix the date for his declaration; the latter was to come first.[123]

Croissy found these proposals little short of outrageous, not least the proposal that Louis should help the English to conquer all of Spanish America. A surviving draft of the proposals, in Clifford's hand, shows evidence of heady excitement. At one point he wrote in the margin: 'if we must presently enter into the war upon the death of the king of Spain, the charge will be defrayed and America His Majesty's'. He wondered if anything should be included about the Dutch plantations in the East and West Indies, but decided against it.[124] Such hopes were wildly unrealistic. Louis may in the past have held out hopes of limited English gains in the Caribbean or the Netherlands, but nothing on this scale. Never renowned for his sense of humour, he declared himself scandalized: Charles, he wrote, expected France to bear all the cost of the war while he made all the gains. An annual subsidy of £800,000 was out of the question; Louis would be satisfied if Charles supplied forty ships (which, with the French fleet, would be sufficient to hold the Dutch at sea) while Louis got on with the serious business of defeating them on land.[125]

Had Catholicity or the strengthening of his authority been Charles's main concern, he would surely have embraced these proposals, which would have involved him in only a token war effort and limited expenditure, and left him free to concentrate on domestic affairs. Charles, however, was adamant that England should play the dominant role at sea. It might seem that this was just a pretext to ask for money, but although Charles put the cost of naval preparations at £1,000,000 a year, and demanded £800,000, he soon declared that he would accept less if Louis supplied some ships. By January he had dropped his demands to £300,000 a year plus forty ships and he eventually accepted about £225,000 and thirty ships. In return, he promised to send 6,000 soldiers to Louis' army, a figure reduced by a secret article to 4,000. Louis carefully avoided committing himself as to the gains Charles might make after some future breach with Spain, or the death of Carlos II, and undertook merely to do what he could for William. He agreed that Charles should receive Walcheren, Sluys and Cadzand and promised some £150,000 (and, if needed, 6,000 men) to support Catholicity. There was friction about the way in which the money was to be paid and about the precise terms on which the fleets should join: yet again the question of the flag proved contentious. Charles and Arlington insisted that Catholicity was the first concern and feigned indifference towards the war, in the hope of extracting better terms, and continued to talk of allowing the emperor to join the Triple Alliance. Meanwhile, Clifford scrutinized the French proposals with exaggerated care, claiming that the English had too often been cheated in the past.[126]

If Charles won some small negotiating victories (for example, on the method of payment) the terms finally agreed were far closer to what Louis wanted than to the proposals that Charles had put forward in December. He still talked of his conversion taking precedence, but the very fact that he had sought money to enable him to prepare for war implied that he saw the war as being at least equally important and he stressed the advantages that he would derive from it.[127] Whatever these might be, they would not be immediate. If he had ever hoped that French subsidies could solve his financial problems, it was now clear that (even with the payment for Catholicity) they would not cover even the cost of his naval preparations. He would thus be faced with the problem of extracting supply from Parliament and loans from the City for a war which was likely to be far from popular.

Charles was clearly well aware of this public hostility to France. When Parliament met in October he ordered that no mention should be made of the intended war; instead, Bridgeman called for money to support the Triple Alliance.[128] The Commons' temper had not improved since the last session. In particular, they resented what they saw as the Lords' attempt to extend their jurisdiction, in Skinner's case, and brought in a bill declaring that the Lords had no jurisdiction as a court of first instance.[129] They then brought in a bill against conventicles, under which any fines levied were not to go to the king, which meant that he would be unable to remit them. Some MPs remarked that those close to the king tried to persuade him that Dissenters were rich and powerful, others reported that Jesuits and Cromwellian officers had been seen at conventicles. Old Cavaliers talked of seditious persons whispering in corners in the House, while Henry Coventry claimed that there were designs to alter the government and to have Parliament dissolved.[130]

With Cavalier MPs clearly disgruntled, Buckingham and the undertakers renewed their attempts to exploit their resentment at the mismanagement of the war. William Garroway and Sir Robert Howard urged the House not to consider supply until all accusations, and the royal accounts, had been fully investigated. The House duly found Carteret guilty of a variety of miscarriages. Ormond's friends sought to profit from the House's ill-temper by impeaching Orrery, but desisted when Charles made it clear he was far from displeased with him; meanwhile, Buckingham and Orrery promised not to attack Ormond.[131] Amid the recriminations, the House somehow found time to agree to a supply of £400,000 – and this despite calls that nothing should be voted until the House was satisfied that previous grants had not been misspent. The sum was, however, a modest one and the House showed its hostility to France by resolving to raise the money by new duties on foreign wines and liquors and on French linen.[132] Before they could proceed further, the dispute with the Lords erupted again. Despite the king's pleas for moderation, the peers rejected the Commons' judicature bill and brought in one of their own. Charles had intended to adjourn the Houses over Christmas, but on 10 December changed his mind and prorogued them instead. Various reasons were suggested for his decision. Some thought that the jurisdictional dispute would make it impossible to complete the supply bill, others that it would not have passed anyway, as MPs would not agree to any duty that could become perpetual. It was also argued that the supply would be worth little, as the new duties would sharply reduce the volume of imports and thus the yield of existing revenues. The Commons were also on the verge of addressing the king to remove Carteret from his offices and there was a report, probably untrue, that they were about to adjourn themselves without reference to the king. One observer – no friend to the Church – claimed that Charles had been angered by the Commons' measures against Dissent. Croissy claimed that Buckingham was responsible for the prorogation, which followed a renewed attack on Orrery, and that Charles seemed inclined to dissolve Parliament and start anew. Others claimed that Buckingham had not been present when Charles decided on the prorogation and that it was the work of York and Ormond.[133]

The fact that so many reasons could be given for the prorogation was a sad comment on the handling of the session. Charles may well have realized this and that Buckingham and his friends had been responsible for much of the disruption. Urged on by York and Ormond, he decided on resolute action. He summoned the accounts commissioners and declared that he would examine the matter himself and punish those who were at fault. He found no serious irregularities in Carteret's accounts and concluded that those who had attacked him were after his job. Buckingham still claimed that the Commons would give nothing until they were allowed a free rein to enquire into maladministration, but his was now a lone voice, as Castlemaine and Arlington urged Charles to stand firm. When Charles recalled Robartes from Ireland, he ignored Buckingham's claim that Orrery was the obvious successor.[134] Charles also insisted that the Corporation Act and the laws against nonconformist meetings should be enforced[135] and dismissed Henry Coventry and Sir Frecheville Holles from their offices, for opposing his will in the Commons.[136] These measures were widely welcomed as evidence that he would stick (as James advised) to his own party – the old Cavaliers and the Anglicans. He also summoned all MPs to come up promptly when Parliament reconvened in February, thus making clear his intention to appeal over the heads of the troublemakers to the loyal backbenchers.[137]

His strategy was triumphantly vindicated. He told MPs that the accounts showed clearly that no money had been diverted from its proper purpose and that his debts were due to war, not mismanagement. Some erstwhile undertakers tried to raise the issues of maladministration and Skinner's case, but the House resolved to consider the king's speech, and therefore supply.[138] On 19 February it resolved in principle to place a duty on wines for seven years; it refused to allow the accounts commissioners to assess the yield of these duties and generally treated them with scant respect. Those MPs who had been bent on making trouble withdrew in disgust. On the 22nd Charles ordered both Houses to raze from their journals all references to Skinner's case. Delighted that he was at last providing firm leadership, the Commons gladly complied and MPs spent the rest of the day drinking his health on their knees in the royal cellars.[139]

In appealing to the old Cavaliers, Charles had to abandon all thoughts of comprehension or indulgence. A new conventicle bill met with no obstruction from the court. The erstwhile undertakers denounced the 'despotic' powers which it gave to JPs, but won little support. Charles reminded MPs that some nonconformists were hostile to monarchy; the Commons asked him to ensure that the laws against both conventicles and Catholics were fully enforced.[140] The Lords tried to amend the bill, by increasing the number of persons constituting a conventicle from five to ten and by adding a sweeping proviso, to safeguard not only the royal supremacy but also any prerogative exercised by the king or his predecessors. The Commons, fearing that this might allow Charles, or some future king, to dispense with the penalties imposed by the bill, replaced the Lords' proviso with a much more limited salvo for the royal supremacy; they also insisted that a meeting of five persons was a conventicle. The Lords backed down. Sheldon gleefully ordered his clergy to be vigilant and to encourage JPs to suppress all meetings; on a more positive note, they were to be careful to adhere to the Prayer Book services and to set a moral example to their flocks, thus weaning them away from error and schism.[141]

There is no evidence that those who knew of Catholicity disapproved of the conventicle bill. Clifford argued vehemently against the Lords' proviso and Arlington expressed himself very satisfied with the session.[142] York, who had always advocated a firm line against Dissent, now had particular need of the bishops' support. Lord Roos, son of the Earl of Rutland, had earlier secured a legal separation from his wife; they had lived apart for some time and she had borne a son called Ignotus, after the father. Roos now promoted a private bill to allow him to remarry. Buckingham saw this as a possible precedent which Charles could use to divorce the queen. The queen was very alarmed, while James suspected a dark design to deprive his daughters of their claim to the throne.[143] He and twelve bishops entered protests against the decision to give the bill a second reading and his alarm grew when Charles began to attend debates in the Lords. He told Croissy that he was the first king to do so since Henry VIII: James I had been advised against it by his councillors, who did not wish him to be too well informed. Croissy heard that Buckingham was behind it: he had told Charles that York's influence among the peers was too great. Although the king declared that he had no intention of influencing the debates, he made his support for Roos's bill very clear and it eventually passed by eight votes.[144]

Buckingham's hopes and James's fears proved unfounded. Charles was annoyed by the queen's too obvious interest in the case and slept with her even more infrequently than usual.[145] Buckingham's influence, however, was not what it had been. His attempts to show his power and popularity by making trouble in Parliament had failed; his attempts to distract the king through pleasure were no longer effective. The Roos case briefly raised his credit, but overall Arlington, suppler and more reliable, had got the better of him.[146] When Charles adjourned Parliament on 11 April he had much cause for satisfaction. Not only had the Commons voted the wine duties (for eight years rather than seven) but they had passed an Act authorizing the sale of the fee-farm rents, which were to bring in over £650,000 over the next three years. Marvell wrote, with disgust: 'The king was never since his coming in, nay, all things considered no king since the Conquest, so absolutely powerful at home as he is at present, nor any Parliament, or places, so certainly and constantly supplied with men of the same temper.'[147] Charles probably had qualms about the Conventicle Act – it was, as Marvell said, 'the price of money'[148] – and took steps to ensure that it did not lead to disorder. Worried by reports of plots, or of nonconformists planning mass disobedience, he ordered lords lieutenant to send in lists of their deputies and appointed new lieutenancy commissioners for London. When he travelled to Dover in May, to meet Madame, he left James to maintain order in the capital.[149]

By early May, Charles and Louis were close to agreement. The only questions that remained were those of the timing of Charles's declaration and of the war. Charles still insisted that he would announce his conversion – after all Louis had promised him money for it – but seemed in no great hurry. He still insisted, too, that his declaration had to come first, a stance vigorously supported by his brother. After many difficulties raised by her petulant and spiteful husband, Madame arrived at Dover on 16 May, to complete the treaty to which she had contributed so much. Ostensibly, it was just a family visit, but many suspected a deeper design. For Charles, it offered a brief opportunity to see the beloved sister whom he had not seen for nine years. Monsieur had insisted that she should not leave Dover, which Charles thought a miserable town, so they had to make the most of its limited facilities.[150] The treaty was signed on the 22nd. It was studiously vague about future conquests at the expense of Spain and did not make clear whether the war or Catholicity was to come first. Croissy wrote on the 20th that Madame had persuaded Charles that the war was the first priority, but a week later he wrote that a decision would be made only when the court returned to London. This change can probably be ascribed to York, who was eager that Charles should announce his conversion so that he could do the same. Horrified that Madame had changed the king's mind, he argued that a war would run Charles into debt and leave him dependent on Parliament, in which case he would never be able to declare himself a Catholic.[151]

Charles had probably decided long before that the war was the main priority, but he continued to behave as if he intended to announce his conversion: if he abandoned it too easily, Louis might suspect that it had been merely a ruse to secure money. Besides, he needed to win over those councillors who knew nothing of Catholicity or the secret treaty to the idea of war with the Dutch. Much to York's disgust, Madame had reconciled Arlington to Buckingham, who now threw himself into planning a French alliance, of which he fondly believed he was the architect.[152] She returned to France, leaving her brother in floods of tears, and a fortnight later fell critically ill. As she lay dying her husband seized her money and jewels and went through her papers. Abbé Montagu translated those from Charles, but not (fortunately) his final packet which spoke of Catholicity – Monsieur was a terrible gossip. She died in excruciating pain, amid rumours of poison

which the autopsy did not entirely dispel. Despite the rumours, her dis-
traught brother insisted that her work should not die with her: he would
remain firmly allied to France.[153]

By the middle of 1670 Charles had at last achieved his major foreign policy
objective – an alliance with France against the Dutch. The treaty offered
the prospect not only of commercial, colonial and territorial gains from the
Dutch, but – more distantly – huge acquisitions at the expense of Spain.
But, if Charles was to make war on the Dutch, where was the money to
come from? The promised French subsidies would clearly be insufficient.
The new wine duties and the sale of fee-farm rents would help relieve the
annual deficit, but his ordinary revenue still fell short of the £1,200,000
which the Convention had judged necessary to support the government in
peacetime. To fight a war, more money would have to be found. As no one
seriously suggested raising arbitrary taxation, the only viable way was
through Parliament – which had shown itself very hostile to France and to
Popery. Charles had thus committed himself to pursue precisely those lines
of policy which the Commons would most dislike. The House was also
firmly Anglican. As the price of money Charles had agreed to the Conventicle
Act, but he was very fearful that it might provoke a dangerous level of
disaffection: he was far from sharing the confidence (probably justified) of
magistrates and bishops that the threat to public order could be contained
and on 10 June he ordered that all former Cromwellian soldiers should leave
London and Bristol.[154]

If the present House was anti-French and anti-Popish and insisted on a
religious policy which Charles thought dangerous, was there an alternative?
Buckingham had long argued that a new Parliament, containing many more
Dissenters, would vote money in return for religious liberty, which would
anyway bring greater prosperity and so enhance the king's revenue. The
Dissenters' interest in trade might also make them anti-Dutch, while their
anti-Catholicism might be tempered by their gratitude at being freed from
the yoke of the Church. Viewed in this light, the Conventicle Act could be
seen as a blessing – a sharp burst of persecution would make Dissenters
more grateful when it ended. Croissy also thought that Charles, James and
Arlington hoped that disorders provoked by the Act could provide a pretext
to strengthen the army.[155] How seriously Charles considered such an alternative is open to question. To abandon the Anglicans and appeal to the
Dissenters would be a huge risk. Would an election produce a House of
Commons containing far more Dissenters? Would that House respect the
king's prerogatives? Would it welcome toleration for Dissenters (and Catholics)? Above all, would it give money? Conditioned by hard experience to
equate Dissent with sedition, Charles was reluctant to throw himself on the

mercy of such people: better, perhaps, to stick with the Parliament he knew, which had behaved so well in the last session. But that brought him back to the original problem: he had committed himself to an alliance that was bound to be unpopular and he had promised to announce his conversion, which could ruin him if the news ever leaked out. In a polity which depended on the king's tailoring his policies to meet his subjects' expectations, Charles had done just the opposite. A reckoning was bound to come. When it did, it would shatter the basic trust in the king, which had survived the vicissitudes of the 1660s and resurfaced so triumphantly in the last session of Parliament.

The Grand Design

The period after the signature of the Secret Treaty marks a watershed in Charles's reign. Hitherto the Commons had often been irritated and even enraged by evidence of administrative incompetence (to say no worse) and by his intermittent favour towards Dissenters and even Catholics. There had been little evidence, however, that Charles and his advisers wished to overturn the foundations of Church and constitution, to establish Catholicism and absolutism. Despite the disputes about men and measures, MPs had remained deeply respectful of the royal prerogative and willing, indeed eager, to trust the king (if properly advised): hence the almost hysterical joy at the time of the 'going down into the cellar' in February 1670. By the end of 1673 that trust had been shattered and no attempt to revert to the policies of the 1660s could rebuild it. The reasons for this lay less in the French alliance as such than in what many saw as its likely effects within England – 'Popery and arbitrary government'. How did such a perception develop? And how well founded was it?

Part of the answer to both these questions can be supplied by looking at those who had most influence with the king. Much to the delight of the court's critics, the initials of five of his leading advisers made up the word 'Cabal', a word which usually had connotations of secrecy and intrigue, although Clifford used it to mean 'cabinet' or 'inner ring'.[1] Within this group – to which should be added the Duke of York – there was seldom agreement and never a sense of solidarity. The rivalry and indeed enmity of Arlington and Buckingham formed the axis along which most divisions formed. Arlington needed to retain the king's favour in order to support his expensive lifestyle. Despite his fondness for Spain and his Dutch wife, he had committed himself to the French alliance, because that was what Charles wanted, and did his utmost to make it work. However, his habitual caution – some said timidity – made him likely to modify his stance in the face of forthright opposition from Parliament or public. By the end of 1673 his nerve and his health had given way and he sought to withdraw from high-level administration, while preserving both his fortune and a measure of influence on policy. In urging the king to comply where possible with the Commons, he was usually supported by Ormond, the most widely respected of all Charles's councillors.

Buckingham's influence, while not as great as it had been in 1667–9, was still considerable. He would whisk the king off to frolic with actresses and so gain the opportunity to work on him, away from his other courtiers. Croissy thought also that Charles wished to show that nobody had a monopoly of credit, thus maintaining at least the illusion that he was in overall control.[2] Quite how Buckingham used his influence depended on his moods. He vehemently supported the French alliance, partly because he was duped, for a while, into seeing himself as its architect, partly because he nursed visions of the military glory which his father had sought, but never achieved. He also, however, still wished to be popular. He urged Charles to commission more army officers who had seen service under Cromwell. He talked grandly of his influence in the Commons and tried to persuade his London contacts to support the French alliance. He eagerly supported Charles's grant of indulgence to Dissenters: when the Commons attacked it, Buckingham urged Charles to dissolve Parliament and even to defend the indulgence by armed force. If there was any coherent thinking behind his conduct (which is doubtful) it was that the existing House of Commons did not speak for the most powerful elements, politically and economically, in the nation, the Dissenters and old Parliamentarians. He may even have seen himself as a latterday Cromwell, who could dominate Charles II's government as his father had Charles I's: indeed, he held up Cromwell's regime as a model – tolerant, militarily successful and (he believed) popular.[3]

Two other members of the 'Cabal' also had Cromwellian backgrounds. Ashley (eventually created Earl of Shaftesbury), while not ignoring France's growing maritime power, favoured the Dutch War for reasons that were essentially economic. He too supported the Declaration of Indulgence. Given the Commons' hostility towards Dissent, he was prepared (tactically) to endorse the king's use of his prerogative for that purpose, but in general he was wary of the extension of the power of the executive. Lauderdale had no such qualms. Scotland's government rested much more on brute force than England's and Lauderdale's fiery temperament made him impatient of even the limited restraints imposed on the government by Scots law. He let fall expressions which were to cause him a great deal of trouble: for example, that the king's edicts ought to have the force of laws.[4] He was thus more likely than Ashley or Arlington to advocate authoritarian (or 'absolutist') measures. His main sphere of interest, however, was Scotland; his involvement in English affairs was intermittent and tended to be influenced by

Scottish, or personal, considerations. His occasional authoritarian remarks should probably be seen as born of particular circumstances – or of irritation – rather than as evidence of a design to make England's government more like that of France.

And yet someone at court clearly had such a design – or at least such a vision. In December 1671, the Venetian resident, Alberti, began to report that Charles was going to take a firm line with Parliament, demanding money and dismissing it if it refused to give any. His hand would be strengthened by the war, which would enable him to raise more troops; he would grant posts in the army to loyal members of both Houses. If the 1672 campaign went well, the people would support him; if badly, they would be in no position to resist his army. Croissy, too, wrote that the Cabal saw that their safety depended on enhancing the king's power. When Charles prorogued Parliament, Alberti wrote that he had asserted his authority and humbled the Houses.[5] Neither envoy gave the source of his information. The tough, no-nonsense approach and the stress on loyalty would suggest York rather than the pliant Arlington or Buckingham, who wanted this Parliament dissolved. York, indeed, talked in such terms on other occasions but some reports linked calls for firmness with a denunciation of Clarendon's weakness, which is hardly what one would expect of his son-in-law; there is also evidence that York opposed the decision to prorogue, which was taken while he was away with the fleet.[6] A more plausible source is Clifford, who had been no friend to Clarendon and supported the prorogation. The identification is strengthened by Alberti's reference to a conversation with Charles's 'most confidential minister' at a time when Arlington and Buckingham were abroad and Lauderdale was in Scotland. Clifford was one of the few to take Catholicity seriously – indeed, he became a Catholic – and drew up a scheme of military preparations, albeit to guard against insurrection rather than to coerce Parliament.[7] In fact, expenditure on fortifications remained limited and was concentrated on major naval bases: claims that the garrisons at Gravesend and Windsor would keep London quiet seem far-fetched in the extreme.[8]

It seems clear that there was talk at court of using the war, and the army, to establish a more absolute regime, but reports of such remarks were relatively infrequent and never attributed to particular individuals, even though Croissy, at least, would hardly have disapproved of such designs. Even Alberti remarked that the projects of the English were just talk, not well digested policies.[9] The dearth of hard evidence of a design to establish absolutism is in sharp contrast to the extensive evidence of plans, in both 1672 and 1673, to invade the Dutch Republic. The fact that these plans for a 'descent' on Zeeland never came to anything should not lead us to assume that they were not seriously intended – a cynical pretext to raise an army.

On the contrary, many round Charles believed, as we shall see, that a descent was both desirable and feasible.

In the final analysis, indeed, the main aim of 'the Grand Design' was the war against the Dutch. Most knew nothing of Catholicity and some of those who did soon lost interest. Charles pretended that he was bursting to announce his conversion, but kept finding pretexts to delay it; Louis did not press him. Even without Catholicity, the Design was likely to bring trouble. Charles failed to enlist Parliament's support – indeed, he deliberately misled it – and the Declaration of Indulgence was bound to annoy the Commons. Having failed to extract the necessary money from Parliament, Charles raised a large sum by stopping payments out of the exchequer, thus securing ready cash at the expense of future credit. Such expedients gave hostages to fortune which could be redeemed only by speedy and spectacular success in war: then doubts and suspicions might be forgotten in a warm glow of patriotic fervour. It was a huge gamble. The past record of Charles's government did not suggest that he and his advisers possessed the abilities needed to achieve such success, not least because of their inability to work as a team and because ready money was in such short supply. The gamble would have been substantial even in a politically neutral environment, but then rumours – some wild, others less so – began to seep out about the Secret Treaty. These were given credence by the favour shown to Catholics and by growing suspicions of James's conversion.[10] Fears of 'Popery and arbitrary government' grew to a point where even the most spectacular victories would not remove the public suspicion and dissatisfaction; military failure, on the other hand, could lead to political crisis and even catastrophe.

The Secret Treaty of Dover had been signed (on the English side) by Charles, Arlington, Clifford, Arundell and Bellings; apart from these, only James had known of its contents. If Charles was to prepare for war, others – notably Buckingham, Ashley and Lauderdale – would have to be brought to support a French alliance. Of the three, Buckingham was the most important, because of his capacity for wrecking schemes of which he disapproved. Fortunately for Charles, the duke embraced the idea enthusiastically and rushed off to Paris to negotiate with Louis. He continued to talk loudly of the need for commercial concessions but this, as it turned out, was only talk: although the French discriminated blatantly against English merchants, Buckingham was so eager to conclude his treaty that he allowed himself to be fobbed off with kind words.[11] He had initially proposed to divide the republic between France, England and Louis' German allies, but Arlington persuaded him to scale down his demands to those of the original treaty, plus Goeree and Voorne. Had the English been able to secure all of those islands and towns, they would have controlled most of the province of Zeeland and, even more important, the mouths of the Great Rivers – the Lek and Waal (divisions of the Rhine), the Maas (Meuse) and the Scheldt. Rotterdam would have been effectively cut off from the sea and much of the republic's trade would have fallen into English hands.[12]

In view of their economic and strategic importance, it may seem surprising that Louis agreed that Goeree and Voorne should be added to England's proposed gains, especially as at one stage the English were prepared not to insist on having them.[13] Buckingham was prepared to compromise, partly out of sheer impetuosity, partly because he hoped to command the expeditionary force to Zeeland; the prospect of a gift from Louis to Lady Shrewsbury also helped.[14] Louis, however, was neither impetuous nor unconcerned about details. He gave way on the issue of Goeree and Voorne either because he calculated that the English would never be able to take them or in order to secure what he wanted on other matters. He was surprised that Charles raised difficulties about the command of the fleet, which he thought had been settled by the original treaty: Louis would not agree that a French admiral (as distinct from vice-admiral) should be under York's command, as that might seem to concede English claims to sovereignty in the Narrow Seas. The question of the flag also came up again, as did Charles's claim to the title of 'King of France' and problems of precedence among land commanders.[15]

Most of these problems were settled quickly: far more serious was the one which had remained unresolved when Madame left Dover – should the war, or Catholicity, come first? The fact that this part of the negotiations had to be kept secret from Buckingham, Ashley and Lauderdale enabled Charles to use the need for their approval as a means to extract further concessions: if the negotiations went too smoothly, he argued, some might suspect that they were a sham to conceal a *fait accompli*. He declared himself eager to announce his conversion, but began to suggest that perhaps he could make his announcement and declare war at the same time. His wariness doubtless owed much to fear of losing the money promised for Catholicity; once Louis had agreed that this should be added to the war subsidies, Charles concentrated on trying to improve on the terms already agreed, in return for his agreeing formally that the war should come first. His efforts were rewarded by the provision about Goeree and Voorne; he secretly reaffirmed his intention of announcing his conversion, but there was no statement of when he should do so. Once terms had been agreed, Charles declared himself eager to start the war in the spring of 1671; Louis' German allies could not be ready before the late summer, so it was agreed that the war should begin in the spring of 1672.[16]

Even if Charles now had no intention of announcing his conversion, he felt the need to go through the motions of wishing to do so. He and Arlington talked of the need to secure concessions from Rome to make Catholicism more acceptable to the English and appointed George Leyburn, a leading English priest, to put his case at the Vatican, but Leyburn's instructions, though promised, took a long time to complete. In February 1671 Arlington told Croissy that Charles expected the coming session of Parliament to prove successful, so long as he did not antagonize the Commons by measures in favour of the Catholics, who were too few to offer a viable basis of support; it would be wiser to wait until a victorious war provided him with a stronger army.[17] Clifford and a Benedictine monk, Serenus Cressy, continued to work on Leyburn's instructions, but Charles's interest was at best fitful. When he feared that the Queen of Spain might ally with the Dutch he talked of informing her of his plans for conversion, which Croissy thought most unwise. In the spring of 1672 he asked Louis to send a skilled theologian to advise him about his declaration. Soon after, he revived the plan to send Leyburn to Rome, but Arlington remarked that the impatience of York and Clifford to declare themselves only made Charles more reticent.[18] James's decision to tell Buckingham about Catholicity – the latter, it was said, had just become a Catholic – was especially foolish.[19] By now, however, the war had begun, the Catholicity money had been paid and the French showed little eagerness to press Charles to declare himself; Croissy received Arlington's assurances that he would do so at the end of the summer's campaign with polite scepticism. The following spring Charles recalled Leyburn from Paris and asked Louis to ensure that all papers relating to Catholicity were safely under lock and key. Croissy remarked, euphemistically, that he now saw that the king's declaration would be much delayed.[20]

There had been one other obstacle to the conclusion of the so-called *traité simulé*, which was signed on 21 December 1670. Charles proposed that William should receive as his share of the spoils the great trading province of Holland, which was richer than the other six put together. Louis was prepared at most to install William as governor of the province and Charles's enthusiasm for his nephew cooled after he visited England that autumn. Charles had last seen him as a boy of nine and expected him to defer to his uncle, as head of the family; instead he found him too stubborn, too Dutch and too Protestant. Charles told him that the Protestants had become divided into factions after breaking off from 'the main body' (the Catholic Church). His comment made a deep impression on the young man, but was probably intended more as a political than an ecclesiastical statement. The treaty as signed, like that of Dover, included only a vague undertaking to do whatever was possible for William.[21]

With the treaty completed, Charles prepared for war as vigorously as his limited resources would allow. The French alliance remained secret: Buckingham made exaggerated gestures of hostility to France in order (he said) to disarm suspicion; meanwhile, he accused Arlington of being pro-Dutch.[22] Gradually, the circle of those officially informed of the alliance widened, to include first Rupert and Ormond (in May), then the whole privy council (in December). A new, less secret version of the *traité simulé* was signed in February 1672.[23] There was still friction between the allies. Charles proposed that Louis should contribute more money and fewer ships – he was determined that England should be the dominant partner at sea. Louis replied that he was spending so much money preparing for war that he had none to spare.[24] The French understandably resented Clifford's proposal, supported by Ashley, Buckingham and Lauderdale, that the joint war effort should begin with an attack on those places which were to make up England's share; Louis fobbed them off by offering to keep 2,000 men ready to assist in the descent on Zeeland.[25] Louis was still less impressed by Buckingham's proposal, following reports of a possible Spanish–Dutch alliance, that Louis and Charles should attack Spain's possessions in the West Indies; Louis had been careful to ensure that no explicit reference to the Spanish succession appeared in the treaties. Charles's other advisers were most reluctant to break with Spain, fearing a slump in trade and so in the customs revenue; besides, the recent colonial treaty promised to open up new trading opportunities in the New World.[26]

The most serious interruption to the war preparations came, predictably, from Buckingham. Charles had undertaken to send 4,000 men to Louis' army at his own expense. Buckingham had set his heart on commanding this contingent and so was not well pleased when Montagu proposed that Louis should waive this requirement and be allowed to recruit soldiers in England instead. Louis agreed, at least for the first year of the war; Montagu claimed that he did so because he doubted Buckingham's fitness for command. The duke was livid: he declared that both kings had broken their word to him and that Montagu had made the suggestion in order to spite him. He may have been right: Montagu was an associate of Arlington's. Worse was to come: Buckingham could hardly criticize the decision that Monmouth should command the forces raised for the descent on Zeeland, but the appointment of Ossory as second-in-command was a bitter blow. When the duke finally tackled Charles about this, he responded by complaining of Buckingham's disruptive conduct in Parliament and his favour towards Cromwellians (a point often stressed by Arlington). Buckingham, he added, should not let his yearning for command come before his duty to the state. Rage having failed, Buckingham stomped off into the country to sulk. When he returned to court, he continued to grumble and received visits from the Spanish ambassador. In January he asked if he could command any French regiments sent to join the English army.[27]

Having resolved the question of military command, Charles set out to pick a quarrel with the Dutch. He had a choice of pretexts – a dispute over English settlers being allowed to remove their possessions from Surinam, the asylum granted to English political refugees, the 'insolent' prints and medals which circulated in the republic – but he plumped for the flag, as the issue most likely to win public support. When a yacht was sent to collect Lady Temple from the Hague, its captain was ordered to seek out the Dutch fleet and demand that it salute the king's standard. The Dutch commander refused and, although the authorities at the Hague imprisoned him on his return, court and people took his refusal as an affront. A few weeks later Temple was replaced by the far more uncompromising Downing.[28] He gave out that he would conduct no business until his master received satisfaction. Charles ordered him to insist on the salute, even on the Dutch coasts, and to accept no apologies but play for time while Charles completed his preparations. The States General were now so worried by Louis' mobilization that they were ready to do almost anything to appease the English, but Downing demanded that they should submit unconditionally and then hastily left the Hague before they could do so. Such precipitate action was not what Charles had wanted: he had no wish for hostilities to break out before he was ready, so he sent Downing to the Tower for returning without orders. He still seemed hesitant about declaring war, but then Sir Robert Holmes attacked the returning Dutch Smyrna fleet on the pretext that it had not saluted the king's flag. Ominously the attack failed, but on 17 March 1672 Charles issued his declaration of war.[29]

When Parliament reconvened on 24 October 1670 Charles's alliance with France was still a closely guarded secret. His opening speech was extremely terse; Bridgeman's stressed the usefulness of the Triple Alliance in the face of a possible threat from France. Other spokesmen gave an account of the king's debts and of the cost of the navy, which since 1660 had averaged £500,000 a year. Charles claimed that he would need £800,000 to fit out the fleet next spring, plus an unspecified sum to pay off his debts.[30] During the summer the council had examined the material accumulated by the accounts commission and had decided that, despite his wayward accounting procedures, Carteret had done nothing untoward.[31] The investigations left king and ministers more aware of the costs of government and of the navy. Charles told Croissy that he needed an additional £400,000 a year, quite apart from the cost of arming against the Dutch. Clifford and Downing told the Commons that the crown's debts stood at around £2,000,000, even after valiant efforts to reduce them. The Commons welcomed the offer to inspect the figures produced by treasury and navy officials, but many MPs found them difficult to understand. Some were unsure whether the figures for the royal debts were for interest alone, or included the principal, and many backbenchers, suffering from falling rents, pinned much of the blame on the machinations of the bankers. Nevertheless, ministers' openness did much to convince MPs of the genuineness of the king's needs. Wild claims that as much as £1,000,000 granted earlier had yet to be collected were shown to be without foundation.[32]

The Commons quickly voted that the king should be supplied according to his needs, but the crucial question was, how much? The king's spokesmen tried to keep before MPs the spectre of French attack, although the decision to prohibit the printing of the king's speech (as offensive to France) raised some eyebrows.[33] On 10 December the Commons resolved to raise a supply of about £800,000, but not by a land tax: MPs felt that land already contributed more than its share. The House had already agreed on three new duties which were expected to yield some £400,000: a tax on legal documents, an additional excise on beer and other liquors for six years and new customs duties, mainly on imports from France. The last of these was a response to Colbert's protective tariffs: its purpose was 'not to raise a revenue but to keep out the things taxed'.[34] After the vote of 10 December some way had to be found to raise the remaining £400,000 and the House pitched on a subsidy. The pre-civil-war subsidy had been chronically under-assessed and had proved painfully slow to collect, but it had had the great advantage over the assessment that it fell on net rather than gross income – taxpayers could deduct 'necessary' expenses – and on sources of income other than land, including offices and banking. Nothing showed the Commons' co-operative attitude more clearly than their attempts to make this subsidy work. It was all the more remarkable in view of the House's outrage at a brutal attack by some court bullies (some said by Monmouth's command) on one of their members, Sir John Coventry. The Commons quickly passed a bill against malicious wounding, but then (much to the relief of ministers) returned to the question of supply. If the subsidy eventually produced just under half of its estimated yield of at least £750,000, this reflected not lack of goodwill but the practical difficulties inherent in the tax: income from office or banking was far harder to assess accurately than that from land, and taxpayers, when making returns of their income, were not on oath.[35]

The Commons' stance on religion was less pleasing to the king. Having assented to the Conventicle Act as 'the price of money', he tried to enforce it in order to preserve the peace, but told Croissy that he was persecuting Dissenters only so that they would be grateful for the indulgence he would grant them when he declared his conversion. While one may doubt his commitment to Catholicity, he does seem to have inclined once more towards indulgence: Sheldon's influence at court had noticeably diminished.[36] The Commons' attitude had not changed. When two London Dissenters complained of wrongful imprisonment, the House exonerated the lord mayor and launched an investigation into the working of the Conventicle Act. The upshot was a bill which treated conventicles as riots and laid down punishments for those who evaded payment of fines or who were too poor to pay. More than three months later, in March 1671, it emerged from committee with the riot element removed and with little of the original content remaining, apart from an indemnity for over-zealous officials. Contrary to predictions, the House passed the modified bill, but the Lords received it coolly and the Commons showed little desire to press them to pass it; it was lost with the prorogation.[37]

Meanwhile, the Commons' concern about the growth of Popery was revived by the efforts of Richard Talbot and other Irish Catholics to reverse some aspects of the land settlement. The House drew up an address asking the king to enforce the laws against Popery and to have Talbot arrested. The Lords seemed in no hurry to consider the address, expressing doubts about some of the evidence cited by the Commons. On the day that the Lords finally considered it, a bill against the growth of Popery was brought into the Commons; on the day that the bill passed its third reading, the Lords approved the wording of the address. It seems possible that the bill was designed to push the Lords into endorsing the address, as the lesser of two evils; delays to the beer bill doubtless served the same purpose. Meanwhile, a clause had been added to the Popery bill imposing an oath against taking up arms against the king on the pretext of acting by his authority. In replying to the address, Charles declared that he would enforce the laws, but distinguished between those who had lately changed their religion (and so deserved to feel the full weight of the laws) and those bred as Catholics, who had served the crown loyally in the civil wars. As for the bill, Croissy thought that the clause against taking up arms seemed to be directed against Presbyterians rather than Catholics and did not improve the bill's chances of passing the Lords. Another clause, to prevent the king from dispensing individuals from the penalties of the bill, suggested that MPs' religious anxieties outweighed their respect for the king's prerogatives. The Lords felt it politically inexpedient to reject the bill, but ordered that the penal laws against Catholics should be read in their entirety, thus wasting time while the money bills completed their remaining stages. Even Bishop Cosin thought the bill was a little severe: it too never emerged from committee and was lost with the prorogation.[38]

By mid-March the subsidy bill, the excise bill and the legal proceedings bill had all passed both Houses. The final money bill, for additional customs duties, ran into unexpected snags. At the request of the Barbados sugar refiners, the Lords reduced the duty on white sugar from one penny to five-eighths of a penny per pound. The Commons angrily denied that the Lords had a right to amend money bills; the Lords retorted that they had; the attorney-general explained at length that there were many precedents on both sides. Charles expressed impatience at their wrangling and on 22 April prorogued Parliament.[39] Many saw this episode as a defeat for the court, and Charles was said to be furious with Buckingham for urging the Lords to stand up for their rights. The value of the duties which had been lost was estimated at £100,000, £400,000 and even £800,000.[40]

It is possible, however, that Charles was not sorry to see the bill fail. Apart from new duties on sugar and other goods, it prohibited the import of a variety of manufactures (including gloves, ribbons, furniture and artificial ostrich feathers) – and of brandy. Before the previous summer's adjournment, the Commons had passed a bill to ban imports of brandy; it passed the Lords, but only with amendments to which the Commons would not agree.[41] The contrast between the time taken by the Lords to pass this bill – almost a year – and the swift passage of the subsidy and excise bills (eight and four days respectively) suggests that their lordships thoroughly disliked it. When on 27 March the Commons sent up their bill for additional duties on foreign commodities, the Lords argued that it was unParliamentary to bring in a second bill prohibiting brandy imports while the first was still under consideration. The brandy clause had in fact been added in the expectation that the Lords would reject or drastically amend the brandy bill and the Lords soon dropped their claim that it was unParliamentary, but they continued to argue that it should be omitted. The focus of debate now shifted to the Lords' attempt to reduce the duty on white sugar. The Commons claimed that the Lords could not amend money bills. The Lords responded that to reduce the rate of a tax was not to tax the people and that they had a duty to do what they judged best for the kingdom, which they would be unable to do if the Commons could label any measure a 'money bill'. They had a point: the bill was designed more to discriminate against French commodities than to raise money. Nobody at this stage could predict whether the new duties would increase the king's revenue or, by bringing about a sharp fall in imports, actually reduce it: the figures that were bandied about reflected the habitual optimism of the promoters of revenue bills about their likely yield. The Commons had, indeed, added a clause to compensate Charles for his losses from the ban on brandy imports by means of a new duty on liquors distilled within England, but this was likely to produce far less than the brandy duties. Even if the bill did not harm his revenue, it would not improve his relations with France; he may have decided that any financial advantages would be outweighed by diplomatic disadvantages – but given his outwardly anti-French stance he could not say this openly. The attorney-general's even-handed discussion of the constitutional issues might, therefore, have been designed to keep the dispute alive and Buckingham's swift return to favour may have reflected more than Charles's habitual propensity to forgive: Buckingham and Ashley had urged the Lords to stick to their guns, while Arlington's clients called on the Commons to do the same.[42]

If the foregoing analysis is correct, the court enjoyed almost unblemished success in the session of 1670–1. Seymour, Howard and Sir Richard Temple had all abandoned their opposition and joined Osborne in supporting the court; all three were to receive their rewards: Osborne, a treasurer of the navy, had his already. The Commons had shown hostility to Dissent and Popery, but had been unable to secure an Act against either. It was, indeed, open to question how far the Commons mirrored the views of the nation. Those at court who argued that Dissenters and Catholics made up a majority of the population included not only Buckingham and Ashley, but Serenus Cressy, who saw liberty of conscience as an essential adjunct to Catholicity.[43] It was now ten years since the last general election and it could reasonably be argued that MPs were out of touch with those they represented.[44] A strategy based on a measure of indulgence, therefore, might seem to make sound political sense. Financially, the king's position would seem stronger as a result of the supplies granted in 1670–1: only time would show how far the yield of the subsidy would fall short of the Commons' estimates and that the new duties would do little more than reduce the annual shortfall on the ordinary revenue. The king's debts remained substantial and he had received no additional grant towards the coming war, for the simple reason that he had felt unable to ask for one. On the contrary, he had played on Parliament's fears of France, telling them of Louis' military preparations and of his bringing 40,000 men to Dunkirk for 'manoeuvres'. He had asked for money so that England could be prepared for any eventuality, by which the Commons understood attack by France. A move to include a reference to the Triple Alliance in the preamble to the supply bill was rejected. This, however, implied no hostility to the alliance, but rested on a combination of respect for the king's right to direct foreign policy and backbenchers' fears that if they started meddling with alliances they might be called upon to pay for them.[45] To embark on a war and a religious policy which were so clearly against the sense of the Commons was clearly risky – just how risky remained to be seen.

With Parliament prorogued, king and ministers began to prepare for war. In particular, they took steps to remove two potential obstacles to an effective war effort – lack of money and domestic disaffection. The subsidy and the new indirect taxes would bring in little at first and what Charles really needed was ready cash; this may be one reason why he asked, soon after the prorogation, that Louis contribute money rather than ships.[46] His problems were compounded by the failure of negotiations for a new customs farm.

Collection of the major branches of the revenue was contracted (or farmed) out to syndicates of financiers, who paid over an agreed sum and kept the surplus. The system had the advantages that the farmers made substantial advance payments and were a fruitful source of loans. The major disadvantages were that the farmers, rather than the king, benefited from any sudden increase in trade and they claimed 'defalcations' – substantial reductions in their payments in case of war or natural disaster. In September 1671 Charles's government was on the verge of concluding a new contract, then changed its mind. Some blamed Buckingham, who disliked the proposed syndicate, which included Arlington's brother. A more likely reason was the syndicate's eleventh-hour demand that it could deduct from its payments any losses incurred as a result of war, which would do much to nullify the value of the farm. Charles therefore decided to have the customs collected by officials of his own. In the long run, this was to prove highly advantageous, as trade expanded rapidly, but in the short term it seriously exacerbated his cash-flow problems. Not only did he lose the prospect of a large advance, but he had to repay what had already been advanced in anticipation of the contract. (Much of the repayment was, in fact, in fee-farm rents, but these could not then be sold for cash.) Small wonder that by November the government was desperately short of ready money.[47]

Desperate problems required desperate remedies. On 5 January 1672 Charles told the council that as his neighbours were preparing for war, he was forced to do the same. In matters of self-preservation, normal rules of conduct did not apply, so he was ordering a stop of all payments out of the exchequer until 31 December; the money was to be applied instead to the war. Those to whom payments were due would receive interest at 6 per cent. It was Clifford's idea and, although the majority of Charles's advisers were against it, they had no alternative to offer. Initially it provoked an outcry in the City; bankers refused to repay money which merchants had deposited with them for safe-keeping. Charles acted quickly: he summoned the bankers to the treasury, assured them that their money was safe and demanded that they unfreeze the merchants' deposits; business resumed more or less as usual. In the short term, the Stop brought major advantages. It relieved the crown of the obligation to repay some £1,200,000 assigned on various revenues: as the money came in, it could be spent on the war. It also freed the exchequer from the rigidity of Downing's system of repayments 'in course', under which these could not be delayed and swallowed up an increasing proportion of the revenue. This rigidity also encouraged those holding repayment orders to sell them, at a discount, to bankers, who found such transactions more lucrative than lending directly to the government and so proved reluctant to do so, except at exorbitant interest; the imposed rate of 6 per cent was therefore very favourable to the king. The crown had thus been faced with a crisis of credit at the start of 1672: one report suggested that it was the bankers' refusal to advance money that precipitated the Stop. Even so, with the Stop Charles gave yet more hostages to fortune. It generated no new revenue, while war expenditure would merely add to his debts. If the war was successful, yielding conquests and prizes, then the risk would have been worthwhile and Parliament could be expected to reimburse what Charles had spent. He would be able to take off the Stop at the end of the year, as promised, and pay the bankers what he owed them: any damage to his credit would be only temporary. If the war went badly, however, his debts would increase substantially, his credit would be badly shaken and he would have to face a Parliament angry at having been duped into giving money on false pretences.[48]

The prospect of war revived the government's concern about disaffection. In May 1671 the committee for foreign affairs expressed concern for the Tower, after 'Colonel' Thomas Blood's audacious attempt to seize the crown jewels. Blood's career had been nothing if not colourful: the previous December he had tried to abduct (and perhaps kill) the Duke of Ormond. It came as some surprise when, soon after his escapade at the Tower, he dined with Clifford and had an interview with the king. In July he was released and pardoned and in the following months he persuaded former republicans and Cromwellians (including Cromwell's brother-in-law John Desborough) to make their peace with the government; they were granted pardons in return for promises of good behaviour.[49] Such efforts to reconcile the politically disaffected raised echoes of Buckingham's patronage of former radicals in 1667–8: indeed, it is likely that Buckingham had links with Blood and even that he had encouraged the attack on Ormond.[50] Blood soon extended his activities to religious Dissenters. There had been reports in the summer that the leading nonconformists in the City had been offered liberty of conscience in return for money, which encouraged their brethren elsewhere to meet more openly.[51] Notes made by Arlington's undersecretary, Joseph Williamson, betrayed a deep anxiety. Conventicles were meeting in defiance of the law. The government was going into a war with far less support than in 1665. The old Cavaliers resented the king's failure to reward their services, but Williamson's main concern was the Dissenters: it would be dangerous 'to leave such considerable numbers unsatisfied'. It might be wiser for the king to grant a limited liberty of his own volition, rather than be forced to grant more later. His powers in ecclesiastical matters, wrote Williamson, were more extensive than in civil; he had no need to seek the assistance of Parliament.[52]

In these notes, dated 11 November, lie the essence of the Declaration of Indulgence of March 1672. Ministers tried privately to persuade nonconformists not to meet, or at least to do so more discreetly, but to no avail.

Without a firm order from the king not to meet, the ministers declared that they could not justify their conduct to their congregations. Charles, however, feared that to order the rigorous enforcement of the laws, or to use soldiers to break up conventicles, could provoke serious disorders.[53] The government's fear of disaffection also extended to the newly popular coffee-houses, but as these were not illegal it was uncertain how to suppress them.[54] Charles's lack of confidence in his ability to suppress Dissent doubtless owed much to the arguments of Buckingham and Ashley, but by December Lauderdale and Arlington were also wooing the Dissenters. Ministers held frequent, but separate, meetings with all denominations. There was renewed talk of both comprehension and indulgence and in January Charles told Anglesey of his designs 'for liberty'.[55]

On 6 March, at a meeting of the committee for foreign affairs, Clifford called for a proclamation to suspend the penalties of the laws against religious meetings and then to issue regulations to ensure that this new liberty was not abused. The king, he claimed, had the power to dispense with the Act of Uniformity, but not to change it: in other words, he proposed a limited indulgence, but not a comprehension. The king insisted that the regulation should go hand in hand with the liberty. Private meetings, or conventicles, were dangerous. Meetings should be public; preachers should be authorized by the king and should lose the right to preach if they touched on controversy or matters of state. Clifford was adamant that the regulation should follow the proclamation: only experience could show what was needed. Despite this difference, the closeness of Charles's and Clifford's viewpoints suggests that they had discussed the matter beforehand. Others were more cautious. Ashley and Buckingham stressed the need to ascertain exactly what the king's powers were; Ashley and Lauderdale wished the proclamation to stress the economic benefits of toleration; Arlington, apparently, said nothing. Three days later, the committee returned to the matter and resolved that all penal laws in matters of religion should be repealed when Parliament met; in the meantime, they should be suspended 'as far as the king can do it', which hardly exuded confidence that he legally could. Two days later, the committee drew up the heads of the Declaration, which was approved on the 14th and issued on the 15th.[56]

It began with an assertion that twelve years of persecution had failed to bring about the religious peace and harmony which Charles had long sought to promote. He was therefore making use of 'that supreme power in ecclesiastical matters which is not only inherent in us but hath been declared and recognized to be so by several statutes and Acts of Parliament' to quieten the minds of his subjects and thus promote prosperity. (There was now no mention of Parliament's repealing the penal laws.) The Church's worship and government were to remain unchanged; all holders of benefices had to conform to them. All penal laws were to be suspended, but to prevent 'illegal meetings and conventicles' nonconformists were to meet only in meeting houses licensed by the king; only ministers approved by the king could preach there. Catholics could meet only in private houses. Those who assembled otherwise than as allowed in the Declaration would be severely punished.[57]

The arguments used in the Declaration were essentially pragmatic, perhaps because those were the only kind that the Commons might accept. There was no appeal to principle, just a statement that persecution had failed to eradicate disagreement and a pious hope that indulgence would stimulate the economy. The purpose of the Declaration was not to liberate but to control Dissent, to bring it out of the clandestine, extra-legal twilight in which it had lurked and to ensure that in future nonconformists would meet only in the full light of day, subject to the scrutiny of the king's officials. This reflected Charles's own concern: on 6 March he alone had been adamant that 'regulation' should be linked to indulgence from the start.[58] As for the Catholics, they were apparently not mentioned on the 6th; when Clifford proposed on the 9th that they should be free to worship in their homes, nobody is recorded as objecting. Unlike the Dissenters, they seemed to pose no threat to the state, so their secret meetings could be connived at, whereas any public indulgence would be politically provocative.[59]

Arlington wrote that the government hoped that the Declaration 'will keep us quiet at home whilst we have business to do abroad'. It rested on the assumption that Dissent was strong and had to be propitiated; for those who shared that assumption, the lack of disorder when the war began was an indication that it was serving its purpose. There were, however, some ominous signs. Bridgeman refused to seal it, as he doubted whether the king legally possessed the power that he claimed. The lack of the Great Seal made little practical difference, although one judge was said to have refused to accept the Declaration as law.[60] Anglicans, naturally, disliked it. Some of the bishops asked for an explanation of certain aspects, but were told that none was needed. John Tillotson, a future archbishop, preached a rousing and much applauded anti-Catholic sermon at court; Charles refused to command that it be printed, on the grounds that it was too 'controversial'. He tried to persuade Sheldon to prohibit anti-Catholic preaching, but the archbishop refused to forbid his clergy to defend the Protestant religion. Arlington's brother-in-law, Sir Robert Carr, remarked that only the fact that it was the king's pleasure could make him 'relish' the Declaration; he hoped that the 'fanatics' would now be satisfied and not prove as ungrateful as in the past, a view shared by that hammer of the Westmorland Dissenters, Daniel Fleming.[61] Their pessimism was justified. Self-styled agents for the Dissenters, like Dr Nicholas Butler, argued that licences should be issued without any restrictions and that the government should make it easier for those who had qualms about applying (such as Quakers and Fifth Monarchists) to obtain them. Others, like Blood, seemed more concerned to exact money in return for procuring them.[62] What aroused most anxiety, however, was the inclusion of the Catholics. For Charles, this was a matter of rewarding a loyal group of people and doing something to earn the money paid for Catholicity (although Croissy had advised against issuing the Declaration). Some, however, claimed that the Catholics, who could worship in secret, had been granted more than the Dissenters. The concessions to them seemed more sinister in the light of other developments. There had already been rumours that the French alliance was designed to establish Popery. Louis' treaty with the Elector of Cologne gave the good of Catholicism as the main reason for making war on the Dutch. When James went to the fleet without taking communion at Easter, there were rumours that he had abjured Protestantism. In short, the Declaration gave yet more hostages to fortune. When Parliament met in April for a formal renewal of the prorogation, a surprisingly large number of MPs appeared: feelings, or rather anxieties, were running high.[63]

Charles sought to make all the political capital he could from the Declaration. The committee for foreign affairs promoted a series of addresses of thanks, with each denomination thanking the king separately: 'by that means they will be still kept from having an understanding' and each would be dependent on the king's grace for the continuance of their liberty. The Presbyterians were to address together, so that those who favoured comprehension would join with those who did not 'and so the design of the Presbyterian comprehension &c will be lost'. Charles had now decided that indulgence, not comprehension, was the way to draw the sting of nonconformity.[64] There followed orders to release from gaol Dissenters imprisoned merely for nonconformity, as distinct from (say) non-payment of tithes. Leading Presbyterians (and a few Independents) received pensions from the crown.[65] The licences, conceived as an instrument of stringent control, were in practice granted virtually on demand.

This escalation of concessions to Dissent reflected not tolerance but fear. Alberti remarked that Charles regarded his people as hostile and had strengthened the guard around the court.[66] The magistrates of the shires seem mostly to have respected the Declaration, but with misgivings. Uncertain exactly what was allowed, they tended to give Dissenters the benefit of the doubt, even if they refused to produce licences, and as the central government sent no details of the licences it had issued it was impossible to check on the Dissenters' claims. Clearly, many JPs felt resentful, especially those berated by the more aggressive nonconformists.[67] Only occasionally did the Anglicans hit back. A group of Oxford students disrupted a meeting, arguing with the preacher, upon which Arlington sent a strong reprimand to the vice-chancellor. Undeterred, the students took to groaning and crying 'amen' loudly, which drove 'the brethren' to find new premises, protected by a fierce dog, whereupon the scholars brought a fiercer 'conformist dog', which killed its rival.[68] Such incidents are evidence of a resentment, suppressed for now, which would find its voice when Parliament met – unless Charles could deflect it by military success. Everything, therefore, hinged on the conduct of the war.

Charles had had last-minute doubts about declaring war, which owed less to fears that Louis might not follow suit than to the conclusion of a defensive alliance between Spain and the Dutch, at Brussels, in November 1671.[69] In a desperate attempt to prevent ratification of the treaty, Charles sent to inform the Spanish queen mother of his intention to convert to Catholicism, a course of action proposed by Arlington and opposed by Croissy. The latter pressed Charles to be ready to declare war against the Spaniards if they helped the Dutch: Louis still kept open the option of making war against Spain instead of against the Dutch and derived great pleasure from bullying the hapless authorities in Flanders, who he hoped could be provoked into some rash action which could justify further French conquests in the region. Only Buckingham, who talked wildly of conquests in the West Indies, seemed prepared to envisage war against Spain. York was sure that the Spanish threats were mere bluff; Arlington thought it was necessary to frighten the Spaniards with talk of war, but to go no further. Charles, meanwhile, was reassured by the Spanish queen's response to his plans for conversion. His declaration of war included a promise to respect the Treaty of Aix-la-Chapelle (and thus to preserve the Spanish Netherlands) and he told Alberti that his interests were identical with those of Spain.[70]

Charles's hesitations were not born of a lack of commitment. He sent out a fleet larger than he was obliged to by treaty and threw himself wholeheartedly into the organization of the war. Buckingham, Clifford and Arlington offered to serve as volunteers on the fleet.[71] It soon became apparent, nevertheless, that any qualms which Charles may have felt would have been fully justified. His subjects showed little enthusiasm, their reservations about the war being strengthened by Dutch propaganda. It was difficult to recruit seamen. Many, even at court, declared that the real purpose of the war was to destroy Protestantism. By May Charles, deeply alarmed, bemoaned his brother's headstrong eagerness to avow his conversion and kept finding new pretexts for delaying his own.[72] Seen in this context, the remarks reported by Croissy and Alberti about establishing absolutism seem like whistling in the dark.[73] The best that Charles could hope for was to come out of the war without too much damage to his authority and his honour.

For Louis, success was not slow in coming, Carefully avoiding Spanish territory, his huge army passed through the bishopric of Liège, crossed the Rhine near Cologne and, in the first week of June, swept into the republic from the east. The direction and scale of the assault took the Dutch by surprise; their army 'collapsed like a bad soufflé'.[74] Five of the provinces were quickly overrun, leaving only Holland and Zeeland. The States General offered to cede all their territory south of the Great Rivers, which would have left them powerless to oppose French expansion in the Southern Netherlands, plus a large indemnity. Louvois and the generals urged Louis to demand more, including freedom of worship for Catholics and an annual embassy to give Louis humble thanks for having granted them peace. Such arrogance proved misplaced. The Dutch were badly shaken, but still had their pride. The French had not taken the two richest provinces, which were soon rendered inaccessible, as the dikes were cut and the countryside flooded. Louis, however, remained confident that they would have to come to terms before the winter frosts came and opened the way for his armies to march to Amsterdam. He returned to Paris to await developments.

Charles's advisers were far less confident: Arlington told Croissy that there were more grounds for fear than hope. Money was desperately short and Charles enquired tentatively whether the pope or the French clergy might be persuaded to contribute to the costs of Catholicity.[75] The war at sea started badly. Only fog prevented the Dutch from attacking the English fleet before the French contingent could join it. Charles proposed that the fleet should sail close to the Dutch coast to prevent their fleet from coming out and to let the people see that its commanders dared not fight: two could play at fomenting domestic disaffection. In fact, the fleets met in the bloody battle of Sole Bay on 28 May. As they limped back to port for repairs, both sides claimed to have had the better of the fray, but it was now clear that there would be no quick English victory. The English public criticized the French for failing fully to engage the enemy and York for inadequate leadership, but the duke successfully resisted moves to have Rupert appointed commander in his place. Charles did not regard his brother as the brightest of mortals, but wished to maintain his honour (and that of the family) and was confident that, unlike the obstreperous Rupert, he could maintain good relations with the French commanders.[76]

News of Sole Bay was soon followed by that of Louis' invasion of the republic. The contrast between the supine performance of the French fleet and the dazzling success of the French armies aroused jealousy and suspicion. Charles and Arlington, while stressing their commitment to the alliance, told Croissy that it was politically necessary to receive the proposals which the States General now sent. Buckingham, so recently the leading 'hawk', urged Charles to accept the Dutch proposals before Louis overran the whole of the Netherlands: how far this sudden change was due to James's telling him of Catholicity we shall never know. Buckingham's influence, however, was not what it had been: he was less a senior adviser than a capricious, spoilt child who needed to be kept occupied and happy. It was decided to send him to Louis' military headquarters to concert a joint response to the Dutch proposals – and to send Arlington to keep an eye on him.[77] Although Charles and Arlington still stressed their determination to continue the war, they were clearly alarmed by Louis' successes and by his proposals, first, that Charles should accept money in lieu of towns and, second, that (if William were to receive Holland) Louis should exchange his conquests for Breda and Brabant. Such an exchange would give him control of the southern side of the mouth of the Great Rivers and so reduce the commercial and strategic usefulness of Zeeland, which the English still hoped to conquer. The committee of foreign affairs showed itself suspicious of both Louis and William. It still hoped for the whole of Zeeland, but agreed to settle for Flushing, Brill and Sluys as 'cautionary towns'; William should have Holland and Louis should be accommodated elsewhere. If these demands proved unattainable, the war would have to continue: after such great expenditures and such great expectations, they would have to have *something* to show for it. Moreover, as Charles remarked, it would be fatal to lose both France and Holland, as Clarendon had done. It was therefore decided to prepare for a descent on Zeeland.[78]

There can be no doubting Charles's determination to make territorial gains on the European mainland. Not only was he very conscious that he had gained nothing from the war, but his dislike of the Dutch had ripened into pathological hatred: the republic, he declared, must no longer pretend to be a state. Louis, however, had no wish to see the English installed on continental soil, nor did he see why he should help them secure territories which they seemed unable to conquer for themselves. Besides, to add England's territorial demands to those Louis had already made would inevitably retard his expected peace with the Dutch. Having failed to interest Charles in either an indemnity or conquests outside Europe as an alternative to his towns, Croissy suggested that he should switch his attention from Sluys and Cadzand to Delfzijl, at the mouth of the Ems, with good access to the north of the republic and to Germany – and well away from the Great Rivers. Charles visibly brightened; he later told Croissy that he had persuaded the council to accept this change of objective, but that Clifford and Buckingham still pressed for Sluys, Cadzand, Brill and Flushing.[79]

Meanwhile, Buckingham and Arlington made their way to Louis, via Rotterdam. They found the Dutch people friendly, but William, now emerging as the leading figure in the republic, stubborn and intractable. William, for his part, was perplexed by Buckingham, who one day offered to settle on William's terms (agreeing with him that it was not in England's interest to make France more powerful) and the next told him defeat was inevitable and urged him to put himself wholly in Charles's hands. The two envoys met Louis at his camp at Heeswijk and signed a treaty renewing the alliance. Neither king was to make peace without the other; Louis was to press for the Dutch to make concessions to the English which in some respects would be more extensive than those envisaged in Charles's treaties with Louis. These included recognition of the salute due to the flag; the banishment of regicides and others active against Charles's government; £1,000,000 in 'reparations' for the cost of the war; and a tribute of £10,000 a year for the right to fish around the English coasts. William was to receive the sovereignty of as much of the republic as should remain after the demands of France and England had been satisfied: at the least, the post of stadhouder was to be hereditary within the House of Orange. On the other hand, England was now to receive the five places mentioned in the *traité simulé* only as guarantees for the execution of the rest, not in permanent possession.[80] The fact that Louis should commit himself to securing so much suggests that he had been alarmed by Croissy's reports that Charles had received overtures from the Dutch. It also seems likely that he was far more willing to press for reparations (which could be scaled down), the flag and commercial concessions than for the outright cession of parts of Holland and Zeeland, which (as Pomponne, Louis' new foreign minister, told Arlington) would be quite impossible.[81]

The embassy strengthened Charles's commitment to Louis and his distrust of William. He ordered Arlington and Buckingham, on their way home, to warn Monterey, the Spanish governor in Brussels, to withdraw his troops from Dutch fortresses. Charles still hoped that William would come round to his way of thinking: he assured him that he could establish him in a position of unassailable power and expressed irritation and bewilderment at the young man's failure to follow his advice. When an exasperated mob lynched de Witt and his brother, Charles hinted that the same fate might befall William if he did not come to terms; it was in William's interest, he suggested, to ensure that Charles should possess sufficient power within the republic to protect him against his enemies. William, however, was no coward and nobody's puppet. Gradually, he rallied the Dutch people, gathered allies and rebuilt the republic's demoralized army. If Charles and Louis wanted to take the republic, they would have to fight for it.[82]

Once Arlington and Buckingham had returned, Charles began to prepare in earnest for the descent, although Shaftesbury thought that, in the last resort, he would settle for less than the original demands: something for the fishing, more modest reparations and two cautionary towns 'for their performance and good behaviour'. The invasion force was to consist of 8,000 men, plus the 2,000 whom Louis had promised to hold in readiness. The smallness of this force reflected both limited resources and a confidence that the people of Zeeland would welcome the English as liberators. Some had, in fact, approached Charles and had been assured that they could have William as their stadhouder if they so wished. Charles ordered James to detach as many ships as he could spare to ensure the success of the descent 'without which we shall lose the reputation and advantage of this summer'.[83] The lack of confidence which that remark betrayed became manifest when the committee for foreign affairs discussed William's insistence that England should receive no towns in perpetuity. With the exception of Buckingham, the committee agreed to specify a period of ten years. The newly appointed secretary, Henry Coventry, remarked that it would be rare for a peace to last so long and, if it did not, England would keep the towns. Arlington was less sanguine. He knew at first hand the French hostility to any permanent cessions and argued that it would be impossible to continue the war for another year; some show of moderation was therefore needed to justify the government's conduct to the world. Charles, too, supported the change of objective, expressing concern that Louis might make a separate peace. As the campaigning season was now almost over, the decision to press on with the descent smacked less of hope than of desperation: at the very least, fear of invasion might make the Dutch more amenable.[84]

As the summer neared its end with no prospect of English military success, friction developed between Charles and Louis. Each complained that the other pitched his demands too high: Louis argued that Charles's insistence on towns in Zeeland was an insuperable obstacle to a settlement, but Charles could ask for no less if he was to convince his people that the war had not been an abject failure. The brutal fact, however, was that he lacked the resources to mount a full-scale invasion. The damage inflicted on his fleet by a storm and the safe return of the Dutch East India fleet added insult to injury.[85] After that, talk of seeking out and fighting the Dutch fleet was merely foolhardy.[86] Charles's frustration was exacerbated by new disputes about protocol at the entry of the Earl of Sunderland, his new ambassador in Paris, and by news that Louis had sent to the Rhine the 2,000 men he had promised to keep ready to assist the descent; by now, however, it was so late in the season that Charles saw no point in complaining.[87] Starved of victory, his priority now was to limit the political damage done by the war.

If he were to stand any chance of this, he needed a face-saving peace, but William would make no concessions while there was a prospect of a Parliament, which he expected to press Charles to settle with the Dutch. Arlington, who had more cause than most to fear Parliament's wrath, urged Charles to prorogue it until the new year. Charles sounded MPs about the possibility of supply and talked boldly, but unspecifically, of raising money elsewhere.

Money certainly had to be found somehow, to pay off the fleet: Arlington's request for a French loan was rejected. In mid-September the committee of foreign affairs resolved, after much debate, to prorogue Parliament until 4 February. Charles's reasons for the delay were diplomatic: 'The French', he said, 'will have us or Holland always with them and if we take them not, Holland will have them.' If Parliament met and began to 'dog and rogue the French and the alliance' Louis would close with the Dutch and England would be isolated. He hoped that if, by February, it could be shown that the Dutch had rejected reasonable terms, Parliament would support the war.[88]

Such an argument possessed a certain superficial logic but it smacked of an excuse to put off the day of reckoning: it is hard to accept Alberti's claim that the prorogation struck a great blow for the king's authority.[89] The disadvantages of the war became clearer and clearer: Dutch privateers played havoc with English merchant shipping.[90] The need to raise troops for the descent also raised the issue of martial law. Neither statute nor the common law recognized the legality of the army or provided means of punishing mutiny and desertion. Kings had traditionally, in wartime, established martial law, by virtue of their prerogative: the king had a right, indeed a duty, to do whatever was necessary for the defence of the realm. Martial law applied equally to soldiers and civilians, and courts martial could impose the death penalty on soldiers for offences normally triable in civilian courts. This was justified by the argument that civilian justice was far too slow: drastic methods were needed to maintain discipline in wartime. In 1628 the Petition of Right declared illegal the use of commissions of martial law under which the king's subjects (soldiers and sailors) could be executed otherwise than by the law of the land. Martial law was not, however, the only means whereby the king could maintain discipline in the armed forces. He could also, as commander in chief, issue articles of war, which applied only to the military, but could also be enforced by courts martial. These could not impose severe penalties, at least in England: overseas garrisons, like Tangier, were another matter. Although the relationship between courts martial and common law courts was never fully defined, a rough *modus vivendi* developed, whereby the former dealt with strictly military offences, imposing no sentence more severe than cashiering, while soldiers who offended against the common law were tried in civilian courts.[91]

In June 1672 Bridgeman refused to seal a commission for 'martial law' on the grounds that it would contravene the Petition of Right. The committee for foreign affairs resolved to ask Serjeant Ellis 'how he can find it lawful'; Shaftesbury was to speak to Solicitor-General North. Their answers cannot have been encouraging, because it was not until September that the 'articles of war' came before the committee. York complained that they did not allow for the death penalty, except where it was already prescribed by common law: if the council of war was not expressly allowed to impose the ultimate penalty, it would never do so, as shown by the experience of the navy. Clifford, in a somewhat confused reply, seemed to claim that the king had the right to dispense with the Petition of Right. The law officers were asked whether, despite the Petition, the king could issue a commission of 'martial law'. Attorney-General Finch agreed that such a commission had been issued in 1639, but that had been during an 'intestine war'. With a fine ignorance of history, he doubted whether the Petition had been drawn up in time of war. He insisted that soldiers should be subject to civilian courts for offences against the common law and that all disputes between soldiers and civilians should be triable in civil courts. It was agreed that a commission should be issued, which was to operate only in wartime and to cover only those in pay. Even then the committee had second thoughts, deciding that separate commissions should be issued to each colonel or garrison commander.[92]

Finch had thought that, as drafted, the commission ought to prove unexceptionable. He was wrong. The varied terminology used by Williamson in the committee's minutes mirrored a common confusion between 'articles of war' and 'martial law', the latter widely seen as illegal since the Petition of Right. The very fact that troops were being raised led to wild speculation about the use to which they might be put, among not only habitual critics of the government but even the bishops.[93] In these circumstances, it is not surprising that no commission for martial law was ever issued.[94] After the Commons expressed great alarm about the army in the spring of 1673, ministers became even more cautious. By June of that year articles of war had been printed which provided for a court martial, presumably under the restrictions suggested by Finch. The reaction, among soldiers and civilians, was so hostile that a month later nobody had dared to put the articles into execution. There was particular alarm about a 'horrid oath' in which each soldier undertook to obey his officers 'in all they shall command me for His Majesty's service'. Some did indeed appreciate that the common law alone could not maintain military discipline, but 'our Parliament men and lawyers do not care to hear of martial law'. These fears of 'martial law' might bear little relation to the government's intentions, but it had no choice but to bow to them. The articles were never issued and the officers had to maintain discipline as best they could.[95]

A further source of anxiety was the renewed prospect of war with Spain. Louis had been careful to avoid hostile acts, but his success against the Dutch had alarmed Brussels and Madrid. Arlington had always insisted that a breach between England and Spain would be fatal. Not only would it add new complexities to the peace negotiations, but it would be very unpopular in the business community; he therefore became increasingly eager for peace. Buckingham, perhaps just for the pleasure of differing with Arlington, professed to view the prospect of war with Spain with equanimity; others argued that Charles should embark on such a war only if there were prospects of substantial gains, in Flanders or the Caribbean. In December news came that an army, led by William and Monterey, had attacked the French-held town of Charleroi, which many (including Charles) thought a breach of the Treaty of the Pyrenees. Charles, Arlington and Clifford were most relieved when the siege was lifted and expressed hopes that the Dutch might now reduce their demands. They still accepted that they were obliged to help Louis against Spain, but insisted that such help should stop short of open war. Croissy insisted that Louis intended only limited hostilities against Spain in the Netherlands, sufficient to prevent them from helping the Dutch: he wanted no more English talk of partition or of subsidies. Only Buckingham, avid for conquests (this time in Flanders), urged Charles to declare war.[96]

The threat of war with Spain and the chronic shortage of money made it impossible to delay Parliament any longer. As the meeting loomed nearer, the court closed ranks. Bridgeman had long seemed timid, objecting to the Declaration of Indulgence and the articles of war. The last straw came with his refusal to seal a royal declaration that creditors could not constrain bankers for the repayment of the principal, but only for the interest. He was dismissed in November and replaced by the more resolute Shaftesbury, who was given the more prestigious title of lord chancellor.[97] Meanwhile, Clifford's rise (he had been raised to the peerage in April) was crowned by his appointment as lord treasurer, much to the chagrin of his former patron, Arlington (although the two were soon reconciled). Buckingham, meanwhile, was temporarily in disgrace for having tried to seduce Nell Gwynn.[98]

The crown's continuing cash-flow problems led Clifford to extend the Stop until 1 May, despite earlier assurances that it would end in December.[99] Such an action was not likely to improve Parliament's temper. Arlington, after sounding MPs, expressed every confidence, but Croissy was sceptical. Charles tried to reassure the churchmen, telling Sheldon to order his clergy to catechize the young and to proceed against unlicensed schoolmasters; the archbishop still instructed his bishops to come up in force for the session. Charles remarked that MPs' attitudes suggested that the Dutch had been spending money liberally among them – yet again, he seemed unable to consider the possibility of spontaneous and principled opposition to his policies. Croissy, more realistically, blamed James's conduct for much of the hostility shown by MPs, but comforted himself with the thought that, if bribery failed to change their minds, Charles could always dissolve. In such circumstances, talk of asking for a land tax of £1,200,000, plus the bill for additional duties on imports which had been lost in the previous session, must have seemed wildly unrealistic; so must the issuing of commissions to raise eight new regiments – how were they to be paid for? As so often, then, Charles's ministers approached a session of Parliament with something akin to dread.[100]

When Parliament assembled on 4 February, Charles's opening speech contained a mixture of defensiveness and defiance. As far as the war was concerned, the nation's honour and interest were at stake: had he missed this opportunity 'perhaps I had not again ever met with the like advantage'. The Declaration was designed to secure peace at home while he made war abroad. It did not harm the Church; the liberty granted to Catholics was much narrower than that accorded to other Dissenters and was the least he could do to reward the former's loyalty. He was, therefore, determined to maintain the Declaration. He dismissed as frivolous claims that the land forces he had raised 'were designed to control law and property'; he did not yet have enough and intended to raise more in the coming year. He asked for money for the war and to pay his debts and concluded that he would preserve liberty, property and the Protestant religion.[101]

The Commons considered the king's speech on the 7th. To the court's surprise and delight, they voted an eighteen months' assessment at £70,000 a month, sweeping aside complaints that some counties were rated too highly. It seemed too good to be true, and it was. Some of the court's critics, like Garroway and Thomas Lee, feared that without the bait of a substantial supply the king might dissolve Parliament.[102] It soon became clear that this time 'the price of money' would be the withdrawal of the Indulgence, plus new measures against Catholicism. MPs were now obsessed with the dangers of 'Popery' to a point where they were prepared to modify their attitude towards Dissent. In the previous session they had passed yet another bill against conventicles; now they were ready to allow Dissenters a measure of indulgence, albeit within stringent limits. They would thus secure, in part, the declared objective of the Declaration, in a manner which raised no constitutional difficulties – and gave nothing to the Papists. MPs of many shades of opinion argued that the Declaration was illegal: it suspended forty Acts of Parliament, which could be repealed only by statute. Attorney-General Finch told the House that the king's counsel had not been consulted about the Declaration; he argued that the king could dispense only with penalties that were due to him and that (whatever the Declaration claimed) there was no difference between the king's ecclesiastical and his secular prerogative. Staunch Cavaliers like Sir Giles Strangways were as outspoken as such habitual critics of the court as Henry Powle. One remarked that the Indulgence 'has done him [the king] more harm among his father's friends than good to those indulged'. While professing great respect for the king, MPs expressed great anxiety about the possible misuse of the powers he had claimed by some future monarch – a reference, perhaps, to his brother. The House resolved to drawn up an address to show that penal laws in matters of religion could be repealed only by Act of Parliament.[103]

Faced with the Commons' stance, the committee for foreign affairs considered two possible courses of action. The first was to try to have the substance of the Declaration – both a grant of indulgence and an assertion of the king's dispensing power – confirmed by statute (as had originally been intended). The second was to try to set the Lords against the Commons, on the grounds that the Commons had not invited the peers to concur with their resolution. The committee was confident that the Lords would declare the Declaration legal. The Commons would then back down; if not, the deadlock between the Houses would frustrate any further attempts to overturn it. Some members of the committee claimed, indeed, that the agitation in the Commons was intended to undermine the king's authority: talk of religion was a blind. The committee resolved to pursue both courses at once, but not to consult the judges, who were likely to rule against the Declaration: far better to rely on the king's influence among the peers.[104] Either way, York, Shaftesbury, Buckingham, Clifford and Lauderdale insisted that Charles must stick to the Declaration. Burnet even cited reports that the three last named had advocated using armed force to intimidate Parliament, but in the original draft of his *History* he expressed scepticism about these stories. After the assault on Sir John Coventry, he wrote, Charles had decided to eschew violent methods, but it is possible that Lauderdale talked of assistance from Scotland if need arose.[105] Arlington, however, doubted whether the Lords would uphold the dispensing power and insisted that Charles should not jeopardize supply. He was supported by Secretary Coventry, who (as a strong Churchman) disliked the Declaration on principle. Charles came to share Arlington's point of view: 'The only fear', he declared, 'is stopping our money and disappointing us of the fleet. . . . We must stand to what we can stand to.'[106] Torn between fear for his prerogative and fear of losing the money, Charles delayed his reply to the Commons until the 24th. Then he told them that the crown's ecclesiastical prerogatives had never been questioned before and existed only to secure the public peace. He made no claim to suspend laws protecting liberty or property, or to change the Church's doctrine and discipline – in other words, he aimed at indulgence, not comprehension, and would gladly assent to any bill to that end.[107]

The Commons remained unsatisfied. MPs argued that if Charles could suspend statutes, invoking the plea of 'necessity', liberty and property would never be safe; the legislative power resided in king, Lords and Commons, not just the king. As it was clear that Charles's attempt at conciliation had failed, many of those around him urged him to dissolve Parliament rather than sacrifice his prerogatives; Charles, in a fit of bravado, talked of doing so. Arlington, however, insisted that the king had to have money at all costs; besides, the Declaration was so unpopular with everybody except the Catholics that his own servants would desert him if he tried to maintain it.[108] Charles decided to make one last effort and told the Lords of his offer to the Commons. The Lords welcomed his proposal to resolve the matter by legislation and set up a committee, to which Clifford presented a bill to grant the king the powers claimed in his Declaration, if he did not possess them already. This would have stood no chance of passing the Commons, however, and the committee never put it before the House. What the court had really wanted was a clear statement from the Lords that they regarded as a breach of privilege the Commons' decision to address the king without informing them; and this the peers seemed disinclined to make. The Commons tactfully sent up their latest address, against the growth of Popery, for the Lords' concurrence. Having played his last card, Charles bowed to the inevitable and sent Coventry to inform the Commons that he had torn the seal off the Declaration, rendering it null and void.[109]

As the news spread, wrote Coventry smugly, 'the streets shin'd with bonfires as if there had been a second Restoration'.[110] The mood at court was less euphoric: York grumbled that Charles's weakness would ruin him. Croissy claimed that it was Louis' advice, and the promise of French troops to assist his designs after peace had been made, which had finally persuaded the king to abandon the Declaration. He added, however, that Charles and his advisers had told him that they would take up Louis' offer only in the direst necessity: to use foreign troops could prove counter-productive.[111] French influence may indeed have proved decisive, but it seems more likely that the crucial factor had been the need for money to continue the war: Charles had committed himself too far to back down without a humiliating loss of face. He stressed to the Houses that, now that he had cancelled the Declaration, he expected them to respond by expediting the supply bill. The prevailing feeling in the Commons, however, was that other measures should be completed first, notably the test bill and the bill to relieve Dissenters.[112] The former was designed to weed out of office the few Catholics who had managed to evade the existing legal obstacles to their employment. To the requirement that they take the oaths of allegiance and supremacy was added a new 'test': a declaration against a variety of Catholic tenets, including transubstantiation – the belief that in the eucharist the bread and wine were transformed into the body and blood of Christ. All office-holders were to take communion according to the Anglican rite at least once a year. With the exception of some bishops, who disapproved of using the holy sacrament as a test for secular office, the Lords raised no major objections until Clifford denounced the bill as a 'monstrum horrendum'. He told York that he had not intended to speak until God had suddenly inspired him to do so; others, however, claimed that he had discussed with Charles what he planned to say and was flabbergasted when Charles, on Arlington's advice, disavowed his speech. The Commons were outraged – there was talk of an impeachment – and any prospect of major amendments to the bill disappeared.[113] Once the test bill had passed, the money bill was quickly completed and Charles adjourned the session on 29 March. As it neared its end, the Commons presented addresses on other issues – the favour shown to Papists in Ireland, abuses in the quartering of soldiers – but firmly rejected proposals to delay supply until other grievances had been redressed. The Commons stressed this point in one of their addresses to the king: they preferred, they said, to trust in his goodness. After a difficult session, they doubtless felt that a gesture of goodwill was required.[114]

Perhaps the strongest indication of the changing temper of the Commons was the bill for the relief of Dissenters. The Commons resolved to bring in such a bill on 14 February, immediately after drawing up their first address against the Declaration. Many MPs, however, had reservations. Some denounced Dissenters' political principles – 'the Presbyterians will ever be for a commonwealth' – while others argued that any liberty should be temporary, so that it could be withdrawn if it was abused. The question of comprehension proved equally divisive. Sir William Coventry argued that it would unite Protestants against the threat of Popery; his brother Henry replied that a garrison was not strengthened by bringing in people infected with plague. Emotions ran high, with talk of Charles I's murder.[115] The bill eventually passed the Commons on 19 March. It laid down that the relief should be for one year only and that Dissenters were to meet only in meeting houses, licensed by the JPs at quarter sessions, with the doors open. Preachers were not to attack the doctrine of the Church of England and were to take the oaths of allegiance and supremacy and to subscribe those of the Thirty-nine Articles which dealt with doctrine. The bill provided for the repeal of the clause in the Act of Uniformity requiring beneficed clergymen to swear their unfeigned assent and consent to everything in the Prayer Book. The clause relating to the Covenant was to be modified. Ministers had been required to declare that it imposed no obligation on themselves or others; now they were to speak only for themselves and only those who had subscribed the Covenant were to be required to renounce it.[116]

Compared to the Declaration, the bill offered a very restricted liberty. The insistence on the doctrinal articles would exclude Baptists: Article XXVII prescribed infant baptism. The requirement that teachers take the oaths would exclude Quakers. Many Presbyterians would be unwilling to renounce the Covenant, even in these more moderate terms. And, of course, the liberty was to be for a limited period. The bill, in fact, exuded hostility and suspicion. It stipulated that Dissenters should not use nonconformity as a pretext to avoid onerous local offices and it was linked to another to promote catechizing within the established Church. The Lords proposed a number of amendments which would have brought it much closer to the Declaration – above all, that the king should be given the power to dispense with the laws against Dissent. He, not the JPs, was to license meeting houses, for a period of a year and from then to the next session of Parliament. The Lords also wished to omit all reference to the Thirty-nine Articles and to the oaths of allegiance and supremacy, leaving it to the king to judge the teachers' (political) acceptability. The Lords thus wished to give statutory backing to the dispensing power and to allow a wider indulgence than that envisaged by the Commons. On the other hand, they had no interest in comprehension or in weakening the requirement to renounce the Covenant. The Commons refused point-blank to allow the king to dispense with the laws: it would be a dangerous precedent and would make the Dissenters directly dependent on the king. JPs, not the king, should issue licences, because they were responsible for law and order in the localities. The Commons argued that those who refused the oaths did not deserve liberty, nor did those who differed from the Church in fundamentals: if that were once conceded, even the Papists might be indulged. The only discretion they were prepared to allow the king was that of issuing proclamations to restrict (but not to extend) the liberty allowed by the bill. The Commons defended the proposal to amend the requirement to renounce the Covenant, saying it would strengthen the Church by encouraging as many 'as may consist with its safety' to come into it.[117]

Clearly, the Lords' amendments represented an attempt by the court to secure the substance of the Declaration, and of Clifford's abortive bill, in another form. After giving his assent to the test and money bills, Charles stayed in the Lords until seven o'clock, hoping that the Dissenters' bill would be completed, and decided to end the session only when it became clear that the Commons would not budge. It is possible that he decided to adjourn, rather than prorogue, in order that this bill could be completed next session. Croissy may have reflected the view current at court when he wrote that the Anglicans had offered concessions to win the Dissenters' support against the Catholics, but had reneged on them once they secured the Test Act. Others were delighted. The debates on the Covenant had aroused strong emotions: 'I will never receive the blood of my saviour', declared Henry Coventry, 'from that hand that stinks with the guilt of the blood of my great master.' Soon after the prorogation Bishop Morley wrote that the bill would have established schism by law: he was against any comprehension which did not require exact subscription to all the articles and canons – which would hardly be a comprehension at all.[118] The failure of the bill left the Dissenters' status uncertain. Morley thought that they would worship openly until firmly ordered to desist. The council decided to leave the matter open until Parliament met. In the meantime, it required Dissenters to worship peacefully and magistrates to keep the peace.[119]

If, as seems probable, the Indulgence had been designed mainly to maintain peace at home during the war, such indeterminacy would not have displeased the king. True, he had been forced to withdraw the Declaration, but outwardly this had been his voluntary act; no statute had been passed to limit his use of the dispensing power. The Test Act did no more than close the last small loopholes in the legal exclusion of Catholics from office; if the requirement to take Anglican communion bothered some Dissenters, it would not have upset Charles. When he adjourned Parliament, he could not have foreseen the embarrassment soon to be caused by York's and Clifford's decision to lay down their offices rather than take the test. If the concessions which he had made could be seen as less than disastrous, on the positive side he had secured a grant of money sufficient to enable him to continue the war. By the time Parliament reconvened, he might well be able to win its admiration, and financial support, by means of either impressive victories or an honourable peace. Yet again, his fate hung on the fortunes of war.

Two days after the adjournment, the committee for foreign affairs agreed a set of terms, similar to those in the Treaty of Heeswijk, on which Charles could make peace. The first priority was to acquire towns: either Flushing and Ramekens or Helvoetsluys and Goeree, plus the wherewithal to sustain them. This marked a substantial climb-down from the objectives of the previous year and it was not spelled out whether Charles hoped to gain these towns in perpetuity or as guarantees for the performance of other articles in a treaty; given the fact that this demand was given pride of place, the former seems the more likely. Next came the flag ('take care to word it well') and then reparations of £500,000, half the previous year's figure. Of this, £200,000 was to be paid at once, the remainder over six years, so it would do little to solve the king's financial problems. As before, the Dutch were to pay a small annual tribute for the fishing – again, sovereignty counted for more than money – and William was to be perpetual stadhouder. The English were to be free to leave Surinam; English 'traitors' were to be banished from the republic and trade (especially outside Europe) was to be regulated to the satisfaction of both nations.[120]

It was one thing to draw up a shopping list of demands, quite another to get them accepted. Charles used the usual seventeenth-century combination of diplomacy and force. At the peace congress at Cologne, plenipotentiaries pursued ponderous and intricate negotiations, which could be transformed at any time by changes of military fortune or shifts in the domestic politics of the participating states. The very success of Louis' arms had alarmed other states and his attempts to deter them, by violence, from aiding the Dutch proved counter-productive. Gradually William cobbled together an anti-French coalition, including Spain, the emperor and various German states. Louis withdrew his forces from the republic and the focus of the war shifted to the Spanish Netherlands and Germany. Charles, and his war aims, became peripheral to Louis. England remained a valuable ally, especially at sea – the English fleet might even be used to protect French ports against Dutch or Spanish attack – and Louis certainly did not want Charles to join his growing list of enemies. Even so, Louis was unwilling to offer more than the limited naval help stipulated in the treaties, plus maybe some diplomatic assistance at Cologne – but never to the extent of jeopardizing his wider aims. Any satisfactory outcome to the war would thus depend on England's own efforts.[121]

Charles was well aware of these changes. He continued to profess his determination to stick to France, not least because he feared Louis might join with the Dutch if he did not, but he found that his interests and Louis' increasingly diverged. Louis kept pressing him to break with Spain, arguing that the Spanish (and Dutch) would come to terms only if he took a firm stand. The most Charles would do was sign a paper stating that, in his opinion, the attack on Charleroi absolved Louis from his treaty obligations towards Spain; having done so, he was most reluctant to make his opinion public.[122] Later in the year some of his advisers urged him to consider Spanish proposals which were designed to pave the way for a separate peace with the Dutch, but Charles would not hear of it.[123] Soon after, the Spaniards concluded an offensive and defensive alliance with the Dutch and declared war on France. Though they did not, for the moment, declare war on England as well, the danger remained that Charles could be drawn deeper and deeper into a more and more extensive war. To make matters worse, the Dutch plenipotentiaries at Cologne found endless pretexts to delay their responses to Charles's proposals. They knew that sooner or later he would have to recall Parliament: time was on their side.[124]

The greatest single source of friction between Charles and Louis was the former's insistence on gaining some Dutch towns. For a while there were hopes that Zeeland might voluntarily accept English rule; the Zeelanders were promised freedom of religion and English protection against the French and offered the choice of retaining their existing government or being accorded representation in Parliament. (Needless to say, Croissy was not told of this.)[125] Croissy was, however, told that Charles insisted on having the towns. 'I would rather part with all my money than lose the towns,' he declared.[126] As months passed without military success, his insistence that he needed towns to satisfy his people became ever more plaintive. Louis replied that the Dutch, Swedes and other powers would never agree to allow England to control both sides of the North Sea; although he did not mention it, he was of the same opinion.[127] At the end of July, Charles reluctantly agreed to drop this demand, provided he received compensation. Desperate to save face at home, he now placed most emphasis on the flag, upon which (wrote Coventry) the people were 'very tender'; the secretary was not, however, optimistic about the prospect of persuading other powers to recognize England's claims. Charles's servants complained that Louis pitched his demands too high and that the Dutch were inflexible, while Charles was being eminently reasonable. Unfortunately rectitude and reason – even if they had been on England's side – were no substitute for power.[128]

Military might could not be conjured out of thin air. On the eve of the war the army had numbered less than 8,000 officers and men, stationed mostly in garrisons around the English coast and in foreign outposts such as Tangier. Few of these could be deployed for the descent, for which Charles raised a further 10,000 officers and men.[129] The men would mostly be raw recruits, very different from those who made up the fighting machine built up by Le Tellier and Louvois. Strong commanders and competent officers would be needed to train them for active service, but such commanders were in short supply. York was eager to command the expeditionary force: he loved soldiering and hoped to redeem himself after his less than glorious performance at sea the previous year; Charles had, indeed, decided that Rupert should command the fleet that summer. York was certainly competent, and loyal, but now that his conversion was widely suspected he was a political liability. There had been broad hints in Parliament that, if he ever became king, he might rule more despotically than his brother had done. There was talk of his being attacked and even excluded from the succession when Parliament reconvened and it was noted that he again failed to take communion at Easter.[130] Talk of Charles's divorcing the queen had died down since the Roos affair. Charles was so preoccupied with his latest mistress, Louise de Quérouaille, that he rarely visited Cleveland; he created Louise Duchess of Portsmouth in August 1673. When the queen fell seriously ill in February, it had seemed that he might soon be free to remarry; her recovery led Shaftesbury and others to propose that a divorce bill should be brought into Parliament. As Charles did not respond positively, nothing was done; but in the following months there was renewed talk of legitimating Monmouth.[131]

Although the arguments against appointing James to command the invasion force were extremely strong, in May Charles appointed him 'generalissimo' and commanded him to prepare to transport the troops across the sea. He soon had second thoughts: he told James that he was reluctant to put his life at risk. He may also have been worried by rumours that James spoke of using the army to subjugate Parliament.[132] James continued to press his claim, arguing that the Test Act would not apply outside England. The judges advised otherwise and by mid-July he had given up hope. He continued to attend the committee of foreign affairs and, although he had resigned the post of lord admiral, he and Charles still directed the admiralty, with orders going out in the king's name.[133]

Under the commission issued to James in May, Buckingham was to be lieutenant-general. He threw himself wholeheartedly into his new duties and rushed to recruit soldiers in his native Yorkshire. Angry that few volunteers came forward, he urged Charles to order the lords lieutenant to impress some of the militia, which would have been widely regarded as illegal. Told that men were reluctant to volunteer because of fears of Popery, Buckingham suddenly began to attend church with unwonted assiduity, 'but the people hearken as little to his devotion as ... heaven to his prayers'.[134] Returning south, he tried hard to instruct his men, which led some to cry him up as a great general, but others were more sceptical. John Dryden remarked that the duke was the only man in Charles's kingdoms who did not know that he was unfit to command an army; he would not be satisfied until he had failed in Zeeland as disastrously as his father had done at La Rochelle. His eagerness to be popular with his men owed much to the appointment of Count Schomberg, a German with long experience in the French service, as lieutenant-general. James had pressed for Schomberg's appointment, largely in order to spite Buckingham, who responded by trying to whip up hostility to this 'Frenchman'. Schomberg, for his part, refused to work with one who was so patently inept. As York had no doubt hoped, Buckingham resigned his commission as lieutenant-general, but he was still colonel of a regiment and continued to posture in front of his men, using 'Frenchified' terms which they could not understand. Soon after, he resigned his colonelcy as well; his regiment remained at Blackheath when the others marched to the coast.[135]

With so much confusion at the top, the auguries for the descent were far from good. Money, as always, was short; the Stop was extended again. Discipline was poor: soldiers who were reprimanded for being drunk retorted that their officers were drunk too. Although articles of war had been drawn up, the officers did not dare to make use of them. Schomberg was disliked as a foreigner and quarrelled with Rupert, who grew more prickly and capricious with age. The Count, indeed, found the English war effort a shambles. Rupert had no intention of working harmoniously with the French. Most of the captains in the fleet were loyal to York and hated

Portrait, after the school of Peter Lely, of Charles as a young man.

Catherine of Braganza, by Lely: her sheltered upbringing did nothing to prepare her for life at Charles's court, but her greatest problem was her failure to produce children.

Charles in his coronation robes (1661), by John Michael Wright: a posed portrait of the sort which always tried the patience of a King who never liked sitting still.

The Earl of Clarendon by Lely: a pompous and portentous figure, he had no sympathy for his master's frivolity and love of pleasure.

The King at thirty-five: a miniature by Samuel Cooper, which captures his languorous cynicism far more successfully than more formal portraits.

A Dutch print of 1672, showing Louis XIV running after Charles with a handful of gold while French troops devastate the Dutch Republic. In fact, financial gain was not Charles's main reason for making war on the Dutch.

Pope-burning processions developed in both number and scale in the 1670s. Those on 17 November (Elizabeth's accession day) in 1679 and 1680 displayed a whole range of anti-Popish stereotypes and linked current fears of Popish plotting to those of the English Protestant past.

(A) Clifford: Sir Thomas Clifford (after Lely), an obscure squire who became a baron and Lord Treasurer before resigning in 1673.

(B) Arlington: Henry Bennet, Earl of Arlington (after Lely), the smoothest and best loved of the courtiers, and Charles's leading adviser on foreign affairs for more than a decade.

(C) Buckingham: George Villiers, Second Duke of Buckingham (by Lely), brilliant, vindictive and utterly unreliable, the companion of Charles's childhood, he exercised a powerful and erratic influence on the politics of Charles's reign.

(D) Ashley: Anthony Ashley Cooper, First Earl of Shaftesbury (after John Greenhill), a man whose many changes of direction in the shifting politics of his age earned him the (ironic) nickname of 'Little Sincerity', he ended his days as Charles's most implacable enemy.

(E) Lauderdale: John Maitland, First Duke of Lauderdale (by Jacob Huysmans), imperious, irascible and brutal, his rule in Scotland achieved what Charles most wanted – to keep the country quiet.

Charles in the 1670s: another posed portrait by Godfrey Kneller, but one that is noticeably less stiff and awkward than that of 1661, with an expression of amused detachment.

Rupert; many were more concerned with their own honour, profit or private vendettas than with the common good. As for the king, he showed little sense of urgency, unless pressed by others, and seemed unable to remember what he was told.[136]

Even as the troops marched from Blackheath to Yarmouth, and Schomberg began to instil the rudiments of discipline, the prospects for the descent, never good, were deteriorating. Hopes that the Zeelanders would welcome the English as liberators had always been naive, but the prospect of French military aid had seemed more solid: Croissy expected to be asked if Louis would renew his offer of 2,000 men to assist the invasion.[137] At the very least, Charles needed to have a French force within striking distance of Zeeland, to put pressure on the Dutch and perhaps come to his aid, but as the summer wore on, the focus of the French war effort shifted further and further away, first to Maastricht, then to the Mosel. Charles politely accepted Louis' reasonings, but others grumbled that the prospects for the descent were being ruined by the faithless French.[138] Louis argued that the invasion plans were unrealistic: the places which Charles planned to attack would be inaccessible because of the water defences. Besides, to keep a large fleet close to the Dutch coast would be both difficult and dangerous.[139] Charles vacillated, one day declaring his determination to press ahead, the next moaning that all was lost and that he had to make peace. His subjects were clearly weary of a war 'entered into' (as Ormond said) 'without the concurrence of the Parliament or the affections of the people'. London merchants complained of the decay of trade; the Spaniards disseminated papers which stated that, if Charles would only break with France, he could have peace on generous terms. Dutch propaganda, notably the highly influential *England's Appeal from the Private Cabal at Whitehall to the Great Council of the Nation ... Parliament*, linked the war to alleged designs to establish Popery and arbitrary government. William, meanwhile, had established contact with a number of the English court's opponents: knowledge of this further soured relations between Charles and his nephew.[140]

Bleak though the position seemed, some continued to call for a descent. Buckingham complained of the 'conspiracy' which had denied him command, but his unquenchable thirst for glory (and, perhaps, hope of rebuilding his political influence) led him to argue that an invasion was feasible. Charles remained irresolute: he rarely summoned the committee of foreign affairs, as its members kept giving him conflicting advice. Early in August, it was reported that plans for the descent had been abandoned. A month later, there was a new plan for an expedition to Helvoetsluys, led by Ossory, but this too was abandoned; Burnet gave as a reason Buckingham's hatred of Ossory, but the main problem, as Charles recognized, was that

England had not won control of the seas.[141] Co-operation between English and French had been hampered by protocol disputes, and Rupert's bloody-mindedness; even when they did work together, as at the Schonveld, they found the Dutch stubborn opponents and could not achieve a clear-cut victory. (Indeed, with the fleet short of men and supplies, both Arlington and Rupert thought that they had been lucky to do as well as they had.)[142] In the next major action, off the Texel, the French commander, the Comte d'Estrées, refused to engage, on the pretext that he had not understood the signals, and the prospect of victory (and so of a descent) was lost. Rupert was livid: the French officers and sailors, he claimed, had been eager to fight, but had not been allowed to do so. An angry public saw this as just one more example of French perfidy and was unimpressed by the (rewritten) official account of the battle, which stated that the French had fought bravely. Charles and Arlington tried to placate Croissy and d'Estrées: in such a parlous situation, Charles could not afford to alienate the one friend he had left.[143]

As the campaigning season neared its sorry end, Charles had to turn his thoughts to Parliament, due to meet on 20 October. Croissy pressed him to postpone it, but Charles insisted that he had to have money. It was unlikely to be an easy session. Any enthusiasm that there had been for the war had been dissipated by the lack of success and it was hard to see that the French alliance served any purpose – unless, as the Dutch insinuated, it was designed to facilitate the establishment of Popery and absolutism within England. An army had been raised, but not used, and a 'Frenchman' brought over to command it; the government had also planned to introduce 'martial law'. Such suspicions had been compounded by the resignations of Clifford and York. The former died before the end of the year, but the latter added fuel to the flames by marrying Mary Beatrice of Modena. His first wife had died in 1671, having recently converted to Catholicism, and James was determined that his second should also be a Catholic. As the storm about his religion grew, he hastened to conclude the marriage before Parliament met. It was bound to be controversial: not only were his prospective bride's family clients of France, but it seemed certain that any children they had would be raised as Catholics. If these included a son or sons, these would take precedence over the two daughters of James's first marriage, Mary and Anne, who had been raised as Protestants. As Charles still had no legitimate children, this raised the prospect not only of a Popish successor but of a Popish dynasty; small wonder that there was renewed talk of Charles's divorcing the queen and of James's being excluded from the succession.[144] As the day of Parliament's meeting drew near, ministers rushed to secure pardons under the Great Seal. As for the king, except in moments of lunatic optimism (when he blamed all the Commons' ill-humour on Garroway and

Sir William Coventry), he clearly dreaded the prospect of meeting Parliament again.[145]

When Parliament met, it was widely known that Charles intended to prorogue it. Some gave as a reason a resolution, in March, to grant no more money that session (which, technically, had not ended, as Parliament had only been adjourned). A more pressing reason was that, although James had married his new wife by proxy, she had not arrived in England. The Speaker of the Commons arrived late, expecting to find Black Rod at the door to summon the House to the prorogation; but he was not there. Shaftesbury (who, as lord chancellor, was Speaker of the Lords) deliberately spent time introducing new peers, which gave Powle and the old Cromwellian, Colonel Birch, the chance to propose that the Commons should draw up an address asking that James's marriage should not be consummated. The House approved the motion before Black Rod knocked on the door.[146]

Many suspected that Charles tacitly approved of this move. Some MPs identified with the court had supported it; those who opposed it did so half-heartedly. (The court, however, was in such disarray that little should be read into their conduct.) Publicly Charles declared that he was honour bound to uphold the marriage, but there was much talk of a divorce and the queen expected to be sent away at any time.[147] Sir William Temple wrote that Charles was so uncertain, or 'disguised', that no one could tell what he intended. The former seems the more likely: he had even consulted an astrologer about the most propitious time to call Parliament.[148] When Parliament reconvened on 27 October he denounced the Dutch for arrogantly refusing to make peace; for the nation's safety, he would have to put out a fleet next spring and for this he would need an appropriate supply. He promised to uphold 'the established religion and laws' and referred to their consideration his debt to the goldsmiths. Some thought that his speech, penned by a committee, lacked the coherence of those written by Clarendon, but, whoever had written it, it would not have impressed the Commons. MPs struck out angrily at a variety of targets: the army, martial law, Richard Talbot, even Speaker Seymour (on the grounds that, as a privy councillor, he was not unequivocally the servant of the House).[149] A bill was brought in to distinguish Protestants from Papists, so that no Catholic could be admitted to Parliament, or to any office, or within five miles of the court – yet another reference to York, who was now openly described as a Papist. The House also resolved, by a majority of more than two to one, to draw up an address against the consummation of his marriage.[150]

On the 31st the Commons considered the king's request for supply. MPs alleged that the war had served only to benefit France and to provide a pretext to raise an army. A claim that the House had no grievances was met with howls of derision. Suggestions that Charles was honour bound to adhere to the French alliance were swept aside in a flood of denunciations of France, Popery, the military and corruption. The House resolved to give no money until the end of the eighteen months of the assessment voted in the spring and until the nation had been secured against Popery and Popish counsels. The only glimmer of hope for the court was the addition of a proviso, proposed by Sir William Coventry, 'unless ... the obstinacy of the Dutch shall make a supply necessary'.[151] Three days later the House resolved to draw up an address that the standing army was a grievance. 'These forces were not raised for the war', Powle declared, 'but the war made for raising these people.' The projected descent was dismissed as absurd.[152] Next morning, the Speaker arrived two hours late. Black Rod was already at the door to summon them to the Lords for the prorogation; MPs had no time to resume their debate. Charles told them that any breach between them would encourage the nation's enemies, but that a brief interval (until 7 January) was needed to allow feelings to cool; in the meantime he would take steps to suppress Popery. Grumbling at their wasted journey – the session had lasted only nine days – MPs left for home.[153]

The decision to prorogue had been taken after heated meetings of the cabinet (as the committee for foreign affairs now tended to be called) and of the privy council. After the votes on supply and the army, there seemed no point in prolonging the session: indeed, the main question was whether to prorogue or to dissolve. James urged his brother to dismiss from their offices those who had misbehaved in Parliament and to appoint loyal men in their places: otherwise the nation would rise in rebellion. Others viewed the situation less starkly. Henry Coventry remarked that, great though the people's fears were, with hard work and common sense it might be possible to calm them; the people were much more afraid of disorders than inclined to begin them. Arlington, as always, claimed that by giving the Commons what they wanted Charles could make the nation happy.[154] That, at least, was what he wrote, but he did not believe it. The strain of office and the worsening of his gout had taken their toll. For some months he had been trying to buy the lucrative office of lord chamberlain from St Albans, hoping thus to withdraw from the political front line – and from the drudgery of administration – while continuing to pull the strings of policy-making from a less conspicuous position. York, unkindly, described him as being almost dead with fear.[155] Buckingham, too, feared attack and, anyway, had lost most of his credit with the king, as had Shaftesbury, not least by delaying the prorogation on 20 October. Some ascribed his *volte face* to the loss of the king's favour, but Croissy suspected that he had found out about Catholicity, probably from Arlington.[156] With Clifford dead and Lauderdale away in Scotland, the Cabal was disintegrating. During the summer the balance of power at court had shifted to those who had become disillusioned with the war for reasons of principle (Shaftesbury) or pragmatism (Arlington) or because they had never really approved of it in the first place (Ormond, Rupert, Coventry, Finch and Osborne). Fear of Parliamentary retribution exacerbated the uncertainties and rivalries of court politics. Few had any coherent policy objectives or any compunction about sacrificing others – or the French alliance. Damage limitation and self-preservation were the main priorities, even for York, the one unequivocal advocate of firmness, who was now thoroughly isolated.[157]

Given the government's record over the past two years, and York's conversion, the panic at court was understandable. MPs would naturally wish to identify and punish those responsible for the nation's ills, but (as Coventry remarked) talk of rebellion was wildly exaggerated. Most MPs respected the king's prerogatives – his right to raise soldiers, to conduct foreign policy and to choose his own counsellors. They accepted that the Commons had no right to dictate how he should use those prerogatives, but they did have the right to withhold money until their grievances were redressed. In other words, MPs thought that Charles was morally obliged to frame policies acceptable to his people, while acknowledging that he could not be forced to do so. Effective government depended on mutual trust and the onus was on Charles to take the first steps towards rebuilding it. Similar arguments were used by Sir Thomas Osborne, now Viscount Latimer, who in May had succeeded Clifford as lord treasurer. Charles, he wrote, could not re-establish his position by force, because he lacked the necessary money. He would therefore have to work with a Parliament, which would insist on a firm line against France and Popery; if he kept the present Parliament, it would also prefer action against Dissent.[158]

Not everyone at court saw the conduct of the Commons in this way. York and his friends saw the House as led astray by a small number of 'agitators', who were encouraged by the Spaniards. If Charles would only act firmly against these men, clapping them in gaol, the remainder of the Commons would soon return to their wonted obedience and loyalty. The idea that backbenchers might have minds of their own apparently never occurred to James and his friends, yet they had a point. Charles had failed to reward loyal servants as they expected: it was hard to serve for no more reward than a good conscience, while his habit of buying off the more vocal critics of the court had served only to encourage opposition. York did at least persuade his brother to dismiss Shaftesbury and to appoint Sir Heneage Finch as lord keeper. Charles also talked of dismissing from office MPs who had opposed the court in the last session, including Cornbury and Garroway, but was persuaded by their friends to change his mind. While many, like Latimer, argued that only changes of policy could cure the Commons' ill-humour,

York argued that any such changes would be interpreted as a sign of weakness and would merely encourage the ill-intentioned. Faced with so many difficult choices, Charles became more irresolute than ever, changing his mind six times in as many hours; although he feared (and some said hated) his more resolute brother, he lacked the strength of will to stand up to him or to send him away from court.[159] The one remedy for his predicament upon which almost everyone agreed was a proclamation to enforce the laws against Catholics, although some remarked that there had been too many such proclamations which had not been acted upon.[160]

The failure to extract money from Parliament made it well-nigh impossible to carry on the war, although Croissy claimed that Charles would have enough to set out at least a token fleet in the spring and argued that those who attacked his foreign policy were really seeking to undermine his prerogatives. Louis realized that he would have to scale down his demands: he no longer pressed Charles to declare war on Spain and told Croissy to counter the efforts of the Dutch and the Spanish to induce him to conclude a separate peace with the Dutch, which would leave the allies free to concentrate on the war effort against France. Charles clearly did not want to abandon his ally, partly for reasons of honour, partly because he feared diplomatic isolation and the leaking of the Treaty of Dover.[161] His freedom of manoeuvre was reduced, however, by his lack of money and by the proviso about 'the obstinacy of the Dutch'; this proviso, while keeping alive the possibility of supply, effectively made the Commons judge of whether the Dutch were being obstinate. Eager to maintain the pressure, the Dutch and Spaniards appealed to the Commons and the London public: some of their proposals were in print even before they were formally presented to the king. Ministers countered by canvassing MPs, arguing that the proposals were unreasonable.[162]

In the face of mounting pressure from both inside and outside the court, Charles's resolve weakened. Arlington told him roundly that he had no choice but to make peace; Latimer produced detailed figures to counter Croissy's claims that he could afford to continue the war. York urged him to be firm and blamed his problems on Spanish intrigue. Buckingham talked to Croissy of his zeal to preserve the alliance and sent to ask Louis for money to win over the Commons by bribery (although he later denied having done so); at other times, he called for a dissolution. Louis, perplexed and anxious, sent over Ruvigny to assist Croissy.[163] Beset with conflicting advice, Charles became depressed and confused. By early December Louis accepted that he could not afford to continue the war, but offered only a small sum of money to aid his naval preparations. He still hoped to preserve the alliance, but this seemed less and less likely.[164] Charles agreed to receive proposals from the Spanish, who suggested that the Dutch should concede the question of the flag, together with a mutual restitution of conquests and an indemnity of rather less than £200,000. As Croissy had reported that Charles was ready to drop all his demands except for that of the flag, these proposals must have seemed tempting. Indeed, he welcomed them, but pressed also for a rent for the fishing, a regulation of the East Indies trade and an agreement to allow the English to withdraw from Surinam. He showed no eagerness to grab the money: on the contrary, he agreed that the bulk should go to William to pay what was owing from his mother's marriage portion.[165]

The focus of discussion now shifted from the council to the court and to the taverns and coffee-houses of London. Croissy and Ruvigny lobbied MPs and sought to counter Dutch and Spanish propaganda. Charles had already agreed in principle to allow the Commons to control the spending of any money they voted; the battle was now on to persuade MPs to endorse or reject whatever terms he agreed. He still declared that he would sign nothing until Louis had received satisfaction, but by Christmas Louis accepted that a separate peace was inevitable and told Croissy to assure Charles of his future goodwill. Charles hinted that, with the war increasingly focused on Germany, England could do little to help Louis anyway, while Arlington complained of the deadlock at Cologne caused by Louis' refusal to recognize the Duke of Lorraine as a principal in the war.[166] With the negotiations very much in the public domain, Ruvigny pinned his hopes on a stratagem proposed by Buckingham and Latimer: Charles was to show the Commons the treaty of February 1672 and thus remove fears that it contained provisions contrary to England's religion and liberty. Charles agreed, but such was his irresolution that one of the three had to be with him at all times to bolster his resolution. Buckingham was also preoccupied with self-preservation and courted MPs of all kinds, drinking with the debauched, speaking seriously with the sober and seeking to re-establish his reputation among the devout by taking communion. With Charles changing his mind almost daily about setting the treaty before Parliament, the court approached the session in disarray.[167]

Charles's opening speech was extremely conciliatory. He stressed his care to give satisfaction on religion and property; if any of the money given for the war remained unspent when peace was made, he was willing that it should be appropriated for the navy. He was prepared to allow a committee of both Houses to inspect the treaties he had signed. He thus offered appropriation and a scrutiny of treaties in terms more limited than had at one time seemed likely (although both Ormond and Arlington thought that he had conceded too much). It was not an impressive speech; at times he stumbled over his words, notably when assuring MPs that there were no other treaties.[168] The Commons promptly resumed the discussion of grievances, brushing aside the request for supply with the comment that those who had advised the war should pay for it. While Shaftesbury regaled the Lords with the story of a planned rising of Papists in London, the Commons resolved to ask Charles to have the City militia ready to deal with any tumult.[169] Next day, they considered evil counsellors. Some of the family of the Countess of Shrewsbury had already accused Buckingham, in the Lords, of murdering her husband and ruining her reputation.[170] Now MPs criticized Charles for relying on the advice of Lauderdale and Buckingham rather than that of Parliament. As they warmed to their task, Buckingham was accused of murder, evil counsel, consorting with French ambassadors and sodomy; those around him were said to care for neither morality nor Christianity and to have advised using force against Parliament.[171]

The attack on Buckingham came as no surprise and he rushed to defend himself. It was an inept performance. He could not read his notes, complained of conspiracies against him at court, referred less than gallantly to Lady Shrewsbury and blamed everything on Arlington.[172] Next day Arlington, having first (unlike Buckingham) obtained permission from the Lords, addressed the Commons. Afraid he may have been, but he carried himself with 'much more gravity, recollection and temper' than this rival, answering Buckingham's charges point by point and accusing no one.[173] The Commons had resolved to address the king to remove Buckingham from all employments held during pleasure (in other words, not for life), but voted no such address against Arlington. His enemies continued to allege that he was 'popishly affected'; his friends called for legal charges to be brought, confident that he would be exonerated. At last the House set up a committee to consider possible articles for an impeachment, which effectively ended the attacks on him for the present.[174] Buckingham's credit with the king, meanwhile, had finally been destroyed. Charles was incensed at his revealing details of confidential discussions and dismissed him from court and council and even from the post of master of the horse, which he held for life. Buckingham's abject plea that he might keep the office was swept aside and it was given to Monmouth, who paid Buckingham £4,000 a year compensation.[175] With the Shrewsbury affair rumbling on in the Lords, Buckingham felt that he was in grave danger and talked of retiring to France; in an effort to ingratiate himself with Louis he tried, unavailingly, to secure some consideration for French interests in the peace treaty. A simpler remedy lay at hand: another burst of church attendance and a show of contrition earned him the Lords' forgiveness. He was also reconciled with Shaftesbury and other members of a recognizable group of oppositionist peers who met regularly at Holles's house; it was with such men that his political future – what there was of it – lay.[176]

Many MPs, not least Henry Coventry, found the proceedings against Buckingham and Arlington unedifying; they also impeded discussion of the king's business. When the Commons moved on to a different topic, it was to revive the proposal for a new test for Papists. One stimulus for this was James's failure to take communion at Christmas, plus his initial refusal to take the oath of allegiance, claiming that as heir presumptive he did not have to take it. He told his brother that the Commons were seeking to take over the direction of government.[177] Many MPs, however, saw the new test as a prudent safeguard against possible future Catholic misrule – in other words, that of James. There was talk of Charles remarrying and of Mary marrying William. Fear of arbitrary taxation in the future led the Commons to bring in a bill making it treason to levy moneys not voted by Parliament; steps were also taken to stop future kings tampering with the judiciary. The Lords resolved that in future all children of the royal family should be raised in the Protestant religion and no member of that family should marry a Catholic without Parliament's consent. It was proposed that any who did so should be debarred from the throne, but despite Shaftesbury's eloquence it was clear that most of the peers disliked the idea.[178] In general, however, the momentum of criticism, especially of the army, was unrelenting. Many claimed that the war had been a mere pretext to raise an army and called for the disbanding of all forces raised since 1663, on the grounds that any standing forces other than the militia constituted a grievance. There were also complaints of imprisonment without cause shown, which had provoked few complaints in Parliament in the early 1660s but was now politically unacceptable; there was no mention of money. As Conway wrote: 'Fear of the Duke makes them every day fetter the crown.'[179]

Parliament's conduct did nothing to strengthen Charles's hand in his negotiations with the Dutch, but he had one priceless asset: the Dutch were eager for peace, so that they could concentrate on fighting France. The proposals made through Spain had not been ungenerous. Charles was no longer in a position to demand towns and was now so displeased with William that he had no wish to insist that he be made hereditary stadhouder. (Ironically, his position within the republic was now so strong that this happened anyway.)[180] Charles continued to press for an annual payment for fishing rights, a question of honour rather than money. William had offered to concede this in July 1672; now, in a far stronger negotiating position, he rejected it out of hand. Despite Dutch attempts to play king off against Parliament, however, Charles gained some of his demands, including (apart from the points offered in December) an undertaking to discuss regulations for the East Indies trade. The English were to be allowed to leave Surinam, with their possessions, and the Treaty of Breda was to be confirmed. Charles can have had few qualms about accepting these conditions, but nevertheless asked the Commons' opinion, either to show Louis that he was bowing to irresistible pressure or because he hoped that they might then give money.

The Commons responded warily: though most MPs probably favoured peace, they wished to avoid any suggestion that by endorsing it they were committing themselves to vote money. They therefore refused to approve the Dutch proposals as such, but advised Charles to treat with the States General in order to bring about a speedy peace. They then returned happily to their grievances.[181]

Many of Charles's advisers believed that he had had no option but to make peace. Arlington claimed that Charles had insufficient money even for a defensive war, Henry Coventry that he was no longer useful to Louis – or to himself – and that he was risking ruin for a punctilio of honour. Louis responded with the best grace that he could muster and agreed that Charles's plenipotentiaries at Cologne should act as mediators: anything was better than driving him into the arms of the allies.[182] Two sources of friction remained. The treaty included a secret article that neither power should assist the enemies of the other, in any way. This had been added at the insistence of the Spanish ambassador. Charles claimed that this had been included in the 1662 Anglo-Dutch treaty, to which that of Breda had referred, but Ruvigny disagreed. The Dutch wished Charles to commit himself to recall the British regiments in the French service, so this clause marked a compromise: they were not to be recalled but he was to allow no further recruits in his dominions by the French; the Dutch would be free to replenish their British regiments. Charles and Arlington were, naturally, embarrassed when Ruvigny tackled them about this. Charles hinted that he might not be bound by it, but the question of the British regiments in the French service was to cause him considerable embarrassment over the next few years.[183]

Once it became clear that the Commons would not respond to the peace with a vote of money, even for the fleet, there seemed no point in prolonging the session. The cluster of measures designed to fetter a Catholic successor could not but be distasteful to a king bent on preserving the crown's prerogatives; the same was true of the habeas corpus bill, to restrict the crown's power of commitment, which passed the Commons on 23 February. The proceedings against Arlington stuttered on, fuelled by Cornbury and other irreconcilable enemies.[184] The Lords, meanwhile, discussed a comprehension bill, which would have waived the need for assent and consent and the renunciation of the Covenant. This was probably an attempt to pre-empt a rumoured attempt to move for a more sweeping comprehension bill in the Commons; whatever its origins, Charles was unlikely to welcome it.[185] On 24 February, following news that the Dutch had ratified the Treaty of Westminster, Charles prorogued Parliament until November. He did not consult the committee of foreign affairs, which led to wild stories that James was to be charged with treason. The court's leading critics in the Commons hastily went to ground in the City.[186] Their fears of reprisals were unfounded. Charles had already started to disband the land forces raised for the war. His main priority now was to live within his means – not before time, remarked Henry Coventry. Charles believed that he had survived something close to a rebellion: now he needed to catch his breath and consider what to do next. The Grand Design was dead: dreams of conquest had died with it. Two years of war had produced no gain more substantial than a theoretical recognition, by the Dutch, of England's dominion over the Narrow Seas, which might be gratifying, but did not pay any bills. The money paid in reparations would mostly go straight to William.[187] The price which Charles had to pay for this 'success' was enormous. His old team of advisers had been scattered by death, disgrace and disillusionment. His financial problems had been exacerbated by a new load of debts. The greatest damage, however, was political. Looking back, thoughtful contemporaries saw 1672–3 as a watershed in Charles's reign, in which designs to establish Popery and arbitrary government first became apparent. In February 1674 the secretary to the privy council, Sir Robert Southwell, wrote that the Commons 'are making such bills to hedge in the property, liberty and religion of the subject that nothing is to be trusted to good nature in the future'.[188] Trust, more than ministers or money, was the major casualty of the Third Dutch War. The Grand Design had been Charles's first and only major policy initiative and it had failed. Experience of that failure, and the conviction that it had almost led to a rebellion, helped make Charles a wiser and ultimately more decisive politician.

Peace and Retrenchment?

The Peace of Westminster offered Charles a welcome breathing space. If it did nothing to solve his financial problems, at least it prevented them from becoming even more serious. In time, England was to profit substantially from being at peace while much of Europe was at war: as a neutral power, she could trade with all the belligerents. At the same time, there was a rapid growth in imports from England's burgeoning colonial empire – tobacco from Virginia, sugar from the West Indies, luxury textiles from India. It would take years, however, for this commercial expansion to make an appreciable impact on the king's financial position. In the short term, his first priority was to rebuild his political credibility at home, after the failure of the Grand Design. This would be far from easy. Trust had to be mutual and he felt little inclination to trust his subjects. The recriminations of 1673–4 had revived memories of the civil wars. Charles remained convinced that Dissenters (in his eyes, political subversives) made up a large part of England's population. To make the concessions needed to rebuild trust – for example, to join the alliance against France – might leave him at the mercy of his people. There were also the problems created by his brother's conversion, which Charles often declared to be the source of all his troubles.

Looking back at the controversies of 1673–4, Charles at times blamed a few incendiaries for leading astray a basically loyal Parliament, at others claimed that the whole nation was against him.[1] King and ministers were deeply fearful of revolution from below. They had always tended to overreact to disorders, especially in London. A series of riots in 1668, ostensibly intended to pull down bawdy-houses, ended with the ringleaders' being charged with treason, for taking upon themselves a task which was properly the king's.[2] The government showed similar alarm when London weavers rioted in August 1675, as part of a long-running agitation against new machinery and cheap immigrant labour. It was worrying, wrote Henry Coventry, that unarmed rioters should have been masters of the streets for three days, with the City militia unable to suppress them. Charles sent word from Newmarket that unless those involved suffered quick and exemplary punishment, it would merely encourage rebellion. Coventry thought the riot 'foolish and fantastical', but admitted that it had been alarming. In the end, the government accepted that industrial grievances had not been a cover for political agitation and the ringleaders suffered nothing worse than the pillory.[3] Ministers remained nervous. The council devoted much time to reports of seditious words, such as those of a rather dotty old Cavalier, Sir Philip Monckton, who talked of French and Popish designs to murder the king.[4] At much the same time, at a meeting to elect London's sheriffs, Francis Jenks called on those present to press the king to recall Parliament.[5] Meanwhile, rumours swept the provinces of Frenchmen plotting to set fire to towns: Orrery wrote from Minehead that he had never seen people so scared.[6] Bristol was convulsed by a series of ill-tempered disputes between the corporation and the abrasive Bishop Carleton. The lord keeper suggested that the latter should be moved to a less considerable town; he was translated to Chichester in 1678.[7]

The government's edginess can be ascribed to an awareness of both the unpopularity of some of its policies and the intensity of popular interest in politics. In the latter stages of the recent war, ambassadors had lobbied MPs and put their views before a wider public. Government censorship prevented the publication of newspapers, but not of political pamphlets, some of them smuggled in from abroad, notably *England's Appeal*, by Peter du Moulin, a close associate of William III. Manuscript summaries of each day's proceedings in Parliament circulated widely, as did copies of resolutions and speeches; a proposal that the Commons should ask the king to print their address against the Declaration, and his answer, had been defeated only by the Speaker's casting vote. (In fact they were printed anyway.)[8] In London, news spread less by print and paper than by word of mouth – at the Royal Exchange (where merchants gathered to hear of developments abroad that could affect trade) and in the taverns and coffee-houses. There, in the summer of 1676, 'republicans' calling themselves 'liberty and property men' were said to be casting aspersions on the king's ministers. The first political clubs appeared at this time, including one whose members identified themselves by wearing green ribbons; the practice of wearing coloured ribbons threatened to spread even to the privy council.[9] The government tried to halt this flow of information by maintaining pre-publication censorship, by issuing proclamations against spreading false news and discussing state affairs and by trying to regulate the coffee-houses. Its efforts were less than successful: even Jenks's speech appeared in print.[10]

This concern with public opinion was nothing new, but it became more acute after 1673–4. One reason was the need to rebuild the government's credit, after the Stop and its various prolongations. This, as much as fear of disorder in England's biggest conurbation, explains the government's especial concern with London. The need for the goodwill of the business community led Charles to try to influence elections to senior posts in the East India Company[11] and, at a time of financial stringency, to assign the crown's most reliable revenues as security to repay what was owing to the bankers.[12] But credit was not the only concern: Parliament was greatly influenced by the City and by considerations of trade.[13] MPs attracted the attention of merchant lobbyists, but they were also left in little doubt of the hopes and fears of the Londoners among whom they stayed during sessions. This explains why ambassador Honoré de Courtin went to the exchange to justify France's seizure of English merchant ships as prizes; his example was followed, despite his gout, by Henry Coventry, who felt it imperative to scotch rumours that the Spaniards might confiscate English merchants' goods.[14] As Ruvigny remarked, in England it was not enough to persuade the king: one had to persuade Parliament and people as well.[15]

Faced with a populace which it perceived as hostile, Charles's government was very conscious that its powers of coercion were limited. In London it had to rely on the City trained bands: hence the alarm at their failure to suppress the weavers' riots. The king possessed few guards and the City authorities would not willingly allow them to be used in the City (although they could be deployed in Westminster and the suburbs). Much therefore depended on the co-operation of the City authorities – the lieutenancy, which controlled the militia, and, for day-to-day administration, the lord mayor and aldermen. The annually elected common council played only a limited role in City affairs and Charles vigorously supported the aldermen's resistance to any attempt to extend its competence or to involve it in national politics.[16] Ministers were alarmed by Jenks's attempt to use common hall (the assembly of freemen which elected sheriffs and other officials – and MPs) to launch a call for a speedy meeting of Parliament and by his claim that it constituted the 'main body' of the City.[17] In the counties the king controlled the machinery of law and order. He dismissed JPs who failed to enforce the laws against Dissent, starting with a 'gang' in Middlesex which included Sir Robert Peyton and Sir Edmund Berry Godfrey. As for the judges, most had, since 1668, held their places 'during pleasure' (rather than during good behaviour), which meant that he could dismiss them without showing cause. In 1676 this form of tenure was made general and, for the first time, a judge was dismissed.[18] This is not to suggest that the government regularly interfered in legal proceedings: on the contrary, ministers showed an almost pathological obsession with keeping within the law and with avoiding any suggestion that the military power could dictate to the civil.[19] In these circumstances, notes scribbled by Williamson in 1677, about raising an army with French help or on the pretext of fear of France, represented no more than a pipe-dream: they were not the stuff of practical politics.[20]

In the face of distrust and disaffection, firm leadership was needed, but Charles seemed unable to provide it. He was always more inclined to see the snags inherent in various courses of action than to make a decision and stick to it: willpower was never his strong point. Having been persuaded to make a decision or sign an order, he was often persuaded to change his mind by the next person he spoke to. In their efforts to counteract his pliancy, those in the political know resorted to drastic methods. When the friends of the Lord Lieutenant of Ireland, the Earl of Essex, obtained permission for him to come over to England, they were careful to keep the matter secret until the letter had been sent.[21] Latimer, now Earl of Danby, one day got the king alone in the treasury chamber for three hours and gave strict orders that no one else should be admitted. Later he and his cronies pinned the king in the corner of the bedchamber and talked to him of Ireland.[22] As far as Ireland was concerned, Charles was fully aware that Essex was diligent and honourable and recognized the truth of his claim that Ireland had for too long been plundered to provide rewards for his courtiers, or (as Essex put it) torn like a deer carcase thrown among a pack of hounds.[23] Even so, Charles found it hard to resist the sustained pressure – some might call it bullying – to which he was subjected. Essex was forced to stop grants which Charles had made with insufficient consideration, which merely added to the clamour against him at Whitehall. Reasoned arguments in letters from Dublin were undermined by insinuations in 'private debates' in London.[24]

Faced with such pressures, it is not surprising that Charles resorted to dissimulation and deceit or simply lost interest, none of which made for co-ordination or consistency. He feared irrevocable commitments, preferring to keep his options open and to react to problems as they arose. Ministers' attempts to control access to his person were never wholly successful. He met City politicians, some of them far from friendly to the court, in the lodgings of his clerk of the closet, Will Chiffinch.[25] He found it difficult to concentrate on matters which did not really interest him, so those in credit could instil impressions which were unlikely to be shaken by careful scrutiny; they also distracted his attention when letters were being read to him.[26] During visits to Newmarket, the court became so preoccupied with dogs, horses and amorous intrigues that letters missed the post. Even at the best of times Charles would forget what he had said or written: his promises could not be relied on.[27]

The failure of the Grand Design meant major changes at court. Of the Cabal, only Lauderdale remained in favour; his primary concern was to maintain his control over Scottish affairs, to which end he sought to keep in with the stronger party at Whitehall. Arlington finally took possession of the post of lord chamberlain in September 1674. Despite his talk of age and ill-health, he hoped still to play a major role in foreign affairs. Ruvigny continued to discuss business with him and that winter he and Ossory undertook a mission to William, of which Charles had told neither Lauderdale nor Danby. The mission was less than successful and on his return Arlington found his credit much diminished. He survived attempts to oust him from his post, but failed either to bring down Danby or to re-establish himself as *de facto* foreign minister, although Charles sometimes sought his advice. His staying away from court for three months late in 1675 was a tacit admission that his days in power were over, but he still nourished hopes of recovering his former influence and remained lord chamberlain until his death in 1685.[28]

Arlington's failure to cling to power left Danby as the leading figure at court. Neither secretary played a major role in policy-making. Sir Joseph Williamson was a competent bureaucrat, but not a forceful character. Henry Coventry was an able spokesman in the Commons – even his political opponents respected his integrity – but his sturdy churchmanship and resolute hostility to France meant that he could never be admitted to Charles's innermost counsels. In his late fifties and in poor health, he served out of duty rather than ambition: even in 1674 he wanted to sell his place. He often quarrelled with Danby and remarked that, apart from Ormond, nobody at court thought as he did. He thus remained isolated and unhappy, a relic of old Cavalier values in a more cynical world.[29] Danby, by contrast, was never overburdened with principles. A client of Buckingham's, he came to prominence as a critic of the court, but was then 'taken off' with the place of treasurer of the navy. His diligence impressed York, who supported the proposal that he should succeed Clifford as lord treasurer; Buckingham naturally concurred. Danby was initially slow to get to grips with the responsibilities of his new office, not least because of ill-health, which was to be a recurrent problem. Politically he tried to keep in with all sides, collaborating with York, yet courting popularity in the Commons. Only after the peace did he emerge as a dominant political figure.[30]

Danby was in many ways the antithesis of Arlington. He could argue plausibly and showed sycophancy towards those who could harm him, but contempt towards those who could not. Tough and abrasive, in his dealings with the king he relied as much on force of personality as on force of argument. Power made him arrogant; he would not deign to answer letters – it was almost (remarked Essex) as if he thought himself superior to the king.[31] His favour was founded on his promise to bring order to the royal finances. He sought to establish total control over the treasury and ruthlessly swept aside potential rivals and critics.[32] Initially he pinned his hopes on a campaign of retrenchment and similar schemes recurred during his treasurership. (Concern to save money in England was, indeed, one reason for the crown's predatory attitude towards Ireland.) He tried to ease the crown's cash-flow problems: the last formal Stop of the exchequer ran from March to June 1674, but both before and after that Danby often delayed payments for as long as he could.[33] Such measures were never more than palliatives. The stopping of salaries and pensions provoked squeals of outrage from courtiers and Charles found it hard to resist their importunities. Besides, if the king failed to pay his bills, his credit would be damaged and he would find it harder to borrow. Above all, expenditure still came close to or even exceeded income, thanks to Charles's continued extravagance and the need to service his accumulated debts. More income was required and that meant supply from Parliament.[34]

Danby had set out his programme for dealing with Parliament in December 1673. If Charles wished to keep the present House of Commons 'they must be gratified by executing the laws both against Popery and Nonconformity and withdrawing apparently from the French interest'. A new Commons might favour comprehension or indulgence, but would be no less hostile to France and to Popery, so to get money Charles would have to give satisfaction on these points.[35] That, in essence, remained Danby's strategy, which was to be underpinned by careful Parliamentary management. Spokesmen were briefed, letters were sent to supporters of the court to come up promptly for each session. Those who served well were rewarded, partly by payments from the secret service fund, but more by favourable treatment in the payment of moneys due from the exchequer or by participation in lucrative revenue farms. Such methods raised exaggerated but understandable fears that 'the influence of the crown', the ability to buy support by means of places and pensions, would undermine the Commons' independence and subjugate them to the royal will. Thus while trying to reduce fears of Popery, Danby intensified fears of arbitrary government.[36] His attempts to revert to the 'Cavalier' policies, which had worked so well as recently as 1670–1, won only limited success. He could not fully carry Charles with him, especially on foreign policy, and he could not conjure away the spectre of a Popish successor. He was thus unable to dispel the distrust which had burst forth in 1673 – indeed, in some ways his conduct exacerbated it. His failures did not weaken his credit with the king: they were interspersed with successes and he was always well furnished with excuses and reasons why he would do better next time. On the other hand, his adversarial style, his determination to set Churchman against Dissenter and to give a monopoly of office to men of Cavalier principles, encouraged political polarization, both at Westminster and in the localities.

Gradually Danby established his ascendancy. He defeated Arlington's attempts to cling to power. Ormond and Coventry might dislike his methods, but shared his basic outlook on policy; the same may have been true of

Finch. Lauderdale co-operated with him once it became clear that he was the man in power. Rumours that Buckingham or Shaftesbury might return to favour proved unfounded. Danby's control over payments from the treasury made it profitable to serve him and dangerous to cross him. For his Osborne and Bertie relatives he provided offices, peerages and advantageous marriages; his brother-in-law, Charles Bertie, became secretary to the treasury and manager of the secret service fund. Danby's cynical and mercenary approach to government permeated the entire court: the celebrated 'court wit', Henry Savile, expressed amazement that Charles made Lord Ferrers a peer without his having begged or bribed a minister or a mistress.[37]

This did not mean that Danby directed, or even influenced, all areas of government. At first he showed little interest in foreign policy, but he was increasingly drawn into it by the need to reassure the Commons. Even then, Charles resisted his efforts to turn him against France, just as he resisted all attempts to persuade him to remove Essex; when the earl was finally recalled in 1677, he was replaced not by one of Danby's cronies but by Ormond. Moreover, there was one political figure whom Danby could neither bribe nor bully and that was York. The duke insisted that the opposition to him was motivated by hostility not to his religion but to the monarchy. He urged his brother to take a tough line with Parliament. The English, he claimed, were a restless people, but bore the yoke of authority patiently if they were treated firmly: small wonder that Marvell remarked that, bad as Charles was, he was better than his brother.[38] James had no sympathy with Danby's plan to win Parliament's goodwill by breaking with France and repressing Catholicism and Dissent. On the contrary, he regarded Louis' friendship and support as essential for the survival of the monarchy: the 'malcontents' would not dare to rise while Charles had French backing. His hostility to the harassment of Catholics was natural enough; more surprisingly, in view of his past record, he responded to Danby's intransigent Anglicanism by moderating his attitude towards Dissenters, speaking of them as fellow sufferers under the Anglican lash. How far this change of heart was purely tactical is a moot point; it involved him with some unlikely allies, including Shaftesbury, and there were times when he seemed likely to engage in open opposition to the court. If this did not happen, it owed something to James's stolid loyalty to his brother, but also much to a claim, in a pamphlet of 1677, that Parliament could settle the succession, which made a deep impression on him and revived all his latent distrust of his new allies.[39]

In the years after the Third Dutch War, Charles was continually pressed to follow lines of policy which went against his deepest instincts. The thinking which underlay that pressure was explained to him by Sir William

Temple, in 1674. Charles, said Temple, lacked the power and resources to impose his will on his people by force. He quoted the former Frondeur Gourville, who had said that 'a king of England who is willing to be the man of his people is the greatest king in the world; but if he wishes to be anything more, by God he is no longer anything.' After the Parliamentary attacks on ministers in 1673–4, their successors were only too aware of the need to avoid actions that would leave them open to such criticism. This was not just a matter of self-preservation: many believed, as a matter of principle, that they had obligations to their fellow subjects and the law as well as to the king. 'It hath ever been my aim', wrote Essex, 'so to perform my trust as to render all imaginable compliance to His Majesty's commands and yet withal to preserve myself Parliament proof.' Ministers who neglected the latter harmed not only themselves but the monarchy. 'We cannot but see how many flowers have been cropped from the crown on this score, our kings having been still forced to part with many of their own rights only to save their ministers and furnish precedents to after ages which endanger even the whole frame of the government itself.'[40]

It is unlikely that Charles fully understood such arguments. He assured Temple that he would be 'the man of my people' but his heart was not in it. His distaste for most of the advice he received was one major reason for his indecision. On the other hand, while he shared James's fondness for France, and his distrust of Parliament and people, he shrank from violent and extreme methods. Anxious and confused, he found some solace in his domestic life. His relationship with his wife was now largely formal. He rarely slept with her, but respected her position as mistress in her own household; there was now little talk of divorce and remarriage. The queen had come to terms with her position, and filled her days with innocent amusements – bowls and cards, taking the air and drinking the waters.[41] Charles, meanwhile, was preoccupied with Portsmouth. When she first came to England, she had dreams of becoming queen, but these soon evaporated and her relationship with Charles became as stable as any he enjoyed with a woman. After the tempestuous Cleveland, her lack of malice was soothing and at first she showed little interest in politics, devoting her energies to amassing wealth in England, France and Ireland.[42] Cleveland, meanwhile, lost her remaining influence with the king. She was reported to be pregnant by the Earl of Mulgrave and in 1676 she went to France, claiming that she and her children could live more cheaply there.[43]

Portsmouth soon established a mutually advantageous alliance with Danby: he showed her favour at the treasury, she used her influence with the king on his behalf. Her ascendancy was, however, far from complete. Her health was poor, especially after Charles gave her a dose of venereal disease. Then, late in 1675, a serious rival appeared with the arrival of the

Duchesse de Mazarin, the same Hortense Mancini whom Charles had thought of marrying in 1660. Now separated from her irritating nonentity of a husband, she was still exceptionally beautiful and there were those (not least Ralph Montagu) who hoped that she could become Charles's favourite mistress.[44] Courtiers began to mimic Portsmouth, a sign that her credit was slipping; Charles declared that he would never abandon her, but she was still desperately anxious and fell ill. While she was away taking the waters Mazarin moved into the apartments of Lady Sussex, Charles's fifteen-year-old daughter (by Cleveland) who was in the later stages of pregnancy. These apartments were situated directly above the king's and he could enter and leave them without being seen. When Portsmouth returned, looking thin and drawn, Charles visited both women regularly, but seemed more intimate with Mazarin. In an effort to break the liaison, Portsmouth tried to persuade Lady Sussex to go and live with her husband. She enlisted an unlikely ally in Cleveland and eventually the countess was persuaded first to go into the country, then to join her mother in France, where she was to cause her father further embarrassments. Mazarin remained, however, and Portsmouth at last accepted that she would have to come to terms with her: Courtin held a dinner party at which they were formally reconciled and danced up the stairs, hand in hand.[45]

Charles's relationship with his mistresses was far from a private matter. Their influence was considerable: Courtin was surprised that Louis failed to make use of Mazarin's.[46] The ambassador, who despite his years was very much a ladies' man, knew that by talking to Charles of women he could establish a familiarity which allowed him to lead the conversation on to other matters. Courtin clearly liked the libertine atmosphere of the court; others did not. Nell Gwynn might joke about her rivals; Henry Savile might declare that it would be a national disgrace if a fifteen-year-old French actress (after whom Charles lusted) left England a virgin; but others were more censorious:

> Like a tame spinster in's seragl' he sits
> Besieg'd by whores, buffoons and bastard chits;
> Lull'd in security, rolling in lust,
> Resigns his crown to angel Carwell's trust.[47]

Even those who felt no moral revulsion at his conduct worried about the money he spent on his women. Courtin reported that Charles allowed Portsmouth £16,000 a year and by 1677 she was said to possess jewels and plate to the value of £100,000 – and that at a time when Charles was supposed to be economizing. Although a plan to attack her in Parliament came to nothing, her religion, her nationality and her obvious influence did not improve the court's public image.[48]

The picture given thus far of Charles's court in the years after 1674 has been one of indecision, self-seeking and confusion. Not only did Charles's policies lack consistency, but he seems at times to have lacked interest. At the root of this lay a fundamental lack of sympathy between king and chief minister. Charles may not have liked Danby – not many people did – or his policies, but no one else offered a realistic strategy for tackling his financial and political problems. When we turn to foreign affairs, the picture is very different. It was an area which Charles clearly found more interesting than details of finance and administration. He could deal with ambassadors on a one-to-one basis, which he found much more congenial than either speeches to Parliament or privy council meetings.[49] The knowledge of the continent which he had gained in exile enabled Charles to dominate foreign policy-making in a way that he lacked the desire or the application to do with domestic policy. With the eclipse of Arlington, in fact, he became his own foreign minister. Danby lacked the necessary experience and was guided mainly by considerations of domestic politics. York lacked finesse and his views were distorted by awareness of his own political vulnerability. Diplomacy was thus Charles's personal domain.

There was one final reason for the comparative coherence of Charles's decision-making in foreign affairs. At home his objectives were clear – to avoid political and financial disaster – but the means for achieving them were not. Abroad, he had two main objectives: first, to avoid a breach with France, which could lead to his recurrent nightmare, a Franco-Dutch rapprochement (not to mention the publication of the Dover treaty)[50] and second to defuse his subjects' hostility to France. Both objectives could be achieved if he could bring about peace between the warring powers and from early 1674 until late 1677 Charles pursued that goal with diligence and ingenuity. His methods had to be diplomatic: he had no wish to be drawn into a war that could leave him at Parliament's mercy. He often remarked that both James I and Charles I had made a fatal error in allowing Parliament to ensnare them in war. To all other considerations was added that of honour. Even though Louis had not always treated him well, he had been most reluctant to make a separate peace in 1674 and now, despite Danby's scepticism, he felt that honour prevented him from making war on his former ally.[51] Only the most pressing necessity, and purblind French obduracy, would make him change his mind.

As the number of powers ranged against France had grown, so Louis had extended his operations, which in turn increased the number of his enemies: violence which had been intended as a deterrent had had the opposite effect. Although he had withdrawn almost all his troops from the Dutch Republic, the Spanish Netherlands remained a major theatre of war: indeed, their acquisition had always been his primary long-term objective. At the very least, he wished to create a 'duelling field', a broad area guarded by fortresses, which could serve as a defensive buffer, but also offer easy entry into the remainder of the Spanish Netherlands, or the republic. Only in 1677–8 did he become more concerned with building a rationalized and defensible frontier.[52] Thus in 1674–7 the fears, widely expressed in England, that Louis aimed to conquer the whole of the Netherlands were not unfounded. There was less substance to claims that he aimed at universal dominion, but these were given some credibility by the military aggression he had shown in 1667–8 and 1672–3. This belief led to strident calls to Charles to throw his weight behind the allies: otherwise, it was alleged, Louis would conquer first Flanders, then the republic and then England.

If Charles shared these fears, he kept them to himself. He may not have seen France's armed might as a threat to England; he may still have hoped, with French help, to grab Spanish territories when Carlos died. Whatever the reasons, Charles's sympathies in these years were clearly with France. He allowed Louis to continue to recruit soldiers in his dominions and was most reluctant to recall British troops from the French service. He found the allies' proposed peace terms unrealistic: there was no prospect whatever that Louis could be made to cede all that he had taken since the Treaty of the Pyrenees. He did not accept William's argument that, unless France's frontiers were pushed back to those of 1659, Louis would be able to establish French hegemony over the whole of Europe. Gradually, however, William modified his position. He found his allies unreliable. The Spaniards put less effort into the war in Flanders than he thought they should and the emperor's main interest lay in Germany; the various armies and commanders worked poorly together. Meanwhile, William's position within the republic was not impregnable. The surge of patriotism on which he had risen to power was largely spent by 1675. The French had withdrawn from Dutch territory (except for Maastricht) and the regents of the great cities were weary of a war which seemed now to be fought for the benefit of the allies. Republican suspicions of princely power resurfaced: some argued that William was keeping the war going in order to maintain the army and that one day he would attempt a coup just as his father had done in 1650. Slowly and reluctantly, therefore, William came round to the idea of a peace based on the status quo, but with Louis exchanging some of the towns he had taken for others which were strategically less sensitive. He insisted that the Spanish Netherlands had to remain militarily defensible, to serve as a barrier to protect the Dutch against future French aggression.[53]

If William shifted his ground, so did Charles. In late 1674 and early 1675, when the allies' ambassadors called on him to join them he replied baldly, 'Make peace.'[54] He was, however, anxious to assist the peace process, especially in Flanders.[55] He pressed Louis, as well as William, to let him know the conditions upon which he would settle. When the peace congress a Nijmegen was held up by disputes, Charles took the initiative in resolving them. First, a French client, Prince William von Fürstenberg, had been kidnapped by imperial agents. Louis refused to send plenipotentiaries until he was released; the emperor refused to release him, even to a third party. Charles proposed that the prince's kinsman, the Bishop of Strasbourg, should write to beg Louis to rely on the emperor's assurance that the prince would be released after peace had been concluded. Louis agreed: Charles had found a way for him to back down without losing face.[56] Charles was very irritated when Louis created a further delay by refusing to grant passports to representatives of the Duke of Lorraine. Louis had seized Lorraine in 1670 and did not consider that the duke had any right to send representatives to the congress. Charles proposed that he, as mediator, should issue passports to all the participants, thus removing the need for Louis to recognize the duke. Louis agreed, but the States General did not, so Charles pressed Louis to issue the passports which, in the end, he did.[57]

In his efforts to unblock the peace process Charles occasionally expressed irritation with his former ally and anxiety about the growth of French power. As he struggled to stem the tide of anti-French feeling, he complained increasingly that Louis did not understand his predicament.[58] Louis refused to let him know the conditions upon which he would settle. The Spaniards, he said, had declared war on him, so it was up to them to make the first move. Such a stance might be sound negotiating practice, but it did nothing to facilitate Charles's task as mediator, as Courtin recognized. The ambassador, indeed, complained bitterly of his master's imprudence. Surely, he wrote, he did not intend to conquer all of the Spanish Netherlands, as that would force England to enter the coalition against him. As it was, Louis had allowed Leopold to gain more power in Germany than any of his predecessors: he should return at once to the policy of Richelieu and Mazarin, of setting the princes against the emperor.[59] Louis, however, was confident that if he remained firm either the coalition would fall apart or his enemies would accept his terms. Eager to squeeze the maximum profit from every negotiation, he would not listen to pussyfooting considerations of prudence. Courtin tried in vain to win over Chancellor Le Tellier to his point of view and poured out his heart to Pomponne: 'All this, sir, is only for you. It is dangerous to say what one thinks in the country where you are.'[60]

While Louis' refusal even to hint at possible peace terms irritated Charles (and Courtin), a new source of friction appeared. French privateers arrested English merchant ships, claiming that they were carrying contraband or that they were really Dutch. French admiralty courts usually adjudged them to be lawful prizes; there was no appeal against such verdicts and even if the ships were released they had often been pillaged. Lord Berkeley, Charles's ambassador, was rudely rebuffed when he raised the issue; it did not help that the Paris agent for many English merchants was the ubiquitous Sir Ellis Leighton, who cheerfully accepted bribes from all and sundry but did little to get the ships released. Courtin's instructions echoed Colbert's claim that the English complaints were unreasonable; the ambassador thought otherwise.[61] Only when Charles came under pressure to issue letters of reprisal did the French reconsider their position, embracing York's proposal that passports should be issued to vessels which were genuinely English. Charles also sent John Brisbane to Paris to press for the release of some eighty-five merchant ships. The French tried to insist that passports should be issued only by the king and that two-thirds of the crew of any 'English' ship had to be English; Charles dismissed both demands as unreasonable. As anti-French feeling reached fever pitch and the City refused to lend Charles £40,000 to put down a rebellion in Virginia, French resistance crumbled. Louis issued an ordinance against privateers which Courtin thought very wise: it was better to suffer a few frauds than to provoke Charles into issuing letters of reprisal. In fact, Charles was not satisfied by the ordinance, as it could be revoked at Louis' pleasure. His new ambassador in Paris, Ralph Montagu, put forward a new maritime treaty which Louis eventually (and reluctantly) signed.[62]

Between February 1674 and February 1677 Charles did what he could to facilitate negotiations at Nijmegen, signed a maritime treaty in which Louis conceded more than he wished to and repeatedly pressed Louis to set out the peace terms that he would accept. He gained his first glimpse of success in February 1677, when Louis declared his willingness to agree to a barrier to protect the Dutch Republic, provided he in turn received towns to round off and secure his own frontiers.[63] If Charles had not brought about peace, this was due to the intransigence of William and, above all, of Louis. By late 1676, however, both were coming to accept the need for peace. Temple wrote from Nijmegen that if anyone was now likely to obstruct a treaty it was the emperor, who had made substantial gains from the war. Charles had also engaged in negotiations with the States General about an alliance, to come into effect when the war ended.[64] Such developments rarely, however, figure prominently in accounts of Anglo-French relations in these years, which concentrate instead on payments by Louis to enable Charles to prorogue or dissolve Parliament. The idea apparently originated with York, who had more reason than most to fear attack in Parliament. At first he approached Louis' confessor about the possibility of a French subsidy, then suggested to Ruvigny that Louis should lend Charles somewhere between £300,000 and £500,000. In the spring of 1675, the Commons showed great hostility to France, whereupon Ruvigny suggested that Louis should advance some £200,000 to £300,000, once peace had been concluded. Danby claimed that he could obtain far more from Parliament, but Charles was clearly attracted by the French proposal and offered (through James) to prorogue Parliament until the following April if Louis would give him enough to meet his financial needs. Louis did not part with money easily, but eventually agreed to pay Charles £100,000. At the end of 1676, as another session approached, Courtin thought that there was no point in offering Charles a modest sum to delay it, but added that it was essential that Charles should continue to believe that he could receive money in return for refusing to break with France.[65]

Charles's financial dealings with Louis have often been cited as evidence of a shameful dependence on France. It has been my contention that his friendship towards France rested, not only on his hopes of French subsidies but also on what seemed to him sound diplomatic and geopolitical considerations. If Louis wished him to make sacrifices for his benefit, it was only reasonable that he should be compensated. The giving of subsidies was a normal feature of international relations. Charles was well aware that the Dutch and Spanish ambassadors were entertaining MPs lavishly and there was talk, doubtless exaggerated, of massive bribes changing hands. Ruvigny used similar methods to build up support in the Commons: it was vital, for Louis, that king and Commons should not unite against France. Thus while trying to persuade Charles to delay or dismiss Parliament, the French pursued an alternative strategy of inciting MPs to attack the conduct of his government; his ministers were at least partly aware of this by February 1677.[66] Amid such general cynicism it was perhaps neither surprising nor unduly reprehensible for Charles to accept relatively modest sums for doing what he would probably have done anyway.

The period between the prorogation of February 1674 and the assembling of Parliament in February 1677 is an unusually complex and difficult one, dominated by events on the continent. Concern for the preservation of Flanders came to eclipse even the fear of Popery and arbitrary government, although the two were of course connected. If Charles's domestic policies lacked direction, he showed application and skill in his efforts to bring about peace. He was hampered by the need to argue from a position of weakness. He could not threaten Louis, so sought to persuade him that it was not in his interest to allow pressure to build up within England to a point where Charles would be forced into war. It was a delicate hand to play, but Charles played it with some skill. He had to contend with the truculence and intransigence of both Louis and William and with the court at Madrid, which was influenced more by fear of losing face than by military and diplomatic realities. Faced with such difficulties, his achievements were far from negligible. By February 1677 both Louis and William were coming to accept the need for realistic negotiations. It remained to be seen whether either would move far or fast enough for peace to be concluded, before military events or political pressures within England forced Charles to break with France.

The prorogation of February 1674 was followed by a realignment of forces at court, in the wake of the demise of the Cabal. Danby's claim to financial expertise gave him a head start over his rivals. He quickly joined forces with James, whose strength of character was undoubted and who seemed less of a political liability now that Parliament was no longer in session. Once it became clear that Charles was not going to abandon Lauderdale, despite the Commons' attacks on his conduct, Danby welcomed his offers of co-operation. In June Lauderdale was created an English earl, thus guaranteeing him the right of trial by the House of Lords should he be impeached.[67] This doughty triumvirate, followed at a discreet distance by Lord Keeper Finch, sought to assert its dominance over Charles's government. The three pressed Charles to dismiss Essex, who was too independent for their liking and would not allow the indiscriminate plunder of Ireland and its revenues. Portsmouth added her voice to the calls for Essex's removal, but he was made of sterner stuff than some of his predecessors. He refused to seek Portsmouth's friendship – it cost too much – nor would he place any reliance on the 'little people' at court. Instead, he put his trust in his own integrity and in the king; for once, such trust was not misplaced.[68]

Essex's survival showed that the triumvirate was not all-powerful. York was alarmed to learn that Charles had entertained Carlisle and other lords who had attacked him the previous session, but the chief object of their animosity was Arlington. His suppleness and emollience were the opposite of everything Danby, Lauderdale and above all York stood for. Despite all their efforts, however, reports of Arlington's political demise proved premature. Even after laying down the secretaryship, he regularly discussed foreign affairs with Ruvigny. Danby played no part in such matters until Arlington's secret mission to William at the end of 1674. This led Danby to respond, at last, to Sir William Temple's advice that he should interest himself in the moves to bring about a peace. If, as Danby suspected, Arlington had hoped to use the mission to re-establish his influence, the ploy failed: he returned to find that Danby had done much to undermine his credit in his absence.[69]

Another figure whose star was rising was Monmouth. Hitherto he had been renowned mainly for his dissolute and violent lifestyle, but the Dutch war awakened his (and his father's) military ambitions. These were also encouraged by James, who at that time showed a genuine fondness for the young man.[70] Monmouth served with some distinction with the French army at Maastricht in 1673 and Charles considered sending him to the continent again in 1674. Instead, he began to exercise an informal command over the army at home, in conjunction with James, who was now legally ineligible to hold any military office. At some stage, probably in 1674, Monmouth asked Charles to grant him the title of commander in chief, not to be used at present, but to be held in reserve in case of emergency. York claimed that this was unnecessary: as senior colonel Monmouth already outranked all other officers – there had been no general (in peacetime) since Albemarle died. In retrospect, York saw this incident as evidence of Monmouth's desire to make a push for the crown when Charles died; it seems more probable that he wanted the title for the kudos it would bring. In the end, he had to content himself with two of Buckingham's former posts, as master of the horse and, more incongruously, chancellor of Cambridge University. His relationship with James, meanwhile, became markedly cooler.[71]

For the time being, Monmouth showed no interest in court politics, which for much of 1674 were dominated by the question of Parliament. York and Danby urged Charles to dissolve it and live quietly on his revenues; these, Danby claimed, would be sufficient if Charles would only economize. Others, notably Arlington, claimed that a dissolution would provoke a rebellion and bring down the monarchy. As so often, the more cautious counsel carried the day. A proclamation against the discussion of state affairs, even in private conversation, showed clearly the king's fears of upheaval. It referred specifically to malicious rumours that he intended to dissolve Parliament; there had also been a move to include a promise that it should meet on the appointed day, 10 November.[72] In the end, the proclamation left the matter open and contention now centred on whether Parliament should indeed meet in November or be prorogued again. The members of the anti-French alliance (or 'confederates'), confident that it would press Charles to break with France, were eager that it should convene as soon as possible. Ruvigny urged Charles to delay and was supported by York and Lauderdale, both of whom feared that they would again be attacked. Danby had less cause for anxiety – he had had no part in breaking the Triple Alliance – but the conduct of the last session gave him reason to fear that no minister (and especially no finance minister) would be safe. Besides, he argued that time was needed to revive the royal finances and to find ways of calming MPs' fears of France and Popery, so he too supported a further prorogation.

As far as France was concerned, Danby took no positive action, perhaps hoping that England's withdrawal from the war would prove sufficient. On religion, his alliance with York meant that he had to tread carefully. In March 1674 Charles told the judges to order JPs (yet again) to enforce the laws against Catholics and made it clear that he wished the order to be obeyed. This time magistrates, full of fears of Popery, bestirred themselves and the laws against recusancy (absence from church) were vigorously enforced for the first time in the reign; most of those convicted were Catholics, not Dissenters.[73] The problem of Dissent was more complex. The limitations on the liberty proposed for Dissenters in the Commons' bill of 1673 showed continuing dislike and suspicion; a proposal by a group of nonconformists to offer Charles money to dissolve Parliament showed that they were well aware of this. Their legal position was uncertain: the Declaration had been cancelled, but the licences issued under it had not been withdrawn. In May Arlington wrote that Charles wished conventicles to be suppressed, but JPs remained hesitant: it was possible that by 'conventicles' he meant unlicensed meetings and some complained that fines imposed on conventiclers had been pardoned by a higher authority. Sheldon might assert that the laws were fully in force, but few seemed inclined to enforce them until they saw when, or whether, Parliament would meet.[74]

In June Charles told Ruvigny that he would not dissolve Parliament, but that he would prorogue it until April. He could, he added, do as he would with it: if it persisted in acting unreasonably, he would dissolve it. If he had indeed decided to prorogue, the decision remained secret and, like most of Charles's decisions, it was not irreversible. After sounding MPs, Arlington claimed that the Commons would give money. James was unconvinced by this, but even he was half persuaded that MPs would not impugn his claim to the succession and would be satisfied with only token measures against Catholics. He kept his options open, listening to overtures from Presbyterians and sounding Ruvigny about the possibility of a French loan, to enable Charles to survive longer without calling Parliament. Charles seemed undecided, and it came as a surprise when he informed the council, late in September, of his intention to prorogue.[75] He exulted at having asserted himself so masterfully, but some saw behind the decision James's insistence that firmness would win more support than weakness. The news heartened the Dissenters: they argued that the laws should not be enforced against them, at least until Parliament met, and began to meet openly, amid rumours of a general toleration.[76]

The postponement of Parliament gave Charles a chance to use the winter lull in military operations to try to bring about peace. Although he had offered to mediate between Louis and the confederates, his attitude at first was far from even-handed. He clearly felt ashamed at having been forced to abandon his ally and deeply resented William's dealings with English 'malcontents'. He refused Ossory permission to visit William and allowed the French to make recruits in England, while rejecting a similar request from the Dutch. Coventry claimed that to allow recruiting would be incompatible with Charles's role as mediator; the Dutch were not convinced.[77] There seemed little prospect that his proposed mediation would succeed.

Louis quickly took up his offer, but then his plenipotentiaries left the congress at Cologne, in protest against the kidnapping of Fürstenberg. William insisted that peace could be made only on the basis of the Peace of the Pyrenees. The States General accepted Charles as mediator only in July; even then, their treaty obligations to Spain, and concern for their own safety, committed them to maintaining the Spanish Netherlands as a defensible entity and they pressed Charles to help them to do so. All parties waited on the outcome of the 1674 campaign. Arlington argued that it would be impolitic to reject the Dutch overtures out of hand, but Charles told them to make peace: there was no prospect of his breaking with France.[78] He told the Dutch and Spanish envoys that he had done more for Flanders than for France but that, while Louis had treated him better than he had been obliged to, the Spaniards had been consistently ungrateful.[79]

One obstacle to a better understanding with the Dutch was Charles's resentment of their recent dealings with the English opposition. Williamson patiently gathered information about plans for a revolt as soon as the Dutch fleet appeared off the English coast and Charles demanded, as the price of his friendship, that William should reveal the names of his English contacts.[80] William repeatedly refused, as a matter of honour, to betray those who had sought to serve him; Charles became increasingly irritated by his obduracy.[81] Yet the prospects for co-operation were not as bleak as Charles's public utterances (as reported by Ruvigny) and William's stubbornness might suggest. Charles believed, with some justification, that the Dutch people were eager for peace. Some of his advisers – notably Arlington, Temple and Coventry – were deeply concerned to preserve Flanders; Arlington told Temple that, while playing on William's fears for his own safety, he should also assure him that Charles too shared this concern and was eager to help secure a satisfactory peace. The States General, for their part, were careful not to offend English sensibilities on the matter of the flag.[82] Coventry argued that it was in no one's interest to allow the Spanish Netherlands to be overrun, but also warned Temple to watch for signs of a separate peace between France and the Dutch; Louis had, indeed, proposed such a peace, but William had refused to desert his allies. Charles, meanwhile, asked Ruvigny what terms Louis would accept and revived the proposal for a commercial treaty. Ruvigny thought that the latter was a ruse of Arlington's to make the French even more unpopular, but Charles said it was necessary to silence the complaints of the London merchants and promised to extend the prorogation once the treaty had been completed.[83]

The change of heart was not all on one side. For William the 1674 campaign brought a sorry catalogue of failures. He was exasperated by the Spaniards' half-heartedness and incompetence and by the eccentricity, to say no worse, of the imperial commander, the Comte de Souches. While the

Dutch aimed only to establish an effective barrier between France and the republic, the Spaniards pitched their demands impossibly high. The emperor, who was fighting at others' expense, showed no interest in making peace.[84] In these circumstances William felt impelled to improve his relations with his uncle. He sent Sir Gabriel Sylvius to ask Charles's advice about how best to secure Flanders and proposed that he should come to England that autumn. Charles had no intention of allowing him to come over while Parliament was in session and a few days later announced the prorogation. He was pleased, however, that William had sought his advice and asked what the Dutch and Spanish judged necessary to preserve the Spanish Netherlands; he stressed to Ruvigny that an exchange of towns would be needed to guarantee a secure frontier and again asked what terms Louis would accept. William's reply was non-committal. Arlington claimed that he had been persuaded, by the Spaniards, to see Charles as wholly committed to France. He persuaded Charles to send him to assure William that this was not so and to sound him about his intentions. After much hesitation, Ruvigny told Arlington of the terms upon which he thought Louis would make peace.[85]

Arlington was accompanied on his mission by Ossory, for whom William had great respect, and by William's kinsman Odijk. Arlington clearly hoped to use the mission to strengthen his credit at court, establishing himself as the essential link between Charles and William. He claimed, disingenuously, that William would not confide in Temple, once more ambassador at the Hague, because of his association with de Witt: more to the point, although Arlington did not mention it, was the fact that Temple was linked politically with Danby. Even if Arlington's motives were suspect, however, the mission might still serve a valid purpose. Charles declared himself confident that William would see that he had been wrong to put his trust in the English opposition. He charitably (or patronizingly) blamed William's error on inexperience and insisted that he should make a clean breast of his past misdeeds and accept that he was not to come to England until peace had been concluded.[86] The three envoys were also to offer William the hand of James's daughter Mary, now twelve. James was less than enthusiastic about this proposal, claiming that Mary was too young; in fact, he harboured hopes (encouraged by Ruvigny) that she might marry Louis' son and heir, the dauphin. Charles did not press the matter and there remained some uncertainty as to whether James had agreed that William should be offered her hand.[87]

News of Arlington's mission caused considerable surprise; Danby hastily sent his son to Holland to see what his rival was up to. Temple, too, had known nothing of it, but William kept him fully informed of the negotiations. Arlington found William dry and sullen; William found Arlington arrogant and rude and complained that he treated him like a child. When William asked that the past might be forgotten and that Charles should take him into his protection, Arlington replied that he needed to take Charles into his confidence and accused him of maintaining his contacts with English malcontents even after the Treaty of Westminster.[88] Opinions differed as to the terms to which William might agree. Temple claimed that he was determined to seize this chance to secure the Spanish Netherlands against France once and for all; he would therefore agree to no terms that left the Spanish unable to defend themselves. He thus insisted that Louis should hand over Charleroi, Tournai, Lille, Ath and Oudenarde, all of which Spain had surrendered under the Treaty of Aix-la-Chapelle; he rejected suggestions that, in return, Spain should cede Franche Comté or Cambrai, or that the emperor should settle, unless Louis restored Lorraine (nominally part of the empire) to Duke Charles. Ruvigny, however, declared that there was no question of Louis ceding anything he had acquired under the Treaty of Aix: any discussion should be confined to his subsequent conquests. There seemed, therefore, little basis for negotiation. William had scarcely budged from his insistence on the terms of 1659, except that he now envisaged Spain ceding Aire and St Omer. He claimed that Charles could easily bring Louis to accept reasonable terms, but refused to do so. Arlington, however, wrote that William was bitterly disillusioned with the Spaniards and thought that they might be satisfied if Louis returned Franche Comté, razed Maastricht and exchanged Charleroi, Ath and Oudenarde for Aire and St Omer; Charles considered this proposal unsatisfactory, but at least a basis for negotiation.[89]

The disparities between Temple's and Arlington's accounts of William's position reflected their differing political stances and mutual antagonism; besides, William made it clear that he was speaking only for himself, not for the States General. His intransigence might seem unrealistic in view of his resounding lack of military success, but the Dutch treaty with Spain back in 1673 had been based on pushing France back to the frontiers of 1659. Besides, if he really believed that Charles's influence with Louis was sufficient to bring him to accept reasonable terms, then it followed that Parliament might force him to use that influence. William also believed that there was a real possibility of serious tax revolts within France. He was prepared to do something to win Charles's favour: he sent du Moulin away, but he would not name his English contacts. He received Ossory's proposal that he should marry Mary politely, but said it would first be necessary that she should meet him. Charles claimed that Ossory had exceeded his instructions and Ruvigny suspected that Arlington had the matter raised to provide a pretext to bring William to England.[90]

It would seem that, as Temple claimed, Arlington's mission had been a failure. It did nothing to enhance Arlington's standing at court and Charles assured Ruvigny, with tears in his eyes, that he was as displeased as ever with William.[91] He may have been sincere, but he never found it difficult to summon tears and there is evidence that he was being less than frank to the ambassador. Ossory wrote to his father (to whom he had no reason to lie) that Charles had told him that a marriage between William and Mary was 'the only thing capable of helping the Duke'. York had agreed, on condition that the first proposal should come from William, and was angry with Ossory only because he had been told that Ossory had raised the matter first. Other evidence, however, suggests that that is precisely what he did and it is very possible that Charles had told him to do so, but was reluctant to admit it to his irate brother, especially after the plan had clearly failed.[92] Soon after, Temple wrote that William seemed very favourable to 'the match' and added that he hoped that Charles could arrange a peace on terms similar to those which Temple had recently discussed with Gaspar Fagel, Grand Pensionary of Holland. If he could, they could then consider further co-operation. Temple wrote to Danby that he was sure that there had been little substance to Arlington's negotiations, but Charles showed Ruvigny a draft, brought by Arlington, of a treaty for an offensive and defensive alliance, which was not to operate against France during the present war. Charles rejected it, saying that he could not even think of any such thing until peace had been concluded.[93] Outwardly, he remained as hostile as ever towards William and the confederates. He brusquely told William not to come over when Parliament met and continued to urge the ambassadors of the allies to make peace.[94] Nevertheless, a breach had been made in the wall of mutual suspicion between uncle and nephew. William was beginning to accept that Louis would have to be allowed to keep some of his conquests and the proposed marriage offered the eventual prospect of a closer liaison, perhaps even of bringing England into the war.

Although Charles had announced that Parliament would meet in April 1675, Ruvigny urged him to delay the session, at least until after that summer's campaign, and talked of a Dutch fleet sailing up the Thames to encourage malcontents in the Commons; York again sounded the ambassador about the possibility of money from France. Danby and the king were torn between fear of what Parliament might do if it met and fear of what an outraged populace might do if it did not. In the end, fear of disorder and the need for money tipped the balance. Professing a confidence that he probably did not feel, Charles told Ruvigny that he would dissolve Parliament if it misbehaved, but that he did not think that that would be necessary. This was the best House of Commons he could ever have: some MPs had been led astray, but most would behave well provided their fears were soothed.[95] The leading figures at court took steps to safeguard their position if and when Parliament met. York welcomed overtures from Dissenters, unsure of their legal position following the withdrawal of the Indulgence. As the most prominent non-Anglican at court, he was increasingly seen as the natural protector of nonconformists of all kinds. Hitherto, he had distrusted such people as politically suspect, but he had no doubt of their power: indeed, he seems to have believed that they made up as much as three-quarters of the population. Now that his conversion had given him something in common with them, he convinced himself that, if they were assured of liberty if he became king, they would not support his exclusion. Some, indeed, offered to support his restoration to office, in order to enhance his power at court. He secured pardons from the king for groups of Dissenters in Bristol and elsewhere and was reported to be promoting a new indulgence, which might even include Catholics. He also had a friendly meeting with Holles, Carlisle and other peers who had been active against him in the previous session.[96]

York took such pains to build up support because many urged Charles to sacrifice him or played on his fears of James's power and ambition. Charles denounced such machinations and declared with tears in his eyes that the two of them could never be separated, but James knew him well enough not to rely too much on such protestations.[97] The Duke's open commitment to liberty of conscience was further encouraged by Danby's dealings with the bishops. In October he told Morley that it was necessary to find means to unite the people before Parliament met. His meaning was not initially clear. Everybody (except James) accepted that measures against Popery would be politically essential, but there were many rumours that Charles would promote comprehension (and, some said, indulgence as well). Arlington was reported to be deep in discussion with Blood about this.[98] The bishops, by contrast, argued that the laws against both Popery and Dissent should be vigorously enforced, adding a strong exhortation to suppress libertinism and atheism. It was some weeks before Charles made his decision. York claimed later that Danby and Lauderdale had encouraged the bishops to take this firm stand; it is not clear whether they did so, but Coventry probably did. As late as 27 January Williamson noted that a proclamation to enforce the laws against Papists and conventicles was to include a hint that Charles would gladly grant Dissenters as much ease as Parliament should advise. A week later, however, the privy council accepted the bishops' advice. Native-born priests were ordered to leave the kingdom; the laws against conventicles were to be enforced.[99]

It might seem that Charles had at last accepted the need to place his trust in the Anglicans, but some refused to accept his decision as final. Many believed that the strength of Dissent had grown greatly since the Indulgence. York still urged him to plump for liberty of conscience and persuaded him to tone down the orders issued by the council. Danby and Lauderdale continued to discuss comprehension with leading opposition peers and Morley initiated similar discussions with Baxter and some of his colleagues. These prosposals came to nothing, perhaps because they were opposed by York, who knew that the comprehension of Presbyterians within the Church would weaken the case for indulgence for those outside it.[100] Charles's government was by no means wholly committed to persecution, however. Coventry told the Bishop of Bristol to treat the more peaceable Dissenters gently and so justify severity towards the insolent; he saw no need to seek the help of the county militia. Rumours that Charles did not really want conventicles to be disrupted made magistrates hesitant. Some meetings were disrupted, but most continued more or less unmolested.[101] As for Danby and Lauderdale, having failed to agree terms with the Presbyterians, they found themselves committed, by default, to the Anglicans. It was not something that they had sought. Lauderdale was originally a Presbyterian and had promoted episcopacy in Scotland for reasons that were essentially political; Danby had hitherto shown little sign of enthusiastic Church-manship. Now, however, he urged Charles to launch an enquiry into the workings of the Corporation and Five Mile Acts and remove all 'disaffected' men from the judiciary, the magistracy and the militia. He suggested that recusancy fines should be used to meet the expenses of JPs and militia officers, 'by which they may be made offices of benefit as well as trust'. Coventry, too, appealed to the old Cavaliers; he urged MPs to come up in good time for the session, in letters which talked of the king's 'old friends of the loyal party' and of restoring Church and government to their 'legal state and condition'. How well such a strategy would work remained to be seen.[102]

On 13 April Charles came to Parliament in greater state than usual. He stressed his commitment to securing religion and property, praised the loyalty of the Commons and commended the navy to their attention. Neither he nor Finch asked directly for money: the first priority was to recover the Commons' goodwill.[103] To this end a bill was brought into the Lords, to require all office-holders to swear not to attempt to alter the government in Church or state. The aim of 'Danby's test' was to perpetuate and exploit the divisions of the civil wars and to give Anglicans and Royalists a monopoly of office. It was strongly opposed in the Lords, not only by oppositionist peers and those sympathetic to Dissent, but also by some of the Catholics. York was deeply embarrassed: he strongly disliked the test, but had no wish openly to oppose a measure which his brother wished to pass, as his assiduous attendance at debates made clear. James reduced the danger of the test's being used to his detriment by promoting a resolution that it should be a standing order of the House that neither this bill nor any other could prejudice any peer's right to sit. His stance on the bill lost him the support of those MPs who were sympathetic to Dissent; nothing came of the plan to move in the Commons for his reinstatement to office or of another to have him exempted by name from a new bill against Catholics. The test bill finally passed the Lords at the end of May, but by then there seemed no prospect of its passing the Commons, so it was never sent there.[104]

While the Lords laboured over the test bill, the Commons considered a wide range of grievances. Sir William Coventry's place bill reflected the fear that Danby might use places and pensions to build up an obedient 'court party' in the House.[105] The charges against Lauderdale were revived: Burnet told the House of his remark that the king's edicts were above the laws. It was resolved to draw up an address, begging the king to remove him from his offices. Charles replied that the alleged offences would have been covered by his recent general pardon. It was more than three weeks before the House considered the king's answer. It voted to prepare another address, but it was never completed.[106] An attempt to impeach Danby proved equally ineffectual. The charges, mostly of financial irregularities, were flimsy and (many thought) malicious: Arlington was seen as the moving spirit behind them. They were rejected, but a motion that the House should express its confidence in the treasurer fell flat.[107] Other developments were less pleasing to the court. In an effort to induce the Commons to offer money, Pepys gave an account of the current state of the fleet. MPs responded with claims that money was being diverted from the navy to other, less acceptable uses. A bill was brought in to appropriate the customs to the navy and the House approved an address against anticipating customs revenue (in other words, spending it before it had been collected). The promoters of these measures wished to play on backbench suspicions of mismanagement in order to reduce the king's freedom of financial manoeuvre and so increase his dependence on Parliament. Charles's reply to the address was non-committal: he promised that he would manage his money more carefully in future. Privately, he expressed surprise that Danby could mobilize votes to defend himself, but not to defend the royal revenues. The bill appropriating the customs had not emerged from committee when the session ended.[108]

On 19 April the Commons turned their attention to the British regiments in the French service. Apart from showing concern at the growth of French power, MPs talked of the Protestant interest, of the unfavourable balance in Anglo-French trade and of the risk that the soldiers would be infected with French attitudes. It was resolved to address Charles to recall all his subjects from the French service. Charles assured Ruvigny that he would not allow the Commons to dictate to him, but (as so often) his talk of firmness was not translated into action. He told the Commons that he could not, in honour, recall those who had gone over when he and Louis were allies, but he would recall those who had gone over since the peace and would renew his proclamation against new recruits. When the Commons debated this answer feelings ran high. There were dark hints that the troops had been raised with sinister intent and claims that any obligation which Charles might feel towards Louis (who never adhered to his treaties anyway) should give way before his obligation to his people. Others, however, reminded the House that control of the armed forces and of foreign policy were prerogative matters: if Charles refused to take their advice, they had no choice but to acquiesce. One debate, in a committee of the whole House, ended in a tied vote with MPs putting their feet on the mace to prevent an adjournment. Next day a motion to address for the recall of 'all' the king's subjects from the French service was rejected by a single vote.[109] Ruvigny complained that Charles was weak and would not trust in his own judgement, especially when he refused to recall his subjects from the Dutch service as well. Charles, however, was clearly worried by the depth of feeling shown in debate. He was not unduly concerned about French ambitions in the Low Countries, because Louis had assured him that he intended only a limited campaign there, just sufficient to bring the Dutch and Spanish to make peace. Even so, Ruvigny suspected that, in his heart, Charles envied Louis his successes; those around him, moreover, insinuated that Louis did not want to make peace and did not wish to understand Charles's predicament. By mid-June Charles was expressing a resentment which Ruvigny had not heard before: he alone was standing up for France's interests, against his entire kingdom. He was all the more bitter because he believed that the Commons did not really want war, but merely to reduce him to financial dependence and ruin his ministers.[110]

By mid-May it was clear that the session was not going as Danby had hoped. The test bill proceeded painfully slowly and on the 17th hopes of supply were dashed when the Commons resolved to receive no further bills that session. Moreover, the Houses became embroiled in yet another dispute. This grew out of a suit in Chancery, the case of *Shirley* v. *Fagg*. Dr Shirley had appealed to the Lords, but Sir John Fagg was an MP and the Commons ordered Shirley's arrest on the grounds of breach of privilege. Tempers flared and the Houses devoted far more attention to this case than to the charges against Lauderdale or Danby's test. The flames were fanned by Shaftesbury, Holles and others who wished Charles to dissolve Parliament. Charles tried to persuade the Houses to settle their differences, but some suspected that he himself was implicated in an evil design to discredit Parliament. His soothing words had no effect and on 9 June he prorogued the Houses.[111] As on the last occasion, he took no formal advice before doing so, but this time few would have argued that he had any alternative. Ruvigny urged him not to meet Parliament again that year, but despite tough talk about standing up to the Commons and to the confederates, Charles opted to prorogue only until October.[112]

The session's inglorious outcome damaged Danby's political credit. There were rumours that Shaftesbury and other opposition peers would be taken into favour and the former chancellor had long meetings with York. Danby, however, was nothing if not resilient: in a three-hour meeting he argued away Charles's doubts. Shaftesbury and his friends were forbidden the court and oppositionist MPs were dismissed from office; a doughty old Cavalier, Sir Giles Strangways, was appointed to the privy council.[113] Ruvigny claimed that Charles could survive on his existing revenues, but Danby insisted that these were utterly insufficient and that Charles would have to secure money from Parliament, which meant that he would have to follow policies which MPs found acceptable. Danby rebutted York's arguments for liberty of conscience, but Charles still wished to avoid a persecution so harsh that it could lead to disorder and many nonconformists still met in defiance of the law.[114] The deep fears of France expressed in this session also convinced Danby that he needed to take a much more active interest in foreign policy. He stressed to Charles that French successes in the Low Countries could make the Commons intractable and lead to serious upheavals within England and begged him to seek a rapprochement with the States General. It seems plausible to ascribe Charles's occasional flashes of irritation towards France to Danby's influence, but irritation alone could not turn him against Louis, especially as he believed that reports that Flanders was about to fall were greatly exaggerated. On the other hand, the king would welcome any chance to secure peace with honour. He agreed to make overtures to the Dutch, although it may be doubted whether he expected or even wanted those overtures to succeed.[115]

Another unsuccessful campaign was increasing both William's irritation with his allies and the States General's eagerness for peace: Temple may have been right when he suggested that the Spaniards were so confident that Parliament would force Charles to join the war that they neglected their own defence. Temple and Danby argued that the onus was now on Charles to propose terms upon which peace could be concluded, but Charles refused to propose anything more than a truce, which the allies rejected as doing nothing to remove the threat to the Low Countries. On the other hand, Temple resumed his discussions with William about possible peace terms. Charles also agreed to revive the negotiations with the States General about a defensive alliance, but was slow to send specific proposals.[116] It is impossible to tell whether Charles took these negotiations seriously. He may have undertaken them only under pressure from Danby and Temple or with a view to preventing a new Franco-Dutch treaty. To seek to bring about peace was one thing: to throw in his lot with the Dutch was another and he remained determined that William should not come to England until after peace had been concluded. Overall, king and treasurer clearly did not see eye to eye on foreign policy. It is significant that when Danby was away at Bath, and Temple at the Hague, the king's attitude changed. He no longer complained of Louis's failure to make peace and responded warmly to Ruvigny's suggestion of French financial aid if he were forced to delay meeting Parliament. Louis was ready to offer around £112,500 a year if he agreed to dissolve Parliament. This was hardly a princely sum, but Charles agreed to accept even less, £100,000.[117] The treasurer had known nothing of this negotiation, nor of assurances from a group of Dissenters that Parliament would grant money (they did not say how) if Charles granted liberty of conscience. James welcomed the proposal and so apparently did Charles – talk of a million pounds was certainly enticing – but the king dropped the idea when Danby found out about it and assured him that it would be politically suicidal.[118]

When Parliament met on 13 October Charles urged the Houses to secure 'the Protestant religion, as it is now established in the Church of England', and asked for supply, to enable him to take off the anticipations on his revenue and to build more ships. He had, he confessed, been less frugal than he should have been, but it was three years since he had asked for money for his own use. The Commons would give nothing for the anticipations, but after heated debates resolved to give a sum, not exceeding £300,000, for building ships. There was much talk of extravagance, of pensions and the army. Some claimed that any figures put before them would be designed to mislead; Powle claimed that if they voted money Charles would have no need for Parliament for seven years.[119] Opponents of the court revived the proposal to appropriate the customs to the navy and claimed that all the crown's financial problems stemmed from mismanagement. It was suggested that the money for ships should be lodged in the chamber of the City of London – 'we cannot trust the Exchequer'; the proposal was rejected, but it was agreed that the money should be kept separate and accounted for to the Commons. It was also resolved to join the bill to appropriate the customs to the navy to that raising money for the ships, so that the Lords would have either to accept or to reject both.[120] The Commons aimed a further blow at the king's revenue by threatening to bring in a bill to prohibit imports from France, unless the French reduced tariffs on English manufactures to the level of 1660. Finally, on 8 November they resolved to lay no further charges on the subject that session.[121]

The Commons, then, were prepared to grant money only for ships, and then not much; the court's opponents also tried, with some success, to weaken the king's financial position in other ways. They were able to do so because of the distrust endemic among backbenchers, men who sought power neither as individuals nor for the Commons as a whole, but who suspected that too much from previous grants had been frittered away on pensions, mistresses and royal bastards. They expressed respect for the king's person – a proposal that the House should condemn 'the promiscuous use of women' was ignored – but not for his ministers.[122] There were complaints that some MPs had received letters to come up promptly for the session and others had not. Fear of France had if anything increased: addresses having failed, it was agreed to bring in a bill imposing draconian penalties on soldiers in the French service who failed to return within a given time. Finally, there was anger at a move in the Lords to address the king to dissolve Parliament, which failed by only two votes. Many felt that as their lordships did not need to seek re-election, they had no business to seek to end the present Parliament; it was noted, too, that the address was promoted by a motley group, including York, Buckingham, Shaftesbury and Clarendon formerly Cornbury. As the Speaker had remarked earlier, 'There is a strict conjunction between the fanatic and Papist to dissolve this Parliament.'[123]

Amid the recriminations, Danby could cling to the hope of the bill for money for ships, although the annexing of the bill to appropriate the customs reduced its value to the king. The court's opponents had one more card to play – reviving *Shirley* v. *Fagg*. Charles pressed Shirley not to continue with the case, but he insisted that he had promised certain (unnamed) persons of honour that he would do so. The Lords were reluctant to come to any resolution, but on 17 November the Commons resolved that an appeal against a commoner from a court of equity to the House of Lords was against the liberties of the commons of England. Next day came the motion in the Lords to press for a dissolution. The supply bill had only just received its first reading and it seemed most unlikely that it would ever be completed. On the 22nd Charles prorogued Parliament until 15 February 1677.[124]

The general reaction to the prorogation was one of alarm. Many saw it as tantamount to a dissolution and wondered if Parliament would ever meet again. MPs hurriedly left town and there were reports of preparations for a general election.[125] In fact, Danby had argued against a dissolution on the grounds that it would encourage disorder: he and the king had been worried by the Commons' eagerness to seek public support against the Lords in Shirley's case.[126] The government's nervousness was increased by a run on the bankers, following rumours that Tangier was to be sold to France and that the exchequer was to be shut up again. At the end of December Charles issued a proclamation against coffee-houses and false news.[127] Such measures, however, could do nothing to improve either the government's financial position or its political credibility. The prorogation was predictably followed by a bout of retrenchment which, equally predictably, proved insufficient to put the king back on the road to solvency. The most obvious area for economies was the court, but those affected were also those best placed to complain and to play on Charles's generosity. Danby's habit of delaying payments proved counter-productive when applied to interest payments to goldsmith bankers. Several failed, forcing him to resume payments: York, whose own finances were prudently managed, was especially insistent that this should be done. Overall, a buoyant revenue, plus some transfers from Ireland, ensured that the king's debts grew no worse, but they remained substantial and the additional excise voted in 1671 was due to expire at Michaelmas 1677. It was therefore necessary to prepare, politically, to meet Parliament again.[128]

Danby's failure to secure revenue from Parliament encouraged Arlington to make yet another bid for power, again using his supposed influence with William. He persuaded Charles to send Sylvius to William, deliberately bypassing Temple; Ruvigny, too, did not know the purpose of Sylvius' mission. The ploy failed: William, as usual, kept Temple fully informed of his negotiations.[129] The spotlight returned to the struggle between Danby and York. The former argued that the House of Commons was the most loyal and co-operative that Charles was ever likely to obtain and that it could still be persuaded to give money, if only the king would make the necessary preparations. It was necessary to improve the cohesion of the court party, winning support by means of places and other rewards and ensuring that MPs turned up and voted the right way. But MPs also had to be given the policies they wanted, especially on religion and foreign affairs. York argued that there was no point in persisting with the present House of Commons and that a new one would prove more amenable. It would contain more Dissenters, who would gladly vote money in return for indulgence, which would also reduce the level of disaffection and stimulate the economy. Such a House might also, he hoped, be less hostile to Catholics and to himself. His arguments were supported by Ruvigny, and then by Courtin, who maintained discreet and clandestine conduct with dissatisfied members of both Houses. Unlike York, they expected that a new House of Commons would prove even more critical of the king's government and even less willing to vote money, so that Charles would be unable to make war against France. On the other hand, the French thought (like Danby) that the present Parliament might give money, so their first priority was to try to prevent it from meeting at all; failing that, they would inconspicuously encourage opposition to the court. Thus, on the rare occasions when James expressed confidence in the present Parliament, Courtin alleged that it was bent on ruining both the duke and the monarchy.[130]

As far as religion was concerned, Charles continued to make occasional gestures against Catholicism. Rumour of Popish risings in the summer of 1676 led to renewed orders to enforce the recusancy laws; these led to bitter rows between Danby and York, who now refused not only to take communion but even to attend Anglican services. Danby urged Charles to send him away from court, as he was a political liability; all he could achieve was that the duke was no longer summoned to privy council meetings.[131] The discovery that the Portuguese ambassador had ordered the printing of 900 copies of a book of devotion (after Charles had authorized 100 for the queen's household) led to an order that his embassy chapel be closed to the public. James protested, suspecting that the pugnacious Bishop of London, Henry Compton, was responsible for the order. Danby supported Compton, adding that James's conduct had alarmed the people; Compton pressed the king to order his brother to dismiss his meddlesome secretary, Edward Coleman, who was later to land him in more serious trouble. For the moment Coleman survived, as there was no hard evidence against him, but later in the year revelations that he had sent out 'seditious' newsletters forced James to dismiss him.[132] The council, meanwhile, ordered that none of the king's subjects should attend any ambassador's chapel. The London common council still called on the government to take a firm stand against Popery; on 17 November (Elizabeth's accession day) an effigy of the pope was burned and the pulpits rang with anti-Popish sermons.[133]

As far as Dissent was concerned, Charles continued to order the enforcement of the laws against conventicles, but his ministers warned local officials not to overstep the bounds of legality or to use a degree of severity that might provoke disorder.[134] This pussyfooting approach was not always welcomed in the localities, where hostility between Churchman and Dissenter was growing.[135] On the other hand, Charles reprimanded JPs who were negligent and denied rumours that he did not really want the laws to be enforced. In Norfolk, one of the most divided counties, Lord Townshend, who was tolerant towards Dissenters, was replaced as lord lieutenant by the rabidly Anglican Lord Yarmouth.[136] In London, the authorities claimed that to enforce the laws would disrupt trade; the problems faced by the bankers, many of them Presbyterians, added credence to this argument. Nevertheless, the lord mayor and aldermen eventually began to close the halls where Dissenters usually met.[137] The king's anxiety about London was increased by the Jenks affair, behind which he detected the hand of Buckingham, who now lived in the City and claimed to be a reformed character: he lived frugally and attended church regularly with his wife; rumour had it that he planned to stand for alderman. Shaftesbury, too, was busy: when Charles told him to leave London, the earl replied that his business interests would not allow it. In December, shortly before the annual common council elections, the king ordered the lord mayor and aldermen to ensure that all those chosen were legally qualified, under the Corporation Act. The court was particularly concerned to prevent the election of a group of businessmen earlier alleged to have encouraged the opposition in the Commons.[138]

The king's new-found determination to support the Church was especially welcome to Danby. By June he had won his battle to persuade the king to keep his present Parliament: Charles told Courtin that the Presbyterians were republicans and that Danby had won over 150 MPs since the last session.[139] Charles was persuaded to seek the advice of the bishops, who called for tougher action against Catholics; one report claimed that, among the Dissenters, they advised concentrating on Quakers and Baptists, as the most dangerous politically.[140] The persecution of Dissenters remained sporadic: when raids were ordered in London, the conventiclers were usually tipped off. Early in 1677, with Parliament about to reconvene, Danby tried once more to divide the nonconformists, by proposing to the Presbyterians that they should be allowed meeting houses outside the walls of corporate towns; the offer was rejected. Courtin wrote that the bishops, too, were making overtures to the Presbyterians.[141]

It might seem odd that Danby and the bishops should again be seeking a measure of comprehension, given Danby's proposal to give Anglicans a monopoly of office and the bishops' calls to enforce the Conventicle Act. Baxter saw the bishops' conduct as a cunning ploy to lull the Presbyterians with false hopes, prior to resuming persecution; York saw it as part of a plot to divide non-Anglicans, leaving the Catholics (and radical Dissenters) isolated and vulnerable. Such allegations were probably over-cynical. Some bishops had long tried to bring moderate Presbyterians into the Church. Morley, a Calvinist in theology, had been sent by Hyde to negotiate with them early in 1660 and he was involved in further discussions about comprehension in 1674 and 1675. By then his credibility with the likes of Baxter had worn thin, but the prickly Presbyterian was more inclined to trust some younger divines, such as Stillingfleet and Tenison. Compton, too, was far milder towards Dissenters than towards Catholics.[142] Moreover, to advocate the suppression of conventicles, especially those of the Baptists and Quakers, whose separatism was irrevocable, was not incompatible with encouraging erring brethren to return to the Church. On the other hand, even if some of the bishops supported comprehension in principle, it does not follow that they were prepared to make major concessions in order to achieve it. Morley denounced even the modest comprehension adumbrated in the bill of 1673, declaring that it would have established schism by law: neither conformity to the canons and articles nor the use of ceremonies was negotiable. In other words, he hoped that steady pressure could bring many Dissenters to conformity while the Church remained almost unchanged: small wonder that Baxter thought him insincere.[143]

Before we dismiss as hypocritical Anglican attempts to broaden the Church, several points need to be considered. First, Charles's reign saw the growth within the Church of attitudes which can be described as 'Latitudinarian', even if those who thought in that way did not make up a recognizable 'party'. Men like Stillingfleet and Tenison placed more emphasis on what united Christians (and especially Protestants) than on what divided them and concentrated on broad moral precepts rather than narrow dogmas.[144] Second, whereas Churchmen were soon to see Dissenters as bent on the destruction of the Church, in 1674–7 the nonconformists' main aspiration was to be left alone, which leads us to a third, and crucial, point: in these years, the most immediate threat to the Church seemed to come from Popery. Anglican magistrates showed less zeal to persecute Dissenters than they had in the early 1660s and concentrated on the conviction of Papists.[145] The eirenic Tillotson responded to the Indulgence with an aggressively anti-Catholic sermon at court; his example was followed by many others, with Sheldon's full support.[146] Although many Churchmen felt limited solidarity with non-episcopal Churches on the continent, this was not universally true, especially as fear of a Popish king sharpened a sense of the threat from international Catholicism. In the spring session in 1677, there were moves to curb the power of a future Catholic king over the Church of England. Courtin wrote that Danby offered 'Presbyterians' a limited freedom of worship, but it is possible that he did not grasp the differences between the various denominations: the papers of the lord keeper's son, Daniel Finch – a Churchman who consistently advocated both comprehension and indulgence – contain the outlines of a similar scheme which was to extend to all Protestant Dissenters. (There is, however, no record that a bill to this effect was ever introduced.)[147]

The ambivalence of the attitudes of Charles, Danby and even the bishops towards Dissent was exacerbated by uncertainty about its strength. James, Buckingham and many others had claimed that Dissenters and Catholics together outnumbered conformists: in January 1676 Sheldon decided to put this claim to the test. He ordered his bishops to organize a census: each clergyman was to return the number of conformists, Catholics and 'obstinate' Dissenters in his parish. His avowed aim was to show how statistically insignificant nonconformity really was; incumbents were encouraged to put the figure as low as possible by leaving out the many Presbyterians who occasionally attended Church of England services. Modern scholarship suggests that the resulting figures were, nonetheless, substantially accurate. Danby probably encouraged the census and its findings must have been very acceptable to him. It suggested that, in the province of Canterbury, Dissenters made up less than 5 per cent of the population and (as he told Courtin in July) there were only 12,000 adult Catholics.[148]

The Compton Census (as it came to be known) did not immediately remove Charles's fears of the political threat posed by Dissenters, not least because of their disproportionate strength in towns, especially in London. In many towns, law enforcement was the responsibility of members of an elected corporation, which exercised quasi-independent authority by virtue of a royal charter. By 1676 it was clear that many Dissenters had re-entered municipal office, despite the Test and Corporation Acts; this probably explains the proposal that Presbyterians should open chapels outside corporate towns.[149] Even so, the census discredited the claim that non-conformists outnumbered conformists, one of the major arguments for comprehension and indulgence: Charles showed little interest in either after 1676. It also seems likely that its findings encouraged him to keep the existing House of Commons.

If Danby got the better of the arguments over religious policy, he enjoyed less success in foreign affairs, where so much lay outside his control. His great hope was that Charles would be able to mediate a general peace and to this end he encouraged him to negotiate a defensive alliance with the States General, to take effect either at once or after peace had been concluded. He was heartened by William's ongoing dissatisfaction with the Spaniards' limp contribution to the war effort, but found the prince far from easy to deal with. On one hand, he claimed that his honour would not allow him to settle without Spain; on the other, convinced that Louis would grant whatever Charles asked, he blamed Charles for his failure to secure peace. William also complained that Charles still allowed recruits to be raised in his kingdoms for the French service and deeply resented Charles's patronizing attitude towards him. On a more positive note, Charles now accepted that the Dutch needed a 'convenient' frontier and William was still tempted by the prospect of marriage to Mary. He asked Temple about her and wondered if such a marriage would irreparably damage his standing in both England and the republic. Temple reassured him, as far as England was concerned, but Charles would not allow the prince to come to England and expressed the hope that a chastening defeat would teach the young man not to scorn his elders.[150]

As the 1676 campaign neared its end, serious negotiations resumed. The Dutch ambassador, van Beuningen, revived the idea of a defensive treaty. Charles told Courtin that he would not sign it without Louis' approval, but added that Louis still had not declared the terms upon which he would make peace and that he would soon need something with which to justify himself to Parliament; the mounting tension over the French privateers added to his anxiety. Courtin thought that Charles was a little confused about the French queen's claims in the Low Countries, but the ambassador was sure that, if Louis did not soon put forward terms that Charles thought reasonable, he might lose the will to resist his people. Charles complained of William's coldness and his reluctance to take his uncles into his confidence about the terms upon which he might settle, but on one thing Charles was now adamant: the Dutch must have their barrier.[151] The king's anxiety was increased by Fagel's talk of the Dutch making a separate peace with Louis: if, said Fagel, the loss of Flanders was inevitable, why not make peace now on the best terms they could get and hope that in future Louis' ambitions might be directed elsewhere – towards Germany, or Italy, or England? Charles was not blind to the danger of diplomatic isolation and was nettled that William still believed that he could bring Louis to 'reason'. He was also angered by the intrigues among MPs of the Dutch and Spanish ambassadors, which would make it more difficult for him to do anything decisive. Only James seemed keen on a Franco-Dutch treaty, which he thought would leave Louis free to help Charles to re-establish his authority.[152]

While Charles dithered, Danby pinned his hopes on the defensive league with the Dutch. He hoped to include a promise of mutual assistance against domestic rebellion, which had formed part of the project which Arlington had brought over two years before. He hoped too that the league would encourage the Dutch to agree reasonable terms for a general peace, but progress in that direction was still blocked by Louis' refusal to make proposals. William, meanwhile, brusquely rejected Charles's suggestion of an exchange of towns: he would rather die, he declared, than let Louis have Cambrai, the most advanced Spanish town which Louis had not yet attacked. He would rather lose Flanders by a battle than by a dishonourable peace and he suggested that Charles's proposals originated with Courtin.[153] As Parliament approached, it seemed that all the efforts of Danby and Temple to bring Charles and William together had failed.

If Charles found his nephew stubborn, Louis proved equally difficult. He claimed that he was not obliged to pay the £100,000 he had promised because Charles had prorogued, not dissolved, Parliament and because he had not done so to protect the interests of France. When Ruvigny warned that such a breach of faith would destroy Charles's goodwill towards him, he told the ambassador to hand over as little of the money, and as belatedly, as possible. When Ruvigny paid the money, Charles responded with a proposal for a new agreement: as a first step towards a closer liaison, Charles and Louis should promise not to conclude any treaty without the consent of the other, nor would either give any aid to rebels against the other. Charles rejected Danby's proposal that he should open negotiations with the States General and insisted that the only way to achieve peace was through co-operation with Louis. On the other hand, Charles made it clear that he could see no prospect of peace unless Louis gave up those towns which threatened Ghent and Brussels. Ruvigny urged his master to accept this offer: if Louis rejected an English alliance, the Dutch would not. He added, to Pomponne, that Louis would also have to make the English nation see the value of this alliance, a clear hint that meaningful concessions would be required.[154]

Louis was happy to embrace Charles's proposal, which cost him nothing. From Charles's point of view, it would, if Louis kept his word, guarantee him against a separate Franco-Dutch peace – but it also inhibited him from concluding a Dutch alliance of his own, which explains why Danby agreed to Charles's proposal only with great reluctance.[155] Persuading Louis to make meaningful peace proposals was quite another matter. As the disputes about Fürstenberg and Lorraine dragged on, Charles continued to allow Louis to replenish his British regiments, even in the weeks before Parliament was due to meet. Louis expressed his gratitude, but did nothing to ease Charles's plight.[156] The campaign brought him a crop of captured towns and he was in no mood to talk of handing them back. His inflexibility might make diplomatic and military sense, but, given strident English resentment of the French privateers, it was not politically wise, as Courtin repeatedly told Pomponne. Charles judged it prudent not to allow the new ambassador to make a formal entry, as he feared it could lead to anti-French demonstrations. Louis, however, insisted that it was up to Spain to make the first move. Charles, and Courtin, were bewildered by his attitude: all that was needed, Charles pleaded, was for Louis to make it clear that he was ready to leave a barrier between France and the republic; Courtin feared that one more striking French success would leave Charles unable to resist the wishes of his people. One possible explanation for Louis' conduct was his conviction (apparently instilled by Ruvigny) that there was no possibility that Parliament would give money, in which case Louis had nothing to fear from it.[157]

As 1676 neared its end, calls for war against France became more and more insistent. There were complaints about the privateers, about the 'unfavourable balance', about French discrimination against English manufactures. Coffee-house gossip suggested that France was now more powerful at sea than England. As members of the Houses gathered, Courtin heard that Holles and Shaftesbury would argue that, having been prorogued for more than a year, Parliament was *ipso facto* dissolved. Charles looked worried. James told Courtin that the Commons were basically loyal, but his sincerity must be doubted: he had tried to secure another prorogation only a month before. His position was difficult: he was uncertain which posed the greater threat to his interests – the current House of Commons or a new one, containing more Dissenters. He assured Courtin that Charles had promised never to abandon him and added that he was ready to give guarantees to secure the Protestant religion; he did not specify what these might be, but told the ambassador confidentially that he could not be bound by them if he became king.[158] Despite his outward confidence, James tried not to let Charles out of his sight and renewed his contacts with Dissenters and opposition peers, even Buckingham. He was especially alarmed at news that Danby had renewed his support for comprehension.[159] Charles was fearful and bewildered. No sooner did Louis agree terms for the maritime treaty than news came of Fagel's talk of a Franco-Dutch peace: he begged Courtin to remind Louis of his promise not to make peace without consulting him. With both William and Louis refusing to make any move towards peace, Charles feared a catastrophe when Parliament met.[160]

Then, at the eleventh hour, it seemed that relief was at hand. Louis declared that he agreed that the Dutch should have their barrier, provided he too received the towns he would need to form a defensible frontier. He was ready to cede towns in Flanders, provided he received compensation in Catalonia, Italy or the Indies, and to agree to a lengthy suspension of hostilities against Spain. Not all of this was good news: Charles was worried by the prospect of the French gaining Sicily or a stronger foothold in Latin America. On the other hand, he was relieved that Louis promised to inform him of any overtures he received from the States General and in general he and James responded to Louis' proposals with what Courtin regarded as naive optimism.[161] On other matters, Louis still showed only limited understanding of Charles's position. In December he had authorized Courtin to offer a mere £90,000 to delay the session; Courtin argued that that was impossible: it would be wiser to hold out the offer to persuade Charles to dissolve if Parliament voted no money. As Louis did not authorize this, Courtin fell back on the alternative strategy of encouraging the opposition, although he insisted, sanctimoniously, that he was doing nothing of which Charles could complain.[162] Meanwhile, Danby prepared for the session. He and Lauderdale held long meetings with the bishops, amid talk of new measures against Papists. The affair of the bankers' debt was settled and Charles was reported to have agreed in principle that any money voted by the Commons should be appropriated for ships.[163] Ambassadors scurried hither and thither, coffee-houses and taverns hummed with gossip and intrigue. All England, indeed all Europe waited to see what Parliament would do.

'An Army Without a War'

In the eighteen months following the start of the new Parliamentary session, in February 1677, English politics were heavily influenced by events on the continent. As Louis XIV's armies rumbled inexorably through the Low Countries, and the confederates seemed unable to stop them, alarm mounted in England: after Louis had taken the Spanish Netherlands, where next: the Dutch Republic? England? Pressure mounted for Charles to join the war on the confederates' side, but for many such a remedy was potentially more dangerous than the disease. To make war effectively Charles would need an army: but could he be trusted not to use that army in a bid to establish 'arbitrary government' at home? Even if Charles himself could be trusted, what of those around him? Danby was known to be a hard and cynical political operator: faced with the wrath of Parliament, might he not be tempted to resort to force? Lauderdale had allegedly talked of bringing Scottish troops to England in 1673 and was soon to turn loose a 'host' of wild Highlanders on the recalcitrant Presbyterians of south-west Scotland. And then there was York: a military man, who made enemies easily, who harboured grudges and who professed a religion which many saw as inseparable from absolutism. His right to succeed his brother had already been challenged and in 1677 there were proposals in Parliament to restrict the powers of a future Catholic king: what more natural than for him to use force to safeguard his inheritance?

Fears that the court might use a foreign war as a pretext to raise an army were, in fact, exaggerated, although the idea was occasionally canvassed in these difficult months. The conflicting fears, of French military power abroad and English military power at home, were summed up by the wit who declared that some wanted a war without an army, others an army without a war.[1] They created for Charles a dilemma which often seemed insoluble: the only way out was to secure peace on the continent. Had Louis really been bent on universal dominion, that would have been impossible, but by the summer of 1677 he was prepared to consider reasonable terms. The war had not gone as planned. The attack on the republic had failed; his attempts to deter German states from intervening had proved counter-productive, driving the princes into closer co-operation with the emperor against their common enemy. As a result, the danger of Habsburg encirclement remained: as Spanish power waned, at least in the north, Austrian power grew, so that the main threat to France now came not from the north, but from the east. In 1674 and 1675 German armies crossed the Rhine, into Alsace; in 1676 imperial forces seized one of the key Rhine crossings, Philippsburg. Moreover, as hostilities spread to the Mediterranean and the Caribbean, even France's great resources became stretched: there were serious tax revolts in Brittany in 1675.

In these circumstances, Louis was ready in principle to discuss terms upon which peace might be made in the Spanish Netherlands, the region which most concerned the Dutch and English. His attitude towards it had always been ambivalent: he had been torn between the prospect of easy conquests (and glory) and the more patient strategy of acquiring a large share of the Spanish succession through negotiation, either by a partition treaty with the emperor or by agreeing exchanges with the Madrid government, which was tired of defending its outlying possessions. He had been shaken by the extent of the opposition he had provoked and by the revival of imperial power: by the middle of 1677 he was prepared to settle for a strengthened northern frontier, provided that his honour and reputation were secured, and then to wait for Carlos II to die.

Before 1659 France's northern frontier ran south from Gravelines (by Dunkirk), then swung east, passing south of Arras and Cambrai. It followed few natural boundaries and was far from straight – few European frontiers were – but there were no jutting salients from which either the French or the Brussels government could launch attacks into the other's heartlands. Under the Treaties of the Pyrenees and Aix-la-Chapelle, France gained a strip of land along the Channel coast, a number of largely unlinked towns and territories in the east, towards Luxemburg, and, above all, a great swathe of territory in the centre, including most of Artois and a substantial part of Flanders. This ranged from Arras in the south, past the great city of Lille and its hinterland, to Ath and Courtrai: now French armies could mass within striking distance of Ghent, Bruges and even Brussels. Many at the French court saw the Treaty of Aix as merely an interim agreement and argued that Louis should press on and overrun the remainder of the Spanish Netherlands. Yet these new acquisitions also left dangerous gaps, great corridors through which hostile forces could sweep into France. The first, which included St Omer and Aire, opened the way into Picardy; the second, along the valley of the Escaut (or Scheldt), controlled by the towns of Condé, Valenciennes and Cambrai, opened the way to Paris itself.[2]

While these corridors remained open, Louis was unwilling to discuss detailed terms for a peace in the Low Countries. Then, in a few weeks in the spring of 1677, his armies took St Omer, Valenciennes and Cambrai. Charles was quick to respond to the changed circumstances: in June he sent Louis proposals to establish a more rational frontier than that left by the Treaty of Aix. Louis was to surrender his more advanced, and exposed, possessions: Maastricht was to be returned to the Dutch; Spain was to recover Charleroi, Ath, Oudenarde and Courtrai. No mention was made of St Omer, Aire, Cambrai and Valenciennes, which implied that Louis was to retain them. Disagreement soon focused on a handful of more advanced towns, which Louis claimed he needed to protect those behind them: Tournai and Ypres to cover Lille, Condé to cover Valenciennes; he argued that he needed Charlemont to guard against raids into Champagne. He also staked a claim to Luxemburg, which he later dropped, while Charles later added Valenciennes to the towns which France was to cede.[3]

Charles's proposals were not concerned exclusively with France: he also suggested that Spain should cede Franche Comté to France and that the emperor should return Philippsburg. Later negotiations brought in other territories, notably Sicily. Even so, negotiations were dominated by two concerns: Louis wanted a viable northern frontier, the Dutch wanted a viable barrier. Charles's proposals were designed to satisfy both parties and the areas of disagreement seemed marginal: surely, Charles thought, a town here or there should not stand in the way of a peace which all parties professed to want. If peace took a long time to conclude, this was due, not to any lack of realism or goodwill on Charles's part, but rather to a complex tangle of mistrusts, miscalculations and vanities. Louis always sought to extract the maximum gain from every situation. He enjoyed overwhelming military superiority in the Low Countries: as he took one town after another – even Ghent – he increased the pressure on the confederates. Exulting in his power, he paid little heed to Charles's warnings that if peace was not made the English would rise in revolt: Louis calculated that, if that happened, it would be unfortunate (for Charles), but an England convulsed by civil war could pose no threat to France. He was confident that Parliament distrusted Charles too much to vote money for a war; to make doubly sure, his ambassadors intimated to opposition MPs that Charles talked of war only to provide a pretext to raise an army.

The Spaniards, by contrast, pinned their hopes on Parliament's forcing Charles to make war: for a long time, their envoys in London ignored the king and his ministers and concentrated on the Commons. Some thought that they were so confident that England would join the war that they made little effort to defend themselves; it is possible, however, that they were doing their best, but were hamstrung by disorganization and vast logistical problems. Whatever the reasons for their lamentable military performance, they stubbornly refused to make concessions, convinced that their neighbours could not allow Louis to overrun the whole of Flanders. William's position was even more complex. He more than anyone believed that Louis aimed at universal dominion, so that any peace would be no more than a truce, but he could not halt the French juggernaut. The Spaniards' muddle and broken promises drove him mad, the imperialists were more interested in the Rhineland. Within the republic, the regents complained that war was ruining their trade and muttered about the monarchical ambitions of the House of Orange: increasingly, William came round to the idea of peace because he feared that the States General might make peace without him.

With his enemies so weak and divided, Louis calculated that time was on his side: if he kept up the military pressure, sooner or later they would have to settle on his terms. On one point, however, his calculations proved defective: Charles, against all expectations, began to prepare for war. His preparations were, however, hampered by distrust: many in Parliament suspected that he was seizing the chance to create an army, while Charles feared that the Commons would engage him in a war and then deny him the money he would need to fight it, in order to have him at their mercy. Nevertheless, Charles raised an army and sent much of it to Flanders, but he shrank from formally declaring war against France, thus increasing talk of 'an army without a war'. For all their inadequacies, the war preparations served their purpose. Truculently, Louis agreed to make peace with the Dutch, but by means of a devious diplomatic manoeuvre ensured that Charles, having lost the raison d'être for his army, would lack the wherewithal to disband it. Charles might feel that he had done all that might reasonably be expected on Louis' behalf – and, indeed, a great deal more. Louis, ever the egoist, believed that Charles had let him down and was determined to make him suffer for it. The domestic political legacy of Charles's military and diplomatic efforts of 1677–8 was thus unlikely to be a happy one. Now, at last, he would have to face the consequences of the failure of the Grand Design.

On 15 February 1677, Parliament reconvened. At once, a group of peers – Shaftesbury, Buckingham, Wharton and Salisbury – claimed that it should not have met at all. Citing a statute of Edward III's reign, which stated that Parliament should meet annually, they argued that a prorogation of fifteen months was illegal and that the Parliament was therefore dissolved. Their lordships were unconvinced and sent the four to the Tower: it was one thing to ask the king to dissolve Parliament, quite another to take the matter out of his hands. The four lords put a brave face on it: Buckingham was accompanied by a bevy of footmen in new liveries; Shaftesbury asked that he should be allowed his own cook, which Charles took as a personal affront. The ploy had, however, failed. Holles, whose Parliamentary experience dated back to 1624, had decided, on reflection, not to press the point; Wharton tried to go back on what he had said. In the Commons, some moved to address the king to dissolve, but others argued that it was illogical for those who claimed Parliament was dissolved to propose any action at all. The House was clearly hostile and the matter was allowed to drop.[4]

The initial false move by the opposition lords strengthened the court's position. The Catholic peers, alarmed by the challenge to the king's prerogative, broke with their former allies; York claimed that the move had been designed to overturn all government; backbench MPs recoiled at this factious manoeuvre. It was later claimed that a mob had been brought from Southwark and Wapping to terrorize the Lords into supporting the four peers' proposal, but contemporary accounts suggest that many applauded the decision to send them to the Tower: Buckingham's hopes of popular adulation proved unfounded. Ormond remarked that the four had done Charles more service than any of his acknowledged supporters could have done.[5] Six days after the start of the session, the Commons, vigorously encouraged by the Speaker, voted to grant £600,000 for ships. On 2 March they resolved that this should be raised by a land tax – always the most reliable method – and ten days later they agreed in principle to extend the additional excise for three more years. A proposal to add to the land tax bill a clause appropriating the customs to the navy was defeated by over fifty votes, although it was decided that the money for ships was to be kept separate and accounts were to be sent to the Commons.[6]

Thus far the session had gone well, helped by the court's tact in pressing for the renewal of the additional excise for three years only, so that it would clearly not become permanent; the secretaries had also assured the Commons that Charles would ask for no further supply that session.[7] Securing a vote to grant money was, however, only the beginning. As bills went through their various stages, vigilance was needed to thwart wrecking amendments, like that appropriating the customs to the navy. MPs had to be soothed and wooed. There had been rumours of plans for a bill to exclude York from the succession; Danby had therefore prepared bills to reduce anxieties about a possible Popish successor and Charles insisted that his brother should not oppose them.[8] Two were introduced into the Lords. The first provided for the education of children of the royal family in the Protestant religion, under the supervision of three bishops; any future king who refused the test was to choose bishops only from shortlists drawn up by the existing episcopate. The second set out elaborate procedures for the better conviction of Papists. Those who registered as such, and took the oath of allegiance, were to be free of all penalties apart from the statutory fine of a shilling a week for absence from church. They were not to hold offices, bear arms, come to court without licence or send their children to Catholic colleges abroad. The children of deceased Catholics were to be educated as Protestants. Converts or those who tried to 'pervert' anyone to Catholicism were to suffer the full penalties of the laws. The bill would have produced a modest revenue, but more importantly would clearly have identified Catholics and ensured the gradual erosion of the Catholic community, partly by encouraging apostasy, partly by concentrating the full weight of the laws on converts and on those who refused to register.[9] A future Catholic king would thus have few supporters and conversions would be discouraged.

James had promised his brother that he would not oppose these bills, but did not keep his word: he may, at the time of his promise, have been unaware of the bills' contents and he was alarmed by Halifax's proposal to add a clause against future kings marrying Catholics. Pushed once more into a comparatively oppositionist stance, he renewed his contacts with the Dissenters.[10] Nevertheless, both bills passed the Lords only to be rejected, contemptuously, by the Commons. MPs who were opposed to the Church claimed that the bishops could not be trusted to guard against the threat of Popery. The registration bill was denounced for, in effect, legalizing Catholicism. The Commons produced a much more severe bill, to strengthen the existing laws, and another to exclude Catholics from both Houses (which, in practice, meant from the Lords). Neither stood any chance of passing the Upper House, much to Danby's chagrin: it was in his interest to calm fears of Popery and in the opposition's interest to sustain them.[11]

The bills against Popery were peripheral to the main concerns of both court and opposition. The former was interested above all in supply; the latter wished to force changes of men and measures. If many of the arguments of Henry Powle, or Lord Cavendish, or William Sacheverell were alarmist and unfair, they genuinely believed that evil counsel had destroyed the understanding that ought to exist between king and people and that affairs would not go well until Charles paid less heed to his courtiers and more to his Commons. Their arguments were often supported by the independent and respected Sir William Coventry and won much backbench support. Many MPs accepted that government, or at least the navy, had to be paid for, but were deeply unhappy about some of Charles's policies, especially foreign policies. When it was proposed to prepare another bill to recall Charles's subjects from the French service, the council judged that the torrent of feeling was so strong that it would be futile to oppose it. The bill stuck in the Lords: Charles assured Courtin that Louis could continue to replenish the British regiments.[12]

Even this emotive issue paled into insignificance compared to that of Flanders: Sir William Coventry declared, 'If Flanders be swallowed up, there is nothing betwixt us and France.' He urged the House to press Charles to enter into such alliances as would guard against that danger (without prescribing what those alliances should be). He was supported by Burnet's neighbour, Sir Thomas Littleton, who remarked that Flanders was England's only worry: he was not concerned about Lorraine or Franche Comté.[13] Henry Coventry and Williamson replied that the king could do nothing without money, but the sense of the House was against them and they concentrated on keeping the wording of the address as general as possible, in order to foil those who wished to use the state of Flanders as a pretext to attack evil counsellors: there was wild talk of French pensioners, who kept a gracious king ignorant of his people's wishes.[14] Such talk might seem cynical or hysterical, but reflected a distrust based on many years' bitter experience. As William Garroway remarked, using a phrase that achieved wide currency: 'Our meaning was a real war, not a cheat, a pickpocket war.'[15]

The distrust was not all on one side. Charles could not but be alarmed by remarks such as 'these seven years scarce any addresses have ever been kept'. This implied that he was obliged to comply with the Commons in all things and some MPs, despite professions of respect, spoke as if he were a cipher, with no mind of his own, manipulated by courtiers and ministers.[16] In such circumstances, he naturally suspected that MPs used a feigned concern for Flanders as a pretext to challenge his direction of the government. He was also very conscious of the lobbying and treating of foreign envoys: he expelled two Spanish envoys, Fonseca and Salinas, and declared that they were inciting rebellion. He bitterly denounced van Beuningen and complained of William's lack of respect towards him. Willing and eager, as always, to see opposition as the product of disinformation and conspiracy, Charles blamed the Commons' attitude not on the righteous indignation of country squires but on the bribes and intrigues of foreign envoys. He therefore saw concessions to the Commons as positively dangerous and brusquely advised the confederates to make peace.[17]

While Charles was determined to be resolute, the pressure on him continued to mount. The Lords largely endorsed the Commons' address, adding a commitment to secure Sicily and arguing that the Houses should assure the king of their utmost assistance. Charles, indeed, given the importance of England's Mediterranean trade, thought that the fate of Sicily concerned England more than that of the inland towns of Flanders. Most MPs, however, thought Flanders far more important and many resented any hint of the Lords meddling with supply. If the Lords' amendments had represented a device to sow dissension between the Houses, the design failed. Sir William Coventry headed off an attempt to reaffirm the Commons' sole right to deal with supply and the Lords were persuaded to drop their proposals; they were doubtless encouraged to do so, first, by the vote to continue the additional excise and then by the first reading of the supply bill.[18] Courtin, alarmed, told York that he had been authorized to offer another £90,000 if Charles would dissolve Parliament. In the following weeks, news came of the fall of Valenciennes, Cambrai and St Omer and anti-French feeling reached fever pitch. An unfortunate German was attacked by a crowd of women who had heard him speak French; once he had convinced them that he was a German, they apologized and kissed him.[19] Danby, lured by the scent of money, urged Charles to respond positively to the address, but Charles was wary. Neither money bill had yet passed the Commons. The House had avoided an unequivocal promise to support alliances with money and without such a promise he was reluctant to commit himself; he also resented the Commons trespassing on his right to direct foreign policy. It did not help that the court's spokesmen in the Commons were outdone by their rivals – even Henry Coventry was no match for his brother – so that the court was losing the battle for the hearts and minds of backbenchers. When Charles replied tersely to the address, the Commons resolved to ask him to ally with the confederates, adding (to sweeten the pill) that they would assist him if he were forced to make war and that they did not expect an immediate answer. They did not seek the Lords' concurrence: their aim was less to put pressure on the king than to let him know the sense of the nation.[20]

A few days later, with even York telling Courtin that Louis should be satisfied with his conquests in Flanders, Danby drew up a memorandum. He did not think that Parliament would engage Charles in a war and then deny him money: even if that were to happen, if Charles had an army he would be in a strong bargaining position. Perhaps, indeed, here was an opportunity of 'getting into some condition of arms and money by the consent of the people, who would otherwise not give the one and be jealous of the other'. This, however, was only one of several arguments for preparing for war against France. The main theme of the paper was a familiar one: that Charles should break with France and so regain the goodwill of Parliament and people.[21] Meanwhile, Charles grumbled about the Spaniards and Dutch. In an effort to overcome his reticence, the Commons completed the bill for the land tax and continued to work on that for the additional excise. At last, on 11 April, Charles gave his answer: the international situation was so uncertain that he needed to be able to guard against all eventualities; he would adjourn them briefly over Easter and then expected them to consider the matter further.[22]

It was a tactless response, widely seen as a thinly disguised call for supply: Henry Coventry, indeed, declared that Charles was reluctant to make alliances because he feared that the Commons would not vote the necessary money. MPs resented this argument, and still more that the request for supply should be brought in so late in the session, as the money bill neared completion and after the secretaries had assured the House that no more would be asked. Some complained that Charles clearly did not intend to take them into his confidence; another, more soberly, remarked that the problem was one of 'want of confidence, lest the money should be for some ill intent'.[23] Reluctant to vote further supply, MPs resolved to add to the additional excise a clause to enable the king to borrow £200,000 at 7 per cent: the Commons would reimburse this when they next met and, if necessary, they would also assist the king. Charles replied that without at least £600,000 he would not be able to achieve the ends specified in their address. The Commons declared that it would be improper to vote more in such a thin House. Charles adjourned them until 22 May.[24]

In these exchanges the Commons showed more tact and restraint than the king. The wild men of the opposition had failed to carry the Commons with them; there had been no wrecking amendments to money bills or major inter-House disputes (thanks, perhaps, to the enforced absence of Shaftesbury and Buckingham). This restraint was all the more creditable because – as noted by Daniel Finch and Southwell – the Commons' mood had changed for the worse since the start of the session. Apart from their anxieties about France and Popery, MPs resented what they saw as sharp practice and the absence of the reciprocity which should have existed between king and Parliament: Charles seemed interested only in getting money.[25] Charles told Courtin that he was on bad terms with his subjects because of his attachment to Louis; Courtin again warned Pomponne that unless their master curbed his ambitions in Flanders, Charles would be forced to make war, but added, 'I dare not importune the king [Louis] with such reflections as these, which could displease him.'[26]

Despite Danby's warnings that to ask for further supply might anger the Commons, Charles decided to do so. Henry Coventry argued that without £600,000, Charles would be in no position to act on their addresses. Some MPs, however, were reluctant to vote anything until they knew how it was to be used; others saw the king's warning that this was to be only a short session as subjecting them to undue pressure.[27] Charles denied that he had summoned them only in order to secure money: he promised, on the word of a king, that they would not regret placing their trust in him: it would be their fault if insufficient provision was made for the kingdom's safety.[28] His approach nettled MPs: even Sir Robert Howard complained that a principled refusal to vote money should not be portrayed as distrust of the king, while Sacheverell declared that he would give nothing 'to be in the hands of that council which broke the Triple Alliance and greatened France'. It was resolved to draw up an address for an offensive and defensive league with the States General for the preservation of the Spanish Netherlands. Until this demand was met, the House could not vote supply, but once it had been met, their assistance would be speedy and generous.[29]

The Commons' firm stand owed much to changing circumstances. Rumours abounded that the confederates were making great offers to king and Commons if they would break with France. The City refused to lend until it knew how the money would be spent – and that despite Charles's taking the final steps to ensure that the bankers received what was due to them.[30] The confrontational, authoritarian approach of Charles and Danby had proved counter-productive: only Williamson had voted against the address. When the House began to debate its content, no one denied the need to ally with the Dutch, but some questioned the propriety of seeking to influence foreign policy. Others replied that at the time of the Dutch Wars and the Triple Alliance Charles had informed the Commons of his treaties and intentions before asking supply. Henry Coventry and others replied that such a condescension on his part implied neither that the Commons had a right to be informed, nor that they should dictate to him (especially since they had not first provided the necessary money). Sacheverell brashly claimed that Charles should take the Commons' advice before that of his council; Sir Thomas Lee, with more restraint, claimed that they sought to advise and to persuade, not to dictate. The proponents of the address, realizing that they were on shaky ground in seeking to influence the king on such a 'prerogative' matter, tried to intimidate their opponents with shouts of 'Agree! Agree!', which the redoubtable Sir Jonathan Trelawney likened to 'club law'. The earlier restraint had gone: fear and anger had overcome MPs' sense of constitutional propriety. The Commons resolved by a majority of forty to adhere to the address.[31] Forty to fifty MPs retired to the Speaker's room when the vote was taken. It was not clear what they feared more: the wrath of their colleagues or that of the king.[32]

The debate had revealed divisions among supporters of the court: the friends of Speaker Seymour had strongly supported the address. The council, too, was divided. Some argued that to enter the proposed alliances would commit the king to a war for which he was unprepared and which could end only in disaster. Others argued that war against France was inevitable, so he should begin now, while the people were eager and he could still find allies. As so often, the more timorous counsels carried the day. Charles also rejected James's advice to dissolve Parliament; he refused even to prorogue it, as that would have terminated the proceedings against the four lords in the Tower. On 28 May he told the Commons that their address impinged on his prerogative: if he allowed them to dictate to him even once, no other prince would ever pay any heed to him and he would be left with only the empty name of king. Despite the refusal to grant supply, he would do his best to safeguard the nation's interests. He then adjourned the Houses until 16 July, adding that he would probably not recall them until the winter.[33]

On previous occasions when he had dismissed Parliament Charles had put a brave face on it, saying he had shown who was the master. This time he talked sadly to Courtin of the great harm done by James's conversion and of the suspicions aroused by his own friendship towards France. There seems little reason to doubt that he believed that the Commons really did intend to leave him with only the empty name of king. The talk of France and Popery was, in his eyes, a cloak covering a politically motivated attack on his prerogatives. The anti-monarchical elements in the House had finally thrown off the mask of propriety. This distrust of his people was not new – he had talked earlier of using money voted for war preparations to build up his magazines and forces, in order to secure his position at home. Such remarks raised echoes of Danby's memorandum of 4 April, but were far less frequent than complaints of his sufferings for Louis' sake and expressions of fear that he would be forced to make war. No clear pattern emerges from his utterances: his resolutions were as variable as the weather.[34] Others viewed the Commons' motives less pessimistically. Daniel Finch wrote that the Commons had refused to grant further supply simply because they did not believe that the court really wanted war against France: 'It appears by the whole session that all things against France have gone on heavily and with as much opposition as the court did dare to show.' By delaying the request for money until too late in the session to have it granted, Charles and Danby had lost the House's goodwill.[35] How far Finch's cynicism was justified remained to be seen.

At any other time in the reign, a session which produced a grant of £600,000 and the renewal of the additional excise would have been accounted a success. The former, however, was strictly appropriated to the fleet and the latter merely ensured that Charles's income would not fall. Repayment of the bankers' debt, the Virginia rebellion and douceurs to MPs had weakened his financial position and the duties granted in 1670 were due to expire at Michaelmas 1678.[36] Charles was still ill-equipped financially to prepare for the war which was becoming politically more and more necessary. Indeed, the court's sharp practice had dissipated the goodwill apparent in the early part of the session and made the Commons both more insistent in their calls for war and more reluctant to vote money towards it. Danby argued that Charles was under no obligation to allow Louis to conquer whatever he chose and that he could expect no benefit from France once peace had been made; instead, he said, Charles should work closely with William to secure peace, in return for which he could expect both commercial advantages and Spanish recognition of England's claims on the flag. If, however, the States

General forced William to make peace, the prince might find himself forced to join with France (Charles's recurrent nightmare). In the last analysis, political conditions at home left him only one choice: 'Till he can fall into the humour of the people,' wrote Danby, 'he can never be great nor rich and while differences continue prerogative must suffer, unless he can live without Parliament ... [but] the condition of his revenue will not permit that.'[37]

Charles, however, was prepared neither to break with Louis nor to throw in his lot with his prickly nephew. He was thus trapped in a dilemma from which only peace could release him. As James had pointed out in April, having captured Valenciennes, Cambrai and St Omer, Louis had done enough to secure his frontier. Such thinking underlay the proposals which Courtin forwarded to Louis on 11 June, which were designed to secure both a defensible frontier for France and a barrier for the Dutch.[38] Courtin told Charles and James that these proposals were quite unreasonable, but intimated strongly to Louis and Pomponne that they should be taken seriously. The ambassador warned that the English were being as intractable as ever on the question of the flag, which created a risk of incidents between English and French vessels in the Narrow Seas.[39] Danby, now playing a central role in foreign affairs, was telling Charles that, if he deferred meeting Parliament until the winter, he would need at least £200,000 from France merely to survive financially. The Spaniards were making wild offers and wild threats. At one moment they suggested that England should be given possession of Ostend and Nieuwpoort until they could take Dunkirk or Calais and even that the allies should make war until England regained Normandy and Guyenne; at another they threatened to seize all English goods in Spanish ports, which created a panic among London's merchants. 'The poor Spaniards want counsel as much as power,' commented the Catholic lawyer Richard Langhorne.[40] Most ominous of all, for Courtin, William's confidant Hans Willem Bentinck came to England soon after Parliament ended. York told him that all who wished to force Charles to make war were republicans and advised William to make peace. The duke was, however, far from confident that his brother would resist Bentinck's blandishments and did not let Charles out of his sight.[41]

Louis was at least prepared to respond to Charles's proposals, but his refusal to give up Tournai and Condé, and his demand for Ypres, Charlemont and Luxemburg, suggested that negotiations would be protracted. In general, Courtin's forebodings seemed justified. Bentinck brought a message that William would follow Charles's guidance in all things. Charles, well pleased by this unwonted show of submission, agreed that William could come to England, provided Parliament was not then in session. Bentinck also however proposed, unbeknown to Courtin, a series of exchanges in

Flanders: soon after, Charles made similar proposals to Courtin, which differed only in that Charles did not stipulate that Louis should hand back Valenciennes.[42] As Charles at last began a serious dialogue with his nephew, the arguments for a rapprochement between them seemed ever more compelling. On one hand, despite Courtin's best efforts, Charles did not find Louis' peace proposals reasonable, or his proffers of money adequate. Danby insisted that the proposed sums were paltry and argued that Louis would never stand by Charles as Charles had stood by him. Besides, they would have to find something to set before Parliament. On the other, news came from Nijmegen of attempts to renew the Franco-Dutch treaty of 1662. Courtin assured Charles that any agreement would be confined to matters commercial, but feared that if the provisions about fishing were renewed it would revive Charles's deep resentment of what he had long regarded as Louis' perfidy in signing the treaty in the first place.[43]

Danby played skilfully on these anxieties and resentments. Courtin might sneer that the treasurer knew nothing of foreign affairs, and was guided by Temple, but his influence over his master was very strong. He persuaded Charles to offer Coventry's secretaryship to Temple, but Coventry refused to quit and Temple said he did not want the post anyway. Courtin was unaware that the committee of foreign affairs had, in June, drafted a defensive alliance with the Dutch, reviving van Beuningen's earlier proposal. Temple looked over the draft in July.[44] No further use was made of it, but Charles had it to hand if needed. His next move was to send Clarendon's younger son, Lawrence Hyde, to William, with proposals marginally more favourable to France than those sent to Louis in June. As far as Flanders was concerned, they reproduced Louis' proposals of February. Charles stressed to William the Spaniards' failings and that, while it might be desirable to return to the position of 1659, that was not a practical possibility. Hyde was also to make it clear that Charles had no intention of entering the war. Charles told Courtin that Hyde was to tell William to pay more heed to his uncle in future; in fact, his instructions said no such thing, but stated that Charles was resolved to 'entertain a strict alliance' with William and the States General, after the war was over. Danby, meanwhile, hinted strongly that William might secure better terms if he came over to England.[45]

If negotiating a peace was the obvious solution to Charles's problems, it was bound to be a lengthy process and in the meantime he had to postpone meeting Parliament. When the Houses met on 16 July, he adjourned them again until 3 December: attempts to start a debate were shouted down.[46] Courtin had indicated that if Charles put off Parliament until the winter Louis would give all he could and negotiations for French money now resumed in earnest. Danby insisted that nothing less than £200,000 would do, but Charles was persuaded, by James, to settle for 2,000,000 *livres*, about

£150,000. In return, Charles promised to adjourn until April, by which time it would be too late to prepare for that summer's campaign. He told Courtin that he would tell Bergeijk, the new Spanish ambassador, of his intention so that, deprived of their hopes of a Parliament, the Spaniards would become more tractable. Montagu, once more ambassador at Paris, had been pressing for the full £200,000: he remarked that Charles's willingness to accept less showed how little he valued money.[47] Danby was away from court when the decision was made; his wrath on hearing the news was compounded when he learned that Nell Gwynn had brought Buckingham, newly released from the Tower, to kiss the king's hand. Danby stormed back to court, sent the wayward duke packing and pressed Courtin, and his successor Barrillon, for more money, insisting that more had been promised.[48] When these arguments failed, he persuaded Charles to claim that he had not understood the difference between 2,000,000 *livres* and £200,000; Montagu used the same argument in Paris. Charles, understandably embarrassed, told Barrillon tetchily that he did not wish to discuss the matter and referred him to Danby; Charles, meanwhile, refused to promise not to call Parliament for another twelve months. He suggested more than once that Louis' approach to the peace negotiations was unnecessarily rigid: to ask for Luxemburg, a whole province, was too much and, although Louis might claim that he wanted Ypres only to protect Lille, others might fear that it could serve as a base from which to attack Bruges and Ghent. Charles's relations with Louis were thus less than cordial when William arrived at his court.[49]

At first, with the court at Newmarket, little attention was paid to business. Charles pressed William to abandon the Spaniards, William urged Charles to break with France: each replied that his honour would not allow him to do so. Then, abruptly, William asked for Mary's hand in marriage. Charles neither accepted nor rejected the proposal, but continued to press William about the terms upon which he would agree to a peace. William complained privately that Charles was even more pro-French than he had expected; he did not know that Charles had not, at first, told Barrillon of the proposal of marriage and that he was now arguing more forthrightly than ever that Louis should scale down his demands and, more particularly, abandon all thoughts of Luxemburg. Never a patient man, William threatened to break off negotiations and go home unless he received a straight answer about his marriage proposal. Charles cheerfully gave his consent: he declared that his skill in physiognomy, which had never let him down, told him that William would prove honest; besides, he could be a dangerous enemy. He told Barrillon that this marriage, more than anything else, would remove suspicions that his friendship with France showed that he wished to establish Popery and arbitrary government. James, too, seemed to believe that it would reduce his unpopularity: he declared to the cabinet council that he would never try to alter the established government in Church or state. He told Barrillon that his own wife was young and pregnant: it seemed probable that she would bear him sons and so William would never become king. Charles assured Barrillon that he would show his firmness to France by postponing the next meeting of Parliament until April.[50]

Charles had no objection to Mary's marrying William: he had, indeed, floated the idea three years earlier. Neverthless, he had wished peace to come first, but now he bowed to the pressure of Temple and Danby and the argument that the marriage would defuse hostility to the court. He may have comforted himself with the thought that it would make William more amenable and drive a wedge between the prince and his allies, who would suspect him of sacrificing the common cause to his personal interests. Charles told Barrillon that he was trying to cure William of the belief that Louis' ambitions in the Low Countries were insatiable and that no frontier, no matter how secure, would satisfy him. William was deeply sceptical and must have been agreeably surprised when Louis offered not only to undertake not to attack the Spaniards in Flanders in the event of a future war, but also to accept Puigcerda, in the Pyrenees, in lieu of Ypres; he was even ready to drop his claim to Luxemburg in return for an equivalent elsewhere, perhaps in Catalonia. As William apparently agreed that Louis should retain Franche Comté, the prospects for agreement seemed bright. Charles pressed Louis to cede Courtrai as well and told Barrillon that peace would make him independent of the 'malcontents' among his subjects. His good humour was improved by the wedding of William and Mary. The bride was less ecstatic: when told of her happy fate she wept for a day and a half. Buoyed up by optimism, Charles agreed with William a package of proposals which were to be carried to Louis by the Huguenot soldier, Louis Duras, Earl of Feversham.[51]

As far as Flanders was concerned, the Feversham proposals were those which Charles had put forward in June, except that Louis was also to cede Valenciennes: in other words, these were the terms proposed by Bentinck. They did not constitute an ultimatum. Feversham was to stress the diffi-culties under which Charles laboured, his lack of money and his need to renew the additional excise in 1678; he was then to beg Louis to rescue Charles from the imminent peril of civil war. Charles later claimed that he had been 'outmeasured' by William: the prince had claimed that the States General would agree to no terms which left Tournai and Valenciennes in French hands: this turned out to be untrue.[52] His claim is plausible: Charles was never the toughest or most precise of negotiators and he may well have been out-argued by his single-minded nephew. He seems also genuinely to have believed that Louis would accept his terms: he tended to be swept along by moods of optimism or pessimism and found it easy to believe what he wanted to believe.[53] When he eventually gave Barrillon details of his proposals, however, the Frenchman, horrified, declared that his master would never agree to them, and he was right. Louis refused even to consider them as a basis for negotiation. They were utterly unreasonable, he said; they bore no relation to military reality and would not give France a secure frontier. He would lose more by such a peace than by any war. Although the campaigning season was over he was keeping his armies in the field and would use them to intensify the pressure on the confederates until they saw 'reason'.[54]

Charles was flabbergasted. He does not seem to have considered what to do if Louis rejected his proposals out of hand. He ordered Feversham to press for a positive answer, while Montagu was to argue that it was surely better for Louis to give up 'a town or two' than for Charles and the English monarchy to be ruined by another 'rebellion'. Charles also resolved to meet Parliament in January rather than April, so that he could at least suggest that he intended military action.[55] All the evidence indicates that Charles recoiled from the prospect of war, but others felt differently. On the news that French forces were besieging St Ghislain, between Valenciennes and Mons, Danby declared that Louis was clearly out to complete his conquest of the Low Countries, which Charles could not allow. York complained that Louis ignored all Charles's pleas and claimed that he aimed to establish a universal monarchy. Both Danby and York doubtless calculated that an openly anti-French stance would reduce the risk of their being attacked in Parliament; York also hoped to resume his military career and told Barrillon that here was an opportunity to re-establish the power of the monarchy. Thus while Charles and Montagu begged Louis to make at least a show of negotiating, his ministers began to make serious preparations for war. Danby urged William to help conclude an alliance between Charles and the States General; he assured the prince that Charles would send troops to Flanders, provided they had a port, preferably Ostend, at which to land.[56]

This unwonted show of resolution took the French by surprise. Barrillon believed that Charles did not want war, but that he would be unable to resist his subjects' pressure; he also thought that Parliament would vote the necessary money. Louis' logic might be impeccable, he added, but the English saw things differently; like it or not, Louis would have to shift his ground.[57] Ordered to suspend payment of the money promised earlier, the ambassador feared that an outright refusal would drive Charles into the arms of the Dutch, so he took refuge in excuses. He found himself isolated at court, while Charles made merry with the envoys of the confederates. In time, Barrillon's arguments made an impact. Louvois intimated to Montagu that Charles might be paid good money if Parliament did not meet or if William dropped his demand that Louis should abandon Valenciennes, Condé and Tournai. The French court also seemed to receive favourably

Montagu's suggestion that England should receive a town or two on the continent, but when he spoke specifically of Ostend Louvois seemed alarmed. (Charles, however, declared that such towns would be of no use and would cost a great deal of money.) To Charles, Louis proposed a general truce (which Charles thought would take too long to arrange), but he would not agree to suspend hostilities for two months: the best he would offer was a ten days' suspension of arms and a promise to restore any towns taken after that time. Late in December he dropped his demands for Ypres and Luxemburg, but insisted on retaining Valenciennes, Condé and Tournai and called on Charles to postpone meeting Parliament until at least the end of February.[58]

Louis' attempts at conciliation were too insubstantial and came too late. Having committed himself to prepare for war, Charles found it impossible to retreat. Not only would he have to meet Parliament on 15 January, but it was imperative that he should then be able to announce that he had concluded a treaty with the Dutch. Privately, William had doubted Charles's fixity of purpose. To overcome his reticence, he had assured him that the States General would fall in with his designs and also force the Spaniards to come to terms, but snags soon arose. The Anglo-Dutch treaty was soon drafted, but Hyde, who carried it to the Hague, agreed to unacceptable alterations, which took time to correct. Charles was forced to delay meeting Parliament until the 28th.[59] Meanwhile, although the Spanish ambassador in London, Burgomano, had promised that Ostend would be made available to the English, the authorities in Brussels, despite William's attempts to persuade them, refused to co-operate.[60]

The delays in meeting Parliament and shipping troops to Flanders cannot but have increased suspicions that Charles had no intention of making war. Barrillon, assisted by Ruvigny's son, tried to persuade MPs that Charles merely talked of war to provide a pretext to raise an army. Burgomano continued to urge his friends in the Commons to demand that the king should begin hostilities.[61] Van Beuningen, on the other hand, was pressed by the court to assure MPs that Charles was sincere and that they should vote supply for the war effort.[62] There were other signs, too, that Parliament was indeed to meet. Magistrates were ordered to enforce the Corporation and Conventicle Acts. York reportedly resumed his dealings with the Dissenters, offering a limited toleration in return for the same being allowed to Catholics and for his being readmitted to his offices.[63]

By now, however, domestic issues were secondary. There were two crucial questions: could Charles convince the Commons that he really wanted war and could he win their financial backing for it? It would not be easy, not least because Charles could not fully convince himself. On one hand, he was well aware that Barrillon was encouraging the opposition in Parliament and was displeased that he had not paid over all the money which Louis had promised him. He deeply resented Louis' refusal to abate his demands, even though Charles had defended Louis' interests to a point where Charles claimed, and apparently believed, that he had put his throne at risk. Why, he asked, would Louis not forgo a town or two to save Charles from his father's fate?[64] On the other hand, he hesitated to put himself at the mercy of his Parliament and his people and to throw in his lot with allies as inept and devoid of sense as the Spaniards.[65] Torn between unpleasant alternatives, he vacillated. Orders were issued and then countermanded. At one moment, he would berate Barrillon, the next he would plead with him to press his master to extricate him from his predicament. His confusion was mirrored in Danby's correspondence: to William he wrote of Charles's eagerness for war, to Montagu of the need to find some expedient for peace. As troops were raised for a war which he did not really want, Charles sought advice from a new quarter. Hitherto Portsmouth had shown little interest in public affairs. Now she and Charles pored over maps, looking for alternatives to the Feversham proposals. Louis hinted that he might part with Valenciennes and Condé, but not Tournai; Portsmouth suggested that he might cede all three in return for Ypres. It was all so frustrating, that hopes of peace should be dashed by Louis' concern for just one town. Did this mean, Charles wondered, that Louis wished to resume his conquests in the Low Countries at a later date? Could he believe his assurances to the contrary? He continued to press Louis for money in return for delaying Parliament, but insisted on the need for a peace acceptable to the confederates.[66]

Those close to Charles were well aware of his trouble of mind. Danby wrote of his 'being very unwilling to come to a rupture with France and yet scarce seeing how to avoid it'. Unable to make peace, he drifted towards war, which at least (as he told Barrillon) would be a lesser evil than a general rebellion.[67] Such an attitude was not designed to inspire confidence. Temple, indeed, had refused to become involved in negotiations with the Dutch because Charles's approach was so half-hearted and confused. For him, and for many MPs, a strategy of limiting Louis' ill-gotten gains, rather than trying to make him give them up, was fundamentally unsatisfactory.[68] While Charles vacillated, even his brother, who was much more eager for war, sometimes expressed reservations about the possible outcome and his very eagerness led to suspicions of sinister ulterior motives.[69] In short, circumstances conspired to increase rather than diminish the mistrust which had built up among MPs over the years. It promised to be a stormy session.

When the Houses met, Charles told them that, as all attempts at mediation had failed, he had no choice but to prepare for war, especially since the Spaniards showed so little concern for their own preservation. He had concluded alliances with the Dutch and intended to fit out ninety ships and to deploy thirty to forty thousand soldiers, on the fleet and elsewhere. This would require further taxation, but he was willing 'that such money be appropriated to those ends as strictly as you can desire'.[70] The Commons' response was discouraging. They resolved on an address that Charles should agree to no treaty that would leave Louis in a better condition than in 1659 and that all the confederates should cease to trade with France. The former demand was based on the assertion that nothing less could eliminate the threat which France posed to England. Some argued that the terms already offered to Louis were far too favourable. As for the prohibition on trade, it was claimed that this would bring France to her knees, especially as she would no longer be able to profit from her 'unequal' trade with England. Having said all that, the Commons assured the king of their support.[71]

To Charles such war aims and such a war strategy seemed hopelessly unrealistic; what was said about money did not suggest that the Commons would provide adequately for the war. Even a vote to stage a more dignified burial for Charles I could be seen as an implied criticism of his son. Charles replied, with some irritation, that he had made a league with the Dutch, as they had requested the previous May, when they had also promised their speedy assistance. Now they prescribed additional conditions and expected him to provoke all the world, yet without providing the necessary money. He could not undertake to secure any particular terms and, anyway, decisions on peace and war were his alone.[72] Opposition MPs continued to talk of French counsels and backstairs deals. They demanded to see the treaties and expressed indignation that Charles should have invoked his prerogative: 'I am for it as it is by law,' declared Lord Cavendish, 'but not for "prerogative" to be swayed by ill counsels.' Well aware that the tide of opinion in the House ran strongly in favour of a war with France, opposition MPs sought to direct attention back to fears of 'Popery' at home: Sacheverell declared that he would give no money 'merely' to preserve Flanders.[73] Despite their rhetoric, they did not prevail. The House agreed that ninety ships would be needed and accepted the estimate for the land forces. On 18 February it was resolved in principle to raise £1,000,000 to enable Charles to enter into an actual war against the French king.[74]

At the start of the session Barrillon had wondered if the Commons' hatred of France would prove stronger than their suspicion of the court; it now seemed as if it would.[75] Nevertheless suspicions remained, of the army and of Popery. MPs made it clear that they expected the soldiers raised for the war to be sent abroad, not deployed at home.[76] Danby's abrasive manner and cynical techniques of Parliamentary management had made him many enemies, including some of the ablest orators in both Houses. He had even fallen out with the imperious Speaker Seymour.[77] For a while, the opposition got the better of the debates but lost the substantive votes: some even threatened to withdraw, claiming that bribery had destroyed the Commons' independence. In fact, many backbenchers wanted the war and accepted that it had to be paid for. If the opposition kept plugging away, however, they might nurture the suspicions in MPs' minds to a point where they would vote the other way. Why, they asked, were the new soldiers not sent to Flanders? Why was Charles so often with Barrillon? 'And thus they go on,' wrote Southwell, 'contending and disputing every particular step that is made, having a great number of able and contentious speakers, though they are outdone in votes.'[78] After long debates, it was resolved to prepare an address which, in respectful terms, asked Charles to declare war: the Commons had already completed one supply bill and would pass others as necessary. They urged the king to expel Barrillon and desist from his mediation. The Lords, after a long debate at which Charles was present, substituted for 'immediately' a phrase designed to protect the king's prerogative: 'with all the expedition that may consist with the safety of your majesty's affairs'. The Commons refused to accept the amendment and were preparing for a conference with the Lords when proceedings were interrupted by a short recess.[79]

Money, meanwhile, remained a problem. The million pounds so far voted was much less than was really needed but, given the mood of the House, the court did not dare to ask for more. Moreover, opposition MPs sought to limit its value by proposing that the money be raised by slow and unpopular methods and clogged with unpalatable conditions. Their task was made easier by the ineptitude of the court's spokesmen: Williamson had proposed that the money should not be raised by a land tax. On 27 February the Commons resolved to 'tack' to the bill for a poll tax (itself a slow and over-complicated way of raising money) a clause prohibiting imports from France for three years.[80] Soon after, the Commons added another clause imposing penalties if the money was not spent on an actual war with France. Southwell wondered if the poll bill was really worth having under such conditions. The suggestion that the ban on French commodities would damage the customs revenue was brushed aside and they were described as 'nuisances' so that Charles could not dispense with the ban. While the opposition played on MPs' hatred of France, the secretaries offered little leadership: Coventry was old and tired, Williamson was less than dynamic and neither was fully informed of the most secret negotiations that supposedly fell within their departments: if the court's spokesmen were uncertain of the king's intentions, how could they convince others? Their inadequacies were highlighted by their call for a clause to enable the king to borrow on the credit of the poll money, only to be told that one had already been included.[81] By mid-April the vote for £1,000,000 had produced only the poll tax Act (which was to bring in under £300,000 and at some cost to the customs) plus an abortive proposal to tax new buildings in London, to which the Commons tacked new measures against Popery. As James, Coventry and Williamson all remarked, even on the most optimistic estimates these would bring in much less than £1,000,000, whereas the true cost of the war was likely to run to £2,400,000 a year.[82]

Charles, as always, blamed the Commons' conduct on conspiracy – more particularly, French bribery. Barrillon worked closely with Sacheverell and Lords Russell and Cavendish (from the Commons) and with Holles. These saw no reason why they should not accept money for pursuing a political line which they would have followed anyway. They also held out to James the prospect of restoration to office in return for helping to get rid of Danby. While they could not openly oppose proposals for a French war, they argued that Charles did not intend to fight. Why, they asked, were two hundred of the newly raised troops used to reinforce the king's guards? When Ghent and Ypres fell, their immediate response was to blame evil counsellors for allowing it to happen.[83] Some were clearly ambitious men, frustrated by Danby's refusal to brook possible rivals, and their methods were often far from scrupulous, but it does not follow that they did not genuinely fear 'arbitrary government'. Fearful that the king might abuse his powers, they sought to define those powers more narrowly and slid from a claim that he was morally obliged to inform and consult the Commons to a claim that he was, in effect, bound to follow their advice. Convention dictated that he should not be held personally responsible for his government's misdeeds, which were the fault of his ministers. This fiction, however, could not always be sustained, especially when Charles declared his will in person. Opposition MPs were then reduced to claiming that his speeches were written for him by his ministers and did not represent his own views: as in 1641–2, the king was treated as if he were 'deranged', with no mind of his own. The shift from the conventional platitude that the king was free to accept or reject the Commons' advice to the assertion that he was obliged to accept it was neither clearly articulated nor explicitly argued: most, torn between deep anxiety and an instinctive veneration for monarchy, probably did not even notice that this was happening. Charles, however, did, which was why he defended his prerogative vigorously and talked of being chased from his kingdom.

If Charles derived little cheer from the Commons' conduct, his intended allies proved no more satisfactory. Despite all William's efforts, Villa-hermosa, the Spanish governor at Brussels, refused to hand over Ostend without explicit orders from Madrid. Eventually a compromise was found, the first troops were shipped over and relations began to improve. Villa-hermosa even agreed with William a set of peace terms similar to those sent with Feversham, except that Louis was to retain Valenciennes and Tournai.[84] But as the Spaniards became more amenable so the Dutch became less so. The offensive treaty with the States General had been ratified in January, but the defensive treaty proved more problematical. Charles's difficulties with Parliament and Louis' military successes intensified the desire in the republic for peace. Many doubted if Charles was willing or able to come to their aid: could they trust a king who seemed so irresolute? Fagel declared that they would gladly embrace any peace, no matter how insecure. They began to quibble about the flag and the provision whereby each undertook not to aid those who rebelled against the other. The committee for foreign affairs agreed to drop the stipulation about the flag, but insisted on the clause about rebels, as in the Treaty of Breda. New problems then arose. The towns of Holland were determined to do their utmost to prevent a prolongation of the war. Van Beuningen raised difficulties about the proposed prohibition on trade with France, after pressing for months for this to be included. Despite fears that the Dutch might draw England into war and then make peace and steal her trade, the committee, in desperation, agreed to sign on the Dutch terms, but when Charles tried to initiate negotiations with the Dutch, Spanish and imperial ambassadors about joint action, van Beuningen claimed that he had insufficient authorization to agree to anything.[85]

As the Dutch proved so slippery, Charles concentrated on trying to reach agreement with the Spanish and imperial ambassadors, with a secret proviso that the treaty would be null and void unless the Dutch also joined. They seemed to agree, but then denied that Villahermosa had ever accepted that the terms proposed by William constituted a 'reasonable peace'.[86] With the Commons so truculent and his allies so fickle, Charles shrank from declaring war, yet he felt politically unable to slacken his preparations, so pressed on as fast as his inadequate resources would allow.[87] Yet again, he looked to Louis to rescue him, but Louis was a master of the art of moving the goalposts while the game was in progress. He professed his willingness to negotiate and insinuated that the fate of only one or two towns – maybe just Tournai or Condé – needed to be decided. Yet, as the spring advanced, his position grew stronger. Charles was hamstrung by his inability to secure money from Parliament, the Dutch were desperate for peace. Louis' armies were in the field long before those of the allies. He took Ghent and Ypres with nonchalant ease and promptly stepped up his demands. He now insisted on keeping Ypres, and the Dutch (and even William) saw little alternative to adjusting their position accordingly.[88]

Like everyone else, Charles found Louis' conduct infuriating. He might admire his foresight and envy his not having to deal with a Parliament, but why (he asked) did he keep changing his demands? And why did he insist on keeping towns which he could easily retake later?[89] As he prepared for a war which he did not want, Charles shrank from an irrevocable commitment and pathetically assured Louis of his goodwill. Surely, he pleaded, summoning home a Scots regiment and sending a battalion or two to Ostend could not be construed as acts of hostility.[90] He continued to sound Barrillon about the possibility of French money if he desisted from making war and was forced to dismiss Parliament. Barrillon, experienced diplomat that he was, responded with insinuations and vague assurances which stopped short of specific commitments.[91] So, on 25 March, Danby, at Charles's command, wrote a fateful letter to Montagu, which Charles countersigned. It set out terms which, he hoped, both Louis and the allies would accept, but added that if Charles secured such a peace it would so infuriate his subjects that he would be unable to call Parliament for at least three years. Montagu was therefore to ask Louis to pay Charles 6,000,000 *livres* (about £450,000) a year during that period.[92]

Louis was in no hurry to fall in with these proposals. While he was displeased at the prospect that Charles might, after all, declare war, nothing in the English king's conduct suggested that he was capable of that degree of resolution. When Charles wailed that if he failed to make war his people would rise against him, Louis calculated that such a revolt posed little threat to him, as it would prevent England from undertaking any military offensive on the continent. Louis found Charles's demands excessive: he told Montagu that the English were being more difficult than the Dutch (now ready to make peace on almost any terms) and even the Spanish.[93] Charles, meanwhile, complained petulantly about the way his French cousin was treating him.[94]

Such complaints might relieve Charles's feelings, but they did nothing to extricate him from his predicament. His brother kept telling him that, if they had to face a revolt, it was better to do so when they had an army: indeed, he claimed that here was an ideal opportunity to re-establish the power of the crown once and for all. James may have believed this, but Charles did not want even to think in such terms.[95] Apart from his brother, Charles's only close adviser was Danby. It seemed for a while that Buckingham might regain the king's favour: he accompanied Charles to the Lords and knelt by his side, whispering in his ear, like a witch's familiar. Whereas York and Danby gave unpalatable advice, Buckingham offered 'divertisement' and the prospect of peace, 'therein serving France and pleasing nature'. It soon became clear, however, that Buckingham would not sever his links with the Parliamentary opposition and the comet of his favour declined as speedily as it had risen, leaving Danby in the ascendant once more.[96] Although he transmitted to Montagu Charles's pleas for French money, the treasurer continued to urge his master to tell the Commons whether he intended peace or war: unless he took MPs into his confidence, it would be impossible to regain their trust. Charles was reluctant: 'Then they'll be able to see all that has been done and what we are doing.' He feared that if the Commons were admitted into the *arcana imperii*, they would wrest from him control over the government and reduce him to a cipher. But what was the alternative? The Dutch seemed less and less eager to continue the war, the Spaniards and imperialists were proving reluctant to live up to their earlier assurances and Louis remained deaf to all his pleas. Reluctantly, Charles decided that he had no choice but to follow Danby's advice. After two adjournments, he could delay meeting Parliament no longer. He ordered Williamson to prepare a narrative of the previous fifteen months' negotiations. Like it or not, he was about to take the Commons into his confidence.[97]

On 29 April Finch, now promoted to lord chancellor, gave the Houses a long account of the diplomacy of the last two years, including the Feversham proposals and the treaties with the Dutch, which Charles was ready to lay before Parliament. The king, he said, had sent troops to Flanders and would have sent more, but for certain difficulties (by which he meant lack of co-operation from the Spanish). Now he sought a general alliance against France, but the Dutch were dragging their feet and it seemed probable that they wanted a separate peace. This was a difficult and complex situation and he asked for the Houses' advice as to how to proceed.[98] The Commons' response to this candid exposition was far from what the king had been led to expect. Some MPs who had earlier demanded to be shown treaties now declared that they had no wish to see them; others wished to compare them with copies already circulating in print or complained that they had called for war, but the treaties spoke only of peace. Then the opposition leaders switched the direction of debate. Long-standing fears of the growth of Popery had been rekindled by claims by a disgruntled former JP, John Arnold, that the Marquis of Worcester had been protecting Papists in Herefordshire and Monmouthshire. A feud had developed in this area similar to those in Norfolk and elsewhere, as peers with strong Royalist sympathies sought to extend their power, using the Conventicle and Corporation Acts to harass their enemies. The fact that Worcester was a convert from Catholicism and that there were many Catholics in the region encouraged his enemies to make use of anti-Popery. The Commons had been so perturbed by Arnold's allegations that the committee appointed to investigate them was ordered to continue its labours even during the adjournment. The committee now recommended that the House should lay no further burden on the people until the threat from Popery had been removed. When some objected that this linked two unrelated issues, the old Cromwellian Colonel Birch resorted to a classic anti-Popish tactic: if any member, he cried, was against securing the Protestant religion, he should say so. The House resolved, by a majority of forty, to concur with the committee.[99]

The court was taken totally by surprise. Charles angrily reproached Temple for his 'popular notions' and asked how he could rely on the Commons to support him if he were to declare war on France. The diplomat was for once lost for a reply: he did not judge it politic to say what he really thought – that MPs had good reason not to trust the king.[100] Meanwhile, opposition MPs missed no opportunity to feed backbench suspicions of collusion with France and fears of a standing army. They pressed for more information and demanded to see more documents. They denounced the clause about 'rebels' in the Dutch treaty: who was to define 'rebellion'? The government, they claimed, had done too little too late. The Feversham terms would have given Louis far too much. When ministers invoked the royal prerogative or expressed fears of another civil war, they were merely trying to conceal their misdeeds from legitimate Parliamentary scrutiny.[101] Only Sir William Coventry offered a serious critique of the king's foreign policy, but his was a lone voice of reason amid the wild recriminations and allegations. The previous year Coventry had been able to lead debates: now he could not and he became weary and disillusioned.[102] His argument that the present alliances, while not perfect, should be improved was swept aside by strident demands that they should be abrogated (as not in accordance with the Commons' addresses) and claims that the confederates could easily be brought to agree better terms. The House called for an alliance with the States General, Spain and the emperor, under which all would cease to trade with France and none was to make peace without the others. Soon after, the House resolved on an address to Charles to remove from his counsels those who had advised the answers of 26 May 1677 and 31 January 1678 to the Commons' addresses. They also agreed on an address against Lauderdale.[103]

As reports of the cynical and alarmist tactics of opposition MPs reached the king, they raised in his mind unpleasant echoes of 1640–2: the talk of evil counsellors, the claims that the king's speeches did not represent his own views, the intimidatory use of anti-Popery. Not unnaturally, he assumed that his critics' real aim was to seize power and to leave him (at most) the mere name of king. The fear was not all on one side, however. Barrillon was convinced that the MPs he dealt with were terrified that Charles wished to use his newly raised forces to establish absolutism. As Temple remarked, mutual distrust prevented any concerted action and the Commons' conduct exacerbated Charles's habitual indecision.[104] Convinced that he could never obtain the money needed for an effective war effort, he renewed his attempts to persuade Louis to pay him 6,000,000 livres a year for three years. Louis demanded that he should first commit himself, in writing, to prorogue Parliament and to disband all of his newly raised forces, except for 3,000 which were to remain temporarily at Ostend. Danby, York and even Charles jibbed at the infringement of sovereignty which this implied: calling Parliament and commanding the armed forces were among the king's most cherished prerogatives. Louis, moreover, was prepared to discuss only one payment of 6,000,000 *livres*, spread over three or four years: frankly, he wrote, Charles's services were worth no more. Charles wriggled, but on 17 May he agreed to a treaty which, in effect, obliged him to prorogue Parliament for four months and to disband the army; he would then receive his 6,000,000 *livres*. Nothing was agreed about further payments, but Louis did promise to respect all William's possessions, including Orange.[105]

The French terms were harsh, but (as Charles told Barrillon) he had no option but to make himself wholly dependent on France.[106] There seemed no prospect of his being able to wage war: even the bellicose James now told William that, given the mood of the Commons, the Dutch should secure the best tems they could. Danby and the Dutch envoys in London reached much the same conclusion.[107] Both royal brothers were convinced that the very survival of the monarchy was at stake: the more they conceded to the 'fanatics', in England or Scotland, the more they would demand. Attempts by a group of Scottish lords to undermine his faith in Lauderdale provoked Charles to ferocious rage.[108] Despite all his fears, however, Charles hesitated to sign the French treaty and refused to ratify it: just as he was reluctant to trust Parliament, so he drew back from a step which would destroy all prospect of winning its support. Danby and even York warned him that they would all be ruined if details of the treaty leaked out. Besides, the obnoxious addresses had mostly been carried by small majorities. Given time to reflect, the Commons might yet be brought to see reason. Charles therefore prorogued the Houses for ten days, thus aborting all uncompleted business. In a short speech, he pointedly contrasted the Lords' prudence with the Commons' unseemly addresses.[109] Danby and Finch initially opposed the prorogation, on the grounds that it would anger the Commons and provide the Dutch with a pretext to make peace. They came to support it only as a lesser evil than a dissolution, advocated by York as (he claimed) the only means of preserving the monarchy from ruin.[110]

During the brief recess Charles signed the French treaty and Danby negotiated with opposition leaders about the possibility of money. Charles's opening speech left it to the Houses to decide whether the army should be kept up or disbanded and how it should be paid for. He reminded them that the additional wine duties were due to expire and that the ban on French imports would seriously reduce his revenue. He concluded with a firm warning against driving him to extremities: he would never again assent to a bill which had extraneous clauses tacked on to it.[111] The Commons were clearly torn between their desire to send military aid to the confederates and concern that the necessary forces might be misused at home. Burgomano presented a memorial against disbanding the newly raised forces, but then news came that the Brussels authorities had agreed to make peace. Understandably confused, the Commons asked the king whether there was to be peace or war: if the former, the forces should be disbanded.[112] Charles replied that while the issue remained uncertain it would be imprudent to disband. He reminded the Commons of his request for money and, in particular, of the £200,000 which he had been authorized to borrow on the credit of the additional excise, which they had promised to make good. Before the recess, such a request would have led to an unruly debate, but now MPs were calmer. They resolved to pay off all troops raised since 29 September 1677 but rejected a motion to discharge all forces but the militia. A claim by a lawyer, William Williams, that the king had no right to raise soldiers within England was condemned as nonsense and he was forced to recant his error.[113]

Charles had no objection to paying off the new troops now that he, and almost everyone else, was convinced that peace was imminent. If the Commons gave him the money to pay off his troops, he could then prorogue them for four months, pocket the 6,000,000 *livres* which Louis had promised and enjoy a well-earned rest.[114] His willingness to disband reduced the Commons' fears and, despite the efforts of oppositionist MPs, they turned their thoughts seriously to supply. They agreed to repay the £200,000 which Charles had borrowed and voted a similar sum for the disbandment. On 11 June Williamson passed on a warning from the Dutch ambassadors that it would be unwise to disband before peace had been concluded. Despite attempts to revive fears of a standing army, the House extended the deadline set for disbandment until 27 July, for units in Flanders, and 30 June for those at home.[115] Encouraged, Charles and Danby resolved to make a further push for supply. On 18 June the king told the Houses that the Spanish and Dutch were about to make a peace that would preserve Flanders, of which he was to be guarantor. It would be necessary, however, to be prepared by land and sea to guard against future French aggression. He stressed the smallness of his revenues, compared with those of France, Spain and the Dutch Republic, and the extent of his debts. To enable him to spend the rest of his life 'in perfect confidence and kindness with you and all succeeding Parliaments', he asked them to settle on him, for life, all revenues which he had enjoyed at the previous Christmas (which would include the newly, but temporarily, renewed additional excise and the soon to expire wine duties) together with others to the value of £300,000 a year. He was prepared, in return, to assent to a bill appropriating £500,000 a year to the navy and ordnance, together with any other reasonable public bills.[116]

The speech was a great mistake. Not for the first time, Danby overplayed his hand, asking for additional supply late in the session, as MPs were drifting home. For this very reason, the House had resolved to receive no further motions for supply after that day and MPs reacted angrily to what they saw as sharp practice. There was talk of bribery and 'French' counsels, of mismanagement of money, of threats to Parliament and of Popery and arbitrary power. As opposition (or 'Country') MPs ranted through their repertoire, the court's supporters mostly sat glumly silent: again not for the first time, Danby had neglected to brief his spokesmen. The House rejected out of hand the requests for an extra £300,000 a year and for compensation for revenue lost because of the ban on French imports.[117] After some debate, however, they voted to continue the wine duties for three more years and to raise up to £414,000, to make good the £200,000 and to meet the extraordinary charges on the navy and ordnance. This, like the £200,000 already promised for the disbandment, was to be raised by a land tax. With the poll tax expected to yield £350,000, the Commons could claim that they had just about made good their earlier promise to vote £1,000,000 – and then repeated their resolution that no more was to be raised that session. Country MPs, like Sacheverell and Garroway, now went home, satisfied that they had dashed the king's hopes of a revenue large enough to enable him to subsist without Parliaments.[118]

Despite the failure of Danby's bid for a major addition to the ordinary revenue, the sums granted would alleviate the king's problems, provided peace was concluded at Nijmegen. Just when all seemed settled, however, Louis refused to hand over the towns in Flanders which he had earlier promised to cede, until his ally, the King of Sweden, recovered the territories that he had lost in Germany. Charles was furious: he had just told the Commons that his war preparations had forced the French to make peace. When he informed the Houses, the Lords agreed that Charles should keep up his forces until peace had been concluded, but the Commons voted to press on with the disbandment, arguing that the Dutch and Spanish had left England in the lurch and should take the consequences. Moreover, if the Commons agreed with the Lords that the disbandment should be delayed, more money would have to be found, so that the Lords would, in effect, be impinging upon the Commons' sole right of voting money.[119] Some suspected that this was another trick to get money or keep up the army, but the court was mad for war. 'Whoever is not now in this hot season in a drap de Berry coat with gold galoon enough to load a mule', wrote Henry Savile, 'is not thought affectionate to the government or the army.' York told the committee for foreign affairs that Louis was bent on universal dominion and that only Charles could stop him; he assured William that war was certain if the Dutch would only do their part.[120] Barrillon, naturally, suspected that York had ulterior motives, but others (like Henry Coventry) were talking in much the same terms. The ambassador still doubted whether

Charles wanted war and tried hard to dissuade him, reminding him of his promise of 17 May to disband his army and warning that if he failed to do so Louis would not feel obliged to pay him the 6,000,000 *livres*.[121]

For once his arguments made no impression. Charles complained angrily that the satisfaction of the Swedes had nothing to do with the settlement in Flanders. It would be politically impossible for him to stop transporting troops to Flanders, although he insisted that they would not be used against France; if he disbanded them and then Louis resumed his conquests, he would be driven out of England. All that he had done for Louis apparently counted for nothing. 'There's an end of an old song,' he told the foreign affairs committee. 'By God this is such usage. But I'll say nothing.'[122] Louis did not see things that way. Courtin complained to Brisbane about Mary's marriage, the alliance with the Dutch, the Feversham proposals and the sending of soldiers to Flanders. Charles had broken too many promises: Louis was no longer impressed by his pleas of *force majeure*. What Courtin did not admit was that Charles's military and diplomatic efforts had indeed helped to drive Louis to make peace. The fact that Charles had said as much to the Commons added insult to injury. A few weeks before, Louis had written that Charles's services were of little value to him: now he saw the English king as a positive nuisance and was happy, by this exercise in brinkmanship, to subject him to further political embarrassment.[123]

With his hopes of peace frustrated, Charles saw no option but to try (with Dutch help) to force Louis to come to terms. Temple was sent post-haste to the Hague where he found the States General less resolute than he had hoped. They cannot have been heartened by the Commons' reluctance to postpone the disbandment. MPs were doubtless weary after a long session, but even Sir John Reresby, no enemy to the court, remarked that it was hard to believe the talk of war when Charles and James were so often merry with Barrillon at Portsmouth's lodgings.[124] The House eventually agreed to extend their deadline by a month, but would vote no more money for the soldiers' pay. Once the supply bills had been completed, there was no reason to prolong the session. On 15 July Charles prorogued Parliament; it was eventually to reconvene on 21 October.[125]

Before it met, it was imperative that Flanders should be secured. Charles's court watched anxiously to see if Louis' duplicity would deflect the States General from their gadarene rush towards peace. At the same time, Charles and Danby urged Louis to adhere to the treaty of 17 May, while insisting that the disbandment would have to be delayed for a few weeks.[126] Against all expectations, Temple negotiated a treaty under which the Dutch and English agreed to declare war if France had not handed over the towns in question by 1 August. William warmly applauded Temple's efforts. Williamson complained that the treaty did not specify the two powers' respective military contributions; moreover, the States General agreed to suspend trading with France for one year only – and that by a revocable resolution, not a clause in the treaty. On the other hand, Charles informed William privately that without a further grant from Parliament he would be unable to put most of his troops into the field. Defective as it was on both sides, the treaty achieved its aim. Louis delayed ceding the towns until the ultimatum was about to expire. Then his plenipotentiaries at Nijmegen demanded that those of the States General should sign at once. They had no time to seek authorization from the Hague, where a Swedish agent, primed by Barrillon, spread rumours that Charles and Louis had secretly agreed terms and that the Swedish king wished Louis to hand over the towns. Temple refused to sign, but the Dutch did so anyway. The war was effectively over.[127]

The news merely added to Charles's perplexity. He and his advisers decided that it would be unwise to disband his forces until the peace had been ratified. Money, naturally, was a problem: he sent to the City for a loan, but he could not survive on credit forever.[128] Meanwhile, even though he had thwarted Louis' plans and had failed to abide by the terms of the treaty of 17 May, he, Danby and the new ambassador at Paris, the Earl of Sunderland, resumed the demand that Louis should pay over the promised 6,000,000 *livres*. Louis' response was predictable, as was Charles's indignation at his refusal.[129] Despairing of regaining Louis' goodwill, and fearful that he might resume his conquest of Flanders or conclude an alliance with the Dutch, Charles decided not to recall his forces for the time being. The irregular manner in which the Dutch envoys had signed the treaty at Nijmegen enabled him to claim that his treaty with the States General was still in force. The Dutch, however, were heartily weary of the war and disinclined to place any reliance on a regime as unsteady as Charles's. In September the States General agreed to ratify the treaty.[130] English commentators expressed amazement that they had accepted terms which (they claimed) failed to secure an adequate barrier. William agreed: he was convinced that the renewal of French aggression was only a matter of time. Events were to prove him right, although the form of that aggression changed after 1678. Temple, however, believed that the States General had had no choice. 'Our counsels and conduct', he wrote, 'were like those of a floating island, driven one way or t'other according to the winds or tides.' Their very mutability, indeed, had made them seem more mysterious, indeed sinister, than they really were.[131]

All, however, was not yet settled. Although the Spaniards too had agreed to the terms, they were slow to ratify; Louis, as so often, tried at the last minute to alter what had been agreed. Charles and Danby, saddled with a large army and no obvious use for it, insisted that it should remain in

Flanders until final agreement had been reached; indeed, more men were sent over – they were politically less embarrassing there than they would be at home. Danby told Barrillon that Parliament would insist that Charles should make war on France, but then asked for money from Louis to disband the army. Barrillon was politely sceptical and told his English friends that the court was seeking a pretext to keep it on foot.[132] Charles continued to strive to regain Louis' goodwill, not least because he feared a Franco-Dutch alliance. Barrillon did not discourage him, but continued to press for the army to be disbanded.[133] Charles, however, had little to offer in return for Louis' money, except for an army which, as Barrillon reminded him, had been raised for a war against France. Back in July there had been a bizarre proposal, in St Albans's name, for Charles to supply 10,000 men and fifteen ships to the Swedes, to be paid for by France. This might have helped Louis' ally and gone some way towards paying for the army: but nothing came of it.[134]

The terms finally agreed at Nijmegen left Louis with not only Tournai, Condé and Valenciennes but also Charlemont and Ypres; he also gained Franche Comté, but not Philippsburg. Given Louis' past record, many felt that this would not satisfy him, but others were relieved that he settled for so little: in August Danby had thought that Louis wished to keep all that he had taken in the Low Countries apart from Maastricht.[135] In fact, Louis had settled for less than he wanted mainly because of the substantial forces which Charles had sent to Flanders, but few expressed any gratitude. The Spaniards found underpaid English soldiers unwelcome guests. The Dutch complained that English help was too little and had come too late. Louis was furious at what he saw as a betrayal: his boundless capacity for failing to abide by his promises did not make him tolerant of others who did the same. He did not openly express his anger, and strung Charles along with hopes of money, but informed observers expected him to seek revenge.[136] The Commons, however, were bound to be angry that Charles had failed to disband his new forces, after being given money to do so. His vacillation and duplicity had earned him both Louis' resentment and his people's distrust. He had also given hostages to fortune. He had sought money from France in return for making peace, while declaring to the Commons that he intended to make war. He had also promised to declare himself a Catholic. Many of these dealings remained secret, but for how long? As the summer of 1678 turned to autumn, Charles knew that sooner or later he would have to ask the Commons for money to pay off his now unnecessary army.[137] Amid so many worries, he paid little heed to picaresque stories of plots to assassinate him, with exotic poisons or silver bullets. The allegations were first made by an eccentric parson, Israel Tonge, well known for his anti-Popish fantasies. It transpired that Tonge derived his information from a man who, it was claimed, had been awarded a doctorate of divinity by the great university of Salamanca. On 28 September this august individual appeared before the privy council. His name was Titus Oates.

'Forty-one Is Come Again'

As the hostilities which had begun in 1672 stuttered towards their end, Englishmen's attention focused more and more on domestic affairs and, specifically, on the problem of the 'Popish successor'. If the Papists' alleged designs, so graphically described by Oates, had succeeded, James would have become king. For many, this would have led inexorably to the destruction of laws and liberties, Parliaments and Protestantism. Meanwhile, Danby's reputation was blasted by revelations of his attempts to secure subsidies from France and he was impeached. The hectic two and a half years which followed the outbreak of the Popish Plot saw two crucial struggles. The first was to break Danby's power and to call to account those held responsible for the misgovernment and corruption of the previous decade. The second was to guard against the danger of similar or worse misgovernment by excluding York from the succession. It was this second issue which gave rise to the term often used to describe these years – 'the Exclusion Crisis'.

The fact that his subjects showed so much anger about the past and so much fear for the future demonstrates clearly that Charles had failed to retain the trust and goodwill of the 'political nation' (however one defines that question-begging term). A central contention of this book is that Charles persistently failed to match up to his people's expectations and that the opposition he met with had its roots in disappointment, anger and fear. As we have seen, he saw matters differently. Conditioned by experience of the civil wars, he was inclined to read into criticisms of his government sinister undercurrents which probably were not there. Even Clarendon had blamed the outbreak of civil war on ambitious demagogues, who whipped up hostility to the king by means of cynical allegations of 'Popish plots'. Charles, who in 1641 had been too young to understand much of what was going on, adopted a similar interpretation of those traumatic events. He was always inclined to fear his people, especially the 'giddy multitude' – ignorant and brutal, they were naturally insubordinate but also easily led by agitators, who appealed to their base natures, to their distrusts and hatreds, to their love of violence and plunder. With the help of 'the mob' (the word 'mobile' came into use late in the seventeenth century) the Parliamentary leaders of 1641 had hacked away the pillars of authority in Church and state, not scrupling to turn the world upside down in pursuit of their ends. Loyal ministers were executed on trumped-up charges; the king was stripped of his powers and revenues; and, in the Church, episcopacy was destroyed, conformable ministers were expelled from their livings and free rein was given to wild-eyed sectaries and mechanic preachers.

Such a view of 1641 was, of course, a highly partial one. It took no account of the justified distrust of Charles I's duplicity, flirtations with foreign powers and predisposition to resort to force. Charles II, however, was not inclined to be over-critical of his father or to put himself in others' shoes; on the contrary, he was convinced that the 'republicans' were out to destroy him. In the winter of 1678–9 he re-read the history of 1641. His pre-conceptions were shared by York and (apparently) Danby and were reinforced by the reports of spies sent among the London sectaries and the few surviving civil war radicals.[1] Security was tightened at court to guard, not against the Papists, but against the Fifth Monarchists and other 'fanatics'.[2] Yet if Charles's view of the motives of his critics was highly slanted, there was much in their conduct to give it credence. Indeed, parallels with 1641–2 made good sense because the situation was in many ways similar:

> Men say we act like Forty-two
> Yet none tells thee the reason.
> Yet when the same diseases grow
> Like medicines come in season.[3]

Once again, mutual distrust had grown to a point where a constitution based on co-operation and a mixed sovereign of king, Lords and Commons no longer worked. Forced to choose between securing the rights of the people and respecting the powers of the crown, many opted for the former. Faced with the Lords' refusal to pass bills which it regarded as vital for the preservation of the people and of Protestantism, the majority in the Commons tried to put pressure on the Upper House by mobilizing support 'without doors'. Fear and anger drove many to act against their avowed principles: in desperate circumstances, the end justified the means.

Locked in what they saw as a battle for survival, the Commons' leaders (like their forebears in 1641) had no time for half-measures, faint-hearts or backsliders. Those who questioned the measures they proposed were denounced as Papists, favourers of Popery or 'Papists in masquerade'. The vocabulary of anti-Popery depicted issues (like exclusion) in terms of stark moral opposites – good and evil, Protestantism and Popery. This placed opponents of exclusion (many of whom were, in fact, strongly anti-Catholic) on the defensive and inhibited them from arguing forcefully against measures alleged to be essential for the preservation of Protestantism. Those who most openly opposed the Exclusionist caucus were howled down, called to the bar of the Commons or even expelled from the House. Some of the older opposition leaders found themselves left behind as younger, wilder men began to make the running. These new leaders, some of whom came in in the elections of 1679 and 1681, were less prepared even to go through the motions of professing respect for the king's prerogatives and more inclined to talk of their responsibility to 'the people'. They took care to inform 'the people' of what the Commons were doing (by printing their 'votes') and promoted petitions, instructions to MPs and other popular expressions of support for the Exclusionist cause.

The Exclusionists' populist rhetoric served to increase Charles's anxiety and his vigilance, especially in London 'which is the source of all'. He was perturbed when, just after news of the Plot broke, the City authorities insisted on fixing chains across the streets at night, to impede Popish horsemen – or the king's horse guards.[4] He took care to ensure that the officers commanding the City trained bands were politically reliable and was careful to explain his actions to the lord mayor and aldermen.[5] Remembering the crucial role played by London in 1641–2, he watched anxiously attempts to promote political petitions in the common council and among the citizens in general.[6] The lapsing of the Licensing Act made it far harder to bridle the political press. Exclusionist pamphlets and newspapers proliferated, almost all of them produced in London, which was reported in September 1679 to be 'rotten ripe for rebellion'. The lord mayor and aldermen mostly seemed loyal. Their predecessors of 1641 had been equally loyal, but had then been overthrown by a revolution from below and power passed to a 'committee of safety' set up by the common council: could the same thing happen again?[7]

Of the issues that had precipitated the political breakdown of 1641–2, control of the militia had been the most urgent, because of the need to raise an army to put down the Irish rebellion. This must have been in Charles's mind when he resolved to use his veto (for the only time in his reign) against a bill to allow the calling out of the militia: he would not allow it out of his power for half an hour, he declared.[8] He was equally determined to resist demands to purge the officer corps of the army, navy and county militias, especially as the main 'crime' of many of these officers was to owe their appointment to his brother. Charles had no intention of using the army to coerce his people: indeed, he disbanded the recently raised regiments during the first half of 1679. If he showed a certain reluctance to do so, it was because he felt that without them he would be more exposed to the malice of the 'disaffected' and he was determined not to have unreliable officers foisted upon him in the few units which remained to him. His father had negligently allowed Parliament to meddle with matters of defence when he went off to Scotland in the autumn of 1641; Charles II was not to repeat that mistake.

Looking back, Charles I had believed that his cardinal error, indeed his cardinal sin, had been to sacrifice Strafford: both he and the Lords had agreed to the bill of attainder only under immense popular pressure. The similarities between Strafford and Danby were alarming. Both made enemies easily and often sometimes maltreated their friends and clients. Danby was threatened with attainder, although when he surrendered himself the Commons reverted to an impeachment. In the 1679 Parliament the Commons were far more eager to punish Danby than to prosecute those accused of complicity in the Popish Plot, which led Charles to conclude that they aimed to destroy not Popery but the monarchy.[9] Arguments about how to proceed against Danby led to furious disputes between the Houses, which centred on the bishops' right to take part in trials on capital charges. Those who denied that right argued that it would be improper for men of God to become involved in proceedings which might end in the shedding of blood, but their real objection to the bishops' taking part was more prosaic: it was expected that almost all of them would vote for Danby's acquittal. These disputes raised unpleasant echoes of the bishops' exclusion from the Lords, first by force and then by Parliamentary ordinance, in 1641–2. They had been blamed then for holding up measures (such as Strafford's attainder bill) deemed by the Commons to be vital for the nation's safety. Similar accusations were to be levelled after the Lords threw out the second exclusion bill ('For the bishops, the bishops have thrown out the bill').[10] Meanwhile, as the Anglican clergy appeared more and more forthright in defence of York's title to the crown, the whole clerical order was denounced by Exclusionists (and especially by Dissenters) as favourers of Popery.

For Charles, such developments must have brought back unpleasant memories of pleading for Strafford's life and of stealing furtively out of his father's capital city. At the same time, the very starkness of the threats which he now seemed to face and the growing polarization of the political nation served to clarify the issues facing him. His decision-making had all too often been marred by muddle and vacillation. Now, fighting (as he saw it) for his very survival he showed far greater resolution and a clearer sense of priorities: fear concentrated the mind wonderfully. In addition, in these changed circumstances, some of his former vices became assets. Well aware that he had earlier bowed in the face of pressure, the Exclusionists assumed that he would do so again. This assumption led them to exaggerate their demagogy and populism: in fact, they made no real effort to mobilize anything other than non-violent support until it was too late. Their rhetoric, in short, was not matched by their actions, nor (for most of them) was it underpinned by an ideological commitment to republicanism (or democracy): 'the rights of the people' were invoked for the sake of argument, not actively promoted. There were, it is true, some genuine republicans and radicals among the Exclusionists, but they were few in number and their influence was marginal. Their presence may, indeed, have proved counter-productive: it made it easier to smear the whole movement for exclusion as a revival of the 'Good Old Cause' of the 1650s and gave added impetus to the growing conservative backlash.

A second erstwhile vice which now became an asset was Charles's habit of dissimulation. This had led wise men to place little trust in him, but now it encouraged others to believe what they wanted to believe – that given time, and subjected to sufficient pressure, he would agree to exclusion. Charles bent with the storm, sending James abroad, persecuting Catholics and appointing a new privy council (with Shaftesbury as president). Such compliance naturally nurtured hopes that he might abandon his brother. It was a subtle devious game, which Charles played with some skill, although his appearance of irresolution may at times have come closer than he cared to admit to reflecting his real feelings. At the same time, however, he showed a clear grasp of political realities. He refused to sacrifice his central prerogatives – control over the armed forces, the calling of Parliament and the appointment of ministers and officers. He kept a close watch on London and took care that the machinery of law and order should be in safe hands. His instinct had always been to keep his options open: now he played for time, stringing along those who hoped that he would come to agree to exclusion, while pleading with Louis to provide money to enable him to live without Parliament. Such a strategy was familiar enough, but he also appealed increasingly openly for the support of the crown's 'old friends', the Cavaliers and 'Church of England men'. As the nation became politically divided, so Charles moved towards taking one side unequivocally against the other.

Despite his grand claims, Titus Oates had never been to Salamanca and was not a doctor of anything. He did, however, possess a prodigious memory (with effrontery to match) and, having briefly been a Jesuit novice, sufficient inside information to give his story a certain superficial credibility. The son of a notorious Baptist turned Anglican parson, he was expelled from two Cambridge colleges (apparently for academic insufficiency) but nevertheless took holy orders. He was ejected from his first living for drunkenness and heterodoxy. A brief career as a naval chaplain ended when he was accused of sodomy – a capital offence – and he joined the Jesuits. Little was known of this in 1678, however. The councillors who heard his tale were impressed by his air of gravity, his confidence and his grasp of detail. Henry Coventry wrote that, if Oates was a liar, he was the most skilful that he had ever seen. While accusing the Papists of plotting to murder Charles, Oates was careful to cater for what he saw as the prejudices of the court. There were several references to Catholics seeking to subvert the government in the guise of English Fifth Monarchists and Scots Presbyterians. Although he apparently hinted at first that York might be implicated, he soon realized that this had been unwise and in October declared publicly that James had had no part in it.[11]

Reactions to his story were mixed. Some of the court's enemies regarded Oates's story with suspicion, suspecting that he had been set on by Danby. Barrillon and York did not go that far, but were convinced that he was encouraging Oates to elaborate his story and hoped to use it for his own purposes: the threat from Popery could bring king and Commons together and Danby could resume his stance as champion of Protestantism. If this led the Commons to divert their wrath from Danby to York, so much the better. Barrillon reported also that Danby had again offered a measure of toleration, but only for Presbyterians.[12] Charles was still more sceptical. When he examined Oates, he caught him out several times – he failed utterly to describe Don John of Austria, whom he claimed to have seen often – and some parts of his story were wildly implausible. Of five Catholic peers allegedly commissioned to lead the Popish army, only one (Bellasis) had any military experience and he was virtually crippled by gout. Convinced that the whole story was ridiculous, Charles handed the matter over to the council, confident that if Oates's allegations were fully investigated, they would be found to be insubstantial and no more would be heard of them.[13]

For Charles to wash his hands of the matter was understandable, especially as he wished to spend some more time at Newmarket before Parliament met; but it was unwise. Anti-Popery was a volatile commodity: if handled clumsily, it could blow up in his face, especially as one of those named by Oates was Arundell of Wardour, who had played such an important part in negotiating the Secret Treaty of Dover. Moreover, probably prompted by Danby, Oates added to his growing list of plotters the name of Edward Coleman. The magistrate who had first taken Oates's deposition, Sir Edmund Berry Godfrey, warned Coleman that he had been named, but he did nothing to hide or destroy his papers and they were seized. For some days the councillors were too busy to look at them, but when they did, on 4 October, they were staggered by what they found. Some papers talked of using French money, either to persuade Charles not to call Parliament or to bribe MPs not to attack York and the Catholics. Never given to under-statement, Coleman had written to Louis' confessor: 'We have here a mighty work upon our hands, no less than the conversion of three kingdoms and by that perhaps the subduing of a pestilent heresy which has domineered over part of this northern world a long time.'[14] As Henry Coventry rightly noted, the letters contained little about the Plot, but much presumptuous talk about altering religion and government. Others remarked that the letters dated mostly from 1674–6 and assumed (almost certainly wrongly) that he had destroyed his most recent correspondence, which would have revealed much more. Southwell wrote, with alarm, that the matter was now too big for the council and the judges: it would have to come before Parliament and then God only knew where it would stop, especially as it was clear from the letters (as well as from Coleman's own statements) that York had authorized many of Coleman's negotiations.[15]

Worse was to come. On 12 October Godfrey disappeared. His body was found five days later: despite a clumsy attempt to suggest suicide, he had clearly been murdered. The identity of his killers has remained a subject of speculation, much of it fanciful, from that day to this.[16] What is not in doubt is the public's reaction. The arrests of Coleman, Langhorne and several priests made it clear that something was up. News of Coleman's letters leaked out and had reached Bridlington by the day Godfrey's body was found. (Charles had not yet seen them.) The magistrate's disappearance and death precipitated a nationwide panic. Charles told Barrillon that Godfrey was a fanatic and had probably killed himself, but the general consensus was that he had been murdered by the Papists for taking Oates's deposition. The council responded to the panic by ordering that Papists' houses should be searched for arms: wild rumours of what had been found triggered further alarms. Buckingham, resuming his favourite role as tribune of the people, called for an address to the lord mayor to order the citizens of London to take up arms to defend themselves against the Papists.[17]

Coleman's letters and Godfrey's murder seemed to provide independent corroboration, if not of Oates's story, at least of the sort of design he had described. Fear of Popery and arbitrary government had been running high for many months and had not been diminished by Charles's failure to disband the army. As Southwell wrote, 'it was the preparation of some men's minds and not the witnesses' that made the Plot seem so credible: here was just the sort of Popish design which experience led Protestants to expect.[18] Coleman's letters and Godfrey's murder also ensured that Danby would now be unable to appropriate the Plot for his own purposes. The finding of the body could not, indeed, have come at a worse time. Parliament was due to meet in just four days.

In his opening speech, Charles argued that, until peace had been fully concluded, it would be unwise to withdraw his forces from the Netherlands. He was, however, willing to be advised by the Houses on the matter of troop reductions and to lay before them accounts, to show that his revenue was both inherently inadequate and heavily anticipated. As for the Plot, he would leave it to the law.[19] The Commons showed no inclination to inspect his accounts, nor were they in any hurry to vote money to disband the army. The king's need for money was their best guarantee that the session would not be abruptly terminated and the army's continued existence helped to sustain a high level of anxiety, inside and outside Parliament. Public concern about the Plot also forced Charles to allow the Lords to see some of the relevant documents, after which it proved impossible to deny the same privilege to the Commons.[20] Many MPs were genuinely shocked and alarmed by Oates's story and Coleman's letters, but opposition politicians also found the Plot most useful: it created a renewed sense of panic and provided a fruitful source of new complaints against those in power. New grievances were thus added to old. 'We are now accounting', wrote Southwell, 'for the particulars of many years past.' Accumulated resentment of subservience to France and of 'corruption' and 'the growth of Popery' at home 'make everything break out into harsher resentments than the nature of many things would deserve'.[21]

With the Plot now firmly in the public domain, Charles had no option but to allow the Commons to investigate it. The Plot, however, grew at an alarming rate. Oates continued to dredge new information from his fecund memory and he was joined by others as disreputable as himself (starting with William Bedloe), who realized that informing against the Papists brought both public adulation and hard cash. As few dared openly to doubt the reality of the Plot, sacrifices had to be found to relieve public anxiety. Charles had no qualms about abandoning Coleman to his fate, especially after he told a committee of the Lords that the king, as well as his brother, had authorized his negotiations.[22] The law required that, in trials for treason, there should be at least two witnesses. James was eager to silence Coleman as quickly as possible, but Charles was reluctant to undertake a prosecution unless he was sure that it would succeed and asked the judges if there was sufficient evidence. They replied that to seek to extirpate the Protestant religion was treason, but that they could comment on the evidence only when it was properly presented in court. Charles hesitated and it was not until 27 November that Coleman was brought to trial. By then he had been examined by committees of both Houses and the Commons had asked Charles's permission to publish three of the letters. James had declared to the Lords, on his honour, that he had known nothing of his former secretary's correspondence; he was lying. When, during the trial, Coleman tried to claim that he had acted on orders, the presiding judge told him sharply that such claims were irrelevant. He was found guilty and executed, but the damage he had done outlived him and was not reduced by the conduct of his trial, which looked too much like a cover-up.[23]

If Charles was eager to see Coleman dead, the same was not true of others accused by Oates and his growing tribe of imitators. Charles made no secret of his scepticism concerning their testimony. Having himself heard the evidence used in the trials of those accused of involvement in the Plot, he was reluctant to allow the execution of those convicted on it and told Barrillon that they were innocent. Even Danby remarked, with regret, that the evidence was less full than he had hoped. The judges had to nurse and lead the witnesses in order to secure the convictions that were politically necessary. This same necessity wore down the king's scruples. Having apparently been persuaded by a new witness that Godfrey had been murdered at Somerset House (the queen's residence), he ordered the execution of those convicted of his murder. He hesitated longer about three priests convicted on Oates's evidence and insisted on consulting the judges and some of the bishops. His ministers assured him that the trials had been perfectly fair, but again it took a new witness to convince him. Stephen Dugdale came of a minor gentry family and his apparent respectability, as much as his corroboration of others' evidence, persuaded Charles to allow the executions to go ahead.[24]

Charles could delay the carrying out of death sentences, but otherwise he had little choice but to swim with the tide. He ordered that the laws against Catholics should be enforced and Seymour suggested ways in which they could be tightened up.[25] Such measures had only a limited effect, because 'Popery' implied so much more than mere Catholicism: Country MPs remarked that the greatest danger came not from Papists but from Protestants who favoured Popery. Henry Powle claimed that there had been, since 1660, a 'state plot' to establish arbitrary government: 'if we had not had this army we had not had this plot'.[26] Such claims were made more credible by the revelation that Catholic officers had been granted commissions in one of the recently raised regiments. Furious, the Commons sent Williamson to the Tower for countersigning them; Charles, equally furious, ordered his release: not only was the Commons' right to imprison anyone dubious (except in cases of breach of privilege), but it was highly discourteous to commit a secretary of state to prison without informing the king. Convinced (or so they claimed) that the army posed as great a threat to liberties and religion as the Plot, opposition MPs demanded that it should be disbanded, but that the House should vote no more money for that purpose: such a grant, they claimed, would lead inevitably to a prorogation. Some sought to invoke a right of resistance, against Catholic officers or those commissioned by a Catholic king: under the 1662 Militia Act it was treason to resist anyone bearing the king's commission. Such arguments found little support: they smacked of 'arming the multitude' and revived unpleasant memories of the late 1640s.[27] The House then turned to the militia, whose legality (unlike the army's) was unquestionable and whose members, as ordinary citizens, could be expected to respect liberties and religion. After hearing Bedloe's information, the Commons resolved to address the king to mobilize the militia, one-third at a time, for a total of six weeks, in order to calm the people's fears. The Lords pointed out that under the Militia Act there was no provision for raising money to maintain it for more than twelve days and proposed that a bill should be brought in to allow for this. Despite the Speaker's claim that this was 'against all order', the Commons did so and the bill quickly passed both Houses.[28]

Charles's decision to veto the bill came as a great surprise. Henry Coventry told the Commons that he saw nothing wrong with the bill, but Charles declared that it could be interpreted as requiring the militia to be kept up for the full six weeks: it would thus raise 60,000 men and he would have no power to make them lay down their arms. His fears were not wholly fanciful. He was informed that Shaftesbury and Sir Thomas Meres had said, 'Let us once see the militia up and let them get down as they can,' which Danby claimed was evidence of a plan to use the militia to disarm the army. Both the chancellor and the attorney-general assured Charles that the bill did not violate his prerogative: he preferred to take Danby's advice.[29] London already bristled with armed men. The trained bands were on guard each night; anxious citizens purchased weapons or hired armed porters to protect them; the City set chains across the streets. Alarmist talk abounded: Sir Thomas Player reportedly cried that they could all wake up next day with their throats cut; the governor of the East India Company considered taking his family out of town. Southwell reported that those who pressed for 'reformation' planned to retreat to the City if their designs failed, just as the Commons had done in 1642. Burnet told the king that many hoped that, once the militia had been raised, it would not disband until the demands of both Houses had been met.[30] In short, the reasons for Charles's veto were not legal but political and the Commons' reaction can only have reinforced his conviction that he had been right. MPs complained that he had failed to take their advice and that ministers filled his head with fears of republicans and '41. When one member referred to the 1642 Militia Ordinance he was called a favourer of Popery. Coventry's reminder that the veto was an unquestioned royal preprogative was ignored. The House agreed on an intemperate address against following secret advice contrary to that of Parliament. (It soon had second thoughts and did not proceed with it.) Charles for his part declared that he would readily agree to any bill for the public safety, provided the power of calling and dismissing the militia was left entirely to him. Some denounced this as an attempt to dictate the form of legislation, but the House as a whole welcomed the proposal and set up a committee to frame such a bill: it never reported, which can only have confirmed Charles's suspicions about the motives behind the original bill.[31]

The failure to proceed with the address against secret counsels was indicative of the Commons' volatility. Since 1661 by-elections had brought in some wilder members, like Sacheverell, but the House's changing behaviour owed more to events than to changes of membership. In the charged atmosphere of 'Godfrey's autumn', MPs were living on their nerves and were moved more easily than usual to panic or anger. Moreover, they were torn between the desire to secure the redress of grievances and fear of provoking Charles to dismiss them or even use the army against them. Although they had no wish to end their usefulness by granting money too quickly, they thought it unwise to refuse it too peremptorily. The more astute MPs tried to restrain their more impetuous colleagues, but it was not easy. When Sacheverell denounced the army as illegal, Sir William Coventry replied that the main priority was not to call it names but to be rid of it.[32] The wiser heads could not always divert the House from intemperate actions which they later came to regret (for example, sending Williamson to the Tower), which in turn reinforced Charles's suspicions of the House's intentions.[33]

For most critics of the court, present anger and future fears focused on Danby and York. The two had never been easy allies. Danby saw York's Catholicism and fondness for France as a political liability, York suspected that Danby would gladly sacrifice him (and the Catholics) in return for money from Parliament. The failure to disband the army, and then the Plot, increased their respective senses of vulnerability and their willingness to receive overtures from oppositionist elements, even though they appreciated that those overtures were designed to drive a wedge between them: it would be easier to destroy one if he received no support from the other.[34]

Of the two, James was the more obviously vulnerable, because of his religion and his association with Coleman: his frenzied denials carried little conviction when weighed against Coleman's testimony and the letters themselves. His leading enemies – Shaftesbury, Buckingham, Essex and Halifax – believed that his hostility towards them was so implacable that self-preservation required that they should deprive him of the power to harm them. James had considerable assets, however: he was not a man to break or bend in the face of hostility and as the king's brother and heir presumptive commanded respect and support. Charles found his stubbornness irritating – he remarked that James had neither the conscience nor the understanding of their grandfather, Henry IV of France. But Charles also found it hard to act firmly against him, especially as James insisted that his enemies' true aim was to overthrow the monarchy.[35] James refused to withdraw from court (and so defuse allegations of 'Popish counsels'), calculating (correctly) that Charles would not order him to go. The Commons considered whether to ask Charles to remove James from his presence and counsels, but allowed the matter to drop, as unduly provocative; Charles did, however, order James to stop coming to the committee for foreign affairs.[36] Instead the Commons called for the banishment of Papists from London and brought in a test bill, applying the principles of the 1673 Act to Parliament. The Act excluded the Catholic peers from the Lords, but the Upper House added a proviso excepting James which, to general surprise, was narrowly approved by the Commons. While his Catholic colleagues withdrew, York continued ostentatiously to attend the Lords for the remainder of the session.[37]

Discussion of the threat from Popery led naturally to the issue of the Popish successor. Calling for an address to remove James from his brother's presence, Sacheverell hinted at the need to exclude him from the succession as well, but it was not taken up: the House thought even the address was too provocative.[38] In the same debate, however, Williamson and Hyde hinted at restrictions on a future Catholic king, presumably on the lines of those proposed by the court in 1677. The issue was very much on men's minds, even if they preferred not to address it directly.[39] Proposals for 'limitations' were soon to be made by court spokesmen and by the king himself; Sacheverell again argued the need for exclusion and there was talk of either an exclusion bill or an 'association', like the one in which Elizabeth's subjects undertook to oppose Mary Queen of Scots becoming queen.[40]

No such bill was introduced, but there were two other possible threats to James's becoming king. First, Charles might be persuaded to divorce the queen. In many ways her life had become easier in recent years. Charles showed her a measure of outward politeness, Portsmouth behaved far more correctly towards her than Cleveland had and Nell Gwynn concentrated on keeping Charles happy and living at peace with everyone.[41] With revived public concern about the succession, however, talk of divorce revived and Williamson felt obliged to draw up a list of the advantages of the Portuguese marriage.[42] A more serious threat to the queen came when Oates and Bedloe accused her of complicity in the Plot. They clearly calculated that there was a market for such a story and that Charles would be glad of a pretext to be rid of her. The Commons voted an address asking him to send her away from his person. Some MPs argued that the address was tactless and misconceived and any who expected Charles to welcome it were to be grievously disappointed. The queen, he said, might have some 'disagreeable humours', but she was incapable of doing a wicked thing; after he had treated her so badly, it would be a 'horrible thing' to abandon her. The moves against her, indeed, reinforced his belief that Oates and Bedloe had been tampered with by the court's enemies. The Lords refused to concur with the address. Charles attended the debates and made his opinion clear, but his presence was probably unnecessary: only eight peers, led by Shaftesbury, supported the address.[43]

The threat to the queen was only suspended: the accusations had been made and could be revived. A very different threat to York's claim to the succession came from Monmouth. Before 1678 his political role had been exiguous. There had been a move in 1677 to have him made Lord Lieutenant of Ireland, but it had been taken for granted that a deputy (Conway) would do the real work. The plan had been foiled by York, who persuaded Charles to reappoint Ormond instead.[44] Relations between uncle and nephew worsened in 1678, when York noted that Monmouth's new commission as general described him simply as the king's son, the word 'natural' having been struck out. At York's insistence, the word was restored, but he had then to endure the indignity of Monmouth's being appointed to command the expeditionary force to Flanders, while he stayed at home.[45] Soon after, Monmouth became identified with the Scottish peers who were lobbying for Lauderdale's removal and began to affect popularity, talking of the need to disband the army.[46] He was not yet, however, identified with the English 'patriots': indeed, it was his regiment that contained the Catholic officers about whom MPs expressed such concern. As pressure on York mounted, it became clear that there would be much popular support for Monmouth as an alternative successor. There was little such support in the Commons: an attempt by Cavendish to air his claims met with no response.[47]

Monmouth first signalled his challenge to York by supporting the test bill and by going out before the Lords voted on the proviso exempting York from its provisions. York complained that he spent too much time in the company of men like Shaftesbury, Wharton and Essex (since his recall from Ireland, an open critic of the court); he had also allowed his health to be drunk as 'Prince of Wales'. Monmouth's sidekick, Sir Thomas Armstrong, gave out that Charles would soon declare him his heir. The young duke's popularity deeply offended York, but also made Charles reluctant to reprimand him openly, although he insisted privately that he would never legitimate him. Although increasingly seen as the 'Protestant' alternative to York, he still had minimal support in Parliament and York's continued presence reduced his chances of extending his influence at court. A new House of Commons, or York's removal from court, might, however, transform his prospects.[48]

Danby's position, meanwhile, remained strong. Accusations that he had tried to cover up the Plot carried little conviction; more plausibly, he was blamed for Charles's decision to veto the militia bill.[49] With the political spotlight on York and the Plot, Danby avoided serious attack until December, when trouble came from an unexpected source. Ralph Montagu was ambitious and unscrupulous, even by Restoration standards. After his first stint as ambassador in Paris, he had persuaded Louis to press for his admission to the Order of the Garter, an honour which Charles thought neither his age nor his services merited.[50] Having failed to secure the post of secretary of state, which he thought he richly deserved, he returned to Paris in 1677. He negotiated with an independence that was perhaps unbecoming in an ambassador, but that was not the reason why he was recalled in the summer of 1678. Cleveland had at last persuaded her (and Charles's) wayward daughter, Lady Sussex, to join her at Paris, only for the young woman to succumb to Montagu's charms. Cleveland saw the seduction of the daughter as revenge for his having been rejected by the mother; to make matters worse, Montagu threatened to tell Charles of her own indiscretions with the Chevalier de Châtillon. In a long letter to Charles, she excused this affair by remarking that affairs of the heart can never be governed by reason and that, as her own long liaison with Charles was over, he had no cause to complain. She then launched into a series of allegations against the ambassador: he had called Charles a dull governable fool, who always chose a greater beast than himself to govern him; he had planned to use an astrologer to persuade Charles to dismiss Danby; he had told Louis that Cleveland wished to marry her daughter to the dauphin.[51]

Charles's immediate response was a firm letter to Lady Sussex to move from the convent where she was staying (which had 'no good reputation') to the much more austere Port Royal. When she refused to go, Charles recalled Montagu in disgrace.[52] With her lover gone, the young woman reluctantly obeyed her father, but Montagu was less submissive. Stripped of his post of master of the horse to the queen, he burned for revenge. Shortly before Parliament met in October, he told Barrillon that he could ruin Danby, using his letter of 25 March about pressing Louis to give money in return for proroguing Parliament. Well aware that the ambassador was paying money to opponents of the court, Montagu asked for money to pay out in bribes – and to compensate himself for his loss of office. The French embraced the plan in principle, but (like the opposition leaders) saw disbanding the army as the first priority. To gain the protection of Parliamentary privilege, Montagu secured a seat at Northampton (defeating Temple) and waited for the ideal moment to strike. In the end, his hand was forced, when the council issued a warrant to seize his papers, on the pretext that he had had unauthorized dealings with the papal nuncio in Paris. Montagu took good care that the crucial letters should not be found and placed them before a shocked House of Commons on 19 December.[53]

At a stroke, Danby's political credit was destroyed: the self-styled enemy of France was revealed pleading for French subsidies. Several remarked on the parallel with Coleman's letters. As Charles had countersigned them, his credit was also badly damaged, but he at least was above open criticism.[54]

Danby tried to fight back. Bertie produced two letters from Montagu alluding to Russell's dealings with Ruvigny, but Russell categorically denied the charges, Montagu supported him and the House apparently believed them. (The Commons had shown a similar lack of curiosity when Coleman had talked of paying bribes to MPs on Barrillon's behalf.)[55] Charles vigorously supported the treasurer, dismissing from office MPs who voted against him, including Solicitor-General Winnington and Sir Stephen Fox, the man upon whom the crown's financial credit most depended. Charles could not prevent the Commons from impeaching Danby, but his firmness encouraged the Lords to reject the Commons' request to commit him to prison; he was not even required to withdraw from the House. The wiser heads in the Commons were not inclined to press the matter, especially as the Houses were already deadlocked on the disbanding bill. Charles, however, had had enough. He would not allow Danby to suffer Strafford's fate. On 30 December he prorogued Parliament.[56]

It had not been a successful session. The one supply bill, to raise about £200,000 to disband the army, had not passed. The Commons, distrusting Danby, insisted that the money should be paid, not into the exchequer but into the chamber of London. The Lords claimed that to have another authority handling his revenue would infringe the king's prerogative; the Commons responded that the Lords could not amend money bills, adding tetchily that the money previously voted for disbandment had not been used for that purpose. It is uncertain whether this dispute could have been resolved: opinions differed. Charles, however, found the political arguments for ending the session more compelling than the financial arguments for keeping it going. There were rumours that York or the queen would be impeached, but most of all Charles feared a popular revolt, similar to the one which had brought Strafford to the block. Danby had scraped together much of the money needed for disbandment and Charles was prepared to cut his other expenditure to the bone to make more money available. He assured the lord mayor and aldermen that he would preserve the peace and the Protestant religion and pay off the army. He told Barrillon, too, that he was disbanding the army and pleaded again for financial aid. Meanwhile, a committee of the council continued ostentatiously to investigate the Plot. In general, the year ended, for Charles, on a sombre note. The past, in the shape of James's conversion and his own duplicitous dealings with France, was coming back to haunt him. His ambitions for the new year were limited – peace and a measure of prosperity – but the prospect of his achieving them seemed bleak.[57]

Charles prorogued Parliament in something approaching panic: neither he nor his advisers seemed to have any idea what to do next. All were afraid.

Danby and Williamson had been discredited. Lauderdale was old and tired and his administration was so widely criticized that he had become a political liability. Portsmouth was reviled as a 'French whore'; a crowd at the Temple called York a 'Popish dog'.[58] Williamson was replaced as secretary by Sunderland, a man of few political principles but formidable force of personality. A compulsive gambler for whom office was a financial necessity, he brought his gambler's recklessness into political life, following his hunches to the bitter end. Coventry remained as the other secretary: though his health was poor, Charles would not dismiss him and he was determined to quit only when he chose to do so. Politically, at least, he was an asset: Danby's letters made it clear that Coventry had, as a matter of policy, not been told of the negotiations with France. Charles did offer the secretaryship to Temple, but he would not accept it: the court was full of faction and confusion and he had no wish to clamber aboard a sinking ship.[59]

Amid all the uncertainty, all agreed that something had to be done to calm the people's fears. An enterprising manufacturer sold 3,000 daggers bearing the legend 'Remember Justice Godfrey': ladies carried them for protection against Popish assassins. Charles was still believed to be sceptical about the Plot, but few others were – or at least dared to express scepticism, for fear of being labelled favourers of Popery.[60] Although Southwell wrote that Charles would not bend his conscience in matters of blood, he allowed himself to be persuaded by his judges and councillors that those accused by Oates and Bedloe had had a fair trial, although the latter's performance in court had been lamentable and witnesses brought by the accused cast serious doubts on the former's evidence.[61] If Charles placed little trust in such rogues and adventurers, he was more inclined to believe those with some pretensions to gentility, such as Dugdale and Turberville. After examining a Catholic peer, Lord Aston, Charles declared that he was now convinced that there had been a Plot and would allow the executions to go ahead. How far this apparent change of heart was a matter of bowing to political necessity, we shall never know. He continued to distrust Oates and Bedloe and had them confined to the court, to prevent them from conspiring with political malcontents.[62]

In seeking to calm anxieties, Charles was constrained by the law. The judges told him firmly that the five Catholic peers impeached by the Commons could be tried only in Parliament: Charles had hoped to have them tried quickly in the common law courts.[63] Fear of the army continued unabated. Charles and his ministers were genuinely concerned that Louis might attack England, but their concern was not shared by the Commons: even MPs who were basically friendly to the court opposed any suggestion that the new regiments should be kept on foot any longer.[64] After the prorogation, Charles began to bring his regiments home from Flanders and disband them. He borrowed wherever he could – his frugal brother advanced £100,000 of his own money – but goldsmith bankers and customs farmers were reluctant to lend to a regime in such obvious disarray, even though Holles and other 'patriots', impatient to see the army disbanded, urged them to do so. A dank miasma of suspicion hung over the whole process. Some claimed that the 'honestest' regiments were disbanded first; when the demobilization was held up by lack of money, there were claims that Charles could easily have borrowed enough if he had wanted to. Such suspicions were not entirely unfounded: York was very conscious that the disbandment would leave Charles exposed to invasion and revolt.[65]

After the autumn session, York and Danby knew that they were fighting for their political lives. Each sought to save himself at the other's expense and put out feelers to Holles and the Presbyterians. Shaftesbury, well aware that it would be easier to pick them off one at a time, assured each of them that he would be left alone if only he withdrew his support for the other. (Both, however, were alarmed by Shaftesbury's new-found intimacy with Monmouth.)[66] The most immediate issue was the fate of the Cavalier Parliament. The opposition had long pressed for its dissolution, on the grounds that it contained too many placemen and pensioners; the Presbyterians regarded it as excessively Anglican. Danby naturally opposed the destruction of his carefully constructed 'court party', but York's attitude was ambivalent. He appreciated the members' loyalty, but disliked their rabid anti-Catholicism and hoped that a House containing more Dissenters would prove more tolerant of religious minorities. Even Danby, however, offered the Presbyterians the prospect of a new Parliament.[67]

In mid-January Charles decided to issue a proclamation to extend the prorogation, but then had second thoughts. A petition was circulating in London, urging him to reassemble Parliament. The committee for foreign affairs persuaded him to consult the council. When it assembled Charles told the councillors that he would not ask their advice, as they were more afraid of Parliament than of him, so he had decided of his own volition to dissolve and to call a general election.[68] James claimed that the new Parliament would be better than the old; Charles seemed less sanguine. He refused to endorse any candidates, no doubt well aware that such endorsements could prove counter-productive: he told Barrillon that he would rather depend on Louis than on his people. He attended prayers every morning and evening – presumably as a public relations exercise, rather than with a view to seeking divine guidance.[69] York, whose appreciation of public relations was minimal, played a more active electoral role, but achieved little. Coventry remarked that he did not know if it would be possible to make MPs courtiers when Parliament met, but that he was sure that few courtiers would be elected: there was clearly deep public resentment of the corruption and mismanagement of recent years and Charles's indifference made many suspect that the session would not last long.[70]

The outcry against 'corruption' suggested that the new House of Commons was likely to fall as heavily on Danby as on York. Charles, however, remained convinced that his brother's conversion was the cause of most of his problems and commissioned two bishops to tackle James about his religion. James had long been on friendly terms with Morley, the veteran Bishop of Winchester, and had supported William Sancroft's elevation to Canterbury after Sheldon's death: at the very least, York preferred the diffident Sancroft to the ebullient Compton.[71] The two bishops found York as stubborn as ever: his conscience was clear, he said, and there was nothing to discuss.[72] Danby, happy to parade his Protestantism at York's expense, told the king that he had no choice but to send his brother away: Charles agreed. For once, York's tactic of refusing to go unless specifically commanded failed, but before leaving for Brussels he gained an important victory. At a full meeting of the privy council, Charles dashed the hopes of Monmouth's supporters by solemnly declaring that he had never been married to any woman but the queen.[73]

When James left, he shed many tears, but his brother shed none: he was preoccupied with the prospect of the first new House of Commons for eighteen years. His opening speech was conciliatory: he had ordered the prosecution of those accused of complicity in the Plot, sent his brother away and disbanded as much of the army as he had money for. He asked for money to complete the process; he could, he added, have asked for an addition to his thoroughly inadequate ordinary revenue, but he was 'contented to struggle with that difficulty a little longer'.[74] If the speech generated any goodwill, it was soon dissipated. The Commons again elected Seymour as their Speaker and presented him to the king for his approval, which was usually a formality. In the previous session Seymour had been nominated by privy councillors and Charles had seemed willing that he should continue.[75] To general amazement, Charles rejected him. The Commons, fearing that he might try to tell them who to choose, refused to nominate anyone else. The deadlock lasted for more than a week. A compromise candidate was eventually found, but the session had got off to the worst possible start.

The dispute provoked widespread speculation. Some thought that the court's spokesmen had been slow to name the 'official' candidate. Others noted that Seymour (never renowned for his modesty) had failed to make the usual humble professions of unworthiness to hold such a great office, culminating in a plea to be relieved of the burden, which would have allowed the king to take him at his word. Most, however, blamed Danby, who loathed Seymour and had denounced his conduct.[76] His loathing was wholeheartedly reciprocated, so it was natural that Danby did not want Seymour in such a powerful position for what was likely to be a difficult session, but the furore over the speakership increased both the House's distrust and the animus against him. The day after the new Speaker was admitted, Danby resigned his office; Charles appointed five commissioners of the treasury, including the diligent and respected Essex and Sir Stephen Fox. He also granted Danby a full pardon and promised him a marquisate and a pension of £5,000 a year, neither of which he received in Charles's lifetime. Finch refused to affix the Great Seal to the pardon, so the Earl of Bath did so by the king's express command. Charles told the Commons defiantly that if there was any defect in it he would remedy it ten times over. He had granted similar pardons to other former ministers, including Buckingham and Shaftesbury. He concluded by assuring them that claims that Danby had covered up the Plot were untrue and exhorting them to get on with public business.[77]

Danby resigned because the election of the Speaker showed that he no longer controlled the Commons, but any hope that MPs would be satisfied by his resignation proved illusory. 'All the mismanagements and evil maxims since the Restoration are ripped up and exposed,' wrote Southwell, who added that Danby was now reaping the bitter harvest of his own support for Clarendon's impeachment. Distrust and resentment of 'secret counsels' bred a general agreement on the need for 'reformation', although there was disagreement as to how far it should go.[78] Danby's pardon was interpreted as proof of his guilt. Many thought that he deserved a greater punishment than mere loss of office, but that would require a legal process, which would be blocked by the pardon. They argued, therefore, that the pardon was invalid: the king, they claimed, could pardon offences against himself but not against the public. Besides, impeachment proceedings had been started in December and some claimed that if those impeached by the Commons could be pardoned, it would never be possible to bring wrongdoers to justice. Some hinted at a concept of treason as an offence not against the king (as the law decreed) but against the kingdom, or the people. Charles's speech was brushed aside as not representing his true views and the House resolved, without a dissentient voice, to ask the Lords to commit Danby to custody.[79]

The debates on the nature of treason raised echoes of those of Strafford's attainder. Danby stressed to Charles how dangerous it would be to sacrifice a servant accused only of obeying his master: such a 'downright desertion' had been the prime cause of his father's ruin.[80] Charles, however, was far from certain that he could defend him. Some at court argued that as long as Danby remained near the king, he would be seen as directing the government. When the Lords resolved to arrest the former treasurer, Charles ordered him to flee. The Commons responded with an attainder bill; the Lords effectively transformed it into a bill of banishment, by making the punishment effective only if Danby was found in England after 1 May. For two weeks the Houses were deadlocked. Then, on 15 April, the Lords resolved, by three votes, to accept the Commons' version of the bill. The next day, Danby surrendered himself, at Charles's command, and was sent to the Tower.[81]

Charles faced what seemed an impossible dilemma. On one hand, Danby and York insisted that to sacrifice Danby would lead to the ruin of the monarchy; besides, Charles would not relish Danby's making public his dealings with France.[82] On the other hand, some of his advisers claimed that if the Commons were allowed to give vent to their anger by prosecuting Danby and the five Catholic lords, they would calm down and vote money. Sunderland and Portsmouth argued that conciliation was the only viable option: Sunderland, indeed, told Blood to assure his friends that Charles would fall in with Parliament. Erstwhile oppositionists made their peace: Cavendish kissed the king's hand; Essex became first commissioner of the treasury. Charles put out feelers to Shaftesbury and Halifax, but they suspected that he was also seeing Danby secretly and would not trust him.[83] Charles also sought advice from Temple. The former ambassador had always told the king that he should 'fall into the vein of his people'. As the Commons talked so much of 'evil counsel', Charles should reconstruct his privy council, bringing in men in whom MPs could trust. Apart from Temple, Charles discussed the idea only with Finch, Sunderland and Essex. Most of the proposed names elicited swift agreement, but Charles regarded Halifax as inordinately ambitious. Temple thought Shaftesbury was irreconcilable, but Charles thought that he was 'angry' only because he was out of office: he could not accept that a foundation of principle underlay the little earl's opposition. At last, on 21 April, the new privy council was unveiled, with Shaftesbury as lord president. Finch announced that it would direct all domestic and foreign affairs and hoped that its creation would dissipate suspicions. Portsmouth was fearful at Charles's putting himself into the hands of his enemies, but others remarked that, just as Danby (and Strafford) had at one stage been critics of the court, so others could now be won over. Charles, however, had little faith in his new councillors. 'God's fish,' he told Lord Bruce, 'they have put a set of men about me, but they shall know nothing.'[84]

In 1641 Charles I had refused to make the 'bridge' appointments that might have rebuilt trust between the Commons and himself. Charles II's new council seemed at first sight to be such a 'bridge', but bridges need foundations and Charles had no intention of allowing the council to control decision-making. Shaftesbury, however, saw the presidency as offering a chance to direct the government, while his association with Monmouth guaranteed him extensive popular support. Their supporters were confident that 'Whitehall must render in six months,' but they reckoned without Charles's evasiveness and cunning. The councillors became frustrated: they exercised little real power, but the very fact that they had accepted office reduced their credit in the Commons. The former hammer of the court, Henry Powle, was told to his face that he would have spoken differently had he not been a councillor.[85] In short, the new council proved a red herring, to distract and divide the court's enemies. It bought a little time and served as a gesture of moderation and conciliation, but little more. The muted enthusiasm with which it was greeted in London was well deserved.[86]

When Danby gave himself up, the attainder bill was quietly laid to rest and the Commons reverted to their impeachment. The former treasurer defended himself with skill and determination; his enemies responded by attempting to deter potential supporters from voting for an acquittal. They bragged of turning 'Danbyists' out of office; Charles Bertie was rigorously quizzed about the secret service money; Sacheverell declared that any lawyer who acted for Danby was an enemy to the privileges of the Commons.[87] The Lords were not to be intimidated. They rejected the Commons' assertion that the pardon was illegal – the Commons (unlike the Lords) were not a court of law – and referred the matter to the judges. The Commons responded that to uphold the pardon's validity would be to betray the liberties of the commons of England.[88] Still more contentious was the issue of whether the bishops could take part in the trial. The divisions on the attainder bill had suggested that their votes would hold the balance.[89] Danby's support for the Church and the bishops' support for the prerogative suggested that most would take his side. Their conduct had already led to wild allegations against them: even Compton was accused of favouring Popery.[90] The Commons' arguments cut little ice with the Lords: the precedents were solidly on the bishops' side. To the argument that men of God should not soil their hands with blood (by pronouncing a death sentence) the Lords responded by ruling that the bishops should go out between verdict and sentence. Some of the bishops were prepared to withdraw, but the House – and the king – were adamant that the Lords' privileges should be upheld to the full.[91]

The Lords did not confine themselves to defending their privileges. They accused the Commons of failing to follow up the Plot and argued that the trial of the five lords should precede that of Danby. As Essex remarked, even if Danby were found guilty on all counts, his crimes would not match those of killing the king and changing the government. Sacheverell and others, however, claimed that the pardon was far more important: if it were allowed to stand, the Commons would never be able to call great men to account. MPs also calculated that Charles would not dare to prorogue Parliament while the five lords remained untried.[92] The deadlock suited

Charles well enough: he had no wish for either trial to proceed and the Commons' conduct suggested that they did not believe that the threat from the Papists was as great as they made out. Despite the occasional talk of starting proceedings against them, Danby and the five lords remained comfortably lodged in the Tower.[93]

While the wrangling about Danby went on, other business was not wholly neglected. The fear of Popery gave renewed vigour to projects of comprehension or toleration, to unite Protestants against the common enemy. The Lords passed a bill to distinguish between Catholic and Protestant recusants: Quakers, in particular, were often prosecuted for absence from church. Arguments that toleration would encourage Popery won little support, but the bill proceeded slowly and had not completed all its stages in the Commons when the session ended.[94] When the Commons passed a bill to banish Papists from London, the bishops persuaded the Lords to add a clause that it should extend to all who refused the oaths and test; the amendment was carried by just one vote.[95] Charles showed little enthusiasm for any changes in the law. He withdrew an order to the bishops to tender the oaths to Quakers, but made it clear that he regarded nonconformists (especially their preachers) as subversive. His brother, who not long before had advocated indulgence, now baldly equated Presbyterianism with republicanism.[96]

Far more worrying, from the king's point of view, was the Commons' continued interest in the army. With most of the new regiments disbanded, MPs turned their attention to the officer corps – and to the navy, hitherto regarded with far less hostility. Shaftesbury talked of 'Papists', 'creatures' of the Duke of York, in garrisons and on the fleet. Besides the threat which such men allegedly posed to religion and liberty, others wanted their jobs. This was clearly the motive behind moves to oust Pepys and others from the admiralty, on the pretext that they had been implicated in the Plot: calls for 'reformation' were seldom wholly disinterested. The new privy council offered a platform to many of those most avid for office. They called for a purge of JPs, to ensure that only 'good Protestants' should be magistrates. Charles did not rebut such demands directly, but found pretexts to retain particular JPs, by saying they served good beef or kept fine foxhounds. The attempted purge resulted in few changes.[97]

From his vantage point in Brussels, York found his brother's conduct far from reassuring. The 'republicans', he warned, would not be satisfied until they had stripped the king of his powers. Charles's seemingly compliant response to their calls for changes of office-holders seemed to York wildly irresponsible; conciliation could work only when dealing with people who were prepared to be conciliated. Nevertheless, the challenge which York most feared took a while to materialize. Not until 27 April did the Commons resolve that his religion had encouraged the Plot and that they should take steps to secure themselves. There was talk of the need to put military and civil offices in safe hands, of a right of resistance and of an act of association, but MPs were clearly feeling their way: while stressing the dangers of a Popish successor, they stopped short of an explicit proposal for his exclusion from the throne.[98] Their reticence owed much to fears that such a proposal might lead to a prorogation. On 30 April, when they were summoned to the Lords, many feared the worst. They were pleasantly surprised when Finch offered a wide range of limitations on a future Catholic king: he was to fill major offices in Church and state only in conjunction with Parliament. Finch concluded that Charles would willingly consider any other proposals for their future security, short of depriving James of the succession.[99]

Some found these proposals attractive because they would limit the prerogative far more stringently than exclusion would have done; others opposed them, claiming that their aim was to remove the risk of Popish tyranny, not to transform the monarchy.[100] On 11 May the Commons resolved that exclusion alone could secure the people against the evils which they had such good reason to fear. Against those who argued that it would be illegal or unjust, it was answered (in Burnet's words) that 'government was appointed for those that were to be governed ... therefore all things relating to it were to be measured by the public interest and the safety of the people'.[101] Not all critics of the court wished to press the issue of exclusion. Sir Francis Winnington, embittered by the loss of his post of solicitor-general, regarded the proceedings against Danby and the five lords as the first priority. Both Sir Thomas Littleton and Sir William Coventry opposed the bill, but such elder statesmen found it hard to restrain the younger MPs. Some intimated that, whatever his outward attitude, the king would not be averse to being forced to agree to exclusion. There were also hints that he might divorce the queen or legitimate Monmouth, and even a proposal that James should be impeached. None of these expedients attracted much overt support, but the House resolved to remove from the bill the phrase 'or ever had been a Papist', which would have incapacitated Monmouth. Although the bill met with more opposition than expected, the arguments of its opponents counted for little against weight of numbers and its supporters clamoured for 'the bill, the bill'. On 21 May it passed its second reading and was committed, but the committee (of the whole House) had not begun its work when the session ended.[102]

By now, with the House deadlocked on the issue of the trials, many did not expect the session to last much longer. Informed observers (not least the king) did not think that the Lords, irritated by the Commons' out-spokenness and impatience, would pass the exclusion bill, provided he held firm.[103] The City was restive. The common council promoted an address, which the lord mayor refused to accept, thanking the Commons for their care for the suppression of Popery and promising to stand by them with their lives and fortunes. Danby was quick to warn Charles of the dangerous implications of the address – could the common council be planning to seize control of the City's government, as in 1641–2? Danby thought Shaftesbury was behind it, but Buckingham too had been busy in the City, having gone to ground on hearing that Danby planned to bring a charge of sodomy against him.[104] Presented with an address to call out the militia in the London area, Charles replied in general terms that he would take all possible care to prevent disturbances. He had little to gain from prolonging the session: the bill raising supply to disband the army had already passed. Danby warned of dire consequences if he did not prorogue. York urged him to rely on his own resources and his 'old friends': firmness and thrift would carry him through, especially as Scotland and Ireland were still loyal. The strategy of conciliation advocated by Essex, Halifax and Sunderland had clearly failed: Shaftesbury and Monmouth were driving further and faster than they wished to go. Fear of revolt finally made up Charles's mind: without consulting his new privy council, he prorogued Parliament on 27 May.[105]

The session had not been an unmitigated failure. Charles had been granted supply, albeit much less than he needed: the Commons judged this a lesser evil than delaying the disbandment any longer. The grant was strictly appropriated, but a move to prevent its being paid into the exchequer was easily defeated.[106] The Commons showed only a limited interest in investigating misgovernment and looked only cursorily at the royal accounts, apart from those of the secret service money. On the other hand, pleas for a further supply for the fleet were rejected with something akin to contempt and the House's overall demeanour was suspicious and cantankerous. The one important piece of legislation did not please the king. The Habeas Corpus Act made it much more difficult for the government to circumvent the legel safeguards against imprisonment without trial.[107] In short, Charles had little cause for satisfaction. He was noted to be sullen and thoughtful, as if he was just coming to appreciate the scale of the problems facing him. This was a fight to the finish: 'he had to do with a strange sort of people, that could neither be managed nor frightened'. For the moment, he had to go with the stream: he ordered a full investigation into the Plot and the execution of all condemned priests.[108] In time, however, he would have his revenge.

After the prorogation, Charles was politically isolated. He was saddled with councillors whom he mostly disliked and distrusted: he had not consulted them about the prorogation and, against their advice, had urged the Lords not to back down on the matter of the trials.[109] He did receive other advice.

Danby urged him to issue a declaration comparing the Commons' conduct with that of the Parliament of 1641; York warned with monotonous regularity that if he did not stand firm the monarchy would be destroyed.[110] Charles paid little heed to them, and less to Shaftesbury and Monmouth, who warned that if he did not agree to exclusion and to the removal of all York's creatures from office there would be another civil war. Even so, he hesitated to dismiss Shaftesbury from his post and retained considerable affection for Monmouth. This, and his less than cordial relations with York, encouraged many to believe that he would sacrifice his brother and legitimate his son. Those in the greatest credit, however, were Sunderland and Portsmouth, who argued that concessions were needed to head off a revolt, but that these should stop short of outright capitulation. Their strategy was supported by Essex and Halifax. Both were more moderate by nature than the abrasive Shaftesbury. Essex had a strong sense of loyalty towards the crown – his father had been shot by the New Model in 1648 – while Halifax judged that his best chance of high office lay in working with the king. All the advice that Charles received converged on one point: the imminent danger of rebellion. Of the proposed methods of guarding against it, appeasement appealed more to his cautious temperament than either capitulation or outright defiance, both of which seemed likely to provoke, or encourage, disorder.[111]

While Charles received diverging counsels, the court's opponents were also disunited. Some had weakened their oppositionist credentials by accepting seats on the new privy council. Some old Presbyterians, like Powle, Holles and Littleton, preferred limitations to exclusion, as they wished to curb the monarchy; they showed far less animus than Shaftesbury towards York and the Catholics. Some had been repelled by the Commons' radicalism and refusal to tolerate divergent views; others had become increasingly convinced that desperate ills required desperate remedies. Buckingham now fully committed himself (insofar as that was possible) to a popular role. He spent his days in taverns and coffee-houses and told Barrillon that the party of the people, which he led, was stronger than those of Monmouth or York. He denounced Lord Chief Justice Scroggs in open court as a favourer of Popery and even aired pretensions to royal blood, claiming that his mother was descended from Edward IV's sister.[112]

Faced with so many difficulties, Charles became pensive and moody. Danby complained that he had no idea what Charles was up to; it seems probable that Charles had no idea either. He found relaxation in fishing and affected an indifference to matters political which doubtless masked a deep inner confusion. He accepted the argument of Sunderland, Portsmouth, Essex and Halifax that if he allowed York to return there would be serious disorder and brushed aside James's claim that his return woud dishearten his enemies. James complained that he did not treat him like a brother or a friend, but Charles felt that James's crudely confrontational approach could do no good at this juncture.[113] As so often, Charles sought escape from his predicament by an appeal to Louis. The Commons, he argued, were bent on seizing control of the government; once they did so, they would make war on France. He begged for a few million *livres*, to enable him to subsist without Parliament, but with little success. Barrillon was a subtle and devious negotiator and his access was impeded by the new council's order that ambassadors could see the king only with its permission. Louis still harboured a grudge at Charles's 'deserting' him in 1677–8; indeed, Barrillon remarked that Charles's record suggested that he was liable to renege on any agreement. The ambassador also worried that Charles might tackle him about Coleman's revelations of the bribes paid to MPs. Moreover, Louis felt humiliated by the terms of the peace which was at last completed at Nijmegen in September 1679. He soon began to 'interpret' them, with his usual mixture of cynicism, self-righteousness and brutality. He was therefore not unhappy to see England paralysed by internal dissension: indeed, in terms of value for money, it was better to pay modest sums to Montagu and the opposition than larger sums to the king. Moreover, it cost nothing to dangle before Charles the prospect of a subsidy large enough to dissuade him from coming to terms with Parliament. Not surprisingly, therefore, the negotiations (which at first involved only the king, then Sunderland and finally the up and coming Lawrence Hyde) were slow, complex and, for the time being, abortive.[114]

So long as there remained some hope of French aid, Charles sought to buy time, to defuse popular anxiety and to rebuild his finances, which would make him less dependent on Parliament and less susceptible to popular pressures. He quickly disbanded the remainder of the forces raised in 1677–8, using money borrowed on the personal credit of three of his financial officials, Duncombe, Kent and of course Fox. Essex, as first commissioner of the treasury, imposed rigorous constraints on expenditure and inaugurated yet another programme of retrenchment, cutting the court's food bills and suspending the payment of pensions. This meant that fewer people came to court, which reduced expenditure further; besides, Charles felt no great need for company. Soon, the commissioners assured him that he would have enough to subsist on for a while and even to pay most of the fleet.[115] The disbandment was briefly interrupted by a rising of extreme Presbyterians in Scotland. It soon became clear that the revolt was far less formidable than that of 1639 and it was suppressed by a force commanded by Monmouth. More ominous than the revolt itself was the reaction of some of his councillors. Some urged him to recall Parliament; some claimed that under the pacification signed with the Scots in 1640 troops could be sent from one country into the other only with the consent of both Parliaments; and some argued that under the recent disbanding Act it was illegal to raise new troops. Prominent Exclusionists – Russell, Cavendish, Grey of Wark – refused to accept commissions in the new regiments. Lauderdale's Scottish enemies blamed his misgovernment for provoking the rising; their English allies hoped that the Scots lords would be allowed to put it down, while Essex (who hated Monmouth) made great difficulties about providing him with money. When the forces raised to suppress the rising were disbanded, Essex helped to defeat a proposal that two hundred of the officers should be formed into a special guard for the king: it would, he claimed, reinforce fears of military rule.[116]

Such efforts to deny him soldiers increased Charles's sense of vulnerability. Meanwhile, the lapsing of the Licensing Act made it far harder to control the most potent means of moulding public opinion.[117] In these circumstances, Charles felt impelled to press on with the Plot trials. So far, all had ended in convictions. The next in line was the queen's physician, Sir George Wakeman. Charles feared that the witnesses might take the chance to make allegations against the queen, which could lead to her prosecution or impeachment. As it would be politically inadvisable to discredit the witnesses completely, when their testimony would be needed against the five lords, Charles was concerned that Wakeman's trial should be kept within safe limits. The witnesses were twice summoned before the council and asked what they had to say about the queen. Relieved that their testimony was innocuous, Charles allowed the trial to go ahead. After Oates had given his evidence, Wakeman asked him why, the previous September, he had declared that he had nothing to say against him and failed even to recognize him. Scroggs treated Oates and Bedloe with a rigour absent from earlier trials. The witnesses wavered and the jury found Wakeman and three other defendants not guilty of treason.[118]

The verdict caused a sensation. The Mayor of Hastings gave an interesting twist to the principles of common law, by declaring that if Wakeman had been innocent he would not have been brought to trial. Scroggs was accused of being a Papist and of receiving bribes from the Portuguese ambassador. For many, the verdicts nourished growing doubts about the Plot. Halifax might argue that popular belief in it was such that the government had to act as if it were true; others were less cynical and the acquittals were welcomed at court.[119] Charles, too, was heartened by them. The prorogation had been far from welcome in London and few bonfires were lit to celebrate his accession day, but he now believed that the Plot was 'less credited' and his financial position was improving. Sunderland, Halifax, Essex and Temple advised him to dissolve Parliament: the public mood was changing and a new House would be better than the old one. Charles summoned a select group of councillors to Windsor to discuss the matter, but he, Halifax and Sunderland all failed to sound them out beforehand. Taken by surprise, most (including Finch, Arlington and the Marquis of Worcester) declared against a dissolution. Four days later, Charles peremptorily told the full council of his intention to dissolve. Shaftesbury protested that he had promised to do nothing without the council's advice. Charles replied that he would consult it on other matters, but this was one which lay wholly within the royal prerogative.[120]

The dissolution gave rise to talk of secret counsels, of Danby's influence and of York's likely return; Charles, however, insisted that his brother should remain where he was.[121] Charles expressed optimism about the forthcoming elections; others disagreed and, as so often, the pessimists were proved right.[122] Electors continued to express deep suspicion of the court and hostility to Popery, but there were also much sharper divisions between Church and Dissent than had been apparent in the spring. In 1664 Convocation had given up its right to tax the clergy. Parliament now taxed laity and clergy alike; in return the clergy were allowed to vote in Parliamentary elections. Many threw themselves enthusiastically into the electoral process, thus heightening existing tensions between Church and Dissent: their distinctive dress made their activities especially conspicuous. The bishops' conduct in the Lords, and especially the controversy about Danby's trial, had led to allegations that they were favourers of Popery, but such allegations were by no means confined to the bishops. As one of Lord Yarmouth's correspondents wrote from Norfolk: 'The fanatics since the discovery of the late Popish Plot have made a great advantage by aspersing those who are faithful to the king and Church as being Popishly affected; and when the rabble have once received such an opinion of them, no arguments can prevail to make them believe the contrary.' Talk of conflict between 'the loyal' and 'the disaffected', or between 'the gentry' and 'the rabble', made it clear that English society was now more divided than at any time since the early 1660s.[123]

The beleaguered Churchmen received little support from the king, who judged that to interpose could prove counter-productive. The most he would do was assure individuals that he would stand by his 'old friends'. Without effective leadership, the growing loyalist movement made little impression in elections: even Windsor returned MPs hostile to the court.[124] Nevertheless, the signs of a conservative backlash were encouraging and Charles was soon to receive unexpected evidence that his position was less vulnerable than he had feared. In late August he fell ill of a fever and a few days later he had a severe fit, perhaps a stroke. News of his illness caused great concern: if he died, who would succeed him? Buckingham rushed to court, professing great anxiety for the king's health; Charles replied icily that the duke consorted with people who would gladly cut their king's throat. With Monmouth and Buckingham poised to make their bid for power, the king's fit filled his ministers with panic. Sunderland sent to York to come over: James later claimed that Charles had ordered him to do so; other evidence suggests that the secretary consulted Essex, Halifax, Hyde, Feversham and Portsmouth – all those with most to lose if the court's enemies seized power.[125]

The confusion surrounding York's recall was understandable and perhaps deliberate: Shaftesbury and Monmouth vowed vengeance on whoever was responsible. James found Charles much better, which some ascribed to his having suspended his distrust of physicians. A regime of bleedings and purges had left him weak – he could only crawl around his room – but he seemed cheerful. James apologized profusely for coming without an explicit order, but Charles reassured him and briefed him on recent developments. Others were more guarded in their welcome. Sunderland and his colleagues stressed their part in his return, but claimed that only their careful preparations in the City and among the military had prevented disorder. Charles now had to prepare to meet the new Parliament, so (they insinuated, politely) his continued presence would be something of an embarrassment. James saw things differently: the general revolt which had been predicted if he returned to England had failed to materialize. Instead, many important figures (including the lord mayor and several aldermen) came to kiss his hand. He felt confident and, with the unsurprising exception of Armstrong, was gracious to all.[126]

The warmth of his reception meant that, while James could not persuade his brother to let him stay, he was able to make two important stipulations. He was now to go to Scotland, rather than Flanders, and Monmouth was to be sent away too. The younger duke surrendered his commissions to his father, who promised not to give the place of general to anyone else and allowed him to keep his salary as master of the horse. Charles also gave him a 'very kind' letter and allegedly told him that he would rather York had stayed, so that Monmouth could have stayed too, but that if York had remained in England he would have been impeached. However, when Monmouth declared that he would not be safe in a Catholic country, Charles laughed.[127] Monmouth's supporters played on Charles's fears of an imminent revolt in an effort to persuade him to change his mind. The City was in a state of turmoil: one writer thought it 'rotten ripe for rebellion'. Sir Thomas Player denounced claims in print that the recorder had been sent to compliment York and that the lord mayor would have declared James king had his brother died. The lord mayor denied this in a 'smooth' speech and agreed to double the nightly guard of trained bands. Armstrong consulted busily with Jenks and other 'fanatics', while Monmouth paraded and postured as the Protestant alternative to York, ostentatiously attending church.[128]

Southwell, however, returned to town and found the mood calmer than in many of the provincial towns, then in the grip of election fever. Power remained firmly in the hands of the lord mayor, aldermen and lieutenancy, most of whom were ready to make at least a show of deference towards York. Player tried to rouse the common council with a 'pathetical' speech against Popery, but to no avail. More significantly, in the annual election of sheriffs the Church of England men triumphed over 'the fanatics', although their joy was tempered when Sir Robert Clayton was elected lord mayor a few days later.[129]

Charles, however, remained convinced that rebellion was imminent and that he could not delay meeting Parliament for long; the most he would risk was a short prorogation, to give Barrillon time to conclude a subsidy treaty.[130] Everywhere Charles looked, there was cause for anxiety. Since Wakeman's trial Shaftesbury had ranted about the failure to prosecute the Plot: he seemed bent on provoking Charles to dismiss him, so that he could pose as a martyr, but Charles refused to give him that satisfaction. Oates, stung by Oxford University's refusal to award him an honorary doctorate, declared in a sermon that the Presbyterians were the only sound members of the Church of England and claimed that Shaftesbury would impeach York on a charge of treason. The little earl, for his part, pressed the king to seek a new queen in Germany. Danby, Sunderland and Portsmouth were reported to be terrified of what a new Parliament might do and ready to do almost anything to prevent its meeting. Halifax, reviled and threatened by Shaftesbury, announced that he was ill and went off into the country. When the two rivals for the succession left London, each had a large retinue, but James's was of superior rank: it included eighteen peers, many of them associated with Danby. Monmouth, however, was the people's favourite: his coming was marked by bells and bonfires and those who refused to drink his health were denounced as Papists. It looked as if the battle lines were being drawn for another civil war.[131]

Tory and Whig

The twelve months following the departure of York and Monmouth saw a series of frustrations for the Exclusionists. The second general election of 1679 guaranteed them a comfortable majority in the Commons, but Charles repeatedly prorogued the new Parliament before it could meet. Without Parliament, the court's opponents could neither launch proceedings against evil counsellors nor exclude York from the succession. Frustration bred anger and recourse to more 'popular' tactics: they needed to show the strength of their support in the nation in order to persuade – or force – the king to convene Parliament. They made extensive use of the press, now much freer thanks to the expiry of the Licensing Act, but the key to their strategy was a campaign of petitions that Parliament should meet; some also demanded that it should continue to sit until all grievances had been redressed. The subjects' age-old right to petition their king had been curtailed by the Act of 1661 against 'tumultuous' petitioning. This limited to twenty the number of people who could present a petition and forbade all petitions which had not been authorized by three or more JPs, a county grand jury or the corporation of London; petitions which met these requirements were – or should have been – legal. Exclusionist petitioning showed a sophisticated organization, including the circulation of printed forms for signature, but also involved extensive intimidation. The names of those who refused to sign were carefully noted; counter-addresses were, to put it mildly, discouraged.[1]

The petitions which most worried Charles were those emanating from London: he always saw control of the capital as his highest priority.[2] Until now he had kept a firm grasp on the City's government, thanks to his support among the aldermen, but the common council elections of December 1679 saw significant gains for the court's opponents, which raised unpleasant echoes of 1641–2. The elections were followed by a vigorous attempt to promote a City petition; a grand jury found a true bill, on a charge of riot and sowing discord, against a man who obstructed the collection of signatures. The king ordered Lord Mayor Clayton not to summon the common council, which would almost certainly endorse the petition; Clayton argued that the meeting could not be delayed. The government responded by demanding that all the newly elected councillors should meet the qualifications for office set out in the Corporation Act. Some were removed – reports varied as to how many – and the common council resolved not to support the petition, but only by a narrow margin; had it not been for the votes of the aldermen, it would have been approved.[3] Charles's relations with the lord mayor and aldermen remained outwardly cordial. When James returned from Scotland both brothers dined with the lord mayor and enjoyed a long, convivial evening; it had, however, been necessary to make it clear that any invitation to the king would have to include the duke. Clayton judged it prudent to refuse to offer a similar entertainment to certain 'malcontent' lords.[4] Even so, the tide of public opinion in London was clearly running against the court. In two aldermanic elections, the existing aldermen had to invoke their right to overrule the voters' choice.[5] In June 1680 two outspoken opponents of the court, Bethel and Cornish, were elected sheriffs. The election was set aside, on the grounds that they had not taken communion in an Anglican church within the requisite period, and a fresh election was held. By that time they had remedied the omission and were re-elected, amid riotous and disorderly scenes.[6]

The meetings of common hall in which the shrieval elections took place were not unremittingly hostile to the court: the first rejected as inappropriate calls for a petition that Parliament should sit. Even so, the election of such sheriffs was a serious blow to the court, as they would choose the panels of jurors for London and Middlesex for the coming year. Already a Middlesex grand jury had presented the judges with a petition that Parliament should meet; the judges replied that it was not their function to carry letters and dismissed it.[7] But for this dismissal, the jury would also have presented York as a Popish recusant and Portsmouth as a common prostitute. When a new grand jury was empanelled, the promoters of the presentment refused to proceed, as they regarded the jurors as too favourable to the court, but once the new sheriffs were installed, it would only be a matter of time before such a presentment was approved. A grand jury presentment was not a conviction, but would have considerable political impact. The attempted presentment scared Portsmouth, who decided to sacrifice York in order to save herself. More insidiously, the election of such partisan sheriffs ensured that, within the judicial process, justice would be subordinated to politics.[8]

The two general elections of 1679 and the petitioning campaign divided both metropolitan and provincial society, a process accelerated by the rhetoric of anti-Popery and bitter attacks on the Church and its clergy. The opponents of exclusion were slower to organize, but they too found their voice, in ballads, in pamphlets (notably those of Roger L'Estrange) and in 'abhorrences' – counter-petitions, 'abhorring' attempts to deprive the king of his prerogative of calling and dismissing Parliaments. 'Petitioners' and 'abhorrers' were soon to be renamed 'Whigs' and 'Tories', the former term derived from hard-line Presbyterians of south-west Scotland, the latter from Catholic Irish bandits.[9] The growth of Toryism reflected both scepticism about the continuing danger from Popish plotters and a conviction that Whigs and Dissenters were using the Plot and anti-Popery in order to overturn the established order in Church and state.[10] Cautious and responsible men were alarmed by incidents like a march through Bristol on 30 January – the anniversary of Charles I's execution – led by stout men carrying a trumpet and an axe. Many began to see civil war as a much more immediate danger than the possible actions of a Popish successor – if he ever became king.[11]

This is not to suggest that all opponents of exclusion thought civil war likely. Sir Charles Lyttleton, the governor of Harwich, did not doubt the Whigs' malice, but thought it unlikely that those who blustered in coffeehouses would dare to take up arms or would win much support if they did. Barrillon, too, on reflection thought that most rich and influential men, especially in London, did not want civil war.[12] Nevertheless, fears of chaos were widespread and the growth of the 'loyal party' offered a firm basis of support, should Charles take a firm stand against exclusion. Many pressed him to remove 'the disaffected' from the commissions of the peace and the militia and to enforce the laws against Dissent.[13] Above all, emergent Tories urged the king to look to the towns. As one Kentish knight wrote to Secretary Coventry, the petition that Parliament should meet was:

a factious clandestine paper, surprising [*sic*] all the subscribers of several sects, whose proper nest is the corporations, the seminaries of all separation in church and state. And being by their freedom and privilege electors of burgesses to the Parliament, make a herd, perhaps, of several sorts of people to colour any popular and illegal action that shall arise.[14]

The Tories looked to Charles to give a strong lead against the Exclusionists, but was he prepared to do so? York, of course, had always advocated firmness, insisting to the point of tedium that any hint of weakness would encourage the 'republicans'. Charles, too, feared that exclusion would signal only the start of a comprehensive attack on the monarchy and found it difficult to stand out against his brother's single-mindedness. Charles's consistent rejection of exclusion was, however, founded squarely on self-interest. Even if one chooses not to accept Buckingham's claim that Charles hated his brother, his affection for him was clearly limited. Their temperaments were very different and Charles complained, with good reason, that York's conversion lay at the root of many of his own political problems; he especially resented James's refusal to make even a gesture of conformity to the Church and cannot have been pleased by his insistence on attending the Spanish ambassador's chapel on Good Friday 1680. (He went incognito but, needless to say, he was recognized.)[15] Charles paid heed to James's advice, not because he valued his brother's judgement, but because that advice was echoed by others more astute than himself. The most notable was Lawrence Hyde, brother of York's first duchess. In November 1679 he became first commissioner of the treasury, when Essex resigned. Hyde was never an easy colleague – he was inflexible, abrasive and over-sensitive – but he worked ferociously hard and seemed more likely than anyone to solve the king's financial problems.[16] York could also count on the support of one of the secretaries. Coventry, worn out by age and infirmity, resigned at last: significantly, he sought York's permission before doing so. He was succeeded by Sir Leoline Jenkins, a civil lawyer and diplomat, who proved a poor spokesman in Parliament but a conscientious administrator; he was to play a major part in re-establishing the crown's control over London.[17]

Firmness never came easily to Charles, however, and many around him argued that a policy of firmness was both unnecessary and dangerous. Courtiers, their livelihoods threatened by the retrenchments of Essex and Hyde, pressed the king to abandon his brother and to come to terms with Parliament: a few judicious concessions (they claimed) would untie the Commons' purse-strings and then all would be well. Others, like Temple, had always believed that Charles should fall in with his people's wishes; Essex resigned when he became convinced that Charles was uninterested in being reconciled with the Commons. Halifax, too, affected a principled commitment to moderation, but was so ambitious for power that, while distancing himself from the court's more unpopular measures, he would never sever himself from it. He might storm off to plant carrots and cucumbers on his Nottinghamshire estate, but sooner or later he would return. More formidable, because ever-present, was Sunderland, many of whose friends and kinsmen supported exclusion. Despite his role in James's recall, York came to distrust him, because of his clandestine contacts with the likes of Shaftesbury. The distrust was well merited: Sunderland became increasingly convinced not only that the Commons would give money in return for exclusion, but also that Charles would gladly agree to it, provided he could save his honour by making it appear that he had no option. This view was shared by Portsmouth: already Sunderland's political ally, she was convinced by the attempt to present her as a whore that only by openly dissociating herself from York could she save herself from ruin.[18]

Faced with divergent advice and convinced that his powers and even his life were in danger, Charles became more and more inscrutable.[19] If his words revealed nothing of his intentions, his actions offered no clearer guide. Some showed evidence of firmness. The economies of Essex and Hyde and the credit of Sir Stephen Fox, soon restored to the treasury, materially improved the king's financial position, although opinions differed as to whether he could survive for long without further Parliamentary supply.[20] In January 1680 he recalled James from Scotland; he told the council that he had derived no benefit from his absence. He was gratified by the expressions of popular joy at York's return and went out of his way to show affection towards him, making it clear that he would accept invitations only if James were included.[21] Above all, Charles began to exploit his control of the machinery of law. He dismissed JPs whom he regarded as unreliable – especially those who promoted petitions. The changes were less sweeping than some Tories would have liked, either because Charles's information was defective or because he was reluctant to remove men of great social prominence or Exclusionists who might still be reclaimed. Even so, the changes greatly encouraged 'the Cavalier or Church party'.[22] There were changes, too, among the judges, although (again) fewer than hardline Tories wanted. Since 1676 the judges' patents of appointment had been revocable at the king's pleasure. Four had been dismissed in April 1679, but their replacements were chosen primarily for their legal competence: partisan appointments would have been inappropriate at the time the king was reconstructing the privy council. In February 1680 Charles removed one of the four, Pemberton, together with Sir Robert Atkins: he was moving, gradually, towards a Tory judiciary.[23]

These changes, like the conduct of London sheriffs and Middlesex grand juries, represented a politicization of the legal system. Political battles were fought out in the law courts – especially in the absence of Parliament – and political considerations often determined which laws were enforced, and how. The Plot trials had focused public attention on the judges: Wakeman's acquittal provoked a flurry of accusations of bias and bribery. Two further issues ensured that they remained in the spotlight. After the Licensing Act lapsed, the growing volume of oppositionist pamphlets worried the government. Following the appearance of one which called on Londoners to rise against the threat of Popery, the judges ruled that seditious publications could be seized and those responsible for them committed to gaol and prosecuted. During the first half of 1680 several prominent publishers were charged with publishing 'libels', although the precise legal foundation of the accusations was not made clear. Such prosecutions were no substitute for pre-publication censorship. Their legality was questionable and securing convictions, never easy, soon became impossible: all the major oppositionist publishers operated in London and no jury chosen by Bethel and Cornish would find against them.[24]

It seems likely that some of the judges were reluctant to pronounce on an issue where the king's legal rights were so uncertain. Nevertheless, on 3 May 1680 they declared that he could prohibit all pamphlets, newspapers and other unlicensed works, as tending towards a breach of the peace.[25] The second issue on which the judges were drawn into the political arena was that of petitions. Provided that they complied with the terms of the 1661 Act, it was difficult to argue that these were illegal, however much Charles disliked them. Nevertheless, in December 1679 he issued a proclamation, forbidding the organizing of such petitions as 'contrary to the common and known laws of this land, for that it tends to promote discontents amongst the people and to raise sedition and rebellion'. Apart from a reference to 'a judgment of all the judges of England in the second year of King James', Charles took his stand (as in the orders against unlicensed printing) on the seditious intent which was presumed to underlie the petitions, rather than on the letter of the law. How far he had consulted the judges is uncertain, but it is probable that some were less than convinced that he was acting according to law.[26]

One final legal weapon at the king's disposal was the Corporation Act. In theory, it should have excluded Dissenters from municipal office; in practice, it was unenforceable. Since the mid-1660s Dissenters and former Parliamentarians had seeped back into corporations and the Act was increasingly ignored. This created two problems. First, whereas county magistrates were appointed by the king, most towns governed themselves by virtue of royal charters and their magistrates were members of an elected corporation; the king did not appoint them and could not dismiss him. Second, over four-fifths of MPs sat for boroughs. The general elections of 1679 provided dramatic evidence of the extent to which, since the purges following the passage of the Corporation Act, towns had emancipated themselves from the control of the neighbouring gentry. If Whiggism – or 'disaffection' – was ever to be crushed, the boroughs' autonomy would have to be broken. For the moment, Charles ordered the enforcement of the Corporation Act, but he also asked how far the Act extended – or could be made to extend. Angered by the city of York's less than cordial welcome for his brother, he asked the attorney-general if it would be possible to declare the charter forfeit and to bring the corporation 'under the power of the laws'.[27]

Such evidence of firmness pleased James and the growing Tory party, but Charles would not commit himself unequivocally or irrevocably to one course of action. He continued to hope that the Exclusionists could be deflected, or bought off with moderate concessions, and maintained contact with Shaftesbury and other Whig leaders.[28] He continued to allow investigation of the Plot, even though he was openly sceptical of some of the new witnesses, notably those from Ireland whom Shaftesbury took under his wing. (Charles also reminded the judges to proceed according to law and to inform him fully of the evidence before carrying out sentence of death.)[29] Despite his obvious dislike of nonconformists, now openly shared by his brother, he ordered the judges to proceed severely against Catholics, but to be gentle towards moderate, peaceable Dissenters. This did not end all persecution: 'moderation' and 'peaceableness' could be in the eye of the beholder.[30] Having noted the part played by Dissenters in the election of Bethel and Cornish, he had second thoughts. A brief flurry of persecution followed, but Jenkins was soon holding secret discussions with leading London Dissenters.[31]

Nowhere was Charles's ambivalence more apparent than in his treatment of Monmouth, who returned to England without permission and set himself up as the popular, Protestant alternative to York. Charles responded by depriving his son of his remaining offices, recalling York from Scotland and declaring unequivocally that he had never been married to Lucy Walter. The power of wishful thinking was such, however, that many continued to believe that Monmouth was legitimate or that Charles would make him his heir. These beliefs were encouraged by news, in July, that Charles had been seeing him secretly; York was noted to be gloomy and anxious. As the long-delayed meeting of Parliament approached, pressure mounted on Charles to send his brother away (for his own safety). At length, Charles agreed and York returned to Scotland, convinced that, despite all his promises, Charles would abandon him.[32]

Although Charles and his ministers were preoccupied with domestic affairs, they could not ignore what happened abroad. On one hand, a French subsidy would reduce the need either to call Parliament or to make concessions to the Commons. On the other, a popular foreign policy – in other words, one directed against France – might make the Commons more amenable. The two lines of policy were logically incompatible, but that did not make it any easier for Charles to choose between them. His room for manoeuvre was greatly reduced by the suspicion (to say no worse) with which he was regarded by the major powers of Europe. All things being equal, he would have preferred to close with France, but Louis still deeply resented Charles's 'treachery' of 1677–8 and the 'humiliation' of the Treaty of Nijmegen. In his anger, he dismissed the smooth and skilful Pomponne; his leading foreign policy advisers were now the brutal Louvois and the abrasive Colbert de Croissy, whose own memories of Charles were less than rosy. The new team set out to claim Louis' 'rights', in Alsace and in Flanders, using a mixture of legal chicanery and concentrated military force. The commissioners who met at Courtrai, to 'interpret' the tangled provisions of the Treaty of Nijmegen, found that their deliberations were irrelevant, as Louis helped

himself to what he claimed as his. In these circumstances, England's neutrality (or ineffectuality) was more than sufficient for Louis' purposes: why
waste good money on a king who could do him no harm?[33]

Nevertheless, through much of 1679 Charles hoped for an agreement with
France. What he wanted was money – he dismissed offers of military help
as unnecessary and counter-productive. By mid-October, he and Barrillon
had virtually agreed terms. For three years Charles was to conclude no
alliances without Louis' approval; he was to renounce any existing treaty
which was against Louis' interests. In return, Louis undertook not to attack
the Dutch Republic or the Spanish Netherlands during the same period and
to make no treaty to Charles's prejudice. He would pay Charles 1,000,000
livres (about £75,000) a year for three years, on condition that he did not
call Parliament. If Charles did call Parliament, he undertook that it would
do nothing against France, while Louis would be free to cease payments, if he
so chose. The proposed terms showed clearly the strength of the bargaining
positions of the two kings: Louis was to be left with a much freer hand than
Charles. At the last moment, Charles's nerve failed him. He was reluctant
to commit himself, in writing, not to call Parliament for three years. Not
only would the revelation of such a commitment be politically catastrophic,
but he would need to call one in or after March 1681 to bring to an end the
three-year ban on imports from France. Charles also wished Louis to promise
explicitly to conclude no new treaty with the Dutch – yet again, he was
haunted by the spectre of diplomatic isolation. The negotiations stalled and
each party began to explore other alternatives.[34]

Charles's government had been considering a closer liaison with the Dutch
since at least June. This offered an alternative to the French treaty and
might encourage the French to be more amenable. It would also prove far
more popular with Parliament and public: that, at least, was the argument
used by Sunderland and his uncle Henry Sidney, now Charles's ambassador
at the Hague. It was less than popular in the republic, however. The
republican opposition's long-standing suspicions of William's ambitions,
and English connections, were skilfully fostered by the French ambassador,
d'Avaux. D'Avaux hoped to renew and extend Louis' alliance with the
Dutch and so keep them neutral while he finished his business with Spain
and reinforced his eastern frontier. The ambassador did his utmost to block
any moves towards either an Anglo-Dutch treaty or a guarantee of the
Treaty of Nijmegen, which Louis was so busily reinterpreting. His task was
facilitated by the States General's reluctance to embark on any agreement
with Charles that was not endorsed by Parliament: it seemed futile to ally
with a king who lacked the wherewithal to fight.[35]

In the autumn of 1679, Charles's ministers increasingly feared a new
Franco-Dutch alliance. Sunderland told Sidney to assure William that

Charles would reach no agreement with France without consulting him and
that he had no plans for such a liaison at present. At the same time, he tried
to persuade William that it would be highly dangerous to summon Parliament
at that time. Shortly before Christmas, news came that the States General
had renewed their treaty of 1662 with France. In fact, William proved able
to prevent the conclusion of the agreement, but Charles and Sunderland
reacted angrily to the news: the treaty might be 'defensive', they said, but
in war it was often difficult to tell who was the aggressor. (No doubt Charles
remembered 1665–6.)[36] Charles became even angrier on hearing that Fagel
had shown Sidney a letter from Barrillon to d'Avaux, stating that Charles
wished to prevent a Franco-Dutch alliance only because he wished to ally
with France himself. Charles complained that such a letter could lead to his
being driven out of his kingdom. Sunderland denounced it as a dirty
trick, typical of the French, and argued that the sticking-point in Charles's
negotiations with Barrillon had been Louis' insistence on remaining free to
join with the Dutch. Finding himself unwelcome at court, Barrillon ceased
to discuss the treaty and waited for emotions to cool.[37]

Through much of 1680, despite frenzied diplomatic activity, the position
remained the same: the States General would conclude treaties with neither
France nor England, while negotiations between Charles and Louis were at
best desultory. Charles demanded far more money than Louis was prepared
to pay and insisted that Louis should sign no new treaty with the Dutch.[38]
Anglo-French negotiations were again interrupted as Charles became
worried by Louis' military ambitions in Alsace and, still more, in Flanders.[39]
Having failed to enlist Dutch support against French aggression, Charles's
ministers were reduced to signing a treaty with the Spaniards. He undertook
to send troops to the Low Countries if the Spanish were attacked there; they
promised to hand over cautionary towns. The terms of the treaty reflected
desperation: the king had to have *something* to set before Parliament. Viewed
objectively, it was hardly a realistic agreement. The Spaniards were clearly
unable to defend their Flemish territories – Sunderland had earlier written
of Charles's contempt for their weakness[40] – while his domestic problems
meant that he would be unable to offer Brussels anything more than token
assistance. Sunderland claimed that the treaty was a great coup; others
were sceptical and indeed it was to prove an embarrassment.[41] It further
interrupted Charles's attempts at a rapprochement with Louis. Barrillon
renewed his contacts with the opposition to the court, gleefully informing
them of a secret clause in the Spanish treaty, whereby the two kings promised
mutual assistance against rebellious subjects.[42] York, meanwhile, warned his
brother of the danger that Louis might leak details of the Secret Treaty of
Dover. Louis had, indeed, considered doing so, but Barrillon advised against
it, except in the direst necessity.[43] As the time approached for Parliament to

meet, Charles had little cause for confidence. His hopes of a French subsidy had been dashed, apparently beyond recall. Louis' renewed aggression in the Low Countries threatened to cast him into a political embarrassment akin to that of 1674–8. Despite all his diplomatic efforts, he had nothing to put before Parliament but a potentially costly treaty with a power for which he felt nothing but disdain. At home and abroad, his prospects can never have seemed bleaker.

In September 1679, York left England, confident that his position had been greatly strengthened by his hurried return from Brussels. There had been no disorder and he was now confident that, if Parliament attacked the queen or himself, Charles would dismiss it; he hoped, too, that he had cured Charles of the delusion that the newly elected House of Commons could ever be brought to see reason. He was still, however, worried by the presence of the likes of Shaftesbury on the privy council and, while he expressed complete trust in Sunderland, time was to show that his trust was misplaced.[44] He stayed at Brussels only as long as was necessary to bring home his wife and household, then returned to London to prepare for his journey to Edinburgh. When Shaftesbury heard of his being sent to Scotland, he summoned his supporters on the council and urged them to represent to Charles how dangerous it would be for the duke to remain in Britain; Charles, he added, had promised to do nothing without consulting the council. Frustrated by his colleagues' lack of response, Shaftesbury called for a full debate, but the council resolved to defer discussing the matter; according to one report, he also demanded that York should be committed to gaol until charges could be brought against him. Next day, 14 October, Charles ordered that the earl should be struck off the list of councillors and declared his intention of proroguing Parliament until 26 January.[45]

Charles's actions seemed to mark a sharp break with the policy of conciliation epitomized by the new council. Other changes followed. Essex resigned as first commissioner of the treasury, but remained a councillor. The council appointed a small committee to review the commissions of the peace.[46] Again, however, Charles shrank from irrevocable commitments. Shaftesbury's conduct had been intolerable – indeed, there had been talk of dismissing him even before James's brief return to Brussels – but Charles hesitated to drive so formidable an opponent into unremitting opposition. Sunderland and a London JP, Edmund Warcup, sounded the earl about the terms upon which he might be prepared to resume office. As far as Danby was concerned, Charles stressed that he would abandon neither his own power of pardon nor the bishops' right of judicature. He also refused to sacrifice either York or the queen to the wrath of Parliament. Shaftesbury found such stipulations totally unacceptable. He was determined to force his way into office, on his terms: this was to be a fight to the finish.[47]

If Shaftesbury and his allies were to 'storm the closet', they needed to mobilize popular support, by exploiting Monmouth's charismatic appeal and by promoting petitions. While York returned to London and then made his stately way northwards, Monmouth kicked his heels in Holland. William had no wish to encourage his hopes of the crown, but treated him kindly, in the belief that Charles wished him to do so. The prince was thus greatly surprised to learn that Monmouth had returned to England. Monmouth sought to justify his conduct by the claim that Charles had promised that he could return after the next session of Parliament – and had then postponed its meeting. Many believed that he had been advised to return by a close-knit group of peers, headed by Shaftesbury. On hearing of his return, the Green Ribbon Club ordered that a bonfire should be lit and soon the night sky was ablaze: there were over sixty bonfires between Temple Bar and Charing Cross. Crowds stopped coaches, demanding money to drink the duke's health: if they were denied, they smashed the windows, beat the coachman and called the passengers Papists. There were similar scenes elsewhere. At Chichester, the citizens not only lit bonfires and drank Monmouth's health, but broke into the cathedral and rang the bells, much to the bishop's annoyance.[48]

Whatever his fondness for his son, Charles could not tolerate such flagrant disobedience. Earlier, he had expressed satisfaction that Monmouth had not been at 'the clubs': now he had identified himself unequivocally with the Exclusionists. Monmouth claimed that he had come back to clear his name, following the 'Meal Tub Plot', a clumsy design to turn the Popish Plot against the Presbyterians. His demand that he be brought to trial infuriated his father: Charles declared that if he did not return to Holland, he would never see him again. When Monmouth refused, Charles told him to move out of his lodgings at Whitehall and ordered the guards not to obey him. The functions of the post of master of the horse, which he had been granted for life, were to be performed by commissioners; later he was deprived of it altogether. The importunities of Fox, Nell Gwynn and a bevy of courtiers failed to move the king, but still Monmouth refused to leave the country.[49] Some still wished to believe that Charles would change his mind; Monmouth himself blamed his father's obduracy on the influence of Sunderland and Portsmouth. Charles, however, was now a more resolute man. As it became clear that his anger was not feigned, the crowds attending the duke dwindled. William dissociated himself from his return and Halifax claimed that only Shaftesbury was mad enough to have advised it. It had certainly failed to achieve its object.[50]

As the excitement generated by Monmouth's return died down, the petitioning movement began. On 7 December a group of 'confederate' peers presented Charles with the petition on his way from chapel, although it was thought they would have preferred the first one to come from the London common council. Charles replied that he wished that all were as concerned as he was for the nation's good and peace and that he would consider it. Three days later he announced that Parliament was to be prorogued until 11 November 1680: he brushed aside his councillors' remonstrations, declaring that his mind was made up. On the 12th he issued the proclamation against seditious and factious petitions. Meanwhile, the council committee began in earnest its scrutiny of the lists of JPs.[51] Nevertheless, petition forms continued to circulate. Most referred to the king's speech of 21 April, announcing the new council, in which he had promised to be guided by Parliament. The petitioners' defiance increased Charles's determination that their campaign should not succeed. In response to a petition from Westminster, Charles declared that he was surprised to find a member of the Royalist Gerard family alongside the likes of Desborough. Those who brought the Wiltshire petition were subjected to an outburst of royal rage:

What do you take me to be and what do you take yourselves to be? I admire gentlemen of your estates should animate people to mutiny and rebellion.... You come from a company of loose and disaffected people who would fain set us in troubles.... You would take it ill I should meddle in your concerns and pray do not you meddle with mine, which is so essential a part of my prerogative.[52]

In the case of the Wiltshire petition, Charles could argue that it was less representative than its promoters claimed: they said that they had been commanded by 'the country' to present it, but it had not been approved by the grand jury (as the Act required). The Somerset petition was endorsed by the Green Ribbon Club, which noted that many of the great men of the county had refused to sign it.[53] JPs and army officers who promoted petitions were dismissed and by the end of January the movement had clearly failed. Charles had now decided to prorogue only until April, but he added that he would meet Parliament before November only if events on the continent made it necessary; he also declared his intention to summon York home from Scotland.[54] More Exclusionists resigned from the council: Russell, Cavendish, Capel and Powle saw no point in remaining members of a body which had no influence on policy-making. Charles refused to allow them to give their reasons for resigning; privately, he spoke of them with contempt. It seemed that, unless the Exclusionists were prepared to resort to force, they had no option but to wait until he chose to call Parliament.[55]

Charles's attitude was never, however, as straightforward as it seemed. In December he negotiated secretly with Holles, Littleton and others, who produced a moderate bill, presumably of limitations, which York has said to be ready to accept. Barrillon heard of offers to vote money in return for limitations, the punishment of the plotters and a guarantee that Parliament should meet at least every two years; the queen was to be left alone, but Sunderland and Portsmouth were to be sent away. Shaftesbury still pressed his plan for a divorce, but Holles was against it. It is impossible to say how serious these negotiations were, but it seems improbable that these politicians would have been able to deliver what they promised: once Parliament met, it would produce new demands.[56] Nevertheless, despite his robust response to the petitions, Charles clearly felt a need for conciliation. He ordered that the laws against Catholics should be vigorously enforced and continued to pay lip-service to the reality of the Plot; no doubt, this owed much to ministers' wish to establish their Protestant credentials in the eyes of the public.[57] They also hoped to achieve some success in foreign policy to set before Parliament.[58] Underlying all else, meanwhile, was the uncertainty about the revenue. The scheme of retrenchment which had started the previous autumn would, in theory, yield a comfortable annual surplus: but would the practice match the theory? In a nation where some saw civil war as imminent, could taxpayers be relied upon to go on paying? Would monied men continue to advance the loans on which the crown's day-to-day solvency depended? One judge, Pemberton, claimed that it would be illegal for Charles to continue to collect the additional excise after 24 June; his colleagues (and the lord chancellor) declared that he was wrong. (In fact, Pemberton was correct as far as the three years' duty voted in 1677 was concerned and it duly expired.)[59] This dispute offers yet more evidence of the pervasiveness of political divisions. The divergent views of Essex and Hyde on the state of the revenue were closely related to their attitudes towards calling Parliament. Essex claimed that the revenue was so heavily anticipated that Charles could not survive without Parliament; Hyde, and Fox, insisted that he could survive, provided there was no foreign war.[60]

As winter turned to spring, Charles seemed resolute and determined. Ministers expressed confidence about the revenue and Sunderland declared that the king's affairs were in their best condition for seven years. When York returned to London, there was spontaneous rejoicing, at least in the area around the court.[61] There were no disturbances when Charles fell ill in May, with 'apoplexy', and York was convinced that the City authorities would have proclaimed him king had his brother died.[62] The court's opponents seemed at a loss. Shaftesbury had high hopes that the Irish Plot would enable him to bring down Ormond: he accused the lord lieutenant of planning, like Strafford, to bring Irish troops to subjugate England. The Irish witnesses, however, told their stories badly, in an impenetrable brogue, and time was to show that they would willingly change those stories if the price was right. Moreover, to revive memories of 1641 was a two-edged weapon, reinforcing the growing Cavalier backlash.[63] An assault on one of the

English witnesses, Worcester's old antagonist John Arnold, briefly revived public concern, but in general the credit of both the Plot and Shaftesbury was diminishing.[64] Monmouth, too, found himself out in the cold. He received a tumultuous welcome in Chichester, but the king's warden would not let him hunt in the New Forest. When Charles fell ill, Monmouth sent a message expressing his concern, but his father refused to see him. Charles did all that he could to scotch claims that there was documentary proof of his son's legitimacy in a mysterious black box. A full investigation by the council failed to uncover any evidence of the box's existence and Charles again formally declared that he had never been married to any woman but the queen.[65]

Although Shaftesbury was unable to force Charles to call Parliament, the king and his ministers remained convinced that it would have to meet sooner or later, for both financial and political reasons. They therefore continued to negotiate with opposition politicians, hinting at a deal involving Danby. Parliament was prorogued in April and again in May, but only for short periods: the Dutch had asked that it should not be prorogued for long.[66] Even York came to accept that conciliation, not confrontation, was the way out of the crisis, especially in the light of changes in the public mood: Exclusionist claims to speak for 'the people' were coming to sound hollow.[67] London remained the government's main worry. In March an Exclusionist JP, Sir William Waller (who was soon to be dismissed from office), uncovered a plan by a group of apprentices to burn effigies of the Rump and Cromwell and to pull down conventicles and brothels. It seems probable that these designs constituted an early expression of popular 'Tory' feeling in the capital and an attempt to counter the great pope-burning ceremonies organized by the Exclusionists; no doubt they also reflected a fondness for 'bonfires and ale'. Both the council and the Exclusionists, however, suspected a hidden hand behind them, either 'republican' or 'Papist'; there were also reports that the apprentices had been egged on by Ossory and Feversham. The only result of the council's investigations was an order banning bonfires, even on the king's birthday.[68]

Fears that London was on the verge of revolt were groundless. The City remained quiet when Charles fell ill and in mid-June one writer remarked on the calm and hopeful state of Charles's affairs, especially as the Spanish alliance showed that Charles was taking practical steps to obstruct France's ambitions in Flanders.[69] Nevertheless, events were soon to show that the government's preoccupation with the capital had been thoroughly justified. By the end of the month the court's confidence had been shattered by a petition from Middlesex, the attempts to present York as a recusant and by the London shrieval elections. Charles angrily rejected the petition: he was furious that one of those who presented it was Lord Cavendish, who had been banished from court for refusing to kiss York's hand. Charles reduced the allowances paid to Oates and his colleagues and, when the judges set off on their circuits, he ordered them to ensure that grand juries were composed of well-principled men and to discourage petitions. He also, however, told them to assure the people that Parliament would meet and to be severe against Catholics but not against peaceable Dissenters.[70] It became increasingly clear that his earlier confidence had vanished. Even James, while exhorting his brother to stand firm, told Barrillon that both he and Charles would be ruined unless they threw themselves on Louis' protection; Barrillon, still smarting with resentment of Charles's treaty with Spain, was not inclined to be sympathetic. Charles, meanwhile, had a long secret interview with Monmouth. He clearly found the outcome unsatisfactory and sent word to his son to leave town; Monmouth, following York's example, refused to go without a written order. It was now widely believed that Charles would have to assent to exclusion and abandon his brother to his fate. York was sunk in gloom: according to Barrillon, he believed that only a civil war could save the monarchy and himself.[71]

Sunderland and Portsmouth, too, were convinced that York was doomed; their only concern was to avoid being dragged down with him. In August Charles announced that Parliament would meet in October, but he approached the session with little confidence. Although his hold on the City had been shaken, he still had considerable support among the aldermen and leading citizens and he embarked on negotiations intended to pre-empt any move by the Commons to seek refuge in the City, as in January 1642.[72] He was not well pleased by the election of Sir Patience Ward, a nonconformist sympathizer, as lord mayor, but ordered that there should be no proceedings against him for not having taken communion in the past twelve months. The order caused some surprise, but it was reported that Ward had assured Charles that he was opposed to any alteration in the government. Indeed, despite his religious beliefs, Ward was to give Charles little cause for dissatisfaction: as his predecessor had remarked, it was in the City's interest to remain on good terms with the court.[73] Monmouth, meanwhile, was 'taking the popular air of the country', acclaimed by crowds of 'shabby people', many of whom believed him to be the king's rightful son, but by few persons of quality. He did not see his father again until early October. It was reported that Charles was displeased at his lack of submissiveness: clearly, the duke believed that he would soon be able to dictate his own terms. Others, apparently, believed it too: on the eve of the new Parliamentary session, he was reconciled to Sunderland and Portsmouth.[74]

York, meanwhile, compared himself to a stag at bay. Outwardly he expressed confidence about the coming session: if the Commons misbehaved, Charles would dissolve Parliament and call a new one. Despite pressure from Sunderland and Portsmouth, he refused either to leave court or to take out a pardon for becoming a Catholic, which by law was a capital offence: to show fear, he said, was unmanly. Never renowned for his tact, he insisted on being invited to the Artillery Company's feast, but his reception was notably cooler than that of the previous year.[75] By late September, he expected to be impeached; the best his friends could hope for was that the Commons' conduct would be so extravagant that Charles would be forced to dismiss them.[76] Sunderland, Portsmouth and Essex insisted that he should leave London, preferably for Scotland: indeed, it was reported as early as 19 September that the committee for foreign affairs had agreed that he should go. If he stayed, they argued, Parliament would be unmanageable; if Charles dissolved Parliament to save him there would be civil war. There were reports that most MPs would come up with armed retinues and that the Commons would demand wide-ranging control over the revenue, the armed forces, Scotland and Ireland. Shaftesbury, Monmouth and Russell undertook to do great things if only York were sent away. Charles seemed to accept these arguments and spoke of his brother with great bitterness. York, as always, refused to go without a positive order. He complained that his friends were deserting him and that his brother was hopelessly irresolute, changing his mind with each piece of advice he received; he also strongly suspected that he had again been seeing Monmouth secretly.[77]

York was not, however, as friendless as he claimed to be. On 13 October Charles asked the full privy council whether he should be sent away: it was resolved that he should not. Soon after, Essex, Halifax and the secretaries pressed the duke to withdraw, but he would not do so without a positive order; some now thought that he would be impeached. Portsmouth, Sunderland and Monmouth urged Charles to assert his authority or, better, to abandon York to the wrath of Parliament. On the 16th a majority of councillors was still against sending him away, but Charles decided to do so anyway. He declared firmly that he would agree to no further measures against his brother, as he knew what the consequences would be; James, however, felt betrayed and was particularly angry with Sunderland. The fact that he had a strong power-base in Scotland offered only limited consolation.[78] As he made his sorrowful way northwards, he placed little trust in his brother's resolution. He was not alone. Sidney wrote to William that Charles would not agree to exclusion, but only two weeks before he had written that all the king's advisers insisted that he had no choice but to comply with Parliament. Barrillon remarked that those closest to Charles were more hostile to York than were the most extreme members of the Commons. The ambassador concluded that Charles would not defend his brother to the utmost, but would secure the best terms he could in return for abandoning him.[79] The next few weeks would show whether he was right.

Parliament assembled on 21 October amid more than usual excitement. Charles's opening speech stressed the measures that he had taken with the Spaniards and Dutch and asked for money only for Tangier. He was prepared to agree to any measures which the Houses judged to be necessary for the safety of the Protestant religion – provided that the succession was not changed. The eyes of Europe were upon them: if the session did not have a happy outcome, it would not be his fault.[80] The Commons' response made it clear that they were not interested in foreign affairs: the Spanish treaty was brushed aside with the remark that the Spaniards were Papists.[81] The king's speech, it was claimed, reflected his counsellors' views, not his own. Wild claims abounded: that by an ancient statute the king could not dismiss Parliament until grievances had been redressed; that Parliament could settle the succession; that since the Conquest Acts of Parliament had been the best security for a king's title. 'He who says that the king's power is more than Parliaments have given him', exclaimed Cavendish, with presumably unintended irony, 'is little versed in English story.'[82] They claimed no powers, declared Hugh Boscawen, that were not 'justified by many laws and precedents. And if there were none ...', he added, 'yet I take it that the law of nature and self-preservation would afford us sufficient arguments.'[83]

If MPs played fast and loose with law and history, they showed no more respect for the principles of natural justice. Coffee-house gossip was afforded the same respect as sworn testimony in a court of law. Treason was alleged to be whatever the Commons voted it to be. Winnington, the former solicitor-general, denounced the judges for hindering petitions: 'I will not define the offence, but I think these proceedings do subvert the fundamental laws and so I would go to the utmost severity of judgment.'[84] Others accused of opposing petitions or promoting abhorrences were harshly dealt with: if MPs, they were expelled from the House; if not, they were summoned to account for their conduct and severely censured.[85] On the other hand, leading Whigs were careful to protect other unpopular figures, such as Danby or Portsmouth, from attack.[86] In debate, the adversarial and intimidatory rhetoric of anti-Popery was used ruthlessly: the only question, declared Boscawen, was whether they were to be Papists or Protestants.[87] The argument that exclusion was essential to guard against 'Popery' threw its opponents on to the defensive. They argued that the bill's terms were impractical or unjust, but could not challenge the assumptions upon which it rested. Just in case anyone felt inclined to do so, the Commons impeached a parson from Bristol who cast doubt on the Plot and declared that the Presbyterians were worse than the Jesuits. Indeed, impeachments flew thick and fast in this Parliament.[88] The Commons again resolved to print their votes and several MPs talked of the danger of a popular revolt if their demands were not met.[89] The Parliamentary Exclusionists collaborated closely with their supporters in London. Just before the exclusion bill was carried up – with a great shout – from the Commons to the Lords, the common council petitioned Charles to assent to it. The Commons supported moves to remove Sir George Jeffreys from the recordership of London. The Westminster grand jury presented York as a recusant and asked the judges to beg Charles to heed Parliament's advice. In December, the lord mayor brought the king yet another petition from the City; Charles said that they should mind their own business.[90]

The Commons' demands added up to a comprehensive assault on the royal prerogative. Impeachments and other attacks on ministers threatened the king's right of appointment, as did renewed demands that York's 'creatures' should be weeded out of offices of all kinds. Wild claims that the judges had misinterpreted the law implied that Parliament, or a faction within it, could bend the law to serve their own ends. Denunciations of those advancing money to the crown threatened his credit: if he could not borrow, he would be financially dependent on Parliament. Calls for the relaxation or repeal of the laws against Dissent (above all, the Corporation Act) seemed designed to allow those Charles regarded as disaffected to plot against him with impunity. Claims of an unfettered right (even duty) to petition and denunciations of restrictions of the (Exclusionist) press seemed designed to pave the way for revolution from below. The very fact that the Commons swept aside proposals for limitations reinforced Charles's conviction that exclusion would be only the beginning of the destruction of the monarchy. Memories of the civil war were constantly before his eyes: he told Essex that he would never change the governors of towns at Parliament's behest – he had been there when Hull shut its gates against his father in 1642.[91]

Charles's anxieties were understandable, but were they justified? To some extent, MPs' fears were exploited by politicians avid for office: when the Commons resolved that no member should accept a place without the House's permission, some leading MPs suddenly looked disconsolate.[92] However, the fact that such a vote passed showed that the majority of MPs were not seeking office, but were genuinely angry about past misgovernment and fearful for the future. Their violence was in part the product of frustration and nervous excitement, in part a deliberate ploy to frighten the king into agreeing to exclusion. Experience, reinforced by wishful thinking, suggested that Charles would back down if subjected to sufficient pressure, but in fact the Exclusionists' strategy rested to a considerable extent on bluff: there was little substance behind the sound and fury. The long-feared revolt in London did not materialize. Two days after the Lords rejected the exclusion bill, the annual 17 November pope-burning procession, attended by maybe 100,000 people, passed off peacefully; Lord Mayor Ward and the trained bands maintained order without difficulty. When Charles prorogued Parliament early in January, the members dispersed quietly. Compared with 1641–2, or 1688, there was very little political violence in the years 1679–81. Despite the anger and excitement, the Whigs were not prepared to begin a civil war. After the Commons passed a series of thunderous resolutions on 7 January, Ralph Montagu remarked, pathetically: 'We have nothing left us but votes.'[93]

It is easy to state, with hindsight, that there was no serious danger of insurrection in the winter of 1680–1. There was little reason for Charles to feel confident that this was so: both his own memory of 1640–2 and the arguments of Sunderland and Portsmouth suggested otherwise. The new House of Commons was more extreme than the old. Erstwhile leaders found it hard to get a hearing: it was remarked that MPs started many hares, but caught very few. Shaftesbury, from the Lords, found it harder and harder to control the movement to which he had given so much of the original impetus.[94] Faced with a volatile Parliament, uncertainty about his revenues and (he thought) a hostile populace, Charles was not inclined to take risks. He wanted to believe the assurances of Portsmouth and Sunderland that he would be able to secure money without being forced to agree to the ruin of his brother or the monarchy. Barrillon, however, found him uncertain and lethargic: assurances that he would stick by his old friends carried little conviction, when so many at court clearly favoured exclusion.[95]

After some preliminary attacks on abhorrers, to deter possible opposition, the exclusion bill was brought into the Commons on 2 November. The case for it rested on York's religion; the arguments against it were couched in terms of natural justice and of prudence. Should York be deprived of his birthright without due process of law? Would it be wise to exclude him from the English throne? He would still be king of Scotland and Ireland and, when he set out to recover his throne, he would be helped by powerful Catholic princes. When asked who was to succeed if York did not, the Exclusionists were confused – or evasive. The 1679 bill had laid down that the crown should pass as if James were dead – in other words, to his children. The first draft in 1680 excluded him without naming a successor. After much debate the House agreed on a form of words which tended to favour the claims of Mary (and William) against those of Monmouth, but left some scope for argument.[96] A message from Charles that he would never agree to alter the rightful line of succession was ignored and the bill passed its third reading on the 11th.[97] Next day, the common council presented its petition, asking the king to continue the session and to take all steps necessary to secure the Protestant religion. Charles replied tartly that he did not need to be reminded to take care of religion and warned them to beware of trouble-makers. On the 15th, the bill was brought up to the Lords.[98]

There had been intense speculation about the bill's likely fate in the Upper House. Conway was confident that it would be rejected by at least twenty votes, not counting the bishops, but most saw Charles's attitude as the key. Sunderland and Portsmouth warned him that if he did not let it pass he would be besieged in Whitehall; many MPs put their faith in the lure of money, although there had as yet been no talk of supply. Charles, however, acted with unexpected firmness. When the Commons presented a long address about the succession, he put it in his pocket without saying a word. He sneered openly at the Plot witnesses and told the council that he wanted the Lords to reject the bill on the first reading.[99] He was present throughout the debates and had his dinner and supper sent in. As Shaftes-bury put the case for exclusion, and Halifax that for limitations, Charles made his feelings abundantly clear and so gave the lie to claims that he wished to be forced to cede. When Monmouth expressed concern for his father's safety, Charles talked of the kiss of Judas. Given such a clear lead, the Lords did not hesitate. The bill was rejected by sixty-three votes to thirty.[100]

The king's conduct aroused general surprise. Lady Sunderland declared that he must be mad; other, less biased observers were delighted that he had asserted himself at last.[101] A single victory did not, however, mean that he had won the war. He clearly could expect little good from this Parliament, but he needed a plausible pretext to dismiss it and it seemed politic to take steps to calm popular anxieties about Popery and the Plot. He had already intimated to the Commons that they should proceed with the trials of the five Catholic lords and that the evidence against Viscount Stafford seemed especially strong. Two of the witnesses against him were Dugdale and Turberville, whom Charles found comparatively credible. Moreover, Charles would not wish the Commons to start with Arundell of Wardour, who had been deeply involved in the Secret Treaty of Dover and in Coleman's intrigues. Stafford, by contrast, had been the Catholic peer most actively associated with Shaftesbury and the opposition in 1675–7: indeed, Stafford tried to mention this at his trial, but Shaftesbury quickly silenced him.[102] When the trial started, Charles sent a message to the Commons that the brother of one of those executed earlier had threatened that, if any of the five lords died, Charles would not live six months. He cannot have relished throwing an innocent man to the wolves, but even he must have been surprised that Stafford's defence proved still more inept than the testimony of the witnesses: it seemed almost as if he had given up hope. A majority of peers – including most of those who were his relatives – found him guilty. Charles seemed displeased, but the fact that he had not spoken to any of his servants on Stafford's behalf suggested to some that he had wanted him to be condemned; they may well have been right.[103]

Apart from helping on Stafford's trial, there were few political initiatives that Charles could take. Yet again York was pressed to conform to the Church of England; yet again he refused: as he plaintively remarked, even if he did so few would believe that he was sincere.[104] For the rest, Charles was on the defensive, buying time and hoping that the Commons' extremism would discredit exclusion in the eyes of the public. When the Commons first heard of the bill's rejection they sat mute for almost half an hour, but astonishment soon turned to anger. Some blamed the bishops, others Halifax, not for arguing so ably against the bill – that would have been unParliamentary – but for advising the recent prorogations. Despite the absence of evidence, other than the vaguest of hearsay, Halifax was impeached, as were Seymour, Hyde and several judges. Well aware that these proceedings were intended mainly to defame and to intimidate, the Lords demanded that the Commons produce evidence. This they were in no hurry to do: Capel, indeed, referred to Seymour's impeachment as a 'trivial matter'. The impeachments, nevertheless, served their purpose: Seymour and Hyde ceased to attend the Commons.[105]

Worried by the Commons' anger at the rejection of exclusion, the Lords considered alternative expedients. Limitations on a Catholic king, or James's banishment during Charles's lifetime, were rejected as ineffectual: some claimed that they would change the nature of monarchy. James and William thought these expedients were worse than exclusion. Limitations on the future king could lead to discussion of restrictions on the present one – especially in relation to the armed forces. A second possibility was Shaftesbury's pet project of a divorce: he claimed that Clarendon had always known that the queen was sterile and there was laughter when he said that Charles was clearly still capable of fathering children. The Lords showed little enthusiasm, however, and Charles made his attitude clear by going to sleep with the queen for the first time for months.[106]

Another expedient was an association, which both Charles and James regarded as more dangerous than exclusion. Under it, Protestants would join to defend their religion and liberties if a Papist became king: but might it not seem to legitimate resistance to the present monarch? Shaftesbury first proposed an association on 16 November and the Lords referred it to the judges on the 26th, but it was not until 15 December that the Commons debated the matter. Cavendish proposed that men should be encouraged to adhere to the Protestant heir, as declared by Parliament; all who refused to do so should be ineligible for office. Sir William Jones urged that an association should come into effect in Charles's lifetime, but despite the violent rhetoric of Winnington and others most MPs remained wary. The proposal reopened the question of who was to succeed if York did not. Some suspected that it was designed to give Monmouth control of the armed forces – to serve the interests of a faction rather than to save the nation from Popery. The longer the debate went on, the more MPs became convinced that there was no substitute for exclusion, because that alone could legitimate the resistance which the association would involve. But exclusion had been rejected. Unless the king could be persuaded to wipe the slate clean by a short prorogation, no similar bill could be brought in that session. No association bill was brought in to the Commons; one was drafted in the Lords, but it was never formally read. As so often, a great deal of sound and fury ended with nothing tangible being done.[107]

Moves to improve the lot of the Dissenters also seemed, to Charles, to pose a threat to the crown. It was not until mid-December that the Commons turned their full attention to the Church. The Middlesex grand jury indicted the Bishop of London, under the statute of Praemunire, for holding Church courts, which were also vigorously attacked by some MPs. Bills were brought in for comprehension and indulgence, but were opposed unexpectedly vigorously. Leave was also given to bring in a bill to repeal the Corporation Act, but all this labour brought forth only a bill to repeal an Act of 1593, which required nonconformists to abjure the kingdom on pain of death. (Burnet thought that the penalty had been exacted only once.) It passed both Houses but did not receive the royal assent: Charles ordered the clerk of the Commons not to present it to him.[108]

From Edinburgh York watched these developments with unconcealed alarm. Why, he asked, did Charles not dismiss Parliament? The longer it lasted, the greater the risk that he would be forced to succumb. If York's attitude was straightforward, William's was not. On one hand, he regarded exclusion as unjust and limitations as fatal to the monarchy; on the other, desperate for English assistance against France, he begged Charles to reach agreement with Parliament: he did not specify how. The States General presented a memorial to Sidney, advising Charles to agree to exclusion. (York suspected that Sunderland was behind this.)[109] The secretary, and his ally Portsmouth, soon got over the shock of the rejection of the exclusion bill: by the end of December they again claimed that Charles would eventually agree to it. Some opponents of exclusion, notably Seymour and Halifax, still hoped that the Commons could be persuaded to give money in return for something less. On 15 December Charles told the House of the need to support alliances with the Spanish and Dutch and to provide for Tangier; he would do all that was necessary for the Protestant religion, provided that the right line of succession was not broken. MPs seized on this as a hint that he wished to be persuaded of the merits of exclusion. They resolved, in effect, to give money only when York had been excluded, an association had been passed and the judiciary and the militia had been 'regulated'. Unsatisfactory as these terms might be, the whiff of money encouraged the 'hungry courtiers' to beg Charles to comply. Charles remained inscrutable. Fuelled by more secret negotiations with opposition politicians, rumours circulated that Charles would agree to exclusion, but on 4 January he declared roundly that he would not. The Commons' patience snapped. They could give no supply, they declared, until the exclusion bill passed and resolved that anyone lending money to the crown would have to answer to the Commons for hindering the sitting of Parliament.[110]

Following these resolutions, Charles decided to prorogue. When the news leaked out, the Commons met early on 10 January and resolved that whoever had advised the prorogation, unless it was to facilitate the exclusion bill, was a betrayer of the kingdom and of the Protestant religion and a pensioner of France. They added resolutions that the Papists had burned London in 1666; that customs officials had broken the law by failing to prevent imports from France; that York was responsible for Monmouth's removal from the king; and that the persecution of Dissenters damaged the Protestant interest. The votes were an expression of frustration and impotence. MPs had gambled on forcing Charles to agree to exclusion, but he had called their bluff. Hopes that angry Londoners might take to the streets to protest against the prorogation proved illusory.[111] Despite their talk of resistance, the Whigs had always kept more or less within the law: indeed, they had denounced the judges for misinterpreting the law, and, at least on the issues of petitions and the press, they had a case. The newly elected common council expelled those who were unqualified under the Corporation Act and then produced nothing more subversive than a petition that Parliament should meet when the prorogation ended. Charles replied that it was none of their business and declared his intention to dissolve Parliament. As was now becoming customary, he did not seek the council's advice. One of the few surviving Whig councillors, Salisbury, offered his resignation; Charles replied that nothing would give him greater pleasure than to accept it. He announced that a new Parliament would be held at Oxford in March. There, in a very different setting, the final act of the drama would be played out.[112]

The dismissal of Parliament was followed by sweeping changes in court and council. Portsmouth's political credit had been ruined, despite her pleas that she had done what she judged to be in Charles's own best interests. On a personal level, however, Charles remained as fond of her as ever; there was to be no such escape for Sunderland. He was forced to give up the post of secretary without recovering what he had paid for it – a serious blow for a man with his financial problems. He, Essex and Temple were removed from the privy council; Sunderland's young associate, Sidney Godolphin, was spared for the moment, as Charles believed that he had been led astray by his elders.[113] York was delighted at these changes and at the growth in Hyde's influence, but Charles wrote that his affairs were not yet in a fit state to allow James to return to London and there was yet another attempt to persuade him to abjure Catholicism.[114] Several of those still in favour feared that York, if he returned, would both undermine their credit and persuade his brother to embark on politically dangerous policies. This was especially true of Halifax, whose opposition to exclusion had owed much to hatred of Shaftesbury and nothing to fondness for York; some, indeed, thought that he preferred limitations because they would do more to weaken the monarchy. He had an annoying habit of dissociating himself from policies which could prove unpopular, but this was perhaps understandable in view of the way he had been vilified in the last Parliament and blamed for decisions which had nothing to do with him: a nervous individual, he seems genuinely to have feared civil war. He complained privately of Charles's irresolution and occasionally went off in a huff, but the smell of power always drew him back. He remained an isolated figure, calling for Charles to come to terms with his people, while most of the court supported Tory policies.[115]

Another incongruous figure was Anglesey, lord privy seal since 1672. Whereas Halifax's religion was exiguous, Anglesey had strong Presbyterian leanings. He had long been associated with York. In October 1679, when the council debated whether the duke should go to Scotland or return to Brussels, Anglesey had argued that he should be allowed to stay in London; in October 1680 he opposed his being sent away. He soon changed his tune, voting for exclusion and denouncing Charles's 'dreadful' decision to dissolve Parliament. This abrupt change owed much to accusations that he had been involved in the Meal Tub and Irish Plots: there was even talk of his being impeached. By early February 1681 he was dining with the likes of Monmouth, Armstrong and Lord Grey of Wark and was clearly out of step politically with the rest of the court.[116] As Anglesey's star fell, Seymour's rose. For some years he had been treasurer of the navy and a privy councillor, but his vanity and ambition were not satisfied. Never an easy colleague, he possessed qualities – strength of character and self-confidence – which were in short supply at court. He opposed James's being sent away and hoped to find an alternative to exclusion. When it became clear that the Commons would not compromise, he urged Charles to dissolve Parliament. He brought in Conway to fill the secretaryship vacated by Sunderland and many thought that he was destined for the post of chief minister which he so clearly coveted.[117]

Although Charles was committed to calling another Parliament he had no hope that it would prove more amenable than its predecessors. He had called it at Oxford because, at the last prorogation, there had been rumours that

Parliament might reconvene in the City, as in 1642: the Whigs, as he well knew, relied heavily on their support in the capital.[118] Charles had to call another Parliament because the prohibition on French imports was due to expire after the first Parliament that met after 20 March 1681. Charles convened it on the 21st and the lord chancellor hastened to complete some private business in the Lords so that it could be argued that it was a valid session. Some queried the legality of this procedure, but the determination to hold some sort of session said much for Charles's insistence on adhering to the letter to the law.[119] He could not, of course, admit publicly that the session was to be a charade: indeed, he declared that he would make proposals which no reasonable person could refuse. It soon became clear that he had not decided what these were to be, but he well knew that, in his diplomacy, his hand would be strengthened by holding out the hope that he would be able to reach agreement with Parliament. Privately, he assured York that he would never do so and St Albans told Barrillon that the session would last only a few days. Both Hyde and York tried to wean William from his conviction that agreement could be reached on terms which did not involve the destruction of the royal prerogative.[120]

Charles's firmness was strengthened by the renewed prospect of French money. Through much of the previous session, Barrillon had maintained his contacts with the opposition, seeking to prevent any agreement between king and Commons that could enable Charles to offer effective support to the Spanish and Dutch. Charles, for his part, made no effort to seek French help.[121] The first move towards a rapprochement came from Louis, who began to develop qualms about encouraging men whose principles were so at variance with his own. He was particularly concerned about the peril facing York and the Catholics and by the end of October had ordered Barrillon to assure the duke of his help, should need arise. York responded with polite generalities; not until early January, just before the prorogation, did Barrillon resume negotiations about a subsidy, through St Albans. Despite his brother's pleas for haste, Charles seemed in no hurry. Louis offered 1,500,000 *livres* a year for three years; Charles stuck out for 2,000,000 (about £150,000). Louis also sought guarantees for the safety of York and the Catholics, but Barrillon did not think that this was necessary, nor did he see any point in stipulating that Charles should not call Parliament, since it was so clearly in his interest not to do so. At last, when Charles had already left for Oxford, Barrillon increased his offer; terms were agreed the day after the session began. Charles promised to disengage gradually from his treaty with Spain and that he would not allow Parliament to engage him in any action against France. In return, he was to receive 2,000,000 *livres* in the first year and 1,500,000 in each of the next two. The treaty was purely oral; apart from Hyde nobody – not even Portsmouth – knew of the details.[122]

This treaty was concluded long after Charles had decided to dismiss the second Exclusion Parliament and that the session at Oxford was to be as short as possible. It offered an additional assurance of financial security, but even without it Hyde's economies (unpopular though they were) and the ending of the ban on French imports would have been sufficient to enable him to survive without Parliament.[123] The treaty also marked Charles's effective withdrawal from a role in Europe, although he naturally did not admit this to William. He and Hyde had sought assurances from Barrillon for the security of both Flanders and Strasbourg, but the treaty referred to these issues only in ambiguous terms.[124] Just as the dismissals of Whigs from the council and lord lieutenancies signalled the end of attempts to win over leading opponents of the court, so the treaty marked the abandonment of Sunderland's ploy of winning over the Commons by a 'popular' foreign policy. Both strategies had failed: the nation was too deeply divided, the Commons did not care enough about foreign affairs. Hyde and Jenkins tried to explain this to William. Charles still, they added, had the support of most of the nobility and gentry, the majority of whom had fought for his father: if he stuck to the laws and the Church, they would stick to him. There was no point in trying to be reconciled to the irreconcilable.[125]

The general election, held in February, was vigorously contested, especially by the Whigs, who made even greater use of populist tactics. Pamphlets and petitions proliferated and many newly elected MPs were presented with 'instructions' to insist on exclusion and the redress of grievances. The Tories responded as best they could, but some were reluctant to stand and Charles gave them little encouragement to do so. Jenkins at first thought that the new House would be a little worse than the old one, then that it would be a little better, but either way it did not greatly matter.[126] The government was far more preoccupied with evidence of disaffection, especially in London. Shaftesbury was said to be planning to raise men in Wapping and Southwark. Charles blocked moves to choose Clayton or even Monmouth to command the Honourable Artillery Company.[127] Vigilance was required to thwart politically provocative presentments by grand juries, against York, the queen, the king's guards or Ormond. As far as London was concerned, Charles controlled the appointment of the JPs for Middlesex and ordered them to enforce the laws, especially that against calling the king a Papist. They could not prevent York's being presented as a recusant at the Old Bailey, but the proceedings went no further.[128] The government was also careful to adhere to regular legal procedures at all times.[129]

The run-up to the elections suggested that, with vigilance, the government could maintain order without undue difficulty. There were encouraging signs that some of the Plot witnesses – notably Turberville and the Irishmen – were now ready to inform against their former patrons.[130] Nevertheless, a new witness, Fitzharris, accused York of plotting to kill his brother. He applied to Clayton and the City sheriffs before going to the council and his case was taken up by Shaftesbury and Essex. His information seemed to breathe new life into the increasingly moribund Plot and added to the Whigs' confidence. Convinced that Charles could not survive without money from Parliament, they assembled at Oxford with distinguishing ribbons in their hats and great trains of armed men.[131] Proposals that Mary should act as regent for her father were swept aside: the majority of MPs insisted on exclusion. The new House was, if anything, even more angry and outspoken than the old. MPs demanded to know why the bill repealing the Act of 1593 had not been passed, inveighed against evil advisers and impeached Fitzharris, in the hope that this would forestall any moves either to dissolve quickly or to 'stifle' his information in a hurried trial.[132] The recently dismissed Middlesex JP, Sir William Waller, read a paper 'bespattering' all three Stuart kings and calling on the people to take up arms against the crown. Brome Whorwood declared that Charles was too good a Protestant to hold the views expressed in the king's speech. Several MPs called on the House to follow the wishes of the electors, as set out in their instructions, and the House again resolved to print its votes.[133]

If the Commons' behaviour worried Charles, he did not show it. For some days he had amused himself in the environs of Oxford, with hawking, horse-races and long walks. He told Barrillon that the Commons would soon oblige him to dissolve them. On a visit to the Lords 'to entertain himself', he asked Shaftesbury if he could find an expedient which did not involve exclusion. The earl produced a paper proposing that, if James became king, power should be placed in Monmouth's hands. Charles protested that neither his conscience nor the law would allow that. Shaftesbury responded that a 'court conscience' had never hindered anyone from doing what was in their own best interests; as for the law, Parliament could change that. Charles replied that he was growing more resolute with age – law, reason and (he pointed to the bishops) the Church all supported his opinion. He concluded that he would take better care of the kingdom than those who professed concern for him ever could.[134] Despite his protestations, Monmouth's friends remained confident that he would have to comply with the Commons who, on 28 March, gave the first reading to a new exclusion bill. They were taken completely by surprise when Charles, who had come to the Lords in his ordinary clothes, slipped into his robes and dissolved Parliament.[135]

As the Whigs slunk away from Oxford in a state of shock, Charles returned to Whitehall in a high good humour, with the plaudits of the populace ringing in his ears. While his ministers stressed to William that he had had no choice – the Whigs had expected him to concede everything while conceding nothing themselves – he congratulated himself on being free of

Parliaments at last. In his dissolution speech he had pointedly not promised to call another: he did not need Parliament for money and would call it only if he required legislation. He had no wish to be 'absolute': he told Lord Bruce that a king who was not a slave to five hundred kings was great enough. As the letters to William implied, there was a price to be paid for his emancipation. Without Parliament he could not afford an effective foreign policy, but that was a price that he was well prepared to pay.[136]

In recent years, Charles had often compared his position with that of his father in 1640–2. As he returned for London from the Royalists' capital city, he could not but reflect on the improvement in his condition. His father had been forced to sacrifice Strafford, to assent to swingeing restrictions on his prerogatives and to flee from London like a thief in the night. Charles, by contrast, without sacrificing Danby (or York) and with his powers intact, was returning to London in triumph. The Commons' conduct had been as extreme and outspoken in 1677–81 as in 1640–2. On each occasion, their conduct had provoked a backlash among those who feared that they aimed to overturn the established order in Church and state. In 1640–2 that backlash had created the Royalist party, but by the time it had built up into a major force Charles I's grasp on the machinery of government and on London had been fatally weakened. Charles II, by contrast, remained in control. The Tory backlash, which he was beginning to exploit, was created by painful memories of what had happened in the civil wars as well as by fears of what the Whigs might do. Moreover, the Whigs' populism contained an element of bluff which had not been present in 1640–2: the crowds who surrounded Whitehall, calling for Strafford's blood, were very different to those who wandered tipsily home after the pope-burnings.

The differences between the fortunes of father and of son were due to more than changed circumstances, or luck. Charles I had repeatedly undermined his own efforts to appear moderate and reasonable, the defender of the traditional order in Church and state, by giving clear evidence that he wished to use force and to renege on the concessions that he had made. Charles II did not. He showed a clear grasp of what was essential and what was not, making cosmetic concessions (like the new privy council) but sacrificing neither his prerogatives nor his ministers. He also took his stand firmly on the letter of the law. If his judges bent it occasionally, they did so only to achieve ends that were widely acceptable – the maintenance of order and the suppression of 'disaffection'. There was no repeat of Charles I's cynical misuse of the law for fiscal gain, nor did Charles threaten to use military force against his enemies: the disbanding of the new regiments in the spring of 1679 did much to reduce the political temperature. Respect for the law was deeply engrained in English political culture. The Whigs' flexible – even bizarre – legal arguments did much to discredit them in the eyes of the Tories, as did the shamelessly partisan conduct of London juries. Through his right to appoint judges and county JPs and sheriffs, Charles had some control over the machinery of law, outside London and the larger corporate towns. He also directed the armed forces and the militia and he retained some influence even over the government of London. Given the political necessity of acting through proper legal channels, the reassertion of his authority would be slow and often undramatic. By acting in that way, however, he could be confident of extensive popular support, which would prove far more valuable than brute force.

The Battle for London

'Tis now come to a civil war not with the sword but law and if the king cannot make the judges speak for him he will be beaten out of the field.'[1] Thus an anonymous contemporary summed up the king's position after the Oxford Parliament: if he was to re-establish his authority, he needed to control the machinery of law and order, to appoint reliable judges and secure juries who would give favourable verdicts. He would also have to win the battle for hearts and minds, partly because of the element of popular participation in the legal process (notably on juries), partly because of the subjective element in English law: the king needed to show that his actions were not only technically justifiable but also fair and just. The Whigs had owed much of their popular support to their exploitation of the media; now the Tories hit back, through addresses designed for publication, partisan plays, pamphlets and poems. Of the poems much the most effective was *Absalom and Achitophel*, Dryden's brilliant satire on Monmouth, Shaftesbury and the Whigs; it first appeared on Queen Elizabeth's accession day, a Whig holy day, in 1681 – on the eve of Shaftesbury's trial. The Tories also learned to exploit the demand for newspapers. The first issue of L'Estrange's *Observator*, in April 1681, proclaimed: ''Tis the press has made 'em mad and the press must set 'em right again.' A few months later, one writer remarked that the *Observator* and *Heraclitus Ridens* had done the king more service than all his lawyers and divines put together.[2] The 'Tory reaction' of 1681–5 would have proved far less effective had it not won the support of all conditions of people, from regional magnates like the Marquis of Worcester (soon to be created Duke of Beaufort) to parish clergymen and London apprentices, who burned the Covenant and drank the Duke of York's health. Without their willing co-operation Charles would have been unable to establish such thorough control over the machinery of order or to harass his enemies.

In stressing the importance of popular Toryism, it should be remembered that the Whigs probably enjoyed greater support among the politically aware sections of the population. Popular belief in the Plot remained strong and the Whigs could exploit both anti-Popery and the charisma of Monmouth, seen by many as Charles's true heir. They also enjoyed the support of the great majority of Dissenters, who were a minority in the nation as a whole, but were committed, determined and concentrated in precisely the places which the king found hardest to control, the corporate towns. This is not to suggest that all towns, large or small, were predominantly Whig. Some, like Chester, Bristol or Nottingham, certainly were, but others, like Norwich or Lichfield, were strongly Tory. Even in Whig strongholds there was usually a significant Tory minority, actively supported by the neighbouring Tory gentry.[3] Toryism was also strong in London, but it seems unlikely that the Tories could have gained control over the City without the king's help; the fact that, there as elsewhere, they tended to stress the extent of their support among 'the better sort' suggests that they could not.[4]

The Tories compensated for their inferior numbers by exploiting their increasing control over the machinery of the state. They had no qualms about doing so. They were convinced that, as Ormond put it, the Whigs had sought to destroy the king's prerogative and the people's lives, liberty and property under the pretence of preserving them. 'Arbitrariness', remarked another, could be 'more in the people than in the king'; an address from County Durham talked of a design 'to enslave the people of this nation once more to the tyranny and arbitrary power of their fellow subjects'.[5] Faced with denials of justice by Whig juries, of which the king complained bitterly, Ormond expected the judges to 'extend the law as far as it will go for the preservation of the prerogative and the suppression of factions and factious people'. He was not, he added, suggesting that lives should be sacrificed to reason of state – although that was what the Whigs had done.[6] The Tories saw their measures as being forced on them by the Whigs' violence and extremism. Fear of civil war lingered and there were worries about the condition of urban fortifications.[7] The Tories' prime remedy for the evils they faced was to have loyal men appointed as deputy lieutenants and magistrates. Whatever the militia's military shortcomings, it was the nearest England had to a police force. It could search the houses of the 'disaffected' for arms. At both Nottingham and Bristol the lord lieutenant used it in an attempt to overawe the Whigs in municipal elections; in London the Tories' control of the lieutenancy proved invaluable.[8]

Although militia officers sometimes exceeded their lawful powers, especially during searches,[9] in general the Tories stayed within the letter of the law, but still found ample opportunities for revenge. Tory peers prosecuted individual Whigs for defamation, using actions of *scandalum magnatum* – a practice which had been revived by Shaftesbury, following an election dispute. There were, as we shall see, some treason trials in which the verdicts were heavily influenced by partisan considerations: as one writer noted, 'If anything of Whig or Tory comes in question, it is ruled according to the interest of the party: if in the City of London against the Tories; if in any of the counties, against the Whigs.'[10] Party animosities also led to a renewed persecution of Dissent, which allowed the Tories not only to indulge their thirst for revenge, but also to use the civil disabilities which the law imposed on Dissenters to erode the Whigs' support. Orders were given to enforce the Five Mile and Corporation Acts; the former was aimed especially at nonconformist clergy, while those who failed to meet the terms of the latter were debarred not only from office but also from voting in municipal elections. Despite the remissness of many constables, attempts to suppress conventicles met with more success than hitherto. The recusancy laws were used against Dissenters as well as Catholics. The prisons filled with Dissenters, especially Quakers, whose refusal to swear oaths laid them open to charges of contempt of court. Many died of gaol fever and other diseases in what was by far the severest persecution of the reign. The more extreme sects were not the only ones to suffer: those who failed to take communion at least once a year, as the law required, were excommunicated and so lost the right to plead at law or to vote. Dissenters were removed from offices, in the customs and elsewhere; in some places poor relief was given only to those who attended church.[11]

Much of the animus against Dissenters was political in origin. Charles himself deeply resented the support they had given to Shaftesbury and the Whigs, but his hostility occasionally wavered if there seemed a prospect of securing some advantage from them. He also considered it politically necessary to continue to persecute Catholics.[12] The Anglican clergy, for their part, had played an active part in the politics of the Exclusion Crisis. Political ideas, especially the concept of non-resistance, bulked large in their public pronouncements, to an extent that was to prove highly embarrassing under Charles's successor. For the moment, however, James consistently assured the Church of his goodwill and threats to its interests seemed to come exclusively from Whiggery and Dissent. Not all clerics supported all the measures against nonconformity. Compton had the Presbyterian lobbyist Sir John Baber banished from court, but was said to be unhappy at the use of excommunication as a political weapon. Others, however, believed that a measure of coercion was necessary to maintain purity of doctrine and to impose a wholesome spiritual discipline, 'toleration being certainly destructive of our reformed religion, whether procured by a Lord Clifford or a popular pretence to the uniting of Protestants'. Sancroft and his brethren tried hard to raise the pastoral standards of their clergy and had some genuine cause for the satisfaction they expressed at the increase in the number of Anglican communicants.[13]

In his last years Charles became firmly and unequivocally committed to the Church, which in turn threw its considerable moral and political weight behind the Tory reaction. The Bishop of Exeter rejoiced that the churches were fuller, but added that their task could not be completed until town councils were purged of Dissenters; the Bishop of Norwich agreed and others described corporations as the sole disturbers of the peace.[14] The Whig 'denials of justice' of which Charles and so many others complained stemmed from the predominance of nonconformists on so many corporations: Poole was said to pride itself on its 'true Protestant juries'. As the Corporation Act had failed to prevent this, it was necessary to change the rules under which towns were governed and that meant changing their charters. Once granted, a charter could be confiscated only if it could be proved, by an action of *quo warranto*, that the corporation had failed to abide by its provisions. The threat of such an action might be used in an effort to persuade a corporation to enforce the laws against Dissent, as with Berwick in 1681.[15] As a *quo warranto* could take years to complete,[16] it would have been impractical to proceed against all the refractory corporations: the courts would have been swamped. The king and the local Tories therefore tried to induce a corporation to surrender its charter and petition for a new one. This might involve trickery or bullying, but there could also be the bait of new privileges for the town: the aim was not to deprive it of the right to run its own affairs, but to control the membership of the corporation. New charters gave the king the power to remove any member whom he regarded as 'disaffected', irrespective of whether he had complied with the terms of the Corporation Act. These new charters were at first issued in small numbers: ten in 1682, two in the first half of 1683. Only at the end of 1684 did the trickle develop into a flood. Before then, it is difficult to detect anything resembling a coherent government strategy. The initiative for securing new charters was usually local, often involving peers like Beaufort or Yarmouth. On one point, however, the Bishop of Exeter, the king and most other observers agreed: London was the key to the whole process. Unless Charles could re-establish effective authority over the capital, he would never be master of his kingdom.[17]

Charles emerged from the Exclusion Crisis an older and tireder man: illness and psychological strain had taken their toll. Physically he remained robust – he could still walk nine miles in a morning – but he also tended to nod off and was prone to colds and boils. Hawker's portrait shows a sagging, jowly face: the jaunty moustache has gone and the prevailing impression is of lassitude and of the toll taken by years of debauchery.[18] The king's pleasures were simple – walking, fishing, boating, riding, cards. More than ever he fled the noise and crowds of London for the country: Windsor, if he needed to remain close to the capital, but preferably Newmarket or Winchester. Newmarket had long offered a respite from business – ministers always complained that all the talk there was of dogs and horses – but the delights it offered, as described by Sir John Reresby, were rudimentary:

The king was ... so great a lover of the diversions which that place did afford that he let himself down from majesty to the very degree of a country gentleman. He mixed himself among the crowd, allowed every man to speak to him that pleased, went a-hawking in mornings, to cock matches in afternoons (if there were no horse races) and to plays in the evenings, acted in a barn and by very ordinary Bartholomew-fair comedians.[19]

Compared with the delights of London, the younger and livelier courtiers found Newmarket dull and attendance at court was often thin, but Charles did not mind. In 1682 he began to build a palace at Winchester, where the air was good and the hunting excellent. The fact that the best hunting and many of the best houses around Newmarket belonged to Whigs may have influenced this decision, as may the proximity of Winchester to Portsmouth, which Charles had heavily fortified and which offered an escape route to the continent in case of emergency. Moreover, much of Newmarket was destroyed in a fire in the spring of 1683, but Charles loved the area so much that he continued to spend time there, in conditions which many found unpleasantly spartan. Charles had long aspired to build a new palace. Initially he chose Greenwich, close to his beloved Thames and the dockyards, but away from the smoke and stench of London. He moved the royal observatory there, from the Tower, but building on the site of what became William III's Greenwich Hospital was abandoned because of lack of money. For Winchester, Wren produced a design modelled on Versailles, to which Louis moved his court in that year. Work proceeded apace. Charles stayed several times in the half-finished building, which was nearing completion at the time of his death.[20]

Charles's fondness for the country and its simple pleasures exemplified the domesticity of his last years. The queen's life, of cards and devotions, surrounded by her ladies, was largely separate from the king's. The role of royal consort was filled instead by Portsmouth. She quickly repented of her error in supporting exclusion and broke off her connections with the Whigs. As her influence began to recover, she tried hard to be reconciled to York. He, for his part, was eager to return from his tedious exile and her concern to provide for herself and her children in case of Charles's death offered him an opportunity. He acquiesced in proposals that financial provision should be made for her son out of the profits of the post office, granted to York by Act of Parliament.[21] By the end of 1681 they were reconciled; soon after, York returned to court. Opinions varied on the physical side of her relationship with Charles: Halifax alleged that he had not slept with her for four months, but she was reported to be pregnant in 1682; others claimed that she took other lovers. Charles made his fondness for her apparent on all occasions: allegations that in his old age he preferred wine to women are at best questionable. What was not in doubt was her political influence. When she fell ill late in 1684 the king's affairs ground to a halt. She brought Sunderland back into office and played an active role in foreign policy. She also ensured that Charles provided for her lavishly: he made her son master of the horse – another blow to Monmouth – and granted her £100,000 – over two and a half years – out of the French subsidy.[22]

One of Portsmouth's earliest political allies was Hyde, created Viscount Hyde in April 1681 and, following the death of the poet, Earl of Rochester in November 1682. His position at the treasury made his friendship especially valuable: a common device to relieve the crown's cash-flow problems was to delay payments, especially to those who lacked influence with the treasurer or the king. Such methods were not popular – a partial stop of the exchequer in the spring of 1681 provoked an outcry – but Rochester and his colleagues persisted with the retrenchment which had begun after Danby's fall. Departmental spending was closely monitored and the anticipation of revenue was restricted. The burden of debt remained substantial but manageable, and gradually eased. On the revenue side, the end of the ban on French imports and the continuation of the trade boom of the 1670s boosted the customs. Rochester abandoned Danby's practice of tax farming in favour of direct collection by salaried officials. This had been forced on the crown as far as the customs were concerned in 1671, by the failure to secure an acceptable bid for the farm. Rochester extended the practice to the excise and hearth money, so that the crown – and not the tax farmers – would reap the fiscal benefits of the nation's growing prosperity. The change had the additional advantage of creating, for the first time, networks of salaried employees of the central government throughout the provinces.[23]

High-handed and irritable, Rochester made enemies easily. Courtiers complained that he delayed paying pensions and salaries. Government departments chafed at the treasury's intrusiveness, but Pepys's later claim that retrenchment was a disaster for the navy was at best half true: more ships were put out each spring than during the period of Pepys's ascendancy. Some denounced the evacuation of Tangier, to save money, as the sacrifice of a precious national asset. In fact, the commercial advantages which it had been expected to bring never materialized and, as a base for victualling or careening naval vessels, it proved less useful than Livorno, Cadiz or Port Mahon. Financiers alleged that direct collection would bring the king less profit than farming; Halifax took up their case, accusing Rochester of incompetence and corruption. The subsequent investigations effectively vindicated Rochester's policies and indeed it was no mean achievement that he enabled Charles to survive without Parliament for four years while perceptibly reducing his debts. It is possible that Charles was, at last, learning to live within his means, although Ormond (himself hardly an exemplar of thrift) claimed that he would have become solvent much sooner but for the expense of his bastards and their mothers. (It should be added, however, that he ignored appeals for money from the now impoverished Cleveland.) The palace at Winchester did not come cheap either. The French subsidy gave him some leeway – payments to Portsmouth mostly came from that, or the post office, rather than the regular revenue – and the fact remains that Charles subsisted without resorting to any means of money-raising which could be described as illegal.[24]

No minister, however competent, could survive without allies at court. Hyde was soon on good terms with Portsmouth and began to press for York's return. Charles was reluctant to agree. He had been told that York wanted a showdown with his enemies while Charles was still alive, a prospect which Charles did not relish at all. Portsmouth, convinced that James would never forgive her for supporting exclusion, opposed his return and even Hyde seems at first to have regarded it as impolitic. As the months passed, Hyde won the support of Portsmouth, Seymour and Conway for the duke's coming to court at least temporarily: only Halifax consistently opposed the idea and persuaded Charles to revive the demand that James should first conform to the Church of England. In February 1682, Charles at last sent for his brother. He was supposedly to remain for just a few days, to make over part of the post office profits to Portsmouth's son, but then Charles decided that he should stay.[25] After all the dire warnings that his coming would precipitate a revolt, the duke was widely welcomed, even in London.[26] Re-established at court, he pressed hard to be admitted to the cabinet council. He accepted Portsmouth's assurances that Sunderland had seen the error of his ways and would behave as James wished in future, so the duke began to support his claims to office. James was well aware that Sunderland was an able administrator, with a knowledge of foreign affairs which Conway conspicuously lacked; he could also prove an effective political counterweight to Halifax – the two hated each other. Fortunately for Sunderland's friends, at this point a convenient vacancy appeared. Anglesey, who had been keeping politically dubious company, published a book attacking the conduct of Ormond, and Charles I, in the 1640s. He was deprived of the privy seal and both Halifax and Seymour aspired to succeed him. After much backstairs intrigue, in October Charles gave the place to Halifax, partly as compensation for Sunderland's being allowed to return to court. Seymour, his pride badly bruised, stormed off into the country and was soon removed from the council. In January 1683 Sunderland was made secretary in place of Conway, who was said to be the last person at court to be told.[27]

In a court increasingly dominated by York, Hyde, Portsmouth and the malleable Sunderland, the continued favour of Halifax (whom they all disliked) seemed anomalous. He was also, as we shall see, at odds with the other leading figures at court on foreign policy. He was a difficult colleague: Ormond remarked that he worked well with others only if they complied with his wishes in all things.[28] Nevertheless, he clung to office. His ambition was such that he would shrug off defeats and humiliations in order to remain in power, but it is also clear that Charles wished to retain his services. The king doubtless appreciated the wit which is so apparent in Halifax's writings; he would get few laughs from his brother, and Rochester, while renowned for his wit, had a savage temper and was inclined to drink too much. More important, however, was Charles's determination never to be controlled by a single clique: he wished to hear different points of view and, perhaps, to maintain a healthy sense of insecurity in the minds of his ministers. He also insisted that Ormond, who was loyal but independent-minded, should remain at court rather than return to Ireland.[29]

The policy options facing Charles were now clearer, indeed starker, than at any time in his reign. At home, circumstances left him little choice but to rely on the 'Cavalier and Church' interest. Abroad, his wish to avoid calling Parliament meant that he could follow no policy which carried a serious risk of war. He did not always spell this out. It could be politically wise to receive overtures from Whigs and Dissenters and it would have been diplomatically foolish to state categorically that he had no intention of making war. Charles wished to maintain the impression – and, perhaps, to convince himself – that he enjoyed some freedom of manoeuvre, but in practice his options were limited, which doubtless helps explain the greater firmness and resolution that he showed in these years. Politicians still tried to deny their rivals access to his person and even Hyde expressed doubts as to whether he could be relied upon to adhere to the policies he had adopted. On some issues, such as York's return or Anglesey's replacement, he showed all his old indecision. Halifax often complained of his unreliability, not pausing to consider that if Charles had been rigorously consistent he would not have kept Halifax in office at all.[30] In general, however, disagreement centred on details rather than fundamentals, on means rather than ends. Charles accepted the need for Tory policies, but was not prepared to press forward as far or as fast as some Tories wanted. He did not wish to remove all Whigs from local office, but hoped that the more moderate could be redeemed.[31] He saw the merit of the arguments of men like Jenkins, Chancellor Finch (now Earl of Nottingham) and Sir Francis North (who succeeded Nottingham in 1682) that he should be careful to keep within the law.[32] He also had no wish to call a Parliament, which many Tories wanted him to do, but thought it politic not to say so publicly, especially in view of the delicate situation in the Low Countries.[33] Halifax pressed consistently for Parliament to meet, but even Conway wrote in May 1682 that he expected Charles to summon it soon. By then, however, the foreign crisis was easing and a Parliament became less and less likely. Those closest to the king, indeed, were sure that none would be called.[34]

Except, perhaps, on the issue of calling Parliament, Charles's policies in 1681–3 were more in tune with the wishes of a large section of the political nation than at any time in his reign. Contemporaries remarked approvingly on his new-found firmness. He 'expressed his sense that there is no dallying now and that there ought to be made a clean sweep of such kind of men whose principles are averse to the government'. 'God's fish,' he declared, 'if he did not keep them under they would ruin him.'[35] Early in 1683 Ormond wrote contentedly to his son that all at court were either Tories or 'Trimmers', the latter claiming to combine the Tories' respect for the prerogative and the Whigs' concern for religion and property. The only conspicuous Trimmer at court was Halifax; Rochester, North, Sunderland, Conway and Jenkins were all firm Tories. 'In short,' he concluded, 'if we have good luck we shall be all Tories; if we have bad luck we shall not be all Whigs.'[36]

The Whigs soon recovered from the shock of the dissolution of the Oxford Parliament. A new presentment for recusancy was brought in against York at the Old Bailey and two Whig earls urged the lord mayor to call a common council. Neither move achieved its desired effect. The case against York was transferred to King's Bench and aborted by a writ of *nolle prosequi*. The lord mayor claimed to be ill and when common council eventually met it refused to endorse a petition for a Parliament.[37] This refusal owed much to an address put before the common council by a group of Tories, thanking Charles for his declaration of 8 April. This stressed his efforts to give the Commons satisfaction and recounted a number of their more extravagant resolutions. Charles insisted that he had nothing but affection for Parliaments, but felt constrained to remind his people of 'the late troubles and confusions'. He was sure he could count on the support of all those 'who cannot but remember that religion, liberty and property were all lost and gone when the monarchy was shaken off and could never be revived till that was restored'.[38] Charles I had issued a similar declaration in 1629, but that had been less moderate in tone and had not been accompanied by an order to enforce the laws against Popery. Charles had, indeed, considered some form of self-justification after the previous dissolution, but his advisers had been unable to agree. Now he was determined to appeal to his subjects' loyalty; Sancroft ordered his clergy to read the declaration in their churches.[39]

Local Tories responded with a flood of loyal addresses, like the one presented to the common council: the humour of addressing was now on the other side.[40] Meanwhile, Charles had the few remaining 'disaffected' members removed from the City lieutenancy and ordered the suppression of seditious conventicles.[41]

The Whigs were far from cowed. They claimed that Fitzharris could not be tried in an 'inferior' court once he had been impeached; the Tories responded that the impeachment was of no force as it had not been received by the Lords. Charles, angered by Fitzharris's allegations against his wife and brother, wanted him dead; Bethel and Cornish produced a grand jury with Godfrey's brother as foreman. The judges declared firmly that the alleged impeachment constituted no bar to their proceeding. Faced with Fitzharris's own confession that he had produced a treasonable libel, and with even Sir William Waller testifying against him, the grand jury had no choice but to agree that there was a *prima facie* case against him. Desperate, Fitzharris looked to the Whigs to save him: claiming he had much to reveal, he asked for a private meeting with Essex, Clayton and other luminaries.[42] When he came to trial his counsel included Winnington and the Speaker of the Oxford Parliament, Sir William Williams. Whigs and Tories sat in different parts of the courtroom. Whig peers played to the gallery in an effort to intimidate prosecution witnesses, but the judges and the prosecution lawyers demolished the defence's preliminary legal arguments with little difficulty. Attempts to prompt the accused were thwarted by the officer guarding him, who pushed Williams away so forcefully that the former Speaker ended on his backside. The Whigs tried their utmost to delay proceedings. A grand jury demanded that Fitzharris should tell it what he knew of Godfrey's murder and Fitzharris accused Danby of complicity, hoping that he would then be kept alive to testify against the former treasurer. Others wished to ask what he knew of the Fire, but the judges would not allow it. The day before the trial finally got under way the City sheriffs were fined for failing to prepare a panel of jurors. The jury that they eventually produced was overwhelmingly Whig, but the evidence was so damning that it had little choice but to find Fitzharris guilty. He was finally hanged on 1 July, along with Oliver Plunkett, Archbishop of Armagh, the last victim of the Popish Plot.[43]

Fitzharris's trial was the first in which Plot witnesses accused their former patrons of suborning them. The Whigs still, however, could rely on the partisanship of London juries. The new sheriffs elected in June, Shute and Pilkington, were considered by Tories as bad as their predecessors (who were thanked by common hall for their honest and prudent juries). One beneficiary of their 'honesty' was Lord Howard of Escrick, charged with writing the libel for which Fitzharris lost his life. When an indictment was brought against him, the grand jury seemed inclined to reject it, so the attorney-general withdrew it, to await a more favourable opportunity. Unabashed, the jury presented the clerk of the crown for drawing up the indictment.[44] Another apparent beneficiary was Stephen College, 'the Protestant joiner', who had produced a ballad and print entitled 'The Raree Show', which depicted Charles as an itinerant pedlar. He was accused by several witnesses of planning to seize the king and start an insurrection. The witnesses, headed by Dugdale, had learned their trade in the Plot and many – and not only Tories – found their testimony convincing. The usual batch of Whig lords appeared at the trial and the jury returned a verdict of 'ignoramus', not because there was insufficient evidence but because (they claimed) they did not believe the witnesses.[45] The Whigs' jubilation was misplaced. As some of College's alleged offences had been committed at Oxford, a new indictment was prepared against him there and an Oxfordshire grand jury found a true bill without hesitation. A month later he was convicted and condemned to death: had he come before a London trial jury he would probably have been acquitted. Not for the last time, the Whigs had proved too clever for their own good.[46]

The defiance of Whig magnates, sheriffs and jurors might sustain morale and annoy the king, but it did nothing to bring them closer to their political goals. For that they needed a Parliament and to secure a Parliament they needed to mobilize support 'without doors', above all in London. It was not enough for Whigs to show their allegiance by wearing blue ribbons in the streets: they needed to show that they had the support of 'the body of the City'. But the aldermen, who controlled day-to-day government, were mostly Tories. Only in the occasional meetings of common council and common hall could the strength of Whig sentiment among the citizenry find expression. In May, Charles tried to prevent the lord mayor from assembling common council; when that failed, he hoped that the aldermen would prevent anything untoward.[47] Common council rejected a motion to thank the king for his declaration and approved, by a majority of only fourteen votes, to address the king to call Parliament; most of the aldermen opposed the resolution. It was also agreed that the address should be printed. A similar petition was presented by Fitzharris's grand jury.[48] The chancellor told those who brought the petition that London's common council could not speak for England – and that it had been far from unanimous. The petition was designed, he said, to call into question the king's promise to call frequent Parliaments. He condemned as unconstitutional the demand that Parliament should stay in being until all business had been concluded. He also noted, with distaste, that the petition condemned libels against Parliament, but not those against the king.[49]

Nottingham's response to the petition, and the king's gracious reception of Tory addresses from the City lieutenancy and from Southwark, showed that there was little point in petitioning for a Parliament. Common hall's vote of thanks to the outgoing sheriffs was a gesture of defiance, little more.[50] At least it showed the strength of Whig sentiment in the City, as the government prepared its next move in the courts. The day after Fitzharris's execution, Charles asked if the evidence against Shaftesbury was sufficient to justify a charge of treason. The judges thought that it was and the council ordered that he should be arrested and his papers seized: Charles insisted that this order should be signed by all present. Some of the Irish witnesses now accused their former patron of planning to seize the king at Oxford and the evidence against him was said to be strengthened by an allegedly treasonable 'association' found among his papers. Charles wanted to try the little earl at once, but Nottingham advised him to wait until the new law term, and experience of College's trial gave them further reason to pause.[51] Loyal addresses from thousands of London apprentices showed that Charles had massive support in the City, a support reinforced by gifts of venison and wine, but in a polity of master craftsmen apprentices had no votes. The court won more tangible successes in the defeat of Shute's attempt to be elected an alderman and in the election of Sir John Moore as lord mayor. Many had expected Moore to lose. By custom the aldermen could select one of the two candidates who polled most votes in common hall, but the Whigs were so strong that many feared that both Whig candidates would outpoll Moore, even though he was seen as far from hostile to Dissent. Jenkins enquired whether the king could legally refuse to accept the man chosen. As it turned out, his enquiries were unnecessary, but the shrievalty was still in Whig hands and the time for Shaftesbury's trial was approaching.[52]

Before the trial began, the judges did what they could to counter the probable bias of the grand jury. They delayed the case and considered other expedients, including a commission of oyer and terminer and having the case heard at Westminster, where juries were nominated by the bailiff, appointed by the dean and chapter. They considered ways of excluding Dissenters from the jury, in which they were eagerly supported by the Middlesex JPs, who had earlier proposed that the king should appoint the sheriffs of Middlesex, as he did those of other counties; Charles referred the suggestion to his legal advisers. Shaftesbury was also prevented from indicting for perjury the witnesses who were due to testify against him. He even offered to emigrate to Carolina if Charles would provide for him financially, but the king wanted his head.[53] To a later plea, Charles replied that he would leave Shaftesbury to the law, but the crown's case was questionable, as it rested on words rather than deeds. Was the association treasonable? Had Shaftesbury written or approved it? Moreover, no way had been found to circumvent the sheriffs' power to pack juries. The judges fined the sheriffs for contempt, the king made his displeasure clear, but they remained obdurate.[54] In late October, the attorney-general did not think that any London jury would convict the earl. Charles denounced Whigs and Dissenters, snubbed the sheriffs and complained that he was the only man in England who could not secure justice. Other expedients were considered, but the king at last allowed the indictment to proceed, with little hope of success: the best he could hope for was that Shaftesbury's guilt would be made so clear that he would emerge, in Charles's words, with a bottle at his tail.[55]

When proceedings began on 24 November, the judges had to assign guards to protect the witnesses from a vehemently hostile populace. Even within the courtroom, spectators hissed and shouted as they gave evidence; the usual gaggle of Whig notables, led by Monmouth, Russell, Essex and Montagu, encouraged the tumult. The Irish witnesses swore that Shaftesbury had declared that the people would be justified in taking up arms against the king, but the jury (including one of Godfrey's brothers) declared that it did not believe them. The chief justice reminded them that their task was not to pass a verdict, but merely to decide if there was sufficient evidence for the case to go to trial; he was ignored. The jury's verdict of 'ignoramus' occasioned wide rejoicing: bonfires, despite the lord mayor's efforts, blazed throughout the City; passers-by who refused to drink the earl's health were 'lustily mauled'. The mood at court was sombre. The chief justice had declared after the verdict that it was clear that the king could not obtain justice in London, even if his life was in danger.[56] Charles asked the attorney-general whether the sheriffs and the City could be prosecuted for the disorders that had occurred and whether offences committed in London could be tried by juries from elsewhere. He also ordered that much more vigorous steps should be taken to remove Dissenters from offices. The key to the problem, however, was the City's autonomy and the popular election of the sheriffs. Two days after the fateful verdict, Jenkins wrote that Charles had resolved to be avenged for the insults that he had suffered and was launching a *quo warranto* against London's charter.[57]

The need to avoid calling Parliament, at least until the political foundations of Whiggery had been destroyed, drastically limited Charles's options in foreign policy. Historians often speak of his admiration for Louis XIV and his desire to introduce a 'French' type of government. Charles certainly liked Louis' style – hence his wish to build a mini-Versailles in Hampshire – and he was weary of Parliament's complaints and inquisitiveness, but he lacked the vision, the fixity of purpose and the energy to construct an English 'absolutism'. Advisers like Jenkins and North, not to mention Halifax, would not have supported such a move: they were deeply attached to the existing constitution and were fearful that they might, one day, have to answer to Parliament.[58] Some historians also accuse Charles of subservience to Louis, but that is misleading. In the first half of his reign, Charles deliberately sought Louis' friendship because he wished to prevent Louis closing with the Dutch and because he wanted France to be on his side when Carlos II died. The courtship was not smooth. In 1675–7 Charles had tried all means short of war to curb Louis' ambitions in the Low Countries; subsequently his threat of war had led to strained relations between the two kings. When Louis decided that it was not in his interests for the Whigs to triumph over Charles and James, relations did not dramatically improve. Charles fulsomely expressed his friendship for his cousin, which Louis politely reciprocated, but several sources of friction remained. Charles was well aware of Barrillon's dealings with the Whigs, of which he had first been informed, ironically, by Montagu. His ambassador in Paris, Lord Preston, kept him fully apprised of the dealings of Montagu's former secretary, Falaiseau, and quickly let Charles know that the Whig Hampden had come to Paris with a letter of recommendation from Barrillon. Burnet too, out of favour in England, found a warm welcome at the French court and there were renewed fears of French designs on Ireland.[59] The French remained as ruthless as ever in matters of commerce and Jersey and Guernsey merchants complained of harassment. As Louis' regime stepped up its pressure on the Huguenots, there were stories of the maltreatment of English merchants, like Mr Whiting of Lille.[60] Last but not least, a brief and garbled account of the Secret Treaty of Dover was published at Paris in a history, first printed in Italian, by Abbé Primi. Louis quickly suppressed the book, but Preston noted that it had been licensed by the French authorities and strongly suspected a design to embarrass the English king.[61]

His suspicions were not unfounded. The Treaty of Nijmegen had brought the European war to an end, but Louis wished to ensure England's neutrality as he pursued a more limited and devious policy of territorial acquisition. He pre-empted, in his own favour, the decisions of the commissioners who met at Courtrai to interpret the more recondite details of the treaty. More profitable still was the policy of *réunions*. Between Louis' ancestral dominions and the Rhine lay Lorraine and Alsace, a patchwork of territories held by a motley collection of rulers under a bewildering array of titles, many of which were questionable. The Treaties of Westphalia and Nijmegen had skirted around this jurisdictional labyrinth, so that it offered a lush hunting ground for French lawyers – especially as Louis had the military might to enforce their rulings, and petty German princes and even the emperor, preoccupied with his struggle against the Turk, had not. The *chambres de réunion* in the Parlements of Besançon and Metz awarded Louis parcels of territory, from Montbéliard northwards, which enabled him to consolidate his hold on the region and to strengthen his eastern frontier. Even his most ingenious lawyers, however, failed to find a pretext to annex Strasbourg, but Louvois' forces occupied the city anyway and so brought one of the key Rhine crossings under French control.[62]

The annexations caused anxiety in England and the Dutch Republic, but did not directly threaten the security of either. One decision of the Parlement of Metz, however, clearly did. Having discovered that the county of Chiny, an important part of Luxemburg, had once belonged to the bishopric of Metz, the court ordered its return and that of other territories which had once been its fiefs. As French armies moved in to enforce this order, little was left of the duchy of Luxemburg except the city itself, which was blockaded and seemed unlikely to hold out long. If the French took Luxemburg, they would be able to sweep into the Spanish Netherlands from the east – or up into the republic. William was convinced that, if Louis was not stopped, the republic would be in mortal danger: French control of Luxemburg would tear a gaping hole in the barrier which the Dutch so dearly wanted. Many in England shared this fear and the Spaniards called upon Charles to act on the treaty which he had signed in 1680, under which he promised to send military aid if they were attacked.[63]

In April 1681 the Spanish ambassador formally demanded English assistance. Charles was acutely embarrassed. If he fulfilled his obligations, he would be forced to call Parliament; if he did not, he would encourage suspicions that he had a secret understanding with France. Louis calculated that a combination of the French subsidy and Charles's fear of calling Parliament would keep England neutral. If this calculation proved wrong, he could renew his links with the English opposition or, as a last resort, leak the Dover Treaty. It seemed more likely to prove correct, however, especially in view of the coolness between Charles and William. Charles bitterly resented William's claim that he should somehow have come to terms with Parliament, especially as, when he spelt out the Whigs' demands one by one, William had agreed that all were unacceptable. Charles regarded William's reaction to the Luxemburg crisis as excessive; many in the republic agreed and suspected him of exaggerating the danger in order to build up the army. William thought Charles was either wilfully blind or a French puppet, Charles thought William disobedient and misinformed, notably by Sidney. The prince's decision to appoint Sidney to command the British regiments in the Dutch service added to the friction. William's friends advised him to come over to England to clear the air. He came in July, but went home early, furious that Charles had forbidden him to dine with the lord mayor and sheriffs of London.[64]

After William's departure, York and Hyde stressed to him that domestic reconstruction was Charles's first priority and advised him to accept that the loss of Luxemburg was unavoidable. Others, notably Halifax, disagreed: to allow Luxemburg to fall would, he argued, be politically disastrous. A group of Whigs promised, if Parliament met, to secure a vote of money for the relief of Flanders, without any mention of exclusion. When news came of the annexation of Strasbourg, Charles told Barrillon that there would be a general revolt if he did nothing; he would not call Parliament or enter into a league with the Dutch, but hoped in return that Louis would leave the Low Countries in peace.[65] Halifax, meanwhile, assured William that if Louis clearly violated the peace Charles would call Parliament and join with the Dutch. French military activity in the county of Alost (Aalst), between Ghent and Brussels, added to Charles's anxieties, but Barrillon told him smugly that, provided he did not hold out hopes of English assistance, the Spaniards would soon recognize the justice of Louis' claims. Louis would, however, accept Luxemburg as an 'equivalent' for the rest and suggested that Charles should press the Spaniards to agree.[66] Louis withdrew his troops from Alost, but concern about Luxemburg remained. The Spanish and Dutch ambassadors, supported by Halifax and Seymour, pressed Charles to take action and to call Parliament. Barrillon countered with the bait of a further subsidy, but it was too late. In November Charles assured the two ambassadors that, if Louis used force to violate the Treaty of Nijmegen, he would call Parliament.[67]

Charles gave this assurance reluctantly. His resolution not to call Parliament had been undermined by his advisers. Hyde alone opposed the assurance; York, far away in Edinburgh, was powerless to prevent it. It had the merit of strengthening Hyde's hand in his efforts to persuade the French to ease the blockade of Luxemburg. If the city surrendered, it would clearly have succumbed to force. For Charles's sake, Louis should allow just enough food in to remove any need for surrender; Charles could then claim that Louis was not using force and that he was not obliged to call Parliament. Hyde added that, while the matter remained unresolved, York would not be able to return to court. Barrillon, who was never eager to tell his master unwelcome truths, intimated that he might be wise to comply with Charles's wishes. Louis, however, had no intention of easing the pressure: he exulted in his power and enjoyed humiliating the Spaniards. Hyde was forced to fob off William and the Spaniards with assurances that a diplomatic solution was imminent, while Halifax assured William that Charles would call Parliament if no such solution materialized.[68] For weeks Charles and Hyde writhed, pleading for more time and for provisions to be allowed in. In December Louis granted their requests, but then embarked on further aggression elsewhere in the Netherlands. Even the mild Jenkins denounced the concession as a 'pitiful amusement'; Louis represented it as a great favour. Charles now pinned his hopes on Louis' offer to raze Luxemburg's fortifications, and to abandon his other claims in the Netherlands, if he received the city; he undertook to persuade the Spaniards to cede it, on those conditions, within three months. They, however, refused to make any concessions, confident that public pressure would force Charles to call Parliament and come to their aid. For this reason, they refused to receive the few provisions which Louis allowed through.[69]

It was a serious miscalculation. By the end of January 1682 Charles had made up his mind that he would not call Parliament: if the Spaniards refused to accept the terms he offered, he would leave them to their fate. Catastrophic floods had undermined the resolve of the Dutch, leaving the Spaniards isolated. William claimed angrily that there must be some secret understanding between Charles and Louis and persuaded the States General to urge him to call Parliament. Charles was livid: the move reinforced his suspicions that William was in cahoots with the Whigs. It made him doubly determined to wash his hands of the Spaniards, unless they quickly saw reason. He made one last attempt to persuade Louis to allow troops and provisions into Luxemburg. Barrillon haughtily rebutted his arguments, but warned Louis not to push Charles too far, as he was not a free agent; the fact that the States General did not want war offered an additional reason for Louis to be flexible. Louis, as always, was determined to extract all the advantage he could from his position of strength. He offered a series of expedients to secure his 'rights'; Charles rejected them all. Then, on 12 March, Louis announced that he would withdraw his forces from Luxemburg. He had no wish, he said, to imperil the defence of Christendom against the Turks. He referred the points still at issue at Courtrai to Charles's arbitration.[70]

Charles's failure to take a firm stand against French aggression was seen by many, not least William, as pusillanimous in the extreme. It could equally be argued, however, that from a position of great weakness he had done much to restrain the French king. Charles may have been bluffing when he promised to recall Parliament if Louis used force in the Netherlands, but Louis was bluffing too: he did not want war and so refrained from full-scale military aggression. Furthermore, Louis withdrew from Luxemburg, leaving the points at issue to Charles's arbitration. Charles was delighted that his efforts at damage limitation had succeeded: no one could have predicted that Louis would again occupy Luxemburg two years later. Charles would also have been less delighted had he known that Louis' withdrawal owed little to consideration for his English cousin. He was far more concerned to assuage the hostility of the German princes, in the hope that his son might be elected King of the Romans and so become Holy Roman Emperor when Leopold died.[71]

It soon became clear that, in Louis' eyes, Charles's main task as arbitrator was to persuade the Spaniards to cede Luxemburg, with its fortifications razed, in lieu of Louis' other claims in the Low Countries. In other words, Louis was pursuing the same objective, using diplomatic rather than military methods, a change of approach which greatly reduced the political pressure on Charles at home. The Spaniards were slow to accept his arbitration. They suspected that Charles would prove biased towards France and calculated that they could lose more through arbitration than they would if renewed French aggression forced the Dutch, and even the English, to come to their aid. They sought pretexts for delay: they wished to consult the emperor, they wished the Low Countries and Alsace to be considered together. Charles told them firmly that he would not be dragged into war; privately he suspected William of encouraging them to behave unreasonably.[72] As Louis amused himself by inflicting petty humiliations on the Spanish ambassador in Paris and annexing Orange, William begged Charles to do something to prevent Louis from establishing universal dominion. Charles, however, was reluctant to take any public stand about Orange until he was fully informed of the rights and wrongs of the case, while intimating privately that he hoped that Louis would proceed with restraint.[73]

Towards the end of 1682, Louis began ostentatious military preparations. The Spaniards, he said, were clearly uninterested in a negotiated settlement. Despite pressure from the Dutch, Charles refused to declare either that he would abide by his treaties or that he would not, under any circumstances, make war. He agreed to press Louis to extend the deadline for the acceptance of his arbitration, but Madrid continued to insist that the affairs of the Low Countries and Alsace should be considered together. Charles dismissed this as unrealistic: it would add new complications to problems that were intractable enough already.[74] Matters were not improved by the Spaniards' decision to expel Charles's ambassador, Goodricke, because of a protocol dispute. Charles exclaimed angrily that the Spaniards had tried to undermine the English monarchy since 1660.[75] Louis agreed, perhaps to spite the Spaniards, to extend his deadline, but as he flexed his muscles for further military intervention they became still more reluctant to accept Charles as arbitrator. Charles's patience was wearing thin: he believed that they would see reason only if Louis forced them to do so. The Dutch, too, were increasingly disinclined to become embroiled in war, leading William to make a more submissive approach to his uncle. Charles told him loftily that peace would have been concluded long before had his advice been followed. He suggested that, once the Spaniards had accepted his arbitration, the two of them could work together – with the clear implication that Charles would be the dominant partner.[76] The prospects of Anglo-Dutch co-operation were further damaged by a violent dispute between the two nations in Bantam. York, ever bellicose and anti-Dutch, called for war, but wiser counsels prevailed: Charles had no wish to become involved in a distant conflict which could all too easily spread to Europe.[77]

After the crisis over Luxemburg, Charles was content to let matters drift on the continent. He had no wish to see Louis make major gains in the Low Countries, but still less did he wish to take the Spaniards' side: when they offered him money to make war, he almost burst out laughing. When the Dutch and imperial ambassadors tried to negotiate some sort of peace, Charles told them that Louis would have to be offered 'reasonable' terms. When, in August 1683, Louis prepared to use troops to force the Spaniards to concede his demands, Charles made it clear that he would not come to their aid: they had, he said, brought all their sufferings on their own heads.[78] Besides, he was fully preoccupied with developments at home and it is to these that we shall now turn.

The Whigs watched events on the continent with intense interest, as pressure from abroad seemed to offer the best prospect of a Parliament. During the Luxemburg crisis, Whig leaders assured Charles's ministers that a new Parliament would not behave like the last three.[79] In general, however, once the euphoria of Shaftesbury's acquittal had worn off, the Whigs were more defiant than hopeful; the little earl himself was noted to be very quiet. He started an action of *scandalum magnatum* against a Mr Cradock, who had called him a rebel and traitor. Cradock claimed that he would not receive a fair trial in London; the court agreed and ruled that the jurors must come from at least twenty miles outside the capital; Shaftesbury abandoned the suit.[80] With the end of the Luxemburg crisis, and York's return to court, the Whigs' prospects seemed bleak. Some had already made their peace with the court and there were divisions and recriminations among their leaders.[81] Frustration and a sense of impotence, as well as the growth of popular Toryism, made Whig crowds more violent.[82] There were still limits, however, to the Whigs' defiance of authority. To counter the feast given for York by the Honourable Artillery Company, the Whigs planned a feast in honour of Monmouth, with tickets at a guinea a head, but abandoned the idea when it was forbidden by the privy council.[83]

Amid these reverses, one of the Whigs' few assets was the enduring popularity of Monmouth. He was forbidden the court in December 1681, but despite occasional gestures of defiance still hoped to regain his father's favour. In May 1682 he offered to submit to Charles but not to James. Charles rejected the offer angrily, whereupon Monmouth claimed that it had been made by his friends without his knowledge. He accused Halifax of poisoning the king's mind against him; Charles ordered his servants to have nothing more to do with him.[84] In August there were more rumours that he would be received at court, but that Charles had refused to forgive his friend Shaftesbury. Monmouth therefore reverted to his role as the people's prince. He accepted an invitation to Chester, notorious as a centre of Whiggery and Dissent: Speaker Williams was one of the city's MPs and the radical Whig Henry Booth was both MP for the county and a leading JP.[85] On arrival in Cheshire, Monmouth did the rounds of the Whig landowners and enhanced his popularity by winning a foot race at Wallasey. At Chester he stood godfather to the mayor's daughter and his supporters broke open the church doors and rang the bells to celebrate his coming. Any who showed signs of Toryism were denounced as Papists and had their windows broken. Meanwhile, some eighty Tory gentry and maybe two thousand of 'the vulgar' attended a rival race meeting in Delamere Forest: civil war can seldom have seemed so near. Ormond ordered his son, Arran, to bring more troops to Dublin, ready to be shipped over in case of need.[86] Elsewhere, Monmouth's reception was less rapturous, especially in the Tory stronghold of Lichfield, where he was pointedly snubbed. Retribution, moreover, was not long delayed. A number of those involved in the disorders at Chester were charged with riot, but acquitted by a Whig jury. Charles issued a commission of oyer and terminer, headed by Sir George Jeffreys, to try other 'rioters' and leading Whig JPs were removed from the county bench. The commission was only a temporary expedient; the following year an action of *quo warranto* was started against Chester's charter.[87] Charles also ordered his son's arrest. On the advice of his Whig friends, Monmouth questioned the warrant's legality and at first refused to enter into a recognizance to keep the peace. Charles was livid. The legal proceedings against the duke ended inconclusively, but, although London crowds still chanted his name, it seemed that he had shot his bolt politically. In May 1683 Portsmouth unavailingly tried to reconcile him to his father, who was soon to have yet more cause for displeasure at the conduct of his errant son.[88]

In October 1682 Jenkins wrote to a Cheshire Tory that Charles believed that those who attended Monmouth had something more than horse-racing in mind. At much the same time, it was noted that some leading dissidents (including Anglesey) attended a meeting at Essex's house at Cassiobury.[89] The Whigs' condition was desperate. Defections continued, the persecution of Dissent intensified. The Tories were strengthening their control of the counties and of many towns. Charles's forthright response to Monmouth's 'progress' was ominous; so were signs that he might soon establish control over London. Following the highly contentious election of two Tory sheriffs, Shaftesbury fled to Holland: he could no longer rely on London jurors to protect him from the king's wrath. His precarious health gave way and he died in 1683.[90] His influence among the Whigs outlived him. During the autumn of 1682 there were discussions about a possible rising. Those involved included leading Whigs, like Monmouth, Essex and Russell, but also old Cromwellians and republicans. In June 1683 an oilman named Keeling revealed details of a plan to assassinate Charles and James at Rye House, in Hertfordshire, on their way back from Newmarket. As allegations followed one another in breathless profusion, and some of the accused tried to save themselves at the expense of their fellows, it became difficult to disentangle fact from fiction, and general talk of resistance from specific projects of assassination. It would appear that Shaftesbury had proposed seizing the Tower, during the excitement of the shrieval elections, but had been dissuaded by Essex, Monmouth and Russell, who argued that an unorganized rabble would be no match for the trained bands. It is also clear that neither Essex nor Monmouth would agree to killing the king.[91]

It would seem that, while in theory Essex and Russell endorsed a right of resistance, their discussions had produced only 'embryos of things that were never likely to have any effect'.[92] Charles, however, believed that the evidence was so extensive that it had to be taken seriously. He went out only with an escort of guards and had many of the gates and doors around Whitehall and St James's Park bricked up. He was also, however, concerned to see that justice was done. He kept the witnesses apart and insisted that they should tell all they knew at the first interrogation: he would not have them 'remembering' more once they found out what others had said, nor would he allow leading questions, except to ask if Oates was implicated. His attitude was much more discriminating than that of some of his courtiers: Conway wrote that he was sure all the Whigs had been involved. Charles, however, stressed that he did not believe that Russell had plotted his death, but that he had known of the plans for a rebellion.[93] While York was eager to seize this chance to crush the Whigs and extend the crown's power, Charles became tired of examining witnesses for eight or nine hours a day. He was, however, determined that those he believed guilty should be punished. Russell was clearly implicated, although it was questionable whether his involvement legally amounted to treason. He was condemned to death and Charles rejected all pleas for clemency: he allegedly said that if he did not take Russell's life, Russell would take his.[94] He also wanted the head of Henry Sidney's brother Algernon, an unbending aristocratic republican. The evidence against him was weak – a republican tract had to serve as the second witness that the law required – but, like his old friend Sir Henry Vane, he was executed more for what he believed than for what he had done. The cases of Russell and Sidney showed how ruthless Charles could be towards those he believed were out to destroy him: those who talked of rebellion could also resort to murder. A third casualty was Essex. Despite his family's impeccable Royalism, he had become convinced that Charles was bent on destroying the liberties of the people, who thus had the right to resist him. Sent to the Tower charged with complicity in the Plot, he cut his throat.[95]

For Charles, Monmouth's involvement was the most distressing aspect of the Plot. When the duke protested his innocence, Charles replied that if his wife went every day to a brothel, he would be bound to think her a whore. He insisted that Monmouth's name should be included in the proclamation for the arrest of those accused, but he escaped over the roof. Charles was bitter: even if Monmouth had not plotted against his life, some of those around him (such as Armstrong) clearly had and the duke took Armstrong with him when he went into hiding.[96] While Monmouth's prospects were in ruins, the Plot completed the disintegration of the Whig party. York was restored to the cabinet council. The militia was ordered to search the houses of suspect persons and to seize any arms they found. Charles specified that they should act only as the law prescribed, but many Tory deputy lieutenants were far from scrupulous. The persecution of Dissenters intensified, the surrender of charters accelerated. Whigs might express scepticism about the Plot, but Tories clearly believed in it and the government press ensured that it received maximum publicity. Buckingham and other Whig notables rushed to submit to the king.[97] And these successes were soon to be crowned by the greatest of all: the king's victory over the proud and defiant City of London.

The action of *quo warranto* against London's charter was launched on 21 December 1681, the day of the common council elections. The common council was accused of levying tolls without royal licence and of seditious reflections on the king in its petition of the previous January. The crown's case was not strong: Jenkins doubted whether the corporation could forfeit its rights for the misconduct of one part of it (the common council – or rather a narrowish majority of that body).[98] Legal considerations, however, were secondary: Charles was concerned less with legal rights than with political control. Documents prepared in relation to the action showed clearly that he was interested only in the corporation's membership. He wished to approve or appoint senior officers, including the lord mayor and sheriffs, and that offices relating to the peace should be in the hands of men he could trust. The aldermen were to control the admission of members of livery companies (and so of common hall). He made no claim to meddle with the City's revenues.[99] Charles's strategy towards the City embraced political as well as legal initiatives and depended on winning hearts and minds as well as pursuing the corporation through the courts. He was quite prepared to exploit legal and constitutional rights – not least, the aldermen's traditional veto over resolutions of common council[100] – and to resort to electoral chicanery: why should he be more scrupulous than the Whigs? He also, however, was careful to build up support in the City. Jenkins and Halifax lobbied and organized, Ormond and Bruce lent their prestige and gave wine and fat bucks to Tory clubs and festivities. Without a firm foundation of popular Toryism, the king would never have been able to challenge the Whigs in their greatest stronghold.[101]

Much of the Whigs' support came from Dissenters, so before the 1681 common council elections the lord mayor ordered that the Conventicle and Corporation Acts should be enforced. The Churchmen made modest gains; in one ward the elections were declared void because of the misconduct of the Whig alderman. Tories now outnumbered Whigs, but the balance was held by neutrals and moderates.[102] Neither party would put forward partisan addresses, for fear that they would be rejected. Instead, the common council concentrated on the defence of the charter, in which Whigs played the most active part. Even the aldermen, among whom the Tories had a clear majority, decided that an address congratulating York on his return to London would be unduly provocative.[103] The first major trial of strength came in June, with the shrieval elections. Whereas elections to the common council were often uncontested and were conducted by the aldermen, common hall was a large, 'popular' and potentially unruly body: all members of livery companies had the right to attend. In an effort to prevent the election of yet more rabid Whigs, Lord Mayor Moore revived the ancient custom of nominating one of the sheriffs by drinking his health at a banquet. The government was assured that the Court of Exchequer would uphold the legality of this nomination and anyway the sheriff's year of office would probably be over before the case could be decided.[104]

Faced with this use, or misuse, of authority, the Whigs' only weapon was weight of numbers. When common hall met, the lord mayor declared his nominee, Dudley North, elected; when this was challenged by the outgoing sheriffs, he declared the assembly adjourned. Shute and Pilkington proceeded to hold a poll for both sheriffs, urged on noisily by Armstrong, Grey of Wark and other militant Whigs. Charles was determined to prosecute those responsible for this riot. The sheriffs were sent to the Tower: it was widely noted that they passed through the City with an escort of only four guards, yet no one attempted to rescue them. Their arrest, however, did not solve the problem of how to secure common hall's endorsement of one (or preferably two) Tory sheriffs. A first step was to prepare full lists of liverymen, to prevent the Whigs from bringing in unqualified voters.[105] Legal arguments raged: did the right to adjourn common hall lie with the lord mayor or the sheriffs? Could the lord mayor nominate a sheriff by drinking to him? On 7 July, common hall was reconvened by the recorder, Moore claiming to be ill; the sheriffs continued the poll and declared the Whigs Papillon and Dubois elected. The aldermen, however, reaffirmed the lord mayor's right to nominate one of the sheriffs and the council ordered him to adhere to ancient custom (which presumably meant nominating one sheriff) and to begin the proceedings again.[106]

Common hall reconvened on 14 July and effectively divided into two assemblies. One, under the presidency of Moore, confirmed North's nomination by acclamation and elected Ralph Box as his colleague. In the other, the sheriffs held a poll and declared Papillon and Dubois elected. The court was exultant, but Box, a timid man, chose to pay a fine rather than accept the office and run the gauntlet of his fellow citizens' hostility. The court found another, tougher candidate in Peter Rich. The final showdown came in September, during Monmouth's jaunt to Cheshire. At Moore's request, Charles remained in town while common hall met. The lord mayor called on all those in favour of Rich to raise their hands, declared North and Rich elected and adjourned the assembly. Next day, ignoring the lord mayor's order to disperse, the outgoing sheriffs held a poll and declared Papillon and Dubois elected.[107] The Whigs gathered a crowd of 3,000 to prevent the new sheriffs' being sworn, but were foiled by a large guard of trained bands posted around Guildhall. A few days later, the Whigs suffered another setback in common hall, at the election of the new lord mayor. The court had worried that Pritchard, the Tory candidate, might be defeated, even though the electoral procedure – the aldermen chose one of the two candidates who polled most votes – forced the Whigs to field two candidates against him. The two Whigs both polled a few more votes than Pritchard, but a scrutiny conducted by the aldermen led to a number of Whig voters' being declared ineligible and Pritchard squeezed through.[108]

The court had clearly mobilized all its resources: Jenkins and the new Tory sheriffs were reported to be extremely busy. Charles stayed in town until the poll was well advanced: he had resolved to keep Moore for another year if a Whig was chosen, but much preferred to secure at least the appearance of a regular election. The Whigs, predictably, cried foul; the Tories were delighted. Lord Longford wrote that 'the king has mastered this great beast, the City, and has an opportunity during this honest man's mayoralty to reform and bring them into better obedience for the future'.[109] His rejoicing was premature. Legal moves by the Whigs to have their candidates declared duly elected as mayor and sheriffs predictably failed, although not before Papillon and Dubois had had Pritchard and several aldermen arrested. Fourteen Whigs, including Shute and Pilkington, were found guilty of riot.[110] Yet the Tories' control of the City government was far from secure. They had a comfortable majority among the aldermen, reinforced by the election of two more Tories in 1682. Excommunicates were not allowed to vote, the City clergy were told to mobilize their parishioners and ale- and coffee-house keepers were warned that they could lose their licences if they voted the wrong way. The vigorous enforcement of the Corporation Act gave the Tories a clear majority in the common council elections in December; in May 1683 common council confirmed the lord mayor's right to nominate one of the sheriffs. The Tories' real problem would come when common hall met again, to elect the next year's sheriffs and mayor: would the methods used in 1682 work again? The attorney-general ordered that the oaths of allegiance and supremacy should be tendered to all liverymen, but nobody could predict whether this would weed out enough Whigs to make any appreciable impact on common hall. The triumph of king and Tories would be complete only when Whig voters, in the wards and in common hall, no longer had any influence on the composition of the corporation; and that could be achieved only by securing judgment against the charter.[111]

Throughout 1682 the *quo warranto* proceedings ground slowly on. The government may have hoped that the City could be induced to surrender the charter: only after the first 'riot' in the shrieval elections did the attorney-general put in his response to the City's plea. With the defence of the charter entrusted to Winnington, Williams and other 'true Protestant lawyers', it was clear that the corporation would not give up without a fight.[112] In June 1683, as the time for the shrieval elections approached, the judges declared the charter forfeit. Charles declared exultantly that he was now, at last, king of London.[113] The only question now was whether the corporation would surrender upon terms, or allow the judgment to be entered and the charter seized. Many of its members, including some Tories, believed that to surrender the charter would violate their oaths to uphold the City's privileges, but others feared that if the charter were confiscated the City's property would be forfeit. At length, it was resolved to prepare a petition of submission, which they presented on their knees in the privy chamber, watched by an interested crowd of courtiers and diplomats. Chancellor North told them that Charles would pardon them, but insisted that in future no mayor, sheriff or other officer should serve without his approval and that the City's JPs, like those of Middlesex, should be appointed by the king. These stipulations confirmed that Charles wished to control the personnel, not the conduct, of the City's government; the common council voted by a majority of eighteen to accept a new charter along these lines.[114] When it came to approve the formal document of surrender, however, some had second thoughts. They were especially concerned at the demand that they should concede whatever Charles might see fit to require, a dangerously open-ended commitment. As some Tories wavered, the Whigs turned out in force and the surrender was rejected, again by a majority of eighteen.[115]

Like so many of the Whigs' gestures of defiance, it was a pyrrhic victory. Judgment was entered and the charter declared forfeit. The king issued a commission to eighteen of the former aldermen and eight common coun-cilmen to act as magistrates and to direct the administration; the office of lord mayor was to pass among them, in rotation. The elective element in the City's constitution disappeared, but outwardly much remained the same. The traditional pageantry continued; day-to-day administration remained in the hands of the same sort of people, but their status had changed, from elected representatives to commissioners who could be removed at will. Common hall survived only as the body which elected MPs. It was typical of Charles's regime that it did not try to alter a procedure that was under the jurisdiction of the Commons. It was equally typical that it set out to purge Whigs and Dissenters from the livery companies: in the general election of 1685, four Tory aldermen were returned to Parliament without a contest.[116] Charles's victory over London crowned a series of successes and placed him in a position of power which would have seemed incon-ceivable three years before. True, he was still reluctant to risk calling Parliament, and so could not pursue an active foreign policy, but there now seemed every possibility that he would be able to live out his last years in peace.

14

The End

With the failure of the Rye House Plot and the king's victory over London, the Whigs were broken, politically and psychologically. Some of their leaders were dead or in exile, others crept to make their peace. In May 1684 Lord Wharton came to kiss York's hand. 'I am an old sinner,' he said. 'So you are, my lord,' the duke replied.[1] Several, including Oates, were crushed by actions of *scandalum magnatum*, in which they were condemned to pay damages far beyond their means and imprisoned until they could pay. The persecution of Dissenters intensified. Some were prosecuted for riot, and convicted. The legal system was now wholly in Tory hands. Grand juries called for yet more rigorous measures. In Middlesex, a presentment described nonconformist ministers as the cause of all disorders; the Westminster grand jury called for proceedings against all who had supported exclusion and all who attended church only in order to qualify for office.[2] Tory venom was now directed against Trimmers as well as Dissenters; moderate JPs were presented as 'disaffected'. Clergymen were particularly vociferous against all but true-blue Tories. The committee for ecclesiastical promotions, established in 1681, had shown especial favour to wholehearted supporters of the Duke of York, with the result that by 1684 the upper levels of the hierarchy were more hostile to Dissent than ever before.[3] The subjugation of London continued. Whigs and Dissenters were expelled from hospitals and other charitable institutions; livery companies surrendered their charters and were duly 'regulated'. Tory peers and gentlemen encouraged provincial towns to surrender their charters. The new charters often changed the membership of the corporation or the body of freemen, drafting in Tory squires from the countryside if there were not enough 'loyal' men in the town.[4]

By the end of 1683, Charles and his ministers did not need to encourage the Tory reaction: at times, indeed, they felt impelled to restrain the more zealous Tories. The king felt no inclination to call the Parliament which should, under the Triennial Act, have been summoned by March 1684.

York argued that the Act was of no force: it prescribed no penalties for not calling Parliament and besides there were medieval statutes requiring annual Parliaments which had never been observed. Fearful that a Parliament might generate 'heats', Charles and his advisers quietly let it be known that he would not summon one for the time being.[5] If the Tories felt aggrieved at this, they did not say so. Any delay would work to their electoral advantage, allowing more time to harass Dissenters and procure new charters. Financially secure and with no need to call Parliament, Charles could at last relax and indulge to the full his love of ease; even his physical energy had diminished. Under no pressure from his subjects to intervene on the continent, and lacking the money to do so effectively, he allowed Louis a virtually free hand in his favourite pastime of bullying the Spaniards. His occasional remonstrations were token gestures: Louis listened politely, then carried on as before. Charles was not greatly concerned: he was determined to enjoy whatever span of life remained to him and showed far more concern about Portsmouth's health or the building work at Winchester than about the affairs of Europe.[6]

If Charles was happy to let things drift, others were not. As his vigour diminished, his more diligent and single-minded brother played an increasing role in the government which might soon be his. His influence on policy was seen most strikingly in moves to improve the lot of his fellow Catholics, first in Ireland, then in England. While Charles showed little concern for electoral preparations, York assiduously rebuilt his electoral interest in the Cinque Ports, of which he had been Lord Warden until 1673.[7] Until it was wound up in 1684, the committee for ecclesiastical promotions filled Church preferments with his supporters. He could count on the support of Portsmouth, Rochester and Sunderland and promoted the advancement of Jeffreys, whose ruthlessness and violence were far removed from the cautious legalism of North. The equally cautious Jenkins gave up the secretaryship, ostensibly because of ill-health; his place was taken by one of York's Scots protégés, Lord Middleton.[8]

Faced with his brother's restless energy, Charles showed little inclination to bestir himself. He felt no great affection for James: he had opposed exclusion for his own sake, not his brother's. James's impatience to take over the reins of government irritated him: he remarked tetchily that if James became king he might soon be forced to go on his travels again.[9] In the last analysis, however, Charles lacked the energy or the strength of will to restrain him. He maintained Halifax in office, despite all the attempts of James and his allies to oust him, and he repeatedly urged them to be patient. Nevertheless, by the end of 1684, the direction which affairs would take in the next reign was becoming increasingly clear.

*   *   *

In the autumn of 1683, Charles's general sense of relief and well-being was marred only by distress at the conduct of Monmouth. He had gone into hiding after the Rye House Plot, but in November made a bid to regain his father's favour. The proclamation requiring him to give himself up had set the 26th as the deadline after which he would be deemed an outlaw. His duchess, of whom Charles was very fond, brought a letter of unconditional submission; Charles promised her that Monmouth would not suffer imprisonment, nor would he be forced to testify, provided he confessed all he knew. The duke threw himself at Charles's and James's feet and made a full confession, confirming in essence the evidence against Russell and adding details which Charles had not known. Next day, the 25th, Charles told a special meeting of the privy council that Monmouth had surrendered himself and given full satisfaction: all proceedings against him were to be halted.[10] The king's joy was apparent to all and he was as kind to his son as he had ever been: courtiers who had earlier spoken slightingly of him hastily changed his tune. Soon, however, reports began to circulate that Monmouth's confession had confirmed the existence of the Plot. His Whig friends asked if this was true; at first he was reluctant to reply, but once his pardon had passed – and news of his confession appeared in the *Gazette* – he denied it, vehemently. He would prove a man of honour, he declared; he would not lie or desert his friends.[11]

At the news of his *volte face*, the Whigs were exultant and Halifax was in despair. He had encouraged Monmouth to submit and claimed to have done so at Charles's instigation; it would also, however, be in Halifax's interest to use Monmouth (shorn of his old Whig friends) to counter York's growing influence. Halifax had urged Monmouth not to react to the report in the *Gazette*; now he advised him to write a confession, confirming the reality of the Plot in general terms, without accusing anyone by name. The council rejected the draft put forward by Halifax, but Monmouth refused to sign the more explicit confession drafted by North, Jenkins and Sunderland: it was worse than being called as a witness, he said. Charles then drew up another paper, which Monmouth copied out, under protest: he claimed that it could hang Hampden, but Charles promised that he would not use it for that. However, when asked by his father to acknowledge before the council that he had indeed written the confession, he refused. Charles, hurt and angry, gave him back the paper and banished him from court.[12]

Some Whigs continued to claim that Monmouth had acted with Charles's full approval, but they placed too much reliance on the king's fondness for his son. York, who had been deeply worried by Monmouth's return to court, exulted that he had quite destroyed his father's tenderness for him. Charles was bitter at what he saw as his son's warped sense of honour: he told Barrillon that he had not believed he could have acted as he had. As it was,

Monmouth had sealed Sidney's fate: to re-establish the credibility of the Plot, the sea-green republican had to die.[13] Charles also made it clear that he no longer felt bound by his promise that Monmouth should not be called as a witness. In January, he was summoned to testify against Hampden; rather than do so, the duke went into exile.[14]

In the summer of 1683, while Charles was preoccupied with the Rye House Plot, the eyes of Europe were focused on Vienna, besieged by the Turks. The threat from the east was such that the princes and cities of the Holy Roman Empire, in the Imperial Diet, forgot their differences and their suspicions of imperial power and voted money for a large army. In the international effort against the Turk, Louis XIV was conspicuous by his absence. Although he had lifted the blockade of Luxemburg, he almost certainly hoped that a Turkish victory would open the way for France to crush the Habsburgs once and for all. When the Turks were driven back from Vienna, the rejoicing in France was decidedly muted. The Most Christian King had, indeed, already renewed his aggression in Flanders and his blockade of Luxemburg. He announced that he would desist only if the Spaniards recognized his 'rights', but was still prepared to accept Luxemburg as an 'equivalent'. French artillery pounded helpless Flemish towns and reduced two-thirds of the independent city of Genoa to rubble for having had the temerity to aid the Spanish.[15]

This naked aggression provoked outrage, but little action. The emperor and German princes were busy repelling the Turks, the Dutch were hamstrung by the struggle between William and the States party and Charles was busy investigating the Plot. Barrillon claimed that the sending of troops into the Spanish Netherlands and the exaction of heavy contributions for their subsistence did not amount to an act of war: as soon as the Spaniards saw reason, they would withdraw. Whatever Charles thought privately, he knew he could not afford a war and deeply resented Spanish attempts to drag him into one. James wrote to William that the Spaniards had only themselves to blame and that Louis would have sent troops in sooner had Charles not interposed.[16] William, as usual, was trying to persuade the Dutch that if they did not fight now they would be defenceless against future French aggression: Charles told Barrillon that if his nephew was not careful he could end up suffering the fate of de Witt. William, however, persuaded the States General to honour their treaty with Spain – they sent 8,000 men to Flanders – thus increasing the pressure on Charles to do the same.[17] His response was neither dignified nor honourable, but realistic: he declared point-blank that he was in no position to embark on a war. His only consolation was that an influential section of Dutch opinion, led by Amsterdam, was equally averse to fighting. In December, the Spaniards in desperation declared war on France, but their threats to declare war on England as well were dismissed by Charles and James with the contempt they deserved.[18] On the other hand, despite the urging of York and Sunderland, Charles hesitated to align himself more openly with France, for fear of the political damage that it could do him at home. Barrillon pressed him to order Chudleigh, his ambassador at the Hague, to declare unequivocally that the only viable basis for peace was the acceptance of one or other of Louis' 'equivalents'. Charles had already ordered Chudleigh to work with d'Avaux and to encourage the 'peace party' in the republic, but hesitated to support the French demands so openly or to throw in his lot with William's enemies. Indeed, van Citters, the Dutch ambassador in London, reported that Charles did not really support the French proposals at all.[19]

Barrillon was perplexed: he suspected that Charles, ever eager to please, had suggested more to van Citters than he had intended and added that the Dutchman's French was not good.[20] It is equally possible that, pressed on all sides, Charles said different things to different people. The issue lost much of its relevance when Louis proposed a twenty-year truce as an alternative to the equivalents and warned the Dutch that, if attacked, he would defend himself. Charles welcomed the proposal; William claimed that it would leave the republic at the mercy of France and complained of Chudleigh's dealings with the 'peace party'.[21] In April Louis besieged Luxemburg and threatened to declare war on the Dutch unless they withdrew their troops from Flanders. William was outraged; Charles claimed that it was an understandable response to the Spaniards' stubbornness and expressed relief that the focus of hostilities had moved eastwards, away from Flanders. Chudleigh openly urged the States General to accept Louis' terms, opinion in the republic was running more and more strongly in favour of peace and William's friends expressed fears that his power might be destroyed once and for all.[22]

William's uncles showed no sympathy for his plight. York patronizingly urged him to follow Charles's advice, which was in the best interests of himself and the family. William's relations with Charles were thus extremely poor when Monmouth arrived at his court. Charles had already stressed to his ambassador at Brussels, Bulstrode, that the duke was to be accorded no marks of respect. William, at first, apologized for receiving him, but in time showed more and more open favour towards his one-time rival for the succession, ignoring Charles's and James's expressions of displeasure. William's temper was not improved by the fall of Luxemburg and the conclusion, in August, of the Truce of Ratisbon, whereby the emperor and Spain confirmed Louis in his possession of Luxemburg and Strasbourg for twenty years. He complained bitterly that Chudleigh 'insolently' reprimanded him for receiving Monmouth. He told Bentinck that Monmouth had been pardoned and that he knew that Charles was still fond of him.[23] His continuing open favour to the young duke infuriated Charles. He ordered Chudleigh to have nothing to do with William and considered recalling the British regiments from the Dutch service, for fear that William and Monmouth might use them to foment discontent within England. By the end of 1684 relations between uncle and nephew were colder than they had ever been and Barrillon and d'Avaux did their utmost to ensure that they remained that way.[24]

William's persistent kindness towards Monmouth is not easy to explain. Burnet heard that in 1681 Charles showed William a seal and said that any letter from him which did not bear that seal did not represent his true feelings. This story can be neither proved nor disproved, but either way there seem two possible reasons for William's conduct. The first is anger and contempt at Charles's refusal to oppose French aggression: in the summer of 1684, uncle and nephew seem to have gone out of their way to spite and insult each other.[25] The second is that William really believed that Charles still loved Monmouth. Many in England, and among the British exiles in the republic, had little difficulty in persuading themselves that Charles's outward displeasure was the product of York's malign influence and that, when Charles chose to assert himself, Monmouth would be restored to favour. The duke's brief visit to England at the end of 1684 was seized on as heralding an imminent reconciliation, although there is no evidence that there was ever a possibility. Indeed, Charles's vindictive treatment of Armstrong – kidnapped in Holland, brought to England and executed – did not suggest any kindness for his son.[26] The contention that William genuinely believed that Charles approved of his kindness towards Monmouth is supported by his sending the duke away as soon as he heard of Charles's death.[27]

In terms of foreign policy, Charles's reign ended ingloriously in a bitter family squabble. There was friction with the Dutch over their allowing asylum to British political refugees and a renewal of the disputes in Bantam.[28] There had even been renewed talk of a Franco-Dutch alliance, one of Charles's recurrent nightmares.[29] Barrillon remarked, with something approaching contempt, that Charles saw internal security as his first priority and did not wish to concern himself with foreign affairs.[30] Yet if England seemed unable to exercise a significant influence in international affairs, this did not mean that it lacked the power to do so. Financially and militarily, the government was stronger in 1684 than in 1664 – and vastly stronger than it had been under the early Stuarts. What was lacking was the political will, or rather the political unity, needed to deploy this fiscal and military power. When that unity of purpose was achieved, in the years after 1688, England emerged as a European and indeed a world power.

*   *   *

While Charles's foreign policy showed signs of lassitude and indifference, there was more evidence of dynamism at home. York was restored to the privy council as well as the cabinet council and resumed *de facto* direction of the admiralty, although documents went out in Charles's name. Despite the judges' hesitation, Danby and the surviving Catholic lords were released from the Tower. Many at court had opposed this, fearing that Danby would regain his former power, but he did not.[31] Rochester's dominance at the treasury had increased: two of his fellow commissioners had died and he was seen as lord treasurer in all but name, but he was not content with his lot. He had been deeply hurt by Halifax's accusations of corruption and in March Barrillon reported that he wished to become Lord Lieutenant of Ireland, if age and ill-health forced Ormond to quit. When his enemies, playing on Charles's fear of a single person running the treasury, persuaded him to appoint two more commissioners, Rochester took it as a personal insult. James and Portsmouth talked him out of resigning, but his restiveness strengthened his enemies' hand. As he still seemed determined to quit, James and Portsmouth persuaded Charles to appoint him lord president, a post which he did not want, although Halifax did. Soon after, Charles decided to appoint Rochester lord lieutenant and Halifax lord president.[32]

York would have preferred Rochester to remain at the treasury, but knew that Charles would never agree to his being lord treasurer. He therefore procured the lord presidency and then lobbied hard to have him made lord lieutenant. Rochester wanted the post, but it transpired that York's ideas on Irish policy differed from his. Richard Talbot had returned to court early in 1683 and set out to unseat Ormond. Well aware that Charles's faith in the viceroy would not easily be shaken, he concentrated on the claim that the Irish army was full of 'Cromwellians', who were by definition (he claimed) disaffected. After the Popish Plot, Charles was eager to strengthen the Irish army: he was especially concerned about the Ulster Scots and their links with the militant Covenanters of south-west Scotland. Talbot's arguments were not easily countered. Wild allegations in London were liable to have a greater impact than patient rebuttals from Dublin. As Ormond remarked, it was impossible to vouch unequivocally for the loyalty of every officer, but few now serving had been in the army before 1660 and some of those had earlier served the king.[33] Nevertheless, by the beginning of November 1684 Charles had decided to recall Ormond and, soon after, he agreed that Rochester should succeed him. Arran wrote from London that great changes were intended in Ireland and that Rochester, who feared no odium, was to carry them through. Arran was sure that Rochester had actively sought the post; Ormond was inclined to be more charitable, but sent Arran a copy of a kind letter which Charles had sent him during the Plot, to show that kings had no better memories than ordinary men.[34] The promoters of the change feared that Charles could change his mind, so hastened to make it public. A somewhat petulant letter from Ormond to Rochester was also circulated; Rochester swore that he was not responsible and it seems probable that a copy had been taken, by Sunderland, at the post office.[35]

York had supported Talbot's campaign: he wanted the Irish army in loyal hands and hoped to find some places for Catholics. Rochester wanted the lieutenancy, but did not want to offend Ormond: he stressed that the decision to remove Ormond had been taken before the decision to appoint him. He soon found that he was not to be a free agent. Military commissions, hitherto issued by the lord lieutenant, were now to be issued by Sunderland, as secretary. Not only would this deprive him of a major source of profit, but also the lord lieutenant would have less say in appointments than those who could put their case in London. His credit was also weakened by the production of treasury books from which some pages had been removed, suggesting that he had been implicated in fraud. When Rochester challenged Charles about his intentions for Ireland, the king refused to be drawn. It was clear, however, that James was determined to break the Protestant monopoly of power in Ireland and, once the process started, who could tell where it would stop?[36]

If Rochester's removal did not materially alter the balance of power at court, the rise of Jeffreys did. He had acted as prosecuting counsel in the cases of Fitzharris and College and played a major part in the challenge to London's charter. Created lord chief justice at the age of thirty-four, he presided over the trials of Russell and Armstrong. In September 1684 he joined the cabinet council: Barrillon reported that Charles wanted his legal advice for the vigorous resolutions which it was now intended to take. (As Rochester remarked the same day on Charles's lack of interest in business, one might wonder whose intentions he was referring to.)[37] Jeffreys persuaded, or bullied, a number of northern towns to surrender their charters; with the Earl of Bath pursuing a similar policy in Devon and Cornwall, the issue of new charters accelerated.[38] Jeffreys was also involved in the easing of the persecution of Catholics. In March there were confident reports of an indulgence for both Catholics and Dissenters, but the harassment of the latter continued unabated. Charles had, indeed, put out feelers to the Dissenters from time to time and expressed concern about the number of Catholics in prison. In September, York and Sunderland told Barrillon that Charles wished to release them if he could legally do so. A major debate followed, in which Halifax and North argued against relaxing the laws and Sunderland, Jeffreys and some said Rochester in favour. Jeffreys argued that many of those in gaol had been loyal in the civil wars; North retorted that many 'recusants' were in fact sectaries. Charles listened attentively; he agreed that it would be imprudent to issue a general pardon, but ordered Jeffreys to investigate individual cases.[39] By December Catholics were being released from prison, provided they could produce certificates testifying to their loyalty. Charles insisted that he did not intend a general toleration; James declared that the 'fanatics' did not deserve one.[40] Nevertheless, despite Charles's reluctance and the opposition of North and Halifax, York and his allies were gradually committing the king to policies which marked a clear break with the past and which were to bring untold problems in the next reign.

On 1 February 1685 Charles was in high good humour, even though a sore heel prevented him from taking his usual exercise. The roof of the palace at Winchester was to be sheathed in lead that week. That night, unusually, he slept fitfully. Next morning, as he was being shaved, he suffered a sudden stroke and slumped to the floor, black in the face. By chance one of his physicians, Dr King, was at court: he bled the king, who seemed to recover.[41] He returned to bed and his physicians subjected him to the usual gamut of remedies – purges, vomits, scarifyings and more bleedings. The treatment served only to weaken him, while a surfeit of 'hot' medicines inflamed his throat. By the evening of the 5th he was very ill. His bedchamber was thronged with councillors, courtiers and bishops; James was constantly at his side. At length James whispered to his brother, who replied, 'With all my heart.' York cleared the room and up the backstairs came Fr Huddleston, the priest who had assisted Charles in the escape from Worcester. Charles told the old man that he had saved his body: now he was to save his soul. A consecrated wafer was fetched from the queen's chapel; Charles confessed and received the sacrament and extreme unction. When the waiting crowd was allowed back in, he seemed calmer than before. Weak though he was, he resisted the bishops' entreaties to receive Anglican communion. His physical stamina made the struggle with death long and painful. Just before noon on the 6th he gave up the ghost and his brother was proclaimed King James II.[42]

Death, for kings, was a very public matter and tended to become the subject of myth and wishful thinking. As the reign of his successor unfolded, many claimed that, had he lived, Charles would have reversed the trend towards more Catholic and authoritarian policies.[43] Maybe he would, but there is no solid evidence to support that contention. The overwhelming impression of his last year is that he lacked the will or the energy to hold back his brother. The rumours of poison, which hovered around almost every royal deathbed, seem equally unfounded.[44] On some aspects of the occasion, there is wide agreement. Charles asked his brother to provide for Portsmouth, whom he had loved to the last, and not to let Nelly starve. He also commended to his successor the care of his children – with the significant exception of Monmouth. Burnet wrote that he did not mention the queen, but others reported that when she left the bedchamber, after fainting several times, he begged her pardon and she his. He made no mention of the Church, or of his people.[45]

Altogether more sensational was the news that Charles had died a Catholic: rumours were circulating in London almost at once and James later published what he claimed were two papers of devotion written by his brother. Burnet, convinced that Charles was too intelligent to be persuaded by the Papists' specious arguments, was sceptical of the depth of his conversion, and others agreed.[46] Unlike Buckingham and the poet Earl of Rochester, Charles had shown little sign of repenting of his past sins, although Bruce later claimed that he had recently resolved to give no more countenance to 'loose and buffooning persons'.[47] The very tardiness of the conversion invites scepticism: it seems too much like a last-minute act of insurance. It is possible, however, that in his last years his thoughts had turned to the fate of his immortal soul. He knew he was growing old. York's memoirs for 1682 refer to his conferring at length with Charles about the latter's great scruples about religion. He must also have spoken of them to Portsmouth: as he lay dying, it was she who told Barrillon of his conversion.[48] Reports that he had promised to declare his conversion, either before he fell ill or if he recovered, cannot be proved or disproved. What is clear is that, after receiving the last rites, he felt that he had made his peace with God and approached death with something rather like equanimity.[49]

News of Charles's illness caused great consternation: people filled the streets, waiting for news and many tears were shed when he died. Others seemed less concerned. After the autopsy, which showed that his body was so full of blood that he could not have lived for long, the cadaver was neglected and part of the fatty tissue was allowed to run down a drain. There was no lying in state, no official mourning. The funeral took place with little pomp, in Henry VII's chapel. As was the custom, the officers of the household broke their white staffs and cast them into the grave. The £90,000 which Charles had accumulated for Winchester were diverted to the purposes of the new regime. The palace, still unfinished, was allowed to moulder away. No trace of it remains today.[50]

On 29 May 1660 John Evelyn had watched Charles enter London and had blessed God. A few days after the king's death, the diarist tried to collect his thoughts. Charles had been 'a prince of many virtues and many great imperfections, debonair, easy of access, not bloody or cruel ... an excellent prince, doubtless, had he been less addicted to women'. In public affairs, he had had great opportunities 'to have made himself, his people and all Europe happy ... had not his too easy nature resigned him to be managed by crafty

men and some abandoned and profane wretches'. When he learned of
Charles's conversion, Evelyn regretted still more that he had failed to make
the best use of the many gifts that God had given him.[51] The harsher, more
confrontational style of James II led some to view Charles's reign, in
retrospect, in a more charitable light. The Whigs, however, eager for revenge
for the Tory reaction, tried to depict James's policies as the logical continuation of those of Charles's last years. The Bill of Rights of 1689 mingled
Whig grievances from 1681–4 with Tory grievances from 1685–8. As
England advanced into the very different political world after the Glorious
Revolution, both parties tended to view Charles's reign in accordance with
their own prejudices: the Tories as a golden age of Anglicanism and benevolent monarchy, the Whigs as an awful example of benighted tyranny.[52]
In this book, I have tried to offer a view of Charles uncoloured by either
hindsight or partisan emotion. Like Evelyn, I see him as a king who failed
to make the most of his abilities, through indolence and lack of willpower.
As a politician, he did not possess the most basic of political skills, an ability
to understand the hopes and fears, the ambitions and principles of other
people. And, without understanding, there could be no trust.

Before, as it were, branding Charles II a failure, it is as well to pause.
The demands of a personal monarchy were impossibly heavy. No mere
mortal could know everything and everybody, or make wise and impartial
decisions on all occasions. Louis XIV prided himself on his diligence, the
fullness of his information and his ability to analyse human motivation. He
still made catastrophic miscalculations and ended up with a government
machine over which he exercised less and less personal control. Measured
against more realistic, more human standards, Charles's achievements may
seem less negligible. Unlike his father and brother he kept his throne. If he
won no great victories in war, he suffered no crushing defeats either. His
reign saw a great growth of trade, shipping and empire. Compared with
1640–60 or the period after 1689, taxes were low and the people were
prosperous. Looking back from William III's reign, Halifax felt inclined to
be more indulgent than Evelyn.

A prince neither sharpened by his misfortunes whilst abroad nor by his power when
restored is such a shining character that it is a reproach not to be so dazzled with
it as not to be able to see a fault in its full light. . . . And if all who are akin to his
vices should mourn for him, never prince would be better attended to his grave. . . .
If he loved too much to lie upon his own down bed of ease, his subjects had the
pleasure during his reign of lolling and stretching upon theirs. . . . Let his royal
ashes then lie soft upon him and cover him from harsh and unkind censures; which
though they should not be unjust can never clear themselves from being indecent.[53]

Notes

Abbreviations

Althorp MSS	Althorp papers in the British Library
Arundell MSS	MSS of the Arundells of Wardour, in the possession of the Arundell family
BIHR	*Bulletin of the Institute of Historical Research*
BL	British Library
BN	Bibliothèque Nationale
Bodl	Bodleian Library
Bowman	Bodleian, MS Dep. f 9 (Parliamentary Diary of Seymour Bowman)
BT	Public Record Office, Baschet transcripts of French ambassadors' dispatches (ref. PRO 31/3)
Cal Clar SP	*Calendar of Clarendon State Papers*, 5 vols, Oxford, 1872–1970
Carte MSS	Carte papers in the Bodleian Library
CJ	*Common Journals*
Clar Corr	*Correspondence of Henry Hyde, Earl of Clarendon*, ed. S. W. Singer, 2 vols, London, 1828
Clar MSS	Clarendon papers in the Bodleian Library
Clar SP	*State Papers Collected by Edward, Earl of Clarendon*, 3 vols, Oxford, 1767–86
Cov MSS	Coventry papers at Longleat
CPA	Archives des Affaires Etrangères, Paris, Correspondance Politique, Angleterre
CSPD	*Calendar of State Papers Domestic*
CSPI	*Calendar of State Papers Ireland*
CSPV	*Calendar of State Papers Venetian*
CSPV (cont)	Typescript continuation of *CSPV* for 1676–8: PRO, E/M/21/58
CTB	*Calendar of Treasury Books*
CUL	Cambridge University Library
DCAD	Dean and Chapter Archives, Durham
Dering, *Diary*	Sir E. Dering, *Parliamentary Diary 1670–3*, ed. B. D. Henning, New Haven, 1940
Dering, *Papers*	Sir E. Dering, *Diaries and Papers*, ed. M. F. Bond, London, 1976
DUL	Durham University Library
Eg MSS	Egerton MSS in the British Library
EHR	*English Historical Review*
Exact Coll	*An Exact Collection of the Debates of the House of Commons held at Westminster October 21 1680*, London, for R. Baldwin, 1689
Finch MSS	Finch papers in the Leicestershire RO
FSL	Folger Shakespeare Library

Grey	A. Grey, *Debates in the House of Commons 1667–94*, 10 vols, London, 1769
Harl MSS	Harleian MSS in the British Library
HJ	*Historical Journal*
HLQ	*Huntington Library Quarterly*
HLRO	House of Lords RO
HMC	Historical Manuscripts Commission Reports
HP	*History of Parliament: The Commons 1660–1690*, ed. B. D. Henning, 3 vols, London, 1983
JRL	John Rylands Library
KAO	Kent Archives Office
Lansdowne MSS	Lansdowne MSS in the British Library
Letters	*Letters of Charles II*, ed. A. Bryant, London, 1935
LJ	*Lords Journals*
Morrice	Dr Williams's Library, MS 31P, Entering Book of Roger Morrice
NS	New Series
Nunz Fian	Vatican Archives, Nunziatura di Fiandra
Oates's Plot	Warwickshire RO, CR 1998 (Throckmorton of Coughton MSS), 'Large Carved Box', item 17, unfoliated volume entitled 'Titus Oates's Plot'
OPH	*Old Parliamentary History*, 23 vols, London, 1751–61
PC 2	Privy Council Registers in the PRO
Pforz	University of Texas at Austin, Humanities Research Center, Pforzheimer MS 103c, vol. IX (Bulstrode newsletters)
POAS	*Poems on Affairs of State*, vol. 1 (ed. G. de F. Lord), vol. 2 (ed. L. F. Mengel, jnr), New Haven, 1963, 1965
Prinsterer	G. Groen van Prinsterer, *Archives de la Maison Orange Nassau*, 2nd series, 5 vols, The Hague, 1858–61
PRO	Public Record Office
Rawl MSS	Rawlinson MSS in the Bodleian Library
RB	*Reliquiae Baxterianae*, ed. M. Sylvester, London, 1696
SP	State Papers in the PRO
SR	*Statutes of the Realm*
Stowe MSS	Stowe papers in the British Library
Tanner MSS	Tanner papers in the Bodleian Library
TRHS	*Transactions of the Royal Historical Society*
UCL	University of Chicago Library
Williamson	*Letters Addressed from London to Sir Joseph Williamson 1673–4*, ed. W. D. Christie, 2 vols, Camden Soc., 1874

A Note on References

The aim throughout is to provide references which are unambiguous, but as succinct as possible. Extensive use has been made of the abbreviations listed above. Printed works listed in the Select Bibliography are cited by author and, where necessary, short title. Where possible, manuscript references give page or folio numbers; for unfoliated documents (for example the Althorp MSS) a description is given (usually the name of the writer and addressee) together with the date. An exception to this general rule is the correspondence of the French ambassadors. There are two reasons for this: first, most folios bear two or even three different numbers; second, citing writer, addressee and date makes it possible to consult dispatches either in the Baschet transcripts in the PRO or in the originals in Paris. Where a dispatch can be found in the Baschet transcripts, I have given the relevant bundle number; for those which have not been transcribed, I have given the volume number in Correspondance Politique, Angleterre. For the sake of brevity, I have given the name of the addressee only for letters which were not addressed to Louis XIV; hence, where no addressee is given, they were addressed to the king. Dates given are those used by the writers: new style for foreign ambassadors, otherwise old style.

Chapter 1: A Wandering Prince

1. See R. Lockyer, *Buckingham* (London, 1981).
2. S. A. Strong (ed.), *A Catalogue of Letters and Other Historical Documents at Welbeck* (London, 1903), pp. 188–9. (This is still the most accurate printed version of Newcastle's advice to Charles.)
3. BT 134, Courtin, 26 Nov. 1676; Pepys, III.301; *CSPD 1675–6*, p. 35; Strong, pp. 210–11. See also Pepys, VII.201.
4. Ailesbury, I.91–3; *CSPV 1666–8*, p. 257, *1669–70*, p. 44.
5. Ailesbury, I.96–7; Hartmann, *Madame*, p. 95; Evelyn, IV.409; *HMC 3rd Report*, p. 375; Granville, II.4; Pepys, VIII.116; BN, Fonds Français 15889 fos 375–6; CPA 86, Courtin to Lionne, 15 Aug. 1665; Burnet, *History*, I.330, 356, 439, 448, II.23.
6. Burnet, *Suppl.*, p. 50; Hartmann, *Madame*, p. 108.
7. Strong, p. 183; Burnet, *Suppl.*, p. 50; Ailesbury, I.93.
8. Burnet, *Suppl.*, p. 48; *POAS*, I.424.
9. Clarendon, *Hist.*, IV.22–3 is a little prim on this point.
10. See Clifton, pp. 77–83; Hutton, *Charles II*, pp. 25–6, 188.
11. See Geyl, pp. 44–5, 66–7, 74; Clarendon, *Hist.*, IV.407.
12. BL Add. MS 18982 fo. 177.
13. Nicholas, I.116–17; Clarendon, *Hist.*, V.2–3, 25–8, 31–2, 48–52.
14. Clarendon, *Hist.*, V.50, 64–5; Carte, *Orig. Letters*, I.296, 303–5; *CSPV 1647–52*, pp. 119–20.
15. *Cal Clar SP*, II.32; Carte, *Orig. Letters*, I.322. Hyde himself made proposals to Spain which included large promises of favour for British Catholics: *Cal Clar SP*, II.35.
16. *Letters*, pp. 12, 14; Clarendon, *Hist.*, IV.252–3.
17. Clarendon, *Hist.*, V.105–8; *Cal Clar SP*, II.50–1, 57; *Letters*, pp. 15–16; Nicholas, I.173–4, 186; S. R. Gardiner, *History of the Commonwealth and Protectorate*, 3 vols (London, 1894–1901), I.228.
18. See *Cal Clar SP*, II.83.
19. *Letters*, p. 18.
20. Clarendon, *History*, V.188.
21. *Cal Clar SP*, II.48–9; Clarendon, *Hist.*, V.166–8; Carte, *Orig. Letters*, II.41.
22. Miller, *James II*, pp. 13–15.
23. Clarendon, *Hist.*, V.211, 224 + n., 226–30; *Clar. SP*, III.35–6; *CSPD 1651–2*, pp. 2–3; Carte, *Ormond*, III.625.
24. *Cal Clar SP*, II.119, 124, 128; Gardiner, II.95; Nicholas, I.287.
25. *Clar SP*, III.48, 52; Clarendon, *Hist.*, V.231–7, 315–18; Nicholas, I.298–300.
26. *Clar SP*, III.109 (quoted); *Cal Clar SP*, II.156; Thurloe, I.345.
27. *Cal Clar SP*, II.109, 178, 214–15; Clarendon, *Hist.*, V.257–9, 308–11; Geyl, pp. 108–9.
28. Nicholas, II.7; Clarendon, *Hist.*, V.333–7; *Clar SP*, III.153; *Cal Clar SP*, II.195, 201, 206 (quoted).
29. Clarendon, *Hist.*, V.324–9; *Cal Clar SP*, II.239.
30. Clarendon, *Hist.*, V.331–3; Thurloe, II.128, 146–7, 175–6, 179–80, 268; *Cal Clar SP*, II.337–8, 380.
31. Clarendon, *Hist.*, V.349, 351–2, 354–7, 360; Thurloe, II.586, 678.

32. Burnet, *Hist.*, I.242; Welwood, p. 145; Thurloe, II.586.

33. Thurloe, II.544; Gardiner, III.123; for a claim that Charles attended Mass in 1658; see *HMC 3rd Report*, p. 266; however, the statement is based on hearsay and includes details that are clearly wrong, e.g. that Charles, James, Hyde, Bennet and Ormond were all in Spain in 1658.

34. *Cal Clar SP*, II.394–5, 432–5, III.19; see also, *ibid.*, pp. 35, 106–7, 110, 154.

35. Clarendon, *Hist.*, V.339–40; *Cal Clar SP*, II.320, 383; Brown, p. 109.

36. Nicholas, II.109–13, 128–36; *Clar SP*, II.415–17.

37. *Cal Clar SP*, II.422, 424–5, 428–34; *Letters*, pp. 31–3; Nicholas, II.142, 147–50, 162–4.

38. *Cal Clar SP*, III.364–5, 370, IV.47, 53–4.

39. *Letters*, pp. 30, 40, 44–5; Thurloe, III.659, IV.122, V.8, 388–9, 412; Brown, pp. 115–16, 125–6; Clarke, *James II*, I.266; Carte MS 198, fo. 37; Clarendon, *Hist.*, VI.43–4.

40. Clarendon, *Hist.*, VI.48–51; *Cal Clar SP*, III.143, 223, 370; Clarke, *James II*, I.279–80, 284–7; Carte MS 198 fo. 37; *Clar SP*, III.317–18, 321–4; Thurloe, I.662–4.

41. Clarendon, *Hist.*, VI.78–9; *Cal Clar SP*, III.283; *Clar SP*, III.359; Thurloe, VI.304; *Letters*, pp. 54–6.

42. *Cal Clar SP*, III.357, 393, IV.43–4; Nicholas, IV.264; *Letters*, p. 70; Stradling, *Decline of Spain*, p. 153.

43. *Cal Clar SP*, III.325, 352, IV.175, 199; Thurloe, I.740–4; *Letters*, pp. 60–1; Clarendon, *Hist.*, VI.52–3.

44. *Cal Clar SP*, IV.99, 104, 120, 122.

45. *Ibid.*, 124, 175, 194, 198, 199, 205, 261–2, 278–9; *Clar SP*, III.456, 475.

46. *Letters*, pp. 77–8; A. L. Sells (ed.), *Memoirs of James II* (London, 1962), pp. 290–1; *Cal Clar SP*, IV.474.

47. BT 105, Bordeaux to Brienne 3 and 27 Nov., same to Mazarin 6 and 10 Nov. 1659; Thurloe, VII.770; *CSPV 1659–61*, pp. 97–9; *Clarke Papers*, IV.301; A. Woolrych, 'The Cromwellian Protectorate: A Military Dictatorship?', *History* LXXV (1990), p. 229.

48. Clarendon, *Hist.*, VI.154–6; Gumble, pp. 101–9; Price, pp. 707–25; *CSPV 1659–61*, pp. 57, 59; *Cal Clar SP*, IV.354; *Clar SP*, III.604, 618.

49. *CSPV 1659–61*, pp. 76, 79–80, 83; Mordaunt, pp. 59–61; BT 105, Bordeaux to Mazarin 29 Sept. and 30 Oct., same to Brienne 3 Nov. 1659.

50. *Clarke Papers*, IV.64–6, 75–6, 85–7, 133, 136–9, 275–6; *Clar SP*, III.628; Mordaunt, pp. 59–61.

51. *Clarke Papers*, IV.152.

52. *Clar SP*, III.593–4; Mordaunt, pp. 83, 95–6, 111; *CSPD 1659–60*, pp. 246–8; Carte, *Orig. Letters*, II.256.

53. Pepys, I.125, VII.204, VIII.499, 591; Burnet, *Suppl.*, p. 66; Burnet, *Hist.*, I.152; P. Warwick, *Memoirs of the Reign of Charles I* (London, 1813), pp. 446–7; BN, Cinq Cents de Colbert 478 fos 110–11; BT 111, Cominges to Lionne 28 May 1663; Ailesbury I.9; *Cal Clar SP*, IV.586.

54. BT 105, Bordeaux to Mazarin 15 Dec. 1659; *Clarke Papers*, IV.215–16; Whitelocke, IV.378; Mordaunt, pp. 149–50; *Cal Clar SP*, IV.490.

55. *Clarke Papers*, IV.166, 169, 200, 211, 215–16; *Cal Clar SP*, IV.493–4; Rugg, pp. 13–14.

56. BT 105, Bordeaux to Brienne 22 Dec., same to Mazarin 25 Dec. 1659; BT 106, same to Brienne 1 and 5 Jan., same to Mazarin 5 Jan. 1660; Rugg, pp. 17, 22–3; *Cal Clar SP*, IV.478, 481–2; *Clarke Papers*, IV.212–15, 233–7.

57. Whitelocke, IV.384; BT 106, Bordeaux to Brienne 1 and 8 Jan., same to Mazarin 5 Jan. 1660; R. R. Sharpe, *London and the Kingdom*, 3 vols (London, 1894–5), II.360–3; *Cal Clar SP*, IV.481–2.

58. BT 106, Bordeaux to Brienne 8 Jan. 1660; *CJ*, VII.797–801.

Chapter 2: The Promised Land

1. Gumble, p. 218; *CJ*, VII.801–3, 818, 834.

2. *CJ*, VII.805–6, 812–14; Rugg, p. 30; *Clar SP*, III.654, 682; *CSPV 1659–61*, p. 114.

3. Gumble, p. 226; BT 106, Bordeaux to Mazarin 20 Jan. 1660; Pepys, I.36–8; *CSPV 1659–61*, p. 115; Rugg, pp. 34–5, 37; Lister, III.83–4.

4. Pepys, I.38, 45; Rugg, p. 29; *Clar SP*, III.645. For the petitions, see Rugg, pp. 30ff; *Cal Clar SP*, IV.527, 534.

5. *Clar SP*, III.662–3, 697, 699; *RB*, book I, part II, p. 214; *Cal Clar SP*, IV.582; Carte, *Orig. Letters*, II.310; Nicholas, IV.203.

6. Grimoard, I.323, 325; *Clar SP*, III.667–8, 675, 678; *HMC 7th Report*, p. 462.

7. Pepys, I.47–9; *CJ*, VII.838; Gumble, pp. 235–43; *OPH*, XXII.92–3.

8. *CJ*, VII.813, 823, 841.

9. Price, pp. 762–3; *OPH*, XXII.98–103.

10. BT 106, Bordeaux to Mazarin 22 Feb. 1660; Price, pp. 765–6; Gumble, pp. 244–5; Pepys, I.50–2, 54–5; *CSPV 1659–61*, p. 118; *Cal Clar SP*, IV.560, 566.

11. *CJ*, VII.842–6; *OPH*, XXII.101–2.

12. Price, pp. 770–2; Pepys, I.60–3; Gumble, pp. 260–3; *HMC 7th Report*, p. 462; BT 106, Bordeaux to Mazarin 4 March 1660; *CJ*, VII.842–6.

13. *HMC Ormond*, NS I.333; BL Add. MS 15750 fo. 54; *Clar SP*, III.690; *Cal Clar SP*, IV.574–5, 577–8.

14. *OPH*, XXII.170–2; see also Price, pp. 773–5; BT 106, Bordeaux to Brienne 8 March 1660.

15. *CJ*, VII.872–4.

16. *Ibid.*, 858, 862, 874, 877, 880.

17. BL Add MS 15750 fo. 54; *Clar SP*, III.690; *Cal Clar SP*, IV.577, 588, 593; BT 106, Bordeaux to Brienne 8 March 1660; *HMC 7th Report*, p. 462, 484; *HMC Ormond*, NS I.334–5; *HMC Bath*, II.143; Carte, *Orig. Letters*, II.310; *CJ*, VII.854; Rugg, p. 53.

18. *CJ*, VII.854; *HMC 7th Report*, p. 483; Pepys, I.77, 79; BL Add. MS 15750 fos 55–6.

19. *HMC 7th Report*, p. 483; BT 106, Bordeaux to Brienne 22 March 1660; *Cal Clar SP*, IV.591; Nicholas, IV.194–205; BL Add. MS 15750 fos 55–6; *HMC Ormond*, NS I.335–6; Pepys, I.81–2, 84.

20. *Clar SP*, III.656–8, 660; *Letters*, pp. 81–2; Clarendon, *Hist.*, VI.179–80; *Cal Clar SP*, IV.578.

21. CPA 74, Montagu to Mazarin 13 March, Charles to Montagu 25 March 1660; *Letters*, pp. 81–2.

22. Clarendon, *Hist.*, VI.195–7, 200–1, 225–7.

23. CPA 74, Montagu to Mazarin 13 March 1660; Carte MS 30 fos 550, 561–2, 568–70; Clarendon, *Hist.*, VI.225–6; BT 106, Bordeaux to Mazarin 19 and 22 April, same to Brienne 26 April 1660.

24. *Clar SP*, III.645, 662–3; Mordaunt, pp. 169–70, 178. Mordaunt also sought the queen's help in January: Mordaunt, p. 166.

25. Clarendon, *Hist.*, VI.196–7.

26. *HP*, I.461, 146. See G. Davies, *The Restoration of Charles II 1658–60* (Oxford, 1955), pp. 320–32.

27. *HP*, I.449, 486, II.779–80, III.334.

28. *Clar SP*, III.703, 705, 729–30; *Cal Clar SP*, IV.634, 653, 656.

29. Lister, III.94; Carte, *Orig. Letters*, II.317–18; Rugg, pp. 65–6; BT 106, Bordeaux to Brienne 5 April, same to Mazarin 12 April 1660; *Clar SP*, III.722–3, 726; *Cal Clar SP*, IV.647; Gumble, pp. 278–9; Barwick, pp. 260–3; Whitelocke, IV.408–9; Clar MS 72 fos 44, 59.

30. Clar. MSS 71 fos 156, 198, 72 fo. 50; BT 106, Bordeaux to Mazarin 12 and 19 April 1660; Carte MS 73 fo. 406; *Clar SP*, III.729.

31. PRO, PRO 30/24/3 fo. 62; Clarendon, *Hist.*, VI.202, 226; Rugg, pp. 70–1.

32. Kenyon, *Constitution*, pp. 331–2.

33. Clarendon, *Life*, I.471.

34. Clar MS 72 fos 19–20, 62–3; Staffs. RO, D868/3 fo. 8; *HMC 5th Report*, p. 208; BL Add. MS 11689 fo. 55; *Cal Clar SP*, IV.679–81; BT 107, Bordeaux to Brienne 3 and 6 May, same to Mazarin 6 and 10 May 1660; Pepys, I.118–19.

35. Carte, *Orig. Letters*, II.328–9; *HMC 3rd Report*, p. 89; Dering, *Papers*, p. 37 (this does not mention conditions); Clar MS 72 fos 4, 222.

36. *Clar SP*, III.749 (the date is given as 13 May, but from internal evidence it must have been written on the 4th).

37. CPA 74, Bordeaux to Brienne 17 May 1660; *Clar SP*, III.747–8; Lister, III.500–3 ('The General's Paper'). From the accompanying letter (Clar MS 72 fo. 288) it is clear that this was sent to Hyde without Monk's knowledge: see Abernathy, pp. 58–9 + n.

38. *Clar SP*, III.747–8; Lister, III.100–3; *LJ*, XI.19–20; HLRO, Main Papers 2 April to 14 May 1660 fos 194–203.

39. *HMC 5th Report*, pp. 149, 204; Lister, III.100; *Clar SP*, III.748; Clar MS 72 fos 193, 288; *Cal Clar SP*, V.17–18, 20.

40. CPA 74, Bordeaux to Brienne 17 May 1660; Clar MS 72 fos 234, 432; Dering, *Papers*, p. 40; *HMC 5th Report*, p. 153.

41. Eg MS 2618 fos 69, 75; *Letters*, pp. 90–1. There are other copies of the letter to Morrice in Lansdowne MS 1064 fo. 72; PRO, PRO 30/24/3 fos 97–8.

42. CPA 74, Bordeaux to Brienne 17 May; BT 107, same to same 24 May 1660; Dering, *Papers*, p. 43; *CJ*, VIII.33–4.

43. Clarendon, *Hist.*, VI.224–5; Ludlow, pp. 10–11, 149–50; Carte, *Orig. Letters*, II.341; *Lettres de Mazarin*, ed. P. A. Chéruel and G. d'Avenel, 9 vols (Paris, 1872–1906), IX.608–10; BT 107, Bordeaux to Mazarin, 3 and 7 June 1660.

44. Clarendon, *Hist.*, VI.227–8; Pepys, I.143, 158; *HMC 5th Report*, p. 207; *HMC le Fleming*, pp. 25–6.

45. BL Add MS 18738 fo. 102; Clarendon, *Hist.*, VI.233; Clarendon, *Life*, I.323–6.

46. Evelyn, III.246.

47. Pepys, II.157–8, IV.360; Reresby, p. 194; *CSPV 1661–4*, p. 84; Ailesbury, I.93; *HMC 5th Report*, pp. 169, 170; *Letters*, p. 268; Eg MS 3330 fo. 32; Welwood, p. 149; Buckingham, II.59–60.

48. Pepys, VII.201.

49. *Ibid.*, 218; Ailesbury, I.87; Evelyn, IV.410 (quoted).

50. Buckingham, II.57; Ailesbury, I.93–4; *CSPV 1669–70*, p. 44; Burnet, *Hist.*, II.468.

51. North, *Examen*, p. 657; Buckingham, II.59. See also Clarendon, *Life*, I.504.

52. Pepys, IV.250–1, V.112, IX.192; Ailesbury, I.7–8, 93; Welwood, p. 151; *CSPV 1661–4*, p. 84.

53. Halifax, p. 256; Ailesbury, I.96; BT 121, Croissy to Lionne 31 Jan. 1669; *CSPV 1666–8*, p. 265; *CSPD 1671*, pp. 391–2.

54. Burnet, *Hist.*, II.465–7; Hartmann, *Madame*, p. 203; Eg MS 2618 fo. 108; PRO, SP 78/122 fos 136, 190.

55. Pepys, VI.45; BN, Cinq Cents de Colbert 478 fo. 115; *HMC Heathcote*, p. 48; Lauderdale, I.149–50; Dorset RO, D124, Box 272, 'Analyses and Comparisons of State of Royal Revenue 1618–67', fo. 46; Pepys, VIII.420–1, 449; BL Add MS 29580 fo. 10; for the navy, see Davies, *Gentlemen and Tarpaulins*.

56. Halifax, p. 256; CPA 122, Courtin to Pomponne 2 Feb. 1677; BT 121, Croissy to Lionne 8 April 1669.

57. Burnet, *Hist.*, II.330.

58. *POAS*, II.475–6; Burnet, *Suppl.*, p. 64. See also *POAS*, I.181–3.

59. Pepys, IX.361; BT 121, Croissy 20 Feb. 1669; BT 126, same 28 Sept. 1671; *CSPV*

1671–2, p. 321.

60. BT 121, Croissy 20 Feb. 1669; Pepys, IX.255, 471.

61. Halifax, p. 256; see also Burnet, *Hist.*, I.159–60, 466–8, *Suppl.*, p. 49.

62. BT 122, Croissy 13 May 1669; Reresby, pp. 210, 215; Pepys, VIII.573.

63. Clarendon, *Life*, II.144.

64. *Ibid.*, III.61; BT 121, Croissy to Lionne 7 Feb. 1669; Essex, II.145; BN, Cinq Cents de Colbert 478 fo. 116; Pepys, VIII.356.

65. Buckingham, II.59; Welwood, p. 150; Burnet, *Suppl.*, p. 140.

66. Halifax, p. 255.

67. BT 121, Croissy 31 Jan. 1669.

68. *Letters*, p. 82.

69. Pepys, IX.387; Browning, *Danby*, II.65, 287 (quoted); Buckingham, II.59.

70. Buckingham, II.58; Clarendon, *Life*, II.341; Burnet, *Suppl.*, p. 140, *Hist.*, II.100; Ailesbury, I.92–3; Welwood, p. 151.

71. Clarendon, *Life*, I.419; BT 129, Croissy 23 Nov. 1673.

72. Buckingham, II.58–9.

73. Clarendon MS 71 fo. 71.

74. Clarendon, *Life*, I.362–3, 405–6, II.144–5, III.3; North, *Examen*, pp. 657–8; Burnet, *Hist.*, I.158; *CSPV 1659–61*, p. 297; Haley, *Diplomat*, p. 296.

75. Pepys, VIII.356, 447; Reresby, p. 215; Temple, I.449.

76. Temple, I.462; PRO, SP 104/180 fo. 115.

77. Burnet, *Hist.*, 466–8, II.439.

78. Buckingham, II.59; Welwood, p. 150. The similarity between these two 'characters' of Charles suggests that Welwood may have seen that of Mulgrave/Buckingham, of which there is a manuscript copy in Shaftesbury's papers (PRO, PRO 30/24/6B fos 174–6).

79. Clarendon, *Hist.*, VI.234.

80. Burnet, *Hist.*, II.2.

81. J. R. Western, *Monarchy and Revolution: The English State in the 1680s* (London, 1972); J. Childs, '1688', *History* LXXIII (1988), pp. 398–424.

82. The phrase comes from J. Brewer, *The Sinews of Power: War, Money and the English State 1688–1763* (London, 1989). My debt to Prof. Brewer's work is obvious. For 'absolutism', see Miller, 'Potential for "Absolutism"', J. Miller (ed.), *Absolutism in Seventeenth-Century Europe* (London, 1990); for the navy, see Davies.

83. Ailesbury, I.22, 97; Bulstrode, *Memoirs*, p. 413; Burnet, *Hist.*, I.487–8, II.467, 471; Reresby, pp. 112–13; North, *Examen*, p. 451.

Chapter 3: The King Restored

1. *CSPV 1659–61*, p. 159; BN, Fonds Français 20674 fo. 131; BT 107, Bordeaux to Brienne 17 June 1660; Clarendon, *Life*, I.329–30, 353–5; Bramston, p. 117.

2. *HMC 5th Report*, pp. 154, 194, 205. For demands for money in general, and by Hyde in particular, see *ibid.*, pp. 168, 204; *CSPD 1660–1*, p. 217; *CSPV 1659–61*, pp. 97, 198, 206, 209; Pepys, II.213; R. Spalding, *The Improbable Puritan: A Life of Bulstrode Whitelocke* (London, 1975), p. 229. Hutton, *Charles II*, pp. 142–5, argues that the Royalist claims of neglect were overstated.

3. BT 107, Bordeaux to Mazarin 3 and 17 June 1660; BN, Fonds Français 20674 fo. 131.

4. *CJ*, VIII.172; Clarendon, *Life*, I.358–61, 370–1, 404–6; BT 107, Bordeaux to Mazarin 14 June 1660.

5. BT 114, Verneuil, Cominges and Courtin 21 May 1665; BT 118, Clarendon to Louis 7 Jan. 1668 (in English); BT 107, Crofts to Mazarin 3 Oct. 1660; Clarendon, *Life*, I.405–6, II.327, III.18, 102–4; Burnet, *Hist.*, I.270–1. See also D. Hirst, 'The Privy Council and Problems of Enforcement in the 1620s', *Journal of British Studies* XVIII (1978), pp. 46–66.

6. Burnet, *Hist.*, I.270–2; Macpherson, I.17; Lister, II.23–4n.; Rawdon, pp. 164–5; Pepys,

IX.490; BT 109, Bartet to Mazarin '24 Jan.' (recte 10 Feb.) 1661. (The original is bound in two parts, though with continuous internal pagination: BN, MS Baluze 324 fos 22–5, 36–7; this led Baschet to ascribe the first part to the earlier date).

7. BL Add MS 61483 fos 179, 183.

8. PRO, SP 29/4, no. 77 (III); Clarendon, *Life*, I.419.

9. BT 107, Ruvigny to Mazarin 21 Oct.; BT 108, Bartet to Mazarin 23, 25 and 29 Nov., 2 Dec. 1660; BT 109, same to same 10 Feb. 1661; CPA 74, Montagu to Mazarin 9 Nov. 1660; *Lettres de Mazarin*, ed. Chéruel and d'Avenel, IX.679–80; Miller, *James II*, pp. 44–5.

10. BT 108, Bartet to Mazarin 23 and 29 Nov., 14 and 16 Dec. 1660; BT 109, same to same 3 Jan. 1661.

11. PC 2/54 fo. 26; *LJ*, XI.148.

12. Kenyon, *Constitution*, pp. 331–2; *CJ*, VIII.53, 61, 66. Charles had already (5 June) ordered the lord mayor and aldermen of London to tender the oaths to those who were by law supposed to take them: *CSPD 1660–1*, p. 38.

13. Bowman, fo. 41. See also *HMC 5th Report*, p. 184; *CJ*, VIII.33–4; *CSPD 1660–1*, p. 41.

14. Clarendon, *Life*, I.467–72; *SR*, V.226–34; *CJ*, VIII.135.

15. *Letters*, pp. 100–1; *CJ*, VIII.132–3; *LJ*, XI.109 (Bryant does not include this last sentence in the *Letters*); *HMC 5th Report*, p. 155. See also Hutton, *Charles II*, pp. 171–2.

16. *CJ*, VIII.67, 107; *HMC 5th Report*, pp. 155, 195; *LJ*, XI.121–2; Bowman, fos 128–9.

17. *Letters*, p. 102; *HMC 5th Report*, p. 178.

18. *HMC 5th Report*, p. 174; Staffs. RO, D868/4 fo. 56; *CJ*, VIII.197.

19. Hutton, *Restoration*, pp. 162–3; *Letters*, p. 128; Pepys, III.108, 112; for a comment on Vane's unpopularity among MPs in 1660, see *HMC 5th Report*, p. 154.

20. *HMC Ormond*, NS III.306.

21. M. Ashley, *Commercial and Financial Policy of the Cromwellian Protectorate* (Oxford, 1934), p. 41; for sale prices, see H. J. Habakkuk, 'The Land Settlement and the Restoration of Charles II', *TRHS* 5th Series XXVIII (1978), p. 219. This paragraph and the next draw heavily on Habakkuk's article and on Green, ch. 5, and J. Thirsk, 'The Restoration Land Settlement', *Journal of Modern History* XXVI (1954), pp. 315–28.

22. Lister, III.500–1.

23. *CJ*, VIII.167; *LJ*, XI.170–1.

24. See, for example, *CJ*, VIII.61, 135–6. Monk had received commissions from both the Rump and the restored Long Parliament: see above, p. 17; *CJ*, VII.847.

25. *CJ*, VIII.167; Pepys, I. 249; Clarendon, *Life*, I.333–6, 472–3.

26. *SR*, V.241–2.

27. *CJ*, VIII.42, 49, 57, 71, 80.

28. *Ibid.*, 104, 112, 115, 119, 153, 183, 192 (but it was not included on the list on p. 211); *LJ*, XI.82.

29. HLRO, Parchment Collection, Box 12, Bill for the Confirmation of the Privileges of Parliament, 3 July 1660 (partly printed in J. Miller, *Restoration England: The Reign of Charles II* (London, 1985), pp. 87–8); Lister, III.501.

30. Kenyon, *Constitution*, p. 332.

31. See the discussions in D. Underdown, *Revel, Riot and Rebellion* (Oxford, 1985); K. Wrightson, *English Society 1580–1680* (London, 1982); W. Hunt, *The Puritan Moment* (Cambridge, Mass., 1983); I. Green, 'Career Prospects and Clerical Conformity in the Early Stuart Church', *Past and Present* no. 90 (1981), pp. 71–115.

32. See P. Lake, 'Anti-Popery: The Structure of a Prejudice', in R. Cust and A. Hughes (eds), *Conflict in Early Stuart England* (London, 1989), pp. 72–106; R. Clifton, 'Fear of Popery', in C. Russell (ed.), *Origins of the English Civil War* (London, 1973), pp. 144–67; W. M. Lamont, *Godly Rule* (London, 1969).

33. See especially C. Hibbard, *Charles I and the Popish Plot* (Chapel Hill, 1983).

34. *RB*, book I, part II, p. 217.

35. I shall use the term 'Anglican' although it was not in common use at the time.

36. Ailesbury, I.93; see also Burnet, *Suppl.*, p. 50.

37. Burnet, *Hist.*, I.158–9, 475, II.22.

38. Buckingham, II.55–6; see also the similar passage in Welwood, pp. 148–9; also *CSPV 1661–4*, p. 86; BT 111, Cominges to Lionne 12 April 1663.

39. Burnet, *Hist.*, I.184; *HMC Beaufort*, p. 84; Macray, p. 65; Hutton, *Charles II*, pp. 153–4.

40. Burnet, *Hist.*, I.448–9; Clarendon, *Life*, II.144–5.

41. *Clar SP*, III.571, 613–14.

42. *RB*, book I, part II, p. 218; Burnet, *Hist.*, I.150; *Clar SP*, III.727–8, 738; *Cal Clar SP*, IV.654.

43. Lister, III.501; *HMC 5th Report*, p. 149; *CJ*, VIII.18; *CSPD 1659–60*, p. 433. The reference to 'tender consciences' was added at a late stage, maybe as a gesture towards the wording of the Declaration of Breda: it seems to have borne little relation to the contents of the bill.

44. *Clar SP*, III.747 (for date of the first letter, see *Cal Clar SP*, V.23); Dering, *Papers*, p. 40; *CJ*, VIII.19, 33. Abernathy (p. 61) talks of two bills, but the various references speak only of 'the bill of religion'.

45. Carte, *Orig. Letters*, II.337–9; Clarendon, *Hist.*, VI.231–2. Baxter wrote that Charles was full of assurances of goodwill: *RB*, book I, part II, p. 218.

46. *CJ*, VIII.47, 136; *CSPD 1660–1*, p. 34; *HMC 5th Report*, p. 154; Green, *Re-establishment*, pp. 46–51.

47. Green, pp. 49–60.

48. See Duppa's complaint in Tanner MS 49 fo. 17.

49. *RB*, book I, part II, pp. 229–32; *HMC 5th Report*, p. 168.

50. Bowman, fo. 64; see also *RB*, book I, part II, p. 229.

51. Bowman, fos 62–6, 77–85, 88–9. Bowman has the same conclusion to the debates of both 9 and 16 July, but other sources would suggest that the resolution in question belongs to the 16th (*HMC 5th Report*, p. 155). It seems possible that Bowman became confused, perhaps in writing up the debates from notes. (There is no reference to these proceedings in the journals as they took place in committee.)

52. *CSPV 1659–61*, pp. 173, 176; DUL, Cosin Letter Book 1A, no. 66.

53. Green, p. 27, implies that Hyde approved of the content of these letters. The fact that they are clearly intercepts (neither Montagu's nor Bellings's are in his own hand) would suggest that he was not intended to know of them. Ironically Bellings commented: 'Your letters come very easy and without the least suspicion of being opened': Clar MS 73 fo. 185.

54. Clar MS 73 fo. 175, quoted in extenso, Green, p. 28; could 'Omen' be the king?

55. Clar MS 73 fos 184–5: partly in cipher, deciphered. The fair copy (fo. 182) used by Green (p. 28) differs materially from this rougher copy.

56. Clar MS 73 fo. 196.

57. Green, pp. 29–30; Burnet, *Hist.*, I.307.

58. Green, p. 255 and ch. 4.

59. *HMC 5th Report*, p. 195; Staffs. RO, D868/4 fo. 51.

60. *RB*, book I, part II, pp. 259–64.

61. *Ibid.*, p. 265; *HMC 5th Report*, p. 156.

62. *RB*, book I, part II, pp. 265–76; *CJ*, VIII.172–4; *CSPD 1660–1*, pp. 266–7.

63. B. H. G. Wormald, *Clarendon: Politics, History, Religion* (Cambridge, 1951), section III, esp. p. 312; Seaward, pp. 28–31; K. Feiling, 'A Letter of Clarendon during the Elections of 1661', *EHR* XLII (1927), pp. 407–8. For evidence that he had had a deeper, more intransigent commitment to the Church in the 1640s, see M. Dzelzainis, '"Undoubted Realities": Clarendon on Sacrilege', *HJ* XXXIII (1990), pp. 534–40.

64. Green, ch. 10.

65. *RB*, book I, part II, pp. 276–8.

66. *Ibid.*, p. 279; Lister, III.110–11; Browning, *Documents*, pp. 365–70.

67. *CSPD 1660–1*, p. 350; *HMC 5th Report*, pp. 185, 196; Staffs. RO, D868/4 fo. 55; *OPH*, XXIII.27–30; BT 108, Bartet to Mazarin 10 Dec. 1660.

68. *CSPD 1660–1*, p. 404; BT 108, Bartet to Mazarin 10 Dec. 1660; Marvell, II.6–7 (quotation from p. 6).

69. Carte, *Orig. Letters*, II.225; Clar MS 72 fo. 288; Bowman, fos 50–2, 137–8; Clar MS 73 fo. 208. For an earlier suggestion that Catholics saw Hyde as hostile, see *Clar SP*, III.655. See also Miller, *Popery*, pp. 95–6.

70. *RB*, part I, book II, p. 277; BT 108, Montagu to Mazarin 9 Dec. 1660.

71. PC 2/54 fo. 33; *CSPD 1660–1*, pp. 114, 123, 130, 132, 150, 184–5, 202; *HMC 5th Report*, p. 195; JRL, Legh of Lyme Correspondence, J. Duckenfield to R. Legh 29 July, R. Standish to same 29 Nov. 1660; Coleby, pp. 89–90; C. Russell, *Parliaments and English Politics 1621–9* (Oxford, 1979), pp. 76–8; BL Add. MS 29550 fo. 361.

72. Hutton, *Restoration*, p. 129; Fletcher, pp. 18–19; Coleby, pp. 90–1; Miller, 'Charters', pp. 56–7.

73. BL Add MS 32324 fo. 64. This seems to be the same order as that entered under 'July' in *CSPD 1660–1*, p. 150 (PRO, SP 29/8, no. 188). See also Eg MS 2537 fo. 266.

74. *HMC 5th Report*, pp. 196, 200; *OPH*, XXIII.2, 14–15, 24, 51–3; Marvell, II.2, 7–8.

75. BT 107, Bordeaux to Mazarin 14 and 24 June 1660; CPA 74, Montagu to Mazarin 28 Dec. 1660; *CSPV 1659–61*, p. 231; BN, Fonds Français 20674 fo. 31 (another copy, CPA 74 fo. 692); Childs, pp. 15–16; *LJ*, XI. 237–8.

76. *CJ*, VIII.11, 68.

77. Dering, *Papers*, p. 48; *CJ*, VIII.150; Chandaman, pp. 200–1.

78. *CJ*, VIII.187–8, 193–4; Chandaman, pp. 38–9. The vote (151–149) on 21 November not to include the second half of the excise in the vote on the first did not amount to a rejection as there was no formal proposal to grant it. Chandaman is incorrect to say that this led to the decision to dissolve as that had been taken on the 20th (*LJ*, XI.189).

79. *OPH*, XXIII.24–6; Chandaman, p. 202; BT 108, Montagu to Mazarin 9 Dec., Bartet to same 10 Dec. 1660.

80. On the revenue in general, see Chandaman.

81. The one exception was the vote of £60,000 for indigent Royalist officers, the money for which was (judging from *CJ*) very badly managed.

82. *CJ*, VIII.104, 107; Bowman, fos 96–7; Newton, *House of Lyme*, p. 213.

83. *CSPV 1659–61*, pp. 195–6.

84. *HMC 5th Report*, pp. 158, 195.

Chapter 4: 'Dunkirk and a Barren Queen'

1. Carte MS 32 fo. 368; Pepys, IV.163.

2. *LJ*, XI.148; PC 2/55 fos 49–50; Hutton, *Restoration*, pp. 150–1; Harris, *Crowds*, p. 60; Pepys, II.10–11.

3. Ludlow, pp. 149–50.

4. Both Bennet and Charles expressed confidence in their spies in 1662: Carte MS 221 fo. 7; Hartmann, *Madame*, p. 60.

5. CPA 81 fos 5–6, Newsletter 16 Jan. 1662; Pepys, III.15; BT 109, d'Estrades 26 Sept. 1661.

6. See especially Lister, III.198–201.

7. *CSPD 1660–1*, p. 466, *1661–2*, pp. 92, 156; BL Add MS 32324 fos 108–9.

8. *Life*, I.390–1; Dorset RO, D124, Box 237, item 17 (autobiography of Sir Stephen Fox, unfoliated); BT 109, Bartet to Mazarin 24 Jan. 1661; BN, MS Baluze 324 fo. 153; *HMC 5th Report*, pp. 150, 202; Childs, p. 16.

9. Lister, III.208; BT 110, Battailler to Lionne 31 July 1662; *CSPV 1661–4*, p. 180.

10. *LJ*, XI. 240–3; Burnet, *Hist*, I.282; Clarendon, *Life*, II.97–9; *HMC 5th Report*, p. 208; *CJ*, VIII.256, 278. For the importance of Charles's intervention, see Tanner MS 49 fo. 101; BL Add MS 11314 fo. 27x.

11. *CJ*, VIII.287; *LJ*, XI.315–16; Macray, p. 29.

12. Browning, *Documents*, pp. 63–5; *LJ*, XI.369–70, 382, 495; *CJ*, VIII.395, 447; HLRO, Committee Minutes 1661–4, pp. 117–19, 129, 155, 326–8.

13. Browning, *Documents*, pp. 63–9; *CJ*, VIII.417, 425, 429. The two-year limit was added at a late stage: *SR*, V.433; *CJ*, VIII.435. See also *SR*, V.524, 556, 577.

14. *CSPD 1675–6*, p. 1; Carte MS 70 fo. 447.

15. This paragraph and the next is based on Miller, 'Charters', pp. 56–67. For the warrant, see SP 29/35, no. 18.

16. Browning, *Documents*, p. 793.

17. Eg MS 2043, fo. 23; *CJ*, VIII.324, 339–40; Pepys, II.225; *HMC Beaufort*, p. 51.

18. *CSPV 1661–4*, p. 91; CPA 81 fos 5–6; *LJ*, XI.359; *HMC Beaufort*, p. 52; Pepys, III.15; Rawdon, pp. 150–1; Eg MS 2043 fo. 37.

19. *SR*, V.358–64 (excerpts Browning, *Documents*, pp. 793–5); Western, *Militia*, pp. 12–15; Fletcher, pp. 319–23; Finch MS PP 57(ii), p. 49.

20. BT 109, Bartet to Mazarin 30 Jan. and 7 Feb. 1661; *Clar SP*, III, Supplement, pp. iv–v; *LJ*, XI.242.

21. *HMC 5th Report*, pp. 203–4; Eg MS 2043 fo. 11; *CJ*, VIII.262 (quoted), 273–4.

22. *CJ*, VIII.299, 309, 367–8, 376–8; BL Add. MS 32500 fo. 9; BT 110, d'Estrades 23 March 1662; Chandaman, pp. 77, 87.

23. *Clar SP*, III, Supplement, pp. iv–v; *HMC Finch*, I.154. See also Carte MS 221 fo. 58.

24. Clarendon, *Life*, II.116; Dorset RO, D124, Box 272, State of the Revenue under Southampton, p. 8.

25. Rawdon, pp. 137–8; DUL, Cosin Letter Book 2, no. 70. Clarendon recognized that the access which Charles allowed to Presbyterian ministers held up the settlement of the revenue: Clarendon, *Life*, II.124–5. On the other hand, the hearth money bill passed the Commons very quickly and the House apparently did not try to use it as a bargaining counter: *CJ*, VIII.378, 385.

26. Bowman, fo. 64; PC 2/55 fo. 48. This order dates from five days before Venner's rising, although some claimed that it was a response to it: *CSPD 1660–1*, p. 471.

27. Green, chs 1–6; PC 2/55 fos 48–50; *CSPD 1660–1*, p. 587; *LJ*, XI.242–3.

28. *CJ*, VIII.247, 254, 289; *HMC 5th Report*, p. 207. See also Pepys, II.111.

29. *HMC 5th Report*, p. 151; Staffs RO, D868/3 fo. 38; *CJ*, VIII.299; *LJ*, XI.465; *SR*, V.420. See R. O'Day and A. Hughes, 'Augmentation and Amalgamation', in R. O'Day and F. Heal (eds), *Princes and Paupers in the English Church 1500–1800* (Leicester, 1981), pp. 169–90. Note Dr Green's comment on the clergy's apparently generous leasing policy towards the gentry: Green, pp. 195–201.

30. Seaward, ch. 7, esp. pp. 193–4; Green, ch. 9; Rugg, p. 154; even Baxter recognized, grudgingly and dismissively, the extensive popular support enjoyed by the Church: *RB*, book III, p. 181.

31. A. Fletcher, 'The Enforcement of the Conventicle Acts, 1664–79', in W. J. Sheils (ed.), *Persecution and Toleration* (Studies in Church History, Oxford, 1984), pp. 235–46; Miller, *Popery*, ch. 3.

32. BL Add MS 28053 fos 1–2; *Cosin Corr.*, II.x–xi; *RB*, part I, book II, p. 338; Abernathy, p. 80.

33. Tanner MS 49 fos 146–7; PC 2/55 fos 118, 282–3; Bosher, pp. 214–15, 244–9; Macray, p. 59.

34. *CJ*, VIII.279; Seaward, pp. 166–7; *LJ*, XI.333; *Cosin Corr.*, II.26; Pepys, II.174; BT 109, d'Estrades 26 Sept., Battailler to Lionne 28 Oct. 1661.

35. Rawdon, pp. 137–8; Seaward, pp. 172–4.

36. *HMC 7th Report*, pp. 162–3; Rawdon, pp. 140–3; *CSPV 1661–4*, pp. 124–5; *CJ*, VIII.413; DUL, Cosin Letter Book 2, no. 70; *LJ*, XI.447, 449, 476; Seaward, pp. 174–9.

37. *HMC 7th Report*, p. 484; Carte MSS 31 fo. 602, 32 fo. 3, 47 fo. 359; Clarendon, *Life*, II.143–50; Burnet, *Hist*, I.330–1; J. Owen, *Correspondence*, ed. P. Toon (Cambridge, 1970), pp. 129–30; Pepys, III.186; Tanner MS 48 fos 45, 48; Baxter claimed that the Presbyterians refused to petition: *RB*, part I, book II, p. 433.

38. Green, chs 7–8.

39. Carte MS 47 fo. 3; *LJ*, XI.242–3, 476; see also Clar MS 80 fo. 167; Green. ch. 10.

40. Carte MS 221 fos 9–10.

41. HLRO, Committee Minutes 1661–4, pp. 62–4. (There is another copy in the Newberry Library, Case MS 6 A 20.)

42. *LJ*, XI.276–7, 281, 286, 291; Miller, *Popery*, p. 98; Newberry Library, Case MS 6 A 18, pp. 1–15. (This is marked both 'Bristol's speech to the Lords' and 'a copy of Col. Tuke's paper to be offered to the Parliament, February 1662/3'. It seems to make more sense in the context of 1661, especially as Tuke is recorded as having then made a speech to the Lords.)

43. *LJ*, XI.310–11; Miller, *Popery*, pp. 95–6, 99; see also Clarendon, *Life*, II.108–12; *HMC Ormond*, NS VII.307–9.

44. *CSPD 1670*, p. 643.

45. BT 109, d'Estrades 25 July and 29 Aug. 1661; *CSPV 1661–4*, pp. 85–6.

46. BT 109, d'Estrades to Lionne 1 Sept. 1661; BN, Cinq Cents de Colbert 478 fos 117–18; CPA 75, d'Estrades to Brienne 4 Aug. 1661; *Clar SP*, III, Supplement, p. iii; *CSPV 1661–4*, pp. 212–13.

47. CPA 75, d'Estrades to Brienne, 5 Sept. 1661; BT 109, d'Estrades 26 Sept. 1661; BT 110, Battailler to Lionne 17 July 1662; BT 113, Cominges 29 Sept. 1664; Clar MSS 79 fo. 187, 84 fos 124–5 (misdated 1666). See also Miller, *Popery*, ch. 2 esp. p. 46.

48. *CSPV 1661–4*, pp. 195–6.

49. Rawdon, p. 143; *CSPV 1661–4*, pp. 124–5; *Clar SP*, III.193, Supplement, p. xcix.

50. See Stradling, *Europe and the Decline of Spain*; H. Kamen, 'The Decline of Spain: A Historical Myth?', *Past and Present* no. 81 (1978), pp. 24–50.

51. Mignet, I.118.

52. Hartmann, *Madame*, p. 117; Feiling, pp. 77–8, seems to me to overstate the competence of Arlington and Williamson; many 'state' papers (e.g. those of Coventry and Middleton) continued to end up in private archives.

53. BT 108, Bartet to Mazarin 25 Nov. 1660.

54. Rowen, pp. 18–20; Haley, *Diplomat*, pp. 39–50.

55. Stradling, 'Anglo-Spanish Relations', pp. 23–37.

56. BT 106, Bordeaux to Mazarin 19, 22 and 26 April; BT 107, same to same, 3, 10 and 11 May 1660.

57. BT 107, Bordeaux to Mazarin 17 June and 1 July, Bordeaux to Brienne 14 June and 8 July, Montagu to Mazarin 28 June, Bordeaux's relation 9 Aug. 1660; BL Add. MS 61483 fos 100–1.

58. BT 106, Bordeaux to Mazarin 19 April, Mazarin to Bordeaux 28 April 1660.

59. BN, MS Baluze 324 fos 136, 148, 152–3, 155–6; CPA 74, Mazarin to Crofts 22 Dec. 1660; BT 109, Bartet to Mazarin 12 Jan. 1661.

60. BT 109, Bartet to Mazarin, 7 Feb. 1661; SP 78/115 fos 193–5; BT 110, d'Estrades 20 Feb. 1662.

61. Feiling, pp. 44–9.

62. SP 78/115 fos 193–5; *Clar SP*, III, Supplement, pp. xii–xv; Clar MS 75 fos 77–9; CPA 75, Louis to d'Estrades 24 Sept. 1661.

63. BT 109, Louis to d'Estrades 6 and 16 Sept., 1 Nov. 1661; Jusserand, I.290–1; Clar MS 75 fos 258, 295.

64. Clar MS fos 288–9; Lister, III.126–7.

65. Lister, III.122–3; Clar MS 74 fo. 466.

66. CPA 75 fos 66–7 (St Albans' memorial, 10 July 1661).

67. CPA 75 fos 62–3 (Considerations on the memorial); BT 109, memorial to d'Estrades 13 May, Louis to d'Estrades 5 and 14 Aug. 1661.

68. *Clar SP*, III, Supplement, pp. ii, xi; Clar MS 74 fo. 466; BT 109, d'Estrades 21 July and 15 Aug. 1661; BT 110, same 16 Feb. 1662. Clarendon's speech to Parliament on 19 May 1662 did not mention the Dutch by name, but clearly expressed hostility towards them: *LJ*, XI.475; *CSPV 1661–4*, p. 147.

69. *Clar SP*, III, Supplement, p. viii; Clar MS 74 fo. 466; BT 109, d'Estrades 21 July 1661.

70. Grimoard, I.336–9.

71. Jusserand, I.268–9; *Clar SP*, III, Supplement, pp. x–xii, xiv; BT 109, d'Estrades 21 July, 5 and 16 Sept., Louis to d'Estrades 14 Aug. 1661; Feiling, pp. 98–9.

72. BT 110, Louis to d'Estrades 12 March 1662; Grimoard, I.361–3.

73. Hartmann, *Madame*, p. 36; BT 110, d'Estrades 20 Jan. and 1 Feb., Louis to d'Estrades 22 and 25 Jan., 5 Feb., Lionne to d'Estrades 25 Jan. and 5 Feb. 1662; Grimoard, I.343–5.

74. *Clar SP*, III, Supplement, pp. iv–v, vii–viii.

75. *Ibid.*, pp. xi–xii; BT 109, d'Estrades 4 Aug. 1661; Clar MS 75 fos 77–9 (another copy CPA 76, fo. 77); BT 110, Louis to Cominges 4 Feb. 1663; Clarendon, *Life*, I.517–18, gives a figure of 300,000 pistoles.

76. BT 109, Louis to d'Estrades, 14 Aug., 16 and 23 Sept. 1661; *Clar SP*, III, Supplement, pp. xvi–xvii; Clar MS 75 fos 103–4; Lister, III.206–7.

77. BT 110, Louis to Cominges 4 Feb. 1663; Lister, III.513–17; the 600,000 *livres* apparently never reached the exchequer: Chandaman, p. 48.

78. BT 109, Louis to d'Estrades 14 Aug. 1661; *Clar SP*, III, Supplement, p. xvi; BT 110, d'Estrades 30 March and 5 April 1662.

79. CPA 77, Clarendon to d'Estrades 20 July 1662; Lister, III.210.

80. BT 109, d'Estrades 21 July 1661; *LJ*, XI.475.

81. *Clar SP*, III, Supplement, p. xxv; Grimoard, I.348–9, 359–60, 363; BT 110, d'Estrades 9 and 16 Oct., d'Estrades to Lionne 25 Sept. 1662.

82. BT 110, d'Estrades 27 Oct.; CPA 77, d'Estrades 6 Nov. 1662; Jusserand, I.317–18.

83. BT 113, Ruvigny to Lionne 11 Dec. 1664 (Charles told Ruvigny that Fouquet had put his promise in writing – but did not produce it); BT 114, Cominges 29 Jan., Lionne to Cominges 7 Feb., Ruvigny's relation Feb. 1665; Clarendon, *Life*, I.518–19.

84. BT 114, Verneuil, Cominges and Courtin 24 May; CPA 86, Courtin to Lionne 23 July 1665.

85. Chandaman, pp. 129–30.

86. BT 107, Montagu to Mazarin 28 June, Crofts to same 3 Oct.; CPA 74, Montagu to same 4 and 7 July, 10 Oct. 1660; Carte MS 214 fos 230, 248; Clar MS 73 fo. 196; BL Add MS 61483 fos 229–30.

87. BT 107, Ruvigny to Mazarin 4 Oct.; BT 108, Montagu to same 9 and 16 Dec., Bartet to same 2 Dec. 1660; BT 109, Bartet to same 20 and 24 Jan., 19 Feb. 1661; Burnet, *Hist.*, I.283–4; Clarendon, *Life*, I.505–16; *CSPV 1661–4*, p. 87.

88. Burnet, *Suppl.*, p. 142; Pepys, VIII.356, VI.267; *POAS*, I.424, II.174; Rochester, *Letters*, p. 189. See also Pepys, VIII.368; for Sussex, see the hint in CPA 123A, Courtin to Pomponne 4 Jan. 1677.

89. See J. H. Wilson, *Court Wits of the Restoration* (Princeton, 1948); D. H. Griffin, *Satires against Man: The Poems of Rochester* (Berkeley, 1973); J. H. Wilson (ed.), *Court Satires of the Restoration* (Columbus, 1976), pp. 57–61, 83; Pepys, IV.1, 210.

90. Wilson, *Court Satires*, pp. 38–9 (quoted), 58, 61; Rochester, *Poems*, ed. K. Walker (Oxford, 1984), pp. 76–7; *POAS*, I.424, 426–7.

91. H. Love (ed.), *The Penguin Book of Restoration Verse* (Harmondsworth, 1978), pp. 224–5; Pepys, IV.136–7, 256.

92. Pepys, V.60, VIII.68, 355.

93. *CSPV 1661–4*, pp. 143–4; *Letters*, pp. 126–8; Hartmann, *Madame*, p. 43; *Clar SP*, III, Supplement, p. xxi; Burnet, *Hist.*, I.298–9.

94. Evelyn, III.320–1; *HMC le Fleming*, p. 28.

95. *CSPV 1661–4*, pp. 154, 164; Clarendon, *Life*, II.167–8, 170; Clar MS 76 fo. 287; BT 110, Battailler to Lionne 3 and 10 July 1662; Hartmann, *Madame*, pp. 50–1; Pepys, III.87.

96. Carte MS 31 fo. 559; Lister, III.210; *CSPV 1661–4*, pp. 169, 171–4, 180; BT 110, Battailler to Lionne 4 Sept. 1662.

97. Carte MSS 31 fo. 602, 32 fos 3, 9, 25–6, 36, 40, 67–8, 47 fo. 5, 214 fo. 379; Pepys, III.234–5; *CSPV 1661–4*, p. 169; Clarendon, *Life*, II.177–95.

98. Carte MS 32 fos 40 (quoted), 118; *Letters*, pp. 129–30; Pepys, IV.1.

99. Rawdon, pp. 164–5; *Clar SP*, III, Supplement, p. xcix; Carte MSS 32 fos 3, 9, 47 fos 3, 359, 221 fos 9–10.

100. Lister, III.210, 222 (quoted), 226–8; Carte MS 217 fos 460–1.

101. Carte MSS 31 fo. 559, 32 fo. 35, 217 fo. 460; BT 110, Battailler to Lionne 10 Aug. 1662. The queen mother had earlier been described as Clarendon's protectress: *CSPV 1661–4*, p. 164.

102. Lister, III.223–5; *HMC Finch*, I.221–2; Carte MSS 32 fos 67–8, 47 fo. 379; Pepys, III.227, 245, VIII.534. Clarendon claimed that the queen mother was not responsible for Nicholas's removal: Lister, III.228.

103. Pepys, III.238, 289–91, 302–3; *CSPV 1661–4*, pp. 216–17; Carte MS 47 fo. 18; *HMC Heathcote*, pp. 54–5; BT 110, Battailler to Lionne 14 Dec. 1662, Cominges 15 Jan. 1663.

104. Grimoard, I.363; Pepys, III.229, 237, 248; CPA 77, d'Estrades 6 Nov.; BT 110, d'Estrades 9 Nov., Battailler 30 Nov. 1662; Carte MS 46 fos 12, 20.

105. Browning, *Documents*, pp. 371–4.

106. *CSPD 1661–2*, p. 517; *Life*, I.428; Burnet, *Hist.*, I.333–6; Carte MSS 47 fo. 385, 221 fo. 15; *Cosin Corr.*, II.97; BT 110, Cominges 22 Jan. 1663; Pepys, IV.44.

107. Lister, III.232–3; BT 110, Cominges 22 Jan. 1663; *Cosin Corr.*, II.101–2; *Mather Papers*, pp. 208–9. Hutton, *Charles II*, p. 194, argues that the Declaration not only reflected Charles's views, but was his personal initiative – but he then discusses how others could have influenced it.

108. BT 110, Cominges 22 Jan., 15 Feb. and 19 March 1663; Carte MS 47 fo. 22; *LJ*, XI.478–9; Pepys, IV.50; *HMC 7th Report*, p. 167; DUL, Cosin Letter Book 1B, no. 100.

109. BT 110, Cominges 8 Jan.; BT 111, Cominges to Lionne 8 and 22 March 1663; Pepys, IV.57; Carte MSS 32 fo. 287, 47 fo. 397; *CJ*, VIII.440, 442–3. Clarendon's account (*Life*, II.342–9) of a scheme to allow Dissenters to compound for toleration, inserted under 1665, probably relates to 1663. There is no reference to such a bill in *LJ* for 1665, whereas Clarendon's account of the bill correlates quite closely with that of 1663.

110. *Mather Papers*, pp. 207–8; BL Add MS 40711 fos 6, 43; *HMC Heathcote*, pp. 77–8; Pepys, IV.66–8; *CJ*, VIII.452; BT 111, Cominges 2 and 9 April 1663; HLRO, Committee Minute Book 1661–4, p. 302; *HMC 7th Report*, p. 482.

111. *CJ*, VIII.462–3; *CSPV 1661–4*, p. 241; Carte MSS 32 fo. 357, 214 fo. 471; BT 111, Cominges 19 April and 25 May 1663; *Mather Papers*, p. 208.

112. *CSPV 1661–4*, p. 237; *HMC Ormond*, NS III.47; Lister, III.243–5; BT 111, Cominges 9 and 19 April 1663. See also Burnet, *Hist.*, I.338.

113. Carte MSS 32 fos 390–1, 47 fo. 403; *CJ*, VIII.474, 476; BT 111, Cominges 14 May 1663; Pepys, IV.107, 113–14, 123.

114. *CJ*, VIII.453–4, 478, 481, 498–501; Pepys, IV.103.

115. Carte MS 221 fo. 52; *HMC Ormond*, NS III.47; *HMC Fanshawe*, p. 74; *HMC Heathcote*, pp. 83–4; Clarendon, *Life*, II.211–12.

116. Carte MSS 32 fos 390–1, 597; *HMC Ormond*, NS III.52; see also Pepys, IV.137; BT 111, Cominges to Lionne 22 March, same to Louis 30 April 1663.

117. BT 111, Ruvigny 25 and 28 June, Cominges 5 July 1663; Carte MSS 32 fos 597–8, 679, 34 fo. 777. See also C. Roberts, 'Sir Richard Temple, the Pickthank Undertaker', *HLQ* XLI (1977–8), pp. 137–55. For Bennet's Parliamentary management, see Clarendon, *Life*, II.204–11; Seaward, pp. 98–9.

118. *CJ*, VIII.514–15; Pepys, IV.207–8; BT 112, Ruvigny 12 July 1663; Tanner MS 47, fo. 31.

119. BT 112, Ruvigny 16 July, Cominges 23 and 26 July 1663; Carte MS 32 fos 708–9, 716; *HMC Heathcote*, p. 127; *Life*, I.427; *HMC Finch*, I.302; BN, Cinq Cents de Colbert 478 fos 122–3.

120. Carte MSS 32 fos 709, 732, 36 fos 69–70, 221 fo. 58; BT 112, Bellings to Lionne 24 July 1663; *CJ*, VIII.532; *LJ*, XI.580; Chandaman, p. 145; Western, p. 15.

121. *HMC Ormond*, NS III.64, 68; Carte MSS 32 fos 406, 679, 33 fo. 34; Pepys, IV.220, 230, 272 (but see also p. 238); CPA 80, fos 57–8, 69–70 (unsigned letters of 2 and 13 Aug. 1663).

122. Carte MSS 33 fos 34, 69, 221 fos 74, 77–8; PC 2/56 fos 253–4; Dorset RO, D124, Box 272, 'Analyses and Comparisons of the State of the Royal Revenue 1618–67', fos 43–7; *HMC Ormond*, NS III.78, 174–5; Evelyn, IV.360–1.

Chapter 5: Sword and Fire

1. Pepys, IV.371, V.20–1, 46, 56, VII.8, 100, 159, 326, 336–7; Burnet, *Hist.*, I.436n.; BT 113, Cominges to Lionne 2 Oct. 1664; BT 114, Verneuil, Courtin and Cominges 21 May 1665; CPA 86, Courtin to Lionne 16 and 23 July 1665; Carte MS 34 fo. 459.

2. Pepys, IV.272, 339, 342, 348, 352–3; BT 112, Cominges 1 Nov., same to Lionne 25 Oct.; CPA 86, same to same 29 Oct. and 7 Nov. 1663; Carte MSS 33 fo. 211, 214 fo. 576.

3. Carte MS 46 fo. 250; Pepys, VII.48–9, 411; *CSPD 1665–6*, p. 232; *HMC 6th Report*, p. 337; Clarendon, *Life*, III.59–60.

4. *HMC Ormond*, NS III.120–1; *Hatton*, I.34; see also Pepys, V.56.

5. Stradling, 'Anglo-Spanish Relations', pp. 35–6; SP 78/117 fo. 214; SP 78/119 fo. 203; SP 78/120 fos 67–8; SP 78/121 fo. 83; CPA 85, Courtin to Lionne 1 June 1665; Pepys, VIII.318. For passages left undeciphered, see SP 78/129 fos 137, 180, 188.

6. BT 113, Ruvigny to Lionne 22 Dec. 1664; Pepys, VI.218, VIII.66–7, 121–2; BT 115, Verneuil, Courtin and Cominges 8 Sept. 1665.

7. Dorset RO, D124, Box 272, 'Analyses and Comparisons of State of the Royal Revenue 1618–67', rear of volume; *ibid.*, Box 235, bundle 1, part 2, 'The State of His Majesty's Revenue 15 February 1664/5'.

8. Haley, *Diplomat*, p. 65; Pepys, V.73.

9. BT 114, Cominges 19 Jan., Verneuil, Courtin and Cominges 24 May 1665; Clarendon, *Life*, III.62–3; Pepys, VI.238.

10. Carte MS 33 fo. 120; BT 112, Cominges 20 Sept. and 26 Nov. 1663; BT 113, Cominges 4 Feb. 1664; Pepys, V.60.

11. *HMC Ormond*, NS III.134; Carte MSS 33 fo. 324, 47 fos 83–4; BT 113, Cominges 17 March 1664; Pepys, V.89.

12. Clar MSS 80 fos 153–4, 81 fos 151–2; BT 113, Cominges 31 March, same to Lionne 27 March 1664.

13. BT 113, Cominges 31 March, same to Lionne 3 and 7 April 1664; Carte MS 76 fo. 7; *HMC Finch*, I.302–4; Hartmann, *Madame*, pp. 97–8.

14. BT 113, Cominges to Lionne 24 Nov. 1664; BT 114, same to same 2 March; CPA 85, same to same 27 April, Bigorre to Lionne 11 June 1665; *HMC Hastings*, II.149.

15. Reresby, p. 66; A. Hamilton, *Memoirs of Count Grammont*, ed. Sir W. Scott (London,

1846), p. 142; North, *Examen*, p. 453; Ailesbury, I.13; *CSPD 1673–5*, p. 188.

16. Pepys, V.345; BT 113, Cominges 3 July 1664; BT 114, same 8 Jan., Verneuil, Courtin and Cominges 27 April 1665; Burnet, *Suppl.*, p. 65; BN, Cinq Cents de Colbert 478 fos 123–5.

17. Burnet, *Suppl.*, pp. 58–60; Burnet, *Hist.*, I.164–8; Christie, I.195–9, 204–12, II, appendix, pp. lix–lx; Haley, *Shaftesbury*, esp. pp. 130–9, 158–9, 738–46.

18. BL Add MS 63057A fos 27–9; Ailesbury, I.14–16; Lauderdale, I.183–4. See also Buckroyd.

19. Pepys, V.73, 345; Clarendon, *Life*, II.341–2, III.110–11, 115; Hatton, I.34; BT113, Cominges 5 June 1664; BT 114, same 8 Jan., Verneuil, Courtin and Cominges 27 April and 21 May 1665; BN Cinq Cents de Colbert 478 fos 123–5; Bodl., MS Add.c.303 fo. 104.

20. Hutton, *Restoration*, pp. 204–6; *CSPD 1663–4*, pp. 444–5, *1665–6*, pp. 25, 113, 115; BT113, Cominges 17 March, Louis to Cominges 20 Feb. 1664; CPA 86, Verneuil, Courtin and Cominges 20 Sept. 1665.

21. BL Add MS 23120 fo. 29; *HMC Ormond*, NS III.117–23, 133; Lauderdale, I.183–4.

22. Hartmann, *Madame*, p. 89; Carte MS 33 fo. 324; Pepys, VI.126; *CSPD 1664–5*, pp. 564–5, *1665–6*, pp. 36–7.

23. Kenyon, *Constitution*, p. 342; PC 2/57 fo. 28; BL Add MS 4182 fo. 22; DUL, Mickleton-Spearman MS 31, fo. 77; *CSPD 1663–4*, p. 646; Cosin, II.108; DCAD, Hunter MS 10, no. 86.

24. Hartmann, *Madame*, p. 89; Pepys, VI.277; *CSPD 1664–5*, pp. 395–6, 492. Childs (p. 19) suggests that the regiments were raised in 1662; it is unclear when they were actually raised; there are certainly commissions dating from before June 1666 but one cannot be certain that the regiments in question ever existed: *CSPD 1665–6*, pp. 303, 454, 489, *1666–7*, p. 320; PC 2/59, p. 66; Dalton, I.23, 63.

25. *CSPD 1665–6*, p. 466; *SR*, V.362.

26. *LJ*, XI.582; Hartmann, *Madame*, pp. 97–8; Browning, *Documents*, pp. 153–4; C. Robbins, 'The Repeal of the Triennial Act in 1664', *HLQ* XII (1948–9), pp. 121–40.

27. *SR*, V.516–20; Browning, *Documents*, pp. 382–4.

28. *CJ*, VIII.621–2; C. Robbins, 'The Oxford Session of the Long Parliament of Charles II', *BIHR* XXI (1946–8), pp. 219–24; *RB*, part III, pp. 3–4. There had been an attempt to impose a similar oath on office-holders in 1663: Seaward, p. 212.

29. *HMC Ormond*, NS III.131–2; *CSPD 1664–5*, pp. 373, 478; *HMC Verulam*, p. 72.

30. Stradling, 'Anglo-Spanish Relations', pp. 99–110; Kamen, 'The Decline of Spain', *Past and Present* no. 81.

31. Jusserand, I.323–7; BT 110, Cominges 25 Jan., Louis to same 4 Feb. 1663; Lister, III.513–17.

32. Grimoard, I.348–9; *Clar SP*, III, Supplement, pp. xxiii–xxiv.

33. Clarendon, *Life*, II.382; CPA 79, Clarendon to Lionne 29 Jan.; BT 110, Cominges 19 Feb.; BT 111, Louis to Cominges 1 April 1663; BL Add MS 61484 fos 170–3.

34. Grimoard, I.377, 379–81; BT 111, Cominges 7 and 14 May; BT 112, same 7 June 1663; Hartmann, *Madame*, pp. 74–5; Clar MSS 79 fos 249, 261–2, 80 fo. 116; CPA 79, Bellings to d'Estrades 22 May 1663.

35. Carte MSS 32 fo. 368, 214 fo. 380; BT 111, Louis to Cominges 18 March and 6 May; BT 112, Cominges 7 June, Ruvigny 28 June 1663; Grimoard, I.379–81; Stradling, 'Anglo-Spanish Relations', pp. 94–7, 132–5.

36. Stradling, 'Anglo-Spanish Relations', pp. 71–2, 91–3, 99–100, 121–6, 135–6; Feiling, pp. 50, 122; BT 112, Ruvigny to Lionne 2 July, Cominges 5 July and 25 Oct., Louis to Cominges 17 Oct. 1663.

37. BT 112, Cominges '11' (recte 21) June and 13 July, Louis to same 7 Oct. 1663; SP 78/117 fos 113–15.

38. *HMC Ormond*, NS III.60–1; BT 112, Louis to Cominges 17 Oct., Lionne to Cominges

2 Dec., Cominges to Louis 3 and 7 Dec. 1663; BN, Fonds Français 10712 fo. 131.

39. SP 78/116 fo. 7; SP 78/118 fos 124, 131, 156, 165; Hartmann, *Madame*, p. 101; BT 113, Cominges 9 June and 18 August 1664.

40. BT 112, Cominges 9 and 12 Nov. 1663; Carte MS 33 fo. 211; *HMC Ormond*, NS III.101–2; Hartmann, *Madame*, p. 83.

41. SP 78/117 fos 193, 204, 210, 217, 220, 228, 230, 234, 238; BT 112, Louis to Cominges 12 Dec. 1663. Charles was equally determined to maintain his rights of precedence at Madrid: Arlington, II.48–9.

42. Hartmann, *Madame*, p. 91.

43. *Ibid.*, pp. 90–2, 96; BT 112, Cominges 10 Dec. 1663; BT 113, Cominges 7 Jan., Lionne to same 21 Jan. and 23 March 1664; SP 78/118 fos 14, 22, 26, 32, 89, 94.

44. BT 113, Cominges 25 Feb. and 17 March 1664.

45. SP 78/118 fos 157, 181, 209, 233; SP 78/119 fo. 67; SP 78/120 fo. 60; Hartmann, *Madame*, pp. 101, 103–5.

46. Hartmann, *Madame*, pp. 105, 111–12.

47. Pepys, V.59; BT 113, Cominges 25 Feb., same to Lionne 4 Dec. 1664; SP 104/73, fo. 121.

48. This paragraph is based on P. Seaward, 'The House of Commons Committee of Trade and the Origins of the Second Anglo-Dutch War', *HJ* XXX (1987), pp. 437–52, and on a seminar paper by Steve Pincus, taken from his Harvard PhD thesis on the ideological context of the first two Dutch Wars. See also Pepys, V.105, 121–2.

49. Carte MS 215 fo. 29; Pepys, V.107, 121–2, 264; BL Add MS 32094 fo. 28; BT 113, Cominges 5 May 1664; Clarendon, *Life*, II.237, 310–11, 337.

50. BT 113, Cominges 5 May, 9 June and 21 July 1664; Hartmann, *Madame*, pp. 102, 106, 111–12.

51. BT 113, Cominges 1 and 22 Sept., same to Lionne 28 July and 8 Sept. 1664; Feiling, pp. 129–32.

52. Hatton, I.37; Hartmann, *Madame*, pp. 111–13; BT 113, Cominges 6 and 9 October, same to Lionne 3 Nov., Lionne to Cominges 22 Oct., Louis to Cominges 8 Nov. 1664; Clarendon, *Life*, II.237–42.

53. Hartmann, *Madame*, p. 118; SP 78/119 fos 128–30.

54. BT 113, Lionne to Cominges 29 Nov., Cominges to Lionne 1 Dec., Ruvigny to Lionne 11 Dec 1664; BT 114, Louis to Cominges 3 Jan. 1665; Hartmann, *Madame*, pp. 133–5, 138–40; Mignet, I.414–15. It did not help the English, in the argument about who was the aggressor, that the Dutch were much quicker to publish their case in French: SP 78/120 fo. 42. (As usual, Holles was kept waiting for the information he needed from London: SP 78/120 fo. 94.)

55. *CJ*, VIII.568; BL Add MS 32094 fos 24–8; Pepys, V.330; *CSPD 1664–5*, pp. 88–9; BT 113, Cominges 22 Dec. 1664; BT 114, same 8 Jan. 1665; Dorset RO, D124, Box 235, bundle 1, part 2, 'The State of His Majesty's Revenue 15 Feb. 1664/5'.

56. BT 113, Lionne to Cominges 29 Nov., Louis to Cominges 27 Dec. 1664; BT 114, Lionne to Cominges and Louis to Cominges 7 Feb. 1665.

57. BT 114, Cominges 8 Jan., same to Lionne 8, 15 and 19 Jan., Ruvigny to Lionne 12 Jan. 1665; Clarendon, *Life*, II.334–5.

58. BT 113, Ruvigny to Lionne 11 Dec. 1664; BT 114, Cominges 29 Jan., Ruvigny's relation Feb. 1665; Hartmann, *Madame*, pp. 142–3.

59. BT 114, Ruvigny's relation Feb. 1665; CPA 85, Courtin to Lionne 23 April 1665; Cov MS 101 fos 24–5.

60. BT 114, Cominges 16 Feb., same to Lionne 16 Feb. and 19 March, Louis to Cominges 22 March, Verneuil, Courtin and Cominges to Lionne 4 May 1665; Pepys, VI.78; SP 78/120 fo. 172.

61. Jusserand, I. 346–74.

62. BT 114, Verneuil, Courtin and Cominges 23 and 27 April, 24 May; BT 115, same 23 July, Holles's memorial 26 Dec.; CPA 86, Courtin to Lionne 19 Aug. and 11 Oct. 1665; Hartmann, *Madame*, pp. 165–6. Clarendon (*Life*, II.382–3) thought that the three ambassadors neither expected nor wanted their negotiation to succeed.

63. BT 114, Cominges 29 Jan.; BT 115, Verneuil, Courtin and Cominges 11 June, 2 July, 21 Aug., 8 Sept. and 13 Oct., Lionne to same 3 Oct. 1665.

64. Hartmann, *Madame*, pp. 160–1; *POAS*, I.44; Pepys, VI.123–4; Clarendon, *Life*, II.395–6.

65. BT 115, Verneuil, Courtin and Cominges 22 June; CPA 85, Courtin to Lionne 22 June; CPA 86, same to same 6 July 1665; Pepys, VI.138–9; Clarendon, *Life*, II.399–403; for the navy and naval strategy, see Davies.

66. Carte MS 34 fos 228–30; Clarendon, *Life*, II.335–6; BT 115, Verneuil, Courtin and Cominges 2 July; CPA 86, same to Lionne 13 Oct. 1665; Pepys, VI.262–4, VII.212, 332–4, 354.

67. Pepys, VI.210, 216, 218, VII.64, IX.476; Dorset RO, D124, Box 272, 'Analyses and Comparisons of the State of the Royal Revenue 1618–67', rear of volume; *HMC Portland*, III.293; Clarendon, *Life*, II.337–41, III.1–33; *HMC 4th Report*, p. 303; Carte MS 34 fos 431, 486; Roseveare, pp. 19–27.

68. *HMC 6th Report*, p. 336; CPA 86, Bigorre to Lionne 15 Aug., Courtin to Lionne 23 Aug. 1665; *CSPD 1664–5*, p. 538; Seaward, pp. 237–41.

69. Carte MS 34 fos 427, 429, 431; BL Add MS 4182 fo. 48; BT 115, Verneuil, Courtin and Cominges 26 Oct. 1665.

70. Carte MSS 34 fos 413, 442, 448, 463–4, 46 fos 217, 219.

71. Pepys, VI.268–9, 276–7, 291, 342; Carte MSS 34 fos 444, 452–4, 484, 488, 516, 47 fo. 428; Clarendon, *Life*, II.464–7, 469–71, 474–6; *CSPD 1665–6*, p. 25.

72. Carte MSS 34 fos 512, 516, 553, 221 fos 98–100; Pepys, VII.10, 184, 186.

73. *CSPD 1665–6*, pp. 228, 243, 438, 482–3; Harl MS 3785 fos 91, 114, 151.

74. BL Add MS 10117 fo. 152, 40712 fo. 3; *POAS*, I.51; Pepys, VII.64, 78, 136, 293.

75. Pepys, VII.152–5, 158, 177; Mignet, I.483n.; Ogg, I.298–302.

76. Pepys, VII.185, 196–7; PC 2/59, pp. 66, 78; *CSPD 1665–6*, pp. 454, 466, 481, 483.

77. Ogg, I.302; PRO, PRO 30/24/4, fo. 132.

78. Clarendon, *Life*, III.88–92; BL Add MSS 11043 fos 117–18, 63057A fo. 157; Pepys, VII.279, 281; Evelyn, III.457; *HMC Hastings*, II.370–2; *HMC Eliot Hodgkin*, p. 306.

79. *CSPD 1666–7*, pp. 99, 127–8; Pepys, VII.281; *HMC Portland*, III.298.

80. Burnet, *Hist.*, I.403; Carte MS 217 fo. 336; Browning, *Danby*, II.14; Pepys, VII.357.

81. Clarendon, *Life*, III.101–2.

Chapter 6: Retribution

1. Carte MS 35 fo. 240; Pepys, VII.307.

2. Pepys, VIII.431–2; Hartmann, *Madame*, pp. 191–3; Burnet, *Hist.*, I.436–7 and 436n.

3. Pepys, VIII.288, 355, 366, 377, IX.219; BT 118, Ruvigny to Lionne 20 Feb.; BT 119, Ruvigny 21 May 1668; BL Add. MS 63057B, fo. 1.

4. CPA 85, Courtin to Lionne 27 April 1665; *CSPD 1664–5*, p. 320.

5. Clarendon, *Life*, III.132–4; *CSPD 1666–7*, p. 186; Pepys, VII.309.

6. Carte MSS 35 fos 101, 105, 72 fo. 97; *LJ*, XII.4; Milward, pp. 20–2, 25, 27–8; Pepys, VII.356; *POAS*, I.106–17.

7. Milward, pp. 27–8; Pepys, VII.330–1, 340, 347–9, 356; Carte MS fo. 105.

8. Carte MS 35 fo. 105; Marvell, II.43–4; Milward, p. 38; Chandaman, pp. 163–4.

9. Pepys, VII.310–11, 416; Carte MS 46 fo. 408; Seaward, ch. 4.

10. Carte MS 35 fo. 118.

11. Pepys, VII.402, 408.

12. *CJ*, VIII.628–9; Milward, pp. 11, 20–2; Pepys, VII.307.

13. Carte MSS 35 fos 105, 120, 124, 126, 148, 217 fo. 336.

14. Carte MSS 34 fos 459–60, 35 fo. 240, 217 fos 346, 354; Rawdon, pp. 220–1; Pepys, VII.376.

15. Carte MSS 35 fos 30, 148, 197, 240, 46 fos 434–5, 438, 47 fo. 138, 215 fo. 318; Pepys, VIII.6.

16. Pepys, VII.351, 356; *CJ*, VIII.647; Milward, p. 39.

17. *CJ*, VIII.655, 659; Marvell, II.47; Pepys, VII.399–400, 402; Carte 46 fo. 412.

18. *CJ*, VIII.660–2, 670; *CSPD 1666–7*, pp. 365–6; Carte MSS 35 fo. 197, 46 fos 434–5; Marvell, II.50; Milward, pp. 81–2. The Lords completed the third reading on 24 Jan.; on 5 Feb. the Commons (much to Charles's annoyance) were reminded of the bill by the Speaker: *LJ*, XII.88; Macray, p. 55.

19. *CJ*, VIII.641–2, 645; *CSPD 1666–7*, pp. 209, 268; Carte MSS 34 fos 459–60, 217 fo. 346; Pepys, VII.343; *HMC 5th Report*, p. 348.

20. Seaward, pp. 255, 284–7; for Brodrick's comment, see Carte MS 35 fo. 191.

21. *CJ*, VIII.628; Carte MSS 35 fos 30, 197, 238, 240, 290, 217 fo. 366.

22. Milward, p. 71.

23. For Arlington's anxieties, see Carte MSS 35 fo. 259, 46 fos 398, 434–5, 438, 440–1; see also Clarendon, *Life*, III.141–5.

24. Carte MS 35 fo. 246. See also *ibid.*, fo. 120; Carte MS 217 fo. 353; Pepys, VII.370, VIII.30, 152–3.

25. *CSPD 1666–7*, pp. 511, 553, 555; Carte MSS 35 fo. 329, 46 fo. 457, 215 fo. 341; Pepys, VIII.86, 93–4; PRO, C115/N3/8560 [I owe this reference to James Robertson]; Browning, *Danby*, II.33–4.

26. Pepys, VIII.299, 302; Althorp MS B6, Richard Graham to Earl of Burlington 29 June and 9 July 1667; Carte MS 35 fo. 502.

27. BT 116, Ruvigny to St Albans 12 Nov., St Albans to Ruvigny 22 Nov.; CPA 88, Ruvigny to St Albans 4 Dec. 1666; Lister, III.443–4; Carte MS 46 fo. 426; Feiling, p. 371.

28. Clar MS 85 fos 84–9; BT 116, Letter for St Albans to write to Charles, and addition, 3 March; CPA 89, Lionne to St Albans 19 Feb. 1667; Mignet, I.521–2.

29. Clar MS 85 fos 100, 102–3; SP 78/123 fos 28–9; Carte MS 46 fos 460–1; Mignet, I.522–3.

30. Clar MS 85 fos 118–19, 121–2, 145–6; Lister, III.453–4; SP 78/123 fo. 56.

31. Mignet, II.43–4; BT 116, Ruvigny to Clarendon 6 April, Lionne to Louis 16 April 1667; SP 78/123 fos 28–9; Haley, *English Diplomat*, pp. 109–13.

32. Mignet, II.43, 57–8, 127–8; Lister, III.455–64; Clar MS 85 fos 107, 217–19, 227, 237–8, 258–9, 301–2, 313.

33. Clar MS 85 fos 299, 301–2, 315, 326; BT 116, Clarendon to Ruvigny 10 June, Lionne to Ruvigny 8 June, Ruvigny to Lionne 11 and 15 June, Ruvigny to Clarendon 15 June 1667.

34. See Anglesey's gloomy letter, Carte MS 217 fo. 374.

35. Carte MSS 35 fo. 372, 46 fos 460–1; Pepys, VIII.12; *CSPD 1666–7*, p. 590; Hutton, *Charles II*, pp. 242–3.

36. Pepys, VIII.121–2, 140, 157–8; BL Add MS 40713 fos 54–5.

37. *CSPD 1667*, pp. 130, 167–8; PC 2/59, pp. 438, 442, 447; CUL, MS Dd.IX.43, pp. 129, 134–5.

38. *CSPD 1667*, pp. 167–8; Carte MS 35 fo. 474; Pepys, VIII.257–8.

39. *CSPD 1667*, pp. 179–83; Carte MSS 46 fo. 491, 47 fos 158, 486; Pepys VIII.274.

40. *POAS*, I.132; see also Pepys, VIII.263; Savile, p. 16.

41. Carte MS 35 fo. 478.

42. CPA 89, fo. 82; Pepys, VIII.264 + n.; *CSPD 1667*, p. 189.

43. Pepys, VIII.282; *POAS*, I.146.

44. Pepys, VIII.263–5; *CSPD 1667*, pp. 189, 196, 198, 199, 205–7, 210, 261; Tanner MS 45 fo. 202.

45. Browning, *Danby*, II.31–4.

46. Carte MS 35 fos 484, 502; Pepys, VIII.283–4, 299, 302.

47. Pepys, VIII.268, 282; Carte MSS 35 fos 476, 484, 46 fo. 492; Clar MS 85 fo. 326.

48. Pepys, VIII.292–3, 328–9; Clarendon, *Life*, III.255–60; Carte MS 47 fo. 160; *CSPD 1667*, pp. 221, 240; Canterbury RO, Diocesan Records, folder W/Z; CUL, MS Dd.IX.43, pp. 136–7, 139–41.

49. Carte MS fo. 461. See also Pepys, VIII.287–8; Clarendon, *Life*, III.240–5, 253–5.

50. Carte MS 35 fo. 522.

51. Pepys, VIII.332. See also *ibid.*, pp. 324–5; *POAS*, I.122, 149.

52. Carte MSS 35 fos 534–5, 549, 650, 220 fo. 259; Althorp MS B6, Graham to Burlington, 9 July 1667; Pepys, VIII.330–2, IX.361; Clarendon, *Life*, III.279–81.

53. Haley, *English Diplomat*, pp. 128–30; Feiling, pp. 224–6.

54. Milward, pp. 83–5; Pepys, VIII.352–3; Tanner MS 45 fo. 204; Carte MSS 35 fos 575, 649–50, 46 fo. 506.

55. Carte MS 35 fos 595, 649; Pepys, VIII.361–2, 366–7; *POAS*, I.134–6.

56. Carte MSS 35 fos 628, 632, 46 fos 516–17, 520, 215 fo. 382; *CSPD 1667*, p. 338.

57. Carte MS 35 fos 650, 535.

58. Carte MSS 35 fo. 535 (quoted), 220 fos 257–8.

59. Pepys, VIII.376; Carte MS 217 fos 398, 402.

60. Clarendon, *Life*, III.282–94; Pepys, VIII.403–4; Carte MS 220 fos 274–5.

61. *Letters*, pp. 204–5; Clarendon, *Life*, III.290–1; Pepys, VIII.403–4, 413–14, 427; Carte MS 46 fos 540–2; Althorp MS C4, Coventry to Savile 3 Sept. 1667.

62. Clarendon, *Life*, III.285–6; Pepys, VIII.402; Carte MS 35 fo. 650; Eg MS 2539 fo. 119.

63. Hartmann, *Madame*, pp. 191–3; Burnet, *Hist.*, I.436–7; BL Add. MS 63057A, fos 162–3.

64. Savile, p. 21; Carte MS 217 fo. 409; BT 116, Ruvigny to Lionne 29 Sept., Ruvigny '8' (recte 10) Oct. 1667; Eg MS 2539 fo. 119.

65. Carte MS 46 fo. 558; PC 2/59, pp. 564, 578–9; *CSPD 1667*, p. 457.

66. *CSPD 1667*, p. 451; PC 2/59, pp. 609–11.

67. Tanner MS 45 fo. 202; Carte MS 35 fo. 650. (The latter refers to Clarendon meeting with the Presbyterians, but it is possible that that is a ciphering error.)

68. *CSPD 1667*, pp. 437, 447, 454–5, 457, 484, 552.

69. Eg MS 2539 fo. 119; Bodl B14.15.Linc., pp. 4–5 [annotated printed book; I am grateful to Gordon Schochet for this reference]; Spurr, p. 933.

70. *RB*, part III, p. 21; Burnet, *Hist.*, I.438–9; BL Add MS 63057A fo. 164.

71. Carte MSS 35 fo. 737, 215 fo. 389, 220 fo. 278; Clarendon, *Life*, III.298–300; Eg MS 2539 fo. 121; BT 116, Ruvigny 6 and '8' (recte 10) Oct. 1667; BL Add MS 40713 fo. 25.

72. *LJ*, XII.115; Marvell, II.57–8; Milward, p. 85.

73. Clarendon, *Life*, III.301–4; Mignet, II.525–7; Milward, p. 328; Pepys, VIII.480, 482; Carte MS 220 fo. 294.

74. BT 116, Ruvigny 28 Oct. 1667; Carte MS 35 fo. 778; see Hartmann, *Madame*, p. 194.

75. BT 117, Ruvigny 2 Nov. 1667; Eg MS 2539 fo. 129; Pepys, VIII.492, 499; Carte MS 220 fo. 301; Milward, p. 95; *CJ*, IX.8–9.

76. Hartmann, *Madame*, p. 196; BL Add MS 63057A fos 165–7; Burnet, *Hist.*, I.452–3, 456–7; Pepys, VIII.433–4, 438, 446–7, 482, 518; BT 116, Ruvigny 28 Oct.; BT 117, same 4 and 11 Nov., 2 Dec. 1667; Macpherson, I.39; Carte MS 36 fo. 25.

77. Grey, I.14, 53; Milward, pp. 102, 110–14; Tanner MS 45 fo. 235; *Proceedings of the House of Commons touching the Impeachment of Edward, late Earl of Clarendon* (London, 1700), pp. 23–4, 28.

78. Milward, pp. 120–5; Eg MS 2539 fos 135–6; BT 117, Ruvigny 21 Nov. 1667.

79. Eg MS 2539 fos 137–40; Pepys, VIII.530, 532–3, 541–2; Carte MS 217 fo. 421.

80. BT 117, Ruvigny 24 and 28 Nov. 1667.

81. Pepys, VIII.544, 559; Carte MSS 35 fo. 873, 46 fo. 573; Carte, *Ormond*, V.58–9; BT 117, Ruvigny 6 Dec. 1667; Clarendon, *Life*, III.329–32; *Clar Corr*, I.648–50.

82. Carte MSS 46 fo. 577, 51 fo. 382, 217 fo. 426, 220 fo. 312; Milward, p. 162; Clarendon, *Life*, III.353–4.

83. Pepys, VIII.512, 560.

84. *Ibid.*, 535, 550; Carte MS 35 fo. 873; BL Add MS 63057A fos 166–7; Hartmann, *Madame*, pp. 196, 205; BT 119, Ruvigny 21 May 1668.

85. See Eg MS 2539 fo. 141.

86. BT 118, Ruvigny 9 Jan. 1668. For Ormond see Carte MSS 36 fo. 31, 215 fos 401, 413, 217 fo. 419, 220 fos 296–7, 344–6; Pepys, VIII.518; Orrery, pp. 312–13.

87. BL Add MSS 36916 fos 37, 56, 63057A fos 170–1; PC 2/60, pp. 81, 108; Carte MS 36 fo. 31; *CSPD 1667–8*, p. 88; Pepys, VIII.584–5, 596–7; Tanner MS 45 fo. 240.

88. Carte MSS 36 fos 104, 149, 217 fo. 433, 220 fos 326–7; BT 118, Ruvigny to Lionne 16 Jan., 13 Feb. 1668; *CSPD 1667–8*, pp. 258–9.

89. BT 118, Ruvigny 26 Jan. 1668; Pepys, IX.26–7; Tanner 45* fo. 254. For forgiveness, see *HMC 7th Report*, p. 486; Pepys, IX.218.

90. *RB*, part III, pp. 22–'34' (recte 26); Bodl B.14.15.Linc., pp. 13–14; Burnet, *Hist.*, I.449–51; BL Add MS 36916 fos 59–60; Pepys, IX.45–6; Milward, p. 179; Spurr, pp. 933–4.

91. *LJ*, XII.181; *CJ*, IX.44, 66, 71, 77; Milward, pp. 214–22, 230–1; Eg MS 2539 fos 167–8, 193; BL Add MS 36916 fos 58, 83, 95; Pepys, IX.180–1; Tanner 45 fo. 280; *HMC 3rd Report*, p. 95; *CSPD 1667–8*, p. 382.

92. Carte MS 46 fos 600–1; Milward, pp. 189–90; Grey I.82–4; Eg MS 2539 fo. 155.

93. Milward, p. 190.

94. Pepys, IX.71; Carte MS 220 fo. 354; BT 118, Ruvigny to Lionne 2 March 1668; North, *Lives*, I.120; Roberts, 'Sir Richard Temple', *HLQ* XLI, pp. 146–50.

95. See BT 118, Ruvigny 15 March 1668.

96. *CSPD 1667–8*, pp. 258–9; Carte MS 36 fo. 212.

97. Carte MSS 36 fos 167, 199, 215 fos 437, 440, 220 fo. 354; Eg MS 2539 fo. 157; Milward, p. 198; Grey, I.84–5, 93–4.

98. Milward, p. 241; BT 118, Ruvigny to Lionne 12 April 1668; Chandaman, pp. 44–5; Witcombe, pp. 84–6, 90.

99. Grey, I.93–4, 148–50; Milward, pp. 220, 285–6; *CJ*, IX.62.

100. Eg MS 2539 fo. 170.

101. Hartmann, *Madame*, pp. 203–4; Carte MS 36 fo. 214; BT 118, Ruvigny 19 March, same to Lionne 22 March 1668.

102. Eg MS 2539 fo. 178; C. Roberts, 'Sir Richard Temple's Discourse on the Parliament of 1667–8', *HLQ* XX (1956–7), pp. 139–40; Carte MS 46 fo. 612.

103. Carte MS 220 fo. 354; Eg MS 2539 fo. 193; Witcombe, pp. 90–1.

Chapter 7: The Treaty of Dover

1. BL Add MS 65138: at the time when I consulted this document, it had not yet been foliated.

2. Printed in Hartmann, *Madame*.

3. Jusserand, II.10–23; BT 116, 'Points du Mémoire pour l'Instruction de M de Ruvigny', August 1667.

4. Mignet, II.514–17, 525–7; BT 116, Ruvigny 19 Sept. and '8' (recte 10) Oct. 1667.

5. BT 117, Ruvigny 17 Nov. and 5 Dec. 1667.

6. Mignet, II.517–21, 523–4, 530–1; BT 116, Ruvigny 24 Oct. 1667.

7. BT 117, Ruvigny 4, 14 and 17 Nov. 1667; SP 78/123 fo. 263.

8. Feiling, p. 372; BT 117, Ruvigny 12 Dec. 1667; SP 78/123 fo. 285; Mignet, II.536–9.

9. Mignet, II.539–46 (another copy SP 78/123 fos 302–3).

10. Mignet, II.373–4, 445; J. Bérenger, 'An Attempted *Rapprochement* between France and the Emperor: the Secret Treaty for the Partition of the Spanish Succession of 19 January 1668', in R. M. Hatton (ed.), *Louis XIV and Europe* (London, 1976), pp. 133–52.

11. BT 118, Ruvigny 12, 19 and 26 Jan., Ruvigny to Lionne 23 Jan. 1668.

12. See Haley, *English Diplomat*, ch. 6.

13. *Ibid.*, pp. 162–6; Mignet, II.549–54, 562–3; Carte MS 46 fos 587, 589.

14. Hartmann, *Madame*, p. 200; CPA 91, Charles to Louis 3 Feb.; BT 118, Ruvigny to Lionne 20 Feb. 1668.

15. CPA 90, Lionne to Ruvigny 25 Feb.; BT 118, Ruvigny 5 March, same to Lionne 5 March and 23 April 1668; Sonnino, pp. 14, 16, 21.

16. Milward, pp. 191–2; Grey, I.85.

17. Haley, *English Diplomat*, ch. 7; Rowen, pp. 27–9; Sonnino, p. 23; Mignet, II.636–9, 644–6, III.5–6.

18. Pepys, VIII.185; BT 121, Croissy '20' (recte 18) Feb., same to Colbert 21 March 1669; *HP*, II.92–3.

19. Pepys, IX.361.

20. BT 122, Croissy 17 June, same to Lionne 30 May 1669; Pepys, IX.558; BL Add MS 28053 fo. 24. For a similar incident, see Pepys, IX.338–9.

21. Hartmann, *Madame*, p. 217; Pepys, IX.336, 341, 361; BT 120, Croissy 15 Nov., same to Lionne 29 Oct. 1668; BT 121, Croissy '20' (recte 18) Feb., 4 and 11 April, same to Lionne 8 April; BT 122, Croissy 29 July 1669; Mignet, III.57–8; DCAD, Hunter MS 9, no. 255; Carte MS 48 fo. 290.

22. BT 119, Ruvigny to Lionne 7 June, Croissy 24 Sept.; BT 120, Croissy 29 Oct. and 15 Nov. 1668; BT 123, Croissy to Lionne 14 Oct. 1669; CPA Supplement 1, fos 400–1 (Arlington to Madame, 30 Aug. 1669); BL Add MSS 36916 fo. 113, 36988 fo. 94; *CSPV 1666–8*, p. 323; Pepys, IX.341; *HMC Buccleuch (Montagu House)*, I.424; *HMC Rutland*, II.10; Hartmann, *Madame*, p. 210.

23. Pepys, IX.347, 361; BT 121, Croissy 28 March 1669.

24. BT 118, Ruvigny to Lionne 16 April 1668; Pepys, IX.253, 258, 280.

25. Pepys, IX.340–1, 349–51; BT 120, Croissy 12 Nov. 1668.

26. Eg MS 2539 fo. 292; BL Add MS 36916 fo. 121.

27. Clarke, *James II*, I.436–7; Macpherson, I.45, 47–8; Eg MS 2539 fo. 292; BL Add MS 36916 fo. 121; BT 120, Croissy 24 Dec. 1668; Carte MS 48 fo. 308. York passed through another anxious period in Feb.–March 1669, just after Ormond's dismissal: Carte, *Ormond*, IV.354–5; Carte MS 50 fo. 18; BT 121, Croissy 28 March 1669; Pepys, IX.506–7, 550–1.

28. BT 118, Ruvigny to Lionne, 20 Feb.; BT 119, same to same 28 June; BT 120, Croissy to Lionne 24 Dec. 1668; Pepys, IX.153; Burnet, *Hist.*, I.456–7.

29. BT 121, Croissy to Lionne 21 and 31 Jan.; BT 122, Croissy 13 May, 19 and '30' (recte 29) Aug.; BT 123, same 17 Nov., same to Lionne 10 Oct. 1669; CPA 97, same to same 8 Jan. 1670; Pepys, IX.417, 536.

30. *HMC Hastings*, II.376; Hartmann, *Madame*, p. 208; Eg MS 2539 fo. 193; Pepys, IX.191.

31. BT 122, Croissy 24 and 27 June, same to Lionne 27 May, 3, 17 and 20 June 1669; CPA 97, same to same 29 June 1670; *HMC 2nd Report*, p. 21; *HMC 6th Report*, p. 365; Hartmann, *Madame*, pp. 249, 257–8; Macpherson, I.51.

32. J. C. Beckett, *The Making of Modern Ireland 1603–1923* (London, 1966), p. 120; for a succinct account of the land settlement see *ibid.*, pp. 118–21.

33. Carte MSS 36 fos 31, 201–2, 46 fo. 618, 47 fos 174, 180, 215 fos 401, 413; Orrery, pp. 312–13; Milward, pp. 246–7; Eg MS 2539 fo. 206.

34. Carte, *Ormond*, V.93. For an expression of Ormond's trust in Arlington, see Carte MS 48 fo. 278; but note Lady Ormond's distrust: *HMC Ormond*, NS III.437.

35. Carte MSS 36 fo. 406, 48 fo. 278, 51 fo. 427; BL Add MS 28040 fo. 4. See also

Macpherson, I.42; BT 118, Ruvigny to Lionne 30 March 1668; McGuire, pp. 297–8.

36. Carte MS 48 fos 280, 290; BT 119, Croissy 10 Sept.; BT 120, same 15 Oct. 1668; *HMC 7th Report*, p. 486.

37. Browning, *Danby*, II.21–3; Carte MS 48 fos 290, 295; BT 120, Croissy 5 Nov. 1668.

38. Rawdon, pp. 233–4; Pepys, IX.340–1; BT 120, Croissy 12 Nov. 1668.

39. Pepys, IX.346–7, 360–1, 375; Eg MS 2539 fo. 276; Carte MS 48 fos 307–8, 311; BT 120, Croissy to Lionne 10 Dec.; CPA 92, same to same, 13 Dec. 1668.

40. Eg MS 2539 fo. 292; BL Add. MS 36916 fo. 121; Carte MS 48 fo. 315. Croissy (who derived much of his information from Leighton) still thought Ormond was doomed: BT 120, Croissy 24 Dec. 1668.

41. Carte MSS 48 fos 327, 331, 51 fo. 433; SP 104/176 fo. 116; BT 122, Croissy 25 Feb. 1669; Burnet, *Hist.*, I.462–3; McGuire, pp. 299–300; Carte, *Ormond*, IV.355–6.

42. BT 121, Croissy 25 Feb., same to Lionne 25 and 28 Feb. 1669; Carte MSS 50 fo. 20, 51 fos 433–4; Clarke, *James II*, I.435; Macpherson, I.51.

43. BT 120, Croissy 25 Feb.; CPA 91, Leighton to Madame 16 Feb. 1669; Carte MSS 37 fo. 296, 48 fo. 335; Pepys, IX.446; *HMC Ormond*, NS III.442.

44. BT 120, Croissy to Lionne 28 Feb. 1669.

45. See the discussion in McGuire, pp. 302–4.

46. *Ibid.*, pp. 304–12.

47. BT 121, Croissy 25 Feb. 1669; Hartmann, *Madame*, p. 236.

48. Carte MS 48 fo. 338; BT 121, Croissy 28 March 1669; Carte, *Ormond*, IV.357; *CSPI 1666–9*, pp. 744, 749–50, 759–60.

49. BT 119, Croissy 10 Sept.; BT 120, same to Lionne 12 Nov. 1668; BT 121, Croissy 7 Feb. 1669.

50. McGuire, pp. 302, 304.

51. Pepys, IX.336, 462, 466–8, 471–2; BT 121, Croissy 14 March, same to Lionne 11 and 21 March 1669; Hodgson, p. 205.

52. PC 2/60, pp. 395–6; Eg MS 2539 fo. 280; Roseveare, pp. 26–45.

53. Carte MS 48 fo. 290; Chandaman, pp. 110, 112.

54. BT 118, Ruvigny to Lionne 30 April; BT 119, Croissy 17 Sept. 1668 (Croissy thought that Buckingham was against a dissolution as he believed he had sufficient influence in the present Parliament); Eg MS 2539 fo. 250; *CJ*, IX.97; Rawdon, pp. 233–4; Carte MS 48 fo. 290.

55. Pepys, IX.347, 360–1, 375; Grey, I.108; Spurr, p. 935n.; BT 121, Croissy 28 March and 15 April 1669.

56. BT 121, Croissy 7 Feb. and 28 March, same to Lionne 11 March and 11 April 1669; Eg MS 2539 fo. 327; Pepys, IX.360; Macpherson, I.51. The initial decision had been taken in December: BT 120, Croissy 24 Dec. 1668; BL Add MS 36916 fo. 122; BL Loan 29/48 bundle 5 – to Sir E. Harley 26 Dec 1668.

57. Pepys, IX.473; *CSPD 1668–9*, p. 320; BT 121, Croissy 25 April, same to Lionne 11 April; BT 122, Croissy 11 and 18 July, same to Lionne 20 May 1669.

58. Christie, II, appendix, pp. v–ix; Eg MS 2539 fo. 305; BT 121, Croissy to Colbert 11 Feb. 1669. There is a rather garbled account of these proposals in Nunz. Fian. 57, fo. 85.

59. Pepys, IX.277 + n.; Eg MS 2539 fo. 236; *HMC le Fleming*, p. 58.

60. PC 2/61, pp. 26, 42, 46; *CSPD 1667–8*, p. 11, *1668–9*, pp. 10–11.

61. *RB*, part III, pp. 36–7.

62. *CSPD 1668–9*, pp. 91, 94–6; Eg MS 2539 fo. 292; BL Add MS 36916 fo. 121; Hodgson, p. 188; Cosin, II.198–201.

63. SP 104/176 fo. 130; Pepys, IX.502; BL Add MS 36916 fo. 134; Tanner MS 44 fo. 101.

64. SP 104/176 fos 139–40. See also BT 121, Croissy 25 April 1669.

65. *CSPD 1668–9*, pp. 294, 350; *HMC 3rd Report*, p. 245.

66. *RB*, part III, p. 51.

67. Numerous copies of the letter survive: *HMC le Fleming*, pp. 64–5; Wynne, II.660; Ipswich and East Suffolk RO, HD 36/2672/12; DUL, Cosin Letter Book 1B, no. 180.

68. BL Add MS 19399 fos 107–8.

69. Harl MS 7377 fo. 6 (another copy Cov MS 7 fo. 227). For another comment on the bishops' influence, see *CSPV 1669–70*, p. 85.

70. Tanner MS 44 fo. 108; BT 122, Croissy to Lionne 27 June 1669; Cosin, II.205–6; BL Add MS 36916 fo. 137.

71. PC 2/61, p. 348; SP 104/176 fo. 178; *CSPD 1668–9*, p. 398; Tanner MS 44 fo. 120.

72. *CSPD 1668–9*, pp. 408, 655.

73. BT 122, Croissy 29 July, same to Lionne 25 July 1669; *CSPV 1669–70*, pp. 84–5; *CSPD 1668–9*, p. 412.

74. *CSPD 1668–9*, pp. 354, 373, 404, 407, 419, 430, 438, 463, 466, 481; BL Add MS 36916 fos 140, 144.

75. Harl MS 7377 fo. 4; *CSPD 1668–9*, p. 466; *HMC 6th Report*, p. 367.

76. See Buckroyd, *passim*.

77. Carte MS 50 fos 58, 62; BL Add MS 21483 fo. 4.

78. BT 122, Croissy 15 and 19 Aug. 1669; Pepys, IX.447–8.

79. BT 123, Croissy to Lionne 10 Oct. 1669; BL Add MS 21483 fo. 4; see also Pepys, IX.472; BL Add MS 28053 fo. 24.

80. Stradling, 'Anglo-Spanish Relations', pp. 258–75, 288–92; Pepys, VIII.453. For evidence of hostility to Spain, see *CSPV 1669–70*, p. 63; BT 122, Croissy 3 June 1669.

81. BT 118, Ruvigny to Lionne 23 April; BT 119, Ruvigny 29 May and 7 June 1668; Dalrymple, II(a), pp. 9–10; Mignet, III.11.

82. SP 78/124 fo. 97. The letter was addressed to Charles, not Arlington, and the postscript asked him to burn it.

83. Mignet, III.14–18; BT 119, Ruvigny to Lionne 14 June 1668 (third letter).

84. Mignet, III.24–39; *HMC Buccleuch (Montagu House)*, I.432.

85. Mignet, III.40–7; Hartmann, *Madame*, pp. 218, 223–5; BT 119, Croissy 1 and 17 Sept.; BT 120, same 26 Nov.; CPA 93, Lionne to Croissy 19 Nov. 1668.

86. BT 119, Croissy 27 Aug. and 10 Sept., same to Lionne 3 Sept. 1668; *CSPV 1666–8*, p. 238.

87. CPA 93, Lionne to Croissy 19 Sept.; BT 120, Croissy 17 Sept., 8, 15 and 29 Oct., 15 Nov. 1668; Mignet, III.52–4.

88. BT 120, Croissy 19 Nov. 1668. See also Mignet, III.57–8; BT 121, Croissy 11 April; CPA 94, same to Lionne 15 June 1669.

89. Mignet, III.58, 60–1; BT 120, Croissy to Lionne 20 Dec.; CPA 93, Louis to Croissy 24 Nov. 1668.

90. BT 119, Account of second private audience, August, and Croissy 17 Sept.; BT 120, Croissy '3' (recte 2) Dec. 1668. See also CPA 93, Louis to Croissy 24 Nov. 1668.

91. BT 119, Croissy 24 Sept., same to Lionne 27 Sept. 1669.

92. BT 121, Croissy 25 April; BT 122, same to Lionne 18 July 1669; *CSPV 1669–70*, p. 58; Hartmann, *Madame*, pp. 254–5.

93. BT 120, Croissy '3' (recte 2) and 17 Dec., same to Lionne 17 Dec. 1668.

94. Hartmann, *Madame*, p. 227; Carte MS 198 fo. 47. There is a fourth name which Macpherson (I.48) read as Bellasis, but it does not look like that; Clarke, *James II*, I.441, mentions only the three named here. Macpherson also substituted 'reconciled' for 'instructed'.

95. Clarke, *James II*, I.441–2; Macpherson, I.50–1.

96. BL Add MS 63057B fo. 22; Miller, *James II*, pp. 57–9.

97. Chandaman, pp. 222–3.

98. BT 120, Croissy '3' (recte 2) Dec. 1668.

99. M. D. Lee, *The Cabal* (Urbana, 1965), pp. 103–4. See CPA 94, Arlington to Madame 20 June 1669.

100. Haley, *Shaftesbury*, p. 270.

101. Carte MS 198 fo. 47; BT 120, Croissy to Lionne 5 Nov. 1668; Hartmann, *Madame*, p. 230; Pepys, IX.397.

102. *HMC Buccleuch (Montagu House)*, I.423.

103. Pepys, IX.361; Eg MS 2539 fo. 292; BL Add MS 36916 fo. 121; BT 120, Croissy 24 Dec. 1668; Clarke, *James II*, I.436–7.

104. Hartmann, *Madame*, pp. 229–30.

105. Mignet, III.64–5, 70–1; BT 118, Croissy to Colbert 15 Nov. 1668; BT 121, Croissy '22' (recte 21), 24 and 31 Jan., '20' (recte 18) and 25 Feb., same to Lionne 29 Jan., same to Colbert 11 Feb.; CPA 94, Lionne to Croissy 13 Feb. 1669; Hartmann, *Madame*, pp. 231–2; BL Add MS 65138 no. 14.

106. BT 121, Croissy 14 Feb.; BT 122, same 2 and 23 May; CPA 93, Louis to Croissy 6 April 1669; SP 78/126 fos 39–41. On St Kitts, Croissy conceded that the English had a strong case: BT 120, Croissy 5 Nov. 1668.

107. Mignet, III.73–5, 77–8; Hartmann, *Madame*, p. 241; BT 121, Croissy to Lionne 1 April; CPA 93, Lionne to Croissy 4 May 1669.

108. SP 78/126 fos 70–2, 122, 151–2, 282; CPA 93, Lionne to Croissy 27 March and 20 April, Louis to Croissy 6 April; BT 121, Croissy 11 April 1669.

109. Hartmann, *Madame*, pp. 236, 241.

110. BT 121, Croissy 15 April 1669; Hartmann, *Madame*, pp. 255, 258; Sonnino, p. 67 + n.26.

111. BL Add MS 65138 nos 1, 2, 4 and 6: summarized Hartmann, *Madame*, pp. 263–6.

112. Hartmann, *Madame*, p. 254; BL Add MS 65138 no. 8; Dalrymple, II(a), pp. 33–7.

113. Dalton, I.102–5 (only twenty-seven new commissions in a whole year).

114. *CTB*, III, *passim*. For Gravesend, see *ibid.*, p. 793; for ruined or inadequate fortifications, see *CSPD 1668–9*, p. 244; Hartmann, *Madame*, p. 292; SP 104/176 fos 241, 255.

115. Lauderdale, II.164; Hutton, *Charles II*, p. 268.

116. BT 121, Croissy 25 April 1669. Clifford, too, thought that it was essential to keep the Anglicans' goodwill: BL Add MS 65138 no. 23.

117. Mignet, III.164; BL Add MS 65138 no. 23; Hartmann, *Clifford*, pp. 153–5.

118. BL Add MS 65138 no. 8; Hartmann, *Madame*, pp. 247, 267–9; see also Davies.

119. Hartmann, *Madame*, pp. 277–81; Mignet, II.545–6; Sonnino, p. 14; CPA 93, Lionne to Croissy 20 April 1669. Louis was prepared to hold out hopes of English gains in the Caribbean as late as March 1669: CPA 93, Louis to Croissy 6 April 1669.

120. BL Add MS 65138, nos 12, 15, 17; Mignet, III.101–6.

121. The draft said £600,000, but £800,000 was the figure in the final version.

122. The draft bears in the margin a note: 'Query: An article concerning W'.

123. The draft is BL Add MS 65138 no. 24; the final version is in Mignet, III.117–23. see also BT 123, Croissy 19 Dec. 1669.

124. BL Add MS 65138 no. 24.

125. Mignet, III.136–8.

126. Hartmann, *Madame*, pp. 293–4; Mignet, III.133, 144–5, 147–51, 158–9, 163–9; BT 124, Croissy 7 and 13 Feb., 7 and 20 March and 24 April; CPA 99, Lionne to Croissy 21 May 1670; Sonnino, pp. 108–9.

127. Hartmann, pp. 292–5.

128. CPA 95 fo. 169, [Leighton?] to —, 6 Nov. 1669; *CJ*, IX.98; *CSPV 1669–70*, p. 110.

129. Lauderdale, II.146–8 and appendix, p. lxxvii; BL Add MS 23132 fo. 137. See also Witcombe, pp. 89–90.

130. *CJ*, IX.101–2; BL Add MS 36916 fo. 150; BT 123, Croissy 17 Nov. 1669; Grey, I.160–2, 174–5; PRO, C115/N3/8568; Marvell, II.91–2.

131. Grey, I.176–7, 183, 204; Marvell, II.91–3; *CJ*, IX.114; Macpherson, I.56; BT 123, Croissy 9 Dec. 1669.

132. Grey, I.186–7; Marvell, II.93–4; BT 123, Croissy 9 Dec. 1669; *CJ*, IX.115.

133. BL Add MS 23132 fo. 175; BT 123, Croissy 21 Nov., 16 and 23 Dec. 1669; Lauderdale, II.169–70; Marvell, II.95–6; Carte MS 37 fo. 101; PRO, C115/N3/8572; Harris, *Sandwich*, II.312 (in the last source, Arlington's name appears on both sides).

134. BT 124, Croissy 2, 6 and 28 Jan., 3 Feb. 1670; BL Add MS 23132 fo. 189; Dorset RO, D124, Box 272, State of the Revenue under the Earl of Southampton, pp. 43–9; *CSPD 1668–9*, p. 625; Marvell, II.314; CPA 102, Croissy to Gravelle 1 Feb. 1670; *RB*, part III, pp. 21–2.

135. *CSPD 1668–9*, p. 616; Tanner MS 44 fo. 183; PC 2/62, p. 92.

136. BT 124, Croissy 8 Jan. 1670; BL Add MS 23132 fo. 202; PRO, C115/N3/8573.

137. Cosin, II.226; *CSPD 1670*, pp. 7–8, 45; *CSPV 1669–70*, p. 149; Steele, I, no. 3531.

138. *CJ*, IX.121; Marvell, II.314; BT 124, Croissy 24 and 27 Feb.; CPA 97, same to Lionne 24 Feb. 1670.

139. *CJ*, IX.124–6; Marvell, II.97–8, 314; BT 124, Croissy 3 and 5 March 1670; Newton, *House of Lyme*, pp. 242–3; BL Add MS 36916 fos. 166–7.

140. *CJ*, IX.123, 125; PC 2/62, p. 139; Grey, I.221–2, 227–8; Marvell, II.100–3, 314.

141. *LJ*, XII.336; Grey, I.227–8, 246–50; Marvell, II.104, 317; DUL, Cosin Letter Book 4A, no. 44; BL Add MS 19399 fos 113–14; Wynne, II.660–1.

142. Grey, I.247; *HMC Various Collections*, II.134.

143. BT 124, Croissy 24 March; CPA 97, same to Lionne, 17 March 1670; Marvell, II.315; Clarendon, *Life*, III.171–7.

144. *LJ*, XII.310–11, 329; BT 124, Croissy 3 April; CPA 97, same to Lionne 31 March and 7 April 1670; KAO, U296/036, under 21 and 24 March; Marvell, II.316–17; BL Add MS 36916 fo. 173; *CSPV 1669–70*, p. 177; Burnet, *Hist.*, I.472–3.

145. CPA 97, Croissy to Lionne 29 June 1670.

146. BT 124, Croissy 20 March and 3 April 1670.

147. *CJ*, IX.139; Chandaman, pp. 113–15; SP 104/176 fo. 231; Marvell, II.315.

148. Marvell, II.315.

149. *CSPD 1670*, pp. 96, 99, 162, 175–7, 221–2, 226–7, 229, 233–7; SP 104/176 fos 231, 233; Cov MS 16 fo. 115; Clarke, *James II*, I.449; BT 124, Croissy 27 May 1670; BL Add MS 36916 fo. 181.

150. BT 124, Croissy 3 and 24 April, 15 and 25 May 1670; Mignet, III.185; *HMC Buccleuch (Montagu House)*, I.469–70.

151. Mignet, III.186–99; BT 125, Croissy 6 and 10 June 1670; Clarke, *James II*, I.448–51; *HMC Dartmouth*, I.61; Macpherson, I.54–5.

152. BT 125, Croissy 10 June 1670; Clarke, *James II*, I.451; Mignet, III.215–19.

153. BT 125, Croissy 16 June, 7 and 17 July; CPA 99, Lionne to Croissy 11 July 1670; Mignet, III.208–13; W. Perwich, *Dispatches*, ed. M. B. Curran (Camden Soc., 1903), p. 96; Carte MS 219 fo. 104.

154. *CJ*, IX.135; *CSPD 1670*, pp. 233–7, 248, 268, 276–7;.BL Add MS 36916 fo. 182; Cosin, II.243; SP 104/176, fos 239, 241; PC 2/62, p. 190.

155. Mignet, III.101–6, 185; Dalrymple, II(a), p. 59; Clarke, *James II*, I.443–4.

Chapter 8: The Grand Design

1. Lauderdale, II.228–9.

2. BT 125, Croissy 28 July 1670; BT 126, same 28 Sept. 1671; Jusserand, II.111–12.

3. BT 125, Croissy 30 Oct. 1670; BT 126, same 5 Nov. 1671.

4. Haley, *Shaftesbury*, pp. 282–5; Burnet, *Hist.*, I.587, 589–90.

5. *CSPV 1671–2*, pp. 143, 188, 202–3, 205–6, 295–6; Dalrymple, II(a), p. 89.

6. Dalrymple, II(a), p. 80; *CSPV 1671–2*, pp. 202–3, 205–6, 295–6; BT 127, Croissy 15 Sept. 1672; *CSPD 1672*, p. 686.

7. *HP*, II.93; SP 104/177 fos 82–3; *CSPV 1671–2*, p. 246; Hartmann, *Clifford*, pp. 153–5; SP 104/176 fo. 255; Hatton, I.70; CPA 100, Croissy to Lionne 2 April 1671.

8. BT 125, Croissy 29 Sept. 1670; BT 126; same 14 July 1671; *CTB passim*.

9. *CSPV 1671–2*, pp. 225, 273; Tanner MS 43 fo. 31.

10. CPA 103, Croissy to Pomponne 18 Feb., memorial to Louis 7 June 1672; *CSPV 1671–2*, pp. 225–6.

11. Mignet, III.215–19; BT 125, Croissy 28 July 1670; *HMC Buccleuch* (*Montagu House*), I.483–5, 487; Perwich, *Dispatches*, pp. 112–14. It was especially necessary that Buckingham should be told as Madame had told Montagu: Sonnino, pp. 114–15.

12. BT 125, Croissy 28 July, 30 Oct. 1670.

13. BT 125, Croissy 23 and 30 Oct., 3 Nov. and 29 Dec. 1670; Mignet, III.247–8, 265–7.

14. Mignet, III.221–2; CPA 99, Louis to Croissy 15 Oct.; BT 125, Croissy 2 Oct. and 4 Dec. 1670.

15. BT 125, Croissy 23 Oct., 29 Dec. 1670; BT 126, same 1 Jan. 1671; CPA 105 fos 29–31 (Croissy to [Colbert?] '4 Feb.' [recte 4 March] 1672); Mignet, III.237–8; see Sonnino, p. 147.

16. BT 125, Croissy 25 Aug., 29 Sept., 2, 16 and 23 Oct., 7, 13 and 17 Nov. 1670; Mignet, III.233–5, 238–40, 250–2, 256–67; CPA 99, Louis to Croissy 12 Nov. 1670.

17. BT 125, Croissy 29 Sept. (2nd letter); CPA 98, same to Lionne 23 Oct.; CPA 99, Louis to Croissy 12 Nov. 1670; BL Add MS 65138 no. 39; CPA 100, Croissy to Lionne 19 Jan. and 23 Feb. 1671.

18. Hartmann, *Clifford*, pp. 318–33; BT 126, Croissy 7 Dec. 1671; BT 127, same 1 March and 9 May 1672; CPA 101, Croissy to Louvois 24 Dec. 1671; CPA 103, Croissy to Pomponne 21 March, 11 April, 30 May, Croissy's memorial 7 June 1672; *CSPV 1671–2*, pp. 245–6.

19. CPA 103, Croissy to Pomponne 30 June 1672; Burnet, *Hist.*, I.562; *HMC 2nd Report*, p. 22.

20. CPA 103, Croissy's memorial 7 June 1672; CPA 106, same to Pomponne 24 April 1673.

21. BT 125, Croissy 18 and 29 Sept., 23 and 30 Oct.; CPA 98, same to Lionne 18 Dec.; CPA 99, Louis to Croissy 2 Nov. 1670; Dalrymple, II(a), p. 79; Burnet, *Hist.*, I.475; Mignet, III.261–2.

22. BT 126, Croissy 18 Feb., 2 April and 8 Oct. 1671.

23. BT 126, same 3 June and 24 Dec. 1671.

24. BT 126, same 28 May 1671; *HMC Buccleuch* (*Montagu House*), I.507–10, 513–14.

25. BT 127, Croissy 14 and 21 Jan., 11 Feb.; CPA 103, same to Pomponne 4 Feb. 1672.

26. BT 125, Croissy 18 Aug.; CPA 99, Louis to Croissy 15 Oct. 1670; BT 127, Croissy 25 Feb. and 1 March; CPA 103, same to Pomponne 25 Feb. 1672; SP 104/177 fo. 11; Stradling, 'Anglo-Spanish Relations', pp. 288–93.

27. *HMC Buccleuch* (*Montagu House*), I.501–3; BT 126, Croissy 28 Sept., 8 and 22 Oct., 2, 5, 9 and 12 Nov., 3 Dec.; CPA 101, same to Louvois 16 Nov. 1671; BT 127, Croissy 1 Feb. 1672; Dalrymple, II(a), pp. 86–7; Mignet, III.655.

28. BT 125, Croissy 2 Oct. 1670; BT 126, 10, 27 and 31 Aug. 1671; Arlington, II.337; Feiling, pp. 287–9.

29. SP 104/175 pp. 406–9; *Letters*, pp. 245–6; Mignet, III.697–8; BT 127, Croissy 11 and 18 Feb., 21 March; CPA 103, same to Pomponne 11 Feb. 1672; Feiling, pp. 339–43.

30. Marvell, II.109–10; *LJ*, XII.352–3.

31. PC 2/62, pp. 209, 246, 265, 285–7.

32. SP 104/176 fo. 255; BT 125, Croissy 29 Sept. 1670; Grey, I.270–1, 281, 314–17; *CJ*, IX.159; Marvell, II.111; DCAD, Hunter MS 7, nos 67, 69; Dering, *Diary*, pp. 30–2, 34.

33. *CJ*, IX.159; Grey, I.271; Marvell, II.111; Dering, *Diary*, p. 27; BT 125, Croissy 22 Nov. 1670; CPA 100, same to Lionne 28 Jan. 1671.

34. Grey, I. 314–17; *CJ*, IX.180; Chandaman, pp. 16–17, 45–6.

35. Chandaman, pp. 165–9, 183–5; Grey, I.323–4, 327; Dering, *Diary*, pp. 36, 58–9; Arlington, II.318; CPA 100, Croissy to Lionne 25 Jan., 9 and 16 March 1671; Clifton, pp. 89–90.

36. *CSPD 1670*, p. 390; BT 125, Croissy 4 June and 29 Sept. 1670; Tanner MS 44 fo. 215; Archives of the Congregation 'de Propaganda Fide', Rome, Scriture referite nei congressi dal 1627 al 1707, Anglia I fo. 656.

37. Witcombe, pp. 106–7; *CJ*, IX.168, 230; *LJ*, XII.479, 483; Marvell, II.120, 132; BL Add MS 36916 fos 200, 216. Some thought that Sheldon, because of his fear of Popery, was now less hostile to comprehension: Mather, p. 219.

38. Dering, *Diary*, pp. 80–1; *CJ*, IX.203–8, 210; *LJ*, XII.434, 438–40, 449–52, 454, 460, 468; CPA 100, Croissy to Lionne 23 March; BT 126, Croissy 2 April 1671; *CSPV 1671–2*, pp. 27, 29–30, 34; BL Add MS 36916 fo. 216; Cosin, II.276. For the bill see *HMC 9th Report, Part II*, p. 2.

39. *CJ*, IX.235, 243–4; Witcombe, pp. 122–5.

40. *CSPV 1671–2*, p. 40; BL Add MS 36916 fo. 221; BT 126, Croissy to Lionne 30 April 1671; DCAD, Hunter MS 7 no. 103 (Sir Gilbert Gerard, who gave the highest figure, was easily confused when it came to figures).

41. *HMC 9th Report, Part II*, pp. 8–9; *LJ*, XII.346, 369, 393, 412, 443, 460.

42. *LJ*, XII.470, 472–3, 486–7, 494–8, 502–5; *CJ*, IX.224; CPA 100, Croissy to Lionne 7 April 1671; Chandaman, p. 17; Haley, *Shaftesbury*, pp. 289–91; BL Add MS 36916 fo. 222; *HMC 9th Report, Part II*, p. 99; Harris, *Sandwich*, II.333–6. The attorney-general gave his report after Charles had announced his decision to prorogue, but he had been asked to look into the matter almost three weeks before – six days before the Lords committee had reported the amendment on sugars: *LJ*, XII.482, 506; SP 104/176 fo. 293.

43. Marvell, II.318; Witcombe, p. 105; BL Add MS 65139 fos 17–24.

44. Note Downing's ill-received remark about MPs sheltering behind their privileges: Dering, *Diary*, pp. 30–1.

45. Dering, *Diary*, pp. 27, 76–7; Grey, I.394; *LJ*, XII.352–3.

46. BT 126, Croissy 28 May 1671. The proposal was revived early in 1672: *HMC Buccleuch (Montagu House)*, I.513–14.

47. BT 126, Croissy 21 Sept. and 23 Nov. 1671; BL Add MSS 29571 fos 145, 152, 29577 fo. 95, 29583 fo. 307; Hatton, I.68; *CSPV 1671–2*, pp. 108–9; *CSPD 1671–2*, p. 66; Chandaman, pp. 26–8.

48. PC 2/63, pp. 144–5; Hartmann, *Clifford*, pp. 214–15; BL Add MS 40860 fo. 22; Arlington, II.347–50; Browning, *Documents*, pp. 353–4; BT 127, Croissy 14 Jan. 1672; *CSPV 1671–2*, pp. 146, 148; Chandaman, pp. 224–8; Haley, *Shaftesbury*, pp. 294–6.

49. SP 104/176 fos 299, 319; Evelyn, III.576; *HMC 7th Report*, p. 464; BL Add MSS 29557 fo. 15, 29577 fo. 107; *CSPD 1671–2*, pp. 65, 105; A. Marshall, 'Colonel Thomas Blood and the Restoration Political Scene', *HJ* XXXII (1989), pp. 566–71.

50. Marshall, 'Thomas Blood', pp. 565–6.

51. BL Add MS 36916 fo. 227; *CSPD 1671*, p. 464.

52. *CSPD 1671*, pp. 554, 562–3.

53. *CSPD 1671*, pp. 562, 568–70, *1671–2*, pp. 10, 27–8, 63, 161–2.

54. *CSPD 1671*, p. 581; PC 2/63, p. 173.

55. *CSPD 1671–2*, pp. 8–9, 44–5, *1660–85 (Addenda)*, pp. 341–2; BL Add MS 40860 fo. 23.

56. SP 104/177 fos 12, 14, 16–17. (Until his elevation to the peerage, Clifford is referred to in this volume as 'Mr Treasurer' (of the Household).)

57. Browning, *Documents*, pp. 387–8.

58. SP 104/177 fo. 12. Note Charles's similarly pragmatic attitude towards Dissent in Scotland and Ireland: Lauderdale, II.223–4; Stowe MS 200 fo. 287.

59. SP 104/177 fos 14, 16.

60. Arlington, II.362; Burnet, *Hist.*, I.535; SP 104/177 fo. 115; *HMC 7th Report*, p. 490.

61. SP 104/177 fo. 22; *HMC Fitzherbert*, p. 271; *HMC le Fleming*, p. 92; Burnet, *Hist.*, I.537; *CSPD 1671–2*, pp. 215, 311.

62. *CSPD 1671–2*, pp. 217–18, 381–2, 589.

63. CPA 103, Croissy to Pomponne 18 and 25 Feb., 28 March; BT 127, Croissy 18 Feb. and 21 April 1672; *HMC Fitzherbert*, p. 271; *RB*, part III, pp. 99–101; *HMC le Fleming*, pp. 90–1; *CSPD 1671–2*, p. 382; *CSPV 1671–2*, pp. 205–6; see also Browning, *Danby*, II.91. York had also failed to take communion at Easter (and Christmas) 1671: CPA, Croissy to Lionne 6 July 1671.

64. SP 104/177 fo. 19; Burnet, *Hist.*, I.536; *CSPD 1671–2*, p. 609; *RB*, part III, pp. 99–101.

65. SP 104/177 fo. 20; *CSPD 1671–2*, pp. 489–90, *1672*, pp. 214–15; Burnet, *Hist.*, I.536; E. Calamy, *An Historical Abridgement of my own Life*, ed. J. T. Rutt, 2 vols (London, 1830), II.468–70.

66. *CSPV 1671–2*, pp. 218, 222.

67. *CSPD 1672*, pp. 26, 264, 271, 284, 457, 536–9, 543, 589, *1672–3*, p. 300.

68. BL Add MS 29571 fo. 151.

69. BT 126, Croissy 22 Oct., 3 and 7 Dec. 1671; CPA 103, same to Pomponne 21 March 1672; Feiling, pp. 325–8.

70. BT 126, Croissy 7 Dec.; CPA 101, same to Louvois 24 Dec. 1671; BT 127, Croissy 25 Feb. and 1 March; CPA 103, same to Pomponne 14 and 30 March 1672; SP 104/177 fo. 11; BL Add MS 29553 fo. 393; *CSPV 1671–2*, p. 188; Sonnino, pp. 161, 166–70.

71. CPA 103, Croissy's memorial 7 June 1672 (another copy BN, MS Français 20768 fos 405–11; printed by Christie); *CSPD 1671–2*, p. 288; Lansdowne MS 1236 fos 205–6; BT 127, Croissy 19 May; CPA 105, same to Colbert 19 May 1672.

72. BT 127, Croissy 21 April and 9 May 1672; *CSPV 1671–2*, pp. 218, 221–2.

73. Dalrymple, II(a), p. 89; *CSPV 1671–2*, pp. 202–3, 205–6, 225–6.

74. Baxter, p. 70.

75. CPA 103, Croissy's memorial 7 June; CPA 105, Pomponne to Croissy 15 July 1672.

76. CPA 103, Croissy to Pomponne 19 May; BT 127, Croissy 16 June 1672; Lansdowne MS 1236 fos 205–7; *CSPD 1671–2*, p. 149; *CSPV 1671–2*, pp. 232–3, 235–6; Hatton, I.91.

77. BT 127, Croissy 20 and 30 June, 9 July; CPA 103, same to Pomponne 30 June, same to (?) 30 June [fo. 282]; CPA 104, Croissy to Pomponne 3 July 1672.

78. SP 104/176 fos 366–7; SP 104/177 fos 57–60; BT 127, Croissy 30 June 1672; *CSPV 1671–2*, pp. 251–2; for a rather different account see BL Add MS 28053 fos 43–5.

79. BL Add MS 29553 fo. 463; BT 127, Croissy 30 June and 9 July; CPA 104, same to Pomponne 7 and 9 July 1672.

80. Hatton, I.93–4; Mignet, IV.46–9; Burnet, *Hist.*, I.568–9; Baxter, pp. 86–9. The reference given by Hutton for this episode (*Charles II*, p. 514, n. 10) is incorrect.

81. CPA 105, Pomponne to Croissy 5 July 1672 (the day before the treaty was signed).

82. CPA 104, Croissy to Pomponne 21 July 1672; *Letters*, pp. 257–9; *CSPV 1671–2*, p. 263; SP 104/177, fos 77–8, 83; Stowe MS 200 fo. 138; *CSPD 1672–3*, p. 37; Baxter, chs 7–8.

83. Lauderdale, II.227–8; SP 104/177 fos 62, 64–8; Harl MS 7006 fo. 168; *Letters*, pp. 253–4.

84. BT 127, Croissy 8 Aug.; CPA 104, same to Pomponne 29 Aug. 1672; SP 104/177 fos 69–70, 77–8; Lansdowne MS 1236 fo. 219; *CSPV 1671–2*, p. 273.

85. *CSPV 1671–2*, pp. 268–9, 274; BT 127, Croissy 18 Aug.; CPA 104, same to Pomponne 4, 11 and 15 Aug. 1672; Stowe MS 200 fo. 106; Lansdowne MS 1236 fo. 217; *Letters*, p. 254; SP 104/177 fos 77–8. For earlier hopes of taking the Dutch East India fleet, see CPA 103, Croissy's memorial 7 June 1672; SP 104/176 fo. 366; *Letters*, p. 253.

86. Clarke, *James II*, I.478–81; *CSPV 1671–2*, pp. 290–1.

87. CPA 104, Croissy to Pomponne 21 and 29 Aug., 12 and 29 Sept. 1672.

88. SP 104/177 fos 77–8, 82–5 [quotations from fo. 84]; BT 127, Croissy 8, 15 and '16' (recte 26) Sept., 4 Oct.; CPA 104, same to Pomponne 12 and 15 Sept. 1672.

89. *CSPV 1671–2*, pp. 295–6.

90. *Ibid.*, p. 274; Stowe MS 200 fo. 270.

91. See the useful discussion in Childs, ch. 4. For the Petition of Right, see Kenyon, *Constitution*, p. 70; L. Boynton, 'Martial Law and the Petition of Right', *EHR* LXXIX (1964), pp. 255–84; C. Russell, *Parliaments and English Politics 1621–9* (Oxford, 1979), pp. 358–9.

92. SP 104/177 fos 59, 91–2, 120.

93. Tanner MS 43 fo. 31.

94. There is reference to such a commission being issued to Rupert in July 1672 (SP 104/177 fo. 66) but there is no evidence that it was ever acted upon.

95. Williamson, I.42, 116–17, 158; Hatton, I.111. Childs, pp. 77–8, conflates the events of 1672 and 1673.

96. *CSPV 1671–2*, pp. 314, 317–18, 328–9; SP 104/177 fos 111–12; BT 127, Croissy 22, 26 and 27 Dec. 1672; BT 128, same 2 Jan. 1673; Stowe MS 200 fos 447, 464.

97. CPA 104, Croissy to Pomponne 23 Nov. 1672; Hatton, I.101–2; see also North, *Lives*, I.115.

98. Clarke, *James II*, I.481–2; Hatton, I.102–3; CPA 104, Croissy to Pomponne 8 Dec. 1672; CPA 106, same to same 23 Jan. 1673; *CSPV 1671–2*, p. 321.

99. *CSPV 1671–2*, pp. 323, 326; *CSPD 1672–3*, p. 266; Hatton, I.99–100.

100. BT 128, Croissy 2 Jan.; CPA 106, same to Pomponne 10 and 23 Jan. 1672; DUL, Cosin Letter Book 1B, no. 189; Harl MS 7377 fos 39, 41–2; Stowe MS 201 fo. 107.

101. *Letters*, pp. 260–1.

102. Dering, *Diary*, p. 112; Grey, II.8–11; Brown, p. 98; Burnet, *Hist.*, II.13–14; BL Add MS 63057B fo. 20; 'A Relation of the Most Material Matters Handled in Parliament', in *State Tracts*, I.30.

103. Grey, II.13–26 (quotation from p. 25); Dering, *Diary*, pp. 114–18; *CJ*, IX.251; Stowe MS 201 fo. 147; BT 128, Croissy 20 Feb. 1673.

104. SP 104/177 fos 143–4, 148; Grey, II.18–20; PRO, PRO 30/24/6B fo. 102; *CSPV 1673–5*, p. 19; BT 128, Croissy 5 March; CPA 106, same to Pomponne 13 March 1673.

105. Burnet, *Hist.*, II.8–9; BL Add MS 63057B fo. 19; Dering, *Papers*, pp. 68–9; Alberti (*CSPV 1673–5*, p. 19) wrote of four pressing Charles to take vigorous measures.

106. SP 104/177 fos 147–8.

107. Grey, II.54–5.

108. BT 128, Croissy 9 March; CPA 106, same to Pomponne 9 March 1673; Grey, II.55–68; Tanner MS 43 fo. 149.

109. Stowe MS 201 fos 216–17, 229, 239; BL Add MS 29571 fos 193–4; BT 128, Croissy 16 March; CPA 106, same to Pomponne 13 March 1673; *LJ*, XII.539–41, 543–4, 547–8; *HMC 9th Report, Part II*, p. 25; Dering, *Diary*, p. 134.

110. BL Add MS 25117 fo. 92. See also *CSPD 1673*, pp. 36–8, 41, 49.

111. *CSPV 1673–5*, pp. 27, 29; Dalrymple, II(a), pp. 93–4; CPA 106, Croissy to Pomponne 20 March 1673.

112. *Letters*, p. 263; Grey, II.108–15; Dering, *Diary*, pp. 139–40; Stowe MS 201 fo. 257.

113. BT 128, Croissy 1 and 3 April 1673; Burnet, *Hist.*, II.7–11; 'A Relation', *State Tracts*, I.31; Grey, II.152–4; Stowe MS 201 fo. 283.

114. *CJ*, IX.276, 278; Grey, II.108–15, 126, 139; Dering, *Diary*, pp. 139–40.

115. *CJ*, IX.242; Grey, II. 38–47 (quotation from p. 41).

116. *CJ*, IX.259; BL Add MS 29571 fo. 192; Stowe MS 201 fo. 188; Grey, II.106; Tanner MS 43 fos 191–4.

117. Tanner MS 43 fos 189–90; Grey, II.165–9, 178–9; Stowe MS 201 fo. 309; *CJ*, IX.280–1; *LJ*, XII.579–80.

118. CPA 106, Croissy to Pomponne 3 April 1673; Newton, *House of Lyme*, p. 253; *CSPD 1673*, p. 101; Tanner MS 42 fo. 7; *CJ*, IX.281; J. Spurr, 'Schism and the Restoration Church', *Journal of Ecclesiastical History* XLI (1990), pp. 408–24, esp. p. 417.

119. Tanner MS 42 fo. 7; PC 2/64, p. 6; Williamson, I.33–4; *CSPD 1673*, pp. 367–9.

120. SP 104/177 fos 152–4. (Charles added another £100,000 to the figure for reparations, to cover moneys owed to William.)

121. BT 128, Croissy 22 June; CPA 107, same to Pomponne 10 July 1673; see Ekberg, pp. 19–46 and *passim*.

122. BT 128, Croissy 20 and 23 Feb., 24 April, 15 May 1673; SP 104/177 fos 142–3, 158–9.

123. BT 129, Croissy 10 Aug.; CPA 107, same to Pomponne 27 July 1673; Stowe MS 202 fos 205–6.

124. CPA 110, Louis to Croissy 15 Sept., 21 Oct. 1673; Stowe MS 203 fos 7, 38, 80, 87.

125. SP 104/177 fos 151, 162; *CSPD 1673*, pp. 175–6.

126. SP 104/177 fos 163–4.

127. BT 129, Croissy 10 and 24 July; CPA 110, Louis to Croissy 18 and 25 July 1673; BL Add MS 25122 fo. 103; Stowe MS 202 fos 205–6; Ekberg, pp. 156–9.

128. BT 129, Croissy 10 Aug.; CPA 107, same to Pomponne 14 Aug. 1673; BL Add MS 25122 fo. 155; Stowe MS 203 fo. 38.

129. See J. Miller, 'Catholic Officers in the Later Stuart Army', *EHR* LXXXVIII (1973), p. 42.

130. *HMC 7th Report*, p. 490; Evelyn, IV.7; Brown, p. 98; Grey, II.21; BT 128, Croissy 17 April 1673.

131. *CSPV 1671–2*, p. 114, *1673–5*, p. 13; Hatton, I.80, 83; BT 128, Croissy 20 Feb., 6 and 17 April 1673; Macpherson, I.68; Nunz Fian 59, fo. 241; BL Add MS 29571 fo. 226.

132. *CSPV 1673–5*, pp. 43, 52–3, 55–6, 68–9; *CSPD 1673*, pp. 243, 255–6; Hatton, I.110; BT 128, Croissy 6 July; BT 129, same 10 Aug. 1673.

133. *CSPD 1673*, p. 374; Williamson, I.55, 60; Stowe MS 202 fos 136–7; BL Add MS 25122 fos 91–2, 122; *CSPV 1673–5*, pp. 73, 76.

134. *CSPD 1673*, p. 243; Morrison, 1st series, I.128; Williamson, I.24, 58 (quoted).

135. Williamson, I.67, 91, 102, 106; *CSPD 1673*, pp. 422–3; Rochester, pp. 88–9; BT 128, Croissy 6 July; CPA 107, same to Pomponne 29 June and 3 July 1673; BL Add MSS 29571 fo. 230, 63057B fos 19–20; Buckingham, II.16–17; Hatton, I.110–11.

136. BL Add MSS 29577 fo. 145, 63057B fo. 20; PC 2/64, pp. 14–15; Williamson, I.88, 158; Hatton, I.111; BT 128, Croissy 24 July; BT 129, same 3 Aug. 1673; *CSPD 1673*, pp. 454–5; Davies.

137. SP 104/177 fo. 102; BT 128, Croissy 1 June; CPA 107, same to Pomponne 22 May, [Pomponne] to Croissy 5 June 1673.

138. Williamson, I.7, 93; BT 128, Croissy 22 June and 10 July; CPA 107, same to Pomponne 12 June and 6 July 1673; BL Add MS 29571 fo. 226.

139. CPA 110, Louis to Croissy 18 and 25 July 1673; Davies.

140. Lansdowne MS 1236 fos 162–3; BT 128, Croissy 17 and 24 July 1673; Stowe MS 202 fo. 268 (quoted); Williamson, I.113–14, 116–17, 122, 144; Haley, *William of Orange*, *passim*.

141. BT 128, Croissy 25 May and 31 July; BT 129, same 10 Aug.; CPA 107, same to Pomponne 22 May and 25 Sept. 1673; Williamson, I.151, 158; Stowe MS 203 fos 1, 13; Burnet, *Hist.*, I.580–1.

142. Hatton, I.100; *CSPD 1673*, pp. 279, 308–9, 333; Lansdowne MS 1236 fo. 206; Stowe MS 202 fos 87, 89; Ogg, pp. 373–4.

143. *CSPD 1673*, pp. 498, 507, 509–10; Williamson, I.170, 174, 191, 194, II.9–10; Hatton, I.114; Stowe MS 202 fos 334–5, 337; *CSPV 1673–5*, pp. 106, 121.

144. Williamson, II.27, 36, 48, 63; *CSPV 1673–5*, p. 161; BT 129, Croissy 2 and 30 Oct. 1673; Nunz Fian 59 fo. 296; Miller, *James II*, pp. 71–4.

145. *CSPD 1673*, p. 567; Williamson, II.46; BT 129, Croissy 30 Oct.; CPA 108, same to Pomponne 19 Oct. 1673; *CSPV 1673–5*, p. 138.

146. Stowe 203 fo. 93; Williamson II.51–3; KAO, U1015 028/1; Dering, *Diary*, pp. 149–51; BL Add MS 29571 fos 249–50; Burnet, *Hist.*, II.30–1; *LJ*, XII.586; *CSPV 1673–5*, pp. 161–2.

147. *CSPV 1673–5*, pp. 161–2; Williamson, II.52; Essex, I.130, 132; Nunz Fian 59 fos 305–7.

148. Essex, I.132 has 'disgusted', but the original (Stowe MS 203 fo. 114) clearly reads 'disguised'; K. Thomas, *Religion and the Decline of Magic* (London, 1971), pp. 312–13.

149. *Letters*, pp. 270–1; Burnet, *Hist.*, II.31–2; Grey, II.184–8; KAO, U1015 028/1; Stowe MS 203 fo. 147.

150. Grey, II.189–97; KAO, U1015 028/1; *CJ*, IX.285.

151. Grey, II.197–215; BL Add MS 29571 fo. 253.

152. Grey, II.215–22 (quotation from p. 220); Dering, *Diary*, p. 160; Williamson, II.59.

153. Grey, II.222–3; KAO, U1015 028/1; *Letters*, pp. 271–2 (misdated 3rd).

154. Stowe MS 203 fos 161, 163; Williamson, II.61–2, 65; Mignet, IV.234, 250; *CSPV 1673–5*, pp. 174–5; BL Add MSS 25117 fo. 144, 25122 fos 164–5 (there is another copy of the latter in Cov MS 83 fo. 205).

155. Williamson, I.79, 81; CPA 107, Croissy to Pomponne 10 July 1673; Arlington, II.448, 465; Burnet, *Hist.*, II.32; Mignet, IV.237.

156. Burnet, *Hist.*, II.32; Mignet, IV.236.

157. Essex, I.131–3, 153–5; BT 129, Croissy 9 Nov. 1673; *CSPV 1673–5*, p. 169; Williamson, II.92.

158. Grey, II.208–9 (speech of Sir Thomas Meres); Browning, *Danby*, II.63–4.

159. BT 129, Croissy 2 and 20 Nov., 7 Dec.; CPA 108, same to Pomponne 20 and 23 Nov. 1673; *CSPV 1673–5*, pp. 176–7; Williamson, II.78; Essex, I.140; Tanner MS 42 fo. 44; Clarke, *James II*, I.487–8; Macpherson, I.69; Burnet, *Hist.*, II.37.

160. Williamson, II.73–4; *CSPD 1673–5*, p. 27; Mignet, IV.240.

161. BT 129, Croissy 2 and 6 Nov., '15' (recte 14) Dec.; CPA 108, same to Pomponne 23 Nov.; CPA 110, Louis to Croissy 11 Nov. 1673; Mignet, IV.230–1, 234–5; Essex, I.154–5.

162. Williamson, II.56–7, 69, 84, 103; Essex, I.159; BL Add MSS 25117 fos 164–5, 25123 fos 1, 5; Stowe MS 203 fos 319–20; BT 129, Croissy 9 Nov. and 7 Dec. 1673; BT 130, Ruvigny to Pomponne 25 Jan. 1674.

163. Mignet, IV.233–5, 239–42; *CSPV 1673–5*, pp. 176–7; BT 129, Croissy 27 Nov., 7 and 11 Dec.; CPA 108, same to Pomponne 30 Nov., 4 Dec. 1673; Jusserand, II.132–9.

164. BT 129, Croissy 11, '15' (recte 14), 21 and 25 Dec.; CPA 110, Louis to Croissy 13 Dec. 1673; Stowe MS 203 fo. 243; *CSPV 1673–5*, pp. 184–5, 187; Mignet, IV.245–6.

165. Stowe MSS 203 fo. 217, 204 fos 1–2, 32–3; BT 129, Croissy '15' (recte 14) Dec. 1673; Mignet, IV.247–50.

166. CPA 108, Croissy to Pomponne 28 Dec. 1673; BT 130, Ruvigny 1 Jan., Croissy 7 Jan. 1674; Jusserand, II.123–4.

167. BT 130, Ruvigny 1 and 11 Jan. 1674; Williamson, II.105–6; Mignet, IV.256–8.

168. *CJ*, IX.287; Mignet, IV.258–9; Essex, I.161.

169. BT 130, Ruvigny to Pomponne 21 Jan. 1674; Grey, II.225–36; BL Add MS 29571 fo. 265.

170. BT 130, Ruvigny to Pomponne 18 Jan. 1674.

171. Grey, II.236–58.

172. Stowe MS 204 fos 25, 38–41; Herts RO, D/EP F49; Grey, II.262–3; Essex, I.162–4.

173. *CSPD 1673–5*, pp. 103–6; Grey, II.274–80; Tanner MS 42 fo. 74 (quoted); Stowe MS 204 fos 51, 61, 67.

174. Grey, II.270, 280, 289–99, 303–17, 321–4, 329; Lauderdale, III.24; Stowe MS 204 fos 92–3, 116; BT 130, Ruvigny to Pomponne 1 Feb. 1674.

175. BT 130, Ruvigny 22 Feb., same to Pomponne 25 Jan. 1674; Stowe MS 204 fos 117, 144, 175, 281; Williamson, II.130–1; BL Add MS 18979 fos 285–6.

176. *CSPD 1673–5*, p. 119; Essex, I.167–8, 170, 173–4; Grey, II.381; BT 130, Ruvigny 19 and 22 Feb., same to Pomponne 29 Jan., 1 and 8 Feb. 1674; SP 78/139, fo. 62.

177. Stowe MS 204 fo. 63; BT 130, Ruvigny to Pomponne 21 and 25 Jan., 1 and 22 Feb. 1674; Williamson, II.106; Macpherson, I.71; *LJ*, XII.606–7; *HMC 9th Report, Part II*, p. 44.

178. Grey, II.233, 415–17; Williamson, II.130, 147–8, 156–7; BT 130, Ruvigny 5, 8, 19 and 22 Feb., same to Pomponne 1 March 1674; Stowe MS 204 fo. 117; *HMC 9th Report, Part II*, pp. 42, 45–6; Lauderdale, III.32–3; Macpherson, I.72; *CSPD 1673–5*, p. 221.

179. Grey, II.281, 366–7, 393; *CJ*, IX.305, 309–10; Essex, I.174 (quoted).

180. BT 129, Croissy 23 Oct. 1673; BT 130, Ruvigny 8 Feb. 1674; Stowe MS 203 fos 140–1.

181. SP 104/177 fo. 69; Stowe 204 fos 30, 53–6, 102, 104–5; BT 130; Ruvigny to Pomponne 25 Jan. 1674; Grey, II.338–40, 343–57; Mignet, IV.264–6, 269; Essex, I.168.

182. BT 130, Ruvigny to Pomponne 12 and 19 Feb. 1674; BL Add MS 25123 fos 19–20, 22; Mignet, IV.267–8; Burnet, *Hist.*, II.41–2; Essex, I.178.

183. BT 130, Ruvigny 22 and 26 Feb. 1674 (the former is partly printed in Mignet, IV.269–71); Temple, I.377.

184. *CJ*, IX.307, 311, 313; Williamson, II.153–5.

185. *RB*, part III, pp. 109, 140; Tanner MS 44 fo. 249; BL Add MS 23136 fo. 198; BT 130, Ruvigny to Pomponne 5 March 1674; *HMC 9th Report, Part II*, p. 44; *LJ*, XII.636, 644.

186. BL Add MS 25123 fo. 26; BT 130, Ruvigny 8 March 1674; *CSPV 1673–5*, p. 232; Macpherson, I.72; Williamson, II.157–8; Stowe MS 204 fo. 252.

187. Stowe MS 204 fo. 193; FSL, MS L.c.22; BL Add MS 25123 fos 26, 29; Essex, I.181; Temple, I.377.

188. Williamson, II.142. See also Ormond's similar comment (BT 135, Courtin 4 Feb. 1677) and, more generally, Burnet, *Hist.*, II.1; Dering, *Papers*, pp. 125–6.

Chapter 9: Peace and Retrenchment?

1. BT 132, Ruvigny 18 Feb. and 27 June 1675; BT 134, Courtin 20 Dec. 1676; *CSPV 1673–5*, p. 595.

2. See T. Harris, 'The Bawdy House Riots of 1668', *HJ* XXIX (1986), pp. 537–56.

3. Harris, *Crowds*, pp. 191–204; see the series of letters in Cov MS 83 fos 86–91 and BL Add MS 25124 fos 39–51. The letter referred to is at Cov MS 83 fo. 86; BL Add MS 25124 fo. 43; *CSPD 1675–6*, p. 259.

4. *CSPD 1675–6*, p. 315, *1676–7*, pp. 194–5, 207; BT 133, Courtin 27 July 1676.

5. Pforz, Coleman to Bulstrode 7 July 1676.

6. *CSPD 1676–7*, pp. 142–3, 161, 165, 179–80, 185–6, 200; Essex, II.65; Cov MS 7 fo. 72.

7. Cov MSS 4 fos 193–4, 229–31, 7 fo. 43, 83 fos 73, 75; *CSPV 1673–5*, pp. 324, 331; *HMC 7th Report*, p. 465; *HMC Portland*, III.348.

8. *CJ*, IX.281. See also 'A Relation' and 'England's Appeal', both printed in *State Tracts*, vol. I (1689); Haley, *William of Orange*, esp. ch. 6.

9. BL Add MS 29571 fo. 324; Eg MS 3330 fo. 5 [most of the names are on the list of members of the Green Ribbon Club, Magdalene College, Cambridge, Pepys Library MS 2875 fos 489–91]; Pforz, Coleman to Bulstrode 6 Oct. 1676; BT 134, Courtin 2 Nov. 1676; CSPV (cont) Sarotti 13 Nov. 1676.

10. *CSPD 1673–5*, p. 238, *1675–6*, pp. 465, 496–7, 500, 503, *1676–7*, pp. 254–6; BT 131, Ruvigny 14 May 1674; Stowe MS 205 fo. 109; PC 2/65, pp. 79–81.

11. *CSPD 1676–7*, pp. 75, 81; *HMC 7th Report*, p. 467; BL Add MS 29555 fos 417–18, 421, 427.

12. CPA 118, Ruvigny to Pomponne 2 April 1676; BT 135, Courtin 22 Feb. 1677; *HMC 7th Report*, p. 467; CSPV (cont) Sarotti 10 April 1676; Pforz, Coleman to Bulstrode 2 Oct. 1676; *CSPD 1676–7*, p. 537; Stowe MS 211 fo. 93; BL Add MS 29556 fo. 116.

13. BT 133, Courtin 14 Sept. 1676.

14. BT 134, Courtin 12 Oct. 1676; BT 137, Barrillon to Pomponne 16 Sept. 1677; BL Add MS 32095 fo. 36. For an earlier example, see Mignet, III.213.

15. CPA 117, Ruvigny to Pomponne 9 Jan. 1676; see also Jusserand II.171–2.

16. PC 2/65, p. 393; Williamson, II.157; Macpherson, I.73; Cov MS 16 fos 16, 19–21, 23–6, 259; *CSPD 1675–6*, pp. 21, 26–7, 31–2, *1676–7*, pp. 388–9; Eg MS 3329 fo. 14; FSL, MS X.d.529(2); *HMC 7th Report*, p. 467; Pforz, Coleman to Bulstrode 2 June and 4 Aug. 1676.

17. *CSPD 1676–7*, pp. 194–5, 255–6; Carte MS 80 fo. 790; Pforz, Coleman to Bulstrode 26 June 1676; Hatton, I.132–3; CSPV (cont) Sarotti 10 July 1676.

18. *CSPD 1676–7*, pp. 11–12; PC 2/65, pp. 123, 335; *HMC Finch*, II.43–6; BL Add MS 25125 fo. 4; Havighurst, pp. 65, 76, 230.

19. Cov MS 5 fo. 85; BL Add MS 25124 fos 87–90, 101–2; *CSPD 1675–6*, pp. 496–7, 500.

20. *CSPD 1677–8*, p. 538.

21. Stowe MS 208 fos 90, 96, 99, 123, 131; Essex, II.32.

22. Essex, II.32–3.

23. Stowe MS 215 fo. 167.

24. Stowe MSS 215 fos 36–7, 97, 216 fos 93, 118–19, 139. Note the comment that impressions seldom lasted long with Charles: BT 132, Courtin 22 June 1676.

25. *CSPD 1675–6*, p. 563.

26. BL Add MS 23136 fos 119, 121, 130; Burnet, *Suppl.*, p. 483; Stowe MS 211 fo. 216.

27. BL Add MS 25123 fo. 66; Lauderdale III.40; BT 131, Ruvigny to Pomponne 10 May 1674; Stowe MS 206 fo. 115.

28. Stowe MSS 205 fos 232, 371, 206 fo. 59; BT 131, Ruvigny 13 Aug., 8 and 19 Nov. 1674; BT 132, same 23 May and 22 July; CPA 117, same to Pomponne 14 Oct. 1675; Temple, I.397–9, 410–11; Essex, I.287–8, II.2.

29. Essex, I.242, 259; *HP*, II.148–53; Stowe MS 206 fos 130, 217.

30. Clarke, *James II*, I.484; Burnet, *Hist.*, II.11–12; Williamson, I.140, 176; Essex, I.150.

31. Burnet, *Hist.*, II.12; Essex, II.83; Stowe MSS 206 fo. 78, 217 fo. 22; BL Add. MS 63057B fo. 32.

32. Stowe MS 214 fos 73–4; *CSPD 1673–5*, p. 185; Hatton, I.122; Cov MS 83 fo. 91; *HMC 7th Report*, p. 492; BL Add MS 25124 fo. 52.

33. Browning, *Danby*, II.64–5; Stowe MS 204 fos 237, 311; BL Add MSS 25119 fo. 37, 25123 fo. 26; Essex, I.181; Williamson, II.37; BT 130, Croissy 1 Jan. 1674; CPA 117, Ruvigny to Pomponne 23 Jan. 1676; PC 2/65, p. 43; *HMC le Fleming*, p. 124; Savile, p. 40.

34. Essex, I.199–200, 259; BT 131, Ruvigny 13 Aug. 1674; Chandaman, pp. 233–6.

35. Browning, *Danby*, II.63–4.

36. Browning, *Documents*, pp. 237–49; Essex, II.63; A. Marvell, 'An Account of the Growth of Popery and Arbitrary Government', in *State Tracts*, I. (1689); see also Burnet, *Hist.*, II.69–70; BL Add. MS 63057B fo. 13.

37. Rochester, p. 175; see also Stowe MS 212 fos 179–80, 208, 227–8; Cov MS 83 fo. 91; *HMC 7th Report*, p. 492; Essex, I.258–60.

38. *CSPV 1673–5*, p. 298; *POAS*, I.269.

39. Clarke, *James II*, I.505; BT 140, Barrillon 26 Sept. 1678. For earlier evidence of friction between York and the Presbyterians, see Stowe MS 209 fo. 209; Essex, II.51; CPA 122, Courtin to Pomponne 11 Jan. 1677.

40. Temple, I.383–4, 415–16; Stowe MS 214 fo. 154.

41. *CSPV 1673–5*, pp. 305, 371–2; CPA 119, Courtin to Pomponne 17 Aug. 1676; CPA 124, same to same 2 Aug. 1677; Cov MS 5 fo. 176.

42. Jusserand, II.111–12; CPA 101, Croissy to Louvois 16 Oct. and 24 Dec. 1671; CPA 107, Croissy to Pomponne 17 July, 7 and 29 Aug. 1673.

43. Essex, I.140; CPA 117, Ruvigny to Pomponne 3 Feb. 1676.

44. Essex, II.50; BT 131, Ruvigny to Pomponne 14 May 1674; CPA 117, same to same 2 and 6 Jan. 1676; Stowe MS 205 fo. 318.

45. Pforz, Coleman to Bulstrode 1 May 1676; BT 132, Courtin 8 June; BT 133, same 2, 6, 9 July, 3 Aug., same to Pomponne 9 and 20 July; CPA 119, same to same 17 Aug.; CPA 120, same to same 30 Nov. and 3 Dec. 1676; CPA 122, same to same 11 Jan., 4 Feb., 4 March; CPA 125, Barrillon to Pomponne 22 Nov. 1677.

46. BT 132, Courtin 8 June 1676; CPA 122, same to Pomponne 11 Feb. 1677.

47. BT 133, Courtin 2 July 1676; CPA 122, same to Pomponne 18 Jan. and 22 Feb. 1677; Rochester, p. 175; *POAS*, I.233 ('Carwell' was Quérouaille, or Keroalle, i.e. Portsmouth).

48. BT 133, Courtin 6 Aug. 1676; CPA 117, Ruvigny to Pomponne, 11 Nov. 1675; Pforz, Coleman to Bulstrode, 15 Jan. 1677.

49. Note his interview with Reresby: Reresby, pp. 111–13.

50. BL Add MS 25123 fo. 116; BT 135, Courtin 16 Jan 1677.

51. Temple, I.404; Burnet, *Hist.*, II.115–16.

52. Ekberg, pp. 112, 116–19 and *passim*.

53. Baxter, chs 10–12.

54. CPA 113, Ruvigny to Pomponne 26 Nov. 1674; CPA 115, same to same 7 March 1675.

55. BT 131, Ruvigny 24 Sept. 1674; CPA 122, Courtin to Pomponne 4 Feb. 1677.

56. Stowe MS 207 fo. 40; CPA 117, Charles to Louis 7 Nov. [fo. 64], Ruvigny to Pomponne 9 Dec. 1675; *CSPD 1675–6*, pp. 544–5.

57. CPA 117, Ruvigny to Pomponne 3 and 17 Feb., Ruvigny to Temple 29 Feb.; CPA 118, Ruvigny to Pomponne 16 March and 9 April; CPA 119, Courtin to Pomponne 17 Aug. 1676; BT 132, Ruvigny 7 May 1676; *CSPD 1675–6*, p. 535; see also Wolf, pp. 248–9.

58. Mignet, IV.352; BT 132, Ruvigny 6 June, 22 July 1675.

59. CPA 121, Courtin to Pomponne 12 Oct.; see also CPA 120A, Louis to Courtin 30 Sept. 1676.

60. CPA 120, Courtin to Pomponne 12 Oct. 1676; CPA 120C, Courtin to Le Tellier '2 or 6' June and Le Tellier's reply [fos 51–2, 64]; see also CPA 119, Courtin to Pomponne 21 Sept. 1676; CPA 120, same to same 5 Oct. 1676.

61. CPA 118, Ruvigny to Pomponne 9 March; Jusserand II.185–7; CPA 120C, Colbert to Courtin 24 July; BT 132, Courtin to Louis and to Pomponne 15 June; CPA 121, Courtin to plenipotentiaries 25 Aug.; CPA 119, Courtin to Pomponne 24 Aug.; BT 133, Courtin 24 Aug. and 14 Sept. 1676.

62. BT 133, Courtin 24 Aug. and 14 Sept.; BT 134, same 12 Oct. and 5 Nov.; CPA 119, same to Pomponne 24 Aug. and 14 Sept.; CPA 120, same to same 9, 23 and 26 Nov., 28 Dec. 1676; BT 135, Courtin 21 Jan.; CPA 122, same to Pomponne 28 Jan. 1677; FSL, MS X.d.529(11) and (3); Browning, *Danby*, II.258.

63. Mignet, IV.435; BT 135, Courtin 11 Feb.; CPA 122, same to Pomponne 11 Feb. 1677.

64. Essex, II.79–81.

65. BT 131, Ruvigny 13 Aug. 1674; BT 132, same 27 Jan.; CPA 116, same to Pomponne 8 Aug. and 9 Sept. 1675; CPA 122, same to same 7 Jan. 1677; Mignet, IV.367–70; Miller, 'Coleman', pp. 263–5.

66. Mignet, IV.333–5; CPA 115, Ruvigny to Pomponne 4 March; CPA 116, same to same 16 Dec. 1675; CPA 122, same to same 22 Feb. 1677.

67. Stowe MS 204 fos 285–6; BT 131, Ruvigny 14 May 1674; PC 2/64, p. 229; *CSPV 1673–5*, p. 263; Essex, I.234.

68. Stowe MSS 204 fo. 208, 206 fo. 155, 214 fos 275, 321; Essex I.241–2, 264–5.

69. BT 131, Ruvigny 7 May, 4 June, 13 and 30 Aug., 8 and 19 Nov. 1674; Macpherson, I.73; Essex, I.228, 236; Stowe 205 fo. 262; Browning, *Danby*, II.447–52; Temple, I.395, 397–8.

70. Pepys, VI.167, VII.411; CPA 100, Croissy to Lionne 9 and 16 March 1671; Buckingham II.20–1; Burnet, *Hist.*, I.453.

71. Clifton, pp. 92–7; *CSPD 1673–5*, pp. 327–8; Macpherson, I.73–4; Clarke, *James II*, I.494–5. Macpherson and Clarke date Monmouth's claim in 1674, although the subsequent account of Monmouth's commission belongs to 1678. For other evidence of friction between the two dukes at this time, about a colonelcy in the guards, see CPA 113, Ruvigny to Pomponne 8 Oct. 1674; Stowe MS 206 fo. 98 [Essex, I.261, has 'Montagu', where it should read 'Mulgrave']; Buckingham, II.23–6.

72. BT 131, Ruvigny 16 April, 7 and 14 May, 13 Aug. 1674; PC 2/64, p. 204; *CSPD 1673–5*, p. 238; Essex, I.228; *HMC 7th Report*, p. 491.

73. PC 2/64, p. 188; Miller, *Popery*, pp. 132–3, 265; FSL, MS L.c.43; Eg MS 1633 fo. 6; *CSPV 1673–5*, pp. 269–70.

74. *CSPV 1673–5*, p. 243; DCAD, Hunter MS 7 no. 114; Tanner MS 42 fos 112, 119; Harl MS 7377 fo. 53.

75. BT 131, Ruvigny 18 June, 30 July, 13 Aug. and 6 Sept., same to Pomponne 9 July; CPA 113, same to same 1 Oct. 1674; Essex, I.241; *CSPV 1673–5*, p. 279; *CSPD 1673–5*, p. 365.

76. CPA 113, Ruvigny to Pomponne 1 Oct. 1674; *CSPV 1673–5*, p. 298; Cov MS 4 fos 193–4; *CSPD 1673–5*, pp. 396, 424, 442, 454.

77. BT 130, Ruvigny to Pomponne 12 March 1674; Carte MSS 47 fo. 245, 70 fo. 423; BL Add MS 25123 fos 59, 63. Orders late in 1674 to prevent recruiting were aimed at levies for the Dutch service: *CSPD 1673–5*, p. 414; CPA 113, Ruvigny to Pomponne 26 Nov. 1674.

78. BL Add MS 25123 fo. 50; BT 131, Ruvigny 14 May, same to Pomponne 21 June 1674; Stowe MSS 204 fo. 285, 205 fo. 386.

79. CPA 113, Ruvigny to Pomponne 6 Aug. 1674.

80. BT 131, Ruvigny 31 May 1674; Temple, I.394; *CSPD 1673–5*, pp. 264, 275, 284, 288, 299; Burnet, *Hist.*, II.54–6; Haley, *William of Orange, passim*, esp. pp. 197–9.

81. Temple, I.394; BT 131, Ruvigny 8 Nov.; CPA 113, same to Pomponne 23 Aug. and 11 Oct. 1674.

82. BT 131, Ruvigny 14 May, same to Pomponne 25 June 1674; Cov MS 2 fos 52–3; Stowe MS 205 fo. 189.

83. BL Add MS 25123 fo. 116 (another copy, Cov MS 83 fo. 64); Temple, I.398; BT 131, Ruvigny 30 Aug.; CPA 113, same to Pomponne 11 Oct. 1674; see also Stowe MSS 206 fos 282–3.

84. Baxter, pp. 114–20; Stowe MS 206 fos 4–5.

85. BT 131, Ruvigny 24 Sept., 8 Nov.; CPA 113, same to Pomponne 1 and 8 Oct. 1674; *CSPD 1673–5*, p. 365.

86. BT 131, Ruvigny 8 Nov.; CPA 113, same to Pomponne 12 and 15 Nov., 6 Dec. 1674; Temple, I.395; Browning, *Danby*, II.451.

87. *CSPV 1673–5*, pp. 197, 310; BT 131, Ruvigny 23 April and 19 Nov. 1674; Macpherson, I.75; Clarke, *James II*, I.500–2; Carte MS 47, fo. 246.

88. BT 131, Ruvigny 19 Nov.; CPA 113, same to Pomponne 22 Nov. 1674; Temple, I.394–7; BL Add MS 32094 fos 325–7.

89. FSL, MS V.b.264, facing p. 530; Stowe MS 206 fos 169–70; Temple, II.315–16; BT 131, Ruvigny 13 Dec. 1674.

90. BT 131, Ruvigny 13 and 20 Dec.; CPA 113, same to Pomponne 10 Dec. 1674; BT 132, Ruvigny to 'Louis' (recte Pomponne) 10 Jan. 1675; Browning, *Danby*, II.454–5; Temple, I.397–8, II.322; Burnet, *Hist.*, II.61–2.

91. Temple, I.397–8; CPA 115, Ruvigny 21 Jan.; BT 132, same to 'Louis' (recte Pomponne) 10 Jan. 1675.

92. Carte MSS 38 fo. 223, 47 fo. 246; Temple, I.397; BT 131, Ruvigny 20 Dec. 1674; Burnet, *Hist.*, II.61–2.

93. Temple, II.321–2; Browning, *Danby*, II.456; BT 132, Ruvigny 7 Feb.; CPA 115, same to Pomponne 21 Feb. 1675.

94. Temple, I.400; CPA 115, Ruvigny to Pomponne 7 and 18 March 1675.

95. BT 132, Ruvigny 27 Jan., 4 and 18 Feb.; CPA 115, same to Pomponne 25 Feb. 1675; *CSPV 1673–5*, pp. 371–2.

96. *CSPV 1673–5*, pp. 307–8, 310–11, 316–17, 321, 324, 326–7, 349, 353–4; *HMC Portland*, III.348; Macpherson, I.75; Essex, I.285; Carte MS 72 fo. 257. For an approach to Catholics by Dissenters in the provinces, see *CSPD 1675–6*, p. 87.

97. *CSPV 1673–5*, p. 321; CPA 115, Ruvigny to Pomponne 3 Jan. 1675; Essex, I.288.

98. Carte MS 72 fo. 229; *CSPD 1673–5*, p. 390; Stowe MS 206 fos 161, 178, 182; *CSPV 1673–5*, p. 312; CPA 113, Ruvigny to Pomponne 20 and 24 Dec. 1674.

99. Carte MSS 38 fo. 232, 72 fo. 253; *CSPV 1673–5*, pp. 348–50, 357–8; Macpherson, I.81; Browning, *Danby*, II.54–5; *CSPD 1673–5*, pp. 548–51, 568, 571, 578; Cov MS 83 fo. 72.

100. *CSPV 1673–5*, pp. 358–9, 363–4, 366–8, 376; Carte MS 38 fo. 252; *RB*, part III, pp. 157–8.

101. BL Add MS 25124 fos 16, 22 (other copies in Cov MS 83 fos 73, 75); Cov MS 7 fo. 43; Dorset RO, D 124, Box 233, bundle labelled Col. T. Strangways, Bishop of Bristol to Strangways 24 Feb. 1675; *CSPD 1673–5*, pp. 590, 595, 602, *1675–6*, pp. 18, 23, 68, 73, 163, 185, 234; *HMC 2nd Report*, p. 22.

102. *CSPV 1673–5*, pp. 390–1; Browning, *Danby*, II.65–6; BL Add MS 25124 fos 27, 29.

103. *Bulstrode Papers*, I.284; *CJ*, IX.314–15; Dering, *Papers*, p. 87; Essex, I.298, II.20; BT 132, Ruvigny 18 Feb. 1675.

104. Macpherson, I.80–1; Burnet, II.74, 76; CPA 116, Ruvigny to Pomponne 2, 9 and 13 May 1675; *LJ*, XII.673; *HMC 9th Report, Part II*, pp. 51–2; *CSPV 1673–5*, pp. 393, 397–8, 401–2, 407; *Bulstrode Papers*, I.289; Campana, I.156; Essex, II.1, 8, 23; *CJ*, IX.317–18; Marvell, II.319–20, 341–2; North, *Examen*, pp. 63–4.

105. Dering, *Papers*, p. 68; *HMC 7th Report*, p. 492.

106. Grey, III.34–9, 107–11, 211–17; Dering, *Papers*, pp. 68–9, 80, 95–6; *CJ*, IX.337, 341, 345, 347.

107. Grey, III.41–9, 85–9; Essex, II.1–2; Dering, *Papers*, p. 77.

108. Grey, III.34–40, 97–102, 175; *CJ*, IX.328; Essex, II.7; CPA 116, Ruvigny to Pomponne 16 May 1675.

109. Grey, III.3–9, 116–29, 134–8; Dering, *Papers*, pp. 65, 81–2, 175–8; *CJ*, IX.333; BT 132, Ruvigny 2 May; CPA 116, same to Pomponne 16 May 1675; Essex, II.8–9; Finch MS PP 37 fo. 35.

110. Mignet, IV.346–52; BT 132, Ruvigny 2 May, 6 and 27 June, 22 July; CPA 116, same to Pomponne 30 May and 10 June 1675; Temple, I.404–5.

111. Dering, *Papers*, p. 87; Marvell, II.156–7; Finch MS PP 37 fos 46, 82; Grey, III.261–2, 275–6; Essex, II.24–7; Haley, *Shaftesbury*, pp. 382–4.

112. Stowe MS 208 fo. 55; CPA 116, Ruvigny to Pomponne 20 June 1675.

113. *Bulstrode Papers*, I.302; Stowe MS 208 fos 59, 61, 100, 109; Essex, II.32.

114. Stowe MS 208 fos 61, 109; CPA 116, Ruvigny to Pomponne 29 July, 1 and 8 Aug., 19 Sept. 1675; Marvell, II.319–20; BL Add MS 25124 fos 33, 38 (copies in Cov MS 83 fos 84–5); *CSPD 1675–6*, p. 234.

115. BT 132, Ruvigny 27 June; CPA 116, same to Pomponne 2 Sept. 1675.

116. Stowe MSS 208 fos 217–18; Temple, I.405, II.335–6; BT 132, Ruvigny 22 July; CPA 116, same 1, 8, 15 and 27 July, 8 Aug. 1675; Browning, *Danby*, II.464–9; Mignet, IV.369–70.

117. FSL, V.b.264, front of volume (Charles to Temple 29 Oct. 1675); CPA 116, Ruvigny to Pomponne 8 May, 2 and 9 Sept. 1675; Mignet, IV.367–70; C.L. Grose, 'Louis XIV's Financial Relations with Charles II and the English Parliament', *Journal of Modern History* I (1929), pp. 187–9.

118. CPA 116, Ruvigny to Pomponne 19 Sept. (partly printed in Mignet, IV.365); CPA 117, same to same 31 Oct. 1675.

119. *CJ*, IX.359, 369; Grey, III.302–11, 323–32, 397–9 (Powle's remark is on p. 331).

120. Finch MS PP 39 fo. 1; Grey, III.317–19, 354–66, 446–59; *CJ*, IX.373–4; Tanner MS 42 fo. 182.

121. *CJ*, IX.365, 370.

122. Grey, III.348; Reresby, pp. 96–7.

123. Grey, III.334–6, 345 (quoted), 366–70; BT 132, Ruvigny 21 Nov. 1675; *CJ*, IX.362, 371; *HMC 9th Report, Part II*, pp. 79, 96–7; Burnet, *Hist.*, II.91; *CSPD 1675–6*, p. 413. For the letters, see *CSPD 1675–6*, p. 302; BL Add MS 25124, fos 61–2.

124. Warwicks. RO, CR 136/B71; BL Add MS 41568 fo. 4; Carte MS 130 fo. 18; CPA 117, Ruvigny to Pomponne 31 Oct., 4 and 7 Nov. 1675; *CJ*, IX.378–9, 381; *CSPD 1675–6*, p. 414.

125. BL Add MS 29555 fo. 261; *CSPD 1675–6*, pp. 414, 457, 460–1; Cov MS 7 fo. 78.

126. CPA 117, Ruvigny to Pomponne 2 Dec. 1675.

127. *Ibid.*, Ruvigny to Pomponne 16 and 23 Dec. 1675; *CSPD 1675–6*, p. 465.

128. PC 2/65, p. 43; BL Add MSS 25119 fo. 37, 29555 fo. 309; CPA 117, Ruvigny to Pomponne 23 Jan.; CPA 118, same to same 30 March and 2 April 1676; CSPV (cont), Sarotti 31 Jan., 6 March and 10 April 1676; *CSPD 1676–7*, p. 22; *HMC 7th Report*, p. 467; Chandaman, pp. 236–8.

129. CPA 117, Ruvigny to Pomponne 9 and 13 Dec. 1675; CPA 118, same to same 30 April and 4 May 1676; Temple, I.410–11.

130. CPA 120, Courtin to Pomponne 14 Dec. 1676.

131. Campana, I.166–7; *HMC 7th Report*, p. 467; CUL Add MS 4878 fo. 624; BT 132, Courtin 8 and 22 June; BT 133, same 20 Aug.; BT 134, same 6 Dec. 1676.

132. Pforz, Coleman to Bulstrode 26 May and 23 June 1676; BT 133, Courtin to Pomponne 6 Aug.; CPA 119, same to same 17 and 31 Aug. 1676; Miller, 'Coleman', pp. 269–70.

133. *CSPD 1676–7*, pp. 349, 388–9; FSL MS X.d.529(2); Pforz, Coleman to Bulstrode 20 Nov. 1676; BT 134, Courtin 3 Dec. 1676.

134. BL Add MS 25124 fos 66–7 (another copy Cov MS 83 fo. 96).

135. *CSPD 1676–7*, pp. 23, 51, 56; Cov MS 7 fo. 66.

136. William Salt Library, Stafford, SMS 454 no. 23; BL Add MS 36988 fo. 109; PC 2/65, p. 123; *CSPD 1676–7*, pp. 45, 56; CPA 118, Ruvigny to Pomponne 9 April 1676; see also J. M. Rosenheim, 'An Examination of Oligarchy: The Gentry of Restoration Norfolk', unpublished PhD thesis, Princeton, 1981, pp. 214–22.

137. William Salt Library, SMS 454 no. 23; *HMC 7th Report*, p. 467; *HMC le Fleming*, p. 125; CPA 118, Ruvigny to Pomponne 30 March 1676; Stowe MS 209 fo. 237; PC 2/65, p. 335; Pforz, Coleman to Bulstrode 4 Dec. 1676.

138. Hatton, I.132–3; BL Add MS 29571 fo. 319; CPA 113, Ruvigny to Pomponne 10 Sept. 1674; BT 133, Courtin 23 July 1676; *CSPD 1675–6*, pp. 559–61, 563, *1676–7*, pp. 449–50; Carte MS 228 fo. 101.

139. Browning, *Danby*, II.45; Hatton, I.128–30; BT 132, Courtin 8 and 22 June 1676; BL Add MS 29571 fo. 311; Essex, II.62–3.

140. Nunz Fian 59 fos 485–6; Essex II.62; Pforz, Coleman to Bulstrode 14 July 1676.

141. Pforz, Coleman to Bulstrode 8 Jan. 1677; BT 135, Courtin 21 Jan.; CPA 122, same to Pomponne 25 Jan.; CPA 126, same to plenipotentiaries 9 Feb. 1677 [fo. 51].

142. *Clar SP*, III.722, 727–8; *RB*, book I, part II, p. 218, part III, pp. 109, 140, 157–8; Burnet, *Hist.*, I.150.

143. Pforz, Coleman to Bulstrode 14 July 1676; Tanner MS 42 fo. 7.

144. See J. Spurr, '"Latitudinarianism" and the Restoration Church', *HJ* XXXI (1988), pp. 61–82; Burnet, *Hist.*, I.321–30.

145. See A. Fletcher, 'The Enforcement of the Conventicle Acts 1664–79', in W. J. Sheils (ed.), *Persecution and Toleration* (Oxford, 1984), pp. 235–46; Miller, *Popery*, pp. 142, 267.

146. *HMC Fitzherbert*, p. 271; *HMC le Fleming*, pp. 90, 92; Burnet, *Hist.*, I.537.

147. BT 135, Courtin 21 Jan.; CPA 122, same to Pomponne 25 Jan.; CPA 126, same to plenipotentiaries, 9 Feb. 1677; Finch MS PP 44, p. 4 (the heads are appended to a long letter about the spring 1677 session).

148. A. Whiteman, *The Compton Census of 1676* (British Academy: Records of Economic and Social History X, Oxford, 1986), pp. xxv–xxviii and Introduction, *passim*; Browning, *Documents*, pp. 411–16; BT 133, Courtin to Pomponne 6 Aug. 1676 (Danby said there were 12,000 in the whole kingdom, not just the province of Canterbury).

149. See the case of Great Yarmouth: *CSPD 1676–7*, pp. 221–2, 232; *HP*, I.325.

150. BL Add MS 28054 fo. 38; Browning, *Danby*, II. 474–5, 481; Temple, I.415–16; CPA 118, Ruvigny to Pomponne 30 April; BT 133, Courtin 3 Sept. 1676.

151. BT 133, Courtin 21 Sept.; BT 134, same 1 Oct. and 10 Dec. 1676; Temple, I.432.

152. Temple, I.432–5, 437–8; BT 135, Courtin '1' (recte 7) and 16 Jan.; CPA 122, same to Pomponne 18 Jan. 1677. For Danby's arguing that Louis could attack England, see BT 132, Ruvigny 9 Jan. 1676.

153. Browning, *Danby*, II.481–3; Temple, I.438–9, 443; see Haley, 'Rapprochement', pp. 622–5; for concern about Cambrai, see CPA 120, Courtin to Pomponne 10 and 17 Dec. 1676.

154. BT 132, Ruvigny 9 Dec. 1675 and 9 Jan. 1676 (the latter is partly printed in Dalrymple, II(a), pp. 99–100); Mignet, IV.375–6; CPA 117, Ruvigny to Pomponne 9 Jan. 1676.

155. Mignet, IV.378–85; Jusserand, II.187.

156. CPA 117, Ruvigny to Pomponne 26 Dec. 1675; Jusserand, II.195–6; BT 132, Courtin to Pomponne 25 June 1676; CPA 122, same to same 18 and 25 Jan., 8 Feb. 1677.

157. Stowe MS 210 fo. 1; CPA 120A, Louis to Courtin 1 Aug. and 30 Sept.; BT 133, Courtin 21 Sept.; CPA 120, same to Pomponne 10, 14 and 17 Dec. 1676; Browning, *Danby*, II.551–2.

158. CSPV (cont), Sarotti 13 Nov. and 25 Dec. 1676; FSL, MS X.d.529(2); BT 134, Courtin 30 Nov. and 10 Dec.; CPA 120, same to Pomponne 14 and 28 Dec. 1676; CPA 123A, Courtin 3 Jan.; CPA 122, same to Pomponne 7 Jan. 1677; Essex, II.86.

159. Tanner MS 40 fo. 37; BT 135, Courtin 21 Jan.; CPA 122, same to Pomponne 11, 14 and 25 Jan. 1677; *CSPD 1676–7*, p. 506.

160. BT 135, Courtin 16 Jan. 1677; Temple, I.437–8.

161. BT 135, Courtin 28 Jan., 4 and 11 Feb.; CPA 122, same to Pomponne 4 and 11 Feb. 1677. For an earlier example of Charles's over-reacting to encouraging news, see BT 134, Courtin 1 Oct. 1676.

162. BT 135, Courtin 22 Feb.; CPA 122, 7 and 14 Jan., 11 and 15 Feb. 1677.

163. Pforz, Coleman to Bulstrode [10] Feb. 1677; *CSPD 1676–7*, p. 542; PC 2/65, pp. 461–4; Finch MS PP 57(ii), p. 22; Stowe MS 211 fo. 93; BT 135, Courtin 22 Feb. 1677.

Chapter 10: 'An Army Without a War'

1. *HMC Ormond*, NS IV.428. For a variant (that some wanted war without money, others money without war) see CSPV (cont), Sarotti 25 Feb. 1678.

2. See the admirable map in H. C. Darby and H. Fullard (eds), *New Cambridge Modern History Atlas* (Cambridge, 1970), pp. 108–9.

3. Mignet, IV.479–97, 514–17, 524–7; BT 137, Barrillon 29 Nov. 1677; see also Wolf, pp. 328–32.

4. Finch MS PP 42, pp. 1–3; Grey, IV.64–72, 81–5; Essex, II.100–2; *HMC 7th Report*, p. 468.

5. BT 135, Courtin 1 March 1677; Finch MS PP 42, p. 3; CSPV (cont), Sarotti 5 March 1677; North, *Examen*, pp. 66–7; *HMC 7th Report*, p. 468; *CSPD 1676–7*, p. 564; Carte MS 130 fo. 189; Essex II.105; Stowe MS 211 fo. 220.

6. Grey, IV.130, 173–7, 180–7, 224–37; *CJ*, IX.392; Finch MS PP 41, pp. 13–21.

7. Grey, IV.173–4, 225; BT 135, Courtin 25 March 1677; Finch MS PP 42, p. 34.

8. Finch MS PP 42, p. 8. See also CPA 120, Courtin to Pomponne 14 Dec. 1676; CPA 123A, Courtin 3 Jan. 1677 (draft); *CSPD 1676–7*, pp. 541–2.

9. Finch MSS PP 42, pp. 5–7, PP 44, p. 3; *HMC 9th Report, Part II*, pp. 82–3.

10. BT 135, Courtin 8 and 15 March 1677; Reresby, p. 121; Finch MS PP 42, pp. 8–9; *HMC 9th Report, Part II*, p. 43.

11. Grey, IV.288–96, 335–40; Finch MS PP 42, pp. 3–5, 8–9, 13; Reresby, p. 121; BT 135, Courtin 15 April 1677; *HMC 9th Report, Part II*, pp. 82–3.

12. BT 135, Courtin 4 and 8 March, 3 May 1677; *CJ*, IX.400–1. See also Essex, II.119.

13. Grey, IV.189–91, 193–4, 196–7, 201; Finch MS PP 42, p. 29. For Littleton, see Grey, IV.121, 128–9.

14. Finch MS PP 42, pp. 29–30; Grey, IV.189–90, 194–6, 199–200; Stowe MS 211 fo. 170.

15. Grey, IV.203. See also *ibid.*, p. 198; Essex, II.110.

16. Grey, IV.199. See also *ibid.*, p. 190.

17. BT 135, Courtin 18 and 29 March, 5, 15 and 19 April, 17 May; CPA 123, same to Pomponne 5 April 1677; Essex, II.111; Reresby, p. 120.

18. Pforz, Coleman to Bulstrode 12 March 1677; *CJ*, IX.396, 398–400; Finch MS PP 42, pp. 30–1; Essex, II.110. For Charles's views on Sicily, see Mignet, IV.482–3; BT 136, Courtin 12 July 1677.

19. BT 135, Courtin 25 March; CPA 123, same to Pomponne 1 and 19 April 1677; Burnet, *Hist.*, II.114.

20. Burnet, *Hist.*, II.115–16; *CJ*, IX.401, 408; Grey, IV.305–15; Stowe MS 211 fos 234–6; Finch MS PP 42, p. 33; Pforz, Coleman to Bulstrode 30 March 1677.

21. Browning, *Danby*, II.66–9; for York's remarks see BT 135, Courtin 12 April and 13 May 1677. It is possible that Williamson's jottings about raising an army date from much the same time as Danby's memorandum and were equally hypothetical: see *CSPD 1677*, p. 538.

22. BT 135, Courtin 15 and 19 April 1677; Grey, IV.343.

23. Grey, IV.345, 350 (quoted); Finch MS PP 42, pp. 33–4; BT 135, Courtin 13 and 17 May 1677.

24. *CJ*, IX.419, 421–3.

25. Finch MS PP 42 fos 33–4; Stowe MS 211 fos 292–3.

26. BT 135, Courtin 22 April; CPA 123, same to Pomponne 22 and 29 April, 6 May (quoted) 1677.

27. Browning, *Danby*, II.67; *CSPD 1677–8*, pp. 138–9; Grey, IV.355–9; Marvell, II.201; BT 136, Courtin 3 June 1677.

28. Grey, IV.361–2.

29. *Ibid.*, pp. 362–74 (quotation from p. 366); *CJ*, IX.424.

30. Pforz, Coleman to Bulstrode 14 May; BT 136, Courtin 3 June; CPA 123, same to Pomponne 3 June 1677; *CSPD 1677–8*, p. 142; PC 2/66, p. 25.

31. Grey, IV.374–88; *CSPD 1677–8*, pp. 144–8; Essex, II.141–2.

32. Grey, IV.388; BT 136, Courtin 7 June 1677.

33. Althorp MS C5, Thomas Thynne to Halifax 27 May; BT 136, Courtin 7 June 1677; *CSPD 1677–8*, pp. 156–8; Grey, IV.389–90.

34. BT 135, Courtin 22 April; BT 136, same 13 and 20 May 1677; BL Add MS 29571 fo. 394. For Danby's memorandum, see Browning, *Danby*, II.68.

35. Finch MS PP 42, p. 37.

36. Grey, IV.173–4; BT 135, Courtin 29 March; BT 136, same 21 June 1677 (Mignet, IV.479–81).

37. Browning, *Danby*, II.70–1.

38. BT 135, Courtin 12 April; BT 136, same 17 and 21 June 1677 (Mignet, IV.482–3).

39. BT 135, Courtin 17 May; BT 136, same 28 June; CPA 123, same to Pomponne 22 April and 28 June; BT 137, same to same 2 Sept. 1677.

40. BT 136, Courtin 21 June (Mignet, IV.484); CPA 123, same to Pomponne 21 June; CPA 124, same to same 5 July; BT 137, Barrillon to Pomponne 9, 13, 16 and 23 Sept. 1677; BL Add MSS 32095 fo. 36, 29556 fo. 220 (quoted).

41. BT 136, Courtin 17 June 1677; Clarke, *James II*, I.503–4.

42. Mignet, IV.485–91; Browning, *Danby*, II.391–3, 485–6; Haley, 'Anglo-Dutch Rapprochement', pp. 625–6, 632–4.

43. BT 136, Courtin 12 and 19 July 1677; Browning, *Danby*, II.269–72; BL Add MS 28040 fo. 36; Jusserand, II.245–6.

44. BT 136, Courtin 26 July and 5 Aug.; CPA 124, same to Pomponne 12 and 22 July 1677; Temple, I.448–50; Haley, 'Rapprochement', p. 634; BL Add MS 28040 fo. 37.

45. BL Add MS 25119 fos 1–5; Haley, 'Rapprochement', pp. 636–7; BT 137, Courtin to Pomponne 2 Sept. 1677; Browning, *Danby*, II.396–7.

46. Grey, IV.391; Marvell, II.353–4.

47. BT 136, Courtin 5 and 16 Aug.; CPA 128, same to plenipotentiaries 6 Aug. 1677; Browning, *Danby*, II.277.

48. BL Add MS 29577 fo. 159; Pforz, Coleman to Bulstrode 30 July; *HMC 7th Report*, p. 469; *HMC Portland*, III.355–6; Clarke, *James II*, I.544–5; Macpherson, I.92; Browning, *Danby*, II.280–1; BT 136, Courtin to Pomponne 19 Aug.; BT 137, same to same 2 and 6 Sept., Barrillon to Pomponne 9 Sept. 1677.

49. Browning, *Danby*, II.284–8, 291–2, 294; CPA 124, Montagu to Pomponne 22 Sept.; BT 137, Barrillon 4, 19 and 25 Oct. 1677.

50. BT 137, Barrillon 28 and 30 Oct., 1 and 4 Nov. 1677; Temple, I.454–5; Hatton, I.151–3; Haley, 'Rapprochement', pp. 640–3.

51. CSPV (cont), Sarotti 5 Nov.; BT 137, Barrillon 8, 11 and 15 Nov. 1677; Temple, I.455–6; Haley, 'Rapprochement', pp. 643–4; Miller, *James II*, p. 85.

52. SP 104/180 fos 115, 266–7; BT 137, Barrillon 29 Nov. 1677; BL Add MS 25119 fos 6–11; Haley, 'Rapprochement', p. 645.

53. BT 137, Barrillon 20 and 22 Nov.; CPA 125, same to Pomponne 21 Nov. 1677. See also CPA 122, Courtin to Pomponne 11 Feb. 1677; BT 138, Barrillon 31 Jan. 1678; Temple, I.457.

54. BT 137, Barrillon 25 and 29 Nov. 1677; Mignet, IV.514–17; SP 104/180 fo. 115.

55. Clarke, *James II*, I.510–11; BL Add MSS 25119 fos 13–20, esp. fo. 14, 28040 fo. 41; BT 137, Barrillon 9 and 13 Dec.; CPA 125, same to Pomponne 9 and 16 Dec. 1677; SP 104/180 fo. 115; Prinsterer, V.356; Haley, 'Rapprochement', p. 646.

56. Browning, *Danby*, II.400, 402–4; Prinsterer, V.360; CSPV (cont), Sarotti 7 Jan. 1678; BT 137, Barrillon 13 Dec. 1677; BT 138, same 7 Feb. 1678; BL Add MS 28040 fo. 41; Campana, I.207, 210. In the light of all the evidence adduced here, I find it hard to accept Dr Hutton's claim (*Charles II*, pp. 346–7) that Charles genuinely wanted war.

57. BT 137, Barrillon 13 and 20 Dec. 1677; BT 138, same 20 Jan. 1678; CPA 125, same to Pomponne 13 Dec. 1677.

58. BT 137, Barrillon 20 and 27 Dec. 1677; BT 138, same 3, 17 and 20 Jan., 7 Feb. 1678; CPA 125, same to Pomponne 23 and 27 Dec. 1677; CPA 127, same to same 10 Jan. 1678; Rochester, p. 174; *HMC Ormond*, NS IV.390; Browning, *Danby*, II.300–2, 304–8, 310–14, 320; Mignet, IV.524–7.

59. SP 104/180 fo. 127; BL Add MSS 25125 fos 39–42, 28040 fos 41, 43, 45–6; Browning, *Danby*, II.400–2, 405–6, 409, 412–13.

60. Browning, *Danby*, II.410–16; BL Add MSS 25125 fo. 45, 28040 fos 46–7; Dalrymple, II.(a), p. 146; BT 138, Barrillon 7 Feb. 1678.

61. *HMC Ormond*, NS IV.387–90; Pforz, Coleman to Bulstrode 7 Dec. 1677; BT 137, Barrillon 16 Dec. 1677; CPA 127, same to Pomponne 27 Jan. 1678; BL Add MS 25125 fo. 45.

62. Browning, *Danby*, II.407; SP 104/180 fo. 129; see also CSPV (cont), Sarotti 14 Jan. 1678.

63. PC 2/66, p. 202; BL Add MS 25124 fo. 130; Herts RO, D/EP 24, —Harwell to (?) 8 Jan. 1678.

64. CSPV (cont), Sarotti 14 Jan.; BT 138, Barrillon 3 Feb. 1678; Browning, *Danby*, II.327. For Charles's knowing of Louis' dealings with the opposition, see *HMC Finch*, II.38; Browning, *Danby*, II.314–15, 319, 325 (the second and third of these were intercepted by the French: there are copies in CPA 127, under the dates 21 and 28 Jan. 1678).

65. BT 137, Barrillon 9 Dec. 1677; BT 138, same 7 Feb.; CPA 127, same to Pomponne 6 Jan. 1678.

66. BL Add MS 29571 fo. 434; *HMC Ormond*, NS IV.390; BT 137, Barrillon 20 Dec. 1677; BT 138, same 17, 24 and 31 Jan., 3 Feb. 1678; Browning, *Danby*, II.328, 331–2; Prinsterer, V.362; *CSPD 1677–8*, pp. 517–18; *HMC Finch*, II.38.

67. Browning, *Danby*, II.326; BT 138, Barrillon 27 Jan. and 7 Feb. 1678.

68. Temple, I.457; see also *HMC Ormond*, NS IV.395; *CSPD 1677–8*, p. 517; Haley, 'Rapprochement', p. 647.

69. BT 138, Barrillon 13 Jan. and 9 March 1678; CSPV (cont), Sarotti 24 Dec. 1677 and 8 April 1678.

70. *Letters*, pp. 288–90. Burgomano was offended by the comment about Spain: BT 138, Barrillon 9 Feb. 1678.

71. Grey, V.18–32, 37–46; *CJ*, IX.430; *HMC Ormond*, NS IV.396–8; *CSPD 1677–8*, pp. 608–9.

72. *HMC Ormond*, NS IV.396–7; BT 138, Barrillon 10 Feb.; CSPV (cont), Sarotti 14 Feb. 1678; *CJ*, IX.431–2.

73. Grey, V.81, 77. See also *ibid.*, pp. 77–95; Carte MS 72 fos 346–7.

74. *CJ*, IX.433, 438, 441.

75. BT 138, Barrillon 9 Feb. 1678; Temple, I.458.

76. Reresby, p. 131; Grey, V.148–53.

77. CPA 123, Courtin to Pomponne 26 April 1677; Finch MS PP 42, p. 20; Althorp MS C5, Thomas Thynne to Halifax 27 May 1677; Haley, 'Rapprochement', p. 631.

78. BT 138, Barrillon 3 March 1678; *HMC Ormond*, NS IV.399; Carte MS 72 fos 359–62.

79. Grey, V.223–48, 261–2; *CJ*, IX.455, 460; Carte MS 72 fos 359–62; Pforz, Coleman to Bulstrode 15 March; CSPV (cont), Sarotti 1 and 8 April 1678; *HMC Ormond*, NS IV.416–20.

80. Browning, *Danby*, II.422; *HMC Ormond*, Old Series I.23, NS IV.405; Grey, V.181–2, 210–13; Marvell, II.220; Pforz, Coleman to Bulstrode 1 March 1678; Chandaman, pp. 169–70.

81. *HMC Ormond*, NS IV.408, 412–14; Dalrymple, II(a), pp. 134–5. For Coventry's exclusion from foreign policy decisions, see Browning, *Danby*, II.279, 303, 308. For uncertainty about the king's intentions, see Browning, *Danby*, II.421; *HMC Ormond*, IV.107; *HMC Finch*, II.41.

82. Dalrymple, II(a), p. 152; Grey, V.181–8, 199–200; *CSPD 1678*, p. 98; BT 139, Barrillon 7 April 1678. The ban on French imports was widely evaded: Burnet, *Hist.*, II.123. See also Chandaman, pp. 152–3, 188.

83. BT 138, Barrillon 9 and 24 Feb., 9 March; CSPV (cont), Sarotti 25 Feb. 1678; Browning, *Danby*, II.341–2; *HMC Ormond*, NS IV.403–4, 408; Campana, I.211–12;

Lauderdale, III.107; Dalrymple, II(a), pp. 131–2, 134–5; Clarke, *James II*, I.513; Grey, V.202–7.

84. BL Add MS 28040 fos 47–8; Browning, *Danby*, II.418–20, 425–8; *HMC Ormond*, NS IV.409; SP 104/180 fo. 146; Dalrymple, II(a), pp. 149–50.

85. BL Add MSS 28040 fos 46, 48–50, 52–4, 56, 28053 fo. 59; Browning, *Danby*, II.415, 430–1, 576–9; SP 104/180 fos 148, 150, 192; Cov MS 83 fo. 133; *CSPD 1678*, pp. 78–9; Temple, I.460–1; *HMC Ormond*, NS IV.136, 422; Dalrymple, II(a), p. 155.

86. BL Add MS 28040 fo. 57; SP 104/180 fos 219–20.

87. *HMC Ormond*, NS IV.410.

88. Temple, I.457–60; Browning, *Danby*, II.339, 350–1, 424–5, 578–9; BT 138, Barrillon 13 and 26 March; CPA 128, same to Pomponne 12 April 1678; *CSPD 1678*, p. 61; BL Add MS 28040 fo. 52.

89. CSPV (cont), Sarotti 15 April; BT 139, Barrillon 18 April 1678.

90. BT 138, Barrillon 9, 10 (two letters) and 21 March 1678.

91. BT 138, Barrillon 14 and 19 Feb., 28 and 31 March 1678.

92. BT 139, Barrillon 4 and 11 April 1678; Browning, *Danby*, II.345–9.

93. BT 139, Barrillon 4, 7, 11, 14 and 28 April 1678; Dalrymple, II(a), pp. 142–3.

94. BT 139, Barrillon 18 April and 5 May 1678; SP 104/180 fo. 231.

95. BT 138, Barrillon 9 and 26 March; BT 139, same 7 April 1678; Dalrymple, II(a), pp. 142–3.

96. Macpherson, I.85; BT 138, Barrillon 19 and 24 Feb. 1678; *HMC Ormond*, NS IV.105–6, 401; Browning, *Danby*, II.341–2.

97. SP 104/180 fos 179 (quoted), 192, 219–20, 231, 235; CSPV (cont), Sarotti 6 May 1678. The narrative is in BL Add MS 28040 fos 35–57. See also CPA 128, Barrillon to Pomponne 24 March 1678.

98. *CJ*, IX.464–6.

99. *Ibid.*, pp. 463–4, 471; Grey, V.279–87 (Birch's comment is on p. 283); Carte MS 72 fos 382–3; *HMC Ormond*, NS IV.422. For Norfolk, see BL Add MS 36540 fo. 27; *CSPD 1678*, p. 45.

100. BT 139, Barrillon 9 May 1678; Temple, I.461.

101. Grey, V.289–90, 292–303, 305–14, '321'[recte 337]–61.

102. *Ibid.*, pp. 297–301; Finch MS PP 42, p. 29; Althorp MS C4, William Coventry to Halifax 19 Aug. 1678.

103. Grey, V.319–34, '321'[337]–61.

104. BT 139, Barrillon 9 May 1678; Temple, I.461–2.

105. Mignet, IV.572–5, 578–81; BT 139, Barrillon 12, 19, 21, 23 and 28 May; CPA 129, same to Louvois 12 May and to Pomponne 19 and 28 May 1678.

106. BT 139, Barrillon 12 May 1678.

107. Dalrymple, II(a), pp. 172–5; Browning, *Danby*, II.422–3; SP 104/180 fos 266–7; Lauderdale, III.146.

108. Dalrymple, II(a), p. 174; BL Add MS 23242 fo. 40; Lauderdale, III.131–2, 139–41, 149–51; *CSPD 1678*, p. 193.

109. BT 139, Barrillon 22 and 23 May 1678; Grey, V.361–82, 390; BL Add MS 18730 fo. 37; *HMC Ormond*, NS IV.425.

110. SP 104/180 fos 278–9; BL Add MS 29571 fo. 472; CPA 129, Barrillon to Pomponne 19 May 1678. Danby wrote to Montagu that Charles was having negotiations with Barrillon of which he (Danby) was not informed: Browning, *Danby*, II.360.

111. SP 104/180 fo. 295; BT 139, Barrillon 30 May 1678; *CJ*, IX.481.

112. Grey, VI.3–13, 16–21; *HMC Ormond*, NS IV.425–8; BL Add MS 25125 fos 51–2.

113. Grey, VI.26–7, 29–31, 35–7.

114. Browning, *Danby*, II.433–4; BT 139, Barrillon 9, 16 and 23 June; CSPV (cont), Sarotti 10 June 1678.

115. *CJ*, IX.488, 493; Grey, VI.71–8, 83–6; *HMC Ormond*, NS IV.431–2.
116. *Letters*, pp. 295–8.
117. Grey, VI.96–105; *HMC Ormond*, NS IV.434–8; BL Add MS 63057B fos 40–1; *CJ*, IX.500; BT 139, Barrillon 29 June 1678.
118. *CJ*, IX.502–3; *HMC Ormond*, NS IV.439–40; BL Add MS 29571 fos 488–9; Chandaman, p. 154. For Charles's hopes of living at his ease, see BT 139, Barrillon 23 June 1678.
119. BT 139, Barrillon 29 June; CPA 129, same to Pomponne 30 June 1678; *CJ*, IX.502, 506; *HMC Ormond*, NS IV.152–3, 440.
120. CSPV (cont), Sarotti 8 July 1678; *HMC Bath*, II.164 (quoted); Temple, I.463–4; *HMC Ormond*, NS IV.160; Dalrymple, II(a), p. 182.
121. BT 140, Barrillon 4, 5, 7 and 11 July 1678; *HMC Ormond*, NS IV.159.
122. BT 139, Barrillon 7, 11 and 14 June 1678; SP 104/180 fo. 365 (quoted).
123. Browning, *Danby*, II.563–4; Mignet, IV.575. See also P. Sonnino, 'Arnauld de Pomponne and the Dutch War', *Proceedings of the Western Society for French History* I (1974), pp. 54–6.
124. Rochester, p. 200; *HMC Ormond*, NS IV.200; Reresby, p. 149.
125. *CJ*, IX.509, 511; *HMC Ormond*, NS IV.161; Morrice, p. 90; Dalrymple, II(a), p. 185.
126. *CSPD 1678*, p. 282; BT 140, Barrillon 18, 21, 23 and 25 July 1678.
127. Browning, *Danby*, II.436–7; *CSPD 1678*, pp. 309–11; Temple, I.464–70; BL Add MS 25119 fos 35–6; BT 140, Barrillon 1 Sept. 1678; K. H. D. Haley, 'English Policy at the Peace of Nijmegen', in J. H. Bots (ed.), *The Peace of Nijmegen* (Amsterdam, 1979), pp. 153–4.
128. Dalrymple, II(a), p. 189; SP 104/180 fo. 409; *HMC 7th Report*, p. 470; Browning, *Danby*, II.532.
129. Browning, *Danby*, II.526–7, 533–4; BT 140, Barrillon 15, 18 and 22 Aug.; CPA 130, same to Pomponne 25 Aug. 1678.
130. Browning, *Danby*, II.437–8, 495–6, 531; Temple, I.473–4.
131. Pforz, Coleman to Bulstrode 9 Aug. 1678; Temple, I.470.
132. BT 140, Barrillon 29 Aug., 12 and 19 Sept.; CPA 130, same to Pomponne 8 Sept. 1678; *HMC Ormond*, NS IV.448.
133. BT 140, Barrillon 8 and 22 Aug., 26 Sept. 1678.
134. Dalrymple, II(a), pp. 178–9; Browning, *Danby*, II.533–4, 537–8, 545–6; BT 140, Barrillon 12 and 15 Sept.; CPA 130, same to Pomponne 29 Aug. 1678 (details are given on fos 245–7).
135. Browning, *Danby*, II.531. The towns which Louis eventually restored included Charleroi, Ath, Oudenarde, Courtrai and Ghent.
136. CPA 130, Barrillon to Pomponne 15 Sept. 1678; Savile, p. 71; *HMC Ormond*, NS IV.195.
137. *CSPD 1678*, pp. 414–15, 418; BT 141, Barrillon 3 Oct. 1678.

Chapter 11: 'Forty-one Is Come Again'

1. Carte MS 39 fo. 1; Burnet, *Hist.*, II.232–3; see also *CSPD 1679–80*, p. 21; Browning, *Danby*, II.85–6.
2. BL Add MS 41568 fo. 35; *CSPD 1678*, p. 497; BT 141, Barrillon 29 Dec. 1678; BT 142, same 5 Jan.; BT 143, same 8 June 1679; Carte MS 72 fo. 429; Burnet, *Hist.*, II.168–9.
3. *POAS*, II.186.
4. *HMC Ormond*, NS IV.536 (quoted); Morrice, p. 95; Carte MS 38 fos 617, 664.
5. D. Allen, 'The Role of the London Trained Bands in the Exclusion Crisis', *EHR* LXXXVII (1972), pp. 287–303; Morrice, p. 104; *HMC Ormond*, NS IV.495; *CSPD 1678*, p. 595.
6. CPA 133, Barrillon to Pomponne 30 Jan.; BT 143, Barrillon 5 June 1679; Browning, *Danby*, II.82–4; *HMC Ormond*, NS IV.515–16.

7. BL Add MS 29572 fo. 156 (quoted); *CSPD 1679–80*, pp. 243–4; *HMC Ormond*, IV.535–6; *HMC 7th Report*, p. 475; Carte MS 228 fo. 103. For other evidence of disorder, see CUL Add MS 4878 fo. 612; *HMC Ormond*, NS IV, p. xx; Harris, *London Crowds*, ch. 7. On London in 1641–2, see V. Pearl, *London and the Outbreak of the Puritan Revolution* (Oxford, 1961), esp. ch. IV.

8. Kenyon, *Constitution*, p. 2; *HMC Ormond*, NS IV.485. Charles I declared in 1642 that he would not allow the militia out of his control for an hour: I. Roots, *The Great Rebellion 1642–60* (London, 1966), p. 57.

9. For Danby, see Savile, p. 78; *HMC Ormond*, NS IV.291. For Charles's views on Strafford, see *HMC Ormond*, NS IV.495.

10. *POAS*, II.375–9. The bill was rejected by thirty-three votes and there were only twenty-six bishops.

11. *HMC Ormond*, NS IV.207; *CSPD 1678*, p. 432; *LJ*, XIII.309; Clarke, *James II*, I.520–1. For Oates's career, see Kenyon, *Plot*, pp. 46–7. For his narrative, see *LJ*, XIII.313–20; *State Trials*, VI.1429–72. Bedloe too exonerated York at first, but later changed his mind; see Rawl MS A136, p. 351.

12. BT 141, Barrillon 10 and 13 Oct. 1678; Clarke, *James II*, I.546; Temple, I.480; Burnet, *Hist.*, II.145, 168.

13. BL Add MS 38847 fo. 205; PC 2/66, p. 396; BT 141, Barrillon 10 and 13 Oct., 7 Nov. 1678; Reresby, p. 153; *HMC Ormond*, NS IV.207; Clarke, *James II*, I.546.

14. 'Mr Coleman's Two Letters to Monsieur La Chaise' [1678], in *State Tracts* (1689), I.145.

15. BL Add MS 25124 fo. 155; *HMC Ormond*, NS IV.212, 380, 457–9; Miller, 'Coleman'.

16. See the discussion in Kenyon, *Plot*, pp. 264–70.

17. BL Add MS 32095 fo. 119; *CSPD 1678*, pp. 451, 462, 562–3; BT 141, Barrillon 20 and 31 Oct. 1678; Kenyon, *Plot*, ch. 4.

18. BL Add MS 38015 fo. 279. See also Miller, *Popery*, pp. 158–9.

19. *CJ*, IX.516.

20. *HMC Ormond*, NS IV.460–1.

21. *Ibid.*, pp. 479–80.

22. CPA 131, Barrillon: Memorial of events in Parliament 8 Nov. 1678; Burnet, *Hist.*, II.167; BL Add MS 63057B fo. 34. Needless to say, the account of Coleman's examination in *LJ*, XIII.307–8, does not mention Charles's alleged approval of these negotiations.

23. *HMC Ormond*, NS IV.458–60, 482–3; BL Add MS 38847 fo. 238; CPA 131, Barrillon to Pomponne 31 Oct. 1678; Grey, VI.149–51; CSPV (cont), Sarotti 11 Nov. 1678; Miller, 'Coleman', p. 272.

24. Carte MSS 38 fo. 682, 39 fo. 1; BT 142, Barrillon 5 and 26 Jan. 1679; *HMC Ormond* NS IV.492–3, 495–7; Browning, *Danby*, II.501; PC 2/67, p. 6; *CSPD 1679–80*, pp. 7, 27. For the trials, see Kenyon, *Plot, passim*.

25. Miller, *Popery*, p. 163; *HMC Ormond*, NS IV.478–9; Grey, VI.264–5.

26. Grey, VI.278, 190; also *ibid.*, pp. 266–7; BT 141, Barrillon 24 Nov. 1678.

27. Grey, VI.172–3, 278–85, 329–35; *CJ*, IX.548; BT 141, Barrillon 8 Dec. 1678; *HMC Ormond*, NS IV.468, 487–9.

28. Grey, VI.212–16, 270–1; Finch MS PP 57(ii), p. 29; *HMC Ormond*, NS IV.475; *CJ*, IX.544–5, 547.

29. Grey, VI.300–4; *HMC Ormond*, NS IV.257–8, 485; Finch MS PP 57(ii), p. 49. For the clause in question see *HMC House of Lords 1678–81*, pp. 64–5.

30. *HMC Ormond*, NS IV.473–4; North, *Examen*, p. 206; Finch MS 57(iii), p. 4; Carte MS 38 fo. 664; Burnet, *Hist.*, II.167–8; BL Add MS 63057B fo. 44.

31. Grey, VI.305–14, 316–20; *HMC Ormond*, NS IV.264–5, 486–7; Finch MS PP 57(ii), p. 51; *CSPD 1678*, p. 554; *CJ*, IX.552.

32. Grey, VI.268–70; Finch MS PP 57(ii), pp. 17–18, 21, 47, 51; Temple, I.480; *HMC Ormond*, NS IV.493.

33. *HMC Ormond*, NS IV.477–8; Finch MS PP 57(ii), p. 32; BT 141, Barrillon 7 Nov. 1678.

34. BT 140, Barrillon 26 Sept.; BT 141, same 27 Oct., 3, 7 and 17 Nov. 1678; *HMC Ormond*, NS IV.466; Reresby, pp. 157–8, 161.

35. BT 141, Barrillon 24 Nov. 1678; Burnet, *Hist.*, II.169; Carte MS 38 fo. 653.

36. Finch MS PP 57(ii), pp. 15–21; Grey, VI.133–49; BT 141, Barrillon 14 [partly printed Campana, I.228] and 24 Nov.; CPA 131, same to Pomponne 21 Nov. 1678; Clarke, *James II*, I.524–5.

37. Clarke, *James II*, I.490; Macpherson, I.79; *HMC Savile Foljambe*, p. 124; CPA 131, Barrillon to Pomponne 1 Dec. 1678; Grey, VI.240–53.

38. Grey, VI.133–48, esp. p. 148, 236; Finch MS PP 57 (ii), pp. 16A–B, 17–18.

39. Grey, VI.136, 140.

40. *HMC Ormond*, NS IV.467, 479; *CJ*, IX.536; Grey, VI.172–3; Reresby, p. 157; Finch MS PP 57(ii), p. 24. For the Association, see P. Collinson, 'The Monarchical Republic of Elizabeth I', *Bulletin of the John Rylands Library* LXIX (1987).

41. CPA 128, Barrillon to Pomponne 17 March; Rochester, p. 189; Burnet, *Hist.*, II.165n.

42. *CSPD 1678*, p. 516; BT 141, Barrillon 24 Nov. 1678.

43. *HMC Ormond*, NS IV.245, 255, 480–1; Finch MS PP 57(ii), p. 47; BT 141, Barrillon 12 Dec. 1678; Burnet, *Hist.*, II.169–70; BL Add MS 63057B fo. 45; Kenyon, *Plot*, pp. 109–15.

44. Essex, II.120–2, 126–8; Clarke, *James II*, I.507; Stowe MS 212 fo. 13; BL Add MS 29571 fo. 392.

45. Macpherson, I.85; Clarke, *James II*, I.497–8; BT 139, Barrillon 2 May 1678.

46. Lauderdale, III.120–2, 152–3, 241–2; BT 139, Barrillon 13 June 1678.

47. CPA 131, Barrillon to Pomponne 21 Nov. 1678; *HMC Ormond*, NS IV.470, 476; Finch MS PP 57(ii), p. 30.

48. BT 141, Barrillon 22 Dec.; CPA 131, same to Pomponne 24 Nov. 1678; Clarke, *James II*, I.525–6, 530; Burnet, *Hist.*, II.168–9.

49. Carte MS 38 fo. 678; *HMC Ormond*, NS IV.470, 486; Burnet, *Hist.*, II.145; Dalrymple, II(a), p. 320.

50. CPA 103, Croissy to Pomponne 7 April 1672.

51. Harl MS 7006 fos 171–6; Burnet, *Hist.*, II.140–1.

52. BL Add MS 21505 fos 32–8; Rochester, pp. 200–1; CPA 130, Barrillon to Pomponne 11 and 18 July, Memorandum about the court 25 July 1678; Hatton, I.167–8; Finch MS PP 57(ii), p. 11.

53. Dalrymple II(a), pp. 193–5; *HMC Ormond*, NS IV.471; Finch MS PP 57(ii), p. 56; PC 2/66, p. 483; *CSPD 1678*, p. 579; BT 141, Barrillon 29 Dec. 1678; BT 142, same 5 Jan. 1679.

54. Grey, VI.355–6; Reresby, p. 163; Burnet, *Hist.*, II.175–6.

55. Grey, VI.152–3, 359–64; Finch MS PP 57(ii), pp. 22, 64.

56. Carte MS 38 fos 682–3; *HMC Ormond*, NS IV.290–1, 491–3, 495; *CJ*, IX.562; BT 142, Barrillon 2 and 9 Jan. 1679. For Fox, see C. Clay, *Public Finance and Private Wealth: The Career of Sir Stephen Fox* (Oxford, 1978).

57. *CJ*, IX.555, 563, 565; BT 142, Barrillon 9 Jan. 1679; Finch MS PP 57(ii), p. 71; *HMC Ormond*, NS IV.494–5; Carte MS 39 fo. 1; Morrice, p. 104; Prinsterer, V.367–8.

58. *HMC Ormond*, NS IV.295, 316; Hatton, I.175; BL Add MS 25358 fo. 139.

59. *HMC Ormond*, NS IV.324–5, 329–30; CPA 133, Barrillon to Pomponne 9 March 1679; Burnet, *Hist.*, II.176–7; Temple, I.479–80. For Sunderland, see J. P. Kenyon's admirable *Sunderland*.

60. BT 142, Barrillon 26 Jan. 1679; Finch MS PP 57(iii), p. 6; Temple, I.332, 479; Carte MS 39 fo. 21. For one who did not believe in the Plot, see *HMC Ormond*, NS IV.329.

61. Carte MS 39 fo. 1; BL Add MS 63057B fo. 47; Kenyon, *Plot*, pp. 126–8.

62. *HMC Ormond*, NS IV.497; BT 142, Barrillon 26 Jan.; CPA 133, same to Pomponne 2 Feb. 1679; Rawl MS A136 p. 106; Hatton, I.173–4; PC 2/67, p. 96. For one item in Dugdale's evidence which Charles is not likely to have believed, see Burnet, *Hist.*, II.180–1.

63. Carte MS 39 fo. 1; CPA 133, Barrillon to Pomponne 16 Jan. 1679.

64. For fear of France, see *HMC Ormond*, NS IV.245, 274, 302; Carte MS 38 fo. 678. For scepticism, even among those friendly to the court, see BL Add MS 29577 fo. 181; Finch MS PP 57(iii), p. 5.

65. BT 142, Barrillon 12 and 19 Jan., 9, 16 and 27 Feb.; CPA 133, same to Pomponne 16 Jan. and 2 March 1679; All Souls MS 171 fo. 6; Dalrymple II(a), p. 206.

66. BT 142, Barrillon 26 Jan. and 9 Feb. 1679; Reresby, p. 168; CUL Add MS 4836 fo. 65; Finch MS PP 57(iii), p. 6; BL Add MS 28053 fo. 133; *Morrison Letters* 1st series, I.181–2; Carte MS 39 fo. 21.

67. BT 142, Barrillon 26 Jan.; CPA 133, same to Pomponne 3 Feb. 1679.

68. Finch MS PP 57(iii), pp. 4–5; BT 142, Barrillon 6 Feb.; CPA 133, same to Pomponne 30 Jan. 1679; Carte MSS 39 fo. 5, 221 fo. 130; *HMC Ormond*, NS IV.308; *CSPD 1679–80*, p. 52.

69. BT 142, Barrillon 12 Jan. 1679; *HMC Ormond*, NS IV.311; Hatton, I.170–1 (but see also p. 172); All Souls MS 171 fo. 12; Carte MS 39 fo. 13; BL Add MSS 29556 fo. 431, 29577 fo. 180.

70. BL Add MS 29556 fo. 431; *HMC Ormond*, NS IV.309, 317, 325; Carte MS 39 fo. 13; Cov MS 7 fo. 148. Some of the comments on the campaign are based on a seminar paper by Mark Knights, which drew on some of the research for his Oxford DPhil. thesis.

71. BL Add 29910 fo. 76; Campana, I.207; *Diary of Dr Edward Lake*, ed. G. P. Elliott, p. 19 in *Camden Miscellany* I (1847); N. Crew, *Memoirs*, pp. 16–17, in *Camden Miscellany* IX.

72. *Clar Corr*, II.466; Clarke, *James II*, I.537–9; Dalrymple, II(a), pp. 213–14.

73. Clarke, *James II*, I.513, 540–1; Macpherson, I.79, 92; BT 142, Barrillon 13 March; CPA 133, same 9 March 1679; *HMC Ormond* Old Series I.27; *Letters*, pp. 304–5; PC 2/67, p. 12. For Danby's attempts to blame everything on York, see Browning, *Danby*, II.90–3.

74. Burnet, *Hist.*, II.184; *Letters*, pp. 305–7.

75. Hatton, I.179–80; *HMC Ormond*, NS IV.346–7, 498.

76. Hatton, I.178–80; *HMC Ormond*, NS IV.346–7, 498–9; BL Add MS 29557 fo. 121; *HMC Finch*, II.47; Burnet, *Hist.*, II.195; CPA 133, Barrillon to Pomponne 23 March 1679; Browning, *Danby* II.71–2.

77. Carte MS 38 fos 617, 683; BT 142, Barrillon 27 March 1679; Browning, *Danby*, II.112–14; Grey, VII.19.

78. *HMC Ormond*, NS IV.xviii–xxi, 359, 500 (quoted).

79. Burnet, *Hist.*, II.196–7; Grey, VII.20–30; *HMC Ormond*, NS IV.500; Carte MS 72 fo. 456. The last item, a speech by Winnington, can also be found in similar form in Lansdowne MS 1064 fo. 77, but doubts were expressed as to whether he actually delivered it: Herts. RO, Gorhambury MSS XII B44.

80. Browning, *Danby*, II.76–7.

81. *HMC Ormond*, NS V.32–3, 38, 48–9; Morrice, p. 154. For a suggestion that Charles sent word that he wished the bill to pass, see CPA 134 fo. 90.

82. Campana, I.265–7; Clarke, *James II*, I.550–2; Dalrymple, II(a), pp. 217–18.

83. Carte MS 228 fo. 151; BT 142, Barrillon 17 and 20 April; CPA 134, same to Pomponne 10 April 1679; BL Add MS 25125 fo. 61; *HMC Ormond*, NS IV.502–3.

84. Temple, I.333–4; Burnet, *Hist.*, II.198–200; PC 2/68, pp. 1–2; BT 142, Barrillon 27 April and 1 May 1679; Ailesbury, I.35.

85. Temple, I.335–8; North, *Lives of Norths*, I.70; North, *Examen*, pp. 75–8; *HMC Ormond*, NS V.57; Grey, VII.268; Sidney, *Letters to Savile*, p. 83; JRL, Legh of Lyme Correspondence, John Chicheley to Richard Legh 31 May 1679.

86. BL Add MS 29572 fo. 119.

87. BT 142, Barrillon 27 April 1679; *HMC Ormond*, NS V.38, 68; BL Add MS 29572 fos 114–16; Grey, VII.221–2, 228–9, 233–6.

88. *HMC Ormond*, NS V.84–6; Grey, VII.227; Morrice, pp. 180–1.

89. Hatton, I.186; *HMC Ormond*, NS V.48–9; Morrice, p. 160.

90. Cov MS 7 fo. 150; Grey VII.150; Morrice, p. 164; *HMC Ormond*, NS IV.510.

91. *HMC Ormond*, NS IV.511, V.97–9, 103–4, 108; Burnet, *Hist.*, II.210, 215.

92. *HMC Ormond*, NS V.88–90, 102–4, 115–16; Grey, VII.292–3, 301, 325–6; *HMC 7th Report*, p. 472; BT 143, Barrillon 5 June 1679.

93. *HMC Ormond*, NS IV.xx, V.116.

94. PC 2/67, p. 131; Morrice, pp. 158, 164; *HMC Ormond*, NS IV.xix; Staffs. RO, D(W)1778/I/i/499; Tanner MS 38 fo. 26.

95. BT 142, Barrillon 4 May 1679; *HMC Ormond*, NS V.55–6, 66–7; Morrice, p. 173; *LJ*, XIII.545, 549.

96. PC 2/67, pp. 123, 131; PC 2/68, p. 20; *RB*, part III, p. 187; Dalrymple, II(a), p. 220. Charles's speech (*Letters*, p. 305) talked of uniting Protestants at home and abroad, but it was not clear whether he meant a religious union, as some thought (Tanner MS 39 fo. 211) or a political one.

97. Grey, VII.64–73, 112–13, 268–70; *HMC Ormond*, NS IV, pp. xxi, 508–9, 513, V.7–8, 106; BT 142, Barrillon 8 May 1679; North, *Examen*, pp. 75–8; North, *Lives of Norths*, I.234–5; Glassey, pp. 41–4.

98. Grey, VII.138–52; *HMC Ormond*, NS IV.506–8. For earlier hints of anxiety about the danger from a Catholic successor, see Grey, VI.437; Pforz, account of proceedings on 12 March 1679.

99. *CJ*, IX.607–8; *HMC Ormond*, NS V.74–5.

100. Burnet, *Hist.*, II.200–2; BL Add MS 63057B fo. 49; Grey, VII.251–2; *HMC Ormond*, NS IV.506, V.96; *HMC Finch*, II.52.

101. Burnet, *Hist.*, II.203. See also Grey, VII.160–1, 243.

102. Sidney, *Letters to Savile*, pp. 67–8; *HMC Ormond*, NS IV.511–17, V.96–9, 110; Sidney, *Diary*, I.2; Tanner MS 38 fo. 26; Grey, VII.238, 313–14; BT 143, Barrillon 1 June 1679; *CJ*, IX.626–7.

103. Ailesbury, I.36–7; BT 142, Barrillon 29 May 1679; Clarke, *James II*, I.533.

104. *HMC Ormond*, NS IV.515–16; Browning, *Danby*, II.82–3; BT 142, Barrillon 20 April; BT 143, same 1 and 15 June, 13 July; CPA 133, same to Pomponne 20 March 1679.

105. BT 143, Barrillon 1, 5 and 8 June 1679; Browning, *Danby*, II.82–3; Campana, I.271; Dalrymple, II(a), pp. 220–1; Clarke, *James II*, I.554; Temple, I.338; *CJ*, IX.617–18; *HMC Ormond*, NS IV.518–20, V.116, 121.

106. *SR*, V.930: *CJ*, IX.598.

107. *CJ*, IX.608–9; *HMC Ormond*, NS IV.514; Haley, *Shaftesbury*, pp. 526–8.

108. Burnet, *Hist.*, II.215–16 (quoted); *HMC Ormond*, NS IV.520–1.

109. BT 143, Barrillon 8 and 19 June 1679; Temple, I.338; Tanner MS 38 fo. 37; *HMC Ormond*, NS IV.520; *HMC 7th Report*, p. 472.

110. Browning, *Danby*, II.84–8; BL Add MS 28042 fos 19–20; Clarke, *James II*, I.554; Dalrymple, II(a), pp. 224–5.

111. BT 143, Barrillon 13 July and 25 Sept. 1679; *HMC Ormond*, NS IV.520, 530; Sidney, *Diary*, I.2, 15; Temple, I.339.

112. BT 142, Barrillon 20 April; BT 143, same 13 July and 14 Sept. 1679; Pforz, — to Bulstrode 22 Sept. 1679.

113. Browning, *Danby*, II.86; Sidney, *Letters to Savile*, p. 131; *HMC Hastings*, II.388; Clarke, *James II*, I.556–8; Carte MS 198 fo. 54; *HMC Dartmouth*, I.36–7.

114. BT 141, Barrillon 17 Nov., 12 and 22 Dec. 1678; BT 142, same 12 Jan. and 8 May;

BT 143, same 6 and 13 July, 3 and 31 Aug., 14 and 21 Sept., 2, 5 and 9 Oct. 1679; CPA 134, same to Pomponne 18 May; CPA 135, same to same 31 July and 3 Aug.; CPA 136, same to same 5 Oct. 1679; BL Add MS 29572 fo. 120. Barrillon first reported Sunderland as involved in the negotiations in his letter to Louis of 31 Aug.; Hyde was first mentioned in that of 9 Oct.

115. *HMC Ormond*, NS IV.520–1, 529, 538, V.147, 151; BT 143, Barrillon 12 June and 6 July 1679; Sidney, *Letters to Savile*, pp. 77–8, 131; Tanner MS 38 fo. 37.

116. *HMC Ormond*, NS IV.522–4, V.133, 136–7; Morrice, pp. 195, 208; Cov MS 16 fo. 110; Temple I.339–40; *HMC 7th Report*, p. 472; *CSPD 1679–80*, pp. 201–2; BL Add MS 25359 fos 69–70; CPA 135, Barrillon to Pomponne 3 Aug. 1679.

117. *SR*, V.577; BL Add MS 25124 fo. 199; *HMC Ormond*, NS IV.528; PC 2/68, pp. 60, 94, 203.

118. Clarke, *James II*, I.558; *HMC Ormond*, NS IV.526, 530, 535, V.140; Morrice, p. 207; Nottingham University Library, MS PwV 51, Blathwayt to Southwell 15 July 1679; Kenyon, *Plot*, pp. 168–76.

119. *HMC 7th Report*, p. 474; Ailesbury, I.31; Temple, I.339; BL Add MS 29910 fo. 114; Burnet, *Hist.*, II.220; Kenyon, *Plot*, pp. 177–8 and ch. 6 *passim*.

120. Carte MS 198 fo. 54; Pforz, — to Bulstrode [end May, but placed before 12 Dec. 1679]; BL Add MS 18730 fo. 57; Temple, I.340–1; *HMC Ormond*, NS IV.530–1, V.119, 152; PC 2/68, p. 168.

121. Althorp MS C5, Sir W. Coventry to Halifax and Sir Thomas Thynne to same, both 12 July 1679; Temple, I.340–1; BL Add MS 29910 fo. 112; Carte MS 198 fo. 54; Barrillon thought Sunderland, Essex and Halifax were responsible for the dissolution: BT 143, Barrillon 24 July 1679.

122. Sidney, *Diary*, I.28; *HMC Ormond*, NS V.152; Althorp MS C5, Thynne to Halifax 12 July 1679; Tanner MS 38 fo. 72.

123. Burnet, *Hist.*, II.210–12; Cov MS 7 fos 150, 152, 164; Morrice, p. 164; Tanner MS 38 fos 22, 45; BL Add MS 36988 fo. 149 (quoted); *A Faithful and Impartial Account of the Behaviour of a Party of the Essex Freeholders* (1679). For similar language in the first 1679 election, again in Norfolk, see Tanner MSS 39 fo. 179, 39* fo. 174.

124. Cov MS 7 fo. 160; Carte MS 39 fos 64, 68; *HMC Ormond*, NS IV.535.

125. Cov MS 2 fo. 177; Hatton, I.189–90; *HMC Ormond*, NS V.191; CPA 135, Barrillon to Pomponne 4 Sept. 1679; Carte MS 228 fo. 121; Clarke, *James II*, I.564–5; Macpherson, I.93–4; Burnet, *Hist.*, II.232; Temple, I.342–3; Reresby, p. 187; *HMC Savile Foljambe*, p. 137. The fact that Charles responded to quinine suggests that the fever may have been malarial.

126. Temple, I.344; Hatton, I.189–93; *HMC Ormond*, NS V.197; Clarke, *James II*, I.567–8; Sidney, *Diary*, I.101; Campana, I.295–6, 299–300; Dalrymple, II(a), p. 247; *HMC Fitzherbert*, p. 21; CPA 135, Barrillon to Pomponne 18 Sept. 1679.

127. Cov MS 6 fo. 127; Clarke, *James II*, I.571–2; Burnet, *Hist.*, II.237; *HMC Ormond*, NS IV.536; Sidney, *Diary*, I.154–5; BT 143, Barrillon 21 Sept. and 2 Oct.; CPA 135, same to Pomponne 28 Sept. 1679. James later claimed (Clarke I.568) that it was Sunderland who proposed that Monmouth should go as well; this is very plausible given the hostility towards Sunderland shown by Shaftesbury and Monmouth. However, James wrote to William that he himself had suggested the idea to Charles (Dalrymple, II(a), p. 248) while Halifax claimed that he had advised it (Warcup, p. 243).

128. Carte MS 228 fo. 103; *CSPD 1679–80*, p. 240; *HMC 7th Report*, p. 475; BL Add MS 29572 fo. 156 (quoted); Hatton, I.194–5; CPA 135, Barrillon to Pomponne 25 and 28 Sept. 1679.

129. *HMC Ormond*, NS IV.535–6; BL Add MSS 29557 fo. 260, 29572 fo. 140; All Souls MS 171 fo. 60; *CSPD 1679–80*, pp. 243–4; *HMC 7th Report*, p. 475.

130. BT 143, Barrillon 2 and 5 Oct. 1679.

131. *HMC Ormond*, NS IV.532–3, 535–9; Carte MS 39 fo. 68; Pforz, John Ellis to Bulstrode 26 Sept. 1679; Temple, I.344; Burnet, *Hist.*, II.236–7; *HMC 7th Report*, p. 475.

Chapter 12: Tory and Whig

1. Browning, *Documents*, p. 66; *HMC Ormond*, NS IV.565; *HMC 7th Report*, p. 496.
2. Carte MS 228 fo. 140; PC 2/68, p. 343; Sidney, *Diary*, I.248.
3. *HMC Ormond*, NS IV.569, 574, 576; BL Add MSS 29572 fo. 180, 29577 fo. 227; Morrice, pp. 246, 248; Carte MS 228 fo. 153; Pforz, — to Bulstrode [23] Jan. 1680; Sidney, *Diary*, I.248; *Hatton*, I.218.
4. *CSPD 1679–80*, pp. 400, 414; Sidney, *Diary*, I.301–2; *HMC le Fleming*, p. 166; BL Add MS 36988 fos 133–4; Hatton, I.224. Clayton had been removed from the commission of the peace for Surrey: BL Add MS 29572 fo. 211.
5. Morrice, p. 258; BL Add MS 29572 fo. 239; UCL MS 268, Godolphin to Bulstrode 16 July 1680.
6. BT 146, Barrillon 8 and 29 July 1680; Prinsterer V.410; *HMC Ormond*, V.349; UCL MS 268, Godolphin to Bulstrode 16 July 1680.
7. UCL MS 268, Godolphin to Bulstrode 25 June 1680; *CSPD 1679–80*, p. 565; Sidney, *Diary*, II.87; Carte MS 39 fo. 160; Burnet, *Hist.*, II.243; *HMC Ormond*, NS V.339–40; BL Add MS 29572 fos 241–2; *HMC 12th Report, Appendix 9*, p. 185.
8. *HMC 7th Report*, p. 479; *HMC Ormond*, NS V.342; Burnet, 'Unpublished Letters', p. 39; All Souls MS 171 fo. 120; Temple, I.349–50; Clarke, *James II*, I.592–3. See also UCL MS 268, Godolphin to Bulstrode 13 Sept. 1680; Morrice, pp. 265–6.
9. *POAS*, II.313–16, 320–6, 328–38; BL Add MSS 29577 fo. 229, 36988 fo. 157; UCL MS 268, Godolphin to Bulstrode 13 Aug. 1680.
10. BL Add MS 29572 fos 205–6; Arundell MSS, Letters to and from Sir John Arundell, Sir T. Chicheley to Sir J. Arundell 5 Jan. 1680; Miller, *Popery*, pp. 176–9.
11. *HMC Ormond*, NS IV.565, 571; Cov MSS 6 fo. 232, 7 fos 184, 194; Pforz, — to Bulstrode 22 March 1680; Reresby, pp. 205, 209; BL Add MS 29577 fo. 281. For rival groups exercising at Bristol, see Tanner MS 37 fo. 31.
12. BL Add MS 29577 fo. 213; BT 143, Barrillon 7 Dec. 1679; BT 144, same 1 Jan.; BT 147, same 21 Nov. 1680; see also Althorp MS C5, Thynne to Halifax 13 June 1680; Prinsterer, V.415.
13. Cov MS 7 fo. 200; *Morrison Letters* 1st series, III.172; Prinsterer, V.393; *HMC Ormond*, MS V.313; Tanner MS 37 fos 17, 114; BL Add MSS 27959 fo. 25, 36988 fo. 157.
14. Cov MS 6 fo. 230.
15. BT 145, Barrillon 22 April; BT 146, same 31 Oct. 1680.
16. *HMC Ormond*, NS IV.559, 578, V.239.
17. BL Add MS 25125 fos 79–80; Cov MS 1 fos 41–2; *HP*, II.643.
18. Temple, I.345; BT 144, Barrillon 15 Feb. and 18 March 1680; Sidney, *Diary*, I.179; Clarke, *James II*, I.591–2; Morrice, p. 276; Reresby, p. 202.
19. BT 146, Barrillon 3 Aug. and 19 Sept. 1680; *HMC Hastings*, II.391; Reresby, p. 208.
20. BL Add MS 29557 fo. 271; *HMC 7th Report*, p. 495; CPA 136, Barrillon to Pomponne 4 Dec. 1679; BT 145, Barrillon 15 April 1680.
21. PC 2/68, p. 370; Arundell MSS, Letters to and from Sir John Arundell, Lady Arundell to Sir John, 26 Feb. [1680]; Burnet, 'Unpublished Letters', p. 30.
22. PC 2/68, pp. 482–4; *HMC Ormond*, NS V.276; BL Add MS 29577 fo. 243; Cov MS 7 fo. 198; Prinsterer V.393. See also Glassey, pp. 49–50.
23. Havighurst, pp. 233, 237; *HMC Ormond*, NS V.273, 275.
24. Crist, ch. 3; P. Hamburger, 'The Development of the Law of Seditious Libel and the Control of the Press', *Stanford Law Review* XXXVII (Feb. 1985), pp. 682–90; *State Trials*, VII.926–33.

25. Crist, pp. 136–8. For another example of the judges' wariness, see Morrice, p. 259. Note the prominent role played in the trials of publishers and printers by the thick-skinned and unscrupulous Scroggs.

26. *London Gazette* no. 1468 (11 to 15 Dec. 1679); PC 2/68, pp. 313, 318; Havighurst, pp. 236–7; for North's role in advising the proclamation against petitions, see North, *Lives*, I.226; Grey, VIII.67–8.

27. Cov MS 6 fo. 230; PC 2/68, pp. 439–40, 455, 471, 519–21; PC 2/69, pp. 25, 33; *HMC Ormond*, NS V.284, 288, 342–3. See also Cov MS 7 fo. 204; *CSPD 1676–7*, pp. 221–2.

28. Warcup, pp. 245–7; BT 143, Barrillon 21 Dec. 1679; BT 144, same 18 Jan. and 14 March; BT 145, same 22 April; BT 146, same 19 Sept 1680; KAO, U1015 O43/5.

29. BL Add MSS 25124 fos 230–1, 29572 fo. 227; BT 145, Barrillon 4, 8 and 11 April 1680; PC 2/69, p. 39; Morrice, p. 259. Note also the order that Gascoigne and Stapleton should be tried by a Yorkshire jury: Kenyon, *Plot*, pp. 197–8; PC 2/68, p. 223.

30. Tanner MS 41 fo. 62; BT 145, Barrillon 3 June 1680; Prinsterer V.422; PRO, PRO 31/9/100A fo. 199; Althorp MS C5, Thynne to Halifax 1 July 1680; Burnet, 'Unpublished Letters', pp. 8, 39; *HMC Ormond*, NS V.342; Morrice, p. 263.

31. Granville, II.51n.; North, *Examen*, pp. 363–4; BL Add MS 29572 fo. 251; Morrice, p. 264; *HMC 7th Report*, p. 479; Tanner MS 37 fo. 114; KAO, U1015 O43/5.

32. Althorp MS C4, Coventry to Halifax 1 May; BT 145, Barrillon 13 June; BT 146, Barrillon 22 July and 24 Oct. 1680; Carte MS 39 fo. 158; BL Add MS 29577 fo. 277; Prinsterer, V.423–4.

33. See Wolf, ch. 25, esp. pp. 495–6.

34. BT 143, Barrillon 2, 9 and 26 Oct., 2 and 30 Nov. 1679; Dalrymple, II(a), pp. 243–4.

35. BL Add MS 25125 fos 70–1; BT 143, Barrillon 13 July; CPA 135, same to Pomponne 14 Aug. 1679; Sidney, *Diary*, I.87–8, 111–12; Sidney, *Letters to Savile*, pp. 150–2; *HMC 7th Report*, p. 476; *HMC Ormond*, NS V.242; Baxter, pp. 178–82.

36. BT 143, Barrillon 9 Oct., 11 and 18 Dec. 1679; BT 144, 1, 8 and 11 Jan. 1680; Sidney, *Diary*, I.187–9; Prinsterer, V.463–4.

37. Sidney, *Diary*, I.211, 219–20, 225, II.74; Prinsterer, V.377–8; BT 144, Barrillon 8, 15, 18, 22 and 29 Jan. 1680.

38. BT 144, Barrillon 5, 12 and 22 Feb., 4 and 11 March 1680; Prinsterer, V.384–5; Sidney, *Diary*, I.157.

39. BT 144, Barrillon 4 March; BT 145, same 29 April, 20 and 23 May, 17 and 27 June 1680; Prinsterer, V.399.

40. Sidney, *Diary*, I.112.

41. *Ibid.*, II.71, 74, 76; BT 145, Barrillon 21, 24 and 27 June 1680; Prinsterer, V.407; Althorp MS C5, Thynne to Halifax 13 June 1680.

42. BT 143, Barrillon 14 Dec. 1679; BT 146, same 1, 18 and 22 July 1680.

43. BT 145, Barrillon 3 June; BT 146, same 22 July 1680.

44. PRO, PRO 31/9/100A fos 197–200; Sidney, *Diary*, I.161, 181.

45. Hatton, I.197–8; CPA 136, Barrillon to Pomponne 16 Oct. 1679; *HMC Ormond*, NS IV.540–2, 545–6; All Souls MS 171 fos 72, 74.

46. *HMC Ormond*, NS IV.558–60, 567, V.239; *HMC 7th Report*, pp. 477, 495; CPA 136, Barrillon to Pomponne 4 Nov. 1679; PC 2/68, p. 304; Temple, I.348–9.

47. Warcup, pp. 245–7; *HMC Ormond*, NS IV.536, V.557–60; Sidney, *Diary*, I.195; CPA 136, Barrillon to Pomponne 23 Nov. 1679.

48. Sidney, *Diary*, I.193n., 195; *HMC Ormond*, NS IV.561; Burnet, *Hist.*, II.238; Pepys Library MS 2875, p. 478; Hatton, I.203–4; BL Add MS 25359 fo. 202; M. M. Verney, *Memoirs of the Verney Family*, 4 vols (London, 1892–9), IV.262; Cov MS 7 fo. 184; Hutton, *Charles II*, pp. 385–6.

49. Warcup, p. 246; *HMC Ormond*, NS IV.561–2, 575, V.244–5; Hatton, I.204–5; BT 143, Barrillon 11 Dec. 1679; BT 144, same 1 Jan. 1680; *HMC 7th Report*, p. 478.

50. BL Add MSS 18730 fo. 63, 29577 fo. 211; BT 143, Barrillon 14 and 18 Dec. 1679; Prinsterer, V.373–4; *HMC Ormond*, NS IV.563, V.247.

51. BL Add MSS 18730 fo. 63, 29572 fo. 173; *HMC Ormond*, NS IV.565–7; Temple, I.346; Morrice, pp. 241–2.

52. Pforz, — to Bulstrode 23 Jan. 1680 (quoted). See also *Letters*, p. 307 (for the speech of 21 April 1679); Temple, I.346; *HMC 7th Report*, p. 496; BL Add MS 29572 fo. 173; *HMC Ormond*, NS IV.574, 576; *HMC le Fleming*, p. 165; Prinsterer, V.374; Jones, *First Whigs*, pp. 116–19.

53. Pforz, — to Bulstrode 23 Jan. 1680; BL Add MS 29572 fo. 253; *POAS*, II.313–16; Hatton I.219; Pepys Library, MS 2875 p. 480. For opposition from the JPs and grand jury to the Somerset petition, see BL Add MS 29577 fo. 229.

54. Sidney, *Diary*, I.252–3; *HMC Ormond*, NS V.276; Carte MS 39 fo. 113; BT 144, Barrillon 5 and 8 Feb. 1680; Hatton, I.220; PC 2/68, p. 370; Morrice, pp. 248–9. York claimed that Charles had assured him that he would stay in Scotland only until January: Clarke, *James II*, I.573–4.

55. Althorp MS C2, Hickman to Halifax 1 Feb.; BT 144, Barrillon 2 Feb. 1680; *HMC Ormond*, NS V.270, 274–5.

56. *HMC Ormond*, NS IV.567; BT 143, Barrillon 21 Dec. 1679; BT 144, same 18 and 25 Jan. 1680.

57. *HMC Ormond*, NS IV.568, V.252, 255–7, 267, 281, 283–5; BT 144, Barrillon 1 and 8 Jan. 1680; Carte MS 228 fo. 153; Clarke, *James II*, I.583–4; Miller, *Popery*, pp. 162–9.

58. BT 144, Barrillon 12 Feb. and 11 March 1680.

59. Sidney, *Diary*, I.188–9 + n.; Carte MS 39 fo. 111; Burnet, 'Unpublished Letters', p. 35 (and see also pp. 7, 10 for a report that the judges were to supply the king's needs between Parliaments); Chandaman, pp. 67–70. It seems at least possible that this ruling may have contributed to Pemberton's dismissal. For a report that taxpayers might refuse to pay, see Cov MS 7 fo. 184.

60. CPA 136, Barrillon to Pomponne 4 Dec. 1679; Hatton, I.212; BT 143, Barrillon 21 Dec. 1679; BT 144, same 8 Jan. 1680. York, of course, agreed with Hyde: Prinsterer, V.387.

61. BT 145, Barrillon 15 April 1680; Sidney, *Diary*, I.286, 292; Arundell MSS, Letters to and from Sir John Arundell, Lady Arundell to Sir John 26 Feb. [1680].

62. *HMC Ormond*, NS V.317; BT 145, Barrillon, 17 and 20 June 1680.

63. BT 145, Barrillon 4, 8, 11 and 15 April 1680; Prinsterer, V.388; *HMC Ormond*, NS V.309, 315; BL Add MSS 25124 fos 230–1, 29572 fos 227, 243, 29577 fo. 255; Sidney, *Diary*, II.87.

64. Prinsterer, V.395; Althorp MS C4, Coventry to Halifax 20 April 1680; Morrice, p. 259.

65. Cov MS 7 fo. 194; Tanner MS 38 fos 126–7; BL Add MS 29577 fo. 251; *HMC Ormond*, NS V.310–11; Althorp MS C4, Coventry to Halifax 27 April and 1 May 1680; Burnet, 'Unpublished Letters', pp. 28, 35; PC 2/69, pp. 1–3.

66. BT 145, Barrillon 22 April 1680; Burnet, 'Unpublished Letters', p. 35; BL Add MSS 15643 fo. 32, 28053 fo. 165.

67. Prinsterer, V.391–5, 415; BT 145, Barrillon 29 April and 20 May 1680; Tanner MS 37 fo. 114.

68. Cov MS 6 fo. 281; *HMC Ormond*, NS V.293, 296; *CSPD 1679–80*, pp. 422–4; Morrice, p. 255; BL Add MS 29577 fo. 249; Warwicks. RO, CR136/B283; BT 145, Barrillon 4 and 11 April 1680; Pforz, — to Bulstrode 26 March 1680; Harris, *Crowds*, pp. 166–8. For Waller's dismissal, see *HMC Ormond*, V.301; BL Add MS 29572 fo. 229.

69. Althorp MS C5, Thynne to Halifax 13 June 1680.

70. *HMC 7th Report*, p. 479; Prinsterer, V.409; Althorp MS C5, Thynne to Halifax 1 July 1680; Morrice, p. 263; *HMC Ormond*, NS V.342–3; North, *Examen*, p. 548; Temple, I.350; Clarke, *James II*, I.592–3.

71. BT 146, Barrillon 1, 15 and 22 July, 19 Aug. [see also Dalrymple, II(a), p. 265] and 30 Sept. 1680; Carte MS 39 fo. 158; BL Add MS 29577 fos 269, 277.

72. Prinsterer, V.415; Clarke, *James II*, I.593–4; BT 146, Barrillon 19 and 29 Aug. and 19 Sept. 1680; see also KAO, U1015 O43/5.

73. Carte MS 39 fo. 211; BL Add MS 29577 fo. 291; Morrice, pp. 266–7; Hatton I.224; BT 147, Barrillon 2 Dec. 1680; Carte MS 222 fo. 232. York had earlier regarded Ward as hostile: All Souls MS 171 fo. 60.

74. UCL MS 268, Godolphin to Bulstrode 3 Sept. 1680 (quoted); Prinsterer, V.418, 421, 423–4; Hatton, I.235–6; BL Add MS 29577 fo. 288; *HMC Ormond*, NS V.449, 458; Dalrymple, II(a), p. 272.

75. BT 146, Barrillon 16, 19 and 30 Sept. 1680 [part of the last is printed in Campana, I.328–9]; Prinsterer, V.415, 422; Hatton, I.235; Carte MS 39 fos 200, 204; Morrice, p. 265.

76. Sidney, *Diary*, II.207; BT 146, Barrillon 7 Oct. 1680; BL Add MS 29577 fo. 281; *CSPD 1680–1*, p. 45.

77. BT 146, Barrillon 7, 21 and 24 Oct. 1680; BL Add MS 28875 fo. 131; Clarke, *James II*, I.594–7; Prinsterer, V.422–3; Hatton, I.238.

78. Sidney, *Diary*, II.109–10; BT 146, Barrillon 24, 28 and 31 Oct. 1680 [for the last, see also Dalrymple, II(a), pp. 269–72]; Clarke, *James II*, I.597–9; *HMC Ormond*, NS V.454; BL Add MSS 28875 fo. 143, 28930 fo. 176.

79. Clarke, *James II*, I.598–9; Prinsterer, V.422–3, 430–1; Dalrymple, II(a), pp. 269, 272.

80. *Letters*, pp. 314–15. See also *HMC Finch*, II.89–90.

81. Grey, VII.375–6, VIII.187, 189, 192; *HMC Beaufort*, p. 109; Temple, I.351.

82. Grey, VII.372–4, 452–3, 458–9, VIII.154 (quoted); Morrice, p. 272; BT 147, Barrillon 16 Dec. 1680.

83. *Exact Coll.*, p. 47.

84. Grey, VIII.21–30, 57 (quoted), 240–1, 251; *Exact Coll.*, pp. 226–8; *HMC Ormond*, NS V.542.

85. *CJ*, IX.642–4, 653, 656, 662; *HMC Ormond*, NS V.497; Ailesbury, I.47; Burnet, *Hist.*, II.250.

86. Morrice, p. 276; *HMC Ormond*, NS V.563; Campana, I.338; BL Add MS 28053 fo. 205.

87. Grey, VII.360–5, 399, 450.

88. *CJ*, IX.695.

89. *Ibid.*, pp. 643, 667, 695; Grey, VII.369, 465–6, VIII.155; *Exact Coll.*, p. 250.

90. Morrice, pp. 276, 279; *HMC Ormond*, NS V.487; UCL MS 268, Godolphin to Bulstrode '13' (recte 15) and 29 Nov., 17 Dec. 1680; *CJ*, IX.653; Macpherson, I.109; Clarke, *James II*, I.634.

91. BT 147, Barrillon 16 Dec. 1680.

92. BT 147, Barrillon 4 and 11 Nov. 1680; BT 148, same 13 Jan. 1681; *CJ*, IX.695–6; Morrice, pp. 288–9; *HMC Ormond*, NS V.514–15, 541–2, 561–2; Grey, VIII.222–3; *HMC Beaufort*, p. 105; *HMC Finch*, II.99–100.

93. BT 147, Barrillon 28 Nov. and 2 Dec. 1680; Prinsterer, V.468; Grey, VIII.262. See also Harris, *Crowds*, ch. 5; Miller, *Popery*, pp. 182–8.

94. BT 147, Barrillon 21 Nov. 1680; *HMC Ormond*, NS V.467; Sidney, *Diary*, II.135; *HMC 7th Report*, p. 496.

95. BT 147, Barrillon 11 Nov. and 16 Dec. 1680; Reresby, p. 202.

96. Haley, *Shaftesbury*, p. 598; Browning, *Documents*, pp. 113–14. See also BT 147, Barrillon 18 and 21 Nov. 1680; *HMC Ormond*, NS IV.475, V.561; *HMC Finch*, II.96; Grey, VII.397–413, 422–8.

97. *CJ*, IX.649, 651; Grey, VII.439–43, 445–59.

98. Morrice, p. 276; *HMC Ormond*, NS V.487; BT 147, Barrillon 25 Nov. 1680.

99. *HMC Ormond*, NS V.486, 488; BT 147, Barrillon 14, 21 and 25 Nov. 1680; Grey, VII.477; Burnet, *Supplement*, pp. 136–8; Clarke, *James II*, I.615; Macpherson, I.107.

100. BT 147, Barrillon 28 Nov. 1680; BL Add MS 63057B fo. 54; *HMC 7th Report*, p. 479; *HMC Ormond*, NS V.490, 496.

101. Sidney, *Diary*, II.125; BT 147, Barrillon 28 Nov. and 5 Dec. 1680; Reresby, pp. 204, 208.

102. BT 147, Barrillon 21 and 28 Nov., 5 Dec. 1680; Morrice, p. 275; *HMC Ormond*, NS V.529; BL Add MS 63057B fo. 57.

103. *CJ*, IX.669; *HMC Ormond*, NS V.513–15, 518–19, 521–2; Warwicks. RO, CR136/B540; Hatton, I.241–2; BT 147, Barrillon 19 Dec. 1680; Ailesbury, I.50–1.

104. Clarke, *James II*, I.627–9; Wynne, II.690–1; *HMC Dartmouth*, I.40 (misdated 1679), 54–5; *Clar Corr*, I.50–1.

105. *HMC Portland*, VIII.15; Grey, VIII.13, 16–17, 21–30; *HMC Finch*, II.97; Burnet, *Hist.*, II.246–7; BL Add MS 28930 fos 203–4; *HMC Ormond*, NS V.497, 506, 524; *Exact Coll.*, p. 242; *CJ*, IX.682, 692, 702.

106. *HMC Ormond*, NS V.488, 490, 499, 502; BL Add MS 28930 fos 203–4; BT 147, Barrillon 28 Nov. 1680; Dalrymple, II(a), p. 306; Clar MS 87 fo. 334.

107. *HMC Ormond*, NS V.490–1, 506; Clar MS 87 fos 331–2; Burnet, *Hist.*, II.252–3; *HMC Finch*, II.97; *CJ*, IX.679–80; Grey, VIII.154–71; *Exact Coll.*, pp. 176, 192–3; *HMC Beaufort*, pp. 100, 110; *HMC House of Lords 1678–88*, pp. 210–11; Prinsterer, V.465–6.

108. BT 147, Barrillon 18 Nov. 1680; *CJ*, IX.680–1, 692; Burnet, *Hist.*, II.267–8; Morrice, pp. 286–8.

109. Sidney, *Diary*, II.120, 143–5; Dalrymple, II(a), pp. 305–7; Prinsterer, V.450–1, 454–6, 461–2, 465–6; BT 147, Barrillon 12 and 26 Dec. 1680.

110. BT 147, Barrillon 16 Dec. 1680; BT 148, same 2, 9 and 16 Jan. 1681; Grey, VIII.189; *CJ*, IX.679–80, 684–5, 699, 702; *Exact Coll.*, p. 190; *HMC Ormond*, NS V.530, 541–2; Burnet, *Hist.*, II.253; *HMC Hastings*, II.391; *HMC Finch*, II.99–100.

111. *CJ*, IX.703–4; *HMC Finch*, II.100–2; Prinsterer, V.468.

112. *Exact Coll.*, p. 149; Grey, VIII.60; Morrice, pp. 293–4; Carte MS 222 fo. 232; Prinsterer V.470–1; BL Add MS 18730 fo. 80; BT 148, Barrillon 30 Jan. 1681; *HMC Ormond*, V.563.

113. BT 148, Barrillon 27 and 30 Jan., 3 Feb. 1681; Sidney, *Diary*, II.159; *HMC Ormond*, NS V.568; Sidney, *Letters to Savile*, p. 7 (misdated 1679).

114. Clarke, *James II*, I.657–61; *HMC Dartmouth*, I.47.

115. Burnet, *Hist.*, II.244; *HMC Ormond*, NS IV.563, 566–7; Temple, I.354–5; BT 144, Barrillon 15 Feb. 1680; BT 148, same 30 Jan. 1681; Reresby, pp. 205, 209–12.

116. *HMC Ormond*, NS IV.545, V.461, 462, 467, 477, 481, 546, 563; BL Add MS 18730 fos 76, 80–1; Grey, VIII.251.

117. Dalrymple, II(a), p. 272; Grey, VII.407–8; BT 147, Barrillon 16 Dec. 1680; BT 148, same 3 Feb. 1681; Sidney, *Letters to Savile*, p. 12 (misdated 1679); see also *HP*, III.412–20.

118. Prinsterer, V.468; Carte MS 222 fo. 232; BT 148, Barrillon 20 and 30 Jan. 1681; Warcup, p. 249.

119. BT 148, Barrillon 10, 20 and 24 Feb., 10, 13 and 31 March 1681; *HMC Ormond*, NS IV.413, VI.8. For other examples of his concern to follow the law, see *CJ*, IX.663; Prinsterer, V.474.

120. Prinsterer, V.472, 477–82; Carte MS 222 fo. 236; Clarke, *James II*, I.663; BT 148, Barrillon 24 Feb. 1680.

121. Dalrymple, II(a), pp. 280–5; BT 147, Barrillon 2 Dec. 1680.

122. Dalrymple, II(a), pp. 277, 291, 293–5, 301–2; Campana, I.346; BT 148, Barrillon 13 and 20 Jan., 13 Feb., 3, 24 and 27 March, 3 April 1681; Clarke, *James II*, I.664–5.

123. See *HMC Ormond*, NS V.541; BL Add MSS 29558 fo. 154, 29577 fo. 307; Clarke, *James II*, I.665–6.

124. BT 148, Barrillon 13 Jan., 27 March 1681; Dalrymple, II(a), pp. 301–2.

125. Morrice, p. 297; BT 148, Barrillon 20 March 1681; *HMC Ormond*, NS V.616–17; Prinsterer, V.474, 479–81.

126. *HMC Ormond*, NS V.579, 604; Temple, I.353–4; Jones, *First Whigs*, pp. 159–73.

127. *HMC Ormond*, NS V.570; Warcup, p. 249; Savile, p. 183; BL Add MS 35104 fo. 6.

128. *HMC Ormond*, NS V.575, 579, 581, 590–2; Luttrell, I.69.

129. BL Add MS 15643 fo. 45; *HMC Ormond*, NS V.542, 546–7, 589, 591, 602, VI.18.

130. Warcup, p. 249; *HMC Ormond*, V.571, 582.

131. *HMC Ormond*, V.609; Burnet, *Hist.*, II.271–2; BL Add MS 29577 fo. 322; BT 148, Barrillon 13 March 1681; North, *Examen*, pp. 100–1; Carte MS 222 fo. 272.

132. *HMC Ormond*, NS VI.5–8, 10; *CJ*, IX.708, 711; Christie, II, appendix, pp. cxiii–cxv; Carte MS 222 fo. 274; Prinsterer, V.488; Grey, VIII.309–32; *HMC Beaufort*, p. 85.

133. Dering, *Papers*, p. 121; Grey, VIII.294, 297, 309, 316–17; *CJ*, IX.708.

134. BT 148, Barrillon 3 and 7 April 1681; *HMC Ormond*, NS V.618, VI.6–8; North, *Examen*, pp. 100, 123–4.

135. BT 148, Barrillon 7 April 1681; *HMC Ormond*, VI.9, 21; *CJ*, IX.712.

136. BT 148, 10 April 1681; Prinsterer, V.488–93; Ailesbury, I.21, 57; *POAS*, II.411.

Chapter 13: The Battle for London

1. *CSPD 1680–1*, p. 660.

2. Crist, p. 184; Tanner MS 36 fo. 106; see also Morrice, p. 353; Oates's Plot, letter dated 26 Jan. 1682; *HMC Ormond*, NS VI.229; D. L. Poole, 'Some Unpublished Letters of Halifax to Burnet', *EHR* XXVI (1911), p. 541.

3. *HMC Ormond*, NS VI.444–5; *CSPD 1682*, pp. 490–1, *Jan.–June 1683*, pp. 95–6.

4. Carte MS 216 fo. 195. Harris, *Crowds*, ch. 7, suggests that the Tories had as much popular support as the Whigs, but his evidence is less than conclusive. It seems possible that he is extending backwards De Krey's conclusions for 1689–1715 (see *A Fractured Society: The Politics of London in the First Age of Party* (Oxford, 1985), but in the immediate aftermath of 1688 it was the Whigs who enjoyed the preponderance of popular support.

5. Carte, *Ormond*, V.161–2; BL Add MS 29558 fo. 357; DUL, Mickleton-Spearman MS 46 fo. 251.

6. Newton, *Lyme Letters*, p. 109; *HMC Ormond*, NS IV.165; Carte MS 50 fo. 229 (quoted); Carte, *Ormond*, V.163–4.

7. *HMC Dartmouth*, I.69, 75, 86; *CSPD 1682*, pp. 342–3; JRL, Legh of Lyme Correspondence, J. Chicheley to R. Legh 13 Dec. 1681; *HMC Ormond*, NS VI.436, 445; *HMC Buccleuch*, I.173; Hatton, II.18.

8. *HMC 7th Report*, pp. 358, 533; *CSPD 1682*, pp. 392, 409, 441; *HMC Ormond* NS VI.31; Luttrell, I.75–6, 83; Morrice, pp. 345, 347; Allen, 'London Trained Bands', *EHR* LXXXVII (1972).

9. *CSPD July–Sept. 1683*, pp. 232–3.

10. Luttrell, I.199.

11. *HMC 7th Report*, p. 405; Oates's Plot, newsletter 12 Oct. 1682; Luttrell, I.232, 242–3, 251, 271–2; PC 2/69, p. 417; Morrice, pp. 318–19, 347, 356; *HMC Ormond*, NS VI.155, 274; Tanner MS 36* fos 212–13; Mather, pp. 498–9; Miller, *Popery*, pp. 265–7; Hutton, *Charles II*, p. 424.

12. *HMC Ormond*, NS VI.155, 185, 237, 242; PC 2/69, p. 386; *An Account of the Convincement of Richard Davies* (Newtown, 1928), pp. 136–7; Tanner MS 36 fo. 67; *CSPD 1682*, p. 356; Morrice, p. 351; Oates's Plot, letter dated 29 Sept. 1681.

13. Tanner MSS 35 fo. 9, 36 fo. 31; Morrice, pp. 329, 347, 351; BL Add MS 29577 fo. 387; Warwicks. RO, CR136/B413 (quoted). See also R. Beddard, 'The Restoration Church', in J. R. Jones (ed.), *The Restored Monarchy 1660–88* (London, 1979), pp. 173–4; G. V. Bennett,

'Conflict in the Church', in G. Holmes (ed.), *Britain After the Glorious Revolution 1689–1714* (London, 1969), pp. 156–7.

14. Tanner MSS 35 fo. 107, 36 fo. 235; *CSPD 1682*, pp. 36, 456.

15. *CSPD 1680–1*, pp. 238–9.

16. For example, the *quo warranto* against Worcester began in 1680 or 1681, but was not completed until the end of 1684: FSL, V.b.302, p. 17; Morrice, pp. 354–5; *CSPD Jan.–June 1683*, pp. 183–4; *HMC House of Lords 1689–90*, p. 298. The process was delayed by negotiations about a surrender in 1681: Althorp MS C1, Windsor to Halifax 10 and 19 Oct. 1681.

17. BL Add MS 27448 fos 141–2; Tanner MS 36 fo. 235; DCAD, Hunter MS 7 no. 136. See the fuller discussion in Miller, 'Charters', pp. 70–8.

18. *HMC Buccleuch*, I.275; *HMC Ormond*, NS V.26, VI.376. Hawker's portrait is in the National Portrait Gallery.

19. Reresby, p. 259.

20. Savile, p. 271; *Hatton*, II.18; BL Add MS 30305 fo. 197; H. M. Colvin, J. M. Crook, K. Downes and J. Newman, *The King's Works V.1660–1782* (London 1976), pp. 144–51, 304–13.

21. BT 148, Barrillon 14 and 17 April; BT 150, same 9 Oct., 20 and 24 Nov. 1681; Clarke, *James II*, I.680–1; Macpherson, I.129.

22. *HMC Ormond*, NS VI.219; Hatton, II.11; Reresby, pp. 247–8; Burnet, *Supplement*, pp. 135–6; Ailesbury, I.85–6; Welwood, p. 146; Campana, I.410; BT 159, Barrillon 6 Nov. 1684; Carte MSS 130 fo. 22, 216 fo. 127; Clarke, *James II*, I.729–30.

23. Chandaman, pp. 72, 102–3, 247–55 and *passim*. For the 'stop' of 1681, see BL Add MS 29558 fo. 252; BT 149, Barrillon 15 May 1681.

24. Chandaman, pp. 102–3, 255, 271–2; Carte MS 70 fos 559, 563; *HMC Ormond*, NS VI.542; North, *Lives*, I.254–6; Bramston, pp. 166–70; J. D. Davies, 'Pepys and the Admiralty Commission of 1679–84', *Historical Research* [formerly *BIHR*] LXII (1989), pp. 44–8. For Castlemaine, see BL Add MS 29559 fo. 97; Carte MS 216 fo. 39. I owe the information about Tangier to a seminar paper by Dr Sari Hornstein, based on part of her doctoral thesis.

25. BT 148, Barrillon 14 and 28 April; BT 150, same 24 Nov. and 18 Dec. 1681; Clarke, *James II*, I.680, 697–9, 702–3, 722–9; *HMC Dartmouth*, I.40–1 (misdated 1679), 65, 69; Macpherson, I.129; *HMC Ormond*, NS VI.271, 327–8, 337.

26. *HMC Ormond*, NS VI.342; Arundell MSS, Bellings Letters, Anne Arundell to (? Sir John) 13 March 1682; Luttrell, I.177; *HMC 7th Report*, p. 479; Oates's Plot, letters dated 27 April and 1 June 1682; BT 151, Barrillon 2 April 1682.

27. BT 152, Barrillon 27 July; BT 153, same 10 Aug. 1682; Burnet, *Hist.*, II.329–30; *HMC Buccleuch*, I.171; *HMC Ormond*, NS VI.324, 355, 40; Carte MSS 70 fo. 559 [also Carte MS 219 fo. 396], 130 fo. 22; BL Add MS 29577 fos 499, 519.

28. Temple, I.354; Carte MS 70 fo. 559.

29. Burnet, *Supplement*, p. 302; Burnet, *Hist.*, I.447n., 465–6; BL Add MSS 63057A fo. 170, 63057B fo. 4; Reresby, pp. 288–90; Halifax, pp. 255–7.

30. *HMC Ormond*, NS VI.59; BT 151, Barrillon 9 Feb. 1682; BL Add MS 29577 fo. 409.

31. *CSPD 1680–1*, pp. 319, 409; Glassey, pp. 53–5.

32. Wynne, II.684–5; *HMC Ormond*, NS VI.452; *CSPD 1680–1*, pp. 384–5, *July–Sept. 1683*, pp. 150, 293; North, *Lives*, I.237; Miller, 'Charters', pp. 79–80.

33. BL Add MSS 27448 fo. 16, 29558 fo. 398, 29577 fo. 421; Althorp MS C1, Windsor to Halifax 16 April 1681; *HMC Ormond*, NS VI.165, 229, 257; Dorset RO, D60/F56 John to Henry Trenchard 1 Oct. 1681; Clarke, *James II*, I.720.

34. Christie, II, appendix, p. cxviii; Reresby, pp. 248–9; BL Add MS 35104 fo. 61; BT 155, Barrillon 2 Aug. 1683; *CSPD July–Sept. 1683*, p. 435. Note Charles's phrase 'a little too Parliamentary': *CSPD 1682*, p. 129.

35. *HMC Ormond*, NS VI.143–4.

36. Carte MS 70 fo. 564 (also in Carte MS 219 fo. 417). See also Carte, *Ormond*, V.161–4; *HMC Ormond*, NS VI.377.

37. Luttrell, I.73; Clarke, *James II*, I.666–7, 675; *CSPD 1680–1*, p. 527; *HMC Ormond*, NS VI.27; Morrice, p. 305; UCL MS 268, Godolphin to Bulstrode 29 April 1681.

38. Browning, *Documents*, pp. 185–8.

39. Tanner MS 36 fo. 7; BL Add MS 15643 fo. 48; Burnet, *Supplement*, p. 106.

40. BL Add MS 27448 fo. 16; Tanner MS 36 fo. 11; *HMC Ormond*, NS VI.48.

41. *HMC Ormond*, NS VI.31; Luttrell, I.75–6, 83; *CSPD 1680–1*, pp. 238–9.

42. BT 148, Barrillon 17 April 1681; BL Add MS 29558 fos 252, 272; Tanner MS 36 fos 19–20; *HMC Ormond*, NS VI.48, 51–2; Oates's Plot, 'Out of my lord Castlemaine's Letters concerning Fitzharris', 2 May 1681.

43. Oates's Plot, M to Mrs Cellier 4, 5 and [17] May; same, 'Out of my lord Castlemaine's Letters', 9 June 1681; *HMC Ormond*, NS VI.59, 74, 80; BL Add MS 29558 fos 265, 272, 276, 309; Haley, *Shaftesbury*, pp. 644–50.

44. Tanner MS 36 fo. 55; Oates's Plot, 'Out of my lord Castlemaine's Letters', 16, 23 and 30 June 1681; *CSPD 1680–1*, pp. 331–2; *HMC 7th Report*, p. 496; UCL MS 268, Godolphin to Bulstrode 24 June 1681. (The accounts of the proceedings against Howard differ somewhat.)

45. *HMC Ormond*, NS VI.95–6; BL Add MS 29558 fo. 357; Morrice, p. 310; Oates's Plot, 'Out of my lord Castlemaine's Letters', [11] July 1681; Haley, *Shaftesbury*, pp. 657–8.

46. UCL MS 268, Godolphin to Bulstrode 15 July 1681; Burnet, *Hist.*, II.283; Hatton, II.7; Haley, *Shaftesbury*, p. 663.

47. Luttrell, I.110–11; *CSPD 1680–1*, pp. 266–70, 272–3.

48. *HMC Ormond*, NS VI.62–3; *CSPD 1680–1*, pp. 277, 279; BL Add MS 29558 fo. 272; Carte MS 222 fos 302–3; UCL MS 268, Godolphin to Bulstrode 16 May 1681.

49. Oates's Plot, 'Out of my Lord Castlemaine's Letters', 16 May 1681; *HMC Ormond*, NS VI.66–7; BL Add MS 29587 fos 68–70.

50. Luttrell, I.87–8; Morrice, p. 307; *CSPD 1680–1*, pp. 331–2; Wynne, II.684–5.

51. BL Add MS 4107 fo. 34; *HMC Ormond*, NS VI.89, 95–6, 149; Oates's Plot, 'Out of my Lord Castlemaine's Letters', [7] July 1681; Hatton, II.3.

52. *HMC Ormond*, NS VI.91, 148–9; Morrice, pp. 309, 311; BT 149, Barrillon 18 Aug. 1681; BL Add MS 29558 fo. 444; *CSPD 1680–1*, pp. 475–6; Burnet, *Hist.*, II.324–5.

53. *HMC Ormond*, NS VI.141, 144–5, 154–5; Luttrell, I.119; BL Add MSS 4107 fo. 35, 29577 fos 370, 392; *CSPD 1680–1*, p. 426; Carte MS 222 fo. 313; Hatton II.7; Morrice, p. 313; Oates's Plot, letter dated 7 Nov. 1681.

54. *HMC Ormond*, NS VI.185, 187–8, 193, 197–8; Hatton, II.8; Morrice, p. 319; BL Add MSS 29558 fo. 472, 29577 fos 382, 386, 63057B fos 60–1; Oates's Plot, CG to — 13 Oct. 1681; Bulstrode, *Memoirs*, p. 331; Burnet, *Hist.*, II.286–92; *The History of the Association* (1682), pp. 20–2.

55. *HMC Ormond*, NS VI.208, 211–12, 215, 220, 226, 229, 234; Oates's Plot, letter dated 7 Nov.; same, Litcot to — 17 Nov. 1681; BL Add MS 29577 fo. 398; BT 150, Barrillon 1 Dec. 1681.

56. Morrice, p. 318; KAO, U1015 O43/6; BL Add MSS 29558 fo. 509, 29573 fo. 401; Bodl, MS Eng Letters d 40 fos 144–5; *HMC Ormond*, VI.236–7; Oates's Plot, letter dated 24 Nov. 1681.

57. PC 2/69, p. 410; Morrice, p. 318; *HMC Ormond*, NS VI.238, 242; Mather, p. 497.

58. BL Add MS 63057B fo. 70; Miller, 'Potential for Absolutism'; *HMC 7th Report*, p. 342.

59. *HMC 7th Report*, pp. 276–8, 334–5, 343–4, 356, 361, 395–7; *CSPD July–Sept. 1683*, pp. 158, 201, 291.

60. *HMC 7th Report*, pp. 266–7, 269, 276, 278.

61. *Ibid.*, pp. 267–70, 355, 404; Dalrymple, II(b), p. 83. For Primi's text, see *A Collection*

of State Tracts Printed on the Occasion of the Late Revolution, vol. I (1705), Introduction, p. 10.

62. Wolf, pp. 499–503.

63. *Ibid.*, p. 501.

64. BT 149, Barrillon 5 and 12 May, 7 and 11 Aug. 1681; Macpherson, I.125; Clarke, *James II*, I.691–2; *HMC Ormond*, NS VI.114–15; *Clar Corr*, I.58–60; Prinsterer, V.504–10; Sidney, *Diary*, II.200, 203; Dalrymple, II(b), pp. 4–6; *HMC Dartmouth* I.65.

65. Prinsterer, V.513, 524; Dalrymple, II(b), p. 39; *HMC Ormond* Old Series I.33; Clarke, *James II*, I.693–4; Macpherson, I.128; BT 150, Barrillon 12 Sept., 5, 9 and 12 Oct. 1681.

66. Prinsterer, V.526–7; BL Add MS 29577 fos 386–7; BT 150, Barrillon 27 Oct. and 10 Nov. 1681.

67. BT 150, Barrillon 3, 6, 17 and 20 Nov. 1681; *HMC Ormond*, NS VI.208–9; Prinsterer, V.531–2; BL Add MS 29577 fo. 394.

68. BT 150, Barrillon 20 and 24 Nov., 1, 11 and 15 Dec. 1681; *HMC Dartmouth*, I.71; Prinsterer, V.534–6.

69. BT 150, Barrillon 1 Dec. 1681; BT 151, same 1, 5, 8, 12 and 15 Jan. 1682; *HMC Ormond*, NS VI.282–3, 522 [misdated 1683].

70. BT 151, Barrillon 9, 16 and 23 Feb., 5 and 16 March; CPA 146, same 2 and 9 March, Louis to Barrillon 23 March 1682; BL Add MS 35104 fos 45–6; *CSPD 1682*, pp. 111–12; *HMC Ormond*, NS VI.307–8, 546–9 [misdated 1683].

71. Wolf, pp. 508–10; CPA 146, Barrillon 29 March; BT 151, same 2 April 1682; *HMC Ormond*, NS VI.349–50; Prinsterer, V.547–8.

72. BT 151, Barrillon 13 April; BT 152, same 15, 22, 25 June, 6 and 23 July; CPA 148, same 5 and 8 Oct. 1682; *HMC 7th Report*, pp. 382, 385.

73. *HMC 7th Report*, pp. 270, 357; *Clar Corr*, II.79; BT 153, Barrillon 17 and 21 Sept.; CPA 148, same 5 Oct. 1682.

74. *HMC 7th Report*, pp. 272, 360, 382; BT 153, Barrillon 2, 5, 9, 11 and 19 Nov.; CPA 148, same 16 and 23 Nov. 1682; Carte MS 70 fos 559–60; BL Add MS 35104 fo. 72.

75. BT 153, Barrillon 26 Nov.; CPA 148, same 17 and 31 Dec. 1682; *HMC 7th Report*, pp. 275, 277, 352, 361, 382; BL Add MS 35104 fo. 83.

76. BT 154, Barrillon 4 and 11 Jan., 22 Feb., 18 and 21 March, 26 April 1683; *HMC 7th Report*, pp. 382, 385; Prinsterer, V.567–70, 577; BL Add MS 35104 fos 45–6.

77. BT 154, Barrillon 15, 19 and 29 April; BT 155, same 6 May; CPA 149, same 20 May 1683.

78. BT 155, Barrillon 1 and 29 July, 2, 9 and 30 Aug.; BT 156, same 6 Sept.; CPA 150, same 2 Sept. 1683; Prinsterer, V.581–3; *HMC 7th Report*, p. 383; Dalrymple, II(b), p. 47.

79. *HMC Ormond*, NS IV.591, VI.260; BT 150, Barrillon 25 Dec. 1681; BT 151, same 8 Jan. 1682.

80. Hatton, II.10; *HMC Ormond*, NS VI.250; Morrice, p. 320; *HMC 7th Report*, pp. 351–2, 372, 405.

81. Althorp MS B6, Dorothy Countess of Sunderland to Lady Burlington 12 May; *HMC Ormond*, NS VI.142, 208, 274, 377, 380–1; Oates's Plot, letter dated 24 Oct. 1681; Hatton, II.17; *CSPD 1682*, p. 356.

82. Harris, *Crowds*, pp. 178–88; *CSPD 1682*, p. 138; *HMC 7th Report*, p. 479; Oates's Plot, letter dated 26 Jan. 1682.

83. Morrice, p. 332; Luttrell, I.179–80; *HMC Rutland*, II.68–9; BL Add MS 29577 fo. 437; PC 2/69, p. 490; Oates's Plot, letter dated 27 April 1682.

84. Hatton, II.12; *HMC Ormond*, NS VI.244 (the date should be 31, not 3 Dec.), 376; BT 151, Barrillon 15 Jan.; BT 152, same 25 May, 4, 8 and 11 June 1682; *HMC 7th Report*, pp. 352, 405; Oates's Plot, letter dated 18 May 1682; Carte MS 216 fos 47, 53, 55; PC 2/69, p. 506; Reresby, p. 266; Bulstrode, *Memoirs*, pp. 320–1.

85. Hatton, II.17, 19; BT 153, Barrillon 3 Sept. 1682; *CSPD 1682*, pp. 342–3; *HMC*

Ormond, NS VI.430; Rawdon, p. 276; Oates's Plot, letter dated 31 Aug. 1682; Carte MS 216 fo. 157.

86. BL Add MS 36988 fos 199, 201; Hatton, II.18; *HMC Ormond*, NS VI.436, 444–5.

87. BL Add MS 29577 fo. 471; *HMC 3rd Report*, p. 96; *CSPD 1682*, pp. 411, 441, *July–Sept. 1683*, p. 190; Carte MS 216 fo. 181; Hatton, II.19–20.

88. CPA 148, Barrillon 5 Oct. 1682; BT 155, same 13 May 1683; Carte MS 216 fos 189–90; Hatton, II.19–20; *HMC Ormond*, NS VI.452; Oates's Plot, letter dated 23 Oct. 1682; *CSPD 1682*, p. 528.

89. Newton, *House of Lyme*, p. 302; Carte MS 216 fo. 206.

90. BL Add MS 29577 fos 483, 501; *HMC 7th Report*, p. 497; Carte MS 216 fo. 216.

91. See the discussions in Burnet, *Hist.*, II.339–49; Burnet, *Supplement*, pp. 109, 111; BL Add MS 63057B fos 69–70. See also Ailesbury, I.73; Evelyn, IV.329, 331; *HMC Ormond*, NS VII.64; Haley, *Shaftesbury*, ch. 30; R. Ashcraft, *Revolutionary Politics and Locke's Two Treatises of Government* (Princeton, 1986), chs 7–8.

92. Burnet, *Hist.*, II.372.

93. Morrice, p. 332; Bulstrode, *Memoirs*, p. 343; BT 155, Barrillon 5 and 8 July 1683; Evelyn, IV.331; Burnet, *Hist.*, II.359; Burnet, *Supplement*, p. 116; Carte MS 219 fo. 482; *HMC Dartmouth*, I.82; Hatton, II.24–5.

94. Prinsterer, V.578; BT 155, Barrillon 15 and 22 July 1683; Hatton, II.31; Burnet, *Hist.*, II.370 + n.; Burnet, *Suppl.*, pp. 127–8; Welwood, p. 138.

95. For Sidney see J. Carswell, *The Porcupine: Algernon Sidney* (London, 1989), chs 14–17 and the forthcoming second volume of the biography by Jonathan Scott. For Essex, see Burnet, *Hist.*, II.345–6; BL Add MS 63057B fo. 70 (note that the manuscript is much fuller, and much less reticent, than the printed version). For Charles's views, see BT 155, Barrillon 12 July 1683.

96. BT 155, Barrillon 19 and 22 July 1683; BL MS 29560 fo. 45; Burnet, *Hist.*, II.355; *HMC 7th Report*, p. 364; Carte MS 219 fo. 482.

97. BT 155, Barrillon 5 July and 9 Aug. 1683; *CSPD Jan.–June 1683*, pp. 339–40, *July–Sept. 1683*, p. 68; BL Add MS 29560 fo. 59; Hatton, II.33–4.98.

98. Wynne, II.684–5; J. Levin, *The Charter Controversy in the City of London 1660–88 and Its Consequences* (London, 1969), ch. 3.

99. *CSPD 1680–1*, pp. 682–3; *HMC Ormond*, NS VI.244.

100. *CSPD 1680–1*, p. 632; Smith, pp. 36–7.

101. *CSPD 1682*, p. 132; Burnet, *Hist.*, II.328–9; BL Add MS 29577 fo. 491; Ailesbury I.64–5; Luttrell I.232; *HMC 7th Report*, p. 356; Smith, chs 6 and 8; Harris, *Crowds*, ch. 6.

102. *HMC Ormond*, NS VI.264, 273–4; BL Add MSS 29558 fo. 537, 35104 fo. 38; *CSPD 1680–1*, p. 638; Smith, pp. 205–11.

103. *HMC Ormond*, NS VI.335–6, 341–2, 347; Morrice, p. 329; Luttrell, I.173.

104. Carte MS 216 fo. 47.

105. *HMC 7th Report*, p. 354; BT 152, Barrillon 6 July 1682; Carte MS 216 fo. 86; Tanner MS 35 fo. 33.

106. Burnet, *Hist.*, II.325–6; UCL MS 268, Godolphin to Bulstrode 8 July 1682; Hatton, II.16; PC 2/69, p. 531; Smith, pp. 187–9.

107. BL Add MS 35104 fo. 66; *HMC 3rd Report*, p. 95; Carte MS 216 fos 171, 173–4, 181; Smith, pp. 190–4; Haley, *Shaftesbury*, p. 700.

108. *HMC 7th Report*, p. 358; BL Add MS 29577 fo. 479; Smith, pp. 199–200.

109. Oates's Plot, letter dated 19 June 1682; *HMC 7th Report*, pp. 262, 358; Carte MS 216 fos 195, 202, 218, 222 (quoted); BL Add MS 29577 fo. 487; Morrice, p. 340; Smith, pp. 201–2.

110. Carte MS 216 fo. 228; Morrice, pp. 346, 357, 365–7; Oates's Plot, letter dated 20 Nov. 1682.

111. Carte MS 216 fo. 79; Mather, p. 511; Oates's Plot, letter dated 19 June 1682; Luttrell, I.242–4; *HMC 7th Report*, pp. 406, 497; Morrice, pp. 346–9, 369; *CSPD 1682*, pp. 522, 557; Smith, pp. 211–13.

112. Carte MS 216 fo. 86; *HMC 7th Report*, p. 359.

113. Morrice, p. 369; BT 155, Barrillon 24 June 1683; Prinsterer, V.577.

114. Bulstrode, *Memoirs*, p. 342; *HMC Ormond*, NS VII.49–50; Morrice, p. 370; Browning, *Documents*, pp. 188–90; *HMC 7th Report*, p. 363.

115. Morrice, p. 376; *HMC 7th Report*, p. 316; Luttrell, I.282.

116. *HMC 7th Report*, pp. 366–7; BT 156, Barrillon 18 Oct. 1683; Morrice, p. 377; *HMC Dartmouth*, I.95–6; Smith, chs 13–14; *HP*, I.314.

Chapter 14: The End

1. Morrice, p. 436.

2. *Ibid.*, pp. 396, 402–3, 415, 428; *HMC Ormond*, NS VII.203.

3. Morrice, pp. 433–4; Tanner MSS 32 fo. 54, 34 fo. 253; R. Beddard, 'The Commission for Ecclesiastical Promotions 1681–4: An Instrument of Tory Reaction', *HJ* X (1967), pp. 11–40.

4. Luttrell, I.288, 295; Morrice, p. 429; *CSPD 1683–4*, pp. 307–8, 360, *1684–5*, p. 80; SP 44/335 fo. 137.

5. BT 155, Barrillon 2 Aug. 1683; BT 157, same 19 March 1684; Burnet, *Hist.*, II.391; *CSPD 1684–5*, p. 22.

6. Ailesbury, I.23; BT 159, Barrillon 6 Nov. 1684; *HMC Ormond*, NS VII.274.

7. *CSPD 1683–4*, pp. 42, 117; *HP*, I.492–3; K. E. Murray, *Constitutional History of the Cinque Ports* (Manchester, 1935), pp. 96–8.

8. Bulstrode, *Memoirs*, pp. 372–3, 378.

9. *Ibid.*, pp. 424–5; Burnet, *Hist.*, II.404.

10. *CSPD 1683–4*, p. 103; Ailesbury, I.81–3; Burnet, *Hist.*, II.400–2; BT 156, Barrillon 8 Nov., 5 and 6 Dec. 1683; *HMC 7th Report*, p. 375.

11. BT 155, Barrillon 6 Dec. 1683; BL Add MS 28930 fo. 266; *HMC Ormond*, NS VII.164; Carte MS 228 fo. 77; Morrice, pp. 392–3, 396; Burnet, *Hist.*, II.402.

12. Reresby, pp. 320, 322–4; *HMC 7th Report*, p. 368; Burnet, *Hist.*, II. 400, 402–3; BT 156, Barrillon 13, 16 and 20 Dec. 1683; Ailesbury, I.84; Carte MS 70 fos 570–1; *CSPD 1683–4*, pp. 153–4. For the paper, see BL Add MS 28875 fo. 321.

13. Dalrymple, II(b), pp. 54–5; *HMC Buccleuch*, I.200; *HMC 7th Report*, p. 368; BT 156, Barrillon 20 Dec. 1683; *HMC Ormond*, NS VII.169.

14. Carte MS 220 fo. 7; BT 157, Barrillon 31 Jan. 1684.

15. Wolf, pp. 509–14; *HMC 7th Report*, pp. 291–3.

16. *HMC 7th Report*, pp. 289, 383; BT 155, Barrillon 30 Aug.; BT 156, same 6 Sept.; CPA 150, same 2 and 19 Sept. 1683; Dalrymple, II(b), p. 47.

17. CPA 150, Barrillon 19 Sept. and 11 Oct. 1683; *HMC 7th Report*, p. 384.

18. BT 156, Barrillon 14 Oct., 23 and 30 Dec. 1683; *HMC 7th Report*, p. 367; Dalrymple, II(b), p. 55.

19. BT 157, Barrillon 3, 16, 17, 20, 24 and 27 Jan. 1684.

20. BT 156, Barrillon 20 Dec. 1683; BT 157, same 27 Jan. 1684.

21. *HMC 7th Report*, pp. 297–8; BT 157, Barrillon 24 Feb., 6, 9 and 26 March 1684; Sidney, *Diary*, II.237–8.

22. BT 158, Barrillon 1, 15, 18 and 25 May 1684; *HMC 7th Report*, pp. 302, 304, 310–11.

23. Prinsterer, V.585–6; BL Add MS 29578 fo. 3; Bulstrode, *Memoirs*, p. 425; BT 158, Barrillon 22 and 29 May 1684; Dalrymple, II(b), pp. 56–7, 62–3; *HMC 7th Report*, pp. 314–15.

24. BT 159, Barrillon, 28 and 31 Aug., 4 and 21 Sept., 16 and 26 Oct., 25 Dec. 1684; BT

160, same 1, 15 and 18 Jan. 1685; *HMC Buccleuch*, I.212; PRO, FO 95/571, d'Avaux 1 and 18 Jan., 1 Feb. 1685.

25. Burnet, *Hist.*, II.404–5; BT 158, Barrillon 31 July; BT 159, same 3 and 10 Aug., 26 Oct., 4 Nov. 1684; Temple, I.479. Baxter, pp. 197–8.

26. Burnet, *Hist.*, II.451–3; Dalrymple, II(b), pp. 62–3; Bulstrode, *Memoirs*, pp. 390–1; BL Add MSS 29578 fo. 15, 38847 fo. 123; Morrice, pp. 445, 450–1; PRO, FO 95/571, d'Avaux 25 Jan.; BT 160, Barrillon 15 Jan. 1685; Welwood, pp. 138–9; Hatton, II.46–7.

27. BL Add MS 41823 fo. 5; Burnet, *Supplement*, pp. 145–6.

28. *HMC Rutland*, II.84; PRO FO 95/571, d'Avaux 25 Jan. 1685; *HMC 7th Report*, pp. 321–2; BT 160, Barrillon 15 and 29 Jan., 5 Feb. 1685.

29. BT 159, Barrillon 21, 24 and 31 Aug. 1684; Morrice, pp. 450–1.

30. BT 160, Barrillon 15 Jan. and 5 Feb. 1685.

31. BT 157, Barrillon 10 and 24 Feb.; BT 158, same 22 May and 8 June 1684; Reresby, pp. 329–31; *HMC Ormond*, NS VII.202.

32. BT 157, Barrillon 19 March; BT 158, same 10, 24, 27 and 31 July; BT 159, same 7 and 31 Aug., 4 and 7 Sept. 1684; *Clar Corr*, I.93–6; *HMC Ormond*, NS IV.595–6; Reresby, p. 344; Carte MS 70 fo. 566.

33. BT 159, Barrillon 4 Sept. and 13 Nov. 1684; *HMC 7th Report*, p. 378; Morrice, p. 360; BL Add MS 29578 fo. 4; *Clar Corr*, I. 96–8, 102–3; *HMC Ormond*, NS VII.310–11.

34. *HMC 7th Report*, p. 378; Carte MS 217 fos 51, 61, 79–80; *HMC Ormond*, NS VII.285–6, 295.

35. *HMC Ormond*, NS VII.284–6, 301–2; *Clar Corr*, I.102–3.

36. Carte MS 217 fos 79–80; BL Add MS 29578 fo. 44; All Souls MS 317, Trumbull's Memoirs fo. 15; Burnet, *Hist.*, II.447–9, 453–4; Burnet, *Supplement*, pp. 134–5; *HMC Ormond*, NS VII.300, 310–11.

37. BT 159, Barrillon 5 Oct. 1684; *HMC Ormond*, NS VII.274.

38. Miller, 'Charters', pp. 78–9.

39. Luttrell, I.303; Morrice, pp. 351, 424–5; North, *Lives*, I.309–14, 427; BT 159, Barrillon 5 and 16 Oct. 1684.

40. BT 159, Barrillon 28 Dec. 1684; BT 160, same [8] Jan. and 8 Feb. 1685; BL Add MS 29578 fo. 42; *HMC Buccleuch*, I.211, 214–15; Luttrell, I.326.

41. Ailesbury, I.23, 86–9; BL Add MS 29560 fo. 48, 53; Burnet, *Supplement*, p. 140; Hatton, II.51.

42. Hatton, II.51–3; Morrice, pp. 454–6; Ailesbury, I.90; Fox, appendix, pp. xii–xv; Burnet, *Hist.*, II.457–9; Burnet, *Supplement*, p. 141; *CSPD 1685*, no. 2143; Campana, II.6–7.

43. North, *Lives*, I.319–20; Ailesbury, I.85–6, 92; Welwood, pp. 138–9; Burnet, *Hist.*, II.451–3.

44. Welwood, pp. 147–8.

45. Morrice, pp. 454–5; Burnet, *Hist.*, II.458–60; Fox, appendix, p. xv; *HMC Egmont*, II.146–7; BL Add MS 34508 fo. 81; H. Ellis, *Original Letters Illustrative of English History*, 2nd edn, 3 vols (London, 1825), III.336–7; Evelyn, IV.408–9; *CSPD 1685*, no. 2143.

46. Burnet, *Supplement*, p. 141; Burnet, *Hist.*, II.459, 472; Evelyn, IV.478.

47. Ailesbury, I.24.

48. Clarke, *James II*, I.736; Fox, appendix, p. xii.

49. Campana, II.6–7; Fox, appendix, p. xiv; BL Add MS 15395 fo. 310; *CSPD 1685*, no. 2143; Burnet, *Hist.*, II.459.

50. BL Add MSS 29560 fo. 48, 29561 fo. 55; Rutt (ed.), *Life of Calamy*, I.116–17; Burnet, *Hist.*, II.460–2; Morrice, pp. 456–7; Hatton, II.54; *HMC Egmont*, II.150–1; Ailesbury, I.92–3.

51. Evelyn, IV.409–11, 478.

52. For a hostile Tory view from 1693, see *HMC 5th Report*, p. 376.

53. Halifax, pp. 265–7.

Select Bibliography

Abernathy, G. R., jnr, 'The English Presbyterians and the Stuart Restoration, 1648–63', *Transactions of the American Philosophical Society*, NS LV, 1965

Ailesbury, T. Bruce, Earl of, *Memoirs*, ed. W. E. Buckley, 2 vols, Roxburgh Club, 1890

Arlington, H. Bennet, Earl of, *Letters*, ed. T. Bebington, 2 vols, London, 1701

Barwick, P., *Life of Dr John Barwick*, London, 1724

Baxter, S. B., *William III*, London, 1966

Bosher, R. S., *The Making of the Restoration Settlement: The Influence of the Laudians*, London, 1951

Bramston, Sir J., *Autobiography*, ed. Lord Braybrooke, Camden Soc. 1845

Brown, T. (ed.), *Miscellanea Aulica*, London, 1702

Browning, A. (ed.), *English Historical Documents 1660–1714*, London, 1953

——, *Thomas Earl of Danby*, 3 vols, Glasgow, 1951

Buckingham, J. Sheffield, Duke of, *Works*, 2 vols, London, 1753

Buckroyd, J. M., *Church and State in Scotland 1660–81*, Edinburgh, 1980

Bulstrode, Sir R., *Memoirs*, London, 1721

Bulstrode Papers, ed. E. W. Thibaudeau, London, 1897

Burnet, G., *History of My Own Time*, 6 vols, Oxford, 1823

——, 'Some Unpublished Letters', ed. H. C. Foxcroft, *Camden Miscellany* XI

——, *Supplement to the History of My Own Time*, ed. H. C. Foxcroft, Oxford, 1902

Campana de Cavelli, E., *Les Derniers Stuarts à Saint Germain en Laye*, 2 vols, London, 1871

Carte, T., *Life of James Duke of Ormond*, 6 vols, Oxford, 1851

——, (ed.), *Original Letters 1641–60*, 2 vols, London, 1739

Chandaman, C. D., *The English Public Revenue 1660–88*, Oxford, 1975

Childs, J., *The Army of Charles II*, London, 1976

Christie, W. D., *The First Earl of Shaftesbury*, 2 vols, London, 1871

Clarendon, E. Hyde, Earl of, *History of the Rebellion*, ed. W. D. Macray, 6 vols, Oxford, 1888

——, *Life*, 3 vols, Oxford, 1827

Clarke, J. S. (ed.), *Life of James II*, 2 vols, London, 1816

Clarke Papers, vol. IV, ed. C. H. Firth, Camden Soc. 1901

Clifton, R., *The Last Popular Rebellion: The Western Rising of 1685*, London, 1984

Coleby, A. M., *Central Government and the Localities: Hampshire 1649–89*, Cambridge, 1987

Cosin Correspondence, ed. G. Ornsby, 2 vols, Surtees Soc., 1872

Crist, T., 'Francis Smith and the Opposition Press in England 1660–88', unpublished Cambridge PhD thesis 1977

Dalrymple, Sir J., *Memoirs of Great Britain and Ireland*, 2 vols, London, 1771–3. (Vol. II is divided into three parts, designated 'Appendix', 'Appendix Part I' and 'Appendix Part II'. For brevity's sake, I refer to these as (a), (b) and (c))

Dalton, C., *English Army Lists and Commissions Registers 1660–1714*, vol. I, London, 1892

Davies, J. D., *Gentlemen and Tarpaulins*, Oxford, forthcoming.

Ekberg, C. J., *The Failure of Louis XIV's Dutch War*, Chapel Hill, 1979
Essex Papers, vol. I, ed. O. Airy, vol. II, ed. C. E. Pike, Camden Soc. 1890, 1913
Evelyn, J., *Diary*, ed. E. S. de Beer, 6 vols, Oxford, 1955
Feiling, K., *British Foreign Policy, 1660–72*, London, 1930
Fletcher, A., *Reform in the Provinces: The Government of Stuart England*, New Haven, 1986
Fox, C. J., *History of the Early Part of the Reign of James II*, London, 1808
Geyl, P., *Orange and Stuart*, London, 1969
Glassey, L. K. J., *Politics and the Appointment of the Justices of the Peace, 1679–1725*, Oxford, 1979
Granville, D., *Remains*, ed. G. Ornsby, Surtees Soc., 2 vols, 1861, 1867
Green, I. M., *The Re-establishment of the Church of England, 1660–3*, Oxford, 1978
Grimoard, Comte de, *Collection des Lettres et Mémoires Trouvées dans les Portefeuilles du Maréchal de Turenne*, 2 vols, Paris, 1782
Gumble, T., *Life of General Monk*, London, 1671
Haley, K. H. D., 'The Anglo-Dutch Rapprochement of 1677', *EHR* LXXIII, 1958
——, *An English Diplomat in the Low Countries: Sir William Temple and John de Witt 1665–72*, Oxford, 1986
——, *The First Earl of Shaftesbury*, Oxford, 1968
——, *William of Orange and the English Opposition, 1672–4*, Oxford, 1953
Halifax, G. Savile, Marquis of, *Complete Works*, ed. J. P. Kenyor, Harmondsworth, 1969
Harris, F. R., *Life of Edward Montagu, First Earl of Sandwich*, 2 vols, London, 1912
Harris, T., *London Crowds in the Reign of Charles II*, Cambridge, 1987
Hartmann, C. H., *Charles II and Madame*, London, 1934
——, *Clifford of the Cabal*, London, 1937
Hatton Correspondence, ed. E. M. Thompson, 2 vols, Camden Soc., 1878
Havighurst, A. F., 'The Judiciary and Politics in the Reign of Charles II', *Law Quarterly Review*, LXVI, 1950
Hodgson, J. C. (ed.), *Northumbrian Documents of the Seventeenth and Eighteenth Centuries*, Surtees Soc., 1918
Hutton, R., *Charles II: King of England, Scotland and Ireland*, Oxford, 1989
——, *The Restoration*, Oxford, 1985
Jones, J. R., *Charles II, Royal Politician*, London, 1987
——, *The First Whigs*, Oxford, 1961
Jusserand, J. J., *Recueil des Instructions Données aux ambassadeurs de la France: Angleterre*, vols I (1648–65) and II (1666–90), Paris, 1929
Kenyon, J. P., *The Popish Plot*, London, 1972
——, *Robert Spencer, Earl of Sunderland*, London, 1958
——, *The Stuart Constitution*, 2nd edn, Cambridge, 1986
Lauderdale Papers, ed. O. Airy, 3 vols, Camden Soc., 1884–5
Lister, T. H., *Life and Administration of Clarendon*, 3 vols, London, 1837–8
Ludlow, E., *A Voyce from the Watchtower*, ed. B. Worden, Camden Soc. 1978
Luttrell, N., *A Brief Historical Relation of State Affairs 1678–1714*, 6 vols, Oxford, 1857
McGuire, J. I., 'Why Was Ormond Dismissed in 1669?', *Irish Historical Studies* XVIII (1972–3)
Macpherson, J., *Original Papers containing the Secret History of Great Britain*, 2 vols, London, 1775
Macray, W. D., *Notes which Passed at the Privy Council between Charles II and Clarendon*, Roxburgh Club, 1896
Marvell, A., *Poems and Letters*, ed. H. M. Margoliouth, rev. E. Duncan Jones, 3rd edn, 2 vols, Oxford, 1971
Mather Papers, Collections of the Massachusetts Historical Soc., 4th Series, VIII, 1868

Mignet, F. A. M., *Négociations Relatives à la Succession d'Espagne*, 4 vols, Paris, 1835–42

Miller, J., 'The Crown and the Borough Charters in the Reign of Charles II', *EHR* C, 1985

——, 'The Correspondence of Edward Coleman, 1674–8', *Recusant History*, XIV, 1978

——, *James II: A Study in Kingship*, repr. London, 1989

——, *Popery and Politics in England 1660–88*, Cambridge, 1973

——, 'The Potential for "Absolutism" in Later Stuart England', *History*, LXIX, 1984

Milward, J., *Diary*, ed. C. Robbins, Cambridge, 1938

Mordaunt, J. Viscount, *Letter Book*, ed. M. Coate, Camden Soc. 1945

Morrison Letters: Autograph Letters in the Collection of Alfred Morrison, ed. E. W. Thibaudeau, 1st Series 6 vols, 2nd Series 3 vols, London, 1883–96 (see also *Bulstrode Papers*)

Newton, Lady, *The House of Lyme*, London, 1917

——, *Lyme Letters 1660–1760*, London, 1925

Nicholas Papers, ed. G. F. Warner, 4 vols, Camden Soc. 1886–1920

North, R., *Examen*, London, 1740

——, *Lives of the Norths*, ed. A. Jessopp, 3 vols, London, 1890

Ogg, D., *England in the Reign of Charles II*, 2nd edn, Oxford, 1956

Orrery, R. Boyle, Earl of, *A Collection of the State Letters of*, London, 1742

Pepys, S., *Diary*, ed. R. C. Latham and W. Matthews, 11 vols, London, 1971–83

Price, J., 'The Mystery and Method of His Majesty's Happy Restoration', in F. Maseres (ed.), *Select Tracts relating to the Civil Wars in England*, London, 1815

Rawdon Papers, ed. E. Berwick, London, 1819

Reresby, Sir J., *Memoirs*, ed. A. Browning, Glasgow, 1936

Rochester, J. Wilmot, Earl of, *Letters*, ed. J. Treglown, Oxford, 1980

Roseveare, H., *The Treasury 1660–1870: The Foundations of Control*, London, 1973

Rowen, H. H., *The Ambassador Prepares for War: Arnauld de Pomponne 1669–71*, The Hague, 1957

Rugg, T., *Diurnal*, ed. W. L. Sachse, Camden Soc., 1961

Savile Correspondence, ed. W. D. Cooper, Camden Soc., 1858

Seaward, P., *The Cavalier Parliament and the Reconstruction of the Old Regime, 1661–7*, Cambridge, 1989

Sidney, A., *Letters to Henry Savile*, London, 1742

Sidney, H., *Diary of the Times of Charles II*, ed. R. W. Blencowe, 2 vols, London, 1843

Smith, A. G., 'London and the Crown, 1681–5', unpublished PhD thesis, Wisconsin, 1967

Sonnino, P., *Louis XIV and the Origins of the Dutch War*, Cambridge, 1989

Spurr, J., 'The Church of England, Comprehension and the Toleration Act of 1689', *EHR* CIV (1989)

State Tracts, 2 vols, London, 1689–92

Steele, R. (ed.), *Tudor and Stuart Proclamations*, 2 vols, Bibliotheca Lindesiana, Oxford, 1910

Stradling, R. A., 'Anglo-Spanish Relations from the Restoration to the Peace of Aix-la-Chapelle', unpublished PhD thesis, University of Wales, 1968

——, *Europe and the Decline of Spain*, London, 1981

Temple, Sir W., *Works*, 2 vols, 1731

Thurloe, J., *State Papers*, ed. T. Birch, 7 vols, London, 1742

Warcup, E., 'Journals, 1676–84', ed. K. Feiling and F. R. D. Needham, *EHR* XL (1925)

Welwood, J., *Memoirs of the most Material Transactions in England for the last Hundred Years*, London, 1700

Western, J. R., *The English Militia in the Eighteenth Century, 1660–1802*, London, 1965

Whitelocke, B., *Memorials of the English Affairs*, 4 vols, Oxford, 1853
Witcombe, D. T., *Charles II and the Cavalier House of Commons, 1663–74*, Manchester, 1966
Wolf, J. B., *Louis XIV*, London (Panther edn), 1970
Wynne, W., *Life of Sir Leoline Jenkins*, 2 vols, London, 1724

Index